· TORQUEMADA ·

Benito Pérez Galdós

TORQUEMADA

Translated from the Spanish by
Frances M. López-Morillas

NEW YORK
COLUMBIA UNIVERSITY PRESS
1986

The translation of this work was made possible by a grant from the Translations Program of the National Endowment for the Humanities.

Columbia University Press is grateful for a grant from the Program for Cultural Cooperation Between the Spanish Ministry of Culture and North American Universities to aid in the publication of this book.

Library of Congress Cataloging-in-Publication Data

Pérez Galdós, Benito, 1843–1920.
Torquemada.

I. Title.
PQ6555.A25   1986   863'.5   85–19560
ISBN 0–231–06228–1 (alk. paper)

Columbia University Press
New York   Guildford, Surrey
Copyright © 1986 Columbia University Press
All rights reserved

Printed in the United States of America

Clothbound editions of Columbia University Press
books are Smyth-sewn.

Designed by Ken Venezio.

CONTENTS

· I ·

TORQUEMADA
AT THE STAKE

ONE

I am going to tell about the journey to the stake taken by that inhuman creature who destroyed by fire so many unhappy lives; some he skewered through the liver with a red-hot poker; others he popped, well larded, into a pot, and frizzled the rest on one side and then the other over a slow fire, with searching, methodical anger. I am going to tell how the cruel executioner became a victim; how the hatred he had aroused turned to pity, and how clouds of curses rained compassion on him: a moving case, a very exemplary case, ladies and gentlemen, worthy of being told for the edification of all, a caution to offenders and a warning to inquisitors.

My friends are already acquainted, through what I have seen fit to tell them, with Don Francisco Torquemada, whom some unpublished historians of our day call "Torquemada the Worse."* Alas for my good readers if they know the implacable stoker of fires that have swallowed lives and fortunes through dealings of any other kind, dealings less innocuous and disinterested than these innocent relationships between narrator and reader! For if they have had anything to do with him in more weighty matters; if they have gone to ask his help in the last throes of pecuniary woe, they had better commend themselves to God and die. Torquemada is the paymaster of that hell where debtors wind up, naked and scorched: men with more needs than means to satisfy them; clerks with more children than paychecks; others avid for a civil service appointment after long periods of unemployment; transferred army officers with huge families and mothers-in-law as well; weak-willed persons who have a good job but are nibbled away by a little

---

*The comparison is, of course, to Tomás de Torquemada (1420–98), who was appointed inquisitor general under Ferdinand and Isabella in 1482. He was noted for the rigor and cruelty with which he carried out the policies of the Inquisition.

wife who gives teas and pawns her very soul to buy pastries; tearful widows who draw a pension from the civil or military credit union and yet are in dire financial straits; people from all walks of life who have never succeeded in solving the numerical problem that is the basis of social existence, and others who are hopeless wastrels and never pay their bills, who either have a screw loose in their heads or are devoid of morals—the tricksters and liars.

Well, all of these, the good and the bad, the hapless and the rascally, each by his own efforts, but always with his blood and bones, built a little fortune for this filthy wretch Torquemada that many a showy gentleman in Madrid might envy—one of those persons with very tight gloves and new outfits for every season, who ask, as if it were a matter of no importance, "I say, how did securities do today?"

In 1868, the year of the September Revolution, Torquemada bought a tenement house on the Calle de San Blas, on the corner of Calle de la Leche. It was a building profitably divided into twenty-four small rooms, which gave him, after discounting some inevitable nonpayment of rent, repairs, taxes, and the like, an income of 1300 reales a month, equivalent to seven or seven and a half percent on his investment. Every Sunday our Don Francisco presented himself there to collect the rents, receipts in one hand and in the other a stick with a staghorn handle. The poor tenants who were unfortunate enough not to be able to pay went about from Saturday afternoon onward with a knot in their stomachs, for the sullen face and stern temperament of their landlord were not in agreement with the idea most of us have of the holiday, the Lord's Day, all surcease and joy. By 1874, year of the Restoration, Torquemada had already doubled the sum he had had on hand at the time of the "Glorious Revolution," and the radical political changes brought him handsome loans and advances. It was a new situation, a fresh page in the ledger, payments secured, honest business done. The brand-new provincial governors who needed to order new clothes, the civil servants of all kinds who hungrily emerged from obscurity, furnished him with a fine harvest. During the whole period of Conservative rule he was quite prosperous because the Conservatives gave him opportunities arising from the ostentation appropriate to a dominant party; and so did the Liberals, with their unsatisfied desires and needs. When the Liberals who had been so long out of power came into the government in 1881, Torquemada's fortunes rose again; he made excellent loans, fat advances, and got on famously. In fact, he was already eyeing another house, not a tenement this time but a good solid building, almost new, in excellent condition for modest tenants; and although it might bring in only three and a half percent at most, looking after it and collecting the rents would give him fewer headaches than the rundown tenement with its Sunday collections.

Everything was going like clockwork for that ravenous ant when suddenly Heaven afflicted him with a tremendous misfortune: his wife died. I hope my readers will forgive me for imparting this news without adequate preparation, for I know that they esteemed Doña Silvia, as did all of us who had the honor of dealing with her and knew her excellent qualities and attributes. She died of inflammation of the bowel, and in praise of Torquemada I am bound to say that he spared no expense on doctors or apothecaries to save the poor lady's life. This loss was a cruel blow to Don Francisco, for, as the couple had lived in holy and hardworking contentment for more than twenty years, both partners' characters had fused perfectly; she had become another self to him, and he the sum and, as it were, recasting of them both. Doña Silvia not only managed the household with masterly economy, but advised her spouse in difficult matters of business, aiding him with her intellectual gifts and experience in moneylending. With Doña Silvia guarding every penny in the house so that it wouldn't get away, and he sweeping in everything that passed by, they formed a couple who never wasted a crumb, a pair who could have served as model to all the ants that live under the ground and above it.

During the early days of his widowerhood Torquemada the Worse was in such a state that he didn't know what was happening to him, doubting that he could survive his better half. He turned even yellower than was his wont, and some gray hairs appeared on his head and in his little tuft of beard. But time did its work, as it has the habit of doing, sweetening the bitterness, filing away imperceptibly at the rough edges of life, and although his wife's memory did not fade from the usurer's mind, his grief was inevitably softened; his days gradually lost their funereal sadness; the sun came out in his soul, re-illuminating the various numerical combinations that existed there; business affairs served to distract the listless business man, and two years later Torquemada seemed to have found consolation; but, be it understood and repeated to his credit, without the slightest desire to marry again.

He had two children left: Rufinita, whose name is not a new one to my friends, and Valentinito, who now appears for the first time. We find that there is ten years' difference in age between them, for the good Doña Silvia had had the misfortune to lose, more or less prematurely, all the intervening babies, and only the first and last survived. At the time of the events I am about to recount, Rufinita had just passed her twenty-second birthday and Valentín was very close to twelve. And, as proof that that brute Don Francisco was born under a lucky star, both his children were—each in his and her own way— real jewels, or like blessings of God showered upon him to console him in his solitude. Rufina had inherited all her mother's domestic capabilities, and managed the house almost as well as she had. Naturally she did not possess her mother's lofty gift in business matters, nor her consummate prudence, nor her sharp eyesight, nor was she possessed of that worthy matron's other faculties of tooth and nose; but in dependability, in modest behavior and acceptable appearance, no girl of her age could surpass her. She was neither vain nor careless of her person; she could not be faulted either for boldness or for diffidence. She had never known what it was to be flirtatious. She had had but one sweetheart from the age when love begins to peep over the horizon until the time she comes into my tale; and this sweetheart, after much lurking about and sighing, showing in a thousand ways the honorableness of his intentions, was admitted to the house shortly before Doña Silvia's death and continued after it, with Rufina's papa's consent, in the same honorable and loving estate. He was a "little medical student," little in every sense of the word, since his height from the ground was the least a man can have; he was studious, innocent, good as gold, and to top it off, he hailed from La Mancha. Their chaste relationship had begun in the fourth year of his studies, and at the time of this account, Quevedito (for that is what he was called) had finished his degree and was launched into the practice of his profession, and they were about to be married. The Worse, satisfied with his daughter's choice, praised her good sense and scorn for vain appearances in attending only to the solid and the practical.

However, if we turn our eyes from Rufina to Torquemada's youthful heir, we will find a better explanation for the vanity instilled in him by his offspring, for (I say this sincerely) I have never known a more beguiling child than Valentín, nor a precocity as extraordinary as his. What a strange thing! Despite his resemblance to his disagreeable father, the boy was extremely handsome, with such an intelligent expression on his face that one gazed at him openmouthed; and such were the charms of his person and character, and his traits of behavior so superior to his age, that to see him, speak with him, and love him dearly was the work of a moment. And what a bewitching gravity he had, though not inconsistent with the characteristic restlessness of childhood! What charm, mingled with a self-possession quite inexplicable in a child of his years! What a divine spark was in his eyes at times, and at others what sweet and mysterious sadness! He was somewhat skinny, with slender but well-formed legs; his head was larger than the norm, with a slightly exaggerated development of the skull. As for his aptitude for study, we can only call it prodigious, to the amazement of his schoolmates and the pride and joy of his teachers. Of this I will speak later on. For the present I need only state that the Worse did not deserve such a jewel—how could he deserve it?—and, were he a man capable of praising God for the good things He had bestowed upon him, the rogue had good reason to stand, like Moses, for many hours with his arms raised to heaven. He did not thus raise them, because he knew that heaven was not going to let fall the kind of plums he was fond of.

TWO

Let us go on to another matter. Torquemada was not one of those usurers who spend their lives multiplying their wealth simply out of the platonic pleasure of possessing it, who live meanly so as not to spend it and, when they die, would like either to take it into the grave along with them or hide it where no living soul can find it. No; Don Francisco might have been such a man at another period in history, but he could not escape the influence of this second half of the nineteenth century, which has almost made a religion out of the decent material needs of life. Those old-fashioned misers who lusted after riches and lived like beggars, and died like dogs on a sleazy pallet full of fleas, with banknotes stuffed into the straw, were the mystics or metaphysicians of usury; their self-love was refined into the pure idea of business dealings; they adored the most holy, the ineffable quantity, sacrificing to it their material existence, the needs of their bodies and lives, just as the mystic places everything below the absorbing idea of salvation. Since the Worse was living in a period that arose out of disentailment, he had undergone, without realizing it, the metamorphosis that has changed the very nature of metaphysical usury, rendering it positivistic; and while it is certainly true, as history witnesses, that during his real period of apprenticeship, between 1851 and 1868, he went about badly dressed and affecting poverty, with unwashed face and hands and constantly scratching his arms and legs as if afflicted with lice, his hat greasy, his cape raveled; though neighborhood annals also state that there was fasting in his house almost all year round and that his wife went out on her errands in a ragged kerchief and a pair of her husband's old boots, it is no less certain that by 1870 or thereabouts the household was run along different lines; that on certain days the good Doña Silvia dressed very smartly; that Don Francisco changed his shirt oftener than once every two weeks; that there was less mutton than beef on his table and that on Sundays a few chicken giblets were added to the pot; that those meals composed exclusively of beans, and on some days dry bread and uncured sausage, were slowly passing into history; that beef-shank stew appeared for supper at certain times, and fish as well, especially at the season when it gets soft and costs less; that veal chops appeared on that table for the first time, along with pig's head, cured at home by Torquemada himself, who was a famous salter of meat; that, in a word and not to be tiresome about it, all the members of the family were beginning to treat themselves decently.

And in Doña Silvia's last years, the change became more noticeable. That was the period when the family first laid eyes on spring mattresses; Torquemada began to wear a fifty-real silk hat; he enjoyed the use of two capes, one of them being of very good quality with scarlet revers; the children were quite well dressed; Rufina had a washstand too pretty to touch, with a blue glass bowl and pitcher, that was never used for fear of spoiling it; Doña Silvia bedecked herself in a fur coat that seemed to be made of rabbit skins, and left the whole Calle de Tudescos as well as the Callejón del Perro green with envy when she went out visiting, adorned with beadwork; in a word, step by step and by dint of pushing and shoving, the family had worked its way into the middle class, our great and good middle class, all needs and pretensions, which grows at such a rate—alas!—that we are losing all our common folk.

Well, sir, once Doña Silvia had upped and died and the household reins were grasped by Rufina, the metamorphosis became still more marked. New reigns, new beginnings. To compare trivial matters with great ones, and the private sector with the public one, I venture to say that to me the situation resembled the Liberals' entry into the government, with their bit of revolutionary bias in everything they do and say. Torquemada represented the conservative ideal; but he gave way—he had no choice!—by adjusting himself to the logic of the times. He faced up to the clean shirt twice a week, to the abandonment of the Number Two cape for daily use, relegating it to nocturnal service, to the total banishment of the Number Three derby, which was incapable of absorbing another spot of grease; he accepted without violent protest fresh tablecloths oftener than once a week, plentiful wine, lamb with green peas (in season), the best fish during Lent, and turkey at Christmas; he tolerated the new set of dishes for special days, the braid-trimmed frock coat, which for him was the last word in elegance; and he had no complaints about the modest finery of Rufina and her little brother, nor the carpet in his sitting room, nor many other signs of progress that were gradually smuggled into the house.

And Don Francisco very soon saw that these novelties were good, and that his daughter was very clever, for—goodness, it seemed an extraordinary thing—my hero went out on the street and felt, in his good clothes, more of a person than before; he even encountered better business deals, more useful and exploitable friends. His step grew firmer, his cough more emphatic; he spoke in a louder voice and dared to assert himself in the café *tertulia*, finding that he had the courage to uphold in these social gatherings any sort of opinion, when previously—no doubt owing to his ragamuffin appearance and habitual affectation of poverty—he had always fallen in with the opinion of others. Little by little he began to observe in himself the powers inherent in his social and financial capabilities; he tapped himself and the sound told him that he was a property owner and a man of means. But he was never blinded by vanity. He was the same man all through, compact and hard, and not fool enough to take one step too many.

There was something in his character that resisted the changes in established practice brought about by the times, and, just as his habits of speech never changed, certain ideas and practices of his trade never altered, either. He retained the mannerism of always saying that the times were very bad, very bad indeed; to lament the imbalance between his miserable profits and the vast amount of work he did; his treacly diction remained, and so did that habit of inquiring after the family whenever he spoke to someone, and saying that he was in poor health, sketching a grimace of distaste for life. His little chin-tuft had already turned yellowish, his mustache was nearer black than white, and both these facial adornments were trimmed so short that they seemed glued on, rather than grown naturally. Apart from his clothing, which was now of improved quality though he wore it no better than before, he was the same man we came to know at the home of Doña Lupe, the Turkey Lady; in his face there was the same strange mixture of the military and the ecclesiastical, the same bilious color, dark and somewhat sleepy eyes, his expression and manner denoting slight effeminacy as well as hypocrisy, his bald spot a little larger and a little cleaner, and all of him crass, slippery, and repulsive, always ready when someone greeted him to offer his hand, which indeed was rather clammy.

He was so proud of Valentín's precocious intelligence that he nearly burst out of his skin. As the boy advanced in his studies, Don Francisco felt his paternal love increasing until it became blind passion. But to the miser's credit be it said that, though he imagined himself physically reproduced in that fragment of his own nature, he recognized his son's superiority and hence congratulated himself all the more for having brought him into being. For Valentinito was a prodigy of prodigies, a sublime piece of divinity that had fallen to earth. And Torquemada, thinking of the future, of what his son must become if he lived, could not imagine himself worthy of having conceived him, and felt in his presence the inborn shyness of matter opposed to spirit.

Do not let it be thought that there is the slightest exaggeration in what I say about that child's extraordinary intellectual endowment. I state with all candor that the boy was made of the most magnificent stuff imaginable, and that he entered the lists of instruction like those extraordinary creative geniuses who are born from time to time, destined to open new paths for humanity. In addition to his intelligence, which peeped forth at an early age like the dawn of a splendid day, he possessed all the charms of childhood: sweetness, grace, and good nature. In sum, the child was wholly lovable, and it is not strange that Don Francisco and his daughter were mad about him. After his earliest years had passed, it was never necessary to punish or even scold him. He learned to read as if by magic, in a few days, as if he had known how from his mother's womb. At the age of five he knew many things that other children find hard to learn at twelve. One day two teachers, friends of mine who have a primary and secondary school, spoke to me about him; they took me to see him, and I was amazed. I never saw so marvelous a show of intelligence, nor such precocity. For, though he rattled off some of his replies pell-mell, demonstrating the efficacy and resources of his memory, the tone in which he gave others showed how well he understood and grasped their meaning.

He knew grammar by rote, but his mastery of geography was that of a grown man. Outside the sphere of school, it was astonishing to observe the confidence of his replies and observations, without a trace of childish arrogance. He was timid and unassuming, seeming not to understand that there was any merit in the skills he displayed, and was surprised that they were regarded and praised so highly. I was told that he gave very little trouble at home. He studied his lessons so quickly and easily that he had plenty of time for his games, which were always very tame and innocent. It was useless to tell him to go out and play with the neighborhood children. Even his pranks were of a quiet kind and consisted (up to the age of five) of covering the wallpaper in the rooms with scribbles and letters, or tearing off a strip of it; or of letting down from the balcony overlooking the street a very long string with the lid of a coffeepot tied to it, paying out the string until it touched a passerby's hat and then hastily pulling it up again. No child was more humble and obedient than he, and because he was perfect in everything, he even wore out his clothing as little as it was possible to do.

But his extraordinary faculties had not yet been demonstrated; they began to appear when he studied arithmetic, and were fully revealed later during his secondary studies. From his earliest years, when he first received elementary notions of the science of quantity, he had added and subtracted from memory figures in the high tens and even hundreds. He did calculations with infallible accuracy, and even his father, who was wonderfully sharp at figuring rates of interest in his head, not infrequently consulted him. When Valentín began his study of high-school mathematics, he instantly revealed all the awesome power of his arithmetical gifts. He did not learn things; he knew them already, and the textbook merely awakened his ideas, opened them, so to speak, like buds that unfold into flowers under the warmth of spring. Nothing was hard for him, no problem frightened him. One day the professor went to his father and told him, "This child is something beyond explaining, Señor Torquemada; either the devil is in him or he is the most wonderful scrap of divinity that has ever fallen to earth. Soon I'll have nothing left to teach him. He is Newton brought back to life, Señor Don Francisco, a genius with an exceptional talent for mathematics, who no doubt is bringing new formulas under his arm to expand the field of science. Remember what I say: when this lad is a man, he will astonish the world and turn it upside down."

It is easy to understand how Torquemada reacted when he heard this. He embraced the professor, and satisfaction spilled out of his eyes and mouth in the form of tears and droolings. From that day forward he was beside himself; he treated his son not with mere love but with a certain superstitious respect. He cared for him as for a supernatural being, placed in his hands by some special privilege. He oversaw his meals, getting terribly upset if the boy displayed no appetite; when he saw him studying he checked the windows to see that no draft got in; he informed himself about the temperature outside before he would let him leave the house, to decide whether he should wear a muffler or his heavy jacket or his gumboots; when he slept, the father walked on tiptoe; on Sundays he took him for a walk or to the theater, and if the little darling had showed an enthusiasm for strange and costly playthings, Torquemada would have wrestled successfully with his stinginess and bought them. But the child prodigy was enthusiastic only about books; he read rapidly and as if by magic, absorbing each page in the wink of an eye. His father bought him a book of travels with many pictures of European cities and wild places. The boy's gravity astonished all the friends of the household, and inevitably there was someone who remarked that he was like a little old man. As for naughtiness, he was exceptionally free of it: he never learned a single ugly word or deed like those that the shameless young sprigs of the present generation know at his age. His innocence and positively celestial grace almost made us feel as if we had met and talked with angels, and his ponderings bordered on the miraculous. Other children, when asked what they want to be when they grow up, say "bishops" or "generals" if they are on the vain side; those who are physically dexterous say "coachmen" or "athletes" or "circus clowns"; those inclined to imitation say "actors" or "painters". But when Valentinito heard the question, he would shrug his shoulders and say nothing. At most, he would answer, "I don't know," and as he said it would pierce his questioner with a luminous, penetrating glance, a vagrant flash of the infinite number of ideas he had in that formidable brain, which in time to come would illuminate the whole earth.

But the Worse, even though he realized that no profession could be lofty enough for his miraculous child, was thinking of having him study engineering, because the law is for shysters. But what kind of engineer? Civil, or military? He soon observed that Valentín was not excited by soldiers, and that, contrary to the general law of childish enthusiasms, he looked on uniforms with indifference. Civil engineer, then. By order of his professor at school, Valentín was placed, before he had finished the secondary course, in the hands of a professor who prepared students for the special professions. This man was dumbfounded as soon as he grasped the boy's colossal intelligence and one day left the class in terror, his hands held up to his head, and, rushing off to find other professors of higher mathematics, he told them, "I'm going to introduce you to the phenomenon of the present age."

And he introduced him, and they marveled, for the boy went to the blackboard and, as if he were scribbling merely in play and to use up chalk, solved very difficult problems. Then he performed a number of computations and mathematical operations from memory, things that even the greatest experts find to be no bed of roses. One of those important professors, in an attempt to fluster him, tossed him the calculus of numerical radicals, and it was as if he had been tossed so many salted almonds. For him, a square root to the nth power was like a hop, skip, and jump for other children. Those wise and learned gentlemen looked at one another dreamily, declaring that they had never seen a remotely similar case.

The scene was indeed interesting and worthy of inclusion in the annals of science: four grave gentlemen of over fifty, bald and purblind from so much study, teachers of teachers, were grouped around that urchin who had to make his calculations on the bottom half of the blackboard, speechless and perplexed with admiration, for no matter how many difficulties they placed in the little darling's way, he tossed them off like water. Another of the examiners proposed homologies, in the belief that Valentín was ignorant of them, and when they saw that he was not, they were unable to restrain their enthusiasm: one of them called him the Antichrist; another picked him up and swung him over his shoulders, and all of them argued about who would take charge of him, all anxious to complete the education of the century's foremost mathematician. Valentín observed them without pride or shyness, innocent and self-possessed, like the child Jesus in the midst of the doctors.

THREE

But enough of mathematics, say I, for I must mention that Torquemada lived in the same house on the Calle de Tudescos where we first met him when Señora de Bringas went to see him in about 1868, to ask him a favor I have now forgotten, and I am in a hurry to present a certain individual whom I have known for some time and of whom I have not made the slightest mention until now: one Don José Bailón, who went nightly to our Don Francisco's house to play a game of checkers or *mus* with him, and whose appearance in my tale is necessary if it is to develop in logical fashion. This Señor Bailón is a priest who hung up his habit in Málaga in 1869, launching himself into a career as a revolutionary and freethinker with such frantic enthusiasm that he could no longer return to the flock, nor would he have been accepted even if he had wished to. The first thing the wretched man did was to let his beard grow, talk his head off in the clubs, write violent diatribes against his fellow clergymen, and at last—operating on the principle of word united to deed—he took to the barricades with an ancient blunderbuss whose flaring muzzle was shaped exactly like a trumpet. Finding him defeated and raging, the Protestants converted him, and adapted him for giving sermons and lessons in their chapel, a task he performed most unwillingly and only to keep body and soul together. He came to Madrid at the time when that excellent couple Don Horacio and Doña Malvina founded their evangelical establishment in the Chamberí district. In return for a modest stipend, Bailón assisted them at the services, preaching sermons that were both sweet and sour, eccentric and tedious. But after a year of this arrangement, I don't know what happened. There was a question of some apostolic liberties taken by Bailón with female converts; it is certain that Doña Malvina, who was a very decorous person, gave him a piece of her mind in bad Spanish; Don Horacio intervened, also denouncing his assistant, whereupon Bailón, who was a man of great spirit in such cases, whipped out a knife as big as all outdoors and went so far as to say that if they didn't get out of his way, he would spill their guts. The poor English couple's panic was such that they ran off screaming and never stopped until they reached the roof. In short, Bailón had to leave that employment, and after an aimless period during which he borrowed money right and left, he wound up on the staff of a little newspaper of radical leanings whose mission in life was to toss firecrackers at all authority: priests, bishops, and the Pope himself. This happened in 1873, and from that period the political treatises on current problems originate, which the ex-priest published in that newspaper and of which he had reprints made; they were arrant nonsense written in biblical style and had, though this seems hard to believe, short periods of success. At any rate, they sold well and got their scapegrace author out of more than one monetary strait.

But all that came to an end; the revolutionary fever and Bailón's leaflets had to go into hiding along with their author, who shaved his beard as a disguise in order to flee abroad. Two years later he turned up in Spain again, with an extremely long mustache extending over part of his beard, like that affected by Victor Emmanuel, and, to find out whether or not he was bringing reports and messages from other political refugees, he was arrested and kept in the Saladero prison for three months. The next year, proceedings against him having been dropped, our man was living in Chamberí and, according to neighborhood gossip, in truly biblical concubinage with a rich widow who owned a flock of goats and in addition an establishment of milk-donkeys. I tell all this as it was told to me, recognizing the fact that this part of Bailón's patriarchal history is extremely murky. But the public and well-known fact is that the widow in question kicked the bucket, and that shortly afterward Bailón appeared to be well provided with money. The establishment and the she-donkeys and goats were his. He rented out everything; he went to reside in downtown Madrid and took to moneylending, and I need say no more to make my readers understand the provenance of his acquaintance and dealings with Torquemada, for it is obvious that the usurer was his teacher, who initiated him into the mysteries of the craft and handled part of his capital for him, just as he had handled that of Doña Lupe the Magnificent, better known as the Turkey Lady.

Don José Bailón was a great tall brute of a man, athletic, heavy-bodied, and strong-featured, a real live anatomical study owing to the opulence of his muscles. Lately he had taken to shaving again, but his face was not the face of a priest or a monk or a bullfighter. He seemed, rather, a Dante gone to seed. A friend of mine who, for his sins, has had dealings with Bailón, says that he is the living image of the Sibyl of Cumae painted by Michelangelo, along with other sibyls and prophets, on the marvelous ceiling of the Sistine Chapel. She seems indeed like an old woman of a titanic race, who bears all celestial angers in her frown. Bailón's profile, and his arms and legs, like ancient tree-trunks; his powerful chest and the postures he was wont to assume, raising a heavy leg and bending his arm, made him resemble those figures that populate the ceilings of cathedrals, sprawling on a cloud. What a pity that it's not stylish for us to go around stark naked, so that this cornice-angel could shine in all his academic elegance! At the time I now introduce him, he was more than fifty years of age.

Torquemada esteemed him greatly, for in their business relationships Bailón made a point of displaying great punctiliousness and even delicacy. And since the renegade priest had such a varied and dramatic history, and knew how to tell it with such verve, touching it up with lies, Don Francisco listened to him enraptured, and considered him an oracle in all questions of lofty import. Don José was one of those people who can take four ideas and a few extra words and put them together in such a way that it seems they know things that they don't, and dazzle the ignorant and credulous. The most dazzled of all was Don Francisco, and, moreover, he was the only mortal who read those ranting leaflets ten years after their publication; it was literature outmoded almost at its birth, and whose fleeting success we cannot understand unless we remember that a sort of sentimental democracy in the style of Jeremiah also enjoyed its short vogue.

Bailón wrote all this foolishness in short paragraphs, and sometimes broke into Holy Writ, as for example:

"Glory to God in the highest, and on earth, peace, etc.," only to go on in the following key:

"The times are approaching, times of redemption, when the Son of man shall be master of the earth.

"The Word planted the divine seed eighteen centuries ago. On a dark and shadowy night it came to fruition. Behold its flowers.

"What is their name? The people's rights."

And perhaps, when the reader was caught unawares, he would toss out a phrase like:

"Behold the tyrant. Accursed be he!

"Incline your ear and tell me from whence comes that vague, confused, strange sound.

"Place your hand upon the earth and tell me why it has trembled.

"It is the Son of man who approaches, determined to recover his primogeniture.

"Why does the tyrant's countenance turn pale? Ah! the tyrant sees that his hours are numbered."

Again, he would start off with the words "Soldier Boy, Where Are You Going?" And in the end, after a great deal of harassment, the reader had not the slightest idea where the soldier boy was going, unless all of them, the author and his public too, were going to the lunatic asylum at Leganés.

All of this seemed very fine stuff to Don Francisco, a man who had read very little. On some afternoons the two moneygrubbers would go for a walk together, chatting animatedly; and though Torquemada was the sibyl in business affairs, in other kinds of knowledge the only sibyl was Señor Bailón. In politics, especially, the ex-priest gave himself very knowing airs, beginning with the statement that he no longer had any desire for conspiracies, for his daily bread was no problem and he didn't want to risk his hide to pull chestnuts out of the fire for a handful of troublemakers. Then he would describe all politicians, from the highest to the most obscure, as a pack of rascals, and calculate to the penny the amounts of money they had looted. He also talked a lot about urban reform, and since Bailón had been in London and Paris, he was in a position to make comparisons. Public hygiene was a concern of both men: the priest blamed everything on "effluvia," and expounded some really outlandish biological theories. He had some grasp of astronomy and music too, and was not ignorant of botany or veterinary science or the art of choosing melons. But nowhere did his encyclopedic knowledge stand out more than in matters of religion. His meditations and studies had permitted him to plumb the great and awesome problem of our whole destiny.

"Where will we end up when we die? Why, we'll be born again; it's as clear as spring water. I remember," he would say, gazing fixedly at his friend and alarming him by the solemn tone he imparted to his words, "I remember having lived before. In my youth I had a vague recollection of that life, and now, by dint of meditation, I can see it clearly. I was a priest in Egypt, understand? Way back in the year I don't know what. Yes, sir, a priest in Egypt. It seems to me that I can see myself in a saffron-colored cassock or vestment and a pair of things like earflaps that hung down on both sides of my face. They burned me alive, because . . . you see . . . there was a priestess I liked in that church, I mean temple . . . a real stunner—understand?—and what eyes! *This* big, and the most wonderful hips, Señor Don Francisco! Well, all that got rather complicated and the goddess Isis and the sacred bull Apis took it very badly. All those priest fellows got into an uproar, and they burned the wench and me alive. What I'm telling you is the truth, as sure as that's the sun in the sky. Concentrate, my friend; stir up your memory; search the cellar and attics of your being, and you will find the certainty that you too have lived in far-off times. That boy of yours, that prodigy, must have been Newton himself, before, or Galileo or Euclid. And as for other things, my ideas are perfectly clear. Heaven and hell don't exist; symbolic pap and that's all. Heaven and hell are here. It's here that we pay, sooner or later, for everything we've done; it's here we receive our reward, tomorrow if not today, if we deserve it; and to say tomorrow is to say the next hundred years. God! The idea of God is a tough nut to crack, and a fellow has to beat his brains out, as I have beaten mine, working away at the books and then meditating. For God"—popping his eyes and making a gesture with both hands that indicated taking in a huge space—"is humanity, humanity, understand? Which doesn't mean that it ceases to be personal. What does personal mean? Listen carefully. Personal is what one is. And the great Whole, friend Don Francisco, the great Whole . . . is all one, because that's all there is, and it has the attributes of an infinitely infinite being. All of us put together make up humanity; we are the atoms that compose the great All; we are a tiny part of God, a minute part, and we are renewed as the atoms of filthy matter are renewed in our bodies. Are you getting the point?"

Torquemada was not getting the point at all, but his interlocutor had got into such a maze that the only way to extricate himself was to stop talking. The sole idea Don Francisco grasped out of all that poppycock was that *God is humanity*, and that it is humanity which makes us pay for our mischief or rewards us for our good works. The rest he couldn't have understood if he were to hang for it. Torquemada's Catholicism had never been very fervent. It is true that during Doña Silvia's lifetime they used to go to mass together as a matter of routine; but that was all. After he had become a widower, the stray ideas about the catechism that the Worse retained in his mind, like useless scraps of paper or jottings, got shuffled around with all that farrago about humanity-God, causing frightful confusion.

If the truth be told, none of these theories stayed for long in the skinflint's noggin, which was always fixed on the sordid reality of his business dealings. But a day came—a night, rather—when those ideas took possession of his mind with a certain degree of tenacity, owing to what I am about to relate. My hero was entering his house at dusk one afternoon in February, having carried out a large number of transactions with varying success and thinking about the steps he was going to take on the morrow, when his daughter, who had opened the door, said the following words to him: "Don't be alarmed, Papa, it's nothing. . . Valentín came home from school feeling ill."

All the prodigy's little upsets frightened Don Francisco very much. The one that was being announced to him might be unimportant, like others in the past. And yet there was a certain tremor in Rufina's voice, a veiled quality, a strange tone, which left Torquemada in suspense and cold with apprehension.

"I think it's nothing serious," continued the young woman. "It seems he had a dizzy spell. It was the professor who brought him home, in his arms."

The Worse stood in the hall as if nailed to the spot, unable to say a word or take a step.

"I put him to bed immediately and sent a message to Quevedo to come as fast as he could," said Rufina.

Don Francisco, emerging from his stupor as if struck by a whip, rushed to the boy's room and saw him in bed with so many bedclothes piled on him that he seemed half suffocated. His face was very flushed, his eyes drowsy. His quietness was more that of a painful stupor than peaceful sleep. The father laid his hand on the innocent prodigy's temples, which were burning hot.

"That ninny Quevedito—confound him! I don't know what he's thinking of. Look, it would be better to call some other doctor who knows more."

His daughter tried to calm him, but he fought off her attempts at sympathy. His son was not an ordinary son, and could not fall ill without an alteration in the natural order of the universe. The grieving father tasted not a bite of his dinner; he did nothing but stride about the house, waiting for the cursed doctor, constantly moving from his room to the boy's and from there to the dining room, where the oilcloth blackboard on which Valentín chalked his mathematical problems appeared before his eyes, burdening his heart. There were still some figures on it left over from that morning, scrawls which Torquemada did not understand, but which almost made him cry, like sad music; a square-root sign, letters above and below, and in another place a network of lines, forming a figure like a many-pointed star with numbers at the tips.

At last, praise be to God! that plaguey Quevedito arrived, and Don Francisco gave him a thorough scolding, for he already treated him like a son-in-law. When the doctor had seen and examined the boy, his expression was not reassuring. You could have strangled Torquemada with a hair when the little doctor, pushing him up against the wall and placing both hands on his shoulders, told him, "I don't like this at all, but we'll have to wait till tomorrow to see if an eruption breaks out. The fever is quite high. I've already told you to take great care with this phenomenal boy of yours. So much studying, so much knowledge, an exaggerated development of the brain! What you've got to do with Valentín is put a bell around his neck, turn him loose in the country in the middle of a flock of sheep, and not bring him back to Madrid until he's quite stupid."

Torquemada hated the country and could not understand that there might be anything good about it. But he made up his mind that if the boy got well, he would take him to some place where there was a pasture, so that he could drink all the milk he liked and breathe pure air. Pure air, as Bailón so well said, was an excellent thing. Ah! Those confounded effluvia were to blame for what was happening! Don Francisco felt such rage that if he had laid hands on an effluvium at that moment, he would have torn it in two. That night the sibyl dropped in to visit his friend and, not surprisingly, repeated the whole harangue about humanity. To Torquemada the priest seemed more enigmatic and annoying than ever, his arms longer, his face harder and more awe-inspiring. When he was alone, the usurer did not go to bed. Since Rufina and Quevedo were sitting up with the boy, he would stay up too. Next to their father's bedroom was the children's, and in it Valentín's bed. The boy spent a very restless night, panting for breath, his skin so hot that it seemed to be on fire, his eyes stunned and glistening, his speech halting, his ideas disconnected, like the beads of a rosary whose string has broken.

FOUR

The following day was all dread and bitter sorrow. Quevedo proffered the opinion that the illness was "inflammation of the meninges," and that the boy was in danger of death. He did not say this to the father but to Bailón, so that he could prepare him gradually. Torquemada and Bailón closeted themselves together and the result of the conference was that they nearly came to blows, for Don Francisco, almost out of his mind with grief, called his friend a liar and a deceiver. The hapless miser's restlessness, nervous agitation, and derangement cannot be described. He was obliged to go out on several errands connected with his unpleasant trade, and every few minutes came home panting, with his tongue hanging out and his derby on the back of his head. He would come in, take a look around, and go out again. He brought the medicines himself, and told the whole story at the apothecary's: "A dizzy spell when he was in class, then a terrible temperature. What good are doctors?" On the advice of Quevedo himself, he called for one of the city's most eminent physicians, who diagnosed the case as acute meningitis.

On the night of the second day, Torquemada, completely exhausted, sank into one of the armchairs in the parlor and stayed there about half an hour, turning over in his mind an ingenious idea—alas—a hard and many-faceted idea that had lodged itself in his brain. "I have failed humanity, and now the filthy slut is presenting the bill with back interest. No! If God, or whoever it is, takes my son, I'm going to be so bad, so beastly! Then they'll see what the real thing is. That's all I needed. Nobody plays games with me. . . But no, what foolishness I'm talking! He won't take him away from me, because I . . . what they say about my never having done good to anyone is a lie. Let them prove it . . . because just saying it isn't enough. And what about all those people I've helped out of tight places? What about that? Because if people have gone telling tales about me to humanity: that I put the screws on, or don't put them on . . . I'll make a test . . . that's right; now I'm really getting my steam up; if I've never done anything good before, I'll do it now, right now, because there has to be some reason for the saying that it's never too late to do good. Let's see: suppose I started praying now, what would they say up there? I think Bailón is mistaken, and Humanity must not be God but the Virgin. Of course, she's a female, a lady. . . . No, no, no . . . let's not pay attention to the materialism of the word. Humanity is God and the Virgin and all the saints put together. Hold on, man, hold on, you're going crazy. The only part I can understand is that, without good works, everything is, as you might say, garbage . . . Oh, my God, what torture, what torture! If You make my son well, I don't know what I wouldn't do; but what magnificent things, splendid things! But who is the scoundrel who says that I haven't a single good work to my name? They want to ruin me; they want to take my son away from me, my boy who was born to teach all the wise men and leave them gasping. And they envy me because I'm his father, because that glory of the world came from these bones and this blood. Envy! How envious this filthy humanity is! I mean, not humanity, because it's God . . . men, fellow humans, us, for we're all great rascals, and that's why the things that happen to us happen . . . We have it coming to us . . . we have it coming to us."

Then he remembered that the next day was Sunday and he had not made out the receipts to collect the rents in his house. After spending half an hour engaged in this operation, he rested for short periods, stretching out on the parlor sofa. Between nine and ten in the morning he went out to make his Sunday collection. What with lack of food and sleep and the terrible grief that was tearing his soul apart, the poor man was positively the color of an olive. His step was faltering and his eyes wandered uncertainly, vaguely, as often sweeping the ground as shooting up to the sky. When the cobbler who had his workshop in the grimy entryway of the house saw the landlord come in, and observed his altered face and drunken walk, he was so startled that he dropped the hammer with which he was driving in tacks. Torquemada's presence in the patio, a most unwelcome apparition that took place every Sunday, produced a real panic that day; while some women hastened to take refuge in their respective apartments, others (who were probably chronically late in paying their rent and had observed the monster's threatening face) left the house entirely. The collection began in the lower rooms, and the mason and the two cigarette-makers paid without a murmur, wishing only to avoid looking at Don Francisco's hated face. They noticed something strange and abnormal about him, for he took the money mechanically and did not examine it with parsimonious care as at other times, as if his thoughts were a hundred leagues away from the important action he was performing; they did not hear his usual grumblings, like those of a snappish dog, nor did he inspect the rooms in search of the broken floor tile or piece of fallen plaster with which to berate the tenant.

When he reached the room of Rumalda, the ironing woman, a widow whose mother lay ill on a pallet and whose three little children were wandering about the patio with their bare skin showing through the holes in their clothes, Torquemada emitted the expected grunt and the poor woman, her voice sad and quavering as though she were about to confess some grave offense before a judge, pronounced the classic phrase, "Don Francisco, today it can't be done. I'll pay another day."

I cannot describe the woman's stupor and that of the two neighbors who were present, when they saw that the skinflint did not spit out a single curse or blasphemy from that mouth of his, and when they heard him say in the most muffled, tearful voice in the world, "No, my dear, I'm not saying a thing. Why, I'm not going to press you. It never entered my head to scold you. What are we to do, if you can't pay?"

"Don Francisco, it's . . ." murmured the poor woman, believing that the fiend was speaking sarcastically and that the attack would follow the sarcasm.

"No, my dear, I haven't said a word. How can these things be expressed? The fact is that you people can't get it out of your heads that I'm, as you might say, a tyrant. Now where do you get the idea that there's no compassion in me, or . . . or charity? Instead of being grateful for what I do for you, you slander me. No, no. Let's understand each other. Rumalda, don't worry; I know you need things, that times are bad. When times are bad, girls, what can we do but help one another out?"

He went on, and on the main floor he met a woman who rarely paid her rent, but who had a high degree of courage in facing up to the fiend. As soon as she saw him coming, judging from the look on his face that he was in a worse temper than ever, she anticipated his harshness with these brazen words: "Listen here, don't you come trying to put the squeeze on me. You know there's nothing here. *Himself* is out of work. D'you expect me to take to highway robbery? Can't you see that there's no furniture in the house, that it's as bare as a charity ward? Where d'you expect me to get the money from? Curse your soul . . ."

"And who told you, you bitch, looselip, bigmouth, that I've come to squeeze you to death? Let's see if one of those hags can say I have no humanity! I dare you to say it to me."

He brandished the cudgel he was carrying, symbol of his authority and evil temper, and the only expressions visible in the circle that had formed around him were open mouths and dumbfounded looks.

"I'm telling you, and all the rest of you, that I don't give a damn if you don't pay me today! For heaven's sake! How do I have to say it to make you understand? Just because your husband's out of work, does that mean I'm going to put the rope around your neck? I know you'll pay me when you can, don't I? Because if it's intent to pay, you have that already. Then why get so worked up about it? Idiots, stupid fools!" (Here he attempted to produce a smile.) "And you thought I was harder than rocks and I let you believe it because it suited me, because it suited me, of course, for God commands us not to put on a show with our humanity! My, what a bunch of harpies you are! Farewell. You" (to the woman), "don't get excited. And don't think I'm doing this so's you'll bless me for it. But just take note that I'm not squeezing you, and to show you how good I am . . ."

He stopped and thought for a moment, putting his hand to his pocket and gazing at the floor.

"Nothing, nothing. God be with you."

And he went on to another apartment. At the next three doors he made his collection without any difficulty.

"Don Francisco, if you'd put a new soapstone in the stewhole, I can't cook anything here. . . ."

In other circumstances this request would have been the signal for a tremendous screaming match, to wit: "Put your bottom in the stewhole, you trull, and build a fire on that," or "Just look at the old tightwad; I hope your money turns to poison on you."

But that day all was peace and sweet accord, and Torquemada granted every favor that was asked of him.

"Oh, Don Francisco!" said another woman, at Number 11. "I have your blasted fifty reales. To scrape them together we've only eaten a few cents' worth of chicken scraps and the same of liver with dry bread. But to keep from seeing that look on your face and hearing your voice, I'd live on French nails."

"Look, that's an insult, an injustice, because if I've pressed you at other times it wasn't because of the materialism of the money but because I like to see people meet their obligations . . . so that it can't be said . . . Everybody ought to have dignity . . . I swear, you have a fine opinion of me! D'you think I'd allow your children, these lambs of God, to go hungry? Go on, forget the money . . . or better still, so you won't take it as a slight, let's divide it and you can keep twenty-five reales. . . You can give them to me another day. You hussies! When you ought to admit that I'm like a father to you, you label me inhuman and I don't know what else! No, I'm telling you all that I respect humanity, that I defer to it, that I appreciate it, and that now and forevermore I'll do all the good I can and then some. So there!"

Astonishment, confusion. The chattering group dogged his heels, whispering comments like, "This scoundrel has had some setback. . . Don Francisco must be off his noggin. Look at the hangman's face on him. Don Francisco with humanity! That must be why that long-tailed star is coming out in the sky every night. The world's coming to an end."

At Number 16, Don Francisco said, "But my dear girl, you slyboots, your little girl was sick and you hadn't told me anything? What am I here on earth for? Frankly, this is an insult I don't forgive. I can't forgive you for it. You're deceitful, and to prove you don't have an ounce of feeling, let's make a bet that you can't guess what I'm going to do? How much do you bet that you can't guess? Well, I'm going to give you money so you can make some stew. There! Take it, and then say I don't have humanity. But you're all so ungrateful, you'll call me all kinds of names, and maybe even curse me. . . Farewell."

In Señá Casiana's room, one of the tenants made bold to ask him, "Don Francisco, you don't fool us. Something's the matter with you. What the devil is in that head, or in that hard heart of yours?"

The wretched landlord sank into a chair and, taking off his derby, wiped his yellow brow and greasy pate with one hand, merely saying between sighs, "It's not a hard heart, dammit! It's not a hard heart!"

As they saw that his eyes were filling with tears and that, as he gazed at the floor, he rested both hands on his stick, leaning the whole weight of his body on it and swaying to and fro, the women begged him to unburden himself; but he must not have thought them worthy of being confidantes of his enormous, lacerating grief. Taking up the money, he said in a hollow voice, "Even if you didn't have it, Casiana, it would make no difference. I repeat that I don't squeeze the poor . . . for I'm poor, too. . . And if anybody says" (here he rose shakily and angrily to his feet) "that I'm inhuman, he lies worse than the official gazette! I *am* human; I take pity on the unfortunate; I help them in whatever I can, because that's what humanity bids us to do; and you all know that if you let humanity down, you'll pay for it sooner or later, and if you're good, you'll have your reward. I swear to you by that picture of the Virgin of Sorrows with her dead Son in her arms" (he pointed to an engraving on the wall), "I swear to you that even if I haven't seemed to be charitable and good, that doesn't mean that I'm not, dammit! And if you need proofs, proofs will be given. Go on, you don't believe it. . . Well, then, you can go to all the devils in hell. Being good is enough for me. I don't need anyone to butter me up. You lousy females, I don't want your gratitude in the least. You can take your blessings and . . ."

Having said this, he rushed out. They all peered after him as he went down the staircase, through the patio, and out the door, waving his arms in such a way that he looked like the devil crossing himself.

FIVE

He hastened toward home, and contrary to his custom (for he was a man who ordinarily would rather walk his legs off than spend a peseta), he took a cab in order to get there sooner. His heart seemed to tell him that he would find good news, the sick boy feeling better, Rufina's face smiling as she opened the door; and in his mad impatience, it seemed that the carriage barely moved, that the horse was lame and that the driver didn't whip the poor animal enough.

"Get on with you, man. Curse the nag! Give him the whip!" he shouted. "Look, I'm in an awful hurry."

At last he arrived; and as he ascended the staircase of his house, panting, he justified his hopes as follows: "Now they can't say that it's because of my wickedness, for I'm not all bad." What a cruel disappointment to see Rufina's face as sad as before, and to hear that "just the same, Papa," which sounded in his ears like a funeral knell! He approached the invalid on tiptoe and looked at him. As the poor child was very drowsy just then, Don Francisco could observe him with relative calm, for when he was delirious and tried to get out of bed, turning terrified eyes from side to side, the father had not the courage to witness so painful a sight, and would flee from the bedroom, shaking and aghast. He was a man who lacked the courage to confront sufferings of such magnitude, doubtless owing to his moral deficiency; he felt fearful, perturbed, and in a sense responsible for so great a calamity and such terrible anguish. Confident of Rufina's exquisite care, the grieving father had no need to stay at Valentín's bedside; indeed, he was something of a nuisance there, for if he stayed he would be sure, in his consternation, to make a mistake in the medicines, giving the poor child something that might hasten his death. What he did do was to keep tireless vigil, to approach the bedroom door every little while to see what was going on, to listen to the child's voice, in delirium or moaning; but if the moans were particularly heartrending or the delirium very pronounced, what Torquemada felt was an instinctive desire to run away and hide with his grief in the uttermost corner of the earth.

That afternoon Bailón, the butcher from downstairs, the tailor from the main floor, and the photographer from upstairs came to visit with him, all of them making great efforts to console him with time-honored phrases; but Torquemada, unable to sustain the conversation on such a sad subject, thanked them brusquely and abstractedly. All he seemed capable of was to sigh gustily, pace up and down, drink long gulps of water, and occasionally crash his fist against the wall. What a terrible business! So many vanished hopes! That flower of the world, cut down and withered! It was enough to drive a man mad. The collapse of the whole universe would have seemed more natural than the death of that fabulous child who had come to earth to illuminate it with the light of his talent. Fine things God did, or humanity, or whoever the accursed being was who invented the world and put us into it! For, if they were going to take Valentín away from him, why had they brought him here, giving him, the good Torquemada, the privilege of having fathered such a prodigy? Fine tricks Providence was up to, or humanity, or the plaguey Whole, as Bailón called it! To take that boy away, that shining light of science, and leave all the fools here below! Did that show common sense? Wasn't there every right to rebel against the ones up there, to berate them and send them packing? If Valentín died, what was left in the world? Darkness, ignorance. And for his father, what a blow! For we can imagine everything that Don Francisco would be when his son became a man and started to be famous, to confound all the sages, to turn the whole of science upside down! In that case Torquemada would be the second most important person in humanity; and, solely for the glory of having fathered the great mathematician, would deserve to be placed on a throne. What an engineer Valentín would make if he lived! Surely he would build railways that would go from here to Peking in five minutes, and balloons to sail the skies, and ships to go right under the water, and other things never seen before or even dreamed of. And the planet was going to lose these easy achievements because of a stupid judgment handed down by the ones who give life and take it away! All pure envy, nothing but envy. Up there, in the invisible spaces of high heaven, someone had decided to make trouble for Torquemada. But . . . but . . . suppose it wasn't envy, but a punishment? Suppose it had been decided this way in order to crush the cruel miser, the tyrannical landlord, the merciless moneylender? Ah! When this idea came into his head, Torquemada felt like running to the nearest wall and smashing himself against it. But he soon reacted, and could think more calmly. No, it could not be a punishment, for he was not bad, and if he had been he would make amends. It was envy, dislike, and ill will that they had for him because he was the father of such a splendid celebrity. They wanted to chop off his future and snatch away the happiness and enormous riches of his latter years, for his son, if he lived, would surely earn a lot of money, a tremendous lot, and that was why the heavens were plotting against him. But (and he thought this sincerely) he would renounce his son's monetary gains, as long as they left him the glory—yes, the glory!—for Torquemada's own earnings were quite sufficient for his business. The last paroxysm of his fevered brain was to renounce all the materialism of his son's knowledge, as long as they let him have the glory.

When Bailón was left alone with him, he told Don Francisco that he had to be philosophical; and as Torquemada did not clearly understand the word's meaning and application, the sibyl explained his idea in the following form: "It's best that you resign yourself, considering our insignificance in the face of these great evolutions of matter—or rather, vital substance. We are atoms, friend Don Francisco, nothing but foolish atoms. Let us respect the dispositions of the vast All to which we belong, and then let sorrows come. That's what philosophy, or religion if you like, is for: to face up to adversity. For if it weren't so, we could not live."

Torquemada accepted it all, except for resigning himself. There was no fountain in his soul from which such consolation could flow, and he did not even understand the concept. And as the other, after having eaten a good dinner, continued to insist on these ideas, Don Francisco felt an urge to give him a couple of punches, destroying in an instant the most expressive profile ever drawn by Michelangelo. But he only stared at Bailón with terrifying eyes, and the other took fright and put an end to his theological ramblings.

During the evening Quevedito and the other doctor spoke to Torquemada in the gloomiest possible terms. They had little or no hope, though they dared not say categorically that they had lost it, and left the door open to the healing powers of nature and the mercy of God. That was a horrible night. Poor Valentín was burning in an invisible fire. His flushed, dry face, his eyes lighted with a sinister glow, his restless tossings and turnings, his abrupt movements in the bed, as if he were trying to flee from something that frightened him, were an appalling spectacle that lay heavy on the heart. When Don Francisco, worn out with grief, approached the opening where the double doors stood ajar and stole a timid glance inside, he thought he could hear in the child's labored breathing a sound like the crackling of his flesh toasting in the fever's fire. He listened to the incoherent phrases of delirium, and heard him say, "x squared, less one, divided by two, plus five x less two, divided by four, equals x times x plus two, divided by twelve. . . Papa, Papa, the characteristic of the logarithm of a whole has as many units, less one, as . . ." No torment of the Inquisition could rival the torture Torquemada suffered as he heard these things. They were stray sparks of his son's astonishing intelligence, hovering over the flames that were consuming him. He fled so as not to hear the gentle little voice, and spent more than half an hour lying on the parlor sofa, clutching his head with both hands as if it were trying to fly off. Suddenly he got up, struck by an idea; he went to the writing desk where he kept his money, took out a roll of coins which were apparently small ones and, emptying it into his trousers pocket, put on his cape and hat, picked up the key, and went out.

He emerged from the door as if in pursuit of a debtor. After walking for a long time, he stopped on a street corner, looked in a confused way from side to side and, like a creditor stalking his victim, resumed his hurried walk. As he walked he could hear the coins jingling against his right leg. His impatience and uneasiness were great, for that night he did not find what so often came to meet him on other nights, annoying and vexing him.

At last—thanks be to God—a beggar approached.

"Take it, man, take it. Where the devil are you all hiding tonight? When nobody needs you, you swarm like flies, and when somebody goes looking for you to help you, nothing's there."

Soon there appeared one of those decent beggars who ask for alms, hat in hand, with tearful courtesy: "Señor, a poor unemployed clerk . . ."

"Here, take some more. That's what we charitable men are for, to help in misfortune. Tell me, haven't you begged from me on other nights? Well, I want you to know that I didn't give you anything then because I was in a great hurry. And another night, and still another, I didn't give you anything because I had no change; but as for the desire to give, I certainly had that."

Naturally the beggar-clerk was in ecstasy and incapable of expressing his gratitude adequately. A little farther on, "the Ghost" emerged from a side street. She was a woman who begs in the lower end of the Calle de la Salud, dressed in black, with a heavy veil covering her face.

"Take it, take it, señora. Now let them tell me that I've never given alms. Don't you think that's a wicked lie? Get along now, you must have collected enough coins for tonight. Anyway, people say that begging as you do, with that veil over your face, you've piled up quite a fortune. Go on home, it's very cold . . . and pray to God for me."

In the Calle del Carmen, in the Calle de Preciados, and in the Puerta del Sol, he gave a small coin to each child who appeared.

"Hey, youngster! Are you begging or what are you doing, standing there like a half-wit?"

This remark was addressed to a little boy who stood leaning against a wall with his hands behind his back, barefoot and with a muffler wound around his neck. The child put out a hand that was stiff with cold.

"Go on, take it. What, didn't your heart tell you that I was going to come along and help you? Are you cold and hungry? Take some more, and run along home if you have one. Here I am to help you out of a tight spot; I mean, to share a crust of bread with you, for I'm poor too, and worse off than you are, you know? Because cold and hunger can be borne; but, oh, my, other things . . . !"

He hastened his step without pausing to look at the mocking expression on the face of the child he had favored, and kept on giving and giving until only a few coins were left in his pocket. As he hurried home in retreat, he looked up at the sky, something alien to his custom, for though he occasionally glanced at it to see what the weather was like, he had never, until that night, really contemplated it. How very many stars there were! And how clear and shining, each in its proper place, millions and millions of beautiful and solemn eyes that cannot see how insignificant we are. What especially took the miser's breath away was the idea that that whole sky could be indifferent to his terrible grief, or rather, ignorant of it. But for all that, as a beautiful sight, how beautiful the stars were! There were small, middle-sized, and big ones; something like pesetas, half-duros and duros. The following thought passed through the celebrated moneylender's mind: "If he gets well, he'll have to make this calculation for me: If we minted all the stars in the sky, how much would they produce at five per cent compound interest in the centuries since all this has been in existence?"

He reached home at about one o'clock, feeling some respite from the anguish in his soul; he went to sleep fully dressed, and the next morning Valentín's fever had abated considerably. Could there be hope? The doctors gave him only vague hopes, hedging their opinion by saying that everything depended on whether the fever rose during the afternoon. The usurer, in a great state of excitement, clutched at that feeble hope as a shipwrecked sailor seizes a bit of flotsam. He would live, he had to live!

"Papa," Rufina told him, weeping, "pray to the Virgin of Carmen and stop talking about humanity."

"D'you think I should? I'm perfectly willing to. But I warn you that without good works you can't trust everything to the Virgin. And there *will* be Christian acts, no matter what it costs; you can be sure of that. Works of charity, that's the whole trick. I'll clothe the naked, visit the sick, console the sorrowful. God knows full well that that's what I intend to do, He knows it full well. Let's not have Him come out with the excuse that He didn't know it. I mean, as for knowing it, He knows it. Now He has to want to do something about it."

The high fever returned that night, and was very severe. Purges and emetics had no effect. The poor child's legs were burned from mustard plasters, and his head was a pitiful sight from the embrocations used to bring out an artificial eruption. In the afternoon, when Rufina cut his hair to relieve his head, Torquemada listened to the clicking of the scissors as if they were cutting into his own heart. They had to buy more ice and put it on the boy's head in bags, and then iodoform had to be brought. The Worse ran these errands with feverish activity, leaving and entering the house at frequent intervals. On his way home after dusk had fallen, as he turned the corner of the Calle de Hita, he met an old ragged beggar wearing a pair of army trousers and no hat, with a tattered jacket thrown over his shoulders that showed his bare chest. A more venerable face could not be found outside the illustrations in *The Christian Year*. Like Saint Peter, he had a bristling beard and a brow full of wrinkles; his pate was shiny and there were two curly white locks at his temples.

"Señor, señor," he said, trembling with intense cold, "look at the state I'm in. Look at me."

Torquemada passed him by and stopped a short distance away; he turned back, hesitated for a moment, and at last went his way. The following idea flashed through his brain: "If only I'd been wearing the old cape instead of the new one."

SIX

And as he entered his door, Torquemada muttered, "Curse me! I shouldn't have let that act of Christian charity slip through my fingers."

He set down the medicine he was carrying and, changing his cape, hurried out again. A little later Rufina, seeing him enter without an outer garment, said in a frightened tone, "But Papa, how forgetful you are! Where have you left your cape?"

"My darling daughter," replied the miser, lowering his voice and assuming a very remorseful expression, "you don't understand the meaning of a good act of charity, of humanity. Are you asking about my cape? Well may you ask. The fact is, I gave it to a poor old man who was almost naked and half dead with cold. I'm like that. I don't fool around when I take pity on the poor. I might seem hard sometimes; but when I soften up . . . I see that I've frightened you. What does a miserable piece of cloth matter?"

"Was it the new one?"

"No, the old one. And now, believe me, my conscience bothers me for not having given him the new one. And it vexes me, too, because I told you about it. Charity shouldn't be shouted from the housetops."

They made no further reference to this, for both had more serious matters to attend to. Rufina was completely exhausted and could hardly stand; for four nights she had not been to bed; but her valiant spirit still kept her on her feet, as diligent and loving as a Sister of Charity. Thanks to the cleaning woman they had in the house, its young mistress could rest at intervals, and the ragpicker of the household stayed in the afternoons to help the cleaning woman with kitchen tasks. She was a little old creature who had collected the garbage and a few leftovers of food *ab initio*—that is, ever since Torquemada and Doña Silvia were married—and had done the same in the house of Doña Silvia's parents. They called her "Tía Roma," I don't know why (but I'm inclined to believe that this name is a corruption of Jerónima), and she was so old, so old and ugly that her face looked like a bunch of spiderwebs mixed with ashes; her squashed and pitted nose was completely shapeless; her round, toothless mouth waxed and waned according to the stretchings of the wrinkles that formed it. Above it, in that muddle of dusty skin, shone two fish-eyes within a circle of watery crimson. The rest of her person disappeared under wrappings of rags and inside her many-times-mended skirt, in which there were scraps of a dress that had belonged to Doña Silvia's mother when she was a girl. This poor woman was greatly attached to the household, whose sweepings she had collected daily for many long years; she had great esteem for Doña Silvia, who had always refused to give anyone else the leftover bones, scraps, and shreds; and she loved the children dearly—chiefly Valentín, before whom she abased herself with superstitious admiration. When she saw him gripped by that terrible illness, which according to her was a rupture of the talent in his head, Tía Roma knew no rest; she went to inquire morning and afternoon; she got into the boy's bedroom and sat for long hours beside his bed, gazing at him silently, her eyes like two inexhaustible fountains that poured tears over the sagging parchment of her face and neck.

The ragpicker left the bedroom to return to the kitchen and, in the dining room, found the master of the house who, seated at the table with his head on his arms, seemed abandoned to profound meditation. Tía Roma, owing to her long association and intimate position in the family, treated him with great familiarity.

"Pray, pray," she told him, standing in front of him and twisting the handkerchief with which she had been attempting to stanch her copious flow of grief, "pray, you really need to. Poor little love, how sick he is! Look, look" (pointing to the blackboard), "such pretty things as he wrote on that black frame of his. I don't understand what it says, but surely it must say that we ought to be good. The little angel knows so much! Maybe that's why God doesn't want to leave him with us."

"What do you know, Tía Roma?" said Torquemada, turning livid with rage. "He *will* leave him with us. D'you think, by any chance, that I'm a tyrant and a scoundrel, as stupid people and a few wastrels and defaulters think? If a man isn't careful, people give him the worst reputation in the world. But God knows the truth. . . It's nobody's business whether I have or haven't done works of charity these last few days. I don't like to be found out and have my good deeds advertised. You pray, too, pray till your mouth goes dry. You ought to have a grand reputation up there, seeing you've never had a peseta in your life. I'm going crazy, and I ask myself if it's my fault that I've earned a few cursed reales. Oh, Tía Roma, if you knew how heartsick I am! Ask God to let us keep Valentín, because if he dies I don't know what will happen. I'll go mad. I'll go out on the street and murder someone. My son is mine, dammit, and he's the glory of the world! If anyone tries to take him away from me . . . !"

"Oh, how awful!" murmured the old woman, choking up. "But who knows? Maybe the Virgin will work a miracle. I'm asking her to, with all the devotion that's in me. Give a push on your side, too, and promise to be at least halfway decent."

"Well, it won't be for want of trying. Tía Roma, leave me . . . leave me alone. I don't want to see anybody. I'm better off alone with my troubles."

Groaning, the old woman went out, and Don Francisco placed his hands on the table and rested his feverish brow upon them. He remained in this posture for I don't know how long, until his friend Bailón made him change it by patting him on the shoulder and saying, "Mustn't lose heart. Let's turn a tough face to misfortune, and not let the slut get us down. Leave cowardice for the women. Compared with nature, with the sublime Whole, we're just bits of atoms who don't know the half of what goes on."

"Go to the devil with your Wholes and all your pap," said Torquemada, his eyes blazing.

Bailón did not insist; judging that the better part lay in distracting him, taking his mind off those somber reflections, he spoke to him presently of a certain business transaction he had in his noggin.

Since the man who had rented his flock of donkeys and goats had annulled the contract, Bailón decided to exploit that industry on a grand scale, setting up a large, modern milk business with prompt home delivery service, fixed prices, a handsome retail store, telephone, etc. He had studied the matter and . . .

"Believe me, friend Don Francisco, it's a surefire deal, especially if we go in for cows as well, because in Madrid, milk—"

"Shut up about milk and about—What have I got to do with she-asses or cows?" yelled the Worse, standing up and looking scornfully at Bailón. "You see what kind of shape I'm in, dammit! Half dead with grief, and you come and talk to me about goddamned milk! Tell me how to fix it so that God will pay attention to us when we ask Him for what we need, talk to me about . . . I don't know how to explain it . . . about what it means to be good and to be bad . . . because either I'm a nitwit or that's one of the things that's a real poser."

"That it is, that it is, by golly!" said the sibyl with a self-important air, shaking his head and rolling his eyes heavenward.

At the moment, Bailón's posture was very different from that of his double in the Sistine Chapel: seated, his hands folded over the knob of his cane, the cane between his legs and both legs crossed at the same angle, his hat pushed back, his athletic body shapeless inside the overcoat with its greasy lapels, his shoulders and collar thick with dandruff. Yet, notwithstanding these prosaic details, the damnable fellow looked like Dante and had been a priest in Egypt! This plaguey humanity with its tricks . . .

"That it is," repeated the sibyl, preparing to enlighten his friend with an opinion of cardinal importance. "The good and the bad, as you might say, light and darkness!"

Bailón's speaking style was very different from that of his writings. This is very common. But on that occasion the solemnity of the example addled his brain so much that ideas came to his tongue in the very form of his literary school.

"Verily, man doubts and is confused in the face of the great problem. What is Good? What is Evil? My son, open your ears to the truth and your eyes to the light. The Good means to love our fellowmen. Let us love, and we will know what Good is; let us hate, and we will know what Evil is. Let us do good to all who hate us, and thorns will turn to flowers. The Just Man said this, and I say it too—wisdom of wisdom, knowledge of knowledge."

"Wisdom, and look out for trouble," muttered Torquemada disconsolately. "I knew that already, because that saying about 'push your neighbor to the wall' has always struck me as brutal. Let's not talk about that any more. I don't want to think about sad things. I say only that, if my son dies . . . heavens, I don't want to think about it . . . if he goes and dies on me, black and white are all the same to me."

At that instant they heard a harsh, strident cry, uttered by Valentín, which left both of them frozen with terror. It was the meningeal cry, like the peacock's crow. This strange encephalitic symptom had begun that morning, and revealed the desperate and horrifying course of the poor mathematical prodigy's illness. Torquemada would have hidden in the center of the earth not to hear that cry: he took refuge in his office, heedless of Bailón's exhortations, and slamming the door on his Dantesque phiz. From the hall they heard him opening the drawer of his work table, and almost at once he reappeared, stowing something in the inside pocket of his coat. He picked up his hat and left the house without a word.

I will explain what this meant and where the wretched Don Francisco was taking himself off to that afternoon. On the very day that Valentín had fallen ill, his father had received a letter from an old and long-suffering client or debtor of his, asking for a loan guaranteed by the furnishings of his house. Relations between victim and inquisitor dated back a long time, and the profits obtained by the latter had been enormous, for the other man was weak, very susceptible, and let himself be flayed, fried, and pickled as though he had been born for nothing else. There are people like that. But extremely bad times came upon him, and the gentleman was unable to recover his note. Almost daily the Worse assailed him, harassed him, put the rope around his neck and gave it a good tug, all without succeeding in extracting from him even the arrears of interest. My readers will easily understand the skinflint's rage when he received the letter asking for a new loan. What a shocking piece of insolence! Torquemada would have answered consigning him to the devil had not the child's illness made him so grief-stricken and disinclined to think of business matters. Two days passed, and along came another anguished missive, a cry *in extremis*, as if requesting extreme unction. In those short lines, in which the victim called upon his executioner's "gentlemanly feelings" and spoke of a debt of honor, he proposed the most frightful conditions, abased himself completely in the hope of softening the usurer's heart of bronze and obtaining an affirmative answer from him. Well, my hero took the letter, tore it to bits, and tossed it into the wastebasket, never giving the matter another thought. His head was in fine condition to be thinking about anyone's obligations and difficulties, be they those of the Holy Word itself!

But then came the occasion I have described, the conversations with

Tía Roma and Don José, and Valentín's cry. It was then that the shylock felt a sort of thrill go through him, the fire of inspiration was kindled in his noggin, and he seized his hat and went straightway in search of his hapless client, who was a respectable though not very intelligent person with an endless string of children and a wife with a craving for elegance. He had occupied good positions both in continental Spain and overseas, and in less than a year the usurer had relieved him of all that he had brought back (which was not much, for he was an honorable man). Then he got an unexpected inheritance from an uncle; but, as his wife had some confounded "Thursdays" which she used to attract and fete the best elements in society, the money from the inheritance had slipped away wonderfully fast and, without the poor man's knowing how or when, had wound up in Torquemada's capacious pocket. I don't know what the dickens got into the money in that household, but it acted like a needle rushing to the magnet of the accursed moneylender. The worst of it was that even after the family was up to its neck, that hussy of a "fashionable" wife was still ordering dresses from Paris, inviting her friends to "five o'clock tea," or thinking up other fripperies of the same kind.

Well then, off went Don Francisco to the house of the gentleman in question, who, to judge from the anguished tone of his letter, seemed to be on the point of winding up in court with all his elegance and his teas, and of exposing a respectable name to derision and dishonor. On the way, the miser felt someone tug at his cape. He turned around . . . and who do you think it was? Why, a woman who looked a very Magdalen with her grief-stricken face and beautiful hair, carelessly covered with a red and blue checkered handkerchief. Her lovely face was up to the highest standard, but already worn by exhausting battles. It was easy to see that she was a woman who knew how to dress, though on that occasion she was in rags, scarcely decent, with a much-mended skirt, a ragged shawl, and boots—heavens, what boots, and how they disfigured that pretty foot!

"Isidora!" exclaimed Don Francisco, looking overjoyed, a rare thing for him. "Where are you going in such a shabby condition?"

"I was on my way to your house. Señor Don Francisco, have pity on us. Why are you so harsh, so unyielding? Can't you see the straits we're in? Haven't you even a touch of humanity?"

"My dear girl, you're mistaken about me. Suppose I told you that

I'd been thinking about you, that I was remembering the message you sent me yesterday by the concierge's son and what you yourself told me day before yesterday on the street?"

"Imagine your not doing anything to help us in our need!" said the woman, beginning to cry. "Martín is dying . . . poor boy . . . in that freezing attic. No bed, no medicines, nothing to cook a miserable stew so I can give him a cup of broth. What agony! Don Francisco, be a Christian and don't abandon us. Of course, we have no credit, but Martín has half a dozen lovely sketches left. You'll see. . . The one of the Guadarrama mountains is beautiful. So is the one of La Granja with those little trees . . . and the one . . . I don't know which one. They're all very pretty. I'll bring them to you. But don't be wicked, and take pity on the poor artist."

"Eh, eh, don't cry, woman! Look, I'm in a terrible situation myself. I have such sorrow in my soul, Isidora, that . . . if you keep on crying I'll break down too. Go home and wait for me there. I'll come in a little while. What? D'you doubt my word?"

"But will you really come? By the Most Holy Virgin, don't deceive me."

"Have I ever deceived you before? You may have other complaints about me, but that particular one . . . ."

"Can I really expect you? How good you would be if you were to come and help us! Martín will be so happy when I tell him!"

"Get along with you, and don't worry. Wait for me, and until I come, pray to God for me with all your strength."

SEVEN

He soon reached his client's home, which was an excellent flat on the main floor, furnished with great luxury and elegance, overlooking the fashionable Calle de San Bernardino. While he waited to be announced, the Worse observed the handsome coat rack and the superb draperies in the drawing room, which could be glimpsed through the half-open door, and such a degree of magnificence brought to his mind the following reflection: "As for the furnishings, they're good. They certainly are good." His friend received Don Francisco in his study, and scarcely had Torquemada inquired after the family when he dropped heavily into a chair, showing signs of great consternation.

"But what's wrong with you?" said the other.

"Don't speak to me, don't speak to me, Señor Don Juan. My heart's in my mouth . . . My son!"

"Poor child! I know he is very ill. But have you no hope?"

"No, señor . . . I mean, hope, what I would call hope . . . I don't know, I'm nearly out of my mind. My head feels like a volcano."

"I know what that is!" observed the other, sadly. "I've lost two boys who were my heart's delight, one at four, the other at eleven years of age."

"But your grief can't be as great as mine. As a father, I'm not like other fathers, for my child isn't like other children: he is a miracle of learning. Oh, Don Juan, my dear Don Juan, have pity on me! Listen. When I received your first letter, I couldn't attend to it. I couldn't think for grief. But I remembered you, and said to myself, 'That poor Don Juan, what a bad time he must be having!' I got your second message, and then I said to myself, 'I'm certainly not going to leave him in that slough of despond. We ought to help one another in our misfortunes.' That's what I thought. It's only that with all the hubbub at home I didn't have time to come or to answer. But today, even though I was half dead with grief, I said, 'I'll go. I'll hurry to take that good friend Don Juan out of purgatory. . .' And here I am, to tell you that even though you owe me seventy thousand-odd reales, which come to more than ninety thousand with arrears of interest, and though I've had to grant you several delays, and—frankly—I'm afraid I'll have to grant you some more, I've decided to make you that loan on the furniture so you can avoid the disaster that's coming upon you."

"It has already been avoided," replied Don Juan, regarding the moneylender with the utmost chilliness. "I no longer need the loan."

"You don't need it?" exclaimed the miser, disconcerted. "Just take note of one thing, Don Juan. I'll give it to you—at twelve percent."

Observing that the other was making negative gestures, Don Francisco rose to his feet and, clutching at his cape, which was slipping off his shoulders, took several steps toward Don Juan, placed his hand on his shoulder and said, "You don't want to deal with me because of that business of whether I'm tightfisted or not. It seems to me that twelve percent . . .! When did you see better terms?"

"The interest seems very reasonable to me, but, I repeat, I no longer need it."

"You must have won first prize in the lottery, for the love of . . ."

exclaimed Torquemada coarsely. "Don Juan, don't joke with me. Do you doubt that I'm speaking to you seriously? Because all that about your not needing it—hell! You? You, who could swallow the whole mint in one gulp, let alone that little bit of money. Don Juan, Don Juan, I want you to know, if you don't know already, that I have my humanity too, like any mother's son, that I have a concern for my fellowman and do good even to those that despise me. You hate me, Don Juan; you detest me, don't deny it, because you can't pay me: that's obvious. Well, so you can see what I'm capable of, I'll give it to you at five . . . at five!"

And, as the other again shook his head negatively, Torquemada became more upset than ever, and raising his arms, which naturally meant that his cape slipped to the floor, he uttered this tirade:

"Not at five either? Listen, my friend, at less than five, damn it all, unless you want me to give you the shirt off my back as well! When were you ever offered a better deal? I don't know what else you can want, you plaster saint. This business is driving me crazy. So you can see, so you can see how far my generosity goes, I'll give it to you with no interest."

"Many thanks, friend Don Francisco. I don't doubt your good intentions. But we've settled the whole matter. In view of the fact that you didn't answer me, I sought out a relative of mine and plucked up the courage to tell him about my unhappy situation. If only I had done so before!"

"Well, your relative has certainly done a fine piece of business. Now he can say that he's baked a mighty thin loaf. If he goes in for many more deals like that . . . Well, you haven't wanted it from me, so it's your loss. And now try to go around saying that I haven't a good heart, when it's you who hasn't got one. . ."

"I? That *is* quite a joke."

"Yes, you, you," said Torquemada indignantly. "Well, I'm off. Some people who really need me are waiting for me elsewhere, where they're expecting my arrival like spring showers. I'm not needed here. Farewell."

Don Juan took leave of him at the door, and Torquemada descended the steps, grumbling, "There's no use trying to deal with ungrateful people. I'm going to see what I can do for those poor young folks. What would become of them without me?"

He lost no time in arriving at the other house, where he was awaited so anxiously. It was on the Calle de la Luna, quite a handsome build-ing, where an architect was the main-floor tenant; families of modest means occupied the floors above, and, just under the roof, a jumble of poor folk lived. Torquemada went up and down the dark corridor look-ing for a door. The numbers on them were useless, for they could not be seen. Fortunately, Isidora heard his step and opened the door.

"Ah, thank heaven for men who keep their word! Come in, come in."

Don Francisco found himself in a room whose sloping ceiling touched the floor on the side opposite the door. Above was a dirty skylight with some of its broken panes stuffed with rags and papers. A tiled floor was covered with occasional scraps of carpet. On one side of the room were an open trunk, two chairs, and a lighted portable stove; on the other was a bed on which lay a man of about thirty years of age, covered with a number of blankets and stray pieces of clothing, half dressed and half wrapped. He was handsome, with a sharp-pointed beard, large eyes, and a beautiful brow, extremely emaciated and slightly flushed about the cheekbones. There was a greenish hollow at his temples and his ears were as transparent as the wax in the votive candles that are hung on altars. Torquemada looked at him without replying to his greeting, and thought to himself, "The poor fellow is more consumptive than Traviata! Poor lad—such a good painter and such a bad head for business. . . He could have earned so much money!"

"You see, Don Francisco, the state I'm in . . . with this cold that doesn't want to go away. Sit down. How grateful I am for your kind-ness!"

"You needn't thank me for a thing. It was the least I could do. Doesn't God command us to clothe the sick, give water to the sorrow-ful, visit the naked? Oh, I get everything mixed up! What a head I have on me! I was saying that us softhearted men are here to help out in misfortune—yes, indeed."

He looked at the garret walls, which were almost entirely covered with a host of landscape studies, fastened to the wall or leaning against it, some of them upside down.

"There are still some very nice things here."

"As soon as I can shake off my cold, I'm going to the country," said the sick man, his eyes alight with fever. "I have an idea—such an idea! I think I'll be well in a week or ten days if you help me, Don Francisco, and then I'll go straightaway to the country, the country . . ."

"The only bit of country you're going to is the cemetery, and soon," thought Torquemada, and added aloud, "Yes, that's a question of a week or ten days—no more. Then you'll go out in a carriage. Do you know your attic's a little chilly? Goodness! Let me wrap myself up in my cape."

"You're going to be surprised," said the sick man, sitting up. "I've started to feel better here. The last few days we spent in the studio— Isidora will tell you—I was terribly ill, so much so that we got frightened and—"

He began to cough so violently that it seemed he would strangle. Isidora hurried to raise him higher, plumping up the pillows. It seemed that the poor chap's eyes would start out of his head, his shattered lungs panted laboriously like bellows that can neither expel nor take in air; he clenched his fingers, and at last lay prostrate and corpselike. Isidora wiped the sweat from his brow, tidied the bedclothes that had fallen to both sides of the narrow couch, and gave him a soothing drink.

"What an awful spasm that was!" exclaimed the artist when he had recovered from his coughing fit.

"Speak as little as possible," Isidora advised him.

"I'll settle things with Don Francisco," said the sick man. "You'll see how we'll come to an agreement. This Don Francisco is a better man than he seems. He's a saint disguised as a devil, isn't he?"

As he laughed he showed his splendid teeth, one of the few attractive features that were left him in his sad decline. Torquemada, assuming the role of a charitable man, told Isidora to sit beside him and placed his hand on her shoulder, saying, "Indeed we will come to an agreement. With you it's easy to agree, Isidorita, because you're not like those other females with no manners. You're a decent person who has come down in the world, but you have that air of refinement, like the true daughter of marquises. I know all about it, and I know that those rascals in the ecclesiastical court took away from you the position in life that you deserved."

"Lord!" exclaimed Isidora, exhaling with a long sigh all the sad and happy memories of her past, which was a veritable novel. "Let's not talk about that. . . Let's get back to reality, Don Francisco. Have you quite realized what our situation is? Martín was locked out of his studio. We had so many debts that we could save only what you see here. Since then we've had to pawn all his clothes and mine, to be able to eat. I have only the clothes on my back. Look, I'm a disgrace! And he has nothing, only what you see on the bed. We'll have to get the most necessary articles out of pawn and take a warmer room, the one on the fourth floor that's for rent. Then we'll light a fire, buy medicine, and at least cook a decent stew every day. A gentleman from the home charity organization brought me two certificates yesterday and told me to go there, where the office is, but I'm ashamed to turn up there looking so dreadful. We people who have been born in a certain position, Señor Don Francisco, no matter how far we fall, never quite reach the bottom. But let's get down to business. For all this that I've just told you about, and so that Martín can get better and go to the country, we need three thousand reales . . . and I'm not saying four so as not to frighten you off. It's the last time we'll ask. Yes, my dear Don Francisco, and we trust in the goodness of your heart."

"Three thousand reales!" said the usurer, assuming the expression of reflective doubt that he employed for cases of charity, an expression that, like those used in diplomacy, was merely a formula for delay. "Three thousand pretty little reales! My dear girl, look."

And, forming a perfect doughnut with his thumb and index finger, he showed it to Isidora and continued as follows: "I don't know if I can spare three thousand reales just at the moment. In any case, it seems to me that you can manage with less. Think it over carefully and lower your figures. I've made up my mind to protect and help you so that you'll have better luck. I'll go to the point of sacrifice, even taking the bread out of my mouth so that you can kill your hunger, but . . . you must see that I have to look out for my interests, too."

"We'll agree to any interest you want, Don Francisco," said the invalid firmly, apparently wishing to end the matter quickly.

"I'm not referring to the materialism of the interest on the money, but to my interests, naturally, to my interests. And I take it for granted that you intend to pay me some day."

"But of course," replied Isidora and Martín in chorus.

And Torquemada said to himself, "You'll pay me on Judgment Day in the afternoon; I know this is money thrown away."

The sick man sat up in bed and said enthusiastically to the money-lender, "My friend, do you think that my aunt, the one who's in Puerto Rico, would leave me in this situation when she finds out about it? I can just see the draft for four or five hundred pesos she's sure to send me. I wrote to her by the last mailboat."

"Probably your aunt will send you five hundred good goddamns," thought Torquemada. And aloud: "You'll have to give me some sort of guarantee, too, that is, I think that . . ."

"Take them! The sketches. Choose the ones you want."

Casting an expert's gaze all around him, Torquemada expounded his thoughts in the following terms: "Very well, my friends. I'm going to say something that will bowl you over. I've taken pity on such poverty. I can't witness misfortune like this without instantly hastening to help. Ah, What kind of an idea did you have of me! Because once before you owed me a little bit and I pressed you and squeezed you, d'you think I'm made of marble? You sillies, it was because then I saw you living high and squandering money, and frankly, the money that I earn with so much effort isn't meant to be thrown away on fancy dinners. You don't know me, I assure you that you don't know me. Just compare the cruelty of those bloodsuckers who locked you out of the studio and left you mother-naked; compare that, I say, with my generosity and this tender heart that God has given me. I'm so good—so good—that I have to congratulate myself and thank myself for the good that I do. You'll see what a stroke of generosity. Look . . ."

The doughnut reappeared, accompanied by these solemn words: "I'm going to give you the three thousand reales, and I'm going to give them to you right now. But that's not the best part, for I'm going to give them to you at no interest. How about it, is that generous or isn't it generous?"

"Don Francisco," exclaimed Isidora effusively, "let me give you a hug."

"And I'll give you another if you come over here," cried the sick man, trying to jump out of bed.

"Yes, come and give me all the hugs you like," said the miser, allowing both to embrace him. "But don't praise me unduly, because these actions are the duty of everyone who looks out for humanity, and there's no great merit in them. Hug me again, as you would your father, and have pity on me, for I need it, too. Here, I'll start to cry if I'm not careful, for I'm so tenderhearted, so . . ."

"My very dear Don Francisco," declared the consumptive, again bundling himself up in his rags, "you are the most Christian, most perfect, most humanitarian person under the sun. Isidora, bring the inkwell, the pen, and the stamped paper you bought yesterday, and I'll make out an IOU."

His companion brought what he asked for, and while the ill-starred young man was writing, Torquemada thoughtfully fixed his reflective gaze upon the floor, with one finger supporting his brow. As he grasped the document that Isidora offered him, he looked at his debtors with a paternal expression and employed the effeminate and treacly register of his voice to tell them, "My dear children, you don't know me. No doubt you think that I'm going to keep this IOU. Well, you're a pretty pair of fools. When I do a work of charity, it's a real one. I put my heart and soul into it. I'm not lending you the three thousand reales; I'm giving them to you, for your pretty faces. Look what I'm doing: zip, zip."

He tore up the paper. Isidora and Martín believed it because they were seeing it, for they couldn't have believed it otherwise.

"That's what I call a real man. Don Francisco, many thanks," said Isidora, much moved.

And the other, covering his mouth with the bedclothes to hold in an incipient fit of coughing, said, "By Most Holy Mary, what a good man!"

"The only thing I'll do," said Don Francisco, rising to his feet and examining the pictures more closely, "is to accept a couple of sketches as a remembrance—this one with the snow-capped mountains and that one with the donkeys grazing. Look, Martín, I'll also take that little seascape and this bridge with the ivy on it, if you don't mind."

Martín's coughing fit had come on and was almost choking him. Isidora, hastening to help him, cast a furtive glance at the pictures and at the scrutiny with which the wily miser was selecting them.

"I accept them as a remembrance," he said, putting them aside, "And if you don't mind, I'll take this other one too. I have to advise you of one thing, however. If you're afraid that these paintings will be damaged by moving, bring them to my house and I'll take care of them, and you can pick them up any day you like. Hey, is that confounded cough getting better? By next week you won't be coughing at all, not at all. You'll go to the country—out there by the bridge of San Isidro. Oh, what a head I have on my shoulders! I was forgetting the main thing, which is to give you the three thousand reales. Come here, Isidorita, look sharp . . . a one-hundred-peseta note, another, another . . ." He counted them out one by one, wetting his fingers with saliva between notes to keep them from sticking together.

"Seven hundred pesetas . . . I haven't a fifty-peseta note, my dear. I'll give it to you another day. You have a hundred and forty duros there, that is, two thousand eight hundred reales.

EIGHT

Isidora almost cried for joy when she saw the money, and the sick man cheered up so much that he seemed to have recovered his health. Poor things, they were so badly off! They had been through such horrible privations and miseries. They had met two years before at the house of a moneylender who was skinning them both alive. They confided their respective situations to each other, sympathized with each other, and fell in love with each other; Isidora slept at the studio that very night. The unlucky artist and the fallen woman made a pact to merge their respective miseries and drown their sorrows in the sweet draught of a truly conjugal intimacy. Love made misfortune easy to bear. They married at the altar of common law, and two days after their union, they were sincerely in love and ready to die together and to share the little good and much greater bad that life would bring them. They struggled against poverty, against usury, and went down to defeat without ceasing to love each other: he was always affectionate, she solicitous and tender; both were a living example of abnegation, of those lofty virtues which shamefacedly hide so that law and religion cannot see them, just as the nobleman dressed in tatters hides from his well-dressed peers.

Torquemada gave them another hug, saying in his syrupy voice, "My children, be good and learn from the example I've given you. Help the poor, love your neighbors, and have pity on me as I've had pity on you, for I am very wretched."

"I know," said Isidora, slipping out of the miser's arms, "that your boy is ill. Poor little thing! You'll see, he'll get well now. . ."

"Now? Why now?" asked Torquemada very anxiously.

"Well . . . what do I know? It seems to me that God must help you, must reward your good works."

"Oh, if my son dies," said Don Francisco in desperation, "I don't know what will become of me!"

"There must be no talk of dying!" cried the invalid, whom possession of the blessed money had exhilarated and excited as much as a dose of the strongest stimulant. "What's this about dying? Nobody's going to die around here. Don Francisco, the boy won't die. I should say not! What's the matter with him? Meningitis? I had a really bad case of it when I was ten years old, and they'd already given me up for dead when I started to mend, and I lived, and here I am, with every intention of living to be old, and I will, because now I'm going to pitch this cold right out the door. The boy will live, Don Francisco, I have no doubt; he'll live."

"He will live," repeated Isidora. "I'm going to pray to the Virgin of Carmen for him."

"Yes, my dear, to the Virgin of Carmen," said Torquemada, raising his handkerchief to his eyes. "I think that's fine. With everyone giving a shove on his side, let's see if among us all . . ."

The artist, beside himself with joy, wanted to pass it on to the afflicted father, and half fell out of bed to tell him, "Don Francisco, don't cry, the boy will live. My heart tells me so, a secret voice tells me so. We'll all live, and we'll be happy."

"Oh, my dear boy!" exclaimed the Worse, embracing him again. "May God hear you! What tremendous consolation you're giving me!"

"You've consoled us too. God has to reward you for it. We'll live, yes indeed we will. Look, look; the first day I can go out, we'll all go to the country, the boy too, and have a picnic. Isidora will fix the food for us, and we'll have a lovely day celebrating our return to health."

"We'll go, we'll go," said the skinflint effusively, forgetting his previous thoughts about the "country" to which Martín would soon be going. "Yes, and we'll have a fine old time, and we'll give money to all the poor folks we meet. What relief I feel since I did that good deed!

No, don't praise me for it. Look here: it occurs to me that I can do you another much bigger favor."

"What is it? Tell us, Don Francisquito."

"It's occurred to me . . . It's not an idea that just came to me. I've had it for some time. It's occurred to me that if Isidora still has the papers concerning her inheritance and the succession of the House of Aransis, we must try to get that matter settled."

Isidora stared at him, half confused and half astonished. "That business again?" was all she said.

"Yes, yes, Don Francisco is right," assented the poor consumptive, who was in an expansive mood, giving himself over almost drunkenly to insane optimism. "We'll try it. Things can't stay as they are."

"I have the suspicion," added Torquemada, "that the people who took part in the suit the first time were either not very clever or were bribed by the old marquis. We must look into it, we must look into it."

"Just as soon as I throw off this cold. Isidora, my clothes, bring me my clothes. I want to get up. How good I feel now! I feel like painting, Don Francisco. As soon as the boy is out of bed, I want to paint his portrait."

"Thanks, thanks. You're very good. All three of us are very good people, aren't we? Hug me again, and pray to God for me. I must be off, for I'm so nervous that I can hardly stand it."

"Come now, the boy is better. He'll be saved," repeated the artist with increasing exhilaration. "Why, I can see him right now. I can't be mistaken."

Isidora prepared to go out to the pawnshop with part of the money, but the poor artist had another, much more acute attack of coughing and gasping, and she had to stay with him. Don Francisco said goodbye in the most affectionate words he knew and, seizing the pictures, departed with them under his cape. As he descended the stairs he said, "Well, now, what a fine thing it is to be good! I feel such a sensation inside, such consolation! If only Martín is right! If only that darling of my heart will get well! Let's hurry home. I'm not convinced, I'm not convinced. This hothead has all the illusions of consumptives in the last stages. But who knows? He's mistaken about himself, for sure, and right about the rest. Where he's going to, and soon, is a niche in the cemetery. But dying people often have second sight, and maybe he's *seen* Valentín's improvement. I must hurry, I must hurry. What a bother these cursed pictures are! They won't say I'm a tyrant and a shylock now, for it's not every day a person does a fine thing like that! Nobody can say that I take out loans in pictures, because if I sold these sketches, no one would give me half of what I paid. It's true that if he dies they'll be worth more, because here in Spain when an artist is alive, nobody gives a damn about him, and when he dies of poverty or exhaustion they praise him to the skies, call him a genius and I don't know what all. It seems as if I'll never get home. How far away it is, even though it's so near!"

He went up the stairs of his house three steps at a time, and Tía Roma opened the door, firing these words at point-blank range: "Señor, it seems the child is a little calmer."

Don Francisco heard this, dropped the pictures, and hugged the old woman all at once. The ragpicker was crying, and the Worse gave her three kisses on the forehead. Then he went straight to the sick boy's bedroom and looked in the door. Rufina rushed toward him to say, "Since noon he's been much quieter. See? It seems the poor angel is sleeping. Who knows—maybe he'll recover. But I daren't have hopes, for fear we'll lose them this evening."

Torquemada was beside himself with dread and anxiety. The poor man's nerves were stretched taut and he could not stay quiet for a moment. At one instant he felt like crying and at the next like laughing. He paced to and fro from the dining room to the bedroom door, from the bedroom to his office, from the office to his sitting room. During one of these flittings he called Tía Roma and, shutting himself into his bedroom with her, invited her to sit down and said, "Tía Roma, do you think the boy will recover?"

"Señor, it will be as God wills, and that's it. I prayed for him last night and this morning to the Virgin of Carmen, with such devotion, I couldn't have prayed harder, blubbering like a baby. Can't you see how red my eyes are?"

"And do you think . . . ?"

"I have hope, señor. As long as he's not a corpse, there has to be hope, no matter what the doctors say. If the Virgin says he'll live, the doctors can go to the devil. Another thing: last night I fell asleep while

I was praying, and I thought the Virgin came right down in front of me and nodded her head, yes. Another thing, haven't you prayed?"

"Yes, woman, of course. What questions you ask! I'm going to tell you something important. Look here."

He opened a secretary in whose drawers he kept papers and valuable jewelry which had come into his hands as pledges for usurious loans; some were not yet his property, others he already owned. He spent a short time opening cases, and the fish-eyes of Tía Roma, which had never looked upon anything like them, lighted up with the splendors that came out of the boxes. As she later told it, there were emeralds as big as walnuts, diamonds that gave off pale rays, rubies like pomegranate seeds, and the finest gold, gold of the very best weight, which was worth hundreds of thousands. After opening a number of cases, Torquemada found what he was seeking: an enormous pearl the size of a hazelnut, with a beautiful sheen, and picking it up in his fingers, he showed it to the old woman.

"What d'you think of this pearl, Tía Roma?"

"It's really beautiful. I don't understand it. It's got to be worth thousands of millions, don't it?"

"Well, this pearl," said Torquemada triumphantly, "is for Our Lady the Virgin of Carmen. It's for her if she makes my son well. I'm showing it to you and letting you know what I mean to do so that you can tell her. If I tell her myself, for sure she won't believe me."

"Don Francisco," said Tía Roma, regarding him with infinite pity, "you must be off your nut. Tell me, for heaven's sake, what would the Virgin of Carmen want with that great big thing?"

"Why, so they can put it on her on her name day, the sixteenth of July. She'll look mighty fine with this on! It was a wedding present to the very honorable marquise of Tellería. Believe me, there aren't many pearls like this one."

"But, Don Francisco, you're acting like a simpleton. D'you really think the Virgin is going to help . . . for that chunk of nothing?"

"Look what a sheen. You could make a brooch out of it and put it on the Virgin's bosom, or on the Child."

"Devil take you! A fine lot of attention the Virgin pays to pearls and all that rubbish! Take my advice; sell it and give the money to the poor."

"Hey, that's not a bad idea," said the miser, putting away the jewel. "You know what you're talking about. I'll follow your advice, although if I'm to be frank, the idea of giving to the poor is foolish, because they spend everything you give them on brandy. But we'll fix things so that the money from the pearl won't wind up in the taverns. And now I want to talk to you about something else. Listen very carefully: d'you remember that once, when my daughter was walking in the outskirts of town with Quevedo and the Morejón girls, she happened to pass by where you live, in the direction of Tejares del Aragonés, and she went into your hut and came back and told me how horrified she was at the poverty and need she saw there? D'you remember that? Rufina told me that the place you live in is a pigsty: a filthy hovel made of mud bricks, old boards, and pieces of iron, with a roof of straw and dirt. She told me that neither you nor your grandchildren have a bed, and that you all sleep on a pile of rags; that the pigs and chickens you raise on garbage are the people out there, and you the animals. Yes, Rufina told me that, and I ought to have felt sorry for you and I didn't. I ought to have given you a bed, because you've served us faithfully; you loved my wife a lot, you love my children, and in all the years you've been coming here you've never stolen so much as a tenpenny nail. Well, then, even if it didn't come into my head to help you then, it has now."

So saying, he walked up to the bed and gave it a good slap with both hands, like the slap one gives to plump up the mattress when making beds.

"Tía Roma, come here. Touch right here. Look how soft. D'you see this wool mattress on top of a spring mattress? Well, it's for you, for you, so you can rest your stiff old bones and sprawl all over it."

The miser expected an explosion of gratitude for such a splendid gift, and thought he could already hear Tía Roma's blessings, when she began to sing a very different tune. Her spiderwebbed face seemed to swell, and from those sighted ulcers that yawned in place of eyes there came a glare of confusion and fright, as she turned her back on the bed and started for the door.

"Let be, let be," she said. "That's a fine thing to come to your mind— to give me mattresses that wouldn't even go through the door of my house! And even if they would go in . . . the devil take them! Just remember that I've spent an awful lot of years sleeping hard, like a queen, and I wouldn't sleep a wink on those soft things. God deliver me from lying down on them! D'you know what I say? That I want to die in peace. When the One with the ugly face comes to fetch me, he'll find me without a penny, but with a conscience that's clean as clean. No, I don't want your mattresses, because your thoughts are in them . . . because you sleep here, and at night when you start turning things over in your head, your thoughts get inside the cloth and into the springs, and there they'll stay, like bedbugs when beds aren't kept clean. The devil take the man and the things he wanted to put over on me!"

The old woman accompanied this speech with very graphic gestures, expressing so clearly with the movements of her hands and flexile fingers how the skinflint's bed was contaminated with his evil thoughts, that Torquemada listened to her with real fury, thunder-struck by such ingratitude. But she continued to spurn the gift firmly and stubbornly.

"That's some lottery prize that's fallen into my lap. Merciful God . . . the idea of sleeping on that! It's not as if I was half-witted, Don Francisco. So at midnight all your thoughts would wriggle out like worms and crawl into my ears and my eyes, driving me crazy and giving me a bad death! Because I know what I'm talking about—you can't fool me. . . All your sins are in there, inside there, all the troubles you give to the poor, your skinflintiness, the interest you suck out of them, and all the numbers that slide around in your brains to pile up money. If I went to sleep in that bed, at the hour of my death, toads with great big mouths would creep first out of one side and then the other, and foul nasty snakes would wrap themselves around my body, and awful ugly devils with great big mustaches and bats' ears—and they'd all grab hold of me to drag me off to hell. Go to the devil and keep your mattresses, because I have a pallet made of rag-sacks, with a blanket on top, that's heavenly glory to sleep on. Even you'd like to have it for yourself. It's a fine bed to sleep on at my ease."

"Then give it to me, give it to me, Tía Roma," said the miser mourn-fully. "If my son lives, I promise to sleep on it all the rest of my life, and eat nothing but the refuse you eat."

"That'll be the day! Now you want to get a toehold in heaven. Oh, señor, to each his own! And what you're saying suits you about as well as earrings on a donkey. And it's all because you're suffering. But if the boy gets well, you'll go back to being worse than Holofernes. Look out, you're getting old. Look out, any day now the One with no skin on his face will turn up, and that's a face you can't swindle."

"But where did you get the idea, you heap of garbage," answered Torquemada angrily, grabbing her by the neck and shaking her, "where did you get the idea that I'm bad, or ever have been?"

"Stop it, let me go, don't shake me. I'm no tambourine. Look, I'm older than Jerusalem and I've seen a lot of the world, and I've known you ever since you first wanted to marry Silvia. And I certainly advised her not to marry you, and I certainly foretold how often she'd go hungry. Now that you're rich, you don't remember the time when you were starting to make money. I do remember, and it seems like it was yesterday when you used to count out the chick-peas for poor Silvia and keep everything under lock and key, and the poor thing was half starved, skinny, and growling with hunger. If it hadn't been for me bringing her an egg or two on the sly, she would have died a hundred times over. D'you remember when you used to get up at midnight to search the kitchen and see if you could find a scrap of food that Silvia had hidden to eat herself? D'you remember that time you found a piece of ham in aspic and half a pastry they'd given me at the marquise's house, and that I brought to Silvia, so she could gobble it up all by herself, without giving you even a little bit? D'you remember that the next day you were raging like a lion, and when I came in, you knocked me down and kicked me? And I didn't get mad; and I came back again, and every day I brought something to Silvia. Since you were the one that did the shopping, we couldn't snitch a thing, and the poor girl didn't even have so much as a morning jacket to put on. She was a martyr, Don Francisco, a martyr; and you hanging on to the money and lending it out at twenty percent a month! And all the while, the two of you didn't eat anything but dried raw fish with stale bread and salad. Thanks to me sharing the things they gave me in rich houses, and one night, d'you remember? I brought a bone of wild boar that you kept putting in the pot for six days running, till it was drier than your cursed soul. I didn't have to bring anything; I did it for Silvia, that I caught in my arms when she was born from Señá Rufinica, who lived in the Callejón del Perro. And what made you so mad was that I used to save things for her and didn't give them to you, the devil take you! As if I had any need to fill your craw, you cur and less than a cur. And now tell me, did you ever give me anything worth a real? She did. She used to give me what she could behind your back. But you, you great bloodsucker, what did you ever give me? Bent nails and house sweepings. And now you come blubbering to me with your doubletalk! A fine lot of attention they're going to pay you up there."

"Listen, you damned hag," said Torquemada furiously, "it's only out of respect for your age that I don't kick you to death. You're a liar, a she-devil, and your whole body is full of lies and tricks. Now you're trying to slander me—after eating my bread for more than twenty years. But I know you, you poisonous vixen; nobody, on earth or in heaven, is going to believe what you've said! The devil's with you and cursed are you among all the witches and gargoyles in heaven—I mean in hell."

NINE

1 orquemada was beside himself with rage and, without observing that the old woman had retired to a prudent distance from the room, kept on talking as if she were still there.

"Scarecrow, mother of spiderwebs, if I catch you, you'll see. . . Slandering me like that!"

He strode up and down the narrow bedroom, and from there to his sitting room, as if pursued by shadows. He beat his head against the wall repeatedly, sometimes so fiercely that the impact could be heard all over the house.

Dusk was falling, and darkness reigned all around the wretched miser, when he heard clearly and distinctly the peacock cry uttered by Valentín in the throes of his raging fever.

"And they said he was better! My dear, dear son. We've been sold, we've been cheated."

Rufina came into the brute's room, weeping, and said, "Oh, Papa, he's so much worse, so much worse!"

"That clumsy fool Quevedo!" screamed Torquemada, raising his fist to his mouth and biting it savagely, "I'll tear his heart out. He's killed the boy."

"Papa, for God's sake don't act like that. Don't rebel against God's will. If He disposes . . ."

"I'm not rebelling, dammit! I'm not rebelling. It's just that I don't want . . . I don't want to give up my son, because he's mine, blood of my blood and bone of my bones."

"Resign yourself, resign yourself, and let's accept God's will," exclaimed his daughter, in floods of tears.

"I can't. I don't feel like resigning myself. This is robbery. Envy, pure envy. What's there for Valentín to do up there in heaven? Nothing, no matter what they say; absolutely nothing. My God, what lies, what a swindle! Talk about heaven and hell and God and the devil and . . . three thousand curses! And Death, that gadabout Death, who passes over so many rascals, so many shysters, so many imbeciles, and has to take a fancy to my son because he's the very best thing in the world! Everything's horrible, and the world is disgusting, a great filthy mess of garbage."

Rufina left the room and Bailón entered bringing a grief-stricken face with him. He had just come from seeing the little patient, who was now on the point of death, with some neighbor women and family friends around his bed. The erstwhile clergyman prepared to comfort the afflicted father at this painful moment, and began by embracing him and saying in a stifled voice, "Courage, my friend, courage. It's at times like these that we recognize strong souls. Remember that great philosopher who expired on a cross, leaving behind the sacred principles of humanity."

"Principles! To hell with your principles! Will you get out of here, you miserable insect? If you aren't the biggest fool and bore and stinker I ever saw! Every time I'm suffering you come out with that jargon."

"Let's take things very calmly, my friend. In the face of Nature's designs, of humanity, of the Great All, what can man do? Man! That ant, more insignificant still, that flea . . . much less than that, even."

"That bugaboo . . . less than that, even . . . that . . . dammit!" added Torquemada with horrible sarcasm, mimicking the sibyl's voice and then brandishing his fist. "If you don't shut up I'm going to break your face in. The great big All and the great big nothing are both the same to me, and the lousy character who invented them. Leave me alone, let go of me, by the cursed soul of your mother, or . . ."

Rufina reentered, led by two women friends who had drawn her away from the heartrending spectacle in the bedroom. The poor girl could no longer stand on her feet. She fell to her knees, moaning, and when she saw her father grappling with Bailón she said, "Papa, for the love of God, don't act like that. Resign yourself. Can't you see I'm resigned? Poor little thing. When I went in there was an instant—oh, dear!—when he regained consciousness. He spoke clearly, and said he saw the angels and that they were calling him."

"My dear, dear son, my darling son!" shouted Torquemada at the top of his lungs, transformed into a savage, a madman. "Don't go. Don't listen to them. They're rascals who are trying to trick you. Stay with us. . ."

Having said this, he fell to the floor in a heap, one leg stretched out stiffly and the other, as well as one arm, contracted. Bailón, despite all his strength, could not hold him down, for Torquemada's muscular force was unbelievable. Simultaneously, a savage roar and foam burst from his contorted lips. The contractions of his limbs and the pounding of his feet on the floor were truly a horrible spectacle; he clawed at his neck until the blood came. He remained in this condition for a long while, held down by Bailón and the butcher, while Rufina, half fainting with grief but with all her wits about her, was consoled and cared for by Quevedito and the photographer. The house filled up with the neighbors and friends who are apt to appear in times of sorrow, pitying and eager to help. At last, Torquemada's fit came to an end; he fell into a deep torpor, so quiet that it seemed like death itself, and four men picked him up and tossed him into bed. Tía Roma, with Quevedito's permission, massaged him with a brush, scraping and scratching away as if she were bringing out a shine.

By this time Valentín had expired. His sister, despite all efforts to dissuade her, went in to see him, kissed him over and over and, aided by her friends, prepared to perform the last duties for the poor child. She was brave, much braver than her father, who when he came to himself after that dreadful seizure and became fully conscious of the total extinction of his hopes, fell into a terrible weakness of body and spirit. He wept in silence and heaved sighs that could be heard all over the house. After a considerable time had passed, he asked to have some coffee and a bit of toast brought to him, for he felt horribly faint. The absolute loss of his hopes brought a kind of repose, a powerful aid toward repairing the exhausted organism. At midnight they had to give him a nourishing concoction of eggs, sherry, and broth, made by the sister of the photographer upstairs and the wife of the butcher downstairs.

"I don't know what's wrong with me," the Worse kept saying, "but the fact is, it seems as if my life is trying to slip away."

The deep sighs and strangled weeping lasted until nearly daybreak, at which time he was assailed by another paroxysm of grief, saying that he wanted to see his son, "to bring him back to life no matter what the cost," and tried to get out of bed in spite of the combined efforts of Bailón, the butcher, and the other friends who were trying to hold him in check and calm him. At last they succeeded in making him lie still, a result owing in no small part to the philosophical exhortations of the disreputable clergyman and the wise sentiments of the butcher, a man of little learning but a very good Christian.

"You're right," said Don Francisco, exhausted and panting for breath. "What else can we do but be resigned? Resigned! It's a journey for which we need no saddlebags. See what good it does a person to be as good as gold, and sacrifice himself for the unfortunate, and do good to all those who can't stand the sight of us. Anyway, the money that I thought I'd use to help a few rascals—money thrown away—would have wound up in the taverns for sure, in gambling houses and pawnshops! What I say is, I'm going to spend all that money on giving my dear son, that wonderful boy, that prodigy who didn't seem to belong to this world, the fanciest funeral Madrid has ever seen. Oh, what a son! Isn't it grief enough that they've taken him away from me? That boy wasn't just a son: he was a little god that the Eternal Father and I shared in the making of. Don't you think I ought to have a magnificent funeral for him? Hey, here it is daylight. Tell them to bring me prospectuses of funeral carriages and black-bordered paper for inviting all the professors."

The poor man got very excited about these projects, which fed his vanity, and by about nine in the morning, he was up and dressed, giving orders calmly and collectedly. He ate a good lunch, received all the friends who came to see him, and told to all the same hackneyed tale:

"Resignation . . . What can we do? It's perfectly clear: whether you become a saint or a Judas it makes no difference as far as their listening to you and taking pity on you is concerned. Ah, pity! A fine hook with no bait on it, for fools to swallow."

And the sumptuous funeral took place, and many people came to it, some of them very important, which was a cause of satisfaction and pride to Torquemada, the only balm for his heartrending grief. That mournful afternoon, when the wonderful child's body had been taken away, there were painful scenes in the house. Rufina, who was moving disconsolately to and fro, saw her father emerge from the dining room with his mustache completely white, and took fright in the belief that it had turned white in an instant. What had happened was this: beside himself, and assailed by a spasm of grief, the inconsolable father had gone to the dining room and unhooked the blackboard on which the mathematical problems were still written. Accepting it as a portrait which faithfully reproduced his adored son's features, he spent a long time kissing its cold black cloth and rubbing his face against it, so that the chalk adhered to his tear-wet mustache and the hapless usurer appeared to have aged suddenly. All present were astonished by this, and some even burst into tears. Don Francisco took the blackboard to his room, and ordered from a gilder the most expensive frame obtainable, the board to be mounted and placed in the most prominent spot in that chamber.

The following day the poor man was attacked, from the moment he opened his eyes, by the fever of earthly business. Since the young mistress was completely exhausted from sorrow and lack of sleep, she could not attend to household matters; the cleaning woman and the tireless Tía Roma took her place, insofar as that place could be taken. And behold, when Tía Roma came in to bring the Grand Inquisitor his chocolate, he was already up, seated at the table in his office and scribbling numbers with a feverish hand. And, because the old witch was on such intimate terms with the master of the house and took the liberty of treating him as an equal, she went up to him, put her cold, fleshless hand on his shoulder, and told him, "You never learn. There you go again, fixing the tools to hang folks. You're going to have bad luck, you old sinner, if you don't change your ways."

And Torquemada shot her a glance that was entirely yellow, for in him this color took the place of the white in other human eyes, and he answered her thus: "I'll do what I damn well please, you miserable gargoyle, old woman older than Methuselah. I'd be a fine one if I had to consult with your stupidity about what I ought to do." Glancing for a moment at the blackboard with the problems on it, he heaved a sigh and continued as follows: "If I'm preparing the tools, that's no business of yours or anybody else's, because I know everything I need to know about this world and the next, dammit! I know you're going to come out with the materialism of pity. To that I say that if I ever did any good deeds, I well and truly got the runaround. Any pity I have from now on, dammit! they can throw right back in my face."

TORQUEMADA
ON THE CROSS

ONE

Well, sir, it was the fifteenth of May, Madrid's great festival day (on this point there is no disagreement in the histories), in the year ——— (this, to be sure, I do not know; whoever wishes to confirm it is at liberty to do so), when that irreparable misfortune occurred, which, moreover, was announced by comets, windstorms, and earthquakes: the death of Doña Lupe, the Turkey Lady, of gentle memory.

And the date of this infinitely sad event is certain because Don Francisco Torquemada, who spent almost all of that day in the house of his friend and crony on the Calle de Toledo, Number — (I don't know the number either, nor do I believe that it matters), relates that late in the afternoon, when the sick woman had dropped off into a healing nap, which seemed a favorable symptom of the end of her nervous crisis, he stepped out onto the balcony to take a breath of fresh air and to rest from the tedious vigil he had been keeping since ten in the morning. He stood there for nearly half an hour watching the endless line of carriages returning from San Isidro's Meadow, making a fiendish racket. There were traffic jams, sudden eddies, and much jostling among the crowd, which spilled over both sidewalks all the way up the street, and incidents befitting the bad temper of those who return from a fiesta, with all the wine and exhaustion of the day turned into fuel for troublemaking. He amused himself by listening to the colorful expressions that bubbled above the tumult like effervescence in a well-shaken liquid, heightened by two hundred thousand squeals from saint's-day whistles, when—

"Señor," said Doña Lupe's servant, giving him such a tremendous clap on the back that the poor man thought the balcony above his head was falling on him, "señor, come here. She's taken another fit. This time I think she's going."

Don Francisco hastened to the bedroom and, indeed, Doña Lupe had

had a seizure. The joint efforts of friend and maid did not suffice to hold her down. The good lady's teeth chattered, a foamy saliva bubbled on her lips, and her eyes rolled inward as if trying to see for themselves that her thoughts were already scattered and flitting about the world. I do not know how long these fierce convulsions lasted. To Don Francisco they seemed interminable, and he feared that the Feast of San Isidro would end and be followed by a very long night, before Doña Lupe was ready for the coffin. But nine o'clock had not yet struck when the good lady became quieter and seemed quite dazed. They gave her a potion to drink, the pharmacological composition of which, like the name of her illness, is not a matter of record. The doctor was sent for, and as the sick woman's limbs lay quiet, a quiet that was the precursor of the grave, with all the life she had left looking out of her eyes, which were again alive and eloquent, Torquemada realized that his friend was trying to speak to him. A slight contraction of the facial muscles indicated the effort she was making to break the lugubrious silence. At last her tongue, spurred by sheer willpower, was loosened, and released a few words which only Don Francisco, with his keen ear and knowledge of what the Turkey Lady was likely to think and say, could understand.

"Rest easy, now," he told her. "We have time to talk all we want about the matter we discussed."

"Promise me you'll do what I told you, Don Francisco," murmured the sick woman, raising one hand as if she wanted to take an oath. "Do it, for God's sake."

"But, señora, do you know . . . ? How can you expect me to . . .?"

"And do you think that I, your faithful friend," said the widow Jáuregui, miraculously recovering all her ability to speak, "am capable of deceiving you? In no case would I advise anything contrary to your interests, still less now, when I see the gates of eternity wide open before me, when I feel the truth, yes, the truth, in my poor soul, Señor Don Francisco, for if my memory doesn't fail me—it was yesterday morning that I received Our Lord."

"No, señora, it was today at ten o'clock exactly," replied he, pleased to correct a chronological error.

"So much the better. Would I deceive you just a tick after I'd taken Our Lord? Listen to the blessed word of your friend, who is already speaking to you from the other world, from the region of . . . of . . ."

Here there was an unsuccessful attempt to give a poetic turn to the phrase.

". . . and I will add that what I'm recommending will be just the thing for both your body and soul, because a good business deal will come out of it and a work of charity besides, in every sense of the word. Don't you believe me?"

"Oh! I'm not saying that . . ."

"You don't believe me . . . and you'll regret it some day if you don't do it. I'm sorry to die before we can have a long talk about this affair! But you stayed ever so long in Cadalso de los Vidrios, and here I was in this miserable bed, eaten up with impatience to lay eyes on you."

"I didn't think you were so poorly. I would have come sooner."

"And I'll die without being able to convince you! Don Francisco, think, heed what I say, for I've always given you good advice. For your information, every dying person is an oracle, and as I die I tell you: Señor Don Paco, don't hesitate for a moment. Close your eyes and . . ."

Pause, owing to a slight relapse. Interlude of visit by the doctor, who prescribed another potion and, as he took his leave, predicted, at the bend in the hall, simply by pursing his lips and shaking his head, a fatal outcome. Interlude of expectancy and despairing massage of the patient's limbs. Don Francisco, feeling weak from hunger, went to the dining room where, in collaboration with the sick woman's nephew Nicolás Rubín, he polished off an omelet with onions in it, which was prepared by the servant in a trice. At midnight, Doña Lupe, motionless and with still watchful eyes, spoke some phrases that made perfect sense but had no correlation with one another; they were choppy, some with no beginning and others with no end. It was as if the manuscript of a scholarly discourse had been torn into a thousand pieces, turning it into scraps of paper which, after having been mixed in a hat, were taken out one by one, as in the well-known parlor game. Torquemada listened to her with deep sadness as he observed how the ideas had taken flight from that brilliant brain, now a ruined and roofless dovecote.

". . . Good works are everlasting riches, the only wealth that goes into the heavenly bank account when we die. At the gate of purgatory they give you a tag with a number, and then, on the day when they let a soul go, they sing out, 'Number so-and-so,' and the soul whose number it is gets out. Life is very short. A person dies when she believes that she's still being born. They ought to give her time to correct her mistakes . . . Isn't it awful? With bread at twelve reales and wine at six, how can anyone expect virtue? The working class wants to be virtuous and isn't allowed. Let blessed Saint Peter order the taverns closed at nine o'clock at night, and then we'll see. I've been thinking it's a good thing to die, because if a person lived forever and there were no burials or funerals, what would the Lord's ministers eat? Twenty-eight and eight ought to be forty, but they're only thirty-six . . . That's because arithmetic has been taught so badly, from time immemorial, in the hands of schoolmasters and assistants who always tend toward meanness, making little sums win and big ones . . . get lost."

She had a short period of lucidity during which, gazing affectionately at her fellow miser, who sat at her bedside like a very scarecrow of silent commiseration, she returned with the same insistence to her former theme.

"Look, I'm dying with the conviction that you'll do it. . . No, don't shake your head."

"I'm not shaking it, Señora Doña Lupe, or if so, I'm shaking it to say yes."

"Oh, how wonderful! What did you say?"

Torquemada repeated it without a twinge of conscience for falsifying his intentions in the presence of a dying person. It was easy to console, with a charitable fib, a person who was not likely to come back and ask him to make good on the unfulfilled promise.

"Yes, yes, señora," he added, "you can die easy—I mean, no, you musn't die, mind you! I mean, you can go off to sleep as peaceful as can be. Now, then, time to sleep."

Doña Lupe closed her eyes, but she lost no time in opening them again with a new idea shining out of them, the last idea, caught in great haste like a forgotten bundle the traveler discovers in a corner at the moment of departure. "I know very well what I'm trying for when I advise you to unite with that family! You must do it for conscience' sake and even, I daresay, out of pure selfishness. Do you know, do you know what might come of it?"

She asked this question so emphatically, waving both arms in the direction of the moneylender's startled face, that he prepared to hold her down, thinking that another attack of delirium, with epileptic convulsions, was about to occur.

"Ah!" added the lady, fixing a maternal gaze on Torquemada, "I can see so clearly what is sure to come of it, because the Lord lets me foresee the things that are good for you, and I foresee that with your help my friends will win their lawsuit . . . as justice demands. Poor family! My Señor Don Francisco will bring them luck. Shoulders to the wheel, and the suit will be won. The other side without a leg to stand on. And you? No, the numbers haven't yet been invented to count the millions you're going to have. . . But you don't deserve it, you're so stubborn and contemptuous of others! What a fine big lawsuit it is! Listen" (here she lowered her voice to a tone of mysterious intimacy), "listen, Don Francisco, when they win it, they'll own all the Valencia market gardens, every last mine in Bilbao, half of Madrid in houses and two-thirds of Havana, in houses too. Item, a strip of land twenty-odd leagues long, from Colmenar de Oreja to I don't know where, and as many shares in the Bank of Spain as there are days and nights in the year; as well as seven big, big steamships, and half the factories in Catalonia, approximately. And on top of that the mailcoach service from Molina de Aragón to Sigüenza, a splendid pantheon in Cabra, and thirty or thirty-five of the very best sugar mills, I'm not sure how many, on the island of Cuba . . . and then add half the money the galleons brought from America and all the tobacco from here, there, and everywhere."

Either she said no more or Don Francisco could not understand the incoherent phrases that followed, ending in a long series of groans. As Doña Lupe fought for breath he paced up and down the neighboring room, his head swimming with the number of Cuban sugar mills and galleons from America that his hapless friend had put into it, with all the exaggeration of a dying woman in the throes of delirium.

She lasted until three o'clock in the morning. Our hero was in the parlor talking to a neighbor woman when Nicolás Rubín, the priest, entered. He was visibly upset but, without losing his pedantry on so solemn an occasion, exclaimed, "*Transit.*"

"Bah! Poor thing, she's finally at rest," said Torquemada, as if congratulating the dead woman on the end of her long suffering.

This does not mean that he did not regret his friend's death; a few minutes after hearing that lugubrious "transit," he felt a great void in his existence. Undoubtedly he was going to miss Doña Lupe very much, nor was he likely to find, around the next corner, anyone who would counsel him about all his affairs with such good sense and disinterestedness. Sad and pensive, measuring with the vague gaze of his spirit the dimensions of that solitude in which he had been left, he wandered through the house giving orders concerning the things that still needed to be done. There was no lack of relatives, kinfolk, and neighbor women who did the last honors for Doña Lupe willingly and with all the affection the dead woman deserved; one saying all the prayers she knew and another helping to dress her in the habit of the Virgin of Carmen. In consultation with Father Rubín, Don Francisco made suitable arrangements for the burial, and when he was sure that everything would be done in accordance with the dead woman's wishes and the family's decorum as well as his own, for he deemed himself such an old and important friend as to be on a level with the family itself, he retired to his home, heaving sighs all the way down the stairs and along the street. Dawn was about to break, and the shrill piping of saint's-day whistles, sounding strident because their glass tubes had broken, could still be heard up and down the dark streets. Don Francisco also heard the dragging footsteps of those who had been up all night, and the light steps of folk who had risen early. Speaking to no one and stopping nowhere, he reached his house on the Calle de San Blas, on the corner of the Calle de la Leche.

T W O

Allowing himself no more respite than five hours abed and another hour and a half to eat breakfast, brush and put on his best black clothes, don his new boots, and cast an eye over his business, the usurer returned to the dead woman's house, suspecting that his presence and authority there would be sadly missed, for Doña Lupe's women friends would muddle everything, and the nephew, the priest, was not a man to solve whatever difficulties might arise. Fortunately, everything was following its normal course. Doña Lupe, laid out in the parlor, was sleeping the first slumber of eternity, surrounded by a restrained and merely dutiful atmosphere of mourning. The relatives had accepted her death calmly, and the maid and the concierge's wife displayed a tendency toward consolation that would become even more marked when the body was removed. Nicolás Rubín was snuffling abstractedly into his breviary, alternating this holy occupation with frequent sallies to the kitchen to ply his stomach with the restoratives that his chronic weakness and the exhaustion of a sleepless nigh; demanded.

Of all the people in the house, the one who expressed the sincerest and most heartfelt grief was a lady whom Torquemada did not know; she was tall, with prematurely white hair, for her still fresh face was that of a woman of forty and did not appear to be consistent with her white hairs, except in the sense that they seemed a mark of elegance and adornment rather than a sign of age. She was well dressed in black, with a hat that struck Don Francisco as one of the most elegant articles of dress he had seen in his life; it was as plain as the nose on your face, he thought, that she was a lady of noble appearance, wearing gloves, her small feet elegantly shod, and all of her person beautifully groomed, decent, and extremely refined, giving off what Torquemada called "a whiff of aristocracy." After she had prayed beside the body for a little while, the unknown woman went into the sitting room, followed by the miser, who was anxious to engage her in conversation and make her understand that he, at least, among so many vulgar folk, could recognize and honor refinement. The lady seated herself on a sofa, drying her tears, which seemed genuine, and when she saw that ungainly figure approaching, hat in hand, she took him for a representative of the family who was doing the honors of the house.

"Thank you," she told him, "I'm very comfortable here. Ah, what a friend we have lost!"

More tears, to which the moneylender responded with a heavy sigh, which he had no trouble in producing from his sturdy lungs.

"Yes, señora, yes. What a friend, what an admirable individual! As for skill in handling things . . . well . . . and as for absolutely honorable dealings, nobody was worthy of untying her shoes. Always on the lookout for profit, and doing everything just right! For me it is a loss . . ."

"And for me?" added the lady in a most disconsolate tone. "In the midst of such trouble, with our horizons closed off on every side, only Doña Lupe consoled us, opened a little chink where we could see a bit of hope shining. Four days ago, when we thought she had recovered from that wretched illness, she did us a favor we can never repay."

To hear someone talk about "never repaying" sounded unpleasant to Torquemada's ears. Could it be that the favor referred to by the noble lady had been a loan?

"Four days ago I was visiting my property in Cadalso de los Vidrios," he said, forming a little round o with thumb and finger of his right hand, "with no suspicion at all that it was serious, and when the nephew wrote to tell me how serious it was, I came running. Poor thing! Ever since the night of the thirteenth, her upper story, that had always gone like clockwork, wasn't functioning any more. No, señora. She was just as likely to tell you things that were gospel truth as to come out with others that the devil himself couldn't have understood. The whole day of the fourteenth she spent talking in a key that would have sent me up the wall, if your humble servant didn't have a head that's solider than an anvil. What confounded madness got into her noggin, when she guessed that death was coming? Just imagine how touched in the head the poor thing must have been when she roped me in, and after recommending me to some lady friends of hers whom she'd lent a few reales to, she insisted on—"

"On your increasing the loan and lowering the interest rate."

"No, that wasn't it. I mean, it was that and something else—a really wild idea—which would have tickled me if it had been a time for joking. Well, these friends of the departed are some ladies whose surname is Aguila, ladies of good family according to what I heard, poor as dirt, as I understand it. Well, Doña Lupe's little joke was that I should marry one of the Aguilas—I don't know which one of them— and till the moment she closed her eyes she had me undergoing the tortures of *Tartarus* with her ravings."

"Ravings, yes," the lady said gravely, "but one can see the nobility of her intentions in them. Poor Doña Lupe! Don't hold something that she said in delirium against her. She was so fond of us! She took such an interest in us!"

Speechless and aghast, Don Francisco stared at the lady without knowing what to say to her.

"Yes," she added kindly, helping him out of the blunder, "those Aguilas are my sister and I. I am the elder Aguila sister—Cruz del Aguila. No, don't be embarrassed. I know that you didn't mean to offend us with your reference to the matter of the hypothetical marriage. Nor am I hurt by the fact that you called us poor as dirt."

"Señora, I didn't know . . . Forgive me."

"Of course, you didn't know me; you have never seen me, nor have I had the pleasure of meeting you . . . until now, for from all appearances, I think I must be speaking with Señor Don Francisco Torquemada."

"At your service," stammered the moneylender, who could have struck himself as punishment for his stupidity. "So you are . . . ? My dear lady; pretend I haven't said anything. What I said about being poor . . ."

"It's true, and it doesn't offend me. As for saying we were poor as dirt, I forgive you for it: it was a passing remark, such as those that even the most well-bred persons might let slip when they are speaking of things they don't know about."

"To be sure."

"And as for the subject of the marriage, let us take it as a joke, or, better still, as the delirium of a dying person. We are as much surprised by that idea as you are."

"And it was a single idea, a fixed idea, that filled up the whole inside of her head; her whole brain seemed to be stuffed with it. And she said it with such seriousness! It wasn't just a recommendation, either, but a supplication, a pleading, as when we ask God to protect us. And I had to promise her that I would, so she could die quietly. You can see what a piece of foolishness . . . I mean, a piece of foolishness in the sense that . . . As for the rest, an honor to me, mind you! Just imagine . . . But I repeat that, to quiet her ravings, I assured her that I would marry not only the elder and younger Aguilas but all the eagles and vultures in heaven and on earth. Naturally, when I saw her so upset, I could hardly do less than fall in with it; but to myself, naturally, I was dragging my feet, for heaven's sake, and not because of the materialism of the marriage, which, as I said, is a great honor for me, but for natural reasons having to do with myself, such as age, circumstances . . ."

"I understand. We ourselves, if Lupe had spoken to us about it, would have answered the same, of course, would have said yes to calm her; and in our own minds . . . Oh, to be married to . . . ! It is not scorn, no. . . But with respect, that at least, with respect to everyone, such jokes are not admissible, no, señor; they are not admissible. And now, Señor Don Francisco . . ."

She rose, holding out her delicate and perfectly gloved hand, which the miser grasped very respectfully and held for a moment without knowing what to do with it.

"Cruz del Aguila . . . Costanilla de Capuchinos, the door just beyond the baker's shop . . . third floor. Please feel entirely at home there. The three of us live alone, my sister and I and our brother Rafael, who is blind."

"May you live so for many years—I mean, no, I didn't know that your brother was blind. Please excuse me . . . Greatly honored."

"I kiss your hand."

"Respects to all the family."

"Thank you."

"And . . . like I say . . . keep well."

He accompanied her to the door, spluttering compliments, but none of those that came to his mind turned out correctly and gracefully, for he was so perturbed that all his channels of speech, which had never been very smooth in any case, seemed to choke up.

"Whew, what a brick I just dropped!" he roared, irritated with himself, shoving his hat backward on his head and pulling up his trousers with a movement of his belly and aided by his hands.

He entered the parlor mechanically, unmindful of the dead woman surrounded by shining candles, and when he saw her, the only thing that occurred to him to say, in his thoughts alone, was, "You! Why didn't you warn me, dammit!"

THREE

All that day the miser was in a very bad mood, unable to banish from his mind his childish agitation in the presence of the lady, whose appearance and aristocratic demeanor entranced him. He was a man very appreciative of good behavior and a sincere admirer of qualities that he himself did not possess, among which, with genuine modesty, he gave first place to easy manners and the social art of compliments. He thought that that confounded Doña Cruz must have gone downstairs laughing her head off at him, and imagined her telling the whole story to the other sister, and both of them laughing themselves sick, calling him an oaf and . . . God knows what they must have called him! Frankly, he had his little speck of self-esteem like any mother's son, and his dignity, and all the trumpery possessions of an individual worthy of occupying a place of honor in society. He had sufficient fortune (well and truly earned by his industry) not to cut a foolish figure in front of anyone, and did not like at all the idea of being a comic figure . . . mind you! It is true that he had been at fault in that day's incident, because he had scoffed at the Aguila ladies, calling them poor as dirt right *in the physiognomy of the face* of the elder of them, a lady who was so well turned out, so polished, in every sense of the word. Ah! As he remembered it, a blush rose to his cheek and he clenched his fists. For, really, he might have suspected that that individual was . . . who she was. And above all, no clever man says contemptuous things about anyone in front of people he doesn't know, for the devil takes over and an embarrassing situation arises when a fellow least expects it. A man has to look out for what he says, on pain of not being able to shove his oar into refined people's society. "I," he said, putting an end to his meditations because the hour had come to convey the corpse to the cemetery, "am pretty canny, pretty canny, I understand everything very well. God didn't make me a fool, nor half a fool, mind you, and I understand the give and take of life. But the fact is that I have no polish, indeed I haven't; as soon as I find myself in front of an important person, I turn into a lout and don't know what to say, or what to do with my hands. Well, I'll have to learn, dammit! Harder things than that are learned, when there's plenty of good will and mother wit. Cheer up, Francisco, new styles for new situations, and it's not good for a rich man to cut a poor figure. The world would be in fine shape if men of influence, men of experience, men who are rolling in money, were laughed at! That can't be, no, no!"

During the long trip to the cemetery, in the monotony of that slow, sad promenade, he was assailed by the same thoughts. He could see in front of him the monstrous, ugly vehicle that was the funeral carriage, pitching and rolling like a ship; his brain was dulled by the slow, interminable noise of the tires on the wheels, leaving tracks on the dusty earth of the neglected roads. Some twenty hired coaches followed the one at the head of the procession, occupied by Don Francisco, Nicolás Rubín, another priest, and a gentleman who was a distant relative of Doña Lupe's, all three of them persons who irritated the usurer very much, and all the more on that occasion because they were so close to him and he could not escape. Torquemada was not a man to be stuffed into a narrow box for such a long time, among people whom he detested, and he constantly shifted position, leaning first on one hip and then on the other. His legs and Nicolás Rubín's legs, his silk hat and the other priest's headgear, were in his way; he was annoyed by the constant smoking and chatter of those three individuals, who seemed not to be able to talk about anything but smuggling and how profligate was the city administration.

Without deigning to toss more than an affirmative word or two into the conversation, to give something to chew on, like a bone, to those poor wretches who possessed no property in Cadalso de los Vidrios nor houses in Madrid, Torquemada continued to turn over in his mind the train of thought begun in the dead woman's house.

"What I say is, I have no polish, and a fellow has to use polish to place himself at the level where he belongs. But how could I have learned anything about good manners when all my life I've only associated with vulgar people? That poor Doña Lupe (may she be in glory) was vulgar, too; is there any doubt about that? I'm not insulting her, no indeed, mind you! A very good person, with a lot of brains, an eye for business that lots of folks would have been glad to have. But she can say what she likes, and I'm not insulting her, as a refined person—not a bit of it! She tried to be, and it didn't quite come off, dammit! It didn't come off. The one thing she hankered for was to be a lady, and it was no good! Even if she did wear shawls imported from Paris, she was about as much of a lady as my grandmother. Ah! For ladies, the one of this morning. That certainly is the genuine article! And it did my friend Doña Lupe no good to look in that mirror. It was too late, too late to learn. Poor woman! As for shrewdness, and inclinations, she had them, mind you, as I'm the first to recognize. But refinement, elegant behavior, bah! After all, like me, she only associated with people of no importance. And what does a fellow hear at the end of the day? Stupidities and garbage. I remember perfectly well that Doña Lupe said "liberry" and "prespiration" and called the Calle de Jacometrezo "Jacometrenzo"; words that, as Bailón told me, aren't pronounced that way. Don't think I'm insulting her by saying this. Anybody can make mistakes in talking when he hasn't had a good start. I kept saying "differience" right up to 1885. But that's what noticing things is good for, listening to how folks talk who know how to talk. The fact is that when a fellow's rich and has earned it by the sweat of his brow, working away here, working away there, it's rotten to have people laugh at him. Rich people ought to give an example, mind you! of good manners as well as good behavior, so that society would go straight and everything would swing along as it ought to. I think it's all right for people who don't have a penny to their name to be stupid and awkward. There's justice in that; it's what they call equilibrium. But for rich people to throw tantrums, for landowners and us folk who pay taxes to be treated like . . . like asses . . . no, no, absolutely not."

The thread of this meditation was still in his mind when they returned from the cemetery, after leaving the great businesswoman's cold remains neatly stowed in a niche in one of the dismal courtyards of San Justo. His three companions in the carriage, still regaling one another with gossip about smuggling, told innumerable anecdotes about how to bring in olive oil, and the battles between the police and the whole brotherhood of smugglers, while Torquemada's imagination wandered after the Aguila lady, and fluctuated between the desire and the fear of seeing her again: desire, because he wanted to make amends for his clumsiness, to appear less of a fool than in their first interview; fear, because undoubtedly the two sisters would burst out laughing when they saw him and make fun of him during the visit. His blackest thought was that he had no choice but to visit them, by express command of Doña Lupe and inescapable obligation. He had arranged with his departed friend to renew a note belonging to the two ladies, adding a certain amount to it. And the new note would not be payable to the heirs of the widow Jáuregui, but to Torquemada, to whom the dead woman had left some funds, for that purpose and others, the proceeds of which would be enjoyed by some of her late husband's poor relatives. It goes without saying that Don Francisco would have to conscientiously carry out any requests of this sort that his business associate had made. The hard part was to carry them out without appearing in the Aguilas' nest, as the dead woman had categorically ordered him to do; and this was the cause of the poor man's dilemma. How should he present himself? Smiling, or down in the mouth? How should he dress? In his Sunday best or the clothes he wore every day? For it was nonsense to think of evading the confrontation by giving the errand to someone else; moreover, it implied cowardice, desertion in the face of danger, and this placed him on bad terms with himself, for his self-esteem always counseled him to accept difficulties, however unwelcome, and not to turn his back on any serious challenge. He resolved, therefore, to confront the Aguilas; and as for his doubts about what to wear, his natural shrewdness triumphed over vanity, suggesting the idea of appearing in his everyday suit, with a nice clean shirt of course, for that vulgar habit of changing his shirt only once every two weeks had not held sway since our hero had begun to have a clear picture of the social scene. In short, he would appear just as he always looked, and would speak as little as possible, answering in simple terms anything that they might ask. If they laughed, let them laugh, dammit! But no, they probably would receive him with all ceremony, in expectation of the favor he was doing them and the aid his visit would bring, for with all their aristocracy and their undeniable refinement, the poor ladies must be awaiting his visit like manna from heaven, as the saying goes.

FOUR

Having chosen an hour that seemed appropriate, our hero made his way to La Costanilla. On such a short street, and with the unmistakable indication of the bakery, the house could not be missed. Don Francisco saw two or three flour-covered men lounging around a door and, in the next building, an antique shop which could better be described as a pawnbroker's. That was the house, third floor. When he glanced at the shop sign, he gave an exclamation of joy.

"I know this dealer. Why, it's Melchor, the one who used to be at Number 5b on the Calle de San Vicente."

I need hardly say that he felt very much like having a chat with his friend before going up for his visit. The dealer lost no time in giving him information about the Aguila ladies, describing them as the most respectable people he had laid eyes on since he had been in the business. They were poor, of course, poor as church mice; but if no one was poorer than they, no one had more dignity either, or more resignation to bear the cross of their poverty. And what refined manners, what a way they had of dealing with people, what a knack of flattering everyone who spoke to them and winning their hearts! This information made the miser feel his fear evaporating, and he hastened upstairs. Doña Cruz herself opened the door. And although she was wearing old clothes (but perfectly decent ones, of course), she seemed as elegant as when he had seen her yesterday, dressed in her best.

"Señor Don Francisco," said the lady, with more pleasure than surprise, for she was no doubt expecting his visit, "come in, come in."

The visitor's first words were clumsy. "How could I have stayed away? How are you? The whole family well? Thanks. It's a pleasure. . ."

And he went through a door that he should not have, and she had to say, "No, no. Through here."

His confusion did not prevent him from observing many things from the very beginning, when Cruz del Aguila ushered him down a passage with three turns in it, to the little parlor. He observed the beautiful head so well wrapped in a colored handkerchief that neither much nor little of the white hair could be seen. He also observed that she was wearing a woolen wrapper, very old but without a spot or rip, with a white kerchief crossed on her breast, all exquisitely clean, and revealing the continual and careful usage of those persons who know how to make their clothes last forever. The strangest thing was that she wore old gloves with stained fingers.

"Excuse me," she said with graceful modesty. "I was cleaning metal."

"Ah, Of course!"

"For you should know, if you didn't know it before, that we have no maid, and my sister and I do everything ourselves. No, don't think I'm complaining about this new privation, one of the many that our unhappy fate has brought us. We have agreed that maids are a calamity, and when one learns to do things for oneself, there are three advantages: first, that one doesn't have to do battle with gawks; second, that everything is done much better and to our own taste; third, that the day goes by without one's noticing it, in healthy exercise."

"Hygienic," said Torquemada, overjoyed at being able to drop a fancy word that fitted the situation so well. And this success cheered him up so much that he seemed like a different man.

"With your permission," said Cruz, "I will continue my task. We are in no position to stand on ceremony, and since you are a person we trust . . ."

"Oh, yes indeed, completely to be trusted! The lady must treat me just exactly like a child. And if she wishes me to help her . . ."

"Goodness! That would be lacking in respect, and . . . Certainly not!"

With the box of cleaning powder in her left hand and a chamois in her right, and both hands gloved, she began to polish the copper knob on one of the doors, and in a twinkling had left it so shiny that it seemed made of fine gold.

"My sister, whom you don't know, will be out in a moment," she said, sighing deeply. "It's sad to say it, but. . . she is in the kitchen. We have to alternate in all the household tasks. When I declare war on dust or clean the metal, she washes the dishes or puts dinner on the fire. At other times, I cook and she sweeps, or washes, or mends clothes. Fortunately we are in good health; work is not demeaning; work consoles and makes company for one, and strengthens dignity as well. We were born to a great position; now we are poor. God has subjected us to this tremendous test. Oh, what a test, Señor Don Francisco! No one knows what we have suffered, the humiliations, the bitterness . . . It's better not to speak of that. But the Lord has sent us, at last, a wonderful medicine, a specific that performs miracles: blessed acceptance. Today you see both of us busy with these tasks which, in former times, would have seemed beneath our dignity; we live in peace, with a sort of quiet sadness that almost—almost—begins to seem like cheerfulness. We have learned, through the hard lessons of reality, to scorn all the vanities of the world, and little by little have come to believe that this honorable poverty in which we live is beautiful, to regard it as a blessing from God."

Within his very scanty repertory of ideas and expressions, the uncouth miser found none worthy of being brought forward to answer that elegant, facile, and unaffected mode of expression. He could only admire and grunt assent, which is the easiest grunt of all.

"You will also meet my brother, the poor blind one."

"Since birth?"

"No, señor. He lost his sight six years ago. Oh, what a sorrow! Such a good lad, destined to be . . . I don't know, whatever he might have wished. Blind at twenty-odd years of age! His illness coincided with the loss of our fortune, to make it even more heartbreaking. Believe me, Don Francisco: the blindness of my brother, that angel, that martyr, is a misfortune to which my sister and I have not yet succeeded in resigning ourselves. May God forgive us for it. To be sure, the blow came to us from above; but I do not accept it, I don't bow my head, no, señor . . . I hold it high . . . though you may disapprove of my irreverence."

"No, señora. Why should I disapprove? The Eternal Father . . . is awful. But do you know what He did to me? It isn't that I throw it in His teeth, mind you! but really, to take all a man's hopes away from him! At least, you haven't lost hope; your little brother can be cured."

"Ah, no, señor. There is no hope."

"But are you sure? There are great *opticians* in Madrid."

The minute he had said it the poor man realized the enormity of his slip of the tongue. Imagine, saying "opticians" instead of "oculists"! He tried to correct himself, but the lady, who apparently had not observed his blunder, gave him an easy outlet in another direction. She asked his permission to leave the room briefly to bring in her sister, a suggestion which suited Don Francisco very well, though doubts very soon began to assail him anew. What would the younger sister be like? Would she laugh at him? If, by some devilish circumstance, she were not as refined as Cruz and took fright on seeing him, so vulgar, so boorish, so . . . ! "Come, it's not as bad as all that," he told himself as he craned his neck to see his reflection in a mirror that hung on the wall opposite the sofa, leaning outward as if it were making a bow. "It's not as bad as all that. . . What I say is, I carry my years very well, and if I felt so inclined, I'd be head and shoulders above all those rascals who have nothing but their appearance to count on."

He was engaged in these musings when he heard the two sisters in the hall, arguing rather energetically:

"As you are, my girl, what does it matter? Can't you see that he comes as a trusted friend?"

"But how do you expect me to go in dressed like this? Let me take off my apron at least."

"What for? Why, we're our own servants and our own employers, and he knows it perfectly well. What does it matter if he sees you looking like that? This is a case when forms don't mean anything. If we were dirty, or not decently dressed, better that no human eyes should see us. But no one could possibly be cleaner than we are, and signs of having worked don't lessen our dignity in the eyes of a person who is so reasonable, so practical, so . . . simple. Isn't that so, Don Francisco?"

As she said this she raised her voice, very near the door, and the thoroughly embarrassed moneylender thought that his best response was to hasten to receive the two ladies gracefully, saying, "Of course, of course; no pretense with me, for I'm as plain and hardworking as any man; and since my earliest childhood—"

He was about to go on to say that he used to clean his own boots and sweep out his room, but the appearance of the second Aguila, which left him dumbstruck and motionless, cut short his words.

"My sister Fidela," said Cruz, tugging at one of her arms until she overcame her resistance.

F I V E

"What does it matter if I see you in working clothes, when I already know that you're ladies, and ladies one hundred percent?" protested Don Francisco, who with each new turn of events was recovering from the terror that paralyzed him. "Señorita Fidela, many years of health. . . Why, you're just fine, dressed like that! Good-looking lasses don't need fancy clothes."

"Oh, excuse me!" said the younger Aguila, all shamefaced and confused. "My sister is like that, to make me come in wearing these rags! With a pair of my brother's old boots, this apron, and my hair not combed."

"I'm a friend of the house, and, mind you! there's no need to stand on ceremony with me, with Francisco Torquemada. And how are you? Are you well? The whole family well? Like I say, good health is the most important thing, and when you have health, everything goes well. I think, just as you do, that there's nothing more tiresome than having maids, for they're usually filthy, gossipy, greedy, and always, always in a flutter about their confounded sweethearts."

During all this small talk, he never took his eyes off the little cook, who was an adorable miniature. Much younger than her sister, the aristocratic type appeared in her in a rather common variation. Her blonde hair, her anemic coloring, her delicate profile, the high-bridged, rather long nose, the clearcut mouth, the noticeably small bosom, the slender figure, all proclaimed the nobly born, pure-blooded lady, without any invigorating intersection of bloodlines, delicate from birth and further weakened by a hothouse upbringing. All this and a bit more was visible under that humble kitchen-maid's appearance, which gave the impression of a disguise invented in a children's game.

Since the poor girl (no longer so much of a girl, for she was twenty-seven or so) had not yet entirely absorbed that dogma of misfortune which prescribes scorn of all pretension, it cost her great effort to present herself before unknown persons in such lowly garb. It was some time before she could recover her composure with Torquemada, who struck her (here between us) as a solemn idiot.

"The gentleman was a great friend of Doña Lupe's," remarked the elder sister.

"Poor thing! What a fancy she took to us!" said Fidela, seating herself in the chair nearest the door and hiding her ill-shod feet. "When Cruz brought the news that the poor lady had died, I felt such sorrow! Dear heaven! We seemed more unprotected than ever at that instant, more alone. The last hope, the last bit of affection seemed to leave us as well, and I thought I saw, off there in the distance, a wrinkled hand, waving" (here she made the motion with her fingers that babies use to wave good-bye) "like this."

"This one," thought the miser, more admiring than ever, "certainly knows how to talk, too. Dammit! What a pair of sweet-talkers they are!"

"But God does not leave us unprotected," said Cruz, making a graceful gesture of negation with her index finger, "and He says no, no, that He does not want to leave us unprotected, though the whole world is bent on doing so."

"And when we find ourselves most alone and swallowed up in darkness, a little ray of sunshine appears and comes in and in, and . . ."

"That's for me. I'm that sunshine," said Torquemada to himself, and aloud: "Yes, ladies; I'm thinking the same thing. Fortune favors the person who works. Just imagine that this delicate young lady has to get into the materialism of a kitchen!"

"And the worst of it is that I'm no good at it," said Fidela. "But thanks to the fact that my sister is teaching me . . ."

"Ah! So Doña Cruz is teaching you? That's fine!"

"That doesn't mean that I'm learning. In the first place, she's no star herself, not at all. I work at it, I do indeed; but I'm very absent-minded, and I do the most awful things!"

"Well, what of that?" said the elder sister gaily. "As we aren't cooking for critical boarders, as this isn't a hotel and we have only ourselves to please, whatever mistakes we make are forgiven beforehand."

"And sometimes because it comes out raw, and other times it's burned, the fact is that we always have fun at table."

"And after all, it gives us a sauce we didn't count on: good cheer . . ."

"Which can't be bought in any shop," said Torquemada, overjoyed at having grasped the figure of speech. "Fine and dandy. Just give me that sauce and I'll sink my teeth into all the bad meals in Christendom. But, Señorita Fidela, you say that you're a bad cook out of modesty. Ah! I'm sure that lots of folks would like . . ."

"No, no. I do it horribly badly. And you can believe me," she added with the animated expression that was perhaps her most visible resemblance to Cruz, "you can believe me when I say that I would like to be a good cook; I'd like it very, very much. Dear me, yes. I think that the culinary art is worthy of the greatest respect, and that its principles should be studied and that it should be practiced seriously."

"Yes, indeed, it should be an important part of education!" assented Cruz del Aguila.

"What I say," added Torquemada, "is that they ought to have a cooking class in schools, and that little girls, instead of all that piano and embroidering of slippers, should learn how to prepare a good Biscayan rice, or fisherman's style tuna."

"I agree."

"So do I."

"Well. . ." murmured the moneylender, bringing both hands down smartly on the arms of his chair, a crude and laconic method of expressing the following sentiments: "My dear ladies, we've wasted enough time chatting. Now let's get down to business."

"No, no. Don't be in such a hurry," said the elder sister with a smile, making a show of friendship that upset the poor man more than ever. "What do you have to do just now? Nothing. We won't let you go away without meeting our brother."

"With the *extremest* of pleasure. I should say so. As for being in a hurry, I'm not. It's just that I wouldn't like to be a bother . . ."

"By no means."

Fidela was the first to rise to her feet, saying, "I mustn't leave the kitchen unattended. Excuse me."

And she hurried out, leaving her sister in an admirable position to sing her praises.

"She is one of God's angels. Because of the difference in our ages, which is no less than twelve years, I am more of a mother to her than an older sister. We are mother and daughter, sisters, and best friends, for the love that unites us is great not only in its intensity, Señor Don Francisco, but in its breadth . . . I don't know if I'm explaining myself properly . . ."

"I understand," remarked Torquemada, though he was completely in the dark.

"I mean that this misfortune, our need, the very energy with which Fidela and I are fighting for existence, has given ramifications to our love. . ."

"Ramifications. Quite so."

"And no matter how much you sharpen your wits, Señor Don Francisco—and they are so sharp already—you can have no idea of my sister's goodness, of her sweetness of character. And with what Christian resignation she has undergone these difficult tests of our misfortune! At an age when young girls enjoy worldly pleasures, she lives in this poverty, this obscurity, resigned and happy. Her abnegation breaks my heart, for it seems like a form of martyrdom. Believe me when I say that if I could place my sister in a different position in life, even at the cost of greater sufferings than those I bear now, I would do so without hesitation. For this unhappy household, her modesty is perhaps the only asset we possess today; but it is also a sacrifice, consummated in silence so that it may be greater and more meritorious; and, truly, I wish that I could compensate for this sacrifice in some way, but" (here she looked confused) "I don't know what I'm saying. I can't express myself properly. Do forgive me for chattering on like this. My brain is always shuffling ideas. Alas! Misfortune is what makes me run on so much that it seems my head is getting larger, yes indeed. I am sure that the skull develops from the exercise of thinking, because of the swelling caused by all the movement inside" (laughing). "Yes, indeed. And it is also undoubtedly true that we have no right to bore our friends. Forgive me, and come see my brother."

Torquemada did not open his mouth on the way to the blind man's room, nor could he have said anything even if he had wanted to, for the noble lady's eloquence fascinated him, and his fascination made him stupid, scattering his ideas into heretofore unknown spaces and rendering the few that remained incapable of expression.

Rafael del Aguila, a motionless and melancholy figure enthroned on a black armchair, was in the best room in the house, a little sitting room with a glassed-in balcony. A very deep impression was made on Torquemada by the sight of the sightless young man, as well as by the supreme sadness of his noble appearance, the gentle and contained resignation of that image, which it was impossible to approach without a certain religious respect.

SIX

I said "image" and I do not withdraw the word, for in color and lines the blind man bore an undeniable resemblance to those saints carved in wood, young martyrs, or handsome Christs praying. This resemblance was strengthened by the absolute serenity of his posture, the inertness of his limbs, the soft, wavy brown beard, which seemed darker against the dead-white skin, as pale as wax, the beauty of his features, which were agonized and deathlike rather than effeminate, and his lack of sight, the absence of visible soul, namely, his glance.

"The ladies have already told me that . . ." stammered the visitor, half startled and half pitying. "Well, I must say that it's a terrible shame that you lost your organ of sight. But, who knows! There are good doctors who—"

"Oh, my dear sir!" said the blind man in a melodious and vibrant voice with a strangely disturbing timbre, "I am grateful for your words of consolation, which, unfortunately, come at a time when there is no hope here to receive them."

A pause ensued, broken by Fidela's entrance with a cup of broth, which her brother had the habit of taking at that hour. Torquemada had not yet released the blind man's hand, as white and slender as a woman's and extraordinarily well-kept.

"All that happens is God's will," said the miser with something halfway between a sigh and a yawn; and, desperately searching in his mind for something appropriate to say, he had the good fortune to find the following words: "In your misfortune, though, fate has compensated you by giving you these two good sisters, who love you so much."

"That is true. Things are never all bad, just as things are never all good," agreed Rafael, turning his face in the direction from which his hearer's voice came.

Cruz cooled the broth by pouring it from the cup to the plate and the plate to the cup. Meanwhile, Don Francisco was astonished to see how clean Rafael was, with his jacket or short dressing gown of light-colored wool, his dark trousers, and red slippers beautifully fitted to his feet. Young Aguila had fully deserved in his time, a time not particularly remote, the reputation of being a handsome youth, one of the handsomest in Madrid. He was distinguished by his elegance and the fastidious perfection of his wardrobe, and when, after he became blind, vanity seemed superfluous and useless from a logical point of view, his kind sisters did not want him to stop dressing and preening himself just as he had done when he could enjoy his handsome face before the mirror. For them, it was a point of family pride to keep him well groomed and elegant, and they would have been inconsolable had they been unable to give themselves this pleasure amid so many privations. Either Cruz or Fidela combed his hair every morning with as much attention as if he were going to a ball; they parted it carefully, trying to imitate the way he used to arrange his handsome locks; and they groomed his beard and mustache. Both enjoyed this operation greatly, knowing how much a meticulous toilette meant to him as a remembrance of his joyous youth; and when they said "How fine you look!" they felt a pleasure that communicated itself to him and flowed back to them, creating a collective pleasure.

Fidela washed and perfumed his hands every day, caring for his nails with exquisite attention, a real masterpiece of her loving patience. And for him, in the shadows of his life, it was a consolation and a joy to feel the freshness of his hands. In general, cleanliness helped to compensate for the darkness in which he lived. Water substituting for light? It might be a scientific absurdity, but Rafael found some resemblance between the properties of these two elements.

I have already said that he was a delicate and very distinguished figure, with a handsome face, beautifully sculptured hands, a woman's faultlessly shaped feet. The idea that their brother, because he was blind and did not go out, had to be badly shod was something the two ladies refused to accept. The elegant daintiness of Rafael's feet was one more mark of breeding, and they would rather have taken the bread out of their own mouths, would rather have suffered the cruelest deprivations, than consent to show the family feet to disadvantage. That is why they had had those elegantly embroidered slippers made, demanding of the cobbler all the resources of his art. The poor blind man could not see his beautifully shod feet, but he felt them, and that was enough for his sisters, who felt a harmony with him in all the acts of existence.

They did not dress him in a clean shirt every day, for this was not possible in their poverty, and moreover he did not need one, for his clothing stayed perfectly clean on that ethereal body for days and weeks on end; but, even though it was not necessary, they changed his clothes assiduously and took great care not to always put on the same cravat.

"Today you're going to wear the blue one with stripes," Fidela would say with ingenuous seriousness, "and the ring with the turquoise in it."

He would agree, and at times showed a kindly preference for another cravat, perhaps because he thought that this would please his sisters more.

The unfortunate man's careful grooming was not the greatest cause of astonishment for Don Francisco in that house, where there was no lack of motives for surprise. He had never seen a cleaner house. You could have eaten off the floors, which were carpeted only in a few places; not a spot of dirt could be seen on the walls; all the metal sparkled. And this marvel was accomplished by people who, according to Doña Lupe's expression, had nothing but the sky overhead and the earth below! What miracles must they perform to keep themselves alive! Where did the money for shopping come from? Did they cheat? By what magic arts must they stretch the miserable peseta, the still more miserable five- and ten-céntimo coins! He would have to see it, to study it, to immerse himself up to the neck in that splendid lesson of life! The moneylender kept thinking about all this while Rafael drank his broth, after having offered some to Torquemada.

"Would you like a little broth, Don Francisco?" said Cruz.

"Oh, no thanks, señora."

"Just see how good it is—the only good thing about our poor diet."

"Thanks. I appreciate it."

"For we can't offer you wine. It doesn't agree with my brother, and we two don't use it for an infinite number of reasons, of which you need understand only one."

"Thank you, Señora Doña Cruz. I don't drink wine either, except on Sundays and days of obligation."

"Just imagine, what a strange thing!" said the blind man. "When I lost my sight I began to hate wine. You would think that wine and light were twin brothers, and that all at once, in a single act of escape, they fled away from me."

Here I must say that Rafael del Aguila followed his sister Cruz in age. He was over thirty-five; but his blindness, which had assailed him in 1883, and his consequent immobility and depression, seemed to have halted the process of aging, leaving him as if embalmed, with the appearance of a man of about thirty. There was no freshness in his face, but neither did he have gray hair or wrinkles; his life seemed to be checked, suspended, resembling as it were the unhealthy, greenish immobility of still waters.

The poor blind man enjoyed pleasant conversation. He talked amusingly about incidents in his life when he could still see, and asked about current happenings. That day they talked about Doña Lupe a little, but Torquemada paid not the slightest attention to what was said of his friend, for his spirit was burdened by confused ideas and reflections about that household and its three inhabitants. He would have preferred to have it out with the two ladies in private, to ask them a thousand questions, to pull from them their confounded economic secrets, which surely constituted a whole body of law, something like the Bible, a supreme code, guide, and beacon of the self-respecting poor.

Although the miser was well aware that he was prolonging his visit more than was seemly, he did not know how to cut it short, nor how to bring up the subject of the note and the money; this, he did not know why, seemed to him a shameful act, like pulling out a revolver and pointing it at the two Aguila ladies. Never had he felt so intensely the shortcomings of his business, for in this and nothing else lay his perplexity; he had always assailed, with a tranquil mind and a firm belief in the rightness of his actions, those who, rightly or wrongly, needed his help to get out of financial straits. Two or three times he put his hand in his pocket, and the sacramental introit, "Well, now, ladies," came to the tip of his tongue, and, an equal number of times, his flagging willpower did not succeed in carrying out the attempt. It was fear, real fear of seeming to lack respect for a family that was as unfortunate as it was noble. As his luck would have it, Cruz took the initiative, either because she understood his difficulty or was anxious to see him go, saying, "If it's all right with you, we'll settle that matter."

They returned to the parlor, and there the business was done quickly, with both sides apparently wishing to tiptoe over it very gingerly. In Cruz this was delicacy of feeling; in Torquemada, the fear he had felt before, and which returned in serious form during the act of settling past and future accounts with these impoverished aristocrats. The idea flashed through his mind of canceling the interest, in view of the three worthy persons' desperate situation. But it was only a flash, a spark, lacking either the intensity or the duration sufficient to produce an explosion in his will. Cancel the interest? Why, he had never done it, nor did he think that he could ever do it under any circumstances. To be sure, the Aguila ladies deserved exceptional consideration, but to be too openhanded with them, mind you, would establish a most lamentable precedent!

And yet his inclination suggested to him, deep in the fiber of his being, that he should cancel the interest. He even had on his lips an awkward attempt to formulate the proposal, but he did not know the word, either elegant or crude, to express such a thing, nor what sort of look he should assume when saying it. Nor could he find a way of bringing such an idea from the dark spaces of his first intention into the bright realms of real fact. And, to his greater torment, he remembered that Doña Lupe had urged something like this upon him. His faithless memory could not determine whether the dead woman had said "cancel" or "lower." Probably it was the latter, for the Turkey Lady was no spendthrift. However, in his perplexity, the miser did not know what he was doing, and the credit operation took place mechanically. Cruz made no remark at all. Nor did Torquemada, who limited himself to presenting the lady with the renewed note for her to sign. The victim exhaled not a sigh, nor could the sharpest observer have seen any change of expression on her noble face. When the business was done, the moneylender's perturbation seemed to increase. Grotesquely taking his leave, he rushed out of the house, bouncing like a ball against the sides of the passage, stepping through a door that was not the one leading to the staircase, catching his coat on the bolt, and descending the stairs at last in a series of leaps, for he had not noticed that the landings were curved, and off went our man down those steps like someone rolling off a precipice.

SEVEN

His confusion and stupefaction did not vanish, as he had expected they would, when he trod the firm ground of the street; rather, the ground did not seem completely dependable. The very houses seemed to totter, unlikely as this sounds, so much so that Don Francisco frequently crossed from one side of the street to the other to avoid having one fall on him, mind you! In the Café de Zaragoza, where he had an appointment with a certain colleague to deal with a foreclosure, in two or three shops that he visited later, on the street, and, finally, in his own house when he dropped anchor there almost at nightfall, a troublesome and tenacious idea, that he pushed away without succeeding in driving it off, pursued him. It attacked him again, as the mosquito in the dark bedroom descends from the ceiling with its buzz and its bite, and the more one tries to shoo it away, the bolder, the more teasing and bloodthirsty the rascal becomes. The wicked little idea ended by producing an inexpressible restlessness which prevented him from dining with his usual solid appetite. It was a poor opinion of himself, a unanimous vote by all the powers of his soul against his behavior that morning. Of course he tried to beat down that judgment with a thousand arguments pulled out of this or that corner of his noddle, but the accusatory idea was much too strong for him and always emerged triumphant. The poor man at last succumbed to the terrifying logical process revealed by the unwelcome idea, and, banging on the table with the handle of his fork, Torquemada addressed the following harangue to himself:

"For Christ's sake—dammit! Little as you may like it, Francisco, admit that you've behaved like a pig today."

He abandoned the not overclean tablecloth without tasting the dessert—which, according to the annals, was Alcarria honey—and, having swallowed the last gulp of Lozoya water, went to his sitting room, ordering his blowsy maidservant to bring him the oil lamp. Pacing from his bed to the balcony (that is, from the middle of the bedroom to the far end of his sitting room, giving an occasional buffet to the glass doors that separated the two rooms and now and then a whack at the curtain to keep it out of his way), he succumbed, as I have said, to the all-conquering idea. For, as he told himself, some occasion was sure to arise when it would be indispensable to make a generous gesture. He had never been generous, nor had he ever done anything but squeeze, squeeze, squeeze. Now it was time to be a little more openhanded, for he had succeeded in amassing, by unrelenting work, a fortune which . . . Well—he was even richer than he thought. He owned houses, land, government bonds, an enormous number of notes, all negotiable, money put out on first mortgages, money lent to military and civilian persons with garnishment of their pay, an account in the Bank of Spain; he had excellent paintings, tapestries, innumerable pieces of very valuable jewelry; he was, to speak clearly and shortly, an affluent man, let us even say a very wealthy man. So what harm could there be in putting himself in a favorable light with the Aguila sisters, as good and refined ladies, perfect ladies, in a word, as he had ever seen? It was time to start behaving like a gentleman, circumspectly and with moderation, mind you! and to present himself to the world, no longer as a leech of a moneylender who does nothing but suck and suck, but as a gentleman of position, who knows how to be generous when he takes the notion. And—what the devil!—it was all a question of a few filthy pesetas; with or without them he would be neither richer nor poorer. In short, he had acted like a pig, and had deprived himself of the satisfaction of having those ladies feel grateful and think more highly of him than the common run of his debtors did. Circumstances had changed for him with the fabulous growth of his wealth; he had a vague feeling that he had risen to a higher social category; whiffs of grandeur and *gentlemanship*, that is, of gentlemanliness, had risen to his nostrils. Impossible to establish himself in that higher state without changing his habits, and without repudiating to some degree all those ignoble arts of miserliness. Why, even in the way of business, he needed a bit more ostentation and openhandedness, even in the way of business, dammit! because when that transformation that he felt in himself had become a little more apparent, events would perforce make it necessary for him to adjust his ways to the new state of affairs. In short, he would have to see how to mend the error he had committed. It was hard, by Christ! because on what sort of errand could he go there again? What would he say to them? Though it may seem strange, the poor man, with all his sharpness of mind, could not find suitable words to express the cancellation of interest. He possessed infinite ways of saying the opposite, but he did not know a word of the language of generosity, even by hearsay.

All evening he continued to torment himself with these ideas. His daughter Rufinita and his son-in-law came to visit, and they attributed his restlessness to reasons that were the exact opposite of the true ones.

"Somebody must have swindled your papa," said Quevedito to his wife as they left the house on their way to the theater, where they were going to see an hour-long performance. "And it must have been a whopper!"

Rufina, arm in arm with her diminutive spouse and well wrapped in her rose-colored shawl, grumbled as she went along the street, "Papa never learns. He squeezes people without mercy, tries to get blood out of stones; he never gives up, never shows any consideration, wouldn't take pity on the Lamb of God, and what's the outcome of it all? That Divine Providence takes a special interest in protecting poor debtors in arrears, and it's a body blow for the nasty moneylender. Papa ought to open his eyes and see that, with the fortune he has, he could play other roles in the world, rise to the sphere of the really rich, wear an English frock coat, and give himself lots of importance. Goodness, to live in a tenement and associate only with idiots, and to dress so plainly! It's not good, not halfway good. True, what does it matter to us? Let him look out for himself; but he's my father, and I'd like to see him live in a different style. As I was saying, Papa squeezes too hard; he chokes the poor and . . . and, well, there's a God in heaven who looks for people who commit injustices, so He can punish them. Of course, He sees that my father's a fiend for collections, and that's where He hits hardest. Heaven knows what happened to Papa today; somebody who won't pay no matter what, and when he went to foreclose he found only a few sticks of old furniture that weren't worth going to law over. Or someone who's had the bright idea of dying, leaving my father dangling; well, I don't know what it can be. What I say is, God can't be one bit pleased that Papa is such an awful man, and He'll tell him, "Hey, look out there!"

EIGHT

After the death of his son Valentín, of unhappy memory, Torquemada had fixed living quarters for himself on the main floor of the tenement house he owned on the Calle de San Blas. By throwing together the two little sitting rooms that looked out on the street, he achieved a reasonably roomy lair, with more chambers in it than he really needed; it was all very cramped, tortuous, and narrow, a real cell block to which he adjusted himself very comfortably, as if he could feel the shape of his body in every one of those tight little rooms. He gave Rufina a flat in another of the houses he owned, for although his daughter and son-in-law were both as good as gold, he was better off alone than even in their good company. Rufinita had begun the practice of interfering in her father's business, preaching him sermons about his avarice, and he didn't stand for that sort of game. To cut them short, and to be able to do exactly as he pleased without irksome intrusions, let each be in his own house, and God—or the devil—in everyone's.

Only three rooms out of all that little labyrinth served the miser for sleeping, receiving visitors, and dining. The rest of his lair was stuffed with furniture, tapestries, and other treasures acquired at auctions or bought for a song from hard-pressed debtors. He never relinquished a single chest of drawers, painting, carving, fan, piece of ivory, or snuff-box without getting a good price for it, and, though he was no artist, a sound instinct and the habit of handling works of art gave him an infallible skill in purchases as well as sales.

A tasteless confusion reigned in the furnishing of the three habitable rooms. To the furniture of the house where the couple had lived in Doña Silvia's time had been added other pieces, some better and some almost worthless, dilapidated, and ridiculous. The carpets had lush Santa Bárbara pieces sewed to strips of wretched felt. But the strangest feature of the great Torquemada's house was that, since his son's death, he had forbidden religious engravings or pictures in his rooms.

Assailed by a ferocious skepticism at the time of that great misfortune, he did not want to see the faces of saints or virgins, not even the face of Our Redeemer, whether nailed to the cross or driving the money-changers out of the temple. Not a bit of it. Out with saints male and female, out with Christs and even the Eternal Father. Out! For all of them, the great and the small, had cheated him abominably, and he wouldn't be the one, dammit! to show them any consideration. And so he cut off all communication with heaven, and all the images in the house, not even excepting the little Virgin of La Paloma herself, so greatly revered by Doña Silvia, were carried to the attic in a big basket, where they were now communing with spiders and mice.

Torquemada was terrible in his fanatical religious hatreds and regarded the Christian faith with the same contempt as all that farrago about humanity and the Great All, which he had been taught by Bailón. The Great All was just as bad a person as the other one, the priests' one, maker of the world in seven confounded days and then—what for? His head swam when he thought of the hurly-burly of things that had happened from the Creation to the day of universal cataclysm and collapse of the spheres, which was the day that the sublime child Valentín had taken flight, as much a son of God as of his father—let them say what they liked—and with as much talent as any Great All or any Most High that they had up there. He firmly believed that his child, snatched up into heaven in spirit and flesh, occupied it from one end to the other, or in the whole expanse of infinite, limitless space. How could anyone understand this business about the land, the air, or whatever they were, never coming to an end! But—what the devil!—without bothering about measurements, he believed implicitly that either there was no heaven or Christ who established it, or that it was completely filled by the soul of that child prodigy for whom earth had been a narrow cell, and all the mathematics that circulate in this world a mere trifle.

And so, with such antecedents, it will be understood that the only image representing divinity in the moneylender's house was Valentinito's portrait, a very skillfully enlarged photograph in a magnificent frame, hanging on the longest wall of the sitting room above a chest of drawers on which were chased silver candlesticks with candles in them, looking very much like an altar. The boy's little face was very expressive. One might call it a speaking likeness, and during his nights of insomnia, the father communicated with him in a language without words, composed rather of signs or communicatory grimaces, of exchanges of glances and a deep sigh, to which the portrait responded with miraculous winks and facial expressions. Sometimes the skinflint was assailed by an indefinable sadness, which he could not explain, for his business dealings were going along like clockwork, a sadness that arose from the depths of that whole internal feeling that has nothing to do with the body. It could only be assuaged by communicating with the portrait by means of a slow, silent contemplation, a sort of trance, during which the poor man was as if struck dumb, open-eyed and unwilling to move from the spot, feeling that time was passing with extraordinary slowness, the minutes like hours and hours like long, long days. Sometimes, when he was perturbed by resistance or arguments with his victims, he soothed himself by cleaning the portrait thoroughly and carefully, dusting it respectfully with a silk handkerchief which he kept for the purpose and which was never used for anything else; placing in perfect symmetry the candlesticks and the mathematics books the boy had used and which served as missals, a toy cart, and a stuffed lamb that he had enjoyed as a baby; lighting all the candles and snuffing them with exquisite care; and spreading on the chest of drawers, as a worthy cloth for that table, a large and beautiful kerchief embroidered by Doña Silvia. Torquemada did all this with a certain gravity, and one night it occurred to him that what he was doing resembled saying mass, for he caught himself making unhurried movements of hands and head that seemed almost sacerdotal.

Whenever he had a stubborn bout of insomnia he would dress and put on his shoes and, after lighting the altar, would engage in conversation with the boy, making little gestures of affection, faithfully recalling his voice and the things he used to say, and extolling, with a sort of inarticulate hosanna—what do you think?—mathematics, infinitely blessed mathematics, supreme science and sole true religion in all the worlds that have ever been and ever will be.

Needless to say, that night, because our man was so overwrought, was one of great solemnity in those peculiar rites. Feeling unable to sleep, he did not even consider going to bed. The maid left him alone. Once the candles were lighted he extinguished the oil lamp, taking it into the next room so that its fumes would not smell up the place, and gave himself over to the practice of his religion. The memory of the Aguila ladies and the vigor with which his conscience made his conduct with them seem unpleasant were mingled with other visions and feelings, forming a strange combination. Mathematics, the science of quantity, sacred numbers, weighed upon his spirit. In his heated brain he thought he heard faraway chants, adding up quantities with music and all. It was an angelic choir. Valentinico's face shone with joy. The father said to him, "They sing well. Who are they?"

Within himself he felt the crash of a great truth, proffered like the blast from a cannon: to wit, that mathematics is the Great All, and numbers the spirits which, viewed from below, are the stars, and Valentinico had all the stars within his being, and hence every bit of the spirit that wanders here and there. It was nearly dawn when Don Francisco gave way to exhaustion and sat down facing the chest of drawers, resting his head on his crossed arms, and they, in turn, upon the chair back. The candle flames grew longer and redder, licking away at their black wicks; the wax guttered, giving off a penetrating, churchly odor. The moneylender fell into a lethargy, or roused himself, for both verbs, though they have opposite meanings, could be applied to the peculiar state of his nerves and brain. Valentín said nothing; he looked sad and sulky, as children do who have not had their way in something they want badly. Nor could Don Francisco have said whether the boy was really looking at him, or whether he saw him in the cloudy dimness of the little nap he was taking on the chair. What is undeniable is that father and son spoke to each other; at least we can be sure, as an absolute fact, that Don Francisco pronounced these or very similar words:

"But I didn't know what I was doing, my darling son. It's not my fault if I don't know how to touch the chord of forgiveness . . . and if I do touch it, it gives no sound, believe me, no sound."

"Well, what I say is," Valentín's portrait must have answered, "you behaved like a real pig. Hurry over there tomorrow and return every cent of the confounded interest."

Torquemada rose to his feet abruptly and, as he snuffed out the candles, said to himself, "We'll do it; we've got to do it. Refund . . . the act of a gentleman . . . a generous gesture! But how do I come up with the gesture? What does a fellow say? How to start off, and with what kind of highflown language? I'll tell them, dammit! that it was a mistake . . . that I slipped up . . . oh, well! that I was ashamed of being ostentatious . . . the truth, the truth first of all . . . that I couldn't find the right word, because it was the first time I ever . . ."

NINE

The first time he had ever canceled interest! He was confused and upset for the rest of the morning, sensing that he was in the presence of a terrific crisis. He descried, as it were, the germ of a different man within himself, like a new being, a mysterious embryo that was already stirring, trying to live on its own within the life of its father. And that brand-new feeling, announcing itself like the stirring of love in someone who loves for the first time, produced a youthful tumult in him, a mixture of joy and fear. He went, therefore, to the house of the Aguila ladies like a man on the threshold of life, who after a thousand vacillations decides to launch his first declaration of love. On the way, he studied his sentences, searching for the words that would have the mellifluous flavor required by the circumstances. Smooth and affectionate words were a great difficulty for him, for those of his usual repertory all sounded harsh and vulgar, like the pounding of iron-shod cartwheels on worn cobblestones.

As on the previous day, he was received by Cruz, who was greatly astonished to see him, and his greeting was extremely awkward. He forgot the whole fancy *dictionary* with which he had come prepared, and when the lady asked him to what happy circumstance she owed the honor of such a visit, the poor man burst forth, under the effects of the spreading anxiety within his soul, and started pouring out, pell-mell, the following stream of ideas:

"Well, look here, Señora Doña Cruz . . . Yesterday, as I'm so absentminded . . . but my intention, mind you! was to give you an indication . . . I'm a considerate man and know how to make distinctions. Believe me, I had quite a bad moment when I became aware, after leaving, of my slip, of my . . . *stupefaction.* You are persons of worth, of great worth, you are most worthy and deserve to have a close friend offer you an indication . . ."

Here he became hopelessly entangled and tried another tack, but he always ended with the "indication" until, taking a hop, skip, and jump—verbally, of course—he fell prostrate on the terrain of pure and concise truth.

"Well, señora, I don't charge interest and wouldn't charge it if the Divine Word commanded me to! And here you have, in good coin, the amount that we discounted yesterday."

A great weight was lifted from him, and he was amazed that the lady made no protest about taking the money he had returned. It might even be said that she expected the gesture, and her gracious and benevolent smile, that of a woman experienced in the manners of society, revealed the satisfaction of a suspicion that had been confirmed. She thanked him gracefully, with none of the whinings of poor folk for whom the receiving and asking of money have become a trade; and, realizing with admirable tact that the subject was a troublesome one for the usurer, since it was out of character for him, she deftly changed the conversation. What bad weather they were having! Goodness, after so much rain, to have that dry cold from the north in the middle of May! And what a disastrous season for the unfortunates who had booths in San Isidro's Meadow! Frankly, the patron saint had not behaved very well this year. From this subject they went on to the sisters' concern over Rafael's ill health. It was undoubtedly a hepatic complaint, the result of his wretched and sedentary life. A period spent in the country, a little trip, a course of alkaline baths, would perhaps be a sure cure; but they could not think of such a thing. With the reticence of good manners, the lady did not harp on the subject of their poverty, so that the other would not believe that she was begging for his help to take the blind man to the baths.

Torquemada's mind had fallen into a brown study about his friends' decorous poverty, and though Cruz was talking about very different things, he could follow her only with an occasional monosyllabic grunt. Suddenly, like a swimmer who comes to the surface breathing deeply after long immersion in the water, the man burst out with this question: "And how goes that lawsuit?"

His imagination reproduced Doña Lupe's tremendous speculations as she lay dying, those galleons loaded with gold, those whole provinces, the Cuban sugar mills, and the incredible accumulation of riches which by rights belonged to the Aguilas, and of which, undoubtedly, they had been deprived by some malefactor. This noble Spain of ours has so much petty thievery in it!

"And how goes that little lawsuit?" he repeated, for the lady had not replied to the first inquiry.

"Well, the lawsuit," replied Cruz at last, "is still in process. It belongs to the court of disputed claims."

"That means that the other party is the government."

"Exactly so."

"Well then, why bother, you'll lose it. The government takes everything. It's the boss. Any coin that falls into its hands, let's not hope for it ever to come out of those confounded coffers. And tell me: is a lot of money involved?"

"Oh, yes indeed! And in the matter of six millions for supplying barley during the first civil war—that was a deal our grandfather made, do you know? Well, in those six millions, the matter is so clear that, if they don't recognize that credit, you might as well say goodbye to justice in Spain."

When he heard the word "millions," Torquemada stood there dumbfounded, and wrinkled his nose with an upward-aimed sniff, a very characteristic gesture of his for expressing the magnitude of things, along with the amazement such magnitude produces.

"And also there are other unresolved questions, other matters. It's a very complicated affair, Señor Don Francisco. My father had his landholdings in La Rioja and on the banks of the Jalón, which were collateral for a loan, seized because of a contract for water supply. The government did not carry out its part of the bargain; it played havoc with the clauses of the rental agreements and impounded the property. Absurd things, Señor Don Francisco, that are seen only in this chaotic country. Would you like to know about the matter in more detail? Then come here one of these nights. In the loneliness and friendless state in which we live, victims of such injustice and outrage, cut off from the society into which we were born and in which we have suffered so many slights and horrible disillusionments, merciful God has given us a consolation, a rest for our souls, the friendship of an incomparable man, a charitable, noble, and generous soul, who sustains us in this struggle and gives us courage. Without that compassionate man, without that angel, our life would be impossible; we would have died of misery by now. He has been the counterweight of so much misfortune. In him we have seen Providence, merciful and beautiful, bringing us an olive branch after the flood and telling us not to forget that hope exists. Hope! It is enough to know that it has not been snatched from the world, to feel it and to live and draw courage from it. Thanks to that good friend, we do not believe that all is lost. We look at the shadows that surround us, and far away we see a tiny light, a tiny light."

"And that gentleman is . . . ?" said Torquemada, in whom curiosity was stronger than the pleasure of listening to the lady talk.

"Do you know Don José Ruiz Donoso?"

"Donoso, Donoso . . . I think I recognize the name."

"He is a very well-known person in Madrid, a mature man, good presence, exuding respectability, the manners of a prince, few words, gentlemanly behavior without affectation . . . Don José Ruiz Donoso . . . Yes, you must have seen him a thousand times. He has been an employee of the Treasury Department, the kind who never lose their positions when there is a change of administration. Nowadays he is retired, with a pension of thirty-six thousand reales, and lives like a patriarch, occupying himself only in caring for his invalid wife and looking after Fidela and me, trying to hasten the wretched lawsuit, in which he couldn't take more interest if it were his own. Ah, he loves us so much, he adores us! He was an intimate friend of our father's, and they studied law together in Granada. He is a very respected man in all of official Madrid; there are no closed doors for him in this ministry and that, nor in the General Accounting Office, nor in the Council of State. All day long you'll find him going from office to office, pushing away at the monstrously heavy cart of our lawsuit, which falls into one pothole today and a different one tomorrow. He knows better than anyone else the whole juridical and administrative keyboard; sometimes he plays in the key of friendly recommendation, sometimes in that of severe authority; one day he throws his arms around Councillor A's shoulders; on the next he gives a tongue-lashing to Officer B, of the General Accounting Office; and that's the way the affair goes, and that's how we know what hope is, and that's the way we live. You may well believe that on the day that Donoso is no longer here to help us, the world will have come to an end for us, and we'll have nothing more to do than to try to have a Christian death that will take us to the other world as quickly as possible."

This eloquent panegyric heightened Torquemada's curiosity and he became wildly impatient to meet Señor Donoso, whom he felt he knew already from the description that had been so skillfully painted for him. He could actually see him, hear him; he was familiar.

"He never misses his nightly visit here, even when it's raining pitch-forks," added the lady. "It is our only tertulia and the sole consolation in this wretched life of ours. I have the feeling that you and he will get on very well. You will meet a man who is very strict in his prin-ciples, straight as a die, absolutely truthful, and has excellent manners without effusiveness, the kind of behavior that is disappearing nowa-days, refinement joined to dignity and an exact feeling for the distance that ought always to be maintained between persons."

"Of course, I'll come," said Don Francisco, feeling overwhelmed in advance by the superiority of the person Cruz had described.

He spun out the visit a little more than courtesy demanded, hoping that Fidela, whom he wanted to see, would appear. He heard her sweet, caressing voice talking with the blind man in the adjoining sitting room as though she were scolding him lovingly. But the little cook did not appear, and at last the skinflint could only depart, con-soling himself for her absence with the firm intention of returning that night.

TEN

Dressed in his Sunday best, he went there between eight and nine, and as he knocked at the door, Señor Donoso was climbing the stairs, coughing and slow of step. They entered the house almost simulta-neously, and in their greeting and introductions to each other it goes without saying that the ease and worldly experience of the family's old friend necessarily contrasted with the new one's clownish awk-wardness. Donoso was a conspicuously bald man, with a military mus-tache that was almost white; his brows were very black, his face grave and ceremonious, like an official emblem that by its mere presence earned the respect of all who saw it; his body and size were rotund and well-proportioned, with a certain formal stiffness, the result of custom and social intercourse; he was dressed with exquisite care, everything very clean from his hairless skull, which shone like a lid of burnished marble, to his well-polished boots without a speck of street dirt on them.

From the very first moment, he fascinated Torquemada, who never took his eyes off him or lost a syllable of what he said, admiring the correctness of the other's appearance and the easy elegance of his conversation. That double-breasted frock coat, so well fitted to the body, was the garment he liked best. That's the way frock coats ought to look—elegant and impressive, *hermetically closed*, not like his, which was as old as the hills and so loose and dowdy that when he walked he seemed like a bat about to take flight. And how about those striped trousers, that fell so gracefully, without bagging at the knees? And everything else, good Lord, everything: the stiff collar-points, white as snow; the calfskin boots, heavy without ceasing to be elegant, and even the monogrammed cigarette case he took from his pocket, to offer him a black-tobacco cigarette, already rolled in expensive paper! Everything, good Lord, everything in Don José Ruiz Donoso proclaimed the gentleman of those times exactly as gentlemen ought to be, as Torquemada had wanted to be ever since this idea of gentlemanship had got itself into his head.

The conversational style, or what Don Francisco described to himself as the *palaver*, enchanted him even more than the clothing, and the poor man scarcely dared to offer a timid opinion on the various things that were discussed there. Cruz and Donoso could talk about anything and rivaled each other in their comments. Both had an inexhaustible repertory of extremely lucid phrases, which Torquemada stored away in his memory to use whenever they came in handy. Fidela spoke little; however, the blind man added his share to every conversation with nervous volubility, and with the wit characteristic of a man who, since he cannot see, has cultivated his imagination.

Giving mental thanks to God for having furnished him a social model so entirely to his taste as Señor Donoso, Don Francisco resolved to imitate him faithfully in that transformation of his personality demanded of him by body and soul; and, more careful to observe than anything else, he allowed himself to intervene in the conversation only to opine as the oracle of the gathering. Goodness, Doña Cruz was an oracle too, and said things that Seneca himself would have been proud of! Torquemada uttered little grunts of approval and ventured a timid phrase or two, with the caution of one who is in constant fear of playing a clumsy role.

It goes without saying that Donoso treated the moneylender as an equal, without indicating in the slightest degree the inferiority of the new friend of the household. His courtesy was very formal, a trifle dry, and he did not indulge in familiarities inappropriate to men of such dignity. Don José appeared to be about sixty years of age, but he was older than that, a good deal older, though he carried his years very well, thanks to an extremely well-organized life filled with precautions. Body and soul were marvelously balanced in that man of unassailable habits, of a probity in which evil tongues had never succeeded in discovering the slightest blemish; he made a religion of method, learned in the bureaucratic form of worship and decanted from administration into all orders of life; his intelligence was perfectly aligned on that median level which constitutes the force called general opinion. Torquemada grasped all this in a moment, with prophetic wisdom: this was his man, his prototype, what he must and would be now that he was rich and worthy of an honorable place in society.

Straying here and there, the conversation turned to the lawsuit. That night, as every night, Donoso brought news. When he had nothing new to say, he touched up what he had said the night before, giving it an appearance of freshness so as to keep his friends' hopes always green, for he loved them dearly.

"At last, the inventory of 1839 has appeared in the Accounting Office. Finding it was no easy task. The official is a friend of mine, and yesterday I gave him a good scolding for his tardiness. The arbitrator of the Council has promised me that he will expedite the verdict on the matter. We can count on a decision before the vacation. I've been able to persuade them not to include the report from the War Office, for that would be an endless story."

And he went on in this vein. Cruz sighed, and Fidela seemed more absorbed in her tatting than in the lawsuit.

"In this Madrid of ours," said Don Francisco, who had found the courage to open up a bit at this stage of the conversation, "lawsuits go on for ever, because those who administer justice pay attention only to influence. If the ladies have influence, they can rest easy. If not, they'll wait a good long time for a decision. The poor plaintiff can have rights as clear as sunshine, but it's no use unless he has good coattails to hang on to."

He had his say and was puffed up with satisfaction at the way his speech fell on the ears of his hearers. Donoso supported his view by rapid movements of his head which produced a dizzying array of sparkling reflections on the shining convexity of his bald skull.

"I know it from my very own personal experience," added the orator with lamentable redundancy. "Oh, what a court, what devil's spawn, a plague out of hell! They smelled flesh; they figured that there was a place to dig their nails in, and they drove me crazy making me wait from one day to the next, and one month to the next, until I sent them to hell and a little farther. Of course, since I wasn't going to let them loot me, I lost, and that's why nowadays I'd rather it all went to the devil than go to court."

Laughter. Fidela looked at him, saying suddenly, "Don Francisco, we know that you have a great deal of property in Cadalso de los Vidrios."

"We know it," added Cruz, "through a woman who used to be our maid and who is from there. She comes to see us now and then, and brings us new wine in October and rabbits and partridges in hunting season."

"I, property? Just a little, just a little."

"How many pairs of animals?" asked Donoso laconically.

"Well, I'll tell you. Most of it is in vineyards. Last year I got fifteen hundred four-gallon jars."

"Well, well!"

"But it sells for only six reales a jar! I hardly get enough out of it to pay for labor and the confounded taxes."

"Don't be so modest," said Cruz. "Farmers are all alike. Always whimpering."

"I'm not whimpering, no, señora. Don't any of you think that I'm discontented with my lot. I have no complaints. Yes, I own things, señora, I certainly do. Why should I deny it, when it's come from the sweat of my brow?"

"Come now, you are tremendously rich," said Fidela in a tone that could easily have been either joking or disdainful, along with a touch of surprise, as if behind her words there were a vague accusation to Providence for having distributed wealth so unequally.

"Easy does it. What's this about tremendously rich? I've got enough, yes indeed, for a pretty good stew in the pot. I have a few houses. And in Cadalso, besides the vineyards, there's a bit of farmland, a bit of grazing land."

"It's going to turn out," observed the blind man jovially, "that with all those bits you have half the world in your pocket. You really ought to share it with us!"

Laughter. Torquemada, slightly annoyed, made haste to say, "Well, all right, ladies and gentlemen, I am rich, relatively rich, which doesn't keep me from being humble, very humble, a very plain man, and I know how to live poorly, with a miserable crust of bread if I have to. Some people who see me dressed without all this fancy business of style think I'm tightfisted. People who know how little I spend on my house and food, and that I don't make a show, and never put on the dog, call me a cheeseparer. Because I don't know what it is to show off, and bragging was never made for me."

When he heard this tirade by Don Francisco, who pronounced it with a certain emphasis, Donoso attracted everyone's attention with an expansive gesture and then pronounced a solemn discourse to which everyone listened with religious attention, and which is worthy of being consigned to paper, for attitudes of the utmost importance to this true story derive from it.

ELEVEN

"Why make a mystery of wealth honestly acquired?" said Donoso gravely, weighing his words and listening to his own idea, so that he was speaker and audience all at once. "Why conceal it with a false sense of humility? That smacks, Señor Don Francisco, of overly-nice manners and of a habit we must banish from our midst if we want to have well-being and progress and to make commerce and industry flourish. And what is the point, Señor Don Francisco, of this exaggerated modesty, these habits of sordid—yes, sordid—economizing, so out of tune with the fortune one has accumulated by one's labor? What is the point of living in apparent poverty when one has millions? And when I say millions I am also talking about thousands, or any other amount. No; every man must live in consonance with his means, and society has the right to demand it of him. Let the day laborer live like a laborer and the capitalist like a capitalist, for if it is shocking to see a poor devil spending himself out of house and home, it is no less so to see a rich man squeezing every penny and living in niggardliness and squalor. No; everyone according to his means. The rich man who lives in poverty, among rude and vulgar people, commits a grave sin, yes, señor; but a sin against society. Society needs to constitute a counterforce to the batterings of the envious proletariat. And what elements are we to use to constitute this force if not the wealthy? For if landowners and persons of independent means hide away underground and conceal what gives them the right to occupy great positions; if they renounce those positions and act like beggars, then on whom, I say, on whom can society rely for her best defense?''

He crossed his arms. No one answered him, for no one dared to interrupt by word or gesture so eloquent a string of remarks. He continued:

"Wealth imposes duties, my dear sir. To be influential yet not to appear as such on the social scene is a grave error. The rich man has the obligation to live in harmony with his means, spending them with proper care and presenting himself to the world in sober brilliance. One's position, my friend, is a very essential thing. Society confers posts on those who should occupy them. Those who flee such positions leave society unprotected and in the hands of bold scoundrels. No, señor; we must be fully aware of the obligations brought to us by every coin that comes into our pockets. If the wealthy man lives in rags, can you tell me how industry is going to prosper? And commerce, can you tell me how it can prosper? Farewell wealth of nations, farewell mercantile movement, farewell exchange, farewell beauty and comfort in the great capital cities, farewell railway network! And there is more. Persons of position constitute what we call the *ruling classes* of society. Who provides the standard for everything that happens in the world? The ruling classes. Who sets up a barrier to revolutions? The ruling classes. Who upholds the standard of morality, of justice, or public and private law? The ruling classes. Do you think that there would be society, and that there would be peace, and that there would be order and progress, if the rich were to say, 'Look here, I just don't feel like being a ruling class; I'll crawl into my hole and dress seven seasons out of date; I won't spend a farthing, like an unemployed clerk; I'll sleep on a pallet full of fleas; I'll just keep stuffing my income into a sock, and society can be left to its own devices, and fight back as best it can against socialism and brawls. And industry can die, for I have no need of it; and commerce can go to the devil; and communications networks can go off and die somewhere. Railways? If I don't

travel, what do I want them for? City planning, hygiene, beautifica-
tion of the cities? What do they mean to me? Police force, justice? Since
I never go to law, since I never infringe the law codes, to hell with
them all.' "

He paused to take breath with trembling lip and heated breast, and
a vague approbatory noise was heard, which did not break out into
applause owing to the excessive respect which the orator inspired in
all present.

Pause. Transition from the serious to the familiar.

"Señor Don Francisco, don't take amiss this tirade that I'm permitting myself to spout at you. Listen to it fair-mindedly, and then, with
your good judgment, you will do as you like. We are speaking as friends
here, and each one says what he thinks. But I am very open, and with
persons whom I truly esteem I speak openly and even heatedly at
times. I know society well. I have lived for more than forty years in
contact with all the eminent people in the country; I have learned a
certain amount; I have no lack of ideas; I know how to appreciate
things; experience gives me a certain authority. You seem to me to be
a very sensitive person, a person of very good judgment, but too much
inside your shell. You are like the snail, always carrying his house
around with him. You must come out of it, live in the world. I'm
allowing myself to tell you how I feel because I only speak like this
to really clever men; I have nothing to say to fools. They wouldn't
understand me."

"Fine, fine," murmured Torquemada who, struck dumb by the terrifying effect of Donoso's admonitions, found no adequate way of expressing his admiration. "You have spoken like Seneca; no, better,
much better than Seneca. It's just that . . . I'll tell all of you . . . Since
I grew up poor, and have always lived meanly, saving everything right
down to my saliva, I just can't get used to . . . What's the straightest
path in the world? Custom . . . and that's the path I take. Me butting
my way into the ruling classes? Me living it up among them? Me showing off and . . . No, it can't be; it just doesn't suit me. I don't understand myself in those terms, that's all."

"That's not showing off, for heaven's sake!"

"There's more affectation, and consequently more 'showing off,' in
pretending to be poor when one is rich."

"It only means giving the truth a chance to show itself."

"It means being what you are."

"Anything else is a deception."

"A lie, a farce."

"It's not enough to be rich, you have to seem rich too."

"Precisely."

"Just so."

These comments, so quickly expressed by all three Aguilas without giving Don Francisco time to respond individually to any of them, set his mind in a whirl. He heard a buzzing in his ears; ideas crept into his mind like a flock of hunted vermin, and reemerged in a crowd to flit about in the air. Stammeringly at first, then in a firmer voice, he expressed agreement with such ideas, assuring his hearers that he had already given them serious thought, and that he realized he was living outside his natural center and class; but how was he to master his diffident and limited character? How was he to learn all at once the thousand things that a person of means ought to know? Instinctively he chose the path of sincerity, after many false starts and reticencies, and even before he thought over whether it would be appropriate to declare his incapacity for refinement, he had already declared and confessed it, like a child caught in a fib. What could he do about it now? What was said was said, and there was no turning back. Donoso attacked him with powerful arguments; Cruz insisted that others even more clumsy than himself were making a princely progress through the world, and Fidela and the blind man cheered him on with gay comments which, though there was an element of mockery in them, were so discreet and so witty that they could not offend him.

By dint of such chatter, the evening came to an end, and Torquemada was so much at ease there that he could almost believe that his acquaintance with the Aguila sisters and Donoso went back a long way, for they were becoming very dear to him. The two friends left the house together and, on the way, chatted to their hearts' content about business, Don Francisco amazed by how well-informed Don José was about these matters and how well he discoursed about interest on capital and other economic affairs.

Alone once more in his burrow, the moneylender remembered word for word the reproof administered by that new friend of his, already his spiritual adviser, for he intended to pursue Donoso's infinitely wise doctrine as best he could. What he had told him about a rich man's duties and the law of social positions was something worthy of being heard kneeling, a little like the Sermon on the Mount, the new law that was to transform the world. The world in this case was himself, and Donoso the Messiah who had come to turn everything topsy-turvy and found a new society on the ruins of the old. During his periods of wakefulness, Don Francisco thought only of the tailor from whom he must order a *hermetically closed* frock coat like Donoso's; of the hatter who would decorate his head; and of other things having to do with clothing. Without wasting a moment, he would have to declare war on his plebeian appearance, on a grubby and vulgar style of dress. He had spent enough time looking like a scarecrow. Refined society was claiming him, like a deserter to its ranks, and there he was going, straightaway, with patent-leather boots and everything else that was appropriate.

But the most astonishing thing was that in a single night of chitchat with those most worthy persons, he had learned more elegant phrases than in ten years of his previous life. From his relationship with Doña Lupe (in justice he had to admit) he had extracted different ways of speaking which he used to great advantage. For example, from her he had learned to say *raise the question, other circumstances being equal, up to a point*, and *in broad terms*. But what did these poor language attempts signify in comparison with the delightful things he had just assimilated? Now he knew how to say *ad hoc* (he pronounced it "edok"), *starting from the principle, admitting the hypothesis, in the vast majority of cases*; and, lastly, the great triumph was being able to call everything "this element" or "that element." He had believed that the only elements were fire and water, and now, lo and behold, it was a very fine thing to say *the conservative elements, the military element, the ecclesiastical element*, and so on.

Next day all things looked different from the way he ordinarily regarded them. "Am I in my second childhood?" he thought, noting within himself a delight that skipped through his whole body, a sort of *joie de vivre* or a pleasant foretaste of happiness. Every acquaintance he saw that day seemed intolerably crude. Some of them even disgusted him. In the Café del Gallo and the Café de las Naranjas, where he had to go in pursuit of a hapless debtor, they seemed hopelessly ill-bred. He met friends who only by God's special grace, it seemed, were not walking on four feet, and some of them smelled horrible. "Get away from me, foul breed," he said to himself, fleeing from contact with those who were his equals and taking refuge in his house, where at least he had the company of his thoughts, some very pretty thoughts, of frock coat and top hat, grave and smiling thoughts with a whiff of cologne about them.

He received his daughter that day with a certain coolness, saying, "My word, you look awful! It even seems to me that you smell bad. You're really very commonplace, and your husband is the most vulgar little fellow I know, *a real number-one vulgarian.*"

TWELVE

It goes without saying that the stars would fail to appear in the vault of heaven before Torquemada would miss the Aguila sisters' tertulia or the company of Señor Donoso, whom he was gradually beginning to imitate, copying his actions and words, the way he put on his hat, the special tone he used to greet someone familiarly, and even the way he walked. A few days sufficed to form a friendship with him. The miser began by running into his model, as if by chance, on the Paseo de Recoletos, where he lived; then he went to see him at his home on the pretext of consulting him about a renegotiable loan he had just been offered, and through Donoso's intervention he later made a mortgage loan under very advantageous conditions. In the evenings the two men saw each other at the Aguilas' house, where the miser had by this time acquired a certain familiarity. He did not feel inhibited there, and observing that he was treated kindly and even affectionately, he basked in the warmth of that household where dignity and poverty were one and the same. And he did not fail to notice a certain difference in the way the four persons of that extremely agreeable society treated him. Cruz was the one who used the most consideration, displaying on every occasion a gentle affability and a desire to please him. Donoso looked upon him as a good friend. In Fidela he thought he noticed a certain coolness and a slightly mischievous tendency, as if, delicately and with the utmost refinement, she sometimes wanted to what is vulgarly called "pull his leg." And, finally, Rafael, though never losing his good manners, always correct and fastidious, took exception to many of the things he said. Slowly it was borne in on Don Francisco that there was a division between the four persons, two on one side and two on the other. Although in some circumstances the division did not exist, and all was brotherliness and concord, suddenly the barrier would go up, and the miser had to stretch his neck a bit to see Fidela and the blind man from his side of it. And they viewed him with a certain reserve, which was the most incomprehensible thing of all. Why that reserve, when he loved them all, and was ready to embark on any humanly possible sacrifice, within the limits imposed by his nature?

Indeed, Cruz had completely captivated him with her affectionate friendliness and the graceful style God had given her in dealing with every question. Little by little, familiarity began to grow, and it was wonderful to see how cleverly the lady could impose her ideas, changing from a friend into a schoolmistress. "Don Francisco, that coat is an absolutely perfect fit. If you didn't move your arms quite so much when you walked, you would be the picture of a diplomat." "Don Francisco, do try to break the habit of saying 'irregardless' and 'keep your eyes peeled.' That way of expressing yourself doesn't sound well on your lips." "Don Francisco, whoever put on your cravat? The cat? One would think that claws, not hands, had been at it." "Don Francisco, take my advice and shave off your goatee; it's half white and half black, so bristly and aggressive-looking that it seems false. Just the mustache, which is going white, will make your face more respectable. You needn't look like a retired noncom. No one will have a better presence than you if you do as I say." "Don Francisco, let's agree that after tomorrow you won't wear a soft collar when you come here. High collar, are we agreed? Either one is or one isn't a person of means, as you say yourself." "Don Francisco, you use too much cologne. Not quite so much, my friend. The minute you come in the street door those whiffs of perfume give warning that you've arrived. Moderation, moderation in everything." "Don Francisco, promise me you won't get angry, and I'll tell you. Shall I tell you? I'll tell you that I'm not at all pleased with your religious skepticism. To say that you 'don't swallow dogma'! Quite aside from the crude way of expressing it, the idea of swallowing dogma is abominable! We must believe, my dear man. What, have we come into this world only to think about miserable money?"

Needless to say, Torquemada was enraptured by these gentle and fraternal reprimands, and lost no time in promising submission to the lady's desires in matters small as well as large, in the insignificant detail of the cravat as well as the grave attempt to embrace blindly each and every religious truth.

Fidela permitted herself to give him the same sort of admonitions, though in a completely different, slightly mocking, tone and with very amusing imaginative touches.

"Don Francisco, last night I dreamed that you came to see us in a carriage, in your own carriage, as a man of means should have. See, dreams are not foolish. The real world is what doesn't make sense in the vast majority of cases. Yes indeed, we heard the noise of the wheels, I went out on the balcony, and there I saw my Don Francisco getting down from the landau, with a footman at the door, hat in hand."

"Oh, what a joke!"

"You said something to the footman, I don't know what . . . in that brusque tone of voice you're apt to use . . . and started upstairs. You were climbing the stairs endlessly. I went to the top of the staircase and saw you climbing and climbing and never getting to the top, for the steps multiplied by hundreds, by thousands, and never came to an end. Steps, endless steps . . . and you were really upset . . . and at the last you were climbing all bent over, terribly bent over, completely exhausted . . . and I was encouraging you. I had the idea of going down to meet you, and the fact is that I did start down, down, never getting close to you, for the staircase grew as much for me going down it as for you climbing up it."

"My word, how tiring, and what strange dreams!"

"That's just like Fidela," said Cruz, laughing. "She always dreams about staircases."

"It's true. All my dreams are about going up and down. I wake up with aching limbs and short of breath. I climb staircases made of paper, staircases made of diamond, on ladders as thin as spiderwebs. I go down steps of molten metal, steps made of snow, and down any number of things that are my own thoughts, set one below the other. Are all of you laughing?"

Indeed they were laughing, Torquemada chiefly, with all his heart, feeling not in the least put off by the slight whiff of satire which seasoned Fidela's conversation like a discreetly used condiment. The feeling aroused in him by the younger of the Aguila sisters was very strange. He could have wished that she were his daughter, or that his daughter Rufina were like her, both being things that could not easily be brought to pass. He regarded her as a child who should never be allowed any initiative in serious matters and who needed to be humored, satisfying her childish whims from time to time. Fidela often said that she adored dolls, and that until the time when poverty had imposed heavy domestic duties on her, she used to indulge herself by playing with them. She still had a few magnificent dolls left from her past as a rich child, and occasionally, in the solitude of night, she would take them out just for fun and chat a while with her speechless friends, remembering the happy times. Furthermore, she admitted that she was greedy. In the kitchen, every time they made some dessert, cooked fruit or anything of the kind, she would taste it before serving it, and the sugar supply had a formidable enemy in the cook. When she was not chewing a stick of cinnamon, she would nibble on lemon peels; she ate noodles raw, and the tenderer leaves of red cabbage, and cheese rinds.

"I'm the house mouse," she would say cheerfully, "and when we had a linnet I used to help him eat the birdseed. I just love to suck a sprig of parsley, nibble on a lima bean or stuff a handful of raw rice into my mouth. I love the hot taste of radish skins, and I'm so crazy about Alcarria honey that I'd go on tasting it, to see if it's good, until I died. As for sugar wafers, I don't know what I'd do for them, for I'd eat every sugar wafer that's made and could be made in the whole world, I like them so, so much. If they'd let me, I wouldn't eat anything but cookies, honey, and. . . I'm sure you can't guess, Don Francisco?"

"Peanuts?"

"No."

"Candied pine nuts?"

"No, not those either."

"Raisins, almond paste, nut brittle, Jordan almonds, tipsy-cakes?"

"I'm tipsy about tipsy-cakes too. But that's not it, that's not it. It's . . ."

"*Chufas*—groundnuts," said the blind man, to put an end to the game.

"That's right. I'm mad about chufas. I'd order that plant to be cultivated all over Spain, and have it sold in all the shops to take the place of chick-peas. And they ought to use orgeat instead of wine! Now, there's something I don't like, wine. How revolting! What won't men invent! To spoil grapes, such a nice fruit, to make that disgusting drink out of them. It really nauseates me, and when people make me drink it, I get sick, I fall asleep, and then I dream the most awful things: that my head is growing, that it grows to be bigger than San Isidro's Church, or that the bed I'm sleeping in is a hurdy-gurdy, and I'm the cylinder full of little bumps that turns and turns to make the music play. No, don't give me wine unless you want me to go crazy.''

What a fine time Donoso and Don Francisco had, listening to the charming girl's original notions! Don Francisco, wishing to show her a pure paternal affection, never went to the tertulia without taking some dainty for the little house mouse. Happily, in the Fúcar passage on the way to the Calle de San Blas there was a Valencian who had a stall where he sold Valencian matting and orgeat. He owed Torquemada a small sum, and the latter never passed by of an afternoon without politely begging him for a cardboard cone of chufas. "It's for some children," he would say. The confectioner on the Calle de las Huertas, an insolvent debtor, paid him interest, for lack of better money, in the form of hard candies, pieces of nut brittle, an egg-yolk sweetmeat or two, honey fritters from Yepes, or Astorga shortcakes, these last an item left over from the previous Christmas and by now a bit stale. The skinflint made little packets of them with colored paper supplied by the confectioner, and by dint of sometimes running to the grocer's shop to acquire a quarter-pound of raisins, or a half-pound of English biscuits, there was never an evening when he went to the tertulia empty-handed. All of it cost him no more than a peseta and a few céntimos every time he had to buy it, and with such scant expense he thought himself a gallant and free-spending man. Exuding sweetness, with all the delicacies in the world in his soul, he would present his little gift to the demoiselle, accompanying it with the most delicate and honeyed expressions that his rude vocabulary could offer: "Well, here's a surprise for us. This is one you didn't expect. They're some things made of fine chocolate, called *pompoms*, with lovely silver paper on them, and better than marzipan." He could not cure himself of the habit of announcing and discussing what he had brought. Fidela would receive the delicacy with a great show of gratitude and childish joy, and Don Francisco was enchanted when he saw her sink her teeth into its delicious center. They were of an ideal whiteness, the evenest, most beautiful, cleanest teeth he had seen in his whole confounded life, teeth so superior in their structure and color that he never thought anything like them could exist in all of humanity. Thinking of them, he would say, "Do angels have teeth, I wonder? Do they bite? Do they eat? There's no telling if they have teeth and molars, those beings who, according to books on religion, don't need to eat. And what's the use of *raising the question?* First we'd have to know if there *are* angels."

THIRTEEN

The friendship between Donoso and Torquemada was rapidly becoming very close, and by early summer, Don Francisco would touch nothing having to do with interest unless he heard the wise opinion of so expert a man. Donoso had expanded his ideas about the lending of money. He no longer confined himself to the narrow area of garnisheeing the pay of civil and military employees, or mortgages on Madrid houses. He learned new ways of placing his money on a larger scale, and was initiated into lucrative operations that carried no risk. Once powerful men, now ruined, entrusted themselves to him for their salvation, which was the same as turning themselves over to him, bound hand and foot; companies in danger of bankruptcy let him have some of their stock at ridiculously low prices in order to assure their dividends; and even the State benignly accepted him. The whole machinery of banking, which had been a mystery to him, was disclosed by Donoso, as was operating on the Stock Exchange, whose advantages and risks he grasped in an instant with unerring instinct. His friend advised him with absolute honesty, and when he said, "Buy Cuban bonds and don't worry," Don Francisco did not hesitate. An unalterable harmony reigned between the two men, and it was an admirable thing that in Donoso's intervention in Torquemada's affairs there always shone the purest disinterestedness. Having put him in the way of two or three business deals of considerable importance, he refused to charge him a broker's commission or anything resembling one.

Along with this transformation in the economic sphere, another transformation, a social one, was taking place, visible in timid changes in dress and carried to its greatest development by slow transitions, so that the great change would not leap to the eye with the crudeness of a music-hall turn. Continued use of the derby tempered somewhat the dazzling appearance of a new outfit of raisin-colored cloth, and the splendors of the brand-new silk hat were obscured and subdued by an overcoat with a somewhat greasy collar, contemporary with the entrance of our valiant troops into Tetuán some twenty years earlier. He was sufficiently intelligent to shun the ridiculous, or to avoid it by skillful combinations. Even so, the metamorphosis was instantly observed by more than one wit in the neighborhoods where most of his chief acquaintances resided, and there was no lack of sneers and poisonous thrusts. Ignoring these, Don Francisco gradually drew away from his traditional associates, and could no longer conceal the coolness he felt toward his friends in the Café del Gallo and in various shops and stores on the Calle de Toledo, a coolness which appeared to some as a more or less openly declared dislike, and to others real aversion. Some found it natural that Don Francisco should want to "live it up," possessing, as he certainly did possess, more than many men who dashed about Madrid in carriages they had not finished paying for, or who lived by crooked and dishonest means. And there was no lack of those who, sadly observing him withdraw from the society in which he had made his first million reales, accused him of being an ingrate and an egotist. . . But he was doing the same as everyone else: after sucking the poor until they had no blood left, he flew higher, toward the homes of the rich.

And if in his habits, especially his habits of dressing, his evolution was marked by signs and characteristics that anyone could see, he progressed still more in his manner of speaking. He had an astonishing capacity for catching on to a phrase, and assimilated Donoso's speech mannerisms with an imitative skill that was incredible at his age. It is true that he often spoiled an idea with crude solecisms, or encountered obstacles of syntax. But even so, he thoroughly fooled those who did not know him, for, shrewdly aware of the dangers of talking too much, he confined himself to the most necessary speech, and this laconism, along with some expression or other that he had picked up from Donoso, made him pass for a profound and thoughtful man. A number of people who met him for the first time at that period regarded him as a very well-informed and serious person, hearing him make these or similar comments: "I have the feeling that the price of barley will be an *enima* in the coming months, on account of the farmers' *expectant attitude.*" Or this: "Señores, I have the feeling" (Donoso's example kept him constantly *having the feeling*) "that there is enough freedom already, and enough universal *sufferance* and more rights than we want. But I ask you: is this enough? Does the nation, perchance, live only by principles? Oh, no. Before the entree, give the nation good-administration stew and balanced-budget soup. That's the real *cock-a-doodle-doo!* That's where the thorn pricks. There. Let the administration manage well and not waste a penny. Let it look out for the taxpayer, and I'll be the first to congratulate myself on my *behalf* as a Spaniard and my *behalf* as a taxpayer." Some said, listening to him speak, "This fellow is a little crude, but how well he talks!" And what an amusing joke, to call suffrage "sufferance"! Needless to say, the judiciousness of his pronouncements and his reputation as a man who was rolling in cash gradually gained friends for him in that sphere where he was trying out his wings. For him, "manifestations" were everything that was being talked about in the world, and he was so taken with the word that he never failed to use it in all circumstances, even if he were to be shot for it. Manifestations were what Cánovas had said in a political speech that was being discussed; manifestations, what was said by the concierge's wife in the house on the Calle de San Blas about whether the children who lived on the fourth floor had or had not pee-peed over the third-floor balconies.

And now that Don Francisco's house has been mentioned, it must be added that the first time Donoso went there, to discuss a large loan that the duke and duchess of Gravelinas were requesting, he was astounded that his friend lived so wretchedly and, taking advantage of the intimacy already established between them, allowed himself to reproach his friend in that fatherly tone which served him so well:

"I wouldn't have believed it if I hadn't seen it, friend Don Francisco. It makes me angry. Take it as you will, but indeed I am angry, yes, señor. Well, now, aren't you ashamed of living in this hovel? Don't you understand that even your financial reputation suffers when you have such a wretched house? What people will say! That you are a close-fisted Alexander, a tatterdemalion skinflint like the ones that are so popular on the stage. Believe me, this favors you not at all. As a man is, so his home should be. It troubles me that a person like yourself doesn't have the reputation he deserves."

"But, Señor Don José, I'm perfectly comfortable here! Ever since I lost my dear son, I've taken a great dislike to the central parts of the city. I live here very comfortably and have the feeling that this house has brought me good luck. But don't think, mind you! that I'm slamming the door on your manifestations. I'll think about it, Don José, I'll think about it."

"Yes, think about it. Don't you believe that instead of going around searching so diligently for a tenant for the main floor of your house on the Calle de Silva, you ought to go and live in it yourself?"

On that big main floor—twenty-three rooms without counting the—! Oh, no. That would be crazy. What would I do in that great palace all by myself, with no needs to speak of—I, who would be quite capable of living happily in a municipal customs booth or in a railway switchman's hut?"

"Take my advice, Señor Don Francisco," added Donoso, catching him by the lapels, "and move to the main-floor flat on the Calle de Silva. That is the natural residence of the man who is listening to my words. Society also has its rights, and it is madness to try to oppose one's individual tastes to them. We have the right to be filthy, miserly, and breakfast off a crust of bread, certainly, but society can and must insist on an appropriate show of opulence. One has to look out for the whole picture."

"But my dear Don José, my personality would get lost in that huge place, and wouldn't know how to behave if I had to live in so many rooms."

"The fact is that you . . ."

Here Donoso paused, as if he dared not proceed with the manifestation he was preparing. But, after a short hesitation, he disposed his legs more comfortably on the not over-soft chair that was serving him as a pedestal, gazed severely on Don Francisco and, gesturing with his cane, which appeared to be a badge of authority, told him, "We are friends. Each of us has faith in the other, owing to a certain compenetration of characters."

"Compenetration!" repeated Torquemada to himself, taking mental note of the lovely word, "I won't forget that one."

"I suppose that you will believe whatever I permit myself to point out to you to be loyal and sincere, inspired by the interest of a true friend."

"Of course, because of the com . . . compenetrance . . . penetration."

"Well, I am of the opinion, friend Don Francisco, and I tell you straight out, plainly, just as things ought to be told you . . . I am of the opinion that you ought to get married.''

Although it did not appear so, his friend's manifestation caused no extraordinary astonishment in Torquemada, but he thought it appropriate to allow surprise to be painted on his face.

"I—marry—at my age? Are you speaking seriously? Christ! Get married. . . That's a big step. As if it were as easy as falling off a log. Am I a young spark?''

"Bah, how old are you? Fifty-five, fifty-seven? What does that matter? You are a mere boy, and the sober and active life you've led makes you every bit as good as all that prematurely gray younger generation out there.''

"Well, strong I certainly am. I don't feel myself getting older. Nobody is in better shape than I am, or . . . I don't know . . . I have the feeling that I wouldn't come up lacking; that is, I think . . . But that's not the problem. What I say is, where would I go at my age with a woman hanging on my arm, or what kind of a figure would I cut as a married man, finding myself, as I do, very comfortable in my *element* as a bachelor?''

"Ah, that's what they all say! Freedom . . . ease . . . the loosed ox. But what about your old age? Who will take care of you then? And that atmosphere of blessed affection—what can take its place when we come to be old? Family, Señor Don Francisco! Do you know what the family is? Can an important person live in this cold, lonely cell, which looks like a room in an inn? Oh, don't you understand, bless you? It is true that you have a daughter, but your daughter will be more concerned for the family she will have than for you. What are your riches good for in the frightful solitude of a loveless home, without little folks, without a faithful and industrious wife? Tell me: what are your millions for? Think about it. Consider that I'm not capable of advising anything that is not honesty itself. Position demands a home, and the home, a family. Society would be in fine shape if everyone thought like you and carried on in such a wildly egotistical way! No, no. We owe ourselves to society, to civilization, to the State. Believe me, one cannot belong to the ruling classes without having children to bring up, useful citizens to offer to that same collectivity which maintains us in its ranks, for children are the coin with which we repay the nation for the benefits we receive from it.''

"But look here, Don José, look here," said Torquemada, pushing back his hat and taking the matter very seriously. "Let's get down to brass tacks. *Starting from the principle* that I happen to draw the marriage card, the great question remains, the real clincher—with whom?"

"Ah! That has nothing to do with me. I've raised the question. I'm no matchmaker. With whom? Look for her yourself."

"But, Don José, look here. At my age, what woman is going to love me, with this figure I cut? That is, I don't cut such a bad figure, mind you! There are worse ones."

"Yes, indeed, there certainly are worse ones."

"With the fifty-six years I'll turn on the twenty-first of September, St. Matthew's day, there's sure to be someone who'd love me for my *dough*, that is, for my capital. But that won't do for me, nor can it do for any sensible man."

"Oh, naturally! I know very well that if you offered your fair white hand, a hundred thousand candidates would appear. But that isn't the point. If you accept my suggestions, which are totally against your remaining single, then search, investigate, grab a lantern, and look around. Ah, you will know how to choose the best of the lot! And they'll be lucky women. My friend knows how to see clearly, and possesses an intelligence that runs circles around everyone else. No, I have no fear that your choice would turn out to be a bad one. Does the person exist who can worthily unite with Don Francisco? Well, if that person exists, let us count on Don Francisco's finding her, though she hide a hundred feet under the ground."

"Goodness, at my age!" repeated the usurer with a slight tone of self-pity.

"Now, don't try to distort the question or go off on the tangent of your age. Your age is the best age of all! For, if you decided to return to the married state, you wouldn't want to leap into the arms of a young, frivolous thing with her head full of foolishness, but those of a woman who has settled down."

"Settled down?"

"And of an irreproachable upbringing."

"But, Don José, the things you say! To come out at this point with the bright idea that I ought to get married. And all for the . . . *collectivity!*" said Torquemada, bursting into laughter like a boy eager for jokes.

"No," replied Donoso, slowly rising to his feet like one who has just performed a lofty social duty. "I am doing no more than pointing out an appropriate solution; I am doing no more than telling my friend what I consider to be reasonable and eminently practical."

They left the house together and spoke no more that day about getting married. But before the week was out, Don Francisco had moved to his enormous main-floor flat on the Calle de Silva.

FOURTEEN

A thousand times he had heard the proverb, "A husband wants a house," but he had never heard that a Christian ought to marry because of the simple fact that he had a house. But when Donoso brought up the matter, he was certainly a little bit right about it. On the nights that followed that memorable conversation, Torquemada was silent and intimidated at the Aguila sisters' tertulia. He was afraid that Don José would start to harp on the subject of marriage in their presence, and frankly, if he were to do so, the object of conversation would turn red as a beet. Even thinking about it made a blush rise to his cheeks. Why was he ashamed of having his possible second marriage discussed in front of Crucita and Fidelita? Had it possibly crossed his mind to take the leap with one of them? Oh, no. They were too refined for him to aspire to any such thing, and even though their poverty placed them extremely low on the social scale, they still preserved that aristocratic something, a perfumed barrier that an old, crude, uneducated man could never cross. No, he never dreamed of such an alliance. If someone had suggested it to him, the man would have believed that he was being laughed at.

One night he spoke to Cruz about Valentinico, and the two sisters showed such an interest in knowing the details of the child prodigy's life and death that Torquemada did not stop talking until very late at night, recounting the sad story sincerely and unstudiedly, in his own words, forgetting all the fancy terms which Donoso let fall and he imitated. He spoke from a full heart, telling of his joys as a father and the bitter cruelty of the disease that had snatched his hope away. He expressed himself with such eloquent warmth and naturalness that the two ladies wept, indeed they wept, and Fidela more than her sister, for she was constantly blowing her nose and holding her handkerchief to her streaming eyes. Rafael also listened quietly to what Don Francisco was saying; but he did not weep, no doubt because it is not appropriate for men, even blind men, to cry. Torquemada did shed a few large tears, as big as chick-peas, as he always did when someone refreshed the sad story in his mind.

And so that my readers may see how human events are intertwined, and how these strands we call living come to be twisted together, as he paced up and down in his room that night before the little altar with its lighted candles, he could think of nothing but the two ladies weeping over the memory of poor Valentinico, and of the very noticeable fact that Fidela had cried more than Cruz did, unquestionably more. The child already knew it, even before his father told him of it. Don Francisco went to bed very late, weary from pacing to and fro and making affectionate gestures in front of the chest of drawers, when in the midst of a half sleep he heard the child's voice very clearly:

"Papa, Papa!"

"What, my son?" he said, jumping out of bed, for he always slept half dressed, wrapped in a blanket.

Valentín spoke to him in that peculiar language of his, understood only by his father, a language that was a very rapid transmission of thought from one pair of eyes to the other.

"Papa, I want to come back to life."

"What, my son?" repeated the skinflint, who had not fully understood, rubbing his eyes.

"That I want to come back to life, why, that I feel like living again."

"Come back to life . . . live again . . . come back to the world!"

"Yes, yes. I can see how happy that makes you. I'm happy too, for I'm telling you that a person gets awfully bored here."

"That means I'll have you with me again, my darling boy!" exclaimed Torquemada, sitting, or rather falling, on a chair as if he were dead drunk.

"I will return to that world."

"Rising again, you might say, just like Jesus Christ; coming ever so neatly out of the perpetual-care tomb that. . . that cost me ten thousand reales."

"No, my goodness, I couldn't do that. What are you thinking of? To come out like that . . . how can you say so? A big boy with the same body I had when I died? Of course not. They wouldn't let me do it that way."

"But that's the way it ought to be. Who says you can't? The Great Big All? Oh yes, I see He has a grudge against me because I say or don't say whatever I like about Him, dammit! But He can't play games with me. . ."

"Be still. . . The Lord Most High is good, and loves me. And because He lets me have my own way in absolutely everything, and now He's told me that I can leave this element, that I can go where you are to convert you and get your devilish heresies out of your head."

"And are you coming to this element?" murmured Torquemada, crouching with his head between his legs.

"To the element of lovely humanity. But what you're thinking, Father, makes me laugh. To believe that I can come out of the grave with the same body I had before! Are we living in biblical times? No, of course not. Now, listen carefully: To go where you are, I have to be born again."

"Born again?"

"To wit, to be born as a little baby, the way we're always born, like the other time I was born, which was not the first time, I repeat, which was not the first time, dammit!"

"Then, my son, I'll get dressed. What time is it? I'll go and call the man-midwife, Don Francisco de Quevedo, Calle del Ave María."

"Not yet. What's the hurry? There's plenty of time for that. You really are stupid, Father."

"Yes, I am. I don't know what's the matter with me. I think it must be almost daylight. The candles give so little light, and I can't see your face very well."

"That's because I'm fading; I don't know what's the matter with me, but I'm fading. I'm getting tinier and tinier."

"Wait. Your mama, where is she?" When he said this, Torquemada, lying stretched out in the middle of the room, looked like a dead man. "I think I heard her cry out. That's what I told you. The pains are starting. We must send word."

"Don't do it, no. I'm so little, I can't even find myself. I have nothing but a soul, and I'm smaller than a grain of rice."

"Now I see nothing. All dark. Where are you?" and as he said this he crawled about the room on all fours. "Your mama isn't here. I had her in my pocket, and she got away. Maybe she's inside the matchbox. Oh, you rascal! You've got her. You're hiding her in your vest pocket."

"No, you have her. I haven't seen her. The Great All told me that she was ugly."

"That she is not."

"And old."

"Not old, either."

"And that He didn't know what her name was, and didn't need to know it."

"I know it; but I won't tell it to you."

"There's time for me to find out."

"*Starting from the principle* that she's who you think she is—"

"That's not the way to say it, Papa. You say: *the mere fact* that she may be . . ."

"That's right: *the mere fact*; I'd forgotten the term. Well, if it is her it will be her, and if not, it won't be. It'll be someone else."

With great difficulty, he rose to a squatting position and, rubbing his eyes, gazed at the altar in stupefaction, saying, "The things that happen to me!"

Valentinico did not answer.

"But is it true that . . . ?" asked Don Francisco, who found himself alone. "I'm cold. I got out of bed without putting my dressing jacket on, and it would be no joke if I caught pneumonia. What I'd like to do now is eat something, for example, porridge or some fried potatoes. But at this hour, how do I *raise the question* with Rumalda about her fixing me a snack? I'd have sworn that my son wants to be born, and that he told me so. But how can I get him born, wretch that I am! I'll go back to bed and sleep a little while, if I can. The whole thing must be a supposition, a *mere fact*. I'll tell Donoso what's happening to me, and he can solve for his very own self this . . . *hypostatis* . . . I mean *hypothesis*. Now, for my son to get born, the first thing we need is a mother; no, first of all a father. Don José wants me to be the father of a family, that is, a person who carries a lot of weight. I can already see Señor Donoso's game, for he respects me, yes, he respects me. But it can't be. Pardon me, my friend, but there's no way under the sun of performing this—what's that word? Oh, yes!—*desideratum*. I thank you sincerely for the *desideratum*, and it tickles my vanity to know that . . . very happy, and to tell the truth I have a few crumbs of *desideratum* myself. But there's an obstacle—that business about so-cial classes. It's easy to say that there are no classes, but as soon as you say it, the confounded classes leap to the eye. Don José, excuse me. Ask me for anything you want, the Bible and all, but don't ask me to do that. The very idea that they might say to me, "Whoa! Get away from here, rabble, you stink," stirs me up and makes me sick as a dog. And it isn't that I smell bad. You know perfectly well that I wash and keep myself clean. And even my breath, which Doña Lupe used to tell me was enough to knock a person down . . . I've cured that by keeping my mouth clean. And ever since I shaved off my goatee, which looked like a rabbit's tail, I look a lot better. Rumalda says I look quite a bit like General O'Donnell when he came back from Africa. So, as for my physical appearance, there's no problem. I have the feeling that, *other circumstances being equal*, I'd have the inside track; that is, if I were more refined and my birth and upbringing more *compatible*. But no, I'm not *compatible*. I don't fit in, I don't adjust. I've got an awfully tough crust; it's scratchy and itchy as sandpaper. It can't be, it can't be."

After a while, he thrashed about in bed, telling himself amazedly, "What do you bet I've been snoring? Yes, I snored. I heard myself let out a snort like people let slip at funerals. Now that's a serious matter. And I ask myself, does Señor Donoso, who's such a gentleman, snore? And those ever-so-delicate ladies, by the Great All-in-All, can it be that they snore, too?"

FIFTEEN

Because of his bad night he was out of sorts and puffy-eyed all next morning, but during the afternoon he was busy as a bee, seeking out bargains at auction sales to furnish his new house decently, though economically. He did not buy a double bed because he already had one, of lignum vitae, acquired cheaply by Doña Silvia. And as Ruiz Donoso felt sufficiently intimate to advise him in those arduous tasks even before Don Francisco had asked for his honest opinion about them, the result was that a large number of objects suitable for use by distinguished ladies were purchased, some of them so strange that Torquemada had no idea what the devil they were good for. Since they had been acquired in different sorts of liquidations, through seizure, bankruptcy, or death, the furnishings were as heterogeneous as can be imagined. But the house was acquiring elegance, and had a rich, high-class appearance. It was impossible not to talk about it during the Aguila sisters' tertulia. Cruz demanded information, made him give explanations and describe every piece, expressing very sensible opinions about the necessary harmony between comfort and elegance.

On one of those afternoons (it must have been a few days after the move), Torquemada and his hero went for a walk, chatting about business. As they were returning from the Retiro Park by way of the Observatory, the conversation turned to the sisters' lawsuit, and Don José, stopping in his tracks, expressed an optimistic opinion about it; but then came the qualifications, a host of drawbacks which stripped his first statement of all its effect. A lot of money had to be spent, and since the ladies had no assets, perhaps—*no perhaps*—they would have to give up their rights simply because they lacked the means to establish them. What a pity! The thing was so obvious! He had exhausted all his actions on behalf of his good friends, all his contacts and, finally, his slender resources. And he was not sorry for it, not at all. The two were so worthy of sacrifice on the part of everyone, of serving them and extracting them from their dreadful situation! But alas, that situation was getting worse, to the point that the ladies and their unfortunate brother would soon have to seek a place in some asylum for the penniless. They now had no sources of income, for all that remained of an untransferable bond had had to be consumed nibble by nibble; they no longer had anything left to sell or pawn.

"As for me," Don José added, downcast and almost on the verge of tears, "I have done everything humanly possible. The expenses of the lawsuit absorb three-quarters of my pension, and here I am, absolutely unable to go on, Don Francisco. The poor drowning victims will have to be left to their fate, for they can't be kept above water even by seizing them by the hair. I'm beginning to be afraid that God has decided to let that whole worthy family drown, and that all our efforts to save them are useless. God wills it so, and, as the absolute master of lives and livelihoods, He will do so."

"No, He won't," said Torquemada obstinately, uttering an oath and following it up with a brisk kick.

"And what can we do in the face of the designs. . . ?"

"The designs can go . . ." (here an unprintable word). "The ladies will win the suit."

"Yes, but. . . you try to guarantee me that we'll get as far as a verdict. I have faith in the rectitude of the Council of State; but quite a lot of time and money must be spent before a decision is handed down, and in the meantime we're going to have to give up the whole matter."

"No, it will not be given up."

"You . . . ?"

"Yes, I, I. *Here I stand* and here I say: on with the dance and with the litigation. It's the least I can do."

"That changes things. Let's be sure about it. You—"

"Yes, I, señor. I, Francisco Torquemada, order and command the lawsuit to go on. What's needed? A big-shot lawyer? Let's find one. What else? Raise a pile of legal paper? Let's go to it! And no talk of giving up. Either you have the nerve or you don't have the nerve. Is their right to the money clear? Then let's get it for them, over the head of Christ himself."

"Fine . . . I think that's just fine," said Donoso, clutching his friend by the arm, for in the heat of his improvised discourse Torquemada had been on the point of being run over by one of the carriages among the large number returning from the Retiro.

They started off along the Paseo de Atocha, towards the Prado, at the hour when the lamplighters were lighting the gas lamps and pedestrians and coach passengers were returning in groups, seeking their evening soup. Near the Museum they saw a cluster of lights on the Paseo del Prado and their nostrils were assailed by the scent of frying olive oil. It was the carnival of San Juan. The evening's excitement was just beginning, and to avoid it, the two good friends started up the Carrera de San Jerónimo, still talking about the same subject, pausing now and then to express a little more quietly the grave matters that came to their lips.

"So, we're in agreement, Señor Don Francisco," said Donoso as they stood opposite the lion statues in front of the Parliament building. "Allow me to congratulate you on your sensitivity, a virtue of which you are one of the rarest examples. I have said sensitivity, and I add abnegation, for great abnegation is needed to face up to such expenses, without . . . well, without obtaining any advantage from them. If you will permit me, I will say that you do wrong, very wrong." (Torquemada said not a word.) "I mean that it does not seem right to me, and that you, excessively modest as you are, do not appreciate your own worth. The ladies' gratitude is enough for you, and frankly, I see no equivalence between the recompense and the service. And it isn't that I am so very positivistic. It's just that it pains me to see you hold yourself so cheap."

As Don Francisco, his eyes fixed on the ground as if he were taking note of the cracks between the cobblestones, made no reply, the other embarked on further clarifications, and when they had almost reached the corner of the Calle de Cedaceros, he stopped in his tracks once again and briskly tore away the veil in this wise:

"Now, we've had enough of playing blindman's bluff with our intentions, Señor Don Francisco! Why are we making a mystery of something that ought to be clear as daylight? I guess what your feelings are. Would you like me to describe your state of mind?"

"Go ahead."

"Well, ever since I had the honor of speaking to you about a delicate subject . . . come now, of the desirability of assuming the married state, the idea has been working in you. Is it or isn't it true that ever since then, you've not stopped thinking about it night and day?"

"It certainly is."

"You are thinking about it, but your extraordinary modesty prevents you from making a decision. You believe that you are unworthy, when you are, quite the contrary, worthy of the greatest happiness! And now, when we have raised the question of carrying forward the famous lawsuit; now, when you are prepared to offer that family a service that cannot be repaid, your sensitivity merely reinforces your hesitation, for if before you felt inhibited to a power of ten, now you are inhibited to a power of two hundred thousand, and you can't stop tormenting yourself with the following argument, which is a real sophism: 'I, who believe myself unworthy to aspire to the hand, etcetera, and now that things are going well, I offer them this service, etcetera, it's even less possible to think of marriage because they and everyone else will believe, etcetera, that I am selling the favor I do them, or that I am buying her hand, etcetera.' Is that what my friend Torquemada is thinking, yes or no?"

"That selfsame thing."

"Well, it seems to me to be a great piece of stupidity, my dear Señor Don Francisco, if you sacrifice such highly noble sentiments before the idol of a misunderstood sensitivity."

He expressed this so elegantly that Torquemada was on the point of shedding tears, he felt so emotional.

"It's just that . . . I'll tell you . . . I . . . it's the way I am. I've never liked to be *above myself*—let's come right out with it—to aim higher than I ought to. It's true that I'm rich, but . . ."

"But what?"

"Nothing, I'm not saying anything. Say it all yourself."

"I know what you fear: the difference in class, in upbringing, their titles of nobility—all that is trifling in these times. Has it passed through your mind that you might be rejected?"

"Yes, indeed. And this character here, though he's of humble stock and not very strong on society folderols because he hasn't had time to learn about them, doesn't want anybody to look down on him, mind you!"

"And the fact that they are poor inhibits you still more, and you say, 'They mustn't think that, just because they're poor, I'm forcing anything on them.' "

"Exactly. It's as if you were walking around inside me with a lantern, recording all the concerns and *sophisms* in the corners of my soul."

They were approaching the Puerta del Sol, where they were to separate, for Donoso lived in the Santa Cruz quarter and Torquemada's way led through the Calle de Preciados. They had to shorten their conversation, for both of them were spurred on by appetite and saw in their imaginations the blessed mealtime stew.

"There's no need to say," remarked Donoso, "that I spoke on my own, both before and now, and that never, never—you may count on it—have the ladies and I ever touched upon the matter. I must remind you, moreover, that poor Doña Lupe (may she be in glory) cherished this project."

"Yes, she did cherish it," replied Don Francisco, enthralled by the phrase, "cherish a project."

"She said something about it to me."

"And to me. To the point that she nearly drove me crazy, the day she passed on."

"It must have been a mania with her, and I know that she said to the ladies . . ."

"Who didn't know me then."

"Precisely; and neither did I. Now we all know each other and, friend Don Francisco, I am going to permit myself . . ."

"What?"

"I'm going to permit myself to propose to you the placing of the whole matter in my hands. Do you think I'll be a good diplomat?"

"The best one God ever sent into the world."

"Do you believe that I will be able to preserve everyone's dignity, both in case of acceptance and in case of rejection?"

"How can there be any doubt about it?"

"Fine! For the moment there's nothing more to talk about. Goodbye, it's getting late."

Donoso took his leave with a firm handclasp, and had not gone six paces when Don Francisco, who had been standing irresolute on the corner of the Ministry of Interior, was assailed by a sudden, piercing doubt. He attempted to call to his friend, but Donoso had already disappeared in the crowd. The miser put his hands to his head, asking himself the following question: "But. . . with which one?" For Donoso had always spoken in the plural: *the ladies.* Was he proposing perchance that Torquemada marry both of them? What the devil! The doubt was enough to drive anyone crazy! Boldly launching himself into the maelstrom of the Puerta del Sol, and weaving and bobbing to avoid the streetcars and to keep from bumping into other pedestrians, he mentally interrogated the Sphinx of his destiny: "But with which one, dammit! Which one?"

SIXTEEN

That night he did not have the courage to go to the tertulia: for if Don José succumbed to temptation and *raised the question* there, face to face, under what chair or table would he hide? And he was not undervaluing himself, not at all; after the conversation with Donoso, he felt himself as much of a man as any other. What? Do money and position mean nothing? Did not one thing make up for the other, that is, the democracy of his origin for the aristocracy of his moneybags? After all, hadn't we agreed that ever-blessed money also constitutes aristocracy? And what if the Aguila ladies came, after all, in a direct line from some high panjandrum, or the king of Babylon? Well, if they came from such, let them come. The fact was that at the present moment they hadn't a penny to their names, and their property was what polite-talking people call a myth—a lawsuit that would be won when there's pie in the sky. So, no silly scruples and no talking yourself down! That precious pair might well beat their breasts, for plums like him didn't fall on them every week of the year! After all, what more could they aspire to? Was the emperor of China's son and heir going to come and propose to Crucita, with her gray hairs, or Fidelita, with her teeth sharpened by all those potato skins she nibbled? Well, he was beginning to understand that he was worth a lot more than he weighed! Begone modesty, begone diffidence, which were caused only by not speaking well and the fear of saying something stupid that would make people laugh. They would not laugh, no indeed, for thanks to his assiduousness he had already learned a host of terms, and used them properly and easily. He knew how to praise things by saying, just at the right moment, "It's beyond all ponderation." He knew how to say, "If I went into Parliament, no one would be better than I at dotting my i's." And even if he didn't know how to say those things—dammit!—his know-how in business, his marvelous ability to get money out of a stone, his economies, his reliability, his clean living habits—were they worth nothing? Let's see if they could pin any kind of vice on him. He didn't drink; he had nothing to do with women; he didn't gamble; he didn't even give himself the inoffensive pleasure of tobacco. So then, what reason would they have for rejecting him? On the contrary, they would be in seventh heaven, and would think that the Most High and all his court were coming through the doors of their house. By reasoning thus, he became calmer, filling himself with boasting and self-confidence. But then the terrible doubt would return: "With which one, Lord, with which one?"

Next morning he was on the verge of writing a little note to Don José Donoso, begging him to resolve that troublesome doubt. But he did not do so. Why bother, when the mystery would soon be dispelled? At last, since the ladies sent a message to his house inquiring after his health (because he had played truant from the tertulia the night before), the poor man had no choice but to go. He all but wanted to. He wasn't afraid of anything, not he! Every man is his own man. If they rejected him, the loss was theirs. No matter how much the incense of vanity had gone to their heads, they could not help knowing that not many men like him would come their way. And goodness knows, the times were not ripe for hesitations and hanging back! *To give only one example,* look at the monarchy coming to terms with democracy, and the two of them eating off the same plate in the tavern of representative politics. And was this example not sufficient? Well, here was another. The aristocracy, an old tree with dried-up sap, could no longer survive unless it was *fertilized* (in the sense of *manured*) by the newly rich common people. And the sweat of the people's brow had brought about some dandy little miracles in the last third of a century! Weren't there a lot of people rolling around Madrid, lolling in carriages, whom he and everyone had once known selling dried beans and salt codfish, or lending money at interest? Were not many who in their childhood had been out at elbow or had gone hungry to buy cheap shoes, lifetime senators and councillors of banks by now? Well and good: to this *element* Torquemada belonged, and he was a fresh example of *the people's sweat fecundating*—he was incapable of rounding off the sentence.

This was what he was thinking as he climbed the staircase in the house of his friends, one might almost say of his wives, for, since in his agitated mind he could not discern which of them was going to fall to his lot, he had a mental picture of matrimony that involved bestowing a hand on each. Cruz opened the door and led him to the parlor as if she wished to speak to him privately. "Penning me up in the parlor like this," thought Torquemada, "smells like *manifestations* to me. Things are really hanging fire now!"

Indeed, Cruz, who had carried into the parlor the lamp which ordinarily lighted the tertulia in the sitting room, shut him up there to manifest to him, with chilly good manners, that Señor Donoso had spoken to them (*them!*) about a subject whose importance could not be concealed either from them or from Señor Torquemada. Unnecessary to say that the ladies felt greatly honored by this . . . indication. So far, it was no more than an indication, but soon it would be a proposition. They were highly honored, naturally. They were grateful with all their hearts for the extremely noble gesture (*gesture*, no less) of their noble friend, and appreciated his noble sentiments (so much nobility was beginning to cloy) for their high worth. But it was not easy to give a categorical reply until some time had passed, for so serious a matter ought to be carefully examined and weighed. The dignity of all concerned depended on it. Don Francisco replied in stumbling, hurried sentences, without saying anything specific, merely that he *cherished the conviction* that . . . and that he had made those *manifestations* to Señor Donoso moved by pity . . . no, moved by a very noble sentiment (by this time we were all too noble for words); that his desire to be acceptable to the Aguila ladies *exceeded all ponderation*, that they should take all the time they wanted to think it over, for that was the way he liked things to be, well thought out and well measured; that he was a very patient man; and that he always *discharged* important matters very slowly and deliberately.

The conference was short. The lady left him alone for an instant, and he paced nervously up and down the room, tormented anew by that doubt which was becoming a regular comic turn, a real music-hall turn. He came to a stop in front of the mirror, and when he saw his reflection could not help rebuking it furiously: "Man, how stupid you are! You still don't know which one it's going to be! Ask, you idiot, ask! It's ridiculous not to know at this stage in the game, although having to ask is perfectly asinine too, dammit!"

The appearance of Señor Donoso put an end to these internal manifestations, and in no time all five persons had gathered in the neighboring sitting room, the ladies nearest the light, Don Francisco next to the blind man, and Donoso seated on the bench in the corner, sitting somewhat apart as if in a show of veneration, so that his words, having to cross a relatively wide space, would sound with greater solemnity. Now that he had lost his fear, Torquemada would, at the slightest provocation, have launched his explosive question into the midst of that noble gathering: "Now then, ladies, let's get to the point, with which of you am I going to get married!" But nothing of the sort happened, for not the slightest reference was made to the ticklish question, and no matter how hard he concentrated, the miser was unable to make out the slightest change in the faces of the two ladies, nor any symptom of emotion. What a strange thing! For it would have been natural for the one—the one it was going to be—to be a trifle upset. Only in Cruz could he observe a bit of animation; in Fidela, perhaps, a shade more pallor. Agreeable as always, the two ladies said nothing to their suitor that he did not know already, from which he deduced that the question of marriage mattered not a whit to either of them, or that they were concealing the agitation that was passing through their minds. What Don Francisco did observe was that it was impossible to get a word out of Rafael all evening. Why was the confounded young fellow so sullen and sunk in his own thoughts? Could there be any connection between that . . . what was the word? . . . ah, *attitude* . . . that attitude and the projected marriage? Perhaps not, for probably his sisters had told him nothing about it.

Cruz was pleasant as always, keeping her distance, every inch a lady and a lady of high degree; Fidela was more informal, tending toward gay familiarity, with touches of daring and more flexibility in conversation than her sister. On this occasion, as on previous ones, they were just as always; but as for the materialism of that project which had stirred up Torquemada's spirit and nerves, they were a pair of equally enigmatic and indecipherable hieroglyphs. Don Francisco was beginning to be very much annoyed by so much hesitation, so much pursing of the lips to show indifference, so much choosing and emphasizing of the blandest words, that were neither fish nor flesh. He was anxious for the end of the tertulia so that he could escape and be at his ease with Don José. Ah, thanks be to God, it was ending at last! "Good night. . . Keep well. . ." On the staircase he did not try to say anything, for the ladies, who had come out to light their way, could have heard him. But as soon as they reached the street, our hero took a firm stand and angrily exploded with the crudeness characteristic of his real self, a crudeness that was preexistent to, and stronger than, the shams of his artificial metamorphosis.

"Would you like to tell me what kind of a damned comedy this is?"

"But, Don Francisco . . . !"

"If they've caught on—damn it to hell—why are they acting so stiff? My God, they can't even let a fellow know they're the least bit happy about it."

"But, Don Francisco . . . !"

"And especially—this is what makes me mad as hell—tell me, tell me right away, which one of the two am I going to marry? Devil take me if I understand it. Dammit, by the Bible and all!"

"Moderation, my dear Don Francisco. And start from the principle that I will not intervene if—"

"I'm not starting from any principle or any conclusion, what the hell, except that I want to know right now!"

"With which one?"

"Yes, with which confounded one! I'm going to find out, by a hundred thousand gross of demons and all the bibles in Christendom!"

"Well, I don't know either, yet. We are at the most delicate point in the negotiations, and if you don't give me full power to act, awaiting the outcome reasonably and calmly, I'll withdraw and you can appoint some other papal nuncio" (trying to make a joke of it) "or deal with the other 'powers' yourself."

"To hell with the powers! I thought . . . Look here . . . it seemed natural" (here he calmed down a bit) "that the most important thing was knowing which branch they were going to hang a fellow on. And so . . ."

"I can't say anything yet about that matter, the importance of which I am the first to recognize."

"Well, I'm in a pretty pickle. You've got to understand that I'm within my rights—*up to a point*—and that any other man, *other circumstances being equal* . . ."

When he observed that Torquemada was putting on his mask of refinement again, Donoso judged him beaten, and inhibited him further by saying, "I repeat that if my efforts are troublesome to you, I hereby hand you my resignation as plenipotentiary minister."

"Oh, no, no! I don't accept it. I mustn't accept it, mind you! I even implore you to withdraw your resignation."

"It's withdrawn" (with a clap on the shoulder).

"Forgive me if my temper got out of hand."

"Forgiven, and we're just as good friends as ever."

They parted in the Red de San Luis, and Torquemada went off grumbling: echoes of the storm were still sounding in his ears, not quite drowned out by the fascination which Don José exercised upon him.

ONE

Cruz del Aguila always rose with the sun, and usually awoke a couple of hours before leaving her bed, lying there in a sort of economic trance, meditating on the difficulties of the day and how to overcome or evade them. She would count her slender resources over and over again, pursuing the insoluble problem of making three out of two and five out of four; and, by dint of turning economic formulas round and round in her heated brain, she succeeded in imparting reality to things that were completely unlikely, and made the impossible possible. She interspersed these calculations with mechanically uttered prayers, and the syllables of her prayers mingled with the syllables of her accounts. Her mind turned toward the Virgin and found itself facing the grocer. At last, her strong will put an end to the advance calculations of the day, all effort, scheming, and supplications for divine aid, for now she must descend to the battlefield, to the struggle with fate on the terrain of practical matters, a terrain bristling with rocks and traversed by fathomless abysses.

Not only was she general-in-chief in that extraordinary war, but the foremost and bravest of the soldiers. The day began, and with the day the battle; years had gone by like this, and that firm will had never flagged. When she measured the long period of time her awful suffering had lasted, the noble lady was amazed by her own indomitable courage, and ended by affirming the human soul's infinite resistance to suffering. The body soon succumbs to physical pain, but the intrepid soul never surrenders; it withstands sorrow even under intolerable pressures.

Cruz was head of the family and her authority could not be challenged; hers was the greatest glory of that heroic campaign, whose laurels she would gather in another life of restitution and justice; hers also was the responsibility for a disaster if the family, devoured by poverty, at last succumbed. Her brother and sister obeyed her blindly and venerated her, regarding her as a superior being, something like a Moses who led them across the wilderness, among a thousand horrible privations and sorrows, with the hope of setting foot at last on fertile and hospitable ground. What Cruz decided to do, no matter what it might be, was like an article of faith for the other two. This submissiveness aided the task of the firstborn Aguila, who could maneuver freely at times of danger without having to bother with opinion from below, for if one day she had said, "I can't go on. Let's all hold each other tight and jump out the window," they would have taken the leap without hesitation.

The use of her faculties in these difficult tasks, repeated day after day, trained Cruz del Aguila's natural ingenuity and it constantly grew more subtle and refined, to the point that all the great intelligences which have enlightened humanity in the government of nations were suckling babes compared to her. For what she did was govern; all the rest was child's play. This meant performing miracles, for to live without means is a miracle; it was a greater miracle to cover all appearances decently, when in fact, under that scab of dignified poverty, gaped the great wound of a rending, horrible, desperate indigence. For all of these reasons, if certificates of heroism were to be given in this world, and awards of preeminence in governing were to be justly distributed, the first title of prime minister and the designation of heroine should have been given to that sublime ant.

When the House of Aguila fell, the flotsam of the shipwreck allowed a tolerable kind of life for two years. The sudden death of their parents had placed Cruz at the head of the little family, and, as disasters followed one another without interruption, like the mace-blows of an implacable Providence falling on their heads, she became intimately acquainted with misfortune; she hoped for no improvement; she saw always before her the long line of disasters, with their hideous faces, waiting their turn to draw closer. The loss of all their landed property affected her very little; it was to be expected. The humiliations, the unpleasant contacts with relatives of near and distant degree, found her heart hardened to them. But the illness and subsequent blindness of Rafael, whom she adored, sent her reeling. That was more than her nature, hardened and tempered like steel as it was, could bear. She swallowed endless griefs without even tasting them. To combat the terrible ailment, she performed the deeds of a heroine, in whose being woman and lion were mingled; and when all hope was lost, she did not die of grief, and observed in her own soul a diamond-like hardness which allowed her to face pressures stronger than can be imagined.

The period when Rafael became blind was followed by another in which their economic straits were gradually becoming very serious. But they had not yet reached the point of indignity; moreover, their loyal and faithful family friend helped them to ride the terrible wave. The sale of a title—the only surviving bit of the Aguila fortune—and of a number of admittedly superfluous objects, enabled them to eke out an existence; but they did live, and there were even occasional nights when, as they rested after rude labors, the two sisters were cheerful and thanked God for the relative good fortune He had given them. This was what we might call the Doña Lupe period, for it was then that they made the acquaintance of the famous moneylender, who, though she began by putting a rope around their necks, later loosened it as she came to know them better, taking pity on that dethroned royalty. From usurious dealings, she passed to benign favor, and from there in a natural progression to sincere friendship, for Doña Lupe was capable of making distinctions. But, not to give the lie to the perverse fate which made the Aguila sisters' existence a tissue of misfortunes, just when Doña Lupe's friendship seemed to presage some happy result, the poor lady had the bad taste to die. One could almost believe she had done it on purpose, simply to annoy.

And at what a miserable juncture did the Turkey Lady take it into her head to go off to the other world! When her illness began to present serious symptoms, the Aguilas were entering what Torquemada, in his zeal to appear refined, would have called *the glacial period* of poverty. Until then they had managed to live by innumerable economies, doing without not only the superfluous things to which they had been brought up but also without those indispensable things which every-one, great or small, is brought up to. They lived poorly, though with-out feeling ashamed, because they could still buy food; but the terrible dilemma was arising of whether to starve to death or eat at the expense of others. They had reached the point of gazing at the heavens, in case some manna was left over from the times of the Hebrews, or of asking for public charity in the least embarrassing way. If the truth must be told, this period of supreme anguish had begun a year earlier; but Don

José Donoso, the household's loyal friend, had held it at bay or concealed it by ingeniously disguised contributions. This peerless man gave the ladies the impression that the sums they received from his hands came from the righting of a judicial wrong; but there was no righted judicial wrong or anything resembling one. Crucita at last discovered this, and her consternation cannot be expressed in words. She did not let Don José know that she knew, realizing that he would be grateful for her silence.

The good Donoso would have continued to practice secret charity if he had had any humanly possible means of doing so. But he too had begun to groan under the yoke of a malign fate. He had no children, but he did have a wife who was, without the slightest doubt, the sickliest woman in creation. In the long catalogue of ailments that afflict miserable humanity, none was ever known that had not lodged itself in her poor body, nor was there a single part of that body which was not a pathological case worthy of study by all the practitioners in the world. Rather than an invalid, the good lady was a school of medicine. Her nerves, her stomach, her head, her limbs, her heart, her liver, her eyes, her scalp, everything in that hapless martyr was, so to speak, in a state of revolution. With so many chronic complaints, suffered for an indefinite time without visible signs of improvement, Donoso's wife eventually assumed a special character, that of a person supremely ailing, proud of her ill health. She believed that she exercised a monopoly over human suffering, to the point that she became vexed when she was told of the existence of anyone else as ill as she. And if a person who suffered from this or that pain or discomfort was mentioned, she—unwilling to be outdone by anyone—would say that she had been attacked by the same thing, but in a worse form. To speak of her ailments, to describe them in leisurely detail, as if she took pleasure in her own suffering, was a form of relief for her which was readily forgiven by all those who had the misfortune of listening to her; and members of the family let her run on all she liked, with that vague whiff of voluptuousness which she inserted into the tale of her shooting pains, dizzy spells, nausea, insomnia, cramps, and gripings. Her husband, who loved her devotedly and had already spent forty years witnessing in his house that compendium of internal pathology, from the times of Galen to the present day, eventually shared the Hippocratic pride of his suffering better half and was not amused when people spoke of ailments unknown to his Justa, or those that remotely resembled his Justa's.

TWO

The first question asked of Don José in the Aguila sisters' tertulia was this: "And how has Justa spent the day?" And in the reply there was always an invariable statement: "Badly, very badly," followed by a comment that varied every twenty-four hours: "Today it was coronary insufficiency." On another day it would be migraine, *bolus hystericus,* or an excruciating pain in the big toe. Every night Donoso enjoyed depicting, with heavy strokes, a painful ailment different from that of the previous night. And though he never spoke of hopes or probabilities of cure, because to be cured would have meant stripping the catalogue of illnesses of all their Dantesque majesty, he did, however, always have something to say about the continuous application of remedies, which were tested by a sort of therapeutic dilettantism, and would continue to be tested as long as there were pharmacies and pharmacists in the world.

With these habits of his wife's and the endless stream of doctors who constantly examined that encyclopedia of suffering, with more scientific enthusiasm than humanitarian pity, Donoso's means were disappearing at a lively rate. He never mentioned any such thing, but the Aguila sisters suspected it, and eventually discovered that their friend, too, had financial problems. Through an indiscreet remark by a close friend of both families, Cruz learned that Don José had contracted a debt, something very unusual in him and at odds with the habits of a lifetime. And to think that she could not come to his aid, returning with interest the favors she had received from him! These sorrows, which each side concealed from the other, coincided with the days of the tremendous economic crisis of which I spoke before, the terrifying creaks that announced the beginning of the end, letting the livid face of poverty show through, no longer shrinking and modestly hiding itself, but naked, tattered, shameless. Rude lack of trust was beginning to show itself in some merchants who supplied the household, which pained the ladies as much as a public flogging. There was no longer the remotest hope of establishing good relations with the landlord, nor was there any possible solution to this much-feared problem. It was no longer possible to struggle, and they would have to succumb heroically, to knock on the doors of provincial or municipal charity, unless the noble victims preferred a triple ration of match heads dissolved in brandy, or unless all three cast themselves into whatever abyss the devil might provide for them.

During these critical days, the solution appeared. The solution! Yes, it was one, and when Donoso proposed it, bringing back memories of Doña Lupe, who had also proposed it as a silly idea that made the ladies laugh, Cruz sat stunned for quite a long while, unsure whether she was hearing the voice of Providence announcing the rainbow of peace, or whether their good friend was making fun of her.

"No, it's no joke," said Donoso. "I repeat that it's not impossible. I've been working out this idea in my head for some time now. I believe that it is an acceptable solution, and, if I'm really put to it, the only possible solution. But, you will say, the interested party will have to show . . . Well, though he has said nothing specific to me, I believe that there will be no difficulty on his side."

Cruz made a gesture of repugnance, and then a gesture of agreement, and then a whole series of gestures and grimaces that demonstrated the perturbation of her soul. It was a solution, indeed it was. If there were no other, and could be no other, what was there to discuss? One does not discuss the floating plank clung to by a drowning man who has already swallowed half the water in the sea. Don José took his leave, and next day returned with the news that his negotiations were going splendidly; that, on the masculine side, one could already venture a resounding "yes." But the "yes" of the feminine *element* was lacking. Cruz, who had a raging volcano in her brain that morning, marked by the reddish spots that burned on her cheeks, waved her arms about like a delirious typhoid sufferer and exclaimed, "Accepted, accepted, since we're not brave enough to kill ourselves."

Donoso did not know whether the lady was crying or raging when he saw her fall into a chair, cover her face with her hands, and then stretch out her arms and throw her head back.

"Quiet, dear lady. To tell the honest truth, I believe that the match would seem acceptable to me under any circumstances. In the present circumstances, I'm of the opinion that it is a superb match."

"I'm not saying that it isn't; I'm not saying anything. Make any arrangements you want to. Bad luck has a horrible sense of humor, don't you agree? What jokes God Almighty plays! Believe me, I can't help regarding all that about immortality and eternal justice from the comic side. What did God do, when He created man, but start an eternal farce?"

"There's no reason to take it like that," said Don José, seeking convincing arguments. "We are confronting a problem. . . The only acceptable solution is, of course, a bit disagreeable, has its ugly side. But the man has qualities; and I believe that if we scratch the rough surface, we'll find a man of merit, of real merit."

Cruz, whose arms were bare because she had been washing clothes, crossed them and dug her nails into them. A little more, and she would have taken off strips of flesh.

"I've accepted; I've already told you that I've accepted," she said firmly, her lower lip trembling. "You know that my decisions are final. What I decide upon, is done."

As he was leaving, assailed by a troublesome doubt, Don José found it necessary to call to her.

"For God's sake don't fly off the handle. We must deal with an extremely important point. To go on with the negotiations and settle the precise terms of the solution with the other party, I have to know . . ."

"What, what else?"

"What I don't know is hardly a small matter. At this stage in the game, neither he nor I knows which of you . . ."

"It's true. . . . Well then, with neither, I mean, with both. No, pay no attention to me. I'll think about that detail."

"You call it a detail?"

"My head is seething. Let me think about it at leisure, and whatever I decide, that will be it."

Don José took his leave and the lady went on washing, without informing Fidela of the secret which the friend of the household had brought. Both sisters performed their domestic tasks with the briskness characteristic of them, the younger gaily, the elder silently. One of the things she found most difficult to resign herself to was the need to go out to shop for food. But she had no choice, for the concierge's wife, who had formerly done them this service, was seriously ill, and Cruz would have died rather than entrust the task to one of her meddling, prying neighbors. To confide the hapless family's economic secrets to persons who were so inconsiderate, so incapable of understanding all the greatness of that martyrdom, would have meant selling herself foolishly. And rather than sell herself, it was preferable to suffer the humiliation of going to the market, to confront insolent market-women and shopkeepers devoid of shame, trying not to be recognized or pretending that she was not recognized. Cruz disguised herself, wrapping a large shawl around her body and a long kerchief about her face; she went out in this guise with her slender store of coppers, which she exchanged for incredibly small portions of meat, vegetables, bread, and perhaps an egg on some days. To go shopping without money, or with less money than she needed, was for so dignified a lady a torture beside which all the tortures invented by Dante in his terrible Inferno paled into insignificance. To have to beg a shopkeeper to extend a bit of credit; to have to lie, promising to pay next week what she was surely not going to be able to give, was an effort of will inferior by only one degree to the effort needed to dash one's brains out against a wall. At times she weakened; but the memory of her poor blind brother, whose only pleasure was the enjoyment of his meals, drove her like a terrible goad to continue on that Way of the Cross. "And then they talk to me about martyrs," she would say to herself as she walked toward the Calle de Pelayo, "and virgins tossed to wild beasts, and others who were flayed alive! I laugh at all that. Let them come here to suffer, to win heaven without making a show of winning it, without drums and cymbals." She would return home panting, her face red as a pepper, exhausted from the colossal effort, which once again had given her an idea of the infinite resistance of the human will. These bitter tasks were followed by the no less bitter one of ar-ranging those bits and pieces of food so that Rafael would have the best part, if not all of them, without discovering that his sisters had not touched a bite. To keep him from realizing the deception, Fidela would imitate the tinkle of the fork, the noise of chewing, and every-thing that could give the illusion that the two sisters were eating. Cruz had already accustomed herself to unbelievable privations, and if Fidela used to nibble a thousand disgusting things out of naughtiness and depraved tastes, she did so now out of conviction, cured of all possible repugnance. In that household, the uses to which a potato could be put would be incredible if faithfully described. Cruz, like the philosopher in Calderón's play, gathered the herbs cast aside by another. Neither of the two had tasted an egg for some time, and to keep Rafael from finding out, the mischievous younger sister would tap an eggshell against the eggcup, imitating with admirable histrionic skill the act of eating a soft-boiled egg. For themselves they made totally unconvincing broths, stews worthy to pass into culinary history as models of nothing pretending to be something. Not even to Donoso did they reveal these miracles of noble poverty, for fear that the good gentleman would do something foolish by sacrificing himself for his friends. Such delicacy in them was excessive; but they felt powerless to sustain these horrendously difficult attitudes for much longer, and at night could not keep up the friendly formality of the tertulia except by tremendous efforts of will.

On that day, which should have been marked by a monument of one color or another because it was the date on which Cruz had accepted Torquemada's proposals in principle, the good lady felt more cheerful. A solution had appeared; good or bad, but a solution after all. To emerge from that dark cavern was now possible, and they ought to be happy about it, even though they did not know where they would go in the end through the crack they saw glimmering in the unyielding rock. As she gave her brother his meal, the lady emphasized even more than on other occasions how good his dinner was that day.

"Today you have just what you like so much: sole *au gratin*. And a delicious dessert, Seville shortcakes."

Fidela tied the napkin about his neck, Cruz placed the plate of soup in front of him, while he groped on the table for the spoon. His lack of sight had made his hearing keener, giving him an ability to notice the slightest variations in the timbre of the voice in the persons around him. The increase in this sense of hearing was so exquisite that on that memorable day he recognized, through her voice, not only his sister's frame of mind but even her thoughts, which she had voiced to no one.

During the times when Cruz went to the kitchen and left him alone with Fidela, the blind man, eating slowly and without much appetite, chatted with his sister.

"What's the matter?" he asked her with some uneasiness.

"Dear boy, what could be the matter? Nothing."

"Something's going on. I know it, I can guess it."

"How?"

"By Cruz's voice. Don't tell me I'm wrong. Something extraordinary is going on in the house today."

"I don't know . . ."

"Wasn't Don José here this morning?"

"Yes."

"Did you hear what they were talking about?"

"No," Fidela said, "but I imagine that they weren't talking about anything in particular."

"I'm not mistaken, I'm not. Something is going on, and it's something very big, Fidela. What I don't know is whether it will bring us happiness or unhappiness. What do you think?"

"I . . . ? Dear boy, whatever it is, more misfortunes can't possibly befall us. It can't be; one's imagination can't conceive of anything more."

"So you suspect that it may be something good?"

"I'll tell you. . . In the first place, I don't think that anything is happening; but if there were something, out of pure logic, by the laws of justice, it must be something good."

"Cruz tells us nothing. She treats us like children. Heavens! And if what is happening is good, she might as well tell us about it."

The appearance of Cruz cut short this dialogue.

"And what are you two eating today?"

"We . . . ? Ah! Something very good. We've brought a fish . . ."

"What's the name of it? Are you going to fix it with rice, or poached with tartar sauce?"

"We'll fix it Madrid style."

"Like bream, with three cuts in the skin and slices of lemon."

"Well, I'm not going to taste it. I'm not hungry," said Fidela. "You eat it, Cruz."

"No, you . . . it was brought for you."

"You, you . . . you eat it all, for goodness' sake!"

"Oh, what a joke!" said the blind man with childlike glee. "You'll have to draw straws."

"Yes, yes."

"Pull two straws out of the matting and bring them to me. Let's see . . . bring them on . . . Now, don't look. I'll cut one of the straws so that the ends will be the same. There. Now I put them between my fingers; don't look, now . . . Aha! The one who draws the long straw is the one who eats the fish. Let's see. . . Ladies, draw."

"I'll take this one."

"And I this one."

"Who won?"

"I have the short straw!" exclaimed Fidela, radiant.

"And I the long one."

"Cruz must eat it, Cruz," cried the blind man, with a seriousness and emphasis inappropriate to so trivial a matter. "And I won't let you wriggle out of it. I'm the boss. Say no more, and eat."

THREE

That was the night when Don Francisco failed to attend the tertulia, which caused no little perplexity, for he was of a punctuality which he himself was wont to call *mathematical*, delighting in the use of a term which seemed to him an extremely felicitous one. What could be the matter, what might be wrong? All was conjecture, fears that he might be ill. When Donoso went home he promised to send a message as early as possible next day, so that they would know what the situation was.

When Fidela, as usual, was helping Rafael undress to go to bed, the blind man said, in a voice so subdued that it was doubtful whether he was talking to himself or to his sister, "There's no doubt, none. Something is going on."

"What are you muttering about?"

"What I told you. I see an event, an extraordinary event, here, hanging over the house, shading it like a cloud so low that you can almost touch it with your hand, or like a great bird with its wings spread."

"But what makes you think such a thing? You're just being captious."

"I say it because . . . I don't know why I say it. When a person doesn't see, a new sense develops for him, the sixth sense, the power of divination, a certain conviction of foreboding, which . . . I don't know, I don't know what it is. I get dizzy just thinking about it. But I'm never mistaken."

Whatever insignificant event that altered in the smallest degree the monotonous regularity of the family's sad existence was reason enough to put Rafael's mind to work, setting in feverish motion his gift for sniffing out events in the mysterious emanations of the atmosphere. The fact that Torquemada had not come that night was sufficient reason to think about an unbalancing of the unchangeable membership of the tertulia, and although Rafael did not miss Don Francisco's presence, he regarded the vacuum left by his absence as something abnormal, which confirmed him in his suspicions or conjectures. And by connecting that absence with acoustic phenomena of the subtlest kind, such as the timbre of his elder sister's voice, he plunged into a labyrinth of hypotheses that would have driven insane anyone whose head was not a regular probability-calculating machine.

"Come now, little one," said his sister, tucking him in, "don't think about foolish things, and go to sleep."

Cruz came in to see if he was properly put to bed, or if he needed something.

"Do you know what?" said Fidela, who always took such things as a joke. "He says that something is going to happen, something very strange and extraordinary."

"Dearest, go to sleep," replied the elder sister, stroking his beard. "We never know what will happen tomorrow. It will be as God wills."

"Then . . . something is up," stated the blind man with quick perception.

"No, dear boy, nothing."

"As long as it's good, let it come," added Fidela perkily.

"Good, yes; think good thoughts. It's high time . . . I think . . ."

"Then . . . it is good?" said Rafael quickly, peering out of the bedclothes.

"What?"

"That."

"What, dear boy?"

"What's going to happen."

"Come now, stop fussing and go to sleep quietly. Who can doubt that God, at long last, must take pity on us? Oh, to think that still greater misfortunes may come! Never; human imagination cannot conceive it. We have reached the farthest limit. Is there or is there not a limit in human affairs? If there is a limit, that is where we are . . . Well! Everybody to bed."

"The limit!" Rafael needed hear no more to spend part of the night spinning and unraveling a word. Limit was the same as frontier, the point or line where one territory ends and another begins. If they were close to the limit, it meant that their life would change completely. How? Why? Fidela, too, believing that she saw a slight nervous excitement in her sister, who was usually so impenetrable and calm, thought that the use of the word limit was not an unimportant thing to say, and began to ponder, opening her spirit to the happy anticipations which were always around her, ready to enter. The poor girl, avid to breathe free of that murky cell of poverty, needed so little to make her cheerful. A passing idea, a word half spoken, sufficed to make her indulge in the innocent game of believing in possible happiness, to see it coming, and to summon it with the very strength of her desire.

"Go to bed," Cruz told her sister with her accustomed gentle authority. And seizing a candle she went to inspect the house, a custom she had acquired following a bad fright they had had soon after moving there. She examined all the corners, got down on all fours to look under the sofa and the beds, and ended by making sure that the bolt was well shot and the windows above the inner patio carefully secured. When she returned to her sister, Fidela was getting undressed preparatory to going to bed, carefully folding her clothing. "Shall I tell her now?" thought Cruz, after laying her ear to the glass door of the sitting room to make sure that Rafael was not stirring. "No, no; it will keep the poor girl awake. I'll tell her tomorrow. Moreover, I fear my brother's sharp ears, for he can hear what one is thinking, let alone what one says aloud."

When she saw that Fidela was praying under her breath, already ensconced in bed, Cruz lay down in the other bed, a very simple operation because the lady was not in the habit of undressing completely. She slept in a petticoat, stockings, and a morning jacket, with a kerchief wound about her head like a bandage. A cotton blanket kept out the cold during the winter months; in summer she used only an old coat that covered her from the knees down. For six months the eldest Aguila had not known the use of sheets.

Once she had put out the light and muttered two or three prayers, the lady dived headlong into that stagnant pool of her poverty-stricken life, feeling that she had the strength to swim a bit. But the pool was uneasy; waves were arising from its depths which tossed the swimmer from side to side, and submerged her with their spirited motion.

"No, Holy Virgin and Eternal Father and all the heavenly powers, not I . . . I am not the one who must make this sacrifice to save us all from death. My sister must do it, she is the one, she is younger; she, who has scarcely had to fight. I am exhausted by this horrible battle with fate. I can't stand any more, I'll fall, I'll die. Ten years of frightful warfare, always on watch, always in the front line, warding off blows, taking care of everything, inventing ruses to gain a week, a day, hours; hiding my grief so that the others would not lose courage; eating thistles and drinking gall so that the others could live! No, Lord, I have done my part; I am relieved from this obligation; my turn is over. Now it's time for me to rest, to quietly rule the others. And Fidela, my little sister, who is coming under fire now in this unknown combat that is going to take place; she is reserve troops; she is young and spirited, and still has rosy hopes. I have none; I am good for nothing, much less for marriage . . . and with that poor scarecrow!"

Here a half-turn in bed and a rapid emergence to the surface from the depths of the waters.

"All things considered, he's not a bad man. I'll take over the job of polishing him, giving his scales a good scraping. He'll be as docile and tame as a little fish. Ah, if my sister is the least bit clever, we'll make of him whatever we like. The solution may be as grotesque as you please, but it is a solution. It's a question of accepting it or letting ourselves die. Of course, it's a little—and a lot—ridiculous. But we're not in a position to pay much heed to what people will say. What have we received from society? Rebuffs and humiliations, when we were not treated with horrible cruelty. Then let's pay no attention to society; let's pretend that it doesn't exist. The same people who criticize us will kiss his hand—indeed they will—because with that hand he signs the checkbook. They will kiss it, to see if something sticks to them. What a joke!"

Another half-turn, and quick immersion in the lowest depths.

"Now if poor little Fidela, who has always been spoiled and a bit stubborn, refuses the sacrifice; if I don't succeed in convincing her; if she prefers death to redeeming the family by such a means, I'll have no choice but to face up to it myself. No, no, I'll convince her; she is reasonable and will understand that she is the one who must drain this cup, as I have had to drain others. But I really feel that I cannot drink it. Besides, I'm old. Surely he'll prefer the other one. But if by some awful mischance he turns to me, or chooses me as if in a game of short straws? How ghastly! I'm forty years old and feel as if I'd lived sixty. Imagine me now in that situation, having to go to bed with that clown, and put up with him, and . . . ! It's out of the question for me to have to do that! Fidela, Fidela, who is scarcely twenty-nine . . . because, good heavens, for the sacrifice to mean anything, something must be born of it. I will raise my nieces and nephews and rule every one of them, large and small, for that is certain. I will not lose my authority. I'll establish a dictatorship. No one will draw breath in the house without my permission, and . . ."

Brief period of sleep and sudden wakefulness, with excitation and tingling all over the body.

"As for that poor man, I promise that I'll polish him. Even now, I teach him things very directly, and . . . really, I have no complaints about the pupil. In his desire to establish himself in a higher sphere than the one he now occupies, he absorbs all the ideas that I throw at him, just as one throws bread to the fish in a pond. The poor fellow is avid for new ideas, for fine manners and elegant language. He's no fool, and is terrified of being ridiculous. Put yourself in my hands, pet donkey, and I'll make you so gentlemanly that people will envy you. When he feels closer to me, I'll take him over, and then we'll see if I do a good job. For the moment, I'll make use of our friend Donoso to let him know that certain things are desirable—little lessons that I can't give him without wounding his pride. Don José will act as my intermediary to make him understand that cultivated people don't eat raw onions. There are some nights, my God, when you have to sit a yard and a half away from the good man, for . . ."

Period of floating in moderately deep waters. Sleepiness, stupor.

FOUR

Early next morning, before Rafael was stirring, Cruz laid hands on her sister and, going with her to the kitchen, a place that was separated from the rest of the house and quiet, and from which, no matter how much Fidela might raise her voice, it could not reach the blind man's delicate ear, without any preparatory or mitigating statements—for that woman of steel was not accustomed to making use of them on really serious occasions—she told her. And very clearly, in short, categorical words.

"I . . . but I . . . !" exclaimed Fidela, opening her eyes as wide as she could.

"Yes, you. There's nothing more to be said."

"I, did you say?"

"You, you! There's no other way. It's necessary."

When Cruz said "It's necessary" in that solemn and authoritarian tone, strengthened and made virile by her constant battle against fate, there was nothing to do but bow one's head. In that house, one obeyed as if under military discipline, or with the wordless submission of the Jesuit rule, *perinde ac cadaver,* "like a corpse."

"Did you think it was something else?" she said after a pause, during which she observed the effects of the blow on Fidela's face.

"Last night I began to suspect it, and I thought . . . I thought that it would be you."

"No, my child, you. So now you know it."

She said this with the cool serenity of a housewife, as if she were ordering Fidela to shell peas or put the chick-peas to soak. Fidela shrugged her shoulders and, fluttering her eyelashes rapidly, replied, "All right."

And she rushed off to her room, quite unaware of where she was going.

Once the stupor of the moment when she heard the news had passed, the lovely young woman's first impression was one of joy, of being able to breathe freely, and of relief in soul and lungs, as if a great boulder that had been weighing on her from time immemorial had been lifted from her. The boulder might have been a terribly heavy hump which at that moment fell off by itself, allowing her to stand straight with her natural grace.

"Marriage," she said to herself, "means a frontier. From this side of it to the other, no more poverty, no more hunger, no more agonies, nor the infinite sadness of this jail cell. I can dress decently, have changes of clothes, primp, go out on the street without dying of shame, see people, have women friends . . . and, above all, relinquish this galley-oar; not to have to go crazy thinking about how to make a squash last for a week's meals, not to count chick-peas as if they were pearls, not to cut and weigh pieces of bread by the gram; eat a whole egg, surround my poor brother with comforts, take him to the baths, go myself, travel, go out in society, move about, be what we were. Oh, we have suffered so much that to stop suffering seems like a dream! Am I really awake?"

She pinched herself and then bustled through the house, mechanically taking up her usual duties; picking up a duster and briskly whisking it at the doors, seizing the broom as well, sweeping . . .

"Don't make much noise," Cruz told her as she passed from the dining room to the kitchen carrying dishes. "I think he's still asleep. Look, I'll sweep a little; you light the fire. Here's the match. Be careful when you light it; we have only three left."

She gave these orders simply, as if she had not exercised her authority moments before in the most serious matter on which it could be exercised. One would have thought that nothing had happened. But Cruz was like that, a very strong character, who arranged for what she deemed necessary by using the same glacial authority in small things as in large ones. The broom changed hands. God knows what Cruz was thinking about as she swept! Fidela, as she lighted the fire, continued to occupy her mind with the pleasant prospect of a change in their lives. A certain amount of time had to pass, during which the kindling ignited and the lazy flame took hold, before the onset of the natural reaction to that feeling of joy, or the awakening from that daydream, disclosing the real outlines of the tremendous change. The flame was licking energetically at the coal when Fidela saw in her mind's eye the image of Torquemada in all his grotesque crudeness. She had often observed him, and had never been able to find in him any of the charms that adorn the stronger sex. But what choice did she have except to resign herself so as to be able to live? Was it or was it not a salvation? Since it was salvation for all three, then she offered herself as a holocaust to the monster and gave herself to him for life. It was some consolation that the others would live happily, though she would suffer terribly from the bitterness of that potion she would be forced to drink.

This idea took away her appetite, and when her sister, with her customary rapidity, prepared the chocolate made with water which served the two as breakfast, Fidela refused to touch it.

"Are you sulking already? Lovely!" Cruz told her, placing on the table the crusts of yesterday's bread which helped them to swallow the unappetizing brew. "What? Are you worried about what I told you? Oh, my child, in this fierce battle we've been waging, when something has to be done, it is done! This obligation has fallen to you, as others have fallen to me, heavy ones at that, and nothing can be done about it. If the three of us are to live, our lives depend on you. And the sacrifice is not going to be as hard as it looks at first sight. It's true that he's not exactly a gallant, shall we say. It's true that he has made a fortune by lending money at horrifying usurious rates, and bears the burden of the scorn and hatred of any number of victims. But oh, Fidela! No one can choose the rock on which to come to shore! The storm has blown us onto this one. What can we do but hold tight? Imagine that we are poor shipwrecked folk floating amid the waves on a rotten plank. We are drowning, the abyss is swallowing us up! And days, months, years pass like this. At last we manage to sight land. Ah, an island! What else can we do but come ashore and give thanks to God? Is it reasonable that, if we are drowning and see land nearby, we should start to argue about whether the island is beautiful or ugly, whether there are flowers on it or nettles, whether it has beautiful birds or lizards and other repellent vermin? It is an island; it is solid ground, and we will go ashore there. We'll try to get along as best we can there. And who knows, who knows whether, if we explore the center of the island, we will find trees and beautiful valleys, health-giving waters and all the good things that we lacked! So you musn't be unhappy. He is a man of a lower class and of humble extraction. But his very inferiority and his desires to be a gentleman will make him more docile, more manageable, and we will succeed in turning him inside out. No matter what you say, I see certain qualities in him; he's not stupid, not at all. If you scratch that rough surface you will find rectitude, sensitivity, and clear judgment. In fact, as soon as you are married, leave him to me. . ." (pause). "Now what are you crying about? Keep your wretched tears for occasions that really deserve them. This is not a misfortune; this, after ten years of horrible suffering, is salvation, a piece of immense good fortune. Think about it and you will understand."

"Yes, I understand it. I'm not saying anything," murmured Fidela, deciding to drink her chocolate, for in the end, hunger was stronger than repugnance. "Do I have to do it? Then we won't talk about it any more. Though the sacrifice were much greater, I would still make it. These are not times for scruples, nor demanding delicacies to eat. I agree with what you said. Who knows whether the island will be less dry and ugly than it seems, seen from the sea!"

"Exactly. Who knows?"

"And whether, once we have been saved, we will be happy to be on it, for that cannot be known. How many women have married thinking that they were going to be very happy, and then it turned out that he was a wastrel and a rogue! And how many go into marriage like a lamb to the slaughter, and then . . . !"

"Quite right. Then they find certain virtues that take the place of physical beauty, and an economic state of affairs which, after all, makes life methodical, pleasant, and agreeable. In this miserable world one must not expect dazzling happiness, which is almost always illusory; it is enough to attain a modest sense of well-being. Bodily needs satisfied: that is the chief thing. To live—and when you say that, you say it all!"

"To live! That's right. Very well, sister, if it depends on me, we will live."

Cruz, rejoicing in her triumph, rose to her feet, and warning her sister not to give the news to Rafael until she had prepared him for it gradually, she disguised herself to go to the market, the obligation which she found most troublesome and which was the most painful for her amid all the burdens of that oppressive existence.

Rafael was calling. Fidela went to see him, and handing him his clothes, encouraged him to get up. That day the young woman was in a good humor and proposed to take her brother for a walk.

"I notice something very strange in the timbre of your voice," the blind man told her after he had risen and his sister had placed the basin in front of him so that he could wash his face. "Don't deny that something is happening to you. You are gayer than on other days. Gay, yes, but emotionally upset. You've been crying, Fidela, don't tell me it's not so; the dampness of tears that you've dried a little while ago is in your voice. You have laughed, either before or after you cried. The vibration of your laughter is still in your voice."

"Oh, for goodness' sake, pay no attention. Hurry, for it's time to comb your hair, and today I'm going to make you as handsome as can be."

"Give me the towel."

"Here."

"What's going on? Tell me all about it."

"Well, there's . . . just a little news."

"See? I told you so last night. Let's see if I can guess. . ."

"Well. . ."

"Has someone been here?"

"No one, dear boy."

"Has a letter arrived?"

"No."

"I dreamed that a letter had come with good news in it."

"Good news can come outside of letters; it comes through the air, by the unknown means that God's infinite wisdom is apt to use."

"Oh, you're really tantalizing me! Tell me quickly."

"First I'll comb your hair. Be quiet, and don't make faces."

"Oh, don't be cruel! Goodness, what torment!"

"Why, it's nothing, my dearest boy. Be quiet. Let me part your hair right. After all, the part is important."

"And speaking of parts . . . What was that business about limits that Cruz was speaking of? I've thought of nothing else all night. Does she mean that we've reached the limit of our suffering?"

"Yes."

"What?" he said, standing up with feverish anxiety. "Tell me, tell me right away. Fidela, don't upset me; don't take advantage of my condition, of this blindness which isolates me from the world and shuts me up in a circle of deceptions and lies. Now that I can no longer see the light, let me see the truth at least, the truth, Fidela, dear sister."

FIVE

"Calm down. I'll tell you all about it," replied Fidela, a bit frightened, hanging on to his shoulders to make him sit down. "It has been a long time since you got so angry."

"It's because ever since yesterday I'm like a gun with a hair trigger. One touch and I'll go off. I don't know what this is . . . a horrible foreboding, a fear. Tell me, has Don José Donoso had any part in this happy change that awaits us?"

"Maybe. I can't tell you for sure."

"And Don Francisco Torquemada?"

Pause. Heavy silence, during which the flight of a fly resounded as if the air were a great sheet of glass scratched by a diamond.

"You don't answer? Are you there?" said the blind man, with great anxiety.

"I'm here."

"Give me your hand. Now, let's see."

"Then sit down and behave sensibly."

Rafael sat down and his sister kissed his brow, leaning toward him, for he was pulling her arm.

"I think you're crying," and he touched her face. "Yes. Your face is wet. Fidela, what is this? Answer the question I asked you. In this change, this . . . I don't know what to call it . . . does that friend of the household, that vulgar man who is making such efforts to be a decent person . . . does he figure in any way as a cause, as a principal agent?"

"And what if he does?" answered the young woman after he had repeated the question three times.

"Don't say any more. You are killing me!" exclaimed the blind man, drawing away from her. "Go away, leave me alone. Don't think that the news has caught me by surprise. For several days a suspicion has been circulating in my mind. It was like an insect biting me inside, eating me up from within. Could there be greater suffering! I don't want to know more: I was right. What a way to find out! But tell me: didn't you bring that man to the house to play the fool, to amuse us with his idiocies?"

"For God's sake, be still," said Fidela, terrified. "If Cruz hears you, she'll get angry."

"Let her hear me. Where is she?"

"She'll be here soon."

"And as for her . . . ! God, You did well to blind me so that I wouldn't see this ignominy. But even if I don't see it, I feel it, I can touch it."

He was on his feet, waving his arms, and would have bumped into the furniture and fallen had not his sister thrown her arms around him, pushing him into the chair almost by force.

"Dear boy, for God's sake, don't act like this. It isn't what you think."

"Yes it is, yes it is."

"But listen to me. Be sensible, reasonable. Let me comb your hair."

Rafael seized the comb from his sister with a brusque movement, and broke it in two.

"Go comb that clown's hair; he needs it more than I do. He must be full of lice."

"Dear boy, for the love of God! You'll make yourself ill."

"That's what I want. I would be better off dead. Then the two of you would have no more responsibility; you'd be free to degrade yourselves to your heart's content."

"Degrade ourselves! But what are you thinking of?"

"No, of course I know that it's a matter of legal marriage. You are selling yourselves, by the good offices or connivance of Holy Church. It comes to the same thing. The shame is no less for that. You must think that our name is a cabbage stalk, and you're throwing it to the hog for him to eat."

"Oh, what wild things you're saying! You're not well, Rafael. You're hurting me dreadfully."

The poor girl began to cry, and meanwhile her brother maintained a grim silence.

"No, I'm not hurting you," he said at last. "I can't hurt you. You are hurting yourself, and my role is to pity you with all my heart and love you the more for it. Come here."

They embraced each other tenderly, and each wept on the breast of the other, with the yearning emotion of those who part forever.

The three Aguilas were united by an immense love. The two women felt for the blind man a love which compassion enhanced to the point of idolatry. He repaid them in the same coin; but even though he adored both of them, there was a subtle difference between his love for Cruz and his love for Fidela. He always regarded the elder sister as a second mother, as a gentle authority which, even though very firmly exercised, reinforced his love. In Fidela he saw only the beloved little sister, his companion in misfortune and even in innocent games. Instead of authority, intimacy, little jokes, tenderness, and a sort of common life, soul joined to soul, in which each of them felt for both. It was a case of Siamese brother and sister, souls united by something more than mere kinship and a spiritual tie. Rafael regarded Cruz with an almost religious veneration; his feelings toward her were those of filial submission and respect. For Fidela he had all the love and delicacy of feeling that had accumulated in his life as a blind man, like a spring which has no outlet and which, working on its own substance, forms a fathomless well.

Unable to stop crying, they could not break away from each others' arms. Fidela was the first to try to end the painful scene, for if Cruz were to come in and see them weeping like this, she would have a very nasty shock. Hastily drying her tears, for she thought she heard the key turning in the lock, she told her brother, "Pretend, dearest. I think she has come in. If she sees us crying, she's sure to be upset. She'll think that I've told you something I shouldn't have."

Rafael said not a word. His head drooping on his breast, his hair falling over his brow in disorder, he resembled a Christ who has just expired, or rather an *ecce homo*, owing to the position of his arms, which needed only a reed clutched in them to make the picture complete.

Cruz looked in at the door, still wearing the disguise she used to go shopping. Pale and silent, she gazed at the two of them and immediately disappeared from view. She needed no more information to realize that Rafael knew about it, and that the effect of the news had been disastrous. Their close association in misfortune, their isolation, and the habit all three had of observing one another constantly had given each member of the hapless family an exceptional sensitivity and the ability to know at a glance what the other two were feeling and thinking. The sisters read Rafael's face as easily as the catechism; he had studied them in the timbre of their voices. No secret was possible among those three clairvoyants, nor was there any second intention they could not discover in a moment.

"It's all in God's hands," said Cruz to herself as she went to the kitchen with her exiguous packages of food.

Tossing her bundles on the table with a weary movement, she sat down and buried her head in her trembling hands. Fidela entered on tiptoe.

"Well," said Cruz, heaving a great sigh, "I see that he knows, and that he took it badly."

"So badly that . . . If you had seen him . . . ! It was horrible!"

"Did you let it slip, by any chance? Didn't I tell you . . . ?"

"Pooh! Why, he knew it already."

"He guessed it. Poor angel! His sightlessness sharpens his wits. He knows everything."

"He doesn't accept it."

"It's his wretched pride of breeding. We have lost it with this tremendous drubbing that Fate has given us. Breeding, family, social class! How insignificant all that seems, viewed from this dungeon where God has kept us imprisoned for so many years! But he retains that pride, the dignity of a name that once was considered glorious, and was glorious. He is an angel of God, a child. His blindness preserves him just as he was in better times. He lives as if enclosed in a glass bell, in the memory of a beautiful past which . . . the very word shows it: 'past' means. . . what will never return."

"I'm very much afraid," said Fidela in a confidential whisper, "that your . . . plan cannot be carried out."

"Why?" asked the other quickly, her eyes blazing.

"Because Rafael can't endure the pain of it."

"Oh, it won't be as bad as that! I'll convince him—we'll convince him. There's no need to give so much importance to a first impression. He'll realize himself that it's necessary. I say that it's necessary, and it will be done."

She emphasized this statement by striking her closed fist on the table, which creaked as the old boards felt the blow, making a paper-wrapped piece of meat bounce. Then the lady sighed as she rose to her feet. You would have said that, by taking in air with all the strength of her lungs, she was inserting a big spoon into her body to extract the energy which, after the colossal expenditure of the last few years, still remained inside. And a great deal did remain; she was an inexhaustible mine of it.

"We mustn't lose courage," she added, taking the piece of meat out of the bloody paper and unwrapping the other packages. "Let's not think about that now, for if we did, we'd go insane. Let's get to work. Look, cut off a piece of the beefsteak. You can fix the rest as you did yesterday. No stew today. Here are the tomatoes . . . a bit of red cabbage . . . three prawns . . . the egg . . . three potatoes. . . . We'll make noodle soup for tonight. And don't go to see him. I'll comb his hair, and we'll see if I succeed in calming him down."

She found him in the same posture, that of an *ecce homo* without a reed.

"What's the matter with you, dear boy?" she said, dropping a kiss on his hair and putting all the affection she could into her voice. "I'm going to comb your hair. Now, then, no tricks. Does something hurt? Are you worried about anything? Tell me about it right away, for you know that I'm here to bring you all the happiness I can. Come now, Rafael, you're like a little child; look, dear boy, it's very late already; your hair isn't combed, and we have much to do."

Alternately chiding and flattering, with the sweetest of words, she was always able to control him. His respect for the elder sister, in whom he had seen, ever since the days of misfortune had begun, a person endowed with supernatural energy and ruling capacity, placed a heavy weight on Rafael's soul and on those impulses toward rebellion that he had shown a short time before. He let her comb his hair. The eldest Aguila, who always rose to the challenge of new difficulties, did not evade the question but tackled it head-on.

"Bah! All that because of what Fidela told you about poor Don Francisco and his aspirations. The poor man is so good; he has taken such a liking to us! And now he's begun to harp on wanting to give a permanent solution to our dreadful situation, to this agony we live in, abandoned by everyone. And it's no use thinking about the lawsuit, which is lost already for lack of means to carry it on. It would be won if we could meet the court costs, but who can think about that? Well, as I told you, that good Don Francisco wants to bring a radical change into our existence; he wants . . . us to live."

As she combed, she felt that under her fingers the poor blind man's head and whole body were trembling. But he said nothing, and after she had carefully parted his hair she went on boldly, presenting the much-feared question smoothly and slowly.

"Poor man! The Canseco family told me yesterday that all those tales about his avarice are false rumors put about by his enemies. A man who does good has enemies who gain strength from the very warmth of his generosity! I'm told that in secret, and even letting himself be flayed alive by gossipers, Don Francisco has righted many wrongs and dried many tears. It's just that he's not one of those men who advertise their works of charity, and would rather be known as tightfisted. Indeed, he actually enjoys being scorned by public opinion. And I say that he's a better man and a better Christian for it. Ah, he has always behaved towards us like a perfect gentleman, and he is, he is, despite his rude outward appearance!"

No reply. Rafael did not say a word, and this disconcerted his older sister, who needed to have him speak, for she was sure that she could get the better of him in a discussion by firing the barrage of her persuasive power at him. But the blind man, no doubt aware that he would emerge the loser in the controversy, took refuge in inertia and silence as though in an unassailable redoubt.

SIX

She was taunting him as the bullfighter does a bull, but he had no desire to emerge from his defensive position. At last, as she finished combing his hair and gave the last touch to the soft, wavy locks that fell over his forehead, she told him a trifle severely, "Rafael, you're going to do me a favor, and it is not a plea, it's more like an order. Don't make me get really angry with you. If Don Francisco comes tonight, I expect that you will treat him with the same courtesy as always, and that you won't come out with any embarrassing gibes. For if the good man has certain hopes, which for the moment I won't describe, it is our business to be grateful for them and in no case to condemn them, whatever the reply we may give to those hopes. Do you understand?"

"Yes," said Rafael without moving.

"I'm sure that you won't place us in a ridiculous position by treating impolitely, in our own house, a person who wishes to help us in a way which for the moment I will not discuss. There's no question of that. Can I be easy in my mind?"

"Good manners, in which I will never be lacking, are one thing; dignity is another, and I can never lack that, either."

"Very well."

"Just as I tell you that I will never betray my good breeding before persons outside the family, no matter who they may be, I also tell you that I will never, never accept that man, nor will I consent to have him enter our family. I have nothing more to say."

Cruz's heart sank, recognizing in her brother's categorical words the iron-hard vein of the Aguila breed, mingled with the invincible pride of the Torre-Auñóns. That dogmatic opinion about the family's dignity was something she had taught Rafael when he was a child, when she, a girl from a rich and noble house, was surrounded by adorers, though her parents had found no man worthy of her exquisite hand.

"Oh, my dear boy!" exclaimed the lady, making no effort to hide her grief. "There are great differences between one time and another. Do you think that we are in those days of prosperity—you don't remember—when we sent you as attaché to the German Legation, to get you away from some friendships that were not very acceptable to the family? My poor boy! Then misfortune came down on our poor heads like a torrential rain that sweeps everything away. We lost all that we had, even our pride. You became blind; you have not seen the transformation of the world and the times. You don't see the painful part of our present abject poverty and the humiliation in which we live. The blackest aspect, the one that cuts to the soul and destroys it most, is the aspect you do not know, cannot know. By the power of imagination, you still live in that brilliant world, full of falsehoods. I can't forgive myself now for having been your teacher in the uncompromising dignity which is as false as all the other baubles that surrounded us. Oh yes, I was the one who put those ideas into your head when you fell in love with the Albert girl, the daughter of honorable bankers, a charming creature and very well brought up, but who we thought would bring us dishonor because she wasn't noble . . . because her grandfather had kept a cap shop in the Plaza Mayor. And I was the one who got out of your head what we called your foolishness; and in the hollow that it left behind, I stuffed a lot of useless nonsense. You still have it inside. And how sorry I am, how terribly sorry, to have been the one who put it there!"

"This case is very different from that one," said the blind man. "I realize that there are times and times. Today I would compromise, but within certain limits. To humiliate oneself a little, well and good, but to humiliate oneself to the point of shameful degradation, to compromise with the crassest kind of vulgarity, and all for what? For material things, for vile self-interest! Oh, my dear sister! That is selling oneself, and I do not sell myself. What is it all about? Simply to eat a little better?"

"To live," said the noble lady energetically, sparks seeming to fly from her eyes, "to live! Do you know what living means? Do you know what it means to fear that all three of us will die tomorrow, to die that death which is out of date now because the world is full of charitable institutions, the most horrible, the most unbelievable death—to die of hunger? What, are you laughing? We are very dignified, Rafael, and with as much dignity as ours I don't think we ought to knock on the door of the hospice and beg a plate of beans for the love of God. That same dignity prevents us from going to the doors of barracks, where they distribute the scraps of offal from the soldiers' mess, and eating that in order to go on living for one more day. Nor does our very dignified character allow the three of us to go out at night and stick our hands out to beg alms, for it would be impossible for us to formulate the words. Well then, my boy, my dear brother, since we cannot do that nor can we accept other solutions that you hold to be dishonorable, there is no solution left but one, and it is for the three of us to gather together and, holding one another tight and begging God for forgiveness, to throw ourselves out the window and smash on the ground below . . . or to seek some other means of death, if the one I've described doesn't seem entirely compatible with your dignity."

Rafael, completely devastated, listened without a word to this sisterly tirade, his elbows resting on his knees and his head buried in his hands. Fidela, curious, drawn by Cruz's raised voice, peeped in at the door as she peeled a potato.

After a little time had passed, and when the elder sister, gathering up Rafael's toilet things, was mentally congratulating herself on the effect caused by her words, the blind man raised his head haughtily and expressed himself as follows:

"Very well, if our poverty is as desperate as you say; if there is no solution for us but death, as far as I'm concerned, let it be so. This minute. I'm ready . . . Let's go."

He rose, groping with his hands for his sister, who did not let herself be caught, and told him from the other side of the room, "As far as I'm concerned, I don't mind, either. Death for me is a rest, a blessing, an enormous good. It has been for your sake that I haven't stopped living. I always believed that my duty was to sacrifice myself and to struggle. But no more, no more. Blessed be death, for it will take me to rest and the peace of my poor bones!"

"Blessed be death, yes indeed!" exclaimed Rafael, carried away by a mad vertigo, a suicidal enthusiasm which showed itself in him by no means for the first time. "Fidela, come . . . Where are you?"

"Here," said Cruz. "Come, Fidela. Is it true that nothing remains for us except death?"

The younger sister said nothing.

"Fidela, come here. Give me a hug. And you, Cruz, hug me too. Lead me; come, the three of us all together in each others' arms. Is it true that you're not afraid? Is it true that we won't turn back, and that, resolutely, as those who place dignity before everything else ought to do, we will take our lives?"

"I do not tremble," said Cruz, embracing him.

"Oh, I do!" murmured Fidela, half fainting; and as she touched her brother with her arms, she fell into the nearby armchair and put her hand to her eyes.

"Fidela, are you afraid?"

"Yes . . . yes," she replied, trembling and abashed, for she had become convinced that they were really going to do it; as for Rafael, he was quite ready.

"She hasn't my courage," said Cruz, "which is even greater than yours."

"Oh, I can't, I don't want to!" declared Fidela, crying like a little girl. "To die, to kill oneself! Death terrifies me. I would a thousand times rather live in the most dreadful poverty, eat cabbage stalks . . . Must we beg for alms? Send me. I will go, rather than throw myself out the window. Holy Virgin, how one's head would hurt when one fell! No, no, don't talk to me of killing ourselves. I can't, no, I can't; I want to live."

This sincere and spontaneous attitude ended the scene, cooling Rafael's enthusiasm for suicide and giving Cruz an admirable prop for carrying the question to the terrain most favorable for her.

"You see, our dear little sister leaves us stuck in the middle of the road, and without her, how can we kill ourselves? We can't possibly leave her alone in the world in such poverty and unprotectedness. From all of this we can deduce, dear brother, baby of the family," and here she caressed him playfully, "that God does not want us to commit suicide just now. Some other day, perhaps, for indeed we have no other choice."

"Ah, but don't count on me," said Fidela, terribly frightened again, and taking it very seriously.

"Let's not talk about that now. So, my young idiot, do you promise to be reasonable?"

"If being reasonable means accepting . . . that, and giving the name of brother to . . . Look, I can't do it; don't expect me to be reasonable. I'm not; I don't know how to be."

"But my dear boy, nothing has happened yet! Why, it's only a rumor, and I don't know how it has come to your ears! But at any rate, I know your opinion and will keep it in mind. Don José will talk to you, and if among us all we agree to reject the proposal, we will also agree among us all what we must do in order to live. Rather, there is nothing more to discuss than the asylum where we will ask for admission. Fidela does not want us to die; you do not want the other. Then it's off to the hospice with our poor bodies."

"To the hospice, then. I will never accept . . . that."

"Fine, that's fine."

"Have Don José come," Rafael suggested. "He will tell us where we can take refuge."

"Tomorrow we'll make the final decision about our fate. And since we still have one day," added the lady with a genial change of tone, "we must take advantage of it. Now, you'll have your lunch. You're going to have what you like best."

"What is it?"

"I'm not going to tell you; I want to surprise you."

"All right; it's all the same to me."

"And after you have lunch we'll go for a walk. It's a perfectly beautiful day. We'll go as far as Bernardina's house, and you'll have a good time there."

"Good, good," said Fidela, "I want to take the air, too."

"No, my dear; you'll stay here. Another day you can go, and I'll stay."

"So I'm going . . . ?" asked Rafael.

"With me," assented the lady, as if to say, 'Today I'm not going to let you out of my sight.' "I have to talk to Bernardina."

"To go out!" exclaimed the blind man, taking deep breaths. "I certainly need to. It seems as if moths had got into my soul."

"Don't you see, my dear idiot, that life is good?"

"Oh . . . that depends!"

SEVEN

If it has not been mentioned before, let it now be said that the Aguilas' former and faithful maid lived in Cuatro Caminos, on the hill that looks westward, beside the Northern Canal. The house, built of paving stones that had formerly served in Madrid, mud bricks, pressed earth, pieces of streetcar track, and old wainscoted doors, was a magnificent hut, adorned peasant-style with pumpkin plants, whose leafy stems grew along the eaves and the rooftop. It occupied the center of a very large rubbish heap with a wall of loose stones around it—material that had come from a quarry—and at intervals there were heaps of garbage and stable straw where a dozen or more good laying hens were scratching, along with a very self-satisfied rooster with golden feathers. At the eastern corner of the wall, looking toward the Tetuán road, was a tumbledown building of only one story, with all the appearances of a guard's house, with a temporary roof and unfinished walls, but its real purpose was quite different. At the door facing the road was a long pole, and at the end of it a sort of enormous star made of black sticks, something like an umbrella with no cloth on it, and underneath, a sign composed of big black blots on white plaster, which read: "Valiente, Fireworks Maker."

It was there that Cándido Valiente, Bernardina's husband, had his workshop; he provided fireworks, on the feast days of their titular saints, to the districts of Tetuán, Prosperidad, Guindalera, and the towns of Fuencarral and Chamartín. Bernardina had served the Aguila ladies in their early period of poverty, until she married Valiente; and such were the good woman's fidelity and loyalty that her mistresses continued to associate with her afterward, and had a relationship of true friendship with her. Cruz made use of Bernardina for delicate commissions about which it was prudent to maintain absolute secrecy; she consulted with Bernardina on grave matters and permitted herself confidences with her that she would have risked having with no one else in the world. Reliability, discretion, and a clear sense of things shone forth in that woman who, though she didn't know how to read or write, could have given lessons in the art of life to a good many upper-class folk.

Her marriage to the fireworks-maker had been until then infertile: miscarriages and nothing more. With the couple lived Cándido's father, a municipal customs agent, an old soldier who had been in the African campaign; he was the great friend of blind Rafael del Aguila, who had a marvelous time listening to him recount his deeds of valor, which in the mouth of their hero were as fabulous as if Ariosto himself sang of them. Were one to keep count of the Moors he had sent to the other world in Los Castillejos, in Monte Negrón, on the plain of Tetuán, and in Wad-Ras, not a sole adherent of Mohammed would have been left on earth as a sample of the breed. Valiente had served in the "Vergara Chasseurs," in the reserve division commanded by General Juan Prim. He had participated in all the actions that took place to protect construction of the highway from Campamento de Oteros to Los Castillejos; and then in Los Castillejos, on that glorious occasion—Christ!—the man would begin and never stop. The "Vergara Chasseurs" always in the front rank, and he, Hipólito Valiente, who was a corporal second class, doing such terrific deeds that they astonished the world. What a day was January 1, 1860! Members of the batallion covered themselves with glory, maintaining themselves in a square, with half their people stretched out on the accursed ground. Until January 14 the battalion could not make contact with the enemy again, and then it was another occasion when they dispatched Moors to their hearts' content. Monte Negrón! That was another of the great battles. And at last came the glorious February 4, the living end, the *neplusuntra* (as he said) of all the battles that ever were and ever will be. All acquitted themselves well, and General O'Donnell better than anyone, with that gift he had of laying everything out so well, and "that great head he had on him," which was the marvel of the universe.

Rafael heard these and succeeding marvels with the greatest enjoyment, undiluted by the suspicion that they might suffer from the vice of exaggeration, if not the poetic lie forged in the heat of enthusiasm. From the time he disembarked in Ceuta until he took ship again for Spain, leaving the Moroccan dogs "with no desire to come back for more," Valiente told the whole story with as much intrepidity in his rhetoric as in his surname, for when he came to a doubtful point, or something of which he had not been an eyewitness, his imagination escaped all bounds and he told the story according to his own ideas, always tending toward the romantic and extraordinary. For Rafael, in the isolation imposed by his blindness, incapable of playing any gallant part in the world that would satisfy the impulses of a noble heart and his chivalrous turn of mind, it was an irreplaceable consolation and joy to hear descriptions of heroic adventures, sublime endeavors of our army, bloody battles in which lives were sacrificed for honor's sake. Honor always first, the dignity of Spain and the splendor of the flag ever placed above any vile self-interest! And, hearing Valiente recount how, without having had a single piece of bread to put in their mouths, those lads went into battle, avid to thrash the enemies of Spain, Rafael became excited and positively glowed with adoration for everything noble and great, and scorn for everything miserable and low. To fight without having eaten! What glory! Not to know fear or danger; not to regard anything but honor! What an example! Happy the men who could follow that path! Wretched and unhappy those who rotted in a do-nothing life, enjoying trifling material things!

As they entered the yard, the first thing that Rafael asked on hearing Bernardina's voice, when she came out to meet them, was, "Is your father off duty today?"

"Yes, señor, he's out there somewhere, fixing a chair for me."

"Take him to your father," Cruz told her, "who will entertain him with tales about Africa, and you and I will go into your house, for we must talk."

The hero of heroes of the Maghreb appeared from behind a heap of garbage; he was a man well along in years, small of stature, muscular and agile despite his age, which was certainly no less than sixty; he looked like a member of a battalion of chasseurs, with a weather-beaten face, close-cropped black mustache, twinkling eyes, and a constant laugh that perpetuated for him the joys of military service. Coatless, his shirt sleeves rolled up, dressed in an old pair of pants from the uniform of Municipal Services, and with his head bare, Hipólito hastened to offer his hand to the young gentleman and took him off to the place where he was working.

"Go on, go on with your work," Rafael told him, seating himself on a three-legged stool with a little help from the veteran. "I already know that you're repairing chairs."

"Well, here we are trying to kill off plaguey idleness, which is a little worm that gnaws like hunger."

Seated on the blessed ground, legs wide apart and the chair between them, Valiente was selecting rushes from a nearby heap and using them to weave a new seat on the framework of the old chair.

"Let's see, Hipólito," said Rafael without further preliminaries, for indeed the old soldier did not need any, "what was that story you started to tell me the other day?"

"Sure! When we were on the bridgehead at Buceta, on the River Gelú, holding it so as to let the wounded cross over . . . ?"

"No, that wasn't it. It was about going through a mountain pass. Moors and more Moors on the heights above . . ."

"Oh, sure! It was the day after Wad-Ras; gosh, that was a dandy little battle! Well, to go from Tetuán to Tangiers, the army had to cross the mountain pass of Fondac. Christ, if it hadn't been for me, I mean for the Vergara Chasseurs! The general ordered us to get up there and throw out the Moorish rabble, and you should have seen us; yessir, you should have seen us. They were really scorching us from up above. But we kept right at it, climbing and climbing. The group we found halfway up the hill—fix bayonets! We really cleaned them up. They came out of the underbrush running in all directions, like rabbits. Once we saw 'em stand up—bam, bam—there was no end to it. I laid out more than fifty of 'em all by myself."

And while our Spanish soldiers so fiercely knocked the descendants of Hagar out of their terrible positions, Cruz and Bernardina, sitting opposite each other outside the doorway, with familiar ease, spoke of less noisy combats, the kind that no historian, great or small, will ever say a word about.

"I need two hens," Cruz had said by way of introduction.

"All the hens the señorita could want. Pick them out now."

"No, you choose them, good fat ones, and don't bring them till I let you know. We absolutely must invite him to dinner one day."

"If you say that, things must be going well."

"Yes, it's all settled. Just before I left home I received a note from Don José, in which he tells me that everything was agreed upon last night, and that the good man is happy as can be. You can't imagine what I have suffered and still suffer. To get to where we are, how many arguments, and what a hard task it has been to fight down repugnance, to hear no voice but the voice of reason, along with another no less serious voice, that of need! But it will be done; there's no other choice."

"And Señorita Fidela . . . ?"

"She's resigned. Really, she hasn't taken it dramatically, as I feared. Probably she'll make the best of things, or understands that the family deserves this sacrifice, which if you really think about it isn't the greatest of sacrifices. There are worse ones, don't you agree?"

"Yes, señorita. The man *is* getting more refined. I saw him yesterday and didn't recognize him, with his fancy top hat just pressed, that was so handsome, and a frock coat. My goodness; anybody would be glad to look like that. When I think how I used to see him, with a three-week-dirty shirt on his back, run-over heels to his shoes, a face like a Jew's in the Holy Week processions, collecting the rents in that tenement he owned across from the reservoir!"

"For Heaven's sake, be quiet; don't bring that up. Mum's the word."

"I mean, he's no longer what he was, and just like his clothes, his temper and his sly tricks may have changed, too."

"Ah! We'll see about that. Those are battles that will have to be fought later."

Both turned, startled by a sound like that of gunfire, which seemed to come from close by . . . Bam, bam, bam!

"Ah!" exclaimed Bernardina, laughing. "It's my father, who's telling the young master about the trouncing they gave the Moors."

"So, as I was telling you, Fidela doesn't worry me: she will submit to anything I decide upon. But this brother of mine . . . the poor blind man! If you knew what he put us through today!"

"He doesn't care for it?"

"Not a bit. So little does he care for it that today he was ready to kill himself. He doesn't accept it, no indeed. Certain ideas are very deeply rooted in him—family feeling, pride of breeding, noble tradition. I too used to feel that, but over the years I have left it behind, caught on the brambles of the path. I've fallen and dragged myself on so many times that vulgarity has had the better of me. My brother keeps up his old attitude as a person of noble descent, enamored of

dignity and a few other things which can't be eaten and which no one
has ever been able to eat in hard times."

"Can Señorito Rafael do anything but what his sisters wish?"

"I don't know, I don't know. I'm afraid that some storm is going to
break out at home. Rafael still preserves the family stubbornness in
his soul, just as precious objects are preserved in museums. But no
matter what happens, we will fight, and since this has to be done,
because it's the only solution, it will be done, I assure you that it will
be done."

The trembling of her lower lip showed the unbreakable resolution
which would turn that intention into a reality, defying all dangers.

"But we must prepare ourselves for events by acting, do you understand? I mean that I have to begin to take measures. Look here. Señor
Donoso wrote me today assuring me that the deal has been made, and
that the man is in a hurry."

"That's natural."

"And he wants to speed things up. Better and better: things that are
hard to swallow should be done all at once, and by surprise. By the
time people take notice, it will be done. I need hardly tell you that
we have to prepare ourselves. That's what I'm told by Don José, who,
understanding the difficulties we would encounter for that preparation
in the dreadful circumstances in which we live, offers me the necessary
funds. Naturally, in the present case, I accept the favor. What a fine
man, what farsightedness, what goodness! I'm accepting, yes indeed,
because I'm sure to be able to repay the loan very soon. Are you getting
the picture?"

"Yes, señora. You'll have to . . ."

"Yes . . . I see that you understand me. We'll have to start getting
things out of . . ."

"You know I'll do anything I can," said Bernardina.

"Starting tomorrow, you'll come to our house every day. We won't
take out everything at once so as not to call too much attention to it.
The most urgent thing is the silverware."

"It's in . . ."

"Well, never mind where it is: it makes no difference."

"Calle de Espoz y Mina. Ten months, if I'm not mistaken."

"Then the bedclothing . . . the clocks . . ."

"Everything, everything. And I thought it was lost! Meanwhile the interest will be mounting."

"Let it mount," said Cruz quickly, wishing to avoid a troublesome and humiliating calculation. "Ah, now that I remember! Tomorrow I'll give you the ten duros I owe you."

"There's no hurry. Don't bother with them. If Cándido finds out, he'll take them to buy powder. Keep them for me."

"No, no. I want to enjoy the pleasure, which had become almost unknown to me, of not owing anything to anyone," said Cruz, her face illuminated by a flash of ineffable joy. "Why, I can scarcely believe it. There are times when I say to myself, 'Am I dreaming? Can it be true that soon I can breathe free of this terrible oppression? Has this death-in-life really ended? Will this change that is about to happen bring happiness, or new misfortunes and new evils to replace those it takes away?'"

EIGHT

The lady said nothing for a little while, her thoughts following the mysterious future, her gaze fixed on the horizon, which was already beginning to be tinged with purple as the sun set among clouds. The almost imperceptible trembling of her lower lip indicated that her will was becoming restive. Yes, she must keep on struggling, struggling without repose; but the conditions of battle and the location of the battleground would no doubt be very different.

"It's late. We must go."

"Are you going in a carriage?"

"I could well afford to return home in a hackney coach today, and my poor legs would be glad of it, but I daren't do so. Such a treat would make Rafael suspicious. We'll go on shank's mare." (Calling) "Rafael, dear boy, it's late," and she went toward him, smiling. "What? Have you taken every last trench? Surely there must not be a Moor left to tell the tale."

"We were 'zactly in Los Castillejos," said the hero of Barbary, rising to his feet, "when Don Juan Prim . . ."

"Our cousin Gaspar de la Torre-Auñón, captain of artillery, died there," remarked Rafael, turning his face in the direction of his sister's voice. "His is the most recent glory of the family. How happy he! So . . . is it time for us to go?"

"Yes, dear boy."

"All right, then . . . quickstep . . . march!"

At that moment the fireworks-maker emerged from his workshop, all covered with soot, his hands black from handling powder, and greeted the guests politely. While Rafael chatted with him about the skyrocket business, and he in turn cursed the industrial crisis that was affecting the entire manufacture of fireworks, particularly the lack of protection afforded by municipal governments to such brilliant industries, and such useful amusement for the public, Bernardina walked ahead of them, accompanying her mistress to the gap in the wall.

"Shall I bring the hens tomorrow?" she inquired.

"No, not yet. Bring me a good tongue from one of the butcher shops in Tetuán, to serve pickled."

"Fine."

"And a good beef tenderloin."

"Would you like some of that good Salamanca sausage?"

"We'll talk about that later."

The fireworks-maker, who had hastily washed his hands, came out to escort them beyond the reservoir. From there to their house, walking alone and arm in arm, the brother and sister had half an hour's walk; it seemed long to her because she was in a great hurry to arrive and short to him for the opposite reason.

Neither Donoso nor Torquemada failed to appear that night, and uneasiness was obvious in the latter, for he did not know what to say or what sort of attitude to assume. He spoke not a syllable about the important matter, for Don José had recommended to his friend a prudent silence about the whole arduous affair. There would be time for explanations later. Rafael was standoffish and glacial for the whole time the tertulia lasted; but he permitted himself no unfavorable comments. Fidela avoided looking directly at Don Francisco, who never took his eyes off her, inwardly congratulating himself on the interesting young woman's chaste modesty, for he felt already that she was his. About halfway through the evening the suitor began to lose his diffidence; he loosened up, made jokes, giving himself airs of a talkative man who knows how to turn a phrase. All of them noticed a spate of fine words which he had learned within the past few days, and which he now launched in the whirl of his speech with the ease imparted only by long practice. His language mannerisms were painfully obvious: if he had to make a remark about the object of something, he said *the objective*, and within a very short time a multitude of *objectives* had been brought into play, sometimes with doubtful applicability, to wit: "I don't know why they water the streets so much, for if the *objective* is not to have dust, *the proper procedure* is to sweep them first. . . But there's nobody like our *municipal government* (he never said "City Hall" any more) to *disarrange* operations." He also revealed a stubborn insistence on making it clear that he knew how to say *hence, ipso facto, the horns of the dilemma, under the terms of*. This last was one of his chief joys, and he considered everything *under* this or that aspect. The ladies also noticed that he was acquiring easier manners; for example, when he took his leave he did so with a certain gentility, and Cruz could not help congratulating herself on his progress. Just as he was leaving he said something to Fidela which did not displease her: it was a gallant phrase that Donoso had no doubt taught him. An expression of joy was visible on that worthy's face, doubtless out of satisfaction for the conquest he had so fortunately made. He had roped the beast, and with subtle worldly arts was turning the beast into a man, a gentleman, perhaps even a personage.

After Rafael had gone to bed, when Cruz and Fidela were left alone, they chatted about the same subject, and the elder sister said, among other things, "Isn't it true that every day he's less of a boor? Tonight he seemed like another man to me."

"To me, too."

"It's his contact with us, the knowledge of his new position. Ah! His association with us carries responsibilities, and he is no fool and tries to learn. You'll see how in the end . . ."

"But oh, dear," observed Fidela with deep sadness, "Rafael does not accept it. If you had witnessed what he said to me just now while he was getting ready for bed!"

"I don't want to know it. Leave him to me; I'll take care of his sulks. Now, go to bed, and let's not think about difficulties, for they will all, all be overcome. I say so, and that's enough."

Rafael was very restless all night long; so much so that Cruz, hearing him muttering to himself, got up and tiptoed barefoot to his bed. He pretended to be asleep when he heard her approaching, and after keeping watch for a long time the lady went back to bed, feeling uneasy. Next day, while Fidela was combing his hair, the blind man mumbled nervously and tried to stand up at every moment.

"For heaven's sake, be quiet! I've already stuck the comb in your ears twice."

"Tell me, Fideli, what do these entrances and exits of Bernardina's mean? She came this morning early, when I wasn't up yet; she went out, came in again, and kept on like that. Now she's coming in for the fifth time. It seems as if she's carrying off and bringing back something, I don't know what . . . What are these errands? What's going on?"

"Dear boy, I don't know. Bernardina brought a tongue."

"A tongue?"

"Yes, to pickle. And by the way, today you're going to have a marvelous beef tenderloin."

"Abundance undoubtedly reigns in the house," said Rafael sarcastically. "But weren't you saying yesterday that the situation is so bad, our need so horrible, that we had no choice but to go into an asylum? How do you reconcile asking for alms with pickled tongue?"

"Come, now; it's a gift from Bernardina."

"And the tenderloin?"

"I don't know! But what does it matter to you?"

"How can it not matter to me? I want to know where these treats are coming from that have been brought so surreptitiously into this house of shameful poverty. Either the two of you don't know what dignity is, or you will have to declare that you've won the lottery. No, don't put me off with excuses: those are the *horns of the dilemma,* as our friend the beast would say. Last night he had such a fund of *dilemmas* and *terms* and *objectives* that it was laughable. Surely you can have no complaint of me. I've respected your ridiculous friend, and haven't wanted to lose my temper in his presence. If I did so I would place myself on his level. No, my good breeding will never cross swords with his lowborn crudeness."

"For heaven's sake, Rafael!" said Fidela, terribly upset.

"No, I can't talk in any other way about that man. When he leaves, the stable smell he leaves behind seems to keep him in my presence. Before he arrives, while he's still climbing the staircase, the odor of onions tells me that he's coming."

"Now, that really isn't true. Don't say foolish things!"

"Why, I recognize that your wild boar tries to be refined and is becoming less of an animal, and he's acquiring a certain resemblance to a person. He doesn't spit into his handkerchief any more, nor does he say *on account of how* or *irregardless*; he doesn't scratch his shins any more; when he did that I felt such repugnance, even without seeing him, and the noise of his fingernails made me as nervous as if I felt them on my flesh. I recognize that there has been progress. Good for you and Cruz. I do not accept him either coarse or fine, and the door that opens to let him into the house is the door I will take to leave it. What can you do, that's the way I am! I can't turn into someone else. I haven't forgotten my mother: I have her right here, and she is speaking to you with my voice. I haven't forgotten my father: I feel him inside me, and what I am saying is what he says."

Fidela could not restrain her emotion and burst out crying, but this did not placate the blind man who, all the more excited by his sister's sobs, continued to attack her as follows:

"You and Cruz can do as you like. I will leave you. I have loved you very much, and still love you; it would be impossible for me to live far from you, Fidela; from you, who are the only joy of this life of mine shrouded in darkness; from you, who are light to me, or something resembling the light I have lost. I will die of grief or loneliness, but I will never authorize by my presence this degradation into which you are about to fall."

"Keep still, for God's sake. We won't do anything. We'll tell him to go to blazes with his millions. I'll work as a seamstress in order to live, my sister will go and be a servant in some priest's house, or with some dignified gentleman. What does it matter? We must live, dear brother. We will sink very low. Does that make you angry, too?"

"No, that doesn't. What infuriates me is that you want to bring that disgusting leech who feeds on the poor into my family. That is what is vile, not honest work. If I had eyes, if I were good for something! But not being good for anything, being a burden and a hindrance, does not take away my dignity, and once again and then again, and a hundred times and a thousand times, I tell you that I will not yield, that I do not consent, that I am simply unwilling to hand you over to the vile beast, and that if you persist, I will go and beg alms on the highroad."

"Jesus, don't say that!" exclaimed the young woman, frightened and hastening to embrace him.

Fortunately Cruz was no longer in the house. When she returned, the crisis was over and Rafael, immobile and silent in his accustomed place, was awaiting his lunch.

"If you only knew what a nice thing I've brought you!" Cruz told him, still with her shawl on. "I'm sure you can't guess!"

The luncheon, prepared by Bernardina, was ready by this time and they served it to him, affecting a happiness which produced in both sisters the most painful smile it is possible to imagine. Rafael ate with reasonably good appetite the tasty, tender beefsteak; but when they offered him a special treat, brought by Cruz herself from the famous House of Lhardy, a piece of truffled boar's head, he brusquely rejected it, saying gravely, "I can't eat it. It smells of onion."

"Of onion? You're out of your mind. And you like it so much!"

"I like it, yes . . . but it reeks . . . I don't want it."

The two sisters looked at one another in consternation. The same scene was repeated that night. Cruz had also brought from the House of Lhardy some very delicious sausages, of which Rafael was extraordinarily fond. He refused to taste them.

"But, dear boy . . ."

"They reek of onions."

"Come, now, don't be foolish."

"It's just that the bad smell of onions seems to pursue me. The two of you have it on your hands. Something that you're carrying in your purse has stuck to you, and it's come into the house, I don't know how."

"I don't want to answer. You are imagining unworthy things, Rafael, which don't deserve to be taken seriously. You have no right to offend your poor sisters, who would give their lives for you a thousand times."

"I'm asking, for the dignity of the family, not your lives but something that is worth a good deal less."

"The family's dignity is safe," replied the eldest Aguila as resolutely as any man. "Are you, perchance, the only repository of our honor, our dignity?"

"I begin to think that I am."

"You are wrong in believing that," added the lady, with her lower lip trembling violently. "You are being very annoying, and a bit impertinent. We tolerate your temper tantrums; but there comes a time, dear boy, when to tolerate them, more patience and calmness is needed than I possess; and remember, I possess a high degree of both. That's enough. Let's consider this matter closed. That is the way I want it, those are my orders . . . my orders, do you hear?"

The unfortunate young man fell silent, and before long, the two ladies were hastily getting dressed in their bedroom, preparing to receive their friends Torquemada and Donoso. When Fidela whimpered a little, her emotions stirred by the storm she had passed through, Cruz upbraided her bitterly:

"Stop being so soft. This is too stupid to be borne. If we give in, he'll infect us with his madness. No, no; we must show energy and confront the scruples of a spoiled young sprig with unbreakable resolution. Take courage, or the scaffolding we've raised with such effort will topple to the ground."

NINE

They had to bring in Don José Donoso to parley with him. The two sisters, confident of the authority of their family friend, shut him up with Rafael and anxiously awaited the results of the conference, no less serious for them than would have been a peace agreement between warring enemy nations. Don José's speech was splendid, and there was no sharp-edged argument that he did not wield with the skill of a diplomatic marksman. Ah, the times were not such that one could pay much attention to inequality of origins! A thousand cases of tolerance could be cited regarding a thousand origins. He, "Pepe" Donoso, was the son of humble farmers in Tierra de Campos, and had married Justina, of the illustrious family of the Pipaones de Treviño and niece of the count of Villaociosa. And in the lineage of the Aguilas themselves, very eloquent examples could be cited. Rafael's own aunt Doña Bárbara de la Torre-Auñón had married Sánchez Regúlez, whose father, people said, had been a saddlemaker in Seville. And in the last instance, good Lord, he must submit blindly to whatever was decided by his sister Cruz, that peerless woman who was fighting heroically to save all three of them from indigence. The skillful negotiator played the tune in various keys, now attacking by way of affection, now by way of fear, and as easily using soft persuasion as solemn threat. But at last, voiceless after so much arguing and with his intelligence drained by the dreadful expenditure of ideas, he had to retire from the field without making any progress. To his specious dialectic, the blind man replied with the uncompromising statements or equally uncompromising negatives inspired by his unconquerable obstinacy, and each disputant was reinforced in his own opinions, the one without winning a handbreadth of territory, the other without losing it, each a firm and absolute master in the field where they were so fiercely contending. Rafael finished his vigorous defensive session by affirming, with heavy blows of his hands on the arm of his chair and on his own thigh, that never, never, never, would he accept that vile pest whom they were stupidly trying to introduce into his honorable family, and he did not hesitate to use very black colors in the brief description he made of the individual in question, emphasizing the ignominy of his sources of wealth, amassed with the blood of the poor.

"But my dear boy, if we're going to insist on everyone's being perfect, you're asking for the moon! I'm going to pick you up off the ground and put you back in the straw of the nest you've fallen from. Yes indeed, because to start to inquire about where wealth comes from is a great piece of stupidity. Come, now. Aren't there plenty of men out there who are lifetime senators and even marquises, with the most impressive coats of arms imaginable? Who remembers that some of them got where they are in the slave trade, and others by sucking up fallen fortunes with usury? You aren't living in the real world. If you were to recover your sight, you would see that the world has progressed and that you have been left behind, with the ideas of your time all dried up in your head. You imagine society according to the standards of your childhood or adolescence, periods of your life imbued by the purest quixotism, and things are not like that, good Lord, not like that at all. Open your eyes; that is, you can't open your eyes; open your spirit wide to tolerance, to the compromises which real life imposes on us and without which we could not live. One lives from general ideas, not from one's own exclusively, and those who try to live exclusively from their own ideas usually end up with them, and their bodies, in a lunatic asylum. There, I've had my say."

Disconcerted and unwilling to go on fighting with an enemy so strongly entrenched in a certain number of strong and immovable ideas, Donoso abandoned the field with his hands to his head, as is commonly said. For him it was an ignominious defeat not to have triumphed over that paltry being, whom in other circumstances and for other reasons he would have reduced with a word. But in the presence of the two sisters he concealed the loss to his pride, soothing them with vague expressions, urging them to carry on, for if the young fellow did not give way for the moment, then time and the logic of events would make him surrender. And in the last instance, good Lord, what could the stubborn aristocrat do against the firm desires of his two sisters, who had such a clear idea of the whole area of life and the paths that were open and those still to be opened? Come, come, courage and forge ahead; they certainly must not subject the good of all three, the *collective good*, to the peevish tantrums of someone who represented no more in the house than an adorable child. Finally: Rafael would have to be treated like a child in these critical circumstances.

Cruz had no peace. While she and her sister hastened to arrange the dining room, setting in their accustomed places the different objects which Bernardina had redeemed and brought from pawnbrokers' shops, they decided to omit, or at least to postpone, the invitation to Don Francisco, for it could easily happen that some disagreeable incident would arise in the midst of the festive occasion. And on that same day, if the chronicles do not lie, Fidela received from her rude suitor a letter which both sisters read and commented upon, finding better grammar and style in it than they could in simple logic have expected.

"No," said Cruz, "there's nothing stupid about him."

"Perhaps some friend who has more practice in writing than he has written it for him."

"No; the letter is his; I would swear it. Those *dilemmas* and *objectives*, and those *aspects* of things, like the *bases* under which he wants to establish your happiness, are the work of his own brain. But the epistle really isn't bad. Last night the poor fellow was even witty. And how much easier he's becoming, and what traits of good sense and shrewd observation he displays! I assure you that there are infinitely worse men, and matrimonial prospects better than he only in deceptive appearance."

Hour by hour the house was losing its poverty-stricken air. Mattresses appeared and curtains returned, wrinkled from their long incarceration, and wearing apparel, now looking a bit old-fashioned, for styles change more quickly than fortunes; the silver table service, for a long time in lamentable emigration, made its appearance, and china and crystal returned, unbroken from long captivity.

Rafael was aware of all that was happening, recognizing the return of the china by its sound and the clothing because of the smell of camphor given off when it was shaken out. Mournful and brooding, he witnessed, if the word can be used in his case, the restoration of the house, that return to the prosperities of former years or to a comfort that would have been a motive for joy in him had the causes of the sudden change been different. But what filled his soul with bitterness was that he did not observe in his sister Fidela the low spirits and consternation that he considered logical in view of the horrendous sacrifice. What an incomprehensible thing! Fidela did not seem to be out of sorts, or even uneasy, as if she had not yet realized the seriousness of the matter, a matter feared even before it was announced. Undoubtedly, six years of poverty had carried her back to childhood, leaving her incapable of understanding anything serious and responsible. This was the way Rafael explained her conduct, for he sensed that she was more affected by childish irresponsibility than ever. In her short periods of leisure, the young woman played with dolls, making her brother take part in this frivolous exercise, and dressed and undressed them, pretending to take them visiting, to the baths, out walking, and to bed; she ate any number of absurd things with them, things that were really more suitable for rag women than flesh-and-blood ones. And when she was not playing with them, her behavior displayed extreme volubility; she did nothing but get excited and run about, laughing for trifling reasons, or bursting into laughter without apparent motive. This made the blind man angry, for, though he had always adored her, he would have wanted her to be more thoughtful in the face of the responsibilities of existence, in the face of that horrible promise to marry a man whom she did not and could not love.

Indeed, the youngest Aguila regarded her coming marriage as simply one more obligation on top of the many that already weighed upon her, something like sweeping floors, peeling potatoes, and ironing her brother's shirtfronts. And she softened the unhappy side of this dark view of marriage by also imagining what it would be like to live without financial problems, to put an end to the horrendous privations and shame in which the family was languishing.

TEN

Rafael understood this with unerring instinct, and spoke to her frankly about it one afternoon when they were alone.

"My dearest sister, you are killing me with that innocent smile, that brainless smile, which are you wearing to the slaughterhouse. You do not know what you are doing, nor where you are going, nor the terrible test that waits you."

"Cruz, who knows more than we do, has ordered me not to feel sad about it. I think that we must obey our older sister blindly, for she is both father and mother to us. What she decides is decided once and for all."

"What she decides! Do we have a case of infallibility? So you accept . . . ? Now there's no hope, I'm losing you. I no longer have a sister. For to think that I'll have to live near you, married to that man, is the greatest insanity imaginable. You are the person I love most in all the world. In you I see our mother, whom you no longer remember."

"Yes, I do."

"Ah, you and Cruz, who have kept your sight, have lost your memory, but in me the recollection of our house is still fresh!"

"In me, too. Oh, our house! It seems to me that I can see it now. Marvelous thick rugs, lots of servants. I could describe Mama's dressing table to you without forgetting a single one of the elegant trifles we used to see on it. Twenty people dined at our house every day; on Thursdays, many more. Ah, I remember it all very well, though I had little chance to live that life, which for all its splendor was a bit sad. It was less than two months after I came back from France that the volcano erupted, the dreadful breakdown came. Happy visions and the impression of ruin are mingled in my memory. Don't think that the disaster caught me by surprise. Without knowing why, I felt it coming. That wasteful life was never to my taste. I well remember that the newspapers called Cruz 'the splendid star of the Aguila salons,' and I don't know what extravagant nicknames they gave me . . . something like a satellite, I don't know . . . foolish things that have left a certain bitter taste in my soul. I remember Mama's death as if it happened yesterday. It was the grief she felt over the family disaster. Don José Donoso took out of Papa's hand the revolver with which he wanted to kill himself. He died of grief four months later. But what is it, are you crying? Do those memories hurt?"

"Yes," said Rafael, "Papa didn't have the stoicism he needed to confront adversity. And besides that, he was a man capable of giving in to certain things rather than be deprived of the comforts he had been born to. Not Mama; Mama wasn't like that. If Mama had lived until our days of poverty, she would have borne them with Christian courage and integrity, without accepting anything humiliating or dishonorable, because in addition to her many virtues, she had a feeling for the dignity of our name and breeding. Among so many misfortunes, I feel something within me that consoles me and gives me hope, and it is that my mother's spirit has been passed on to me; I feel it in myself. This idolatrous cult of honor and good principles comes from her. Take careful note, Fidela: in our mother's family there is not a single thing that is not highly honorable. It is a family which honors our Spanish homeland and humanity itself. From the time of our great-grandfather, killed in the naval battle of Cape St. Vincent, to our cousin Gaspar de la Torre-Auñón, who died gloriously at Los Castillejos, you will see nothing but stories of virtue and strict dedication to duty. Among the Torre-Auñóns there has never been anyone who engaged in that shady business of buying and selling things—merchandise, stocks and bonds, that sort of thing. All of them were gentlemen, hidalgos who lived off the products of their inherited lands, or honorable soldiers who died for king and country, or highly respectable priests. Even the poor members of that breed were always models of nobility. Oh, let me leave this world and return to my world, the other world, the past! Since I can't see, it's very easy for me to choose the world I like best."

"You make me so sad, brother. Say what you will, you cannot choose a world, but must live where God placed you."

"God places me in this one, in mine, in the world of my sainted mother."

"You cannot go backward."

"I go where I please," he said angrily, getting to his feet. "I want nothing from you two, for you are dishonoring me."

"Keep still, for God's sake. You're having another attack of madness."

"I have lost you. You no longer exist. I can see enough to see you

in the arms of that wild boar," screamed Rafael with frantic agitation,
waving his arms wildly. "I loathe him; I can't loathe you; but neither
can I forgive what you are doing, what you have done, what you will
do."

"Darling, dearest boy," said Fidela, throwing her arms around him
to keep him from striking himself against the wall. "Don't be crazy.
Listen . . . love me as I love you."

"Then change your mind."

"I can't. I've given my word."

"Curses on your word and the instant you gave it! Go away; now I
love only God, the only one who does not deceive, the only one who
does not make us ashamed. Oh, I want to die!"

Struggling with him, Fidela managed to guide him into his chair,
where he sat motionless, in floods of tears. It was getting dark. Both
fell silent, and a deep darkness at last covered the sad, silent scene.

After that day, the sisters decided that Rafael ought not to be present
at the tertulia, for if he was greatly embarrassed in the presence of
Donoso and Torquemada, their embarrassment was no less, and they
feared some unpleasantness. During the last few evenings the blind
man had directed some very sharp jabs at his future brother-in-law,
not very well clothed in the polite language of courtesy. The separation of sides was, therefore, inevitable. At Rafael's own suggestion,
they settled him at night in a little room near the front door, which
was the airiest and coolest chamber in the house. Naturally, it was
decided that the blind man should not be unaccompanied during the
evening hours, and rather than leave him alone and bored, the two
ladies would have dissolved the tertulia, closing their door to the only
two persons who attended it. Rafael suggested that a friend for whom
he had a real weakness, the oldest boy of Melchor the pawnbroker,
who lived on the ground floor of the house, should come up and chat
with him. Melchorito was as lively a young fellow as could be found
at his age, which was no more than eighteen; as short of stature as he
was long on brains; lively, affectionate, and with all the patience and
cleverness in the world to entertain the blind man for hours on end
without boring him or getting bored himself. He studied painting at
the Academy of San Fernando, and was not satisfied with becoming a
lesser painter than Rosales or Fortuny. He knew the Prado Museum
like the back of his hand, for he had copied a large number of Murillo's

Virgins which, sold at good or bad prices, provided him with money for boots and a summer outfit; and, as a study in the highest perfections of art, he had "taken on Velázquez" (as he said), copying the head of Aesop and the neck of the Weaving Girl. His description of the museum and the catalogue of all the marvels it contains served to keep Rafael entranced. Remembering what he had seen years before, he saw it again through another's eyes. And out of all that Olympus of painting, the blind man preferred the portraits, where nature was as much admired as art, for in portraits real persons of the past, not imagined ones, lived again. To see and examine portraits, he would retrace all the halls of the museum with his intelligent guide, who lent him his eyes as one might lend a pair of glasses, and both of them were enraptured by those noble figures, living personalities made eternal in art by Velázquez, Raphael, Antonio Moro, Goya, or Van Dyck. On some nights, to vary the entertainment, Melchorito, who was a habitué of the topmost balconies at the Opera and had an excellent musical memory, would give vocal and instrumental concerts, singing to Rafael bits of opera, arias, duets, and full-chorus pieces, not without adding to his singing all the orchestral coloring he could obtain from the most extraordinary manipulations of his mouth. The blind man would contribute some baritone part or simple refrain, for his philharmonic memory was not as great as his taste was refined, and had a marvelous time, to the point of believing that he was in his seat at the Opera, as before he had imagined that he was strolling through the galleries of the museum.

The two ladies' gratitude for the good offices of "the lad from downstairs," and their admiration for his skill, was indescribable, for Rafael was happy in his company and would not have exchanged it for that of all the sages in the world. Cruz often stood, smiling, at the door of the room to watch her brother's radiant face, while the other, red as a turkey-cock, conducted the orchestra, giving the signal to the trombones or coming to grips with the tremolo of the violins. The lady would return to the tertulia saying, "They're in the fourth act of *The Huguenots* now."

And a little later: "There, now, it's over. The queen is leaving, for I can hear the Royal March."

Don Francisco had been informed by Donoso of Rafael's unalterable opposition, but did not give it any importance, so puffed up was the poor man about his coming alliance and the knowledge of having been raised to a higher social status.

"So that young jackanapes," he would say, "doesn't want to accept me as a brother-in-law? *I'm bound to declare* that I don't give a damn about his opposition, and that I've got enough stuff in me to turn up my nose at him and his pride. Give thanks to God that he's blind and can't see; for if he had eyes, I'd soon show him how to see straight and to know who was who. His confounded patents of nobility are only good for me to wipe my nose on. And if I wanted, mind you, I'd have better documents than his and with more confounded folderols of nobility, which would have me descended from the blankety-blank Bible and the Wise Men's star."

Several days went by, and the heat was beginning to be oppressive. Since Torquemada wanted to get to the *new order of things* as soon as possible, the date of the wedding was set for August fourth. The family would move to the Calle de Silva, for which purpose the furnishings had been completed with an extremely elegant dining-room set in walnut, chosen by Donoso, and everything would have gone like greased lightning had not the ladies, and Don Francisco himself, been worried about the attitude of Rafael, who remained stubbornly ensconced in his posture of nonacceptance. There could be no thought of taking him to the couple's house, at least until time had softened his unyielding stand. If Donoso and Fidela trusted in the action of time and the establishment of the *fait accompli*, Cruz felt no such confidence. The three of them constantly discussed the difficult problem, finding no suitable solution, until at last Don José proposed a sort of *modus vivendi* which seemed not a bad idea to his friends; to wit, if Rafael refused to live under the same roof as the usurer, he would take him to his own house, where he would treat him like a son and where his sisters could see him whenever they liked. The solution seemed a sad one, but was accepted as the lesser evil.

One night in July, Rafael and his friend were chatting about modern painting. Melchorito told him that he had at home a very shrewd and witty article about the pictures in the last exposition; the blind man expressed a desire to have his friend read it to him; the other went running off to find the article, and young Aguila was left alone.

The sisters did not notice the departure of "the lad from downstairs," for because there had been no music that night, the silence did not put them on their guard. However, after a while it became too profound not to be noticed. Cruz hastened to the little room. Rafael was not there. She cried out. The others came; they searched for him all over the house, but the blind man did not appear. The idea that he might have thrown himself out of the window onto the patio, or off some balcony into the street, alarmed them momentarily. But no; it could not be. All those apertures were closed. Donoso was the first to discover that the door giving access to the stairs was open. They thought that Rafael and his friend had gone down to the shop. But Melchorito ascended the stairs at that very instant, and he too was astonished by what was happening.

The two sisters went downstairs, more dead than alive with fright, and the two friends of the household followed. In the square outside, a policeman told them that the young blind man had crossed the little garden plot alone, going in the direction of the Calle de las Infantas or the Calle del Clavel. They asked questions of all the people they saw, but no one could give them any information.

Very much upset, they decided to go in search of him. But where? There was no time to be lost. Fidela, with Donoso, would go in one direction; Cruz, with Torquemada, in another. Could the fugitive have started for Cuatro Caminos? That was the likeliest notion. But he might well have gone in a different direction. Melchorito and his father hastily surveyed the neighboring streets. Not a sign; he did not appear.

"Let's go to Bernardina's house!" said Cruz, who had kept calm in the midst of all that despair and confusion. And immediately, like the indisputable general-in-chief she was, she began to issue orders: "Don Francisco, you can't do us any good in this case. Go home; we'll let you know what happens. Fidela, go upstairs. I'll manage by myself. Don José and I will go in one direction; Melchor, father and son, in another; we'll search for him and we simply must find him. What a foolish thing for the boy to do! But he mustn't play games with me. If he is stubborn, I'm more stubborn still. He trying to get lost and I trying to find him, we'll see who wins . . . we'll see!"

ELEVEN

As soon as Rafael found himself alone, he decided to put into practice the plan which had occupied his mind for the past two weeks, and for which he had prepared with all the premeditation of an uncommunicative and crafty criminal. Every night since the idea of flight had occurred to him, he had furtively taken his walking stick and hat to his room and had put a piece of bread in his pocket, which he had procured with many precautions during his meal. Night after night went by as he awaited a favorable occasion, until at last, Melchorito's departure in search of the article of criticism presented him with a perfect opportunity, because, to make things easier, the painter and musician always left the house door open when he went downstairs for a short time, so as not to disturb the ladies on his return.

As soon as he thought that enough time had passed not to meet Melchorito on the stairs, he slipped out as quietly as a cat and, groping along the walls, glided out the door without his sisters hearing him. He descended the stairs as hurriedly as he could and had the good luck that no one in the vestibule saw him leave. Since he knew the streets perfectly, he walked along without the aid of a guide, taking the single precaution of striking the ground with his stick to warn passersby that a blind man was approaching. He crossed the garden in the middle of the square and, reaching the Calle de las Infantas, which seemed to him the most appropriate street for flight, he stayed close to the row of houses on the odd-numbered side of the street and went forward resolutely. To protect himself from pursuit, which would be inevitable as soon as his absence was noted, he thought it prudent to enter the transverse streets, taking a zigzag path. "It isn't at all likely that they'll come looking for me here," he said to himself. "They'll go down San Marcos and Hortaleza, believing that I'm heading for Cuatro Caminos. And while my sisters are going crazy looking for me out there, I'll slip neatly through these parts of the city and then I'll go down to Recoletos and the Castellana."

Oh, what a pleasant sensation of freedom! When his sisters' tyranny had been exercised by them alone, it had indeed been sweet. But with the crude and grotesque ruffian they had introduced into the house, it had become a prison cell, and the most desolate and painful of freedoms was preferable to the gentlest of slaveries.

He walked forward resolutely, pounding his stick on the pavement, not without receiving a bump or two because of the impatience that spurred him and his lack of experience, for it was the first time that he had been out in the streets and squares by himself. Crossing from one side of the street to the other was the most difficult part of his journey. He listened carefully for the noise of carriages, and when he ceased to hear it he would quickly walk into the stream without asking help from the passersby. He would not have resorted to this except in the most extreme of cases, for he felt it humiliating to have to depend on strangers while he still had hands with which to feel and a stick to open a path through the darkness.

When he reached the Paseo de Recoletos he sniffed the coolness of the air that arose from the trees, and his joy increased with the welcome idea of independence in those broad open spaces, for here he could take the direction he preferred without anyone indicating the path to him or telling him to stop. After a short hesitation he headed toward the Paseo de la Castellana by the right-hand sidewalk, and to do this he had to orient himself very carefully, searching with a sailor's caution for the safest course for crossing the Plaza de Colón. His sharp ear told him when the carriages were still some distance away, and he knew how to take advantage of the propitious moment to cross without difficulty. He advanced along the pavement joyfully, breathing in the warm air that was impregnated with vegetable smells and a slight odor of earth dampened by having been watered. More than anything else, he was entranced by sweet freedom, by the fact that he was walking all by himself without clutching the arm of another person, by the certainty that he need not stop until his own will decided to, and that he could be this way all night, bathing his soul and body in the out-of-doors, feeling no other roof over his head than the blessed sky, in which with his soul's eyes he saw a multitude of stars that looked down on him lovingly and inspired him to continue with his pleasant wanderings. Before he would live with Torquemada, the poor blind man would resign himself to all the inconveniences of the vagabond life, with no friend but solitude, with a bench for a bed and the firmament of heaven for a roof. Before he would accept that boorish, lowborn beast, he would accept living off alms. Alms! Neither the idea nor the word frightened him now. Poverty did not debase a person; to ask for public charity, if one had no other recourse, was as noble as contributing toward it. The honest beggar, the wretch who begged to keep himself from dying of hunger, was the favorite child of Jesus Christ, poor in this world, rich with immortal riches in the other. As he thought about this, he ended by *establishing the principle*, as the beast would say, that a dog would be very useful in his honorable profession as a blind beggar. Oh, how he loved dogs! At that moment he would have given a finger off his hand to have a faithful friend to pet, who would go with him silently and vigilantly. Then he thought that, to seek alms effectively, it would be well if he could play something; that is, if he possessed some musical skill. He remembered sadly that the only instrument he could manage was the accordion; but no more than the four notes of "La donna è mobile," and he did not even know how to finish the passage. Well, rather than assault the ears of passersby, it was better not to play anything.

He sat down on a bench, letting time pass in gentle meditation, during which his sisters seemed to be very far away, receding more and more and disappearing into space. Either Cruz and Fidela had died, or they had gone to live in another world that could not be seen from this one. And meanwhile he had formed no plan at all about where to spend the night. He merely thought vaguely that when sleep overcame him he would go and ask hospitality of the fireworks-maker. But no, no, it was better to sleep outdoors, without asking favors from anyone or losing, out of gratitude, that blessed independence which made him master of the world, of earth and sky.

Suddenly he was assailed by an idea that made him shudder. He sniffed the air like a bloodhound seeking the trail of persons or places. "Yes, yes, there's no doubt of it," he said to himself. "Without setting out to do so, without thinking about it, I have come and sat opposite my house, in front of the mansion that my parents owned. I think that I'm not mistaken. The space I've covered from the Plaza de Colón is the exact distance. I've kept my sense of distance, and moreover, I don't know what instinct, or perhaps double vision, tells me that I am here, opposite the palace where we lived during our happy times, so short if I compare them with our unbearable poverty." Tremulous with emotion, he tried to confirm it by touch, and stepped forward, carefully pushing his way through the hedge until he reached a fence, which he explored carefully. His voice knotted in his throat when he achieved the certainty he had been seeking. "These, yes, these," he said to himself, "are the iron bars of the fence. I can see it now, painted dark green, with the points gilded. I know it as I know my own hands. Oh, what times! Oh, mute language of things we love! I don't know what I feel, the resurrection in my soul of a beautiful, sad past, all the sadder now for being past. My God, have You brought me to this place to comfort me or to sink me still deeper in the dark abyss of my wretchedness?"

Drying his tears, he returned to the bench, and burying his face in his hands he brought to his mind, with a blind man's concentration, his vision of the past. "The marquises of Mejorada del Campo live here now," he said, heaving a great sigh. "I can imagine how little the house and garden have changed. How beautiful they were before!" He heard the gates open to let a carriage pass through.

"Surely they must be going to the Opera. My mama always went at that hour, a little late, and arrived for the third act. She never heard the first two acts of operas. We had season tickets for Section 7 on the lower level. It seems to me that I can see the box, and my mama, and Cruz, and our cousins the Rebolledo girls, and that I'm in the second seat of the eighth row. Yes, there I am, there I am, the one I see there, with the fine figure I cut eight years ago. And now I'm coming to my mother's box, and I scold her for not arriving sooner. I don't know why, as I remember it, feelings of boredom rise to my mind. Was I happy then? I'm beginning to believe that I was not."

(Pause) "From where I'm sitting, if I were not blind, I could see the window of my mother's room. It seems that I'm going into it. I wonder what became of those Gobelin tapestries, and that wonderful Old Vienna and Old Saxony porcelain! The storm swallowed everything. We were ruined, but with honor. My mother did not compromise with any sort of ignominy. That is why she died. If only I had died too, so as not to have to witness my poor sisters' degradation. Why didn't they die then? Doubtless God wished to make them undergo all kinds of tests, and in the last one, in the most terrible test of all, they were unable to rise above human weakness, and have succumbed. They surrender now, after having fought so long; and here we have the victorious devil, with permission from Divine Majesty, who is the One who inspires in me this determination not to surrender, preferring solitude, vagrancy, and beggary to degradation. My mother is with me. My father, too, though I don't know, I don't know whether in the present case, if he were alive, he would have let himself be tempted . . . Donoso, formerly a loyal friend and now the corrupter of the family, had a great deal of influence over him. My father became infected with the malady of the times, the fever of business, and, not content with his ample inheritance, aspired to win colossal wealth, like so many others. Involved in dangerous undertakings, his fortune alternately rose and fell. Examples he should never have followed were what ruined him. His brother, my uncle, had amassed a large capital by buying expropriated properties. The curse fell on those who profaned Church property, and my father was swept away by it. I well remember that business was horribly displeasing to Mama, that activity of establishing and destroying credit societies like card houses, that stock-exchange madness, and the disagreement between her and my father was perfectly obvious. The Torre-Auñóns always loathed buying and selling, and underhanded dealings. In the end, events supported the view of my mother, a woman as intelligent as she was pious. She knew that ambition for riches, trying to possess fabulous wealth, is the greatest offense that can be committed against God, who has given us all we need and a little bit more. Too late my father recognized his error, and its recognition cost him his life. Death made everyone equal, leaving us survivors with the conviction that the only truth is poverty, is having nothing. From here I see only presumption, vanity, and the miserable dust which all that grandeur has become; my mother in heaven; my father in purgatory; my sisters in the world, giving the lie by their conduct to what we once were; and I, casting myself alone and unprotected into God's arms, for Him to do with me what He deems best."

TWELVE

(Pause) "How beautiful the garden of my house was! And it must still be beautiful, though I heard that they had sold off a third of it to build apartment houses. How beautiful the garden was and what pleasant hours I've spent in it! It seems that I'm going into the mansion and walking up the marble staircase. There, the splendid suits of armor that my father owned, acquired from the House of San Quintín, relatives of the Torre-Auñóns. In my father's study are gathered Donoso, Don Manuel Paz, General Carrasco, who is mad for business and, sheathing his sword for good, spends all his time putting together railways; the ex-minister García de Paredes; Torres, the stockbroker, and other men of importance. There they talk only of financial deals which I don't understand. I become bored, and they laugh at me; they call me "Don Galaor." They use me to insult diplomacy, which the general calls, parodying Bismarck, "a life of truffles and decorations." I escape from there. It seems to me that I can see the study with its enormous fireplace and on the mantel a magnificent bronze, a reproduction of the Colleone in Venice. On the blinds, the embroidered coats of arms of the Torre-Auñóns and the Aguilas. The carpet, one of the most sumptuous productions of the Santa Bárbara factory, is profaned by the spitting of the stockbroker, who as he goes in and out seems to bring in, and take away in his briefcase, all the financial wealth in the world. And all that is dust and misery now, and the worms are settling business accounts with my father. Torres, the stockbroker, shot himself to death in Monte Carlo three years later, and the general is out there somewhere, utterly wretched as the result of a stroke and able to walk only by hanging on a servant's arm. The only ones left alive are he and Donoso, who is frozen into his self-satisfaction as an administrator, a man I dislike so much, though I'm very careful not to say so to my sisters, for they'd eat me alive."

(Pause) "Oh, how pretty Cruz was, how elegant and proud, with such legitimate and justified pride! We used to call her 'Croisette,' out of the stupid habit of saying everything in French. When Fidela came back from France she enchanted all of us with her chatter. What a delicate being, and what an airy temperament! You would say that she was not made of our miserable flesh, but of subtle substances, like the angels, who have never set foot on the ground. She set hers down by the special grace of God, and you could believe that when we touched her she would dissolve under our hands, turning into impalpable vapor. And now—holy God! Now I see her buried in mire up to her neck. I've tried to pull her out of it. She won't let me. She likes vile matter. Well, she is welcome to it. When I went to the embassy in Germany, which was still a legation then, I left home with the premonition that I wouldn't see my mother again. She was so insistent on my not taking 'Toby,' the Great Dane that my cousin Trastamara gave me. Poor creature! I'll never forget his expression when he saw me leave. He died of some unknown illness two days before my mother. And now that I remember, what ever happened to that good man Ramón, the faithful servant who understood my tastes and whims so well? Cruz told me that he set up a wine business in his home town, and that he has made a fortune selling Valdepeñas wine. He had his savings. He was a very frugal man, though he didn't steal like that scoundrel Lucas, the dining-room footman, who has a railway restaurant now. With the cigars he stole from my father he bought a house in Valladolid, and with what he pilfered in champagne he got enough to start a brewery."

(Pause) "What o'clock is it, I wonder? But what does the hour matter to me, if I'm free and time means nothing to me? My house is still not asleep. I can hear noises in the gatehouse. The servants are having a chat with the gatekeeper, waiting until the lady of the house returns. There, now, I think I hear the carriage. It's the hour when the audience leaves the Opera, a quarter to one if the opera hasn't been a long one. Wagner and his school don't let us out until a quarter to two. There it is. They're opening the gate. The carriage is entering. Why, it seems as if I were back in the times when I was a young blade! The same carriage, the same horses, the night just the same, with the same stars in the sky—for those who can see them. They're closing the gate. The house is going to sleep, like its inhabitants. I actually begin to feel . . ."

Rather than sleepiness, what he began to feel was hunger, and fumbling for the morsel of bread he carried in his pocket, he started to eat his frugal supper, which tasted better to him than all the delicacies that Cruz was accustomed to bring him from the House of Lhardy.

"How frantic my sisters must be, looking for me!" he said, taking leisurely bites. "Go ahead, worry. You've accustomed yourselves to my being a zero, always a zero. Agreed: I'm a zero, but I'm taking myself away, and so you'll be worth less. And I fall back on my dignity as an insulted zero, and, though I'm worth nothing, absolutely nothing to others, I declare myself free and wish to seek my value in my own self. Yes indeed, Señoras de Aguila y de la Torre-Auñón: arrange for your mésalliance to your hearts' content, without worrying about the poor blind man. Ah, you two have your sight, and I have not! My misfortune is recompensed by the immense advantage of not being able to see the beast. You see him, you have him always in front of your noses, and you can never be free of his grotesque mug, which is, after all, your punishment. How good this bread is! Thanks be to God, I've lost that mortifying sensation of the smell of onions when I eat!"

He felt sleepy and was in the act of lying down on the bench, seeking the least uncomfortable position and making a pillow of his right arm, when a poor man approached, dragging one foot behind him as if it were a half-donned boot, and held out to ask for alms, instead of a hand, a naked, angry stump. The beggar's hoarse voice made Rafael shudder; he sat up, saying, "Excuse me, brother. I am poor, too, and if I haven't begged yet it's because I'm not used to it. But tomorrow, tomorrow I'll beg."

"Are you blind, maybe?" said the other, losing hope of receiving alms.

"And at your service."

"Same here."

"If you had come a little sooner I would have given you part of the bread I've just finished eating. But as for money, I can give you none. I have no money on me, no coins large or small. I'm poorer than anyone. I've come, alas, very far down in the world. And you, what are you?"

"What d'you mean, what am I?"

"I mean, are you blind too?"

"No, thank God; I'm only a cripple, but in both legs, and I have no right hand. I lost it in a blasting accident."

"From your voice, I think you are old."

"And you're quite a talker. Hell, just like all blind men, who spit out their souls and their kidneys through their damned mouths!"

"Excuse me if I don't answer you in that vulgar language. I'm a decent person."

"Yeah, I can see that. A decent person! I was one, too. My father owned fourteen pairs."

"Pairs of what?"

"Mules."

"Ah! I thought you meant something really important. Mules, eh? But that's nothing in comparison with what my father had. That palace opposite us, if it could talk, would not let me lie."

"Hell and damnation! Are you going to tell me that that palace is yours?"

"I'm saying that it was. Truly . . . ."

"Shoot, and I'll bet the usurers cleaned you out. Just like me, like my father, who was the oldest son and inherited the land, and because he took money at interest to go into business, he left us poorer than rats."

"Curses on wretched business, on buying and selling! And here we are, the sons paying for the sins of the fathers' ambition. Now we're begging for alms, and you can be sure that those who made us poor pass by without giving us a cent. But God does not leave us comfortless, right? Where one least expects it a charitable person turns up. There are charitable souls. Tell me that there are, for really I would not like to die of hunger on these streets."

"Don't you have a family?"

"My sisters, my good man. But I don't want to have anything to do with them."

"So, the bitches have thrown you out! Hell's fire! Just like me, same as with me."

"Your sisters?"

"No. . . *worser and worser!*" replied the other man in a hoarse, rasping voice which he seemed to extract with great difficulty from the deepest part of his body. "It's my daughters who shoved me out in the street!"

"Ha, ha, ha! Your daughters!" exclaimed Rafael, assailed by a violent desire to laugh. "And tell me: are they ladies?"

"Ladies?" said the other with all the sarcasm that the human voice can express. "Ladies of rags and patches, ladies of the night! They're . . ."

"What?"

"Flat-out whores! So long!"

And off he went, dragging his leg, spitting curses with bestial grunts, drooling like a dog with a cold.

"Poor man. . ." murmured Rafael, lying down on the bench again. "His daughters, from what he said, are . . . What abysses the depths of wretchedness reveal when we descend into them! If I could go to sleep, I would smother in my brain the ideas that trouble me. I'll try. This bench is harder than my bed, but I don't care. It's good to become accustomed to suffering. And heaven knows what I'll have for breakfast tomorrow! What God has in readiness for me, coffee or chocolate or a bit of bread, only He knows. It's out there somewhere. Do not the birds have breakfast? Then there must also be something for me."

He fell into a sort of stupor and had a short dream with very intense visual images. Within a brief time he dreamed that he was in the entrance hall of the neighboring palace, lying on a wooden bench. He saw his father come in wearing a fur overcoat, a wintry circumstance that did not surprise him despite the fact that it was full summer. His father was amazed to see him there, and told him to go out and buy ten céntimos' worth of hazelnuts. What a weird dream! Even in his sleep, he was thinking that the whole thing made no sense. Then the Great Dane ran out howling, with one leg broken and his muzzle covered with blood. At the moment he sprang up to help the poor animal, he woke up. He found that he was on the point of falling off the bench.

His bones ached, the cold was beginning to trouble him, and his stomach did not seem resigned to spending all night in the open with no more nourishment than a piece of bread. To subdue the clamor of the weakling flesh, he set off hastily up the Paseo, bumping against trees and falling flat on his face from two or three falls that he took when he lost his balance. But he succeeded in keeping up his spirits and supporting his body with the energy of his spirit.

"Come now, Rafael, don't be childish; at the first little problem, you're already confused and don't know what path to take. Soon it will be dawn and unless I'm much mistaken, God, who watches over me, will provide me with a charitable soul. I don't hear footsteps—it must be dawn. How alone I am! How will I know whether the sun has risen, or that it's going to rise? Ah, I can hear a cock crowing, announcing the day! It may be an illusion, but it seems to be Bernardina's cock that's crowing. And again, and again. No, there are lots of cocks, all the cocks in the neighborhood who are saying, after their fashion, 'That's enough of night.' What I can't hear yet is the birds' cheerful chirping. No, dawn hasn't come yet. Farther on I can sleep for a while on another bench, and when the birds tell me, I'll leave my lazy featherbed, or rather, my lazy granite bench. Forward, and with courage. Surely none of these little birds that are sleeping innocently in the branches over my head worries the least bit about what he will eat when he awakes. My breakfast is out there somewhere. Charitable souls too are asleep now, and will sleep a little longer; but surely there will be someone who's an early riser."

Near the end of the Castellana, he allowed himself another rest on a bench; but he could not sleep, not even rest his weary bones. Two stray dogs came up to him and smelled and nuzzled him. Rafael tried to keep them beside him with friendly words, but the two animals, who must have been endowed with great penetration and intelligence, realized that they would get little or nothing from him. After both, in leisurely fashion, had infringed the municipal ordinances on the blind man's bench, they went off in search of more profitable adventures.

Rafael rose to his feet as dawn was breaking, its light greeted by the birds, and, rubbing his hands together to provide a bit of heat which would in some sense take the place of food, he started walking and stretching his legs. He had not lost courage, but he was beginning to understand that initiation into the beggar's trade has its drawbacks and that his apprenticeship would inevitably be very hard. How he would have enjoyed a little coffee just then! But charitable souls provided with the precious liquid did not appear. He heard the footsteps of men and animals going toward the center of Madrid: they were carriers, sellers of produce and eggs, who were taking their products to the market. He heard the noise of milk jugs rattling with the movements of the horse that drew the milk cart. How eagerly he would have drunk a glass of milk! But whom, merciful God, could he ask? Country people passed him by without taking notice of him. Surely, if he actually began to beg, someone would give him something. "But the great merit of charitable souls," he thought, "must surely be that they would help me without my having to incur the shame of asking." Unfortunately for him, in that timid attempt at begging, charitable souls showed no desire to help a needy person who did not begin by annoying the passerby with irritating demands for alms. He walked for a long distance in great confusion, without knowing where he was going, and at last, exhaustion and hunger made him decide to ask shelter of Bernardina; but as he made this concession to harsh necessity, he tried to deceive himself into believing in his fortitude by telling himself. "No, I'll only have a sandwich and then move on. To the street once again, to the road."

It was not so easy for him to find his way. But if he felt unwilling to beg for alms, he had no compunction about asking directions. "Am I on the right road for Cuatro Caminos?" This question, repeated and answered innumerable times, was the compass needle pointing to his defeat as he walked through open fields, highroads, and vacant lots, until his tired bones came to rest in the Valientes' barnyard.

THIRTEEN

Bernardina saw him before he had reached the opening in the wall, and came out to greet him with every show of satisfaction, regarding him as a ghost, as someone risen from the dead.

"Give me some coffee," said the blind man in a trembling voice. "It's just that I feel a little weak."

The faithful maid took him inside and, with rare discretion, forbore to tell him that Señorita Cruz had been there three times during the night looking for him, half dead with worry. No time must be lost in sending word to his frightened sisters that he had been found, but it was no less urgent to give the fugitive the breakfast which his pallid face and trembling hands so insistently demanded. Bernardina prepared the coffee with all the haste in the world, and when the blind man was avidly drinking it, she gave instructions to Cándido to keep him there while she went to inform the ladies, who undoubtedly thought that he was dead. The worst of the matter was that Hipólito Valiente, the hero of Africa, was at work that day.

"Since we don't have the old fellow here to keep him spellbound with his stories of battles," said Bernardina to her husband, "keep him entertained as best you can. Tell him anything you can think of; invent big lies. Don't be stupid, now. Anyway, the important thing is not to let him get away. If he tries to leave, hold on to him, even if you have to tie him by one leg."

After his breakfast, Rafael showed no desire for new wanderings. He was so dejected and brain-weary that Cándido had no difficulty in taking him to the firework-maker's shop where he worked. He made him sit on a piece of timber and the good man went on with his task of mixing powder and packing it into the cardboard cylinders that formed the rockets. His constant chitchat, at times as sparkling and noisy as the fireworks he manufactured, did not rouse Rafael from his gloomy silence. There he sat with the expectant silence of a sphinx, his elbows on his knees, his fists supporting his chin, which seemed stuck to them by some freak of nature. He listened to the murmur of Valiente's conversation, an emphatic and erudite praise of the pyrotechnic art; and without taking any of it in, for the firework-maker's voice reached his ears but not his brain, he sank deeper and deeper into meditation, out of which he was abruptly jerked by the arrival of his sister Cruz and Don José Donoso. He heard the lady's voice in the barnyard: "But where is he?" And when he heard her near him, he made no effort to greet her.

Cruz, whose superior intelligence was particularly obvious on critical occasions, understood at once that it would be a mistake to show excessive sternness with the fugitive. She embraced and kissed him tenderly, and Don José Donoso gave him friendly pats on the back, telling him, "All right, all right, Rafaelito. I told everybody that you weren't going to get lost, that this has all been a great joke. Your poor sisters were half dead with worry. But I calmed them down, sure that you would appear."

"Do you know, your little jokes aren't very funny?" said Cruz, seating herself beside him. "For goodness' sake, to keep us in such anxiety all night! But after all, the joy of finding you makes up for our worry, and I forgive your escapade with all my heart. I know that Bernardina has given you breakfast. But you must be sleepy, you poor boy. Could you sleep a little while if you were at home in your very own bed?"

"I don't need a bed," declared Rafael curtly. "Now that I know what hard couches are like, I'm quite at home on them."

Donoso and Cruz had agreed not to cross him, pretending to give in to his demands but planning to win him over later by subterfuge.

"All right, then," said Cruz, "so that you can see that I want everything you want, I won't contradict these new opinions of yours about hard beds. Is that what you like? Splendid. Why am I in the world at all, if not to humor you in everything?"

"Precisely," said Don José, clothing his officiousness in affectionate behavior. "That's what we're all here for. And now, the first thing we have to ask our fugitive is whether he wants to go home in a carriage or on foot."

"I . . . go home?" exclaimed Rafael sharply, as if he had heard the most absurd suggestion in the world.

There was silence in the group. Donoso and Cruz looked at each other, and their looks alone said, "Better not insist. It will make things worse."

"But where could you be better off than in your own house, my dear boy?" said the elder sister. "Just think that we can't bear to be separated from you, at least I can't. If you take the notion to wander about the highroads, I'll do the same."

"Not you. Leave me alone. I can manage by myself."

"Now, let's not have this," declared Donoso. "If Rafael, either for good reasons or by whim, or by personal quirk which I won't discuss at the moment—no indeed, I won't discuss it; if Rafael, I repeat, doesn't wish to return home, I offer him mine."

"Thanks, thanks very much, Don José," replied the blind man, somewhat nonplussed. "I am grateful for your hospitality, but I do not accept it. I would be a very troublesome guest."

"Oh, no!"

"And, believe me, I won't be as well off anywhere as right here."

"Here?"

Donoso and Cruz looked at each other again, and the eyes of both simultaneously expressed the same idea. Indeed, that desire to stay at Bernardina's house was a solution which, for the moment, put an end to the difficulty that had arisen; a provisional solution, which offered space and time to think at leisure about the permanent solution.

"My goodness, what an idea!" said Cruz, hiding her pleasure. "But, dear boy, here! All right, so that you can see how much we love you, I'll compromise; I know how to compromise; you don't, and you make all of us unhappy."

"Compromise is the answer to everything," declared Don José, giving much importance to his dictum.

"Bernardina has a room she can fix up for you. We'll bring your bed. Fidela and I will take turns staying with you. There! Now you see that I'm not stubborn, that I give in and . . . In this life so filled with difficulties, it's best not to take refuge in our own ideas and always to keep in mind those of others, for to believe that the world has been made for ourselves alone is very, very foolish. I, after all, understand that I mustn't go against your wishes in this desire you have to live apart from us. Don't worry, dear boy, everything will be taken care of. Don't get excited. You'll live here, and you'll live like a prince."

"You don't need to bring my bed," remarked Rafael, engaging at last in familiar and affectionate conversation with his elder sister. "Doesn't Bernardina have a folding cot? That's enough for me."

"None of that, none of that. Now it seems that you want to give yourself airs as a hermit. What's the point of these penances?"

"Why, it's no trouble to bring the bed," added Don José.

"As you like," returned the blind man, who seemed happy. "I'll spend my time here going round and round the barnyard, conversing with the cock and the hens; and now and then I'll come and have Cándido teach me the art of making fireworks—don't think for a moment that the art is an easy one. I'll learn it, and even though I don't do anything with my hands, I can certainly suggest any number of ideas to him for combining lighting effects, and loading clusters of rockets, and castles, and all those lovely spark-factories that amuse the worthy public so much."

"Fine, fine, fine," chorused Donoso and Cruz, pleased to see him in such a happy frame of mind.

The lady and the household's faithful friend conferred briefly, out of Rafael's hearing. It was probably something to do with bringing the bed and other objects of domestic use. Donoso said good-bye, embracing the young blind man, who promptly fell back into a brown study, guessing that when his sister was alone with him she would talk to him about the subject that was causing such horrible problems for all of them.

"Let's go away," said Cruz, taking her brother's arm. "I'm afraid of being here, Señor Valiente. It's not that I don't respect your shop, it's just . . . I don't know how anyone can be easy in his mind in the midst of these enormous quantities of gunpowder. Just suppose that, by some awful mischance, a spark should fall . . ."

"No, señorita, it's not possible."

"Be quiet. Just thinking about it makes me feel as if I were already turned into cinders. Come, come, let's get out of here. But we can take a little walk around the barnyard first, if you like. It's a beautiful day. Come on, we'll walk in the shade."

What young Aguila had suspected was true. His elder sister had to talk to him about something very important, a recent inspiration, no doubt, and the latest expedient that had occurred to her considerable intelligence. What could it be?

"What can it be?" thought the blind man, trembling, for all his courage was not equal to his sister's awesome powers of persuasion.

She began by emphasizing the horrible suffering she and Fidela had experienced during the last few days because of their beloved brother's opposition to the proposed marriage to Don Francisco.

"Give it up," said Rafael at once, "and all your suffering will be over."

"That was our idea . . . to give it up, to tell that good Don Francisco to go fly his kite somewhere else, and to leave us in peace. We prefer poverty with peace of mind to the sorrowful life we would lead if there were disagreement with our beloved brother. I said to Fidela, 'You can see that Rafael will not give in. Let us do so, rather than be responsible for his despair. Who knows! It may be that, blind as he is, he sees more than we do. May not his resistance be a sign from heaven, telling us that Torquemada, with the materialism, as he says, of an easy life, will bring us greater unhappiness than we suffer at present?' "

"And what did Fidela say?"

"Nothing; that she has no will of her own; that if I wanted to break it off, she wouldn't stand in the way."

"And what did you do?"

"Well, nothing, for the moment. I consulted with Don José. That was last week. I didn't say anything to you because, since you're so prickly about honor, I didn't want to stir you up about nothing. It seemed better to me not to talk to you about this matter until it was settled in one way or another."

"And what did Donoso think?"

"Donoso? Ah!"

FOURTEEN

"When I tell you that Donoso is an angel come down from heaven! What a man, what a saint!" continued the lady, seating herself on a board beside Rafael, in the best spot in the barnyard. "Look, the opinion of our faithful friend was that we should sacrifice the marriage with Torquemada to keep peace in the family. That's what we agreed upon. But something had already been discussed between him and Don Francisco which he, Don Francisco, had very quickly carried from idea to reality, and when Don José went to see him to propose the definite suspension of matrimonial negotiations, it was too late."

"What happened?"

"Torquemada had done something which had caught us all as if in a trap. It is impossible to escape now, impossible to get out of his power. We are caught, little brother; we can do nothing against him now."

"But what has that scoundrel done?" cried Rafael, beside himself, rising to his feet and brandishing his stick.

"Calm yourself," replied the lady, forcing him to sit down. "What he has done! But goodness, do you think it is something bad? On the contrary, dear boy: because it is good, so excessively good, his act is . . . I don't know how to tell you, it's like a rope that he throws around our necks, making it impossible for us to want anything that he does not want."

"But what is it? I must know," said the blind man with feverish impatience. "I will judge that act for myself, and if it turns out to be as you say . . . No, you're imagining things, and you want me to imagine them too. I don't trust your enthusiasms. What has that ignorant brute done that could lead me not to despise him as I despise him?"

"You'll see . . . be calm. You know as well as I do that our properties in El Salto and La Alberquilla, in the Sierra de Córdoba, were judicially impounded. The syndicate of creditors could not dispose of them because they were bound up with a promissory note that Papa had to give the State. And the wretched State, as long as its right to become their owner was not completely clear (and that is one of the lawsuits we are involved in), could not take our property away from us, but it could take the usufruct. After the properties were impounded, the judge gave the administration of them to . . ."

"To Pepe Romero," the blind man quickly supplied, taking the words out of her mouth, "the husband of our cousin Pilar."

"Who lives there, leading the life of a princess. Oh, what a woman! No doubt because she received so many favors from Papa, she and her scoundrel of a husband hate us. What have we ever done to them?"

"We have made them rich. Do you think that's nothing?"

"And they have done nothing to help us in our poverty. The cruelty, the cynicism, the ingratitude of those people are what have contributed most toward making me lose faith in everything, what makes me believe that humanity is an immense flock of wild beasts. Oh, in this life of unbelievable suffering, I think that God, at least, lets me hate! Rancor, which in ordinary cases is a sin, is not one in my case, nor can it be. Vengeance, a vile sentiment in normal circumstances, now . . . almost strikes me as a virtue. That woman, who bears our name and has spurned us in our misfortune, and that wretch Romerillo who has become rich through dirty business dealings more characteristic of rogues than of gentlemen, live on our property, have the enjoyment of it. They have intrigued in Madrid to make the Council find against the del Aguila estate, for they're dying to have the properties put up for auction."

"To buy them up and keep their hands on them."

"Ah, but that precious pair of horse traders, gypsies by descent without a doubt, has made a great miscalculation! Believe it, because I'm telling you . . . Pilar is worse than he is. She's one of those monsters who frighten people and make them believe that Satan in female form is abroad in the world . . ."

"But let's get to the point. What . . . ?"

"You'll see. Now I can say that the hour of justice has arrived. You can't imagine the joy that fills my soul. God lets me feel rancor, and what is worse, vengeance. What a pleasure, what ineffable bliss, my brother! To trample that rabble . . . to throw them out of our house and our lands without the slightest consideration, like dogs, like base highwaymen! Oh, Rafael, you don't understand such petty thoughts; you are too angelic to understand them! Truly fierce vengeance is an emotion that you rarely find today outside the lower classes of society. But it boils in me, and how it boils! It's true that it is also a feudal sentiment, and in us, persons of noble blood, that sentiment comes to life again; it is the same as justice, brutal justice, as it must have been in past times, as it ought to be also in our time, when the laws are not strong enough to help."

The noble lady rose to her feet, and indeed she was a beautiful and tragic figure. She stamped her foot on the ground two or three times, crushing her enemies in imagination, and God knows that if they had been there, she would not have left a whole bone in their bodies!

"Yes, now I understand," said Rafael, somewhat frightened. "I don't need more explanations. You are hoping to recover El Salto and La Alberquilla. Donoso and Torquemada have arranged to do it, so that you can get the better of the Romeros. Yes, now I see it all very clearly: that precious Don Francisco will recover the properties by placing in the hands of the Treasury Department a sum equal to that of the note . . . for, if I remember correctly, he has to come up with a million and a half reales . . . that is, if indeed he intends . . ."

"He doesn't intend to do it," said Cruz, radiant. "He has done it already."

"Already?"

Rafael was paralyzed with stupefaction for a moment, incapable of saying a word.

"Now tell me whether, after this, it is dignified and decent in us to stand before that gentleman and say, 'Well . . . as for that other matter, nothing doing.' "

A pause which lasted God knows how long.

"But in what form was the liberation of the property made?" the blind man asked at last. "I need to know that. If they're in his name, I can't see . . ."

"No, the property is ours. The deposit is made in our name. Now tell me if it's possible that . . ."

After thinking for a while in silence, Rafael suddenly rose, took a few steps, and, waving his stick, said, "That's not true."

"Are you saying that I'm deceiving you?"

"I repeat that this can't be as you have told it to me."

"Are you saying that I'm lying?"

"No, I'm not saying that you're lying. But you know better than anyone else how to distort things, to gild them when they're very ugly, to sweeten them when they're bitter."

"I have told the truth, believe it or not. And now I'm asking you, can we show this man the door? Do your dignity and your ideas about the honor of the family tell me to dismiss him?"

"I don't know, I don't know," murmured the blind man, turning on his heel and waving both arms over his head. "I'm going crazy. Go away; leave me alone. Do what you like."

"Do you admit that we cannot go back on our word, or refuse the marriage?"

"I admit it, if what you have told me is true. But it isn't; it can't be. My heart tells me that you're deceiving me . . . for good reasons, undoubtedly. Ah! You're so clever . . . cleverer than I, cleverer than the whole family. One has to surrender to you and let you do as you like."

"Will you come home?" said Cruz, stammering a little, for the triumphant joy that filled her soul made her voice thick.

"No, not that. Leave me here, and you go home. I'm very well off in this henyard, where I can go for a walk without having to take anyone's arm, at any hour of the day."

For the moment Cruz did not try to insist. She had obtained victory with her admirable tactic. Her conscience did not trouble her for having lied, because Rafael was a child, and one had to lull him to sleep, as one did to whining children, with pretty stories. The child's tale that the lady had employed so skillfully was only half true, for when Donoso and Torquemada came to an agreement about recovering the Córdoba properties, they had decided that this must be accomplished after the marriage. But Cruz, in her burning desire to hasten toward the *objective*, as the bridegroom would say, felt no scruples of conscience about altering the date of the happy event, since she was using it as an argument to overcome her brother's stubborn opposition. To say that Torquemada had already done what he would do after the wedding by formal agreement? What did that small alteration in the order of events matter, if by means of it she succeeded in eliminating the horrible problem that stood in the way of the family's salvation!

Donoso returned with the news that he had made the necessary arrangements for bringing the bed and the rest of the furnishings from the blind man's bedroom. After the three of them had chatted for a while about things unrelated to the serious matter that was worrying all of them, Cruz took advantage of a moment in which Rafael had become involved in discussions with Valiente about pyrotechnics, and, taking her friend behind the largest heap of garbage and straw in the barnyard, she spat out the following statement:

"Congratulate me, Don José. I've convinced him. He may not want to return home, but his opposition is not, nor can it be, as furious as before. What did I tell you? Ah! Just imagine, in this dreadful conflict I had to use all the ingenuity of my poor intelligence to think of an idea! I believe that God is guiding me. It was an inspiration that I had the moment I arrived here. I'll tell you about it when we have a little more time. And now, the important thing is to activate . . . all that as soon as possible, for fear some complication will arise."

"God forbid. Believe me, no one could be more impatient than he. Just a short time ago he told me that as far as he was concerned, it could be tomorrow."

"As early as tomorrow, no, but it's really hypocritical of us to set the date so far ahead. Between now and the fourth of August, many things can happen, and . . ."

"Then let's put the date forward."

"Yes, let's do that. What has to be done might as well be done soon."

"Next week . . ."

"Oh, not so fast!"

"Then the following week."

"That seems very late to me. You're right; next week. What's to-day?"

"Friday."

"Then Saturday of next week."

"Fine. You tell him . . . propose it to him like an idea of yours."

"He'll be no little pleased about it. As I told you: as far as he's concerned . . . tomorrow. And to return to our young dissident, do you think that he won't give us any trouble?"

"I hope not. The fact that he wants to come and live here is made to order for us. We have absolute confidence in Bernardina: she will take care of him exactly as we would. Fidela and I, taking turns, will come to keep him company; in addition, I'll see to it that Melchorito, that good lad, comes here a few afternoons to sing operas to him."

"That's splendid . . . but . . . and this is the serious part: does he know that his sisters are moving to the Calle de Silva?"

"He doesn't know it. But he will find out. So? Are you afraid that he won't want to go live in that house?"

"Yes, I certainly am!"

"He will live in it. I guarantee that he will live in it," said the lady; and her lower lip trembled dreadfully, as if it were trying to detach itself from her noble face.

FIFTEEN

Slowly, like all much-desired dates, that day at last arrived, a Saturday to be more specific, the day before or two days before (the histories are not entirely clear about this) the Feast of Santiago, patron saint of Spain. The wedding took place in the church of San José, without ostentation, early in the morning, as a somewhat furtive ceremony to which no one wished to draw attention. The only guests were Donoso, Rufinita Torquemada and her husband, and two other gentlemen, friends of the Aguila sisters who took their leave outside the church. Don Francisco was wearing a *hermetically closed* frock coat and gloves so tight that they made his fingers look like sausages and gave him terrible trouble when he tried to take them off. Since it was the hottest part of the summer, everyone, the bride included, constantly passed their handkerchiefs over their faces. The bridegroom's seemed to be covered with oil, so much did it shine, and to make matters worse, he exhaled odors of onion every time he breathed, for at midnight he had eaten, at one sitting, a platter of cold meat with onions, his favorite dish. The odor struck Cruz's nostrils as soon as she laid eyes on her brother-in-law, and she had to conceal her anger to keep from exploding, especially when she saw how badly the onion odor went with the fine words the prideful moneylender was uttering, whether or not they were appropriate. Fidela looked like a corpse, for—one would think the devil had had a hand in it—on the previous night she had drunk some juice of unripe grapes because she was so uncomfortably hot. The drink affected all the liquids in her body, and she fell ill so inconveniently that the wedding was within a hairbreadth of being called off. But Cruz administered I don't know what mitigating drug in veterinary-sized doses, thanks to which there was no need for a postponement; but the poor young woman looked dreadful, her color came and went, she perspired from every pore and was unable to breathe easily. Thank goodness the ceremony was short, for if not she would surely have fallen in a faint. There came a moment when the church and all its altars began to turn round and round the chief actress in the drama, and if her husband had not clutched her firmly, she would have fallen to the floor.

Cruz could not be easy until the ritual was complete, so as to go home, loosen Fidela's corset, and get her to rest. They all went to the new domicile in two carriages, and on the way Torquemada fanned his wife with her own fan, saying from time to time, "This is nothing, it's the *stupefaction*, the emotion, the heat. This is some summer we're having! Within two hours no one will be able to cross the Calle de Alcalá on this side of the street, which is the one with the *solarcism*. It's not so bad in the shade."

Once in the house, Cruz's first impression was horribly disagreeable. What disorder, what lack of taste! Good things placed haphazardly, and among them innumerable dreadful objects that would have to be consigned to the flames. Romualda, the old hag, Don Francisco's servant, came out to receive them in a grease-spotted skirt, shuffling in house slippers, hair wild and uncombed, with the revolting appearance of a servant in some low inn. In his servants, as in everything, the noble lady saw reflected the tightfistedness of the house's owner. The manservant reeked of cheap tobacco, with a butt stuck behind his ear, and spoke with a most vulgar and low-life accent. My God, what a kitchen, in which an ancient, bleary-eyed scullery woman was helping Romualda! No, no, that could not be. She would soon arrange things differently. Happily, the luncheon on that classic day had been ordered from an eating-house by recommendation of Donoso, whose admirable good sense and foresightedness were everywhere evident.

Fidela did not feel better even after her corset and all the other fastenings that confined her body were loosened. She tried to eat; but she had to leave the table, assailed by violent spasms of vomiting which left her completely empty. They had to put her to bed, and neither of the two parts into which the luncheon was divided was cheerful, owing to that wretched nuisance of the bride's indisposition. Fortunately, there was a *practitioner* in the house. This was the name Torquemada gave to his son-in-law, Quevedito.

"What's the matter with you that you can't cure her for me right away? So much for your practice and the blankety-blank Bible."

He wandered from the dining room to the bedroom and back again, quarreling with everyone, mixing up names and persons, calling Romualda Cruz, and telling his sister-in-law, "Go to the devil."

Quevedito gave orders to let the invalid rest, for she seemed to be developing a fairly high fever. Cruz also prescribed rest, silence, and darkness, and was unable to resist scolding Torquemada for the noise he was making by needlessly going in and out of the bedroom. Cruz had never heard such squeaky boots in her life, and those accursed soles squeaked and groaned so loudly that the lady could do no less than issue a quiet recommendation to the master of the house. A short time later he appeared in some old cloth slippers, full of holes and completely shapeless.

They went on with the luncheon, and Don Francisco and Donoso did honor to the dishes served by the proprietor of the eating-house. The bridegroom believed that he could not suitably celebrate a day as solemn as this unless he drank heavily, for, as he said, to spend a reckless sum on champagne and then act like a poor frightened fellow would never do. Whether he drank it or not, he had to pay for it. The point was to use it up so that the stomach's credit would at least equal the pocketbook's deficit. For this double-entry and purely economic reason, rather than out of the vice of drunkenness, the skinflint drank copiously, though it was only on very rare occasions that he trespassed against sobriety.

When the meal was over, Don Francisco decided to inform Cruz about the particulars of the house, and to show her everything, for Donoso had already discussed with him the need to place his illustrious sister-in-law at the head of domestic government. The man was completely disheveled, his face looking as if it had been crudely painted crimson, his eyes sparkling, his hair standing on end, and his mouth exuding an odor of alcohol that would have knocked you down. Cruz's stomach was churning, but she made the best of the situation. Don Francisco led her from room to room, saying one foolish thing after another, praising the furnishings and carpets exorbitantly and with specific references to what they had cost him; he gesticulated, laughed stupidly, sat down heavily on the chair seats to test the softness of their springs; he spat and then scuffed the saliva with his well-worn cloth slippers; he drew open and then closed the curtains with infantile glee; he banged on the beds, adding to all these extravagances the crassest of comments.

"You've never in your life seen anything so gorgeous. And how about this? Doesn't it make you drool with pleasure?"

From one of the wardrobes he took out a number of well-used garments, smelling of camphor, and tossed them one by one on a bed for Cruz to see.

"Just look at this satin skirt. My Silvia bought it for a song. It's gorgeous. Touch, touch . . . She only wore it one Holy Thursday and the day we were godparents of the wedding in Cerro de la Paloma. Well, so you can see how much I appreciate you, Señora Doña Cruz, I'm generously giving it to you. You can fix it up, and you'll circulate around Madrid looking like a real stunner. All these dresses belonged to my departed. There are two made of silk; sure, they're a little bit old, because they belonged to a lady-in-waiting at the Palace before . . . four of merino and fine flannel, all of them gorgeous, bought at auction sales for bankruptcy. Fidela can call on a cheap dressmaker to fix them and bring them up to date, for it's time to economize, dammit! Just because a fellow's rich, that doesn't mean, mind you! that he can throw his blessed money away. Economy, lots of economy, my Señora Doña Cruz, and anybody who's lived on starvation rations ought to be a past mistress at saving money . . . I mean . . . anyone who's lived like Tío Alegría's dog, who had to lean against the wall to get the strength to bark."

Cruz pretended to agree, but inwardly she was raging, telling herself, "I'll get even with you, you miserable skinflint!"

As he showed the noble lady the bedroom intended for her, the moneylender said, "You'll be able to spread out in here. I'll bet you can hardly believe it, eh! Used to those miserable little rooms in that house of yours, And if it hadn't been for me, mind you! you and your sister would still be rotting there. You must think God's come to pay a visit. But now that I've given up the rent on this fine main-floor flat because I'm occupying it myself, we've got to economize on the confounded food, and on clothes. I don't want any luxuries here—see?—because I think I've already spent enough money on the wedding outfits. No more of that, no more—dammit! I'll decide on a sum and you've got to stick to it! We've got to cut down; that's the *objective*, or the *obit*, to cut it shorter."

He burst into uncouth laughter after having said all these foolish things, almost forgetting the elegant terms that he had learned; he snapped his fingers or pulled his hair, adding some new vulgarity or unconsciously making fun of fine language: "Because I *cherish the conviction* that we mustn't *slacken* the purse strings, mind you! *I start from the principle* that we should have an extra course at table only on Thursdays and Sundays, because, as our friend Donoso says, administrative laws have come *to fill a void*. I have come to fill the void in your stomachs . . . that is . . . don't pay any attention to this materialism . . . it's a joke."

Cruz found it hard to conceal her revulsion. Donoso, who had stayed at the table after the meal chatting with Rufinita, went off to look for the pair who were inspecting the house, joining them at the moment when Torquemada was showing Cruz the famous little altar, with Valentín's portrait turned into a religious image, wax candles on either side. Don Francisco stood in front of the picture, saying, "See, my fine fellow, how neatly everything's been done. Here's your aunt. She's not old, no indeed; pay no attention to the materialism of the white hair. She's really beautiful, and noble on all four sides because she's descended from the wisdom tooth of some playing-card king or other."

"That will do," said Donoso, trying to lead him away. "Why don't you rest for a little while?"

"Leave me alone, damn it all! Don't be a bore or a spoilsport. I've got to tell my little boy that we're all here. Your mama is sick. That's a big fat nuisance! But don't worry, my darling boy, I'll *get you born* soon. You're better-looking than they are. Your mother will take after you . . . I mean you'll take after your mother . . . no, no. I want you to be the same one, otherwise, I'll get unmarried."

Quevedito came in, announcing that Fidela had a very high fever and that he could not predict anything until next morning. They all went to her bedroom and, after putting her to bed, placed hot-water bottles at her feet and prepared some drink or other to appease her thirst. Don Francisco kept getting in the way, interfering in everything, giving the most absurd orders and saying at every instant, "Christ, by Christ, is this what I got married for?"

Donoso carried him off to the study, forcing him to lie down until the effects of his alcoholic spree had passed; but there was no way he could be kept on the sofa for more than a few minutes, and he was off again to bother his sister-in-law, who was looking at the room where she wished to install Rafael.

"Look here, Crucita," he said, assuming a tone of grotesque intimacy, "if your little knight-errant of a brother doesn't want to come here, then he needn't come. I'm not begging him to come, and I won't do anything to bring him, mind you! for my *sup-position* is no lower than his. I'm noble; my grandfather castrated pigs, which is, no matter what they say, a very well regarded profession in . . . *civilized countries*. My ever-so-great-granduncle the Inquisitor toasted heretics and kept a butcher shop to sell chops made of people-flesh. My grandmother, a certain Doña Whatsername, read cards and divined secrets. She was called the universal witch. So now you see."

It was impossible to put up with him any longer. Donoso seized him by one arm and, taking him into the next room, made him lie down by force. A short time later, the snores of the Inquisitor's descendant thundered through the house.

"Drat the man!" said Cruz to Don José as they sat together at the bedside of Fidela, who lay in a deep feverish slumber. "He's unbearable today."

"As he's not used to drinking, the champagne did him harm. The same thing happened to me the day I got married. And now you, my friend, proceeding skillfully with the tactics you use so well, will make of him anything you like."

"My God, what a house! I'll have to turn every bit of it upside down. Tell me, Don José, haven't you said to him already that it will be indispensable to keep a carriage?"

"I've told him. That change will come in time, but so far, he's a bit rebellious about it. Everything will come to pass. Don't forget that you must do things step by step."

"Yes, of course. The most urgent task is to bring some decency into this great barn, where there are a lot of good things that don't show up well at present because there's so much disorder and dirt. Those servants he's brought from the Calle de San Blas can't stay on here. And as for his plans for economy . . . I'm economical; misfortune has taught me to live with little or nothing. But shameful economies must not be seen in the house of a rich man. For the sake of Don Francisco's own dignity, I intend to declare war on all these penny-pinching practices that stick to his soul like a scab, like leprosy, and people like us must not become contaminated with it."

Fidela stirred, and everyone inquired with the liveliest interest about her state of health. She ached in all her bones, had a splitting headache, and a very sore throat. Quevedito's diagnosis was a light attack of tonsillitis: a matter of a few days in bed, well covered, diet, something to make her sweat, and a mild antifever medication. Cruz was relieved of her worries, but as she was not quite easy in her mind, she decided not to leave her sister; she sent Donoso off to Cuatro Caminos to see Rafael and tell him about this unforeseen accident.

"Perhaps some good will come of this unfortunate incident," said Cruz, who took advantage of every circumstance to serve her lofty ends, "if we can manage to bring Rafael here, with the lure of his dear sister's illness. My dear Don José, when you speak to him about it, exaggerate a tiny bit."

"And a large bit, if by doing so we can bring the whole family together."

And off went Don José like the wind, after taking a look at his friend, who continued to snore outrageously.

SIXTEEN

That day was an extremely sad one for the poor blind man, who from very early in the morning had been tormented by the idea that his sister was even then getting married. As he was not sure of the hour, at every hour of the day and in all their instants, he saw her getting married and remaining a prisoner forever in the arms of the monster he loathed so much, who in an evil hour had been taken to the Aguilas' home by the officious Don José. The fireworks-maker made tremendous efforts to distract him: he suggested taking him for a walk all along the Lesser Canal as far as La Moncloa, but Rafael refused to leave the barnyard. At last the two of them went into the workshop, where Valiente had to finish a fireworks display for the day of San Agustín, and there they spent a tedious morning, one of them talkative, the other sad and disconsolate. That day Cándido took it into his head to praise the firework-maker's skill—raising it to the category of a noble art with beautiful ideals—and its correspondingly great importance. He complained of the scant protection afforded by the government to pyrotechnics, for in all of Spain there is not even a bad school where the manufacture of fireworks is taught. He took pride in being a master of that art and, with a little official help, would do wonders. He insisted that fireworks could and should be a branch of the Ministry of Education. If it were to subsidize him, he would provide, on any important occasion, a performance that would astonish the world. Why, he would undertake to present the whole history of Spain in fireworks. The shapes of castles, wheels, baskets, fountains of light, mortars, star-showers, whirligigs, combining all these with the colors of the lights, would allow him to express every episode in our country's history, from the Visigoths' arrival to the departure of the French during the War of Independence.

"Believe me, Señorito Rafael," he added in conclusion, "with powder you can say anything you like, and to do things that even powder can't, we have any number of salts, compounds, and exploders that are just the same as speaking in verse."

"Listen, Cándido," said Rafael abruptly and showing very great interest, which contrasted with his previous disdain for pyrotechnic marvels, "do you have any dynamite?"

"No, señor; but I have protoxide of mercury, which is an exploder I use to make cherry bombs and light webs."

"And does it explode?"

"Horrendously, señorito."

"Cándido, by all you hold most dear, make me a rocket which, when it explodes, will destroy—I don't know—half the world. Don't be frightened by seeing me like this. The powerlessness in which I live inspires a madness in me like what I've just expressed . . . and I don't believe . . . I repeat it, knowing it to be madness: I want to kill, Cándido" (here he rose to his feet, tremendously excited), "I want to kill, because only by killing can I do justice. And I ask you, how can a blind man kill? Not with a knife or a firearm. A blind man does not know where he is wounding, and when he thinks he is wounding the culprit, he may be cutting an innocent person to pieces. But what I say, as I think and think about it, is that a blind man can find cunning ways of doing justice. Cándido, Cándido, take pity on me and give me what I ask."

Valiente looked at him, terrified, with his hands buried in the heap of black powder, and if he had suspected before that the young master was not right in the head, he had no doubt now that he was hopelessly mad. But suddenly a violent crisis took place in the unhappy young man's spirit, and by a rapid transition he passed from epileptic anger to the deepest tenderness. He burst out crying like a child, felt his way to the black, cobwebby wall and leaned his arms upon it, hiding his head between them. Valiente, confused and not knowing what to say, cleaned the powder off his hands by wiping one against the other and thought of his explosives and the need to put them in an absolutely safe place.

"Don't judge me harshly," Rafael told him after a short interval, drying his tears. "I have these attacks . . . anger . . . fury . . . wanting to destroy, and since I can't . . . since I don't see . . . But pay no attention to me, I don't know what I'm saying. There, it's all over now. . . I'm not going to kill anyone. I resign myself to this helpless, terribly sad darkness, to being a useless manikin, without willpower, feeling what honor is and being unable to express it. Keep your bombs and your exploders and your explosives. I don't want to use them. I can't use them."

He sat down again and, in a mournful voice which had a prophetic intonation about it, finished expressing his thoughts as follows:

"You, Cándido, who are young and have eyes, must see wonderful things in this society made vile by business and positivistic attitudes. What goes on today, because it is so strange, allows us to foresee what is going to happen. What is happening today? The indigent populace, envious of the rich, threatens them, terrifies them, and wants to destroy them with bombs and diabolical devices of death. After this will come something else, which you will see when the smoke of these battles has lifted. In the times that are to come, ruined aristocrats, dispossessed of their properties by middle-class usurers and traders, will feel impelled to take revenge. They will want to destroy that selfish breed, those gross and vicious members of the bourgeoisie who, after absorbing the assets of the Church, have become masters of the State, who monopolize power and wealth, and want for their coffers all the money of rich and poor alike, and for their marriage beds the women of the aristocracy. You will surely see it, Cándido. We, the masters who, even though they are like me, have eyes to see where they are wounding, will hurl explosive machines against that whole crowd of vile, irreligious peddlers, who are eaten up with vice and sated with base enjoyments. You will see it, you will surely see it."

Donoso entered at this point, but the tirade was finished and the blind man received his friend with jovial remarks. Don José informed him very briefly of the situation, telling him of the marriage and Fidela's illness, which had unexpectedly disturbed the nuptial cheer, resulting in . . . Despite his practiced oratory, Don José did not know how to end the sentence, and repeated "resulting in" three or four times. The idea that he must exaggerate Fidela's illness, thus failing to tell the truth, as Cruz had repeatedly urged him to do, inhibited him.

"Resulting in . . ." repeated Rafael. "For whom and in what sense?"

"In despair—no, not so bad as that—in sadness. Just imagine: gravely ill on the day of the wedding! Or, at least, ill enough to cause great anxiety. Who knows, it could be creeping pneumonia, scarlet fever, smallpox . . ."

"Has she a fever?"

"Very high, and the doctor does not yet dare to make a diagnosis, until he sees how things are progressing."

"I will make the diagnosis," the blind man said haughtily, and without showing any sorrow for his afflicted sister.

"You?"

"I. Yes, señor. My sister is dying. There you have the prognosis and the diagnosis, and the treatment, and the fatal outcome. She is dying."

"Oh, it's not as bad as that!"

"She is dying, I say. I know it, I guess it; I cannot be mistaken."

"Rafael, for the love of God!"

"Don José, for the love of the Virgin. Ah, that is the answer, the only rational and logical one. God in His infinite wisdom could do no less than dispose it thus."

He paced to and fro like a madman, a prey to insane agitation. Don José could not forgive himself for having imparted the news, and tried to soften it by all the means which his facile speech suggested.

"No, it is useless for you to try to deny signs, inspirations that come from on high. How do they come to me, how is this mysterious decree of the divine will communicated to me? I know it. I understand. My sister is dying; have no doubt of it. Why, I can see it now; it had to be like this! What must be, is."

"Not always, my dear boy."

"This time it will be."

They succeeded in calming him by taking him out for a walk in the yard. Don José suggested carrying him off to see the sick woman, but he resisted this, withdrawing into silent melancholy. After charging Bernardina and the Valientes to redouble their vigilance and not to lose sight of the unfortunate young man, Donoso returned fleet-footed to the Calle de Silva, to tell Cruz what was going on in Cuatro Caminos; and such was the good gentleman's generosity that he did not grow weary from walking from the center to the extreme north of Madrid, like a water-carrier, in order to be useful to the last descendants of the illustrious families of del Aguila and de la Torre-Auñón.

Cruz would have liked to be two persons in order to attend to Fidela as well as the blind man, and though she did not want to leave the one, she ardently desired to see the other, and to soothe his troubled mind with arguments and endearments. At last, at about ten o'clock at night, when Señora de Torquemada had hardly any fever and was quiet and rested after her illness, the elder sister decided to leave the house, taking with her the family's "crying towel," and a fast hackney coach transported them to Cuatro Caminos. Rafael was deeply asleep

His sister saw him in bed. She learned from Bernardina that nothing untoward was occurring and returned to Madrid and the huge, untidy, chaotic house on the Calle de Silva.

Next afternoon, when the blind man was in the barnyard sitting on a stone in the shade of a prodigious mound of garbage, with no company but that of the cock, which regarded him haughtily, and that of several hens, which, paying him no attention, scratched at the ground, he received a visit from the indispensable Donoso, who came to greet him, very carefully instructed by the intrepid Cruz.

"What news?" asked the blind man.

"None," said Don José laconically, measuring his words, for the lady had recommended that these be few and explicit. "Your sister Fidela wishes to see you."

"But . . . how is she?"

The "crying towel" was about to say something, for the habit of eloquence was stronger than the demands of discretion. But he restrained himself and, mentally apostrophizing his noble lady-friend, merely said, "Don't ask me anything; I know nothing. I only know that your sister wishes to see you."

After a long pause, during which his head remained at the least possible distance from his knees, Rafael rose to his feet and said resolutely, "Let's go."

Now, it happened that Don Francisco Torquemada was in excellent spirits that day; his head was clear, his senses acute, and all his faculties in good working order. For, having emerged from the shadowy stupor which his alcoholic prank at the wedding luncheon had induced during the afternoon and evening, he did not remember a blessed thing he had said and done in those hours of mindless perturbation, and thus had no reason to be ashamed of anything. Cruz did not make the slightest allusion to such disagreeable matters, and he went out of his way to show himself gallant and obsequious with her, agreeing with whatever observations she made to him about the organization and governance of the household. The noble lady, with supreme skill, had not touched more than the surface with her soft reforming hand, saving deeper matters for the future. Naturally this Torquemadian state of mind coincided with a return of fine words, all the acquisitions of the last few days used pell-mell, as if he feared that the words and phrases which he did not use immediately would necessarily escape his memory. Among other things, he said that he defended Romualda's presence only *under the aspect of fidelity*; but not *under any other aspect. The new order of things* deserved his *concurrence.* Nor need his sister-in-law fear that, pretending to agree, he would oppose her later with *Machiavellianisms* foreign to his character. He did ask that she let him know what she was doing, so that there would not be conflicting orders, because he, mind you, did not like to *infringe laws,* or indeed to infringe anything, for goodness' sake! It was true that the house did not look like a gentleman's house; a good many *elements* were lacking in it; but his sister-in-law, a *model* of intelligence and good taste, etc., had come to *fill a void.* Any *project she might cherish* needed only to be brought to his attention, and it would be *amply* discussed, although he accepted it *before the fact—in principle.*

At this point the doorbell rang. It was Donoso with Rafael. Cruz took him in her arms, kissing him repeatedly. The blind man said nothing and let himself be led inside the house, from room to room. When he heard Fidela's voice gaily chatting with Rufinita, young Aguila shuddered.

"She's better already. She's coming along, my dear; she's coming along beautifully," the eldest sister told him. "What a fright she gave us!"

And Quevedito, sincerely and in good faith, hastened to give his opinion in this wise:

"Why, it was nothing . . . a chill . . . a minor matter. She's fine, perfectly fine. It's only as a pure precaution that I haven't let her get up yet."

At the door of the connubial bedroom stood Torquemada, rubbing his hands together with a satisfied expression, his feet shod in elegant slippers that had just been brought to him from the shop. He welcomed the blind man, for which purpose the latest fine phrase he had learned was exactly right:

"Ah!" he exclaimed, "the *beau ideal!* At last, Rafael! The whole family together again . . . the *beau ideal!*

· 3 ·

TORQUEMADA
IN PURGATORY

· PART I ·

ONE

The licentiate Juan de Madrid, that diligent and malicious chronicler of *The Sayings and Doings of Don Francisco Torquemada*, tells us that Cruz del Aguila waited no less than six months before reestablishing in her house the splendor of former days and surrounding herself with honorable and agreeable society, demonstrating her consummate discretion in this as in everything, lest it be said, mind you! that she was progressing with famished haste from the direst poverty to a good table and a joyous exchange of visits. Another no less serious chronicler, "Archpriest Florián," author of *The Garland of Good Dinners and Labyrinth of Tertulias*, dissents from this opinion and places on the day of Epiphany the first formal dinner offered by the noble ladies in their domicile on the Calle de Silva. But this might well be an error in dating, forgivable in one obliged to appear in so many different dining rooms in the course of a day by virtue of his occupation. And we see the former opinion corroborated in that most erudite volume, *Dispatches on the Culinary Art*, by Maestro López de Buenafuente, who, while discussing a brand-new way of preparing partridges, maintains that the first time this dish appeared at table was in the course of a supper given by that noble couple, the Torquemadas, on the tenth day of February in such-and-such a year of the Christian era. No less scrupulous in historical references is that "Cachidiablo" who signs his name to the *Ordinances of Dressing Well*, for, when describing a sumptuous party in the house and gardens of the noble marquises of Real Armada, on the day of Our Lady of Candelas, he states that Fidela Torquemada wore an elegant outfit the color of dried apricots, with Brussels lace. Through these and other bits of news, gleaned from the best sources of information, we may be sure that until a full six months after the wedding the Aguila sisters did not begin to soar above the narrow space to which their sad fate had so long reduced them.

Nor need we compare at any length the most respectable writers on society affairs to feel certain that the Aguila ladies remained in obscurity for a certain period of time after their change of fortune, as if embarrassed. "Mieles" does not mention them until well into March, and "El Pajecillo" names them for the first time when he lists the tables set up to receive charitable contributions on Holy Thursday, in one of the most aristocratic churches of this capital. To find specific news of periods closer to the marriage, we must have recourse to the above-mentioned Juan de Madrid, one of the most active—and at the same time most ironic—historians of high society, a man as tireless in his eating habits as in describing opulent tables and splendid soirees. This chronicler carried a commonplace book in which he noted all the phrases and turns of speech he heard from Don Francisco Torquemada (with whom he had become friendly through Donoso and the marquis of Taramundi), and set down with scrupulous attention to dates the transformed usurer's progress in the art of conversation. Through the licentiate's papers we know that, beginning in November, Don Francisco was saying at every moment: *that's the way history is written, velis nolis, the revolutionary wave,* and *let's be fair.* A month later he was defacing these absolutely ordinary forms of speech with new acquisitions of insufficiently assimilated phrases and terms, such as *to recapitulate, mannerisms, at the present historical moment,* and *Machiavellianism,* applied to things that had nothing Machiavellian about them. Toward the end of the year, the good man acquired polish by correcting, with great accuracy, the absurd phrases he had used before, for he observed and learned everything good that came to his ears with an astonishing capacity for assimilation, acquiring very fine expressions such as: *I have no objection to stating . . . I abide by the logic of the facts.* And though it is indeed true that his lack of basic education, as the licentiate judiciously observes, sometimes caused him to put his foot in his mouth just when he was speaking best, it is also true that his conscientiousness and the care he exercised in acquiring forms of speech led him to accomplish real grammatical miracles in a very short time, and to play a not unworthy role in gatherings of refined persons, some of whom were superior to him in general knowledge and education, but no better than he in the gift of holding forth on some well-worn subject of controversy—*within the grasp,* as he said, *of the most ordinary intelligence.*

It is an incontrovertible fact that Cruz allowed all of September and part of October to pass before she proposed any alteration in the house's architectural arrangements to her brother-in-law; but there came a day when, with all the smoothness in the world, conscious that she was digging the first trenches for a formidable siege, she put forward the idea of tearing down two walls to make the living room larger, converting it into a drawing room, and making the dining room into a grander *banquet hall*. This was the word used by Don Francisco, softening it with jokes and japes; but the lady was not intimidated, and replied to her brother-in-law as follows: "I'm not saying that we're princes, nor am I of the opinion that our house is the royal palace, as you say. But modesty does not obviate comfort, Señor Don Francisco. I'm willing to admit that, for the present, the dining room is suffi- ciently large. But can you guarantee that it will be so tomorrow?"

"If the family increases, *as we have the right to expect*, I won't say no. Bring on more dining room, and I'll be the first to make it bigger when the need is there. But the living room . . ."

"The living room is simply absurd. Last night, when the Taramundis and the Real Armadas were there with your friends the stockbroker and the money changer, we were like sardines in a basket. I was ner- vous and terribly embarrassed, expecting the moment when someone would have to sit on someone else's lap. You may think that such a cramped room is seemly for a man whose home is visited by persons of the very best society. As for me, what do I care? I only want to live in a corner, with no more social contacts than two or three close women friends. But you, a man like you, destined for . . ."

TWO

"Destined for what?" asked Torquemada, holding a biscuit soaked in chocolate up to his mouth without tasting it, which shows that he was having breakfast at that moment. "Destined for what?" he re- peated, seeing that Cruz, smiling, avoided giving him an answer.

"I'm not saying anything, nor will I waste my time in demonstrating what is perfectly obvious, the inadequacy of this room," said the lady, who, as she moved around the oval table, pretended not to find suffi- cient space between the sideboard and the chair occupied by Don Fran- cisco. "You, as owner of the house, will do as you please. The day that we have a guest, and it is very likely that we will have if we are to repay the social favors offered us by others, and when I say a guest, I might as well say two or four . . . well, on that day I'll have to eat in the kitchen. No, don't laugh. There you go with your same old story, that I exaggerate, that I . . ."

"You are *exaggeration personified*," replied the miser, downing another biscuit. "And since I *make a boast of* the fact that I'm the golden mean *personified*, I put everything in its proper place, and refute your arguments as of the present historical moment. As for tomorrow, I won't say . . ."

"What will have to be done in a great rush and hurry tomorrow ought to be done slowly today," said the lady, resting her hands on the table, just as Don Francisco was finishing his breakfast. She knew in exactly what terms his reply would be couched, and waited quietly, with an expression of smiling confidence on her face.

"Look here, Crucita. Since my marriage I have been *realizing*—yes, that's the word—realizing *a series of transactions*. You've proposed changes that knock the habits of my whole life into a cocked hat; for instance—but why bother with examples and to wits? The fact is that my sister-in-law proposed and I opposed. Finally I compromised, for, as our friend Donoso very well says, to live is to compromise. I've accepted a little bit of what was proposed to me, and you gave up a *trifle*, or a couple of *trifles*, of your plans. The golden mean—*in the vernacular*, prudence. The Aguila sisters are not going to say that I haven't tried to please them, going back on my own self, as you might say. To keep my dear wife and yourself happy, I've given up coming to dinner in shirt sleeves, which was very much to my taste on hot days. Then you insisted on bringing in a twelve-duro cook. Scandalous! You'd think we were archbishops! So I compromised and hired the cook we have, eight big fat duros, and though it's true that she makes us wonderful dishes, she'd be well paid at half the wages. So that my lady-wife and my lady-wife's sister won't be up in arms, I've stopped eating that salad of cold meat and onions last thing at night, before I go to bed, because, I admit it, the smell of onion shouldn't precede me, opening a path before me like a squadron leader. *To recapitulate*: I've also compromised regarding that little footman for running errands and brushing my clothes, though to tell the truth there are days when I brush not only my own clothes but his, too, so as to save him a scolding. But anyway, I'll let the little fellow with the buttons pass, though if I'm not mistaken, he doesn't give enough service to justify the amount he eats. I observe everything, my lady; I often take a turn around the kitchen while the servants—*in the vernacular*, the help— are eating, and I've seen that that angel-child gobbles enough food for seven, apart from the bad turn he does the family by getting the maids in this house and the whole neighborhood all stirred up. Anyway, you two want it, so let it be. *I adopt this attitude* so it can't be said that I am *intransigence personified*, and to show that I'm absolutely jus- tified, for now, in refusing, as I do refuse, to pull down walls, *etcetera*, for this business of spoiling the building flies in the face of logic, of common sense, and the comfort of all, *both foreign and domestic*."

Cruz answered him cheerfully, pretending to submit to the family's chief authority, and went to the bedroom of her sister, who did not rise until later. Both of them chatted gaily about the same subject, agreeing that this concession, and others as well, would be obtained from Don Francisco by waiting for a favorable occasion, as they had been able to observe during the time they had been living with him. Torquemada, after stuffing himself with a good dose of the morning paper, *La Correspondencia*, went to see his wife, newspaper in hand, stepping softly to keep from making a noise and pushing his black silk skullcap to one side to scratch his cranium. Cruz lost no time in going to wake the blind man and bring him his breakfast, and husband and wife were left alone, she in bed and he pacing up and down the bed- room.

"And how are you?" Don Francisco asked her with genuine affec- tion. "D'you feel stronger today?"

"I think so."

"You must try taking a little walk. Now, if you insist on going in a carriage, I'm not opposed, mind you! But you'd do better to go out infantry-style, with your sister."

"We'll go on our own little feet," replied his wife. "We'll go to the Taramundi sisters' house, and to come home, they'll bring us in their landau. That way you'll avoid the expense."

Torquemada said not a word. Whenever discussions arose about changes that would upset Don Francisco's well-studied budget, Fidela took his side, either because she wanted to observe faithfully the law of matrimonial harmony or because, with feminine instinct and almost without realizing what she was doing, she was cultivating strength on the field of her own weakness, giving ground in order to triumph and retreating only to conquer. This is the more likely explanation, and the historian of these annals feels almost sure of it, adding that there was no shade of premeditated malice in that stratagem, a pure product of feminine nature and the situation in which the younger Aguila sister found herself. After three months of marriage, the impression of the first few days had not disappeared for her; that is, that her new state was a liberation, a happy ending to the grinding poverty and humiliating obscurity of those accursed years. Married, she could dress decently and groom herself as her upbringing demanded, eat as many sweetmeats as she wished, go out walking, see an occasional theatrical performance, have women friends, and enjoy those amenities of life which least affect the spiritual order. For the most important thing, after so long a period of poverty and anguish, was to breathe, be nourished, to reestablish the animal and vegetative functions. Her pleasure in the change of environment, so favorable for her bodily life and to some extent for social life, did not allow her to see the empty spaces which that marriage might cause in her soul, spaces already existing in incipient form, like the pulmonary lesions of tuberculosis, which cause scarcely any pain when they first begin to form. It must be added that Fidela, during the long period of suffering in the best years of her life, had lost in delicacy and sensitivity all that she had gained in subtleties of imagination, and was in no condition to gauge accurately her spouse's rude manners and tediousness. Her lymphatic nature allowed her to bear what would have been unbearable for a different temperament, and her skin, apparently so delicate, inwardly was not wholly sensitive to the rough shell of the man whom society had bestowed on her, in agreement with Holy Church, to share her life, home, and bed. It is true that from time to time she thought that she vaguely sensed those voids or caverns that were forming within her; but she paid no heed, or, motivated by a compensatory instinct (and instincts are what we are dealing with), defended herself against that premonitory misgiving—how do you think?—with wheedling behavior. By acting more like a spoiled child than she really was, by cultivating in herself infantile habits and sulkings in which she simply accepted all her sister's and husband's actions, she avoided thinking about that whole probable and possible aspect of empty spaces. And so, as a married woman, she was greedier and more capricious than she had been as an unmarried one; she made faces like a peevish child; she caused unnecessary trouble by constantly shifting objects that were easy to carry; she passed her time in affectations of laziness that increased her congenital weakness; she also affected a certain scorn for everything practical and a horror of the heavy duties of the household; she prolonged her toilet to an incredible degree, spending eternities at her dressing table; she craved perfumes, which for her were a new sweetmeat, no less desired than bittersweet chocolates; she loved to have her husband treat her with exaggerated affection, and called him her little donkey, running her hand over his back as if he were a big pet dog, and saying, "Tor, Tor . . . come here . . . out . . . come . . . your paw . . . give me your paw!"

And Don Francisco, to humor her, would offer his hand, which for that purpose (and for many others) was indeed a paw, and the poor man took a great deal of pleasure in so whimsical a style of marital affection. That morning nothing of the kind occurred; they chatted for a while, both praising the delights of walking, and at last Fidela told him, "You needn't keep a carriage for my sake. I should say not. All that expense to save me a bit of weariness! No, no, don't even think about it. Now, for you it's a different story. It's not at all the thing for you to go to the Exchange on foot. You lower yourself, believe me that you lower yourself, among businessmen. And I'm not the one who says it, my sister says so, who knows more than you do. Donoso says so too. I don't like to have them thinking bad things about you, or have them calling you a cheeseparer. I can get along very well without that luxury; you can't dispense with it, because, really, it's not a luxury but a necessity. There are things as fundamental as bread . . ."

Don Francisco was unable to answer her because he was informed that the stockbroker was awaiting him in his office, and he hastened thence, turning over in his noggin these or similar ideas: "That damned carriage! In the end I'll have to *take the plunge—velis nolis*. It's not the idea, not at all, of that sweet little wife of mine, who never has anything to say about spending more money. The other one, the boss, she's the one who wants to travel on wheels. Nor have I any use for that contraption, which—now that I remember—is also called a *vehicle*. Oh, if I could have one without that despot, Cruz, knowing it! But no, dammit! It'll have to be for everyone, and my wife first of all, on very soft cushions so she won't come to grief, especially if we have an heir. . . Because, though they've said nothing, *I observe the logic of the phenomenon*, and tell myself, 'We have an heir.' "

THREE

The things God accomplishes! That rascal Torquemada had extraordinary luck in everything, and never touched a transaction that did not turn out like a charm, with neat and safe profits, as though he had spent his life doing good works and Divine Providence wanted to reward him hugely. Why did fortune favor him, when his methods of getting rich had been so base? And what kind of Providence is it which understands *the logic of the phenomenon* thus, as the miser had remarked in connection with something quite different? No one can fathom the mysterious relationship between the moral life and the financial, or business, life, and the theory that such currents are going to enrich the arid ground where the flower of goodness does not and cannot grow. This is why the poor and honest majority believes that money is crazy; it is why holy religion, confounded by the monstrous iniquity with which currency is distributed and stored away, and, not knowing how to console us, does so with disdain for riches, which for many is a fool's consolation. At any rate, be it known that Donoso's foresighted friendship had surrounded Don Francisco with very honorable persons who could assist him in increasing his hoard. The stockbroker, who was his associate in the buying and selling of shares, was a man of the most exquisite honesty in addition to possessing an astonishing capacity for work. Other go-betweens who offered him discounts on notes of hand, shares on margin, and a host of deals whose honorableness no one would have dared to put to the test, were nevertheless the best of their ilk. It is true that they, with their good mercantile sense of smell, understood from the very first day that Torquemada was not easily gulled, and perhaps the foundations of their ethical behavior rested upon this, together with the fact that Don Francisco, a man of extraordinary perspicacity in such dealings, guessed their thoughts before they were revealed in words. It was from this reciprocal knowledge, from this interpenetration of desires, that perfect agreement among cronies resulted, as well as a fat profit from their operations. And here we are in the presence of a fact that explains the monstrous gifts of mad luck and the paradox that scoundrels do grow rich. We must not talk so much about blind fortune, or believe the fable that she goes about with bandaged eyes. That is an invention of cheap symbolism! It is not so, no indeed. Nor need we admit that Providence protected Torquemada simply to infuriate all poor and sentimental honest men. It was—let us speak plainly—it was that Don Francisco had a talent of the first magnitude for business, an aptitude nurtured during thirty years of apprenticeship in small-scale moneylending, and later developed on a very large scale in a broader milieu. The education of that talent had been hard, amid privations and horrendous battles with undependable humanity, and from it he drew a very profound knowledge of people, solely in the area of needing to have, or not needing to have, patience, obvious appreciation of a certain percentage, tenacity, and exquisite calculation of opportunity. These qualities, later applied to large-scale operations, were polished and acquired a formidable development, as Donoso and the other powerful friends who were gradually added to the circle soon observed.

All of them acknowledged him to be an uncultivated man, vulgar and sometimes brutally egotistical; but at the same time they saw that he had a masterly eye for business, a completely reliable knack which gave him irrefutable authority, so that although all of them considered themselves his betters in general life, they deferred to the ruffian in that specialized branch of *give and take*, and listened to him as to one of the Church fathers—father of a financial church, that is. Ruiz Ochoa, Arnáiz's nephews, and others, who through Donoso's good offices began to frequent the house on the Calle de Silva, chatted with the moneylender, making a show of superiority to him; but really they were spying out his thoughts in hopes of appropriating them. They were the swineherds and Torquemada the pig who, by sniffing the ground, uncovered the hidden truffles, and the place where they saw him rooting was a sure stroke of business.

And so, as I say, Don Francisco went to his office, where he remained for some quarter of an hour, giving instructions to the stockbroker, and then returned to immerse himself in the morning papers, reading matter that interested him greatly at the time, for it offered him real revelations in the intellectual sphere and opened immense horizons before his eyes, which till then had been fixed on objects located no farther away than his nose. He read everything concerning politics with mild interest, seeing in politics, as is common among men greatly attached to business, nothing more than a futile comedy whose only object lay in offering advantages and satisfactions to vanity to a few hundred persons; he read the telegraphic dispatches with profound attention because all those things that went on in foreign parts seemed more important to him than things here, and because the names of Gladstone, Goschen, Salisbury, Crispi, Caprivi, and Bismarck sounded very grand, revealing a breed of personages on a larger scale than ours; he dwelt with delectation on the chronicle of news of the day, crimes, beatings, scenes of love and vengeance, escapes by prisoners, second-story jobs, burials and funeral services for persons of prominence, swindles, derailments, floods, etc. In this way he found out about everything, and incidentally learned new and elegant *clauses* to introduce into his conversation.

But what he skimmed over like a cat on hot coals were the articles concerning anything connected with literature and art, for there indeed he was uncomfortably in the dark; that is, he did not understand a syllable, nor did the justification for writing such twaddle enter his head. But since he saw that everyone, in ordinary conversation, gave genuine importance to such matters, he never said a single word to the discredit of those liberal arts. It was certainly true that no one was more discreet than he in *the new order of things*, and he had the priceless gift of silence whenever some subject of which he felt himself ignorant was being discussed. He proffered his agreement only in monosyllables, allowing, as it were, glimpses of a very concentrated intelligence which does not wish to squander its substance. Until then, *artists* for him had been barbers, masons, printing compositors, and master cobblers; and when he observed that among cultured people the only true artists were musicians and dancers, and to some degree also those who write verses and paint daubs, he made a mental note to inform himself at length about that whole *jumble*, so as to be able to say something that would allow him to pass for a man of enlightenment. For his pride grew stronger by the hour, and the idea that he might be taken for a fool disturbed him greatly, with the result that recently he had taken to reading the articles of criticism in the newspapers with great care, trying to get some substance from them, and no doubt would have made something of them had he not stumbled at every moment over innumerable terms whose meaning he was unable to digest.

"Dammit!" he said on a certain occasion. "What does this business about *classic* mean, I wonder? What terms these gentry use! I've heard tell of the *classic* stew and the *classic* mantilla, but I can't see what something classic, when they're talking about poems or plays, has to do with chick-peas or Almagro lace. The fact is that these fellows who spout off such *infusions* about the big and little of literary things always talk in code, and the devil himself couldn't understand them. And then all this about *romanticism*, what can it be? What sauce do you eat that with? And I also wish somebody would explain the *aesthetic emotion* to me, though I imagine it's something like a person's having a fit. And what does *realism* mean, for it's nothing to do with the realm or any damned thing like that!"

For nothing in this world would he have ventured to express his doubts to the superior knowledge of his wife and sister-in-law, for he feared that they would laugh in his face, like the time when the devil tempted him, being in a state of great confusion, and he took and said to them, "What does *secretions* mean?"

Lord, what peals of laughter, what ridicule and embarrassment they put him through with their *mannerisms* of educated people!

He interrupted his reading to go to his wife's room, determined to get her on her feet, for Quevedito recommended taking measures to combat her indolent habits, which increased her lymphatic temperament. As he went down the hall he heard somewhat angry voices coming from the room adjacent to the living room, which was the chamber occupied by Rafael. Since, as a general rule, no one ever heard the blind man raise his voice in the house, for his laconism was so pronounced that he seemed to have lost the use of speech along with that of sight, Don Francisco became a bit alarmed and applied his ear to the door. Greater than his alarm was his astonishment when he heard the blind man laughing very heartily, it must have been for some inappropriate reason, for his sister was reproving him severely, the volume of her indignation rising as high as that of his peals of laughter. The skinflint could not understand where the devil such noisy jubilation came from, for Rafaelito had not laughed once since the wedding, and his face was a study in melancholy, always gazing inward and listening to himself from within. Torquemada retreated from the door, saying to himself, "The Knight of Good-for-Nothing and Grand Duke of Useless has waked up in a good humor today. All the better. May God keep him happy and then we'll have peace."

FOUR

What had happened was that when Cruz entered her brother's room that morning with his breakfast, she found him not only awake but seated on his bed preparing, like a man summoned from home by urgent business, to dress himself.

"Quick, quick, give me my clothes," he told his sister. "Do you think this is any time to start the day, when the sun came up at least six hours ago?"

"How do you know when the sun comes up and goes down?"

"How could I not know? I listen to the cocks crowing, and there's no lack of them in this neighborhood. I measure time by those clocks of nature, more accurate than man-made ones, which are always slow. And to be still more sure, I notice the morning carts, the cries of market women and old-clothes sellers, the scissors grinder, the peasant from the Alcarria with his honey, and, as for hearing everything, I hear it when they slip the newspaper under the door."

"So you haven't slept this morning?" asked his sister with tender solicitude, hugging him. "I don't like that, Rafael. It has been going on for a great many days. Why do you goad your imagination during the hours when you ought to be resting? You have plenty of time during the day to make your plans and amuse yourself by seeing how many of the things you propose turn out."

"Everyone lives at the hour he can," answered the blind man, lying back in bed again but with no intention of making up for lost sleep. "I live alone with myself, in the silence of the dark morning, better than I do with the two of you in the noise of the afternoon, with visits that bore me and an occasional roar from the wild buffalo who roams about the house."

"Goodness, there you go," said the lady, becoming irritated. "Hurry and have your breakfast. Lack of food upsets your head a little and demoralizes you, stirring up bad thoughts and repressing good ones. What do you think of my figure of speech? Drink your nice chocolate and you'll see how you turn human, indulgent, and reasonable, and all that horrid anger, injustice, and hatred for people who have done you no harm will go right out of your head."

"All right, my dear, all right," said the blind man, sitting up again and beginning to laugh. "Bring on that chocolate which you say will reestablish military, I mean intellectual, discipline in my brain. It's funny."

"Why are you laughing?"

"Why, because I'm happy."

"You, happy?"

"Are we going to take that attitude? Look, my dear, for four months you've been preaching at me about my low spirits, because I don't talk, because I don't feel like laughing, because I'm not amused by the thousand little tricks you invent to distract me. Good Lord, you drive me crazy. 'Rafael, laugh. Rafael, be in a good mood.' And now that my soul is bubbling with laughter and it slips out through my eyes and mouth, you scold me. Which will you have?"

"I'm not scolding you. I'm surprised by this immoderate laughter, which is not natural, Rafael. Come now, it isn't true happiness."

"I swear that it is, that at this moment I feel happy, that I'd like to see you laugh along with me."

"Then tell me the cause of this happiness. Is it some original idea, something you've thought about? Or are you simply laughing mechanically?"

"Mechanically? No, my dearest sister. Happiness is not something you can wind up like a watch. Happiness springs from the soul and makes itself known by this vibration of the facial muscles, by this—I don't know how to say it. Well, I'll drink my chocolate so that you won't be angry."

"But stop laughing for a moment and don't keep me standing here with the tray in one hand and a slice of bread in the other."

"Yes, I recognize that it's a useful thing to be fed; more than useful; necessary. See? I'm not laughing any more. See? I'm eating. I really have quite an appetite. There. Dear sister, happiness is one of God's blessings. When it arises from within, it means that some angel has lodged inside us. Generally, after a night of insomnia, we get up in a devilishly bad humor. Why is it just the opposite for me, although I haven't slept a wink? You don't understand this, nor will you unless

I explain it to you. I'm happy because . . . but first I must tell you that I spend the wee hours calculating future probabilities, a very amusing pastime. See? I've finished the chocolate. Now for the glass of milk—delicious. Well, to calculate the future, I take human figures, I take past events, I set them out on the playing board, and I make them advance according to the laws of logic."

"My dear boy, will you please stop making your head spin with these absurdities?" said the lady, frightened by her brother's mental confusion. "I see that you oughtn't to be left alone even at night. Someone will have to be with you, always, and talk to you, amuse you, tell you stories in your hours of insomnia."

"Silly, how awfully silly you are. Why, no one amuses me as much as I do myself, and there can be no stories more piquant than those I tell myself. Would you like to hear one? Listen. In a very faraway kingdom there were two poor little ants—sisters. They lived in a little hole—"

"Be quiet. Your stories make me uneasy. I'll have to stay with you at night, even though it means missing my sleep."

"You would help me calculate the future, and when we got to the discovery of truths as amusing as those I discovered last night, we would laugh together. No, don't be angry because I'm laughing. This joy of mine comes from far too deep for me to restrain it. When a person laughs very hard, tears come to his eyes, and since I never cry, I have such a lot of weeping inside me that many a person would like to have it on hand for a day of mourning. Go on, let me laugh a lot, for if you don't I'll explode."

"That's enough, Rafael," said the lady, believing that she ought to be severe with him. "You're like a child. Are you by any chance making fun of me?"

"I ought to be doing so, but I'm not. I love you, I respect you, because you're my sister and have my interests at heart. Though you have done things I don't like, I recognize that you aren't a bad person, and I feel sorry for you—yes, don't laugh now—I'm sorry for you because I know that God is going to punish you, that you're sure to suffer horribly."

"I? Good heavens!" exclaimed the noble lady, suddenly frightened.

"Because logic is logic, and what you have done will have its reward,

not in the life to come but in this one, for, since you're not bad enough
to go to hell, you will have to purge your sins here, here on earth."

"Oh, you're not well, my poor little brother! I, sinful! I, punished
by God! You're returning to the same old subject. I, the martyr, the
slave of duty, who has fought like a lioness to keep you from indigence,
punished—why?—for doing a good work. Has God said that it's a bad
thing to do good and save poor creatures from death? Bah! Now you're
not laughing. How serious you've become! It's because a little common
sense on my part has brought yours back."

"I've become serious because just now I'm thinking about something
very sad. But let's drop the subject. To return to what we were talking
about before and the reason for my laughter, I must tell you that you
won't hear me insult your worthy brother-in-law again; I don't say
'my' because he isn't mine. I will not pronounce a single offensive
word against him, because I eat his bread, we all eat his bread, and it
would be beneath our dignity to insult him after he has fed us. The
shameless ones are ourselves, I more than you, for I was proud of being
inflexible and maintaining a gentleman's idea of dignity. But at last,
how shameful! Excusing myself with my blindness, I ended by accepting from my sister's husband both his hospitality and these slops you
give me, and I call them slops with apologies to the cook, because only
morally, do you understand? morally, the food in this house is like the
free soup that is given, in an immense vat, to poor beggars at the doors
of convents. So you see, I don't insult him, and when I laughed, I was
not laughing at him and his ridiculous ways, which you are gradually
correcting so he won't make you look foolish, because that man will
speak like a human being in the end, he's so good at studying and
taking note of your teachings; I say, I'm not laughing at him, nor at
you, but at me, at myself. And now I'm starting to laugh again. Stop
me. All right, I'll laugh as much as I like, and, laughing, I assure you
that I've guessed the future, and I see as clearly as the soul's light, the
only light that lightens me; I see that, by compromising and compromising, by letting events take their course, high priest of blessed inertia, in the end I will adjust myself to the despicable opulence of this
life, will consciously flout dignity. If this is not comic, highly comic,
it's because humor has fled our planet. Imagine me accepting this
dishonor, witnessing the two of you sunk in such baseness and believ-

ing it not only beyond help, but even natural and necessary! Imagine me conquered by mere habit and adjusted to the poisonous atmosphere that you two breathe! Confess, dear sister, that this is enough to make anyone die laughing, and if you can't join in the joke now, it must be because your soul is proof against humor, understood in its true meaning and not in the meaning given it by your fine brother-in-law the other day, when he spoke about what a lot of *humors* there were in the fireplace."

It was during this part of the scene that Rafael's peals of laughter reached their height, and that was the moment when Torquemada heard the noise from outside the door.

FIVE

"You simply mustn't be allowed to speak in that way," said the elder sister, hiding the anxiety which her brother's wild laughter was arousing in her mind. "I've never seen you in such a stupidly joking mood, nor heard you say foolish things in such bad taste, Rafael. I don't recognize you."

"The family's metamorphosis had to show up in me somehow. You've become serious and I've become lighthearted. Eventually we'll all be grotesque, more grotesque than he is, for you'll manage to touch him up and put a shine on him. Well, all right, I'll get up; give me my clothes. I say that society will some day see in him a man of a certain worth, the sort of man who is called 'serious,' and in us a group of poor pretentious folk who have made fools of themselves out of hunger."

"I don't know how I have the patience to listen to you. I ought to spank you like a naughty child. Here, get dressed; wash in cold water to clear your head."

"That's what I'm going to do," replied the blind man, already on his feet and preparing to cool his head in the basin. "And since there's no help for it, the things that have happened must be accepted, and we'll have to plunge up to our necks in the filth that you . . . well, that fate has brought us. Now you can see that I'm not laughing, though it's not for lack of wanting to. I'll speak to you seriously, despite what the amusing side of the matter calls for. And this is proved by the hint of satire that is noticeable—haven't you noticed it?—that is noticeable, I repeat, in the speech of all the persons who have renewed their friendship with us, after the interval caused by our misfortune."

"I haven't noticed that," said Cruz resolutely, "and there's no such satire except in your unbridled imagination."

"It's because you're dazzled by the sparkle of this tawdry opulence and don't see the truth of social opinion. Though I'm blind, I see it better than you do. Very well, let me rub my face and head a bit, and I'll tell you something that will shock you very much."

"It would be better for you to say nothing, Rafael, than to drive me wild by making such absurd judgments on the most natural events in life. Here's the towel. Dry yourself well. Now, sit down, and I'm going to comb your hair."

"Well, I wanted to tell you . . . My head is clear now, but the fact is that I'm about to burst out laughing again, and have to restrain myself if I'm not to explode . . . I wanted to tell you that when shame is lost, as we have lost it . . . ."

"Rafael, for the love of God!"

"I say that it's best to lose it all at once, to tear this sore spot out of one's soul and face the shameful fact barefaced. At most, one ought to use the rouge of good manners on one's face, once one has lost the blessed blush that distinguishes worthy persons from unworthy ones," he said, trying to hold in his laughter. "You, who have made all this happen, must go on to the end. Don't stop with success half achieved. Begone scruples, begone any delicacy of feeling, for they would be false by now. Haven't you succeeded yet in making the master give you a carriage, so that you can advertise in all the streets and promenades the sale you've made of . . . ? Ouch! Don't tug at my hair. You're hurting me."

"It's because you make me nervous. You poor thing, so delicate and ailing, who can't be punished with a slap!"

"I was saying that the sale . . . All right; I take back the word. Ouch! But you'll do very well to wheedle a carriage out of him. That man, spluttering fine words along with vulgar ones, will champ at the bit that you've placed in his mouth, with your intelligence and your authority. In exchange for the social advantages you use to feed his peacock's pride—no, not a peacock, just an ordinary turkey, the kind that's fattened for Christmas with whole walnuts—in exchange for these social advantages, he'll give you everything you ask for, cursing of course, for avarice is built into his bones and soul, but he'll give way if you know how to handle him, and I should say you do know how! And you'll manage to get the season ticket to the Opera, and the Comedia, and the social gatherings and dinners on certain days of the week. Sate yourselves with riches, with luxury, with vanity, with all the garbage that has replaced the refined delicacy of pure and noble sentiments. Let him pay you what you are worth. Don't leave a single one of the pesetas that business—business as filthy as the soul of the damned—keeps bringing into his coffers! The minute the blessed peseta comes in, the two of you will whisk it away to spend it on furbelows, all sorts of food, public and private amusements, objets d'art, fine furnishings. Be hard on him; maybe he'll kick the bucket and you two will be left with everything, for that must be your game."

"Rafael, not another word," said the lady, trembling with anger. "I have listened to your foolish ranting with all my blessed patience, but it's about to be exhausted. You think it is inexhaustible; that is why you abuse it. But it isn't, indeed it is not. I can't stay with you any longer. Pinto will finish dressing you," and she called him, "Pinto . . . my dear . . . What are you doing?"

The little footman came rushing in at once, laden with clothing that the tailor had just brought.

"I was just getting Señorito Rafael's new suit. The tailor says he'd like to see it on him."

"Then have him come in." And to Rafael, "Here's something to occupy you for a bit. I'll come back to see you with the new suit on, and if any part of it doesn't look well, we'll return it so that he can change it." And to the tailor, "Come in, Balboa. He must try everything. You know already that this gentleman is very particular and demanding about his clothes. He continues to have a sense of good cut and fit, just as if he could see them." And to Pinto, "Come now, what are you doing? Take off his trousers."

"Yes indeed, Señor Vasco Núñez de Balboa," said Rafael, once more showing signs of nervous jocosity. "It's sufficient for me to try on a garment to recognize by touch, by the feel of the cloth, the smallest defects in the tailoring. So don't bring me careless work, relying on my blindness. Bring on the trousers. And by the way, friend Balboa, my sister and I were saying just now . . . has my sister gone?"

"Here I am, my dear. I think those trousers fit you very well."

"They're not bad. Well, I was saying that I need more clothes, Señor Balboa. Another lightweight outfit, an overcoat like the one Morentín wears—you know, don't you?—and three or four pairs of summer trousers, light ones. What does my lady sister say to that?"

"I? Nothing."

"I thought you were protesting about this passion of mine for lots of good clothes. And I'm telling you that some of our change of fortune ought to trickle down to me. And I'll tell you something else: I want a tailcoat. What do I want it for, pray? I know what I want. I need a tailcoat."

"Good heavens!"

"Now you know it, Vasco Núñez. Has my sister gone?"

"Here I am . . . and all my patience with me."

"I'm very glad. Mine has evaporated, leaving behind something else that I'd rather not name. In the hollow that is left, a burning appetite for material goods has taken root. It's not my fault, nor am I the one who has brought this soft demoralization into the house. So, Master Tailor, the tailcoat as soon as possible. And you, dear sister . . . But has she gone?"

"Just this minute, yes. . . the lady left," said the tailor timidly, "and I thought she was the least bit annoyed with you."

And it was true that the lady had left the room not only to escape that torture, but because she suspected, with some reason, that her presence was what excited the unhappy young man. She left him there, with Pinto and the tailor, the whole time the fittings and taking off and trying on of clothing lasted. At luncheon time Don Francisco came home and found his sister-in-law with swollen eyes, full of sighs, and obviously downhearted.

"What's wrong, what's going on?" he asked her, greatly alarmed.

"This was all we needed. I assure you, my friend, that God is trying to test me too severely. Rafael is ill, very ill."

"But this morning he was laughing like a loon."

"Precisely—that's the symptom."

"Laughing—a symptom of illness! Well, well, every day a fellow discovers some strange things in this *new regime* you two have brought me. I've always seen a sick person cry, either because something hurt him or because he couldn't let off steam somewhere. But to have sick people laugh like mad is the only thing left for me to see."

"The best thing," remarked Fidela, taking her place at the table and observing her husband with a serene and gentle expression, "would be to call on a doctor who's a specialist in nervous illnesses—the sooner the better."

"Specialist!" exclaimed Torquemada, suddenly losing his appetite. "That is, some stuck-up, highfalutin doctor who, after leaving your brother worse off than before, will charge us some *emoluments* that'll split us down the middle."

"We simply can't allow this neurosis to develop," said Cruz, taking her seat.

"This what? Ah, sure, neurosis *fiddlededosis*. Look here, Cruz, what my son-in-law can't do won't be done by any of those practitioners who give themselves importance by beggaring the human race, after filling our *classic* cemeteries with corpses."

"Don't be tiresome, dear Tor," argued Fidela sweetly. "We must call on a specialist, two specialists, even three."

"One is enough," said Cruz.

"No, it's better to bring a whole flock of doctors here," added Don Francisco, recovering his appetite. "And after they've finished treating him, we'll all go to the poorhouse in El Pardo."

"You are exaggeration itself, my dear sir," Cruz told him gaily.

"And you are *Machiavellianism* in person, or personified. And, in parenthesis, dear ladies, that eight-duro cook may be the eighth wonder of the world, but she doesn't fool me. I think these kidneys taste burned."

"Why, they're delicious."

"Romualda, whom you dismissed because she combed her hair in the kitchen, did them better. Well, I resign myself to this order of things, and we'll compromise."

"Done," said Fidela, running her hand over her husband's shoulder. "Instead of calling in the three specialists . . ."

"Only three? Why don't you say the three plagues of Pharaoh, and the medical-pharmaceutical plague of locusts?"

"Instead of calling in a specialist, we'll take Rafael to Paris so that Charcot can see him."

SIX

"And who's that quack?" asked Torquemada when he had swallowed the piece of meat which, as he heard the word "Charcot," had got stuck in his throat and seemed not to want to move either up or down.

"He isn't a quack. He's the most eminent authority in Europe on brain disorders."

"Well," said the skinflint, striking the table smartly with the handle of his fork, "I . . . I'll tell the most eminent authority in Europe to go jump in the lake . . . and if he wants rich patients, let him go and treat his slut of a mother."

"Goodness, the things you say!" remarked Fidela with gentle severity and soft indulgence. "Francisco, for heaven's sake . . . Look, dear dummy, on the trip to Paris we'll kill two birds with one stone."

"No, I don't want to kill birds with either one stone or two."

"We'll take Rafael so that Charcot can see him."

"If seeing him were all he did . . . Maybe if we sent his picture . . ."

"I tell you that we'll treat Rafael, and incidentally you'll see Paris, which you've never seen."

"Nor do I need to."

"No? Don't you think it's a bit much, when people speak of great cities, to have to say, 'Well, gentlemen, I've seen nothing but Madrid . . . and Villafranca del Bierzo'? Don't pretend to be a yokel, for you're not. Paris! If you saw Paris, you'd expand your circle of ideas."

"My *circle of ideas*," said Torquemada, avidly picking up the phrase, which struck him as very nice and was filed away in his archive of expressions, "isn't a narrow sleeve that anyone has to stretch for me. Every man in his circle, and God in every man's, as the saying goes."

"And once in Paris," added his wife, trying to tease her husband gently, "we wouldn't return home without doing a little trip around Belgium, or on the Rhine."

"Oh yes, we're in fine shape for little trips."

"Why, that's very cheap . . . And we'd go to Switzerland too."

"Oh, sure, and to Ventas de Alcorcón."

"Or we could do the trip to the Bavarian Palatinate, to Baden and the Black Forest."

"Sure, and the White Forest trip, and then we'll go to the North Pole and Patagonia, and come home by way of the Big Dipper. And when we got here, I'd have to ask for a job as a municipal day laborer to feed my family, or as a policeman."

The two ladies greeted this witticism with open laughter, and Cruz put an end to the argument in the most reasonable manner:

"All that talk of the trip is a joke of Fidela's to frighten you, Don Francisco. We don't need to resort to Charcot. These are fine times to

be spending money on journeys and consultations with European eminences! What Rafael chiefly needs is to be amused, to take the air
often, to go for long rides far from the dreadful noise of these streets."

"Well, now, to tell the honest truth, my fine lady, that's another
reason to have a carriage. In the end, I'll have to put up with the
vehicle."

"Why, we haven't said a thing about a vehicle," said Fidela, half
serious and half joking.

"To go for long rides away from here . . .! Oh yes, Rafael's going to
be cured by the jiggling of the carriage. All right, off you go, and don't
stop till you get to Móstoles."

"The carriage," said Cruz in the authoritative tone which, on the
few occasions when she used it, brooked no reply, especially when it
was accompanied by the trembling of her lip, "you will have to have,
and you will have it, I assure you, not for us or for our brother, for we
are well accustomed to using our feet, but for yourself, Señor Don
Francisco Torquemada. It is unsuitable for a man of your standing and
respectability to walk the streets like a menial."

"Ah, my fine friend!" exclaimed Don Francisco in a very loud voice
and in a tone both jocose and irritable. "Don't you try to wheedle me
with that soft soap you're trying to give me. *Let's be fair*: I'm a humble
man, not an *entity*, as you say. Let's have no more of entities and . . .
bibles. All you're doing with that double-talk is *giving rise* to expense.
I don't *give rise* to anything but economy, and that's why I have a
piece of bread to put in my mouth. But with the attitude you two are
taking, we'll soon have to borrow it, and I don't want to tell you. . .
Debts in my house . . . never! If bankruptcy, *in the vernacular* poverty,
comes, you, my dear Crucita, are to blame. So, a carriage! Well, there
will be a carriage, not for me, for I know how to earn my blessed keep
by using the coach of San Francisco, my patron saint—my own two
feet—but for you, so you can put on all the airs that go with your new
entity."

"But I haven't asked for . . ."

"You haven't? You're better at begging than a mendicant friar! Not
a day passes that you don't wangle something out of me! Pulling down
walls, demolishing half the house to make drawing rooms. If it isn't
the dressmaker it's the tailor, or the upholsterer, or the shopowner, or
the almighty Bible. And now, because little brother feels like laughing,

I'm going to have to cry, and all of us will cry together. I can see an *uninterrupted series* of whims and hence new expenses. He has to be amused; and since he likes music so much, we'll have to bring the orchestra of the Opera here, and that good-for-nothing with the little stick who gives the signal for what they have to play." (Laughter) "A practitioner has to be brought in. Well, bring on the whole San Carlos Medical College, and let the fees rain down. Juan, Pedro, and Diego have to be invited, all the friends who come to talk to him, some of them poets, others ne'er-do-wells. And there go twelve or fourteen places at table, and a pile of special dishes to fill the hungry bellies of those *para* . . ."

The word, which, because it was of recent acquisition, could not be pronounced without a certain degree of preparation and study, stuck in his throat.

"Parasites," Fidela told him. "Yes, some of them are. But we can't avoid inviting them occasionally, for we don't want them to go around commenting on whether or not there's tightfistedness in this house."

"Our friends," remarked Cruz, "don't say that. They are most distinguished persons."

"I'm not questioning their *distinguishability*," said Torquemada, but I *profess the principle* that every man jack of 'em ought to eat in his own house. Do I go and eat in other people's houses?"

"I must say, my dear husband," Fidela told him, running her hand over his back, "that you're really very amusing today. Why, I don't want you to spend money. Why, we don't need a carriage, or luxuries, or foolishness. Go on, keep your little savings, you rascal. Do you know what Ruiz Ochoa said last night? That you'd made thirty-three thousand duros in a month."

"What an awful thing to say!" exclaimed the usurer, rising impatiently to his feet with his coffee merely tasted. "He must have said it as a joke. And with those wild tales he *gives rise* . . . yes, *gives rise* to your exaggerated ideas about what I'm worth. Well, I'm leaving before I get upset. *To recapitulate*: we have to economize. Economy is the poor man's religion. We'll hang onto the obol, for nobody knows what will happen tomorrow, and things may come along that demand this one and that one and all the other obols in the world."

Grumbling, he went to his office, picked up his hat and stick— which, to be more specific, had a staghorn handle much polished by use—and went out to *discharge* his business. Until he had walked all the way to the Puerta del Sol and beyond, the ideas aroused by the lively dispute with his wife and sister-in-law were bubbling away in his noggin, and he continued to aim an irresistible argument in their direction:

"Because you two, with all your *Machiavellianism*, are not going to make me change my system of spending only a minimum part, a *considerably minimum* part, of what I earn. So there! Since you don't have to exercise yourselves to bring it home, you have no idea how much effort it costs. I'd only spend more than we agreed on in case of an heir. That's true, an heir demands any amount of *considerable* expense. That's why Valentinico told me last night, when I fell asleep in my room with my head heated up by working so hard on those blessed numbers, he said to me, he says, 'Papa, don't let go of a cent until you know whether I'm going to be born or not. Those plaguey Aguila women are fooling me—maybe today, maybe tomorrow—and I can't stay like that, with one foot in eternity and the other in that life. Goodness, this gets tiresome. One's whole body, or one's whole soul, hurts, for though the soul has no bones, it has joints . . . and even if it has no flesh or tendons, it tickles, and even with no blood it has fever, and even with no skin, it wants to scratch.' "

SEVEN

The two sisters spent nearly all day trying to bring Rafael's disturbed brain back to normal, and hence corrected his wild words with sensible ones, and his illogical laughter with reasonable and pleasant seriousness. Fidela achieved better results than Cruz because she had more patience and sweetness, and because she had a certain power of suggestion over her brother, the origin of which eluded her, although she clearly recognized its effects. As the afternoon drew to a close, when the two were weary of the struggle, though satisfied with its good results, for Rafael was beginning to talk more sensibly, a reinforcement arrived for which both sisters were very grateful, and they went joyfully to greet him.

"Hello, Morentín, thanks be to God!"

"Goodness, you certainly make yourself scarce these days!"

"Do come in. I don't know how many times this brother of ours has asked about you today."

He was a young man-about-town of some thirty-three years of age, handsome with a rather cloying kind of good looks, a blond beard, large eyes, abundant hair already showing signs of premature baldness, medium height, carefully and very conventionally dressed. After greeting the two ladies with the ease of frequent social contact, he went and sat down beside the blind man, and giving him a pat on the knee said, "Hello there, you rascal, how are you?"

"Today you must stay to eat with us. . . No, excuses will not be accepted. Don't play your usual tricks on us."

"They're expecting me at my Aunt Clarita's house."

"Well, Aunt Clarita can wait in vain. How selfish she is! No, we won't let you out of our hands. Protest all you like, and start resigning yourself to the inevitable."

"We'll send a note to Clarita," said Fidela, settling the matter, "and we'll tell her that we've kidnapped you."

"Very well. And add in your little note that you take upon yourselves the responsibility for my absence. And if there's any shrieking . . ."

"We'll answer by shrieking still louder."

"Agreed."

Pepe Serrano Morentín had formerly been Rafael's inseparable friend, and a fellow student in university days. Although that friendship seemed to have died during the period of awful poverty, and it was very rarely that the two young men saw one another and refreshed their student memories with friendly exuberance, that was only because the Aguila sisters shunned all visits, hiding away in their sad and lonely lodgings as if they believed that they were paying tribute to the dignity of their impoverished state. The change in their material existence opened the doors of their hiding place, and of all the friendships that were gradually restored at that time through the mediation of Donoso, Ruiz Ochoa, or Taramundi, none was more agreeable to the poor blind man than that of his beloved Morentín, who knew how to handle him better than anyone else and to inspire a very profound liking in him amid the indifference or scorn he seemed to feel for the whole of humankind.

Fidela and Cruz, aware of this preference, or rather, of Morentín's absolute control over the poor blind man's will, regarded his visit that day as a providential appearance. And because they knew that Rafael liked to chat at length with his friend, to tell him his sorrows, to engage him in discussions in which humor was mingled with the subtlest psychology, sometimes skirting somewhat risqué areas, they decided to leave them alone once the conventional greetings had been exchanged, for thus they would have a rest from guard duty and the blind man would feel more at ease.

"My dear Pepe," Rafael told him, inviting Morentín to sit beside him, "you have no idea how opportune your visit is. I want to ask your advice about something—an idea—which barely occurred to me yesterday; and today, the minute you came in, when I heard your voice, well, it flashed into my mind as though it had come there all at once, colliding with all the other ideas in my brain and frightening them off and chasing them away . . . I can't explain it to you."

"I understand."

"Does an idea sometimes strike you in that way and with such insistence?"

"Of course."

"I disagree. With you, they enter hooded in hypocrisy. You don't know they're inside until they bare their faces and raise their voices. Morentín, today I'm going to talk to you about a very delicate matter."

"Very delicate?"

As he said this, the friend of the household felt a sudden blow in the cardiac region, like a warning, like an alarm, like what in slang is described by the ugly expression "smelling a rat." Now more than ever, we must give some information about this Morentín, and examine and identify him as exactly as possible.

He was a bachelor, of lower-class extraction on his father's side and aristocratic on his mother's, hence a hybrid socially like almost all the present generation; excellent manners, well suited to the present state of society, which his ample fortune made him consider the best of all possible worlds; complacent because he had been born handsome and possessed the qualities which usually excite no envy; without sufficient intelligence to feel the painful attractions of an ideal, without sufficient coarseness of spirit to be unaware of intellectual pleasures; lacking the great satisfactions of triumphant pride, but also the sorrows of the ambitious man who never reaches his goal; a man possessing neither vices nor virtues in high degree, for he was neither a saint nor a wastrel and thought himself happy living comfortably on his income, representing in Parliament one of the more docile rural districts, enjoying precious freedom and a good English horse to go riding on. Well liked by everyone, but without arousing extreme affection in anyone, he considered himself free of all burning passions, for he had never even felt political passion, and though he was affiliated with Cánovas's party, he realized that he could just as easily have belonged to Sagasta's if things had chanced to turn out that way; nor did he have a lively passion for any art, nor for sport. Although he rode for two or three hours every day, he had never been carried away by enthusiasm for horses, nor by the fever of gambling, nor of women, apart from a certain degree of involvement that never reaches the point of drama or exceeds the limits of a discreet, elegant, and urbane kind of love affair. In a word, he was very much a man of his time, or of his day, spiritually equipped with a sort of gilded commonplaceness, with a dozen and a half ready-made ideas of the kind that seem to come from the factory in little labeled packages, fastened with an elastic band.

Morentín enjoyed a reputation for judiciousness, since he was never out of harmony with what we might call the social orchestra, nor did he contract debts or become involved in scandals, except for a duel or two of a ritual kind, with the token scratch, formal reconciliation, and lunch to follow; nor did he ever feel deep happiness, nor bouts of devastating depression, taking from all things what he could easily extract from them for his private profit without risking the tranquillity of his existence. He respected religious faith without possessing it himself, and while he had no profound acquaintance with any particular branch of knowledge, he knew enough about all of them to offer an acceptable opinion, always within a circumstantial or fashionable framework. And in the moral sphere, Morentín defended decent behavior both in public and in private, but this did not mean that he was free of the mild relaxation of morals that is scarcely felt by those who live with it.

He was one of those cases, not so very rare to be sure, of a satisfied life, for he possessed moderate wealth, was rightly considered to be enlightened, and his society was very agreeable to ladies. The height of his ambition had been to be a member of Parliament, simply to exhibit the office, with no pretensions to a political career or fame as an orator. If he needed to speak as a member of some commission or other, he spoke, and spoke well, without floods of oratory but performing his job satisfactorily. The perquisites of his position satisfied his pride. Lastly, in the sentimental area, his ambition centered on having some married woman fall in love with him. If this woman were a lady, so much the better. But his aspirations stopped at the frontiers of scandal, for indeed this was something that he did not care for in the least, and everything went well, and very much to the gallant's taste, until a drama began to loom. Dramas were not to be thought of; he abhorred them in real life just as in the theater, and when from his theater seat he saw the actors weeping or brandishing daggers, the poor man became quite nervous and felt like going out and asking the ticket-seller for his money back. And, to complete the picture, even the rascal's vanity as a cool and successful adulterer had been satisfied, and he had nothing left to aspire to or to ask from God . . . or whomever it is one asks for such things.

EIGHT

"Yes, a most delicate matter and a very serious one," repeated the blind man. "First of all, my sisters aren't around?"

"No, my dear chap. We're alone."

"Go look out the door, to see if there's anyone in the hall."

"No one's there. You can talk all you like."

"I've been thinking about it ever since last night. How anxious I was for you to come! And this morning, the rage, fear, and sadness I felt showed up in stupid laughter, which alarmed my sister. I wasn't crazy, no indeed, nor will I ever be. I was laughing as condemned souls must laugh, those who are incorrigible mockers. Their punishment must consist of being tickled by devils with red-hot wire brushes."

"Eh? What foolishness! Are you starting all over again?"

"All right, all right; don't be angry. I want to ask you something. But look here, Pepe: you must promise to behave to me with a sincerity and loyalty stronger than any reticences. You must promise to answer what I ask you as you would answer your confessor if you have one, or God himself if God were to wish to explore your conscience, pretending that He did not know it."

"You're very emotional. Speak up, for really you're killing me with suspense. What is it?"

"I'll wager you can guess."

"I? Not a clue."

"And do you also promise not to get angry, even though I say . . . things that are awfully strong, things that, if they frighten you when you hear them, must frighten you still more when spoken by my lips?"

"Goodness, you *are* in a fine mood today," replied Morentín, disguising his uneasiness. "For in the end—I can see it now—you're going to come out with some joke or other."

"You'll soon see. The question is so serious that I'm not going to even start to formulate it without a bit of preamble, so here goes: José Serrano Morentín, your country's representative, landowner, man-about-town and sportsman, tell me: at the present moment, how does society stand on the question of morality and decent behavior?"

His good friend burst out laughing, sure now that Rafael, as on other occasions, after portentously announcing a ticklish question, was going to come out with some jest.

"No, don't laugh. You'll soon become convinced that this is no joke. I'm asking you whether, in the time that I have lived away from society, inside this jail cell of my blindness where hardly a flicker of social life enters, whether private behavior and the ideas of men and women about honor, conjugal fidelity, etcetera, have changed. I imagine that there is no change. Am I right? Yes. For in my time, which is also yours, back in the days when you and I circulated in the world, enjoying ourselves as much as we could, ideas about serious questions of morals were quite anarchic. You will remember that you and I, and our friends, were not excessively scrupulous, nor were we straitlaced, and we felt no respect whatever for marriage. Is this true, or isn't it?"

"It's true," replied Morentín, who was beginning to feel suspicious again. "But what's the point of all this? The world is always the same. There were young men of dubious virtue before us, and in our time we didn't try to improve behavior. Youth is youth and morality keeps on being morality, despite the transgressions that are committed either in intent or in deed."

"That's what I want to talk about. But I believe that our times were more depraved than previous or subsequent ones. I remember that we believed as an article of faith, for sin also has dogmas imposed by frivolity and vice. . . we believed that it was our obligation to make love to every married woman who came into our path; we believed that we were making use of a right inherent to our arrogant youth, and that the couple we ruffled almost ought to be grateful for it. Don't laugh, Pepe. Look, this is serious, very serious."

"Yes, it seems to be turning into a sermon. My dear Rafael, I assure you that if we were back in that historical moment, as somebody I know would say, your holy word would work marvels on the consciences of any number of scamps. But, my boy, the world has changed a great deal, and nowadays we have so much morality that extramarital fun and games have become a myth."

"That's not true. Now, just as formerly, men—especially if they are in that period between youth and middle age—proclaim principles that are entirely contrary to the good organization of the family. Today, for instance, among profligates like you the principle must be quite valid—I call it a principle the better to explain how strong it is—the principle that a woman united by an indissoluble bond to an old, ugly, disagreeable, coarse, avaricious, and brutal man, is justified in consoling herself for her misfortune with a lover."

"My dear chap, that has never been believed either formerly or nowadays."

"Justified, yes indeed, by the circumstantial morality that you men of the world profess, a law that allows all of you license to dishonor, rob, and commit any number of infamies. Don't deny it. There are indulgences, clothed in pious pity, for the woman who finds herself in the situation I have described, perhaps sacrificed to family interests. . ."

"But what is the point of all this, Rafael?" said Morentín, by this time on his guard and thoroughly upset, wanting by all possible means to cut short a question that was becoming very disagreeable to him. "Let's talk about pleasanter things, things that are more to the point, not dragged in by the heels, or. . ."

"Oh, nothing is more to the point than this!" shouted Rafael, who, although he had spoken quietly until now, was becoming very excited, moving his hands and feet restlessly, stammering as he spoke, for he was reaching the point of confrontation. "I need not seek examples, or theorize stupidly, for painful reality has proved me right. I am going to deal with fact, Pepe, and now I need all your sincerity and all your courage."

"My dear chap, why don't you go to the devil?" said Morentín angrily, as though trying to stifle the discussion. "I have come here to pass a pleasant hour with you, not to discuss fantastic abstractions."

"What. . . are you leaving?" (rising to his feet).

"No, I'm still here" (preventing him from getting up).

"One moment more, one moment, and then I'll leave you in peace. I'll sit down again. Please go and see if my sisters are anywhere around."

"No, but they might come in."

"Then before they come, I will tell you that inflexible logic, the logic of real life, which derives one fact from another fact as the child is derived from the mother, and the fruit from the flower, and the flower from the tree, and the tree from the seed . . . that logic, I say, against which our imagination is powerless, has revealed to me that my unhappy sister . . . What a sad thing it is to reveal these shameful realities within our own family, but it is sadder still to be stupidly unaware of them! I am blind insofar as sight is concerned, but not in perception. With the eyes of logic I see more than anyone else, and to them I add the lens of experience to see all the more. Well, I have seen, how shall I tell you? I have seen that my poor sister is firmly caught in that principle, let us call it so, and that, encouraged by the indulgence of society, she allows herself. . ."

"Be quiet! This simply cannot be tolerated!" exclaimed Morentín furiously, or speaking as if he were furious. "You are insulting your sister vilely! Have you lost your reason?"

"I have not lost it. I have it here inside me, and very securely. Tell me the truth. Confess it. Be large-spirited."

"What have I to confess to you, you wretch, and what do I know about your rantings? Leave me alone, leave me alone. I can't stay with you, or be with you, or listen to you."

"Come here, come here," said the blind man, seizing his arm and clutching it with so much nervous strength that his fingers felt like pliers.

"No more of this foolishness, Rafael. What kind of raving is this?" (Struggling with him), "I tell you, let me go."

"I won't let go of you, no I won't" (holding him all the tighter). "Come here. I'm standing up too, and you'll drag me along stuck to you, like your remorse. Deceiver! Libertine! Listen, I want to call you that to your face, since you haven't the courage to confess it!"

"Liar, lunatic! I? What are you saying?"

"That my sister . . . I won't repeat it, no . . ."

"A lover . . . what utter rot!"

"Yes, yes, and that lover is you. Don't deny it. How well I know you. How well I know your tricks, your loose morals, your hypocrisy. Illicit love affairs, so long as they don't give scandal. . ."

"Rafael, don't make me angry. I don't want to be hard on you. You deserved . . ."

"Confess it, be large-spirited."

"I can't confess something that's an invention of your sick mind. Come now, Rafael, let me go."

"Then confess it to me."

Their arms entwined, both of them panting and furiously angry, Rafael trying to grip his friend with nervous strength, the other defending himself without much effort so as not to cause a noisy scene, Morentín won out in the end, forcing the blind man to fall exhausted into his chair and holding him down so that he could not move.

"You are a criminal and you haven't the courage of your crime," said Rafael breathlessly, in a stifled voice. "Confess, for God's sake."

"I swear to you, I swear to you, Rafael," answered the other, softening his voice as much as he could, "that you have invented and expressed a tremendous falsehood."

"It's true, at least in intention. . ."

"Neither in intention nor in anything at all. Calm yourself. I think your sisters are coming."

"My God! I see it so clearly, so clearly!"

Despite Morentín's caution, he could not prevent some slight echo of the quarrel from reaching the vigilant ear of Cruz, who hurried to the scene and, as she entered the room, must have understood from the pallor of their faces and their hesitant speech that some disagreement had arisen between the two good friends, and that the reason for it was undoubtedly a really serious one, for neither of them was wont to lose his serenity or his ready, courteous, joking tone when they were discussing philosophy or music or horse-breeding.

"Nothing, it's nothing," said Morentín in answer to the lady's astonishment and her questions. "It's simply that this chap has some strange ideas."

"This Pepito is so stubborn!" murmured Rafael, in the tone of a spoiled child. "Not to want to confess to me. . ."

"What?"

"For heaven's sake, Cruz, pay no attention to him," replied his friend, quickly recovering himself and composing his voice, manner, and facial expression. "It's only foolishness. Did you think that we had fallen out?"

Cruz looked from one to the other, but with all her intelligence was unable to guess the nature of the dispute.

"I can well imagine. So much passion over Wagner's music or Zola's novels."

"That wasn't it."

"Then what was it? I need to know. (To Rafael, running her hand over his head and smoothing his hair) "If you don't tell me, Pepe will."

"Don't worry, he won't be the one to tell you."

"Imagine, Cruz, that he's called me a hypocrite, a libertine, and I don't know what else. But I'm not angry with him. I got a bit angry about . . . well, about nothing. We won't speak of the matter again."

"I stand firm on everything I said," stated Rafael.

"And I swear to you, and swear again, once and a hundred times, that I am not guilty."

"Of what?"

"Of the crime of *lèse nation*," answered Morentín easily, clothing the lie with a gently mischievous air. "This chap insists that I am an accomplice . . . imagine, Cruz, nothing less than an accomplice of those who have taken the Quirinal's side against the Vatican on the question of competition between the two embassies. Have someone bring the *Parliamentary Proceedings*. Ah, send Pinto to my house to fetch it! It will show that I chose to vote my conscience. The party chief left the matter open, and naturally, I . . ."

"You could have said that at the outset," replied the blind man, falling in with the formula of deception.

"I've always felt the same. 'Vatican forever.' "

Not entirely satisfied by the explanation, her mind assailed by doubts and apprehensions, the lady left the room. Morentín went after her, confirming what he had said before, but even this did not set her mind at rest, and she constantly foresaw new complications and disasters.

NINE

At nightfall, when the lamps had been lit, Serrano Morentín sought compensation at Fidela's side, in her sitting room, for the dreadful afternoon his friend had given him. After that painful experience he certainly deserved the pleasure of a moment's conversation with Señora de Torquemada, who was friendly to him as to everyone, a woman who possessed, among other charms, that of a certain childish spoiledness or innocent compliance that harmonized very well with her delicate figure and her face, as colorless and transparent as porcelain.

"What have you sent me here?" she said, unwrapping a package of books she had received that morning.

"Look and see. It's all there is for the moment. French and Spanish novels. You read very fast, and if you're to be properly supplied, production of such goods will have to triple both in Spain and France."

Indeed, in the spiritual sphere her congenital inclination toward sweetmeats took the form of a taste for novels. Since her marriage, with no work to do in the household, for her sister and husband wished her to be absolutely idle, her old appetite for narrative reading had redoubled. She read everything, good and bad, without making fundamental distinctions, devouring thrillers as well as analytical novels or those with a love interest or devoted to character study. She read rapidly, sometimes skimming over page after page, yet never failing to grasp the substance of what those pages contained. She usually guessed the outcome before reaching the end, and if this offered no novelty in working out the plot, she would leave the book unfinished. The strangest thing about her burning enthusiasm was that she divided real life and the novel into two completely different areas; that is, novels, even those of a naturalistic bent, constituted an imaginary, conventional world, the product of inventors of fictional, deceptive, and fantastic things, though this did not prevent them from being quite pretty sometimes and having a remote resemblance to truth. Between novels that tended to describe real things and the actual truth of life, Fidela always saw an abyss. One day when she was talking about this with Morentín, who because of his (in some sense) professional culture served as an oracle in a household where no one knew more than he did, the lady upheld a theory that the oracle greeted as a critical idea of the first magnitude.

"Just as in painting," she had said, "there should be only portraits, and everything that isn't portraits is secondary painting, so in literature there should be nothing but memoirs, that is, narrations about what has really happened to the person who writes. For my part I can say that I am in ecstasy when I see a good portrait by a master hand, and when I read memoirs, even if they are as boring and fatuous as those of Chateaubriand, I can't put the book down."

"Very good. But tell me, Fidela, what do you find in music that could be the equivalent of portraits and memoirs?"

"In music? How should I know? Pay no attention to me, I'm terribly ignorant. Well, in music . . . the music of birds."

On that afternoon, or rather that night, after she had read the titles of the novels and, when Morentín was recommending to her—following the dominant fashion of the time—the latest work by a Russian writer, Fidela abruptly cut off the young authority's harangue, interrogating him as follows:

"Tell me, Morentín, what do you think about our poor Rafael?"

"I think, my dear friend, that his nerves are not a model of control, that as long as he lives in this house, seeing, or rather sensing, around him persons who . . ."

"Say no more. My brother is very peculiar about that. My husband treats him with the greatest deference and doesn't deserve, indeed he does not, this antipathy which is beginning to turn to loathing."

"It's not only beginning, it exceeds the greatest loathing, frankly speaking."

"But you, my dear man, you, who are his friend and have a certain influence over him, must impress on him . . ."

"I do influence him all I can, and preach at him, and scold him . . . to no avail. Your husband is a good man . . . at heart. Isn't that true? Well, I tell him so in every tone I can muster. Goodness, were Don Francisco to hear the praises I sing about him, and had to pay me for them somehow . . . No, I'd never aspire to have him pay me what they're worth in money."

"Nor do you need it. You're richer than we are."

"I, richer? Even if you swore that I was, I wouldn't believe it. My wealth consists in adjusting myself to what I have, in my lack of ambition, in the few little ideas I've been able to put together, partly by reading and partly by living. Well, spiritually speaking, my capital is not to be despised, my friend."

"Have I ever despised it?"

"Yes, you have. Did you not tell me on Saturday that I am wedded to material things?"

"I didn't say that. You have a bad memory."

"But how can one forget what you say, even if you say it as a joke?"

"Come, let's not twist things! I said that you know nothing of the school of suffering, and that when a person has not followed that road, my friend, which is hard and painful, and its steps won with blood and tears, one does not acquire knowledge of the spirit."

"Quite so; and you added that I, fortune's darling, and knowing grief only by hearsay, am a magnificent animal."

"Good heavens!"

"No; don't go back on your words."

"Yes, I said an animal; but in the sense of . . ."

"There's no other sense. You said that I'm an animal."

"I meant . . ." (laughing) "what an awful man! An animal is something that has no soul."

"Precisely the opposite. A.. ni.. mal, with *anima*, with a soul."

"Is that what it means? Well then, oh dear! I'll go back on what I said. I'll retract, I'll take back the word. But what silly things I say, Morentín! Pay no attention to me, all right?"

"But I'm not the least bit annoyed. Why, on the contrary, I like to have you insult me. And returning to the order of the day, where do you get the idea that I know nothing about pain?"

"I wasn't referring to toothache."

"Moral pain, pain of the soul."

"You? You wretch, how presumptuous ignorance is! What do you know about that? What calamities have you suffered, what loss of loved ones, what humiliations, what shame? What sacrifices have you made, what bitter pills have you had to swallow?"

"Everything is relative, my dear friend. It's true that if I compare myself with you, there's no contest. That is why you are a splendid, superior creature and I a miserable beginner. I know very well that with the little I am learning in that school, I am not, like the person who is listening to me, worthy of admiration, of veneration."

"Yes, yes, flatter me outrageously, I'm sure I deserve it."

"A person who has passed through such terrible trials, who has purified her will, first in martyrdom and then in sacrifice, is indeed worthy of reigning in the hearts of all those who love what is good."

"More flattery, more. I love adulation, or rather, logical and rightful homage."

"And as rightful as it is in the present case."

"And I'm going to tell you something else, for I'm very honest and say everything I think. Don't you believe that modesty is perfectly foolish?"

"Modesty?" (taken aback). "Why do you say that?"

"Because I'm pushing aside that stupid mask of modesty to be able to say . . . well, shall I say it? . . . to be able to state that I am a very, very worthy woman. Oh, how you'll laugh at me, Morentín! Pay no attention to me."

"I laugh at you! You, as a superior being, are as a matter of course excused from having modesty, that adornment of mediocrity that's like a schoolgirl's uniform. Yes, be immodest and proclaim your extraordinary worth, for here are we faithful to say 'amen' to everything, as I do say it, and to go out into the world proclaiming at the tops of our voices that we must adore you for your spiritual perfection, for your mastery of suffering, and for your incomparable beauty."

"Look here," said Fidela, bursting into charming peals of laughter, "I'm not offended because people call me beautiful. To speak more plainly, no woman is offended by it, but others hide their pleasure with disclaimers and protests, made necessary by that wretched modesty. But I'm not like that; I know I'm pretty. Ah! Pay no attention to me. My sister is right when she says I'm a child. But yes, I am pretty, not a prodigy of beauty, no, not that . . ."

"Yes, you are, beautiful beyond all exaggeration, with such a distinguished, aristocratic figure . . ."

"Really?"

"That there's no other to equal or even resemble it in Madrid."

"Really, isn't there? But what am I saying! Pay no attention to me."

"Because of all those traits of soul and body, and because of many others that you do not display, with the exquisite modesty of your character, Fidela, you deserve to be the happiest person in the world. For whom ought happiness to be, if not for you?"

"And who tells Señor Morentín that it won't be for me? Does he think I haven't sufficiently earned it?"

"You have earned it, and won it in principle, but you do not yet possess it."

"And who has told you that?"

"I tell myself, for I know it is true."

"You don't know anything. Bah! Now that I've lost all shame, I'm going to tell you something else, Morentín."

"What?"

"That I'm very clever."

"That's news."

"Cleverer than you, lots cleverer."

"Infinitely more? For goodness' sake! Why, you are quite capable, with so many perfections, of driving the whole human race mad, starting with me for practice' sake."

"Well, if you continue to be sensible for a little while longer, you will recognize the fact that you don't know what happiness consists of."

"Show me, for I proclaim you mistress of the subject. I know very well what happiness would consist of for me. Shall I tell you?"

"No, because you might say something different from my idea of happiness."

"How do you know, when I haven't told you yet? And, especially, why should it matter to you if my ideas about happiness are foolish? Just imagine that. . ."

The sentence was abruptly broken off by the sound of a slow, heavy foot, of shoes squeaking on the carpets. And lo and behold, Torquemada entered the sitting room, saying, "Hello, Morentinito. And how are the folks at home? I'm glad to see you."

TEN

"Not as glad as I am to see you. We were beginning to miss you, and I was just telling your wife that business matters have kept you away from home today until later than usual."

"We're about to have dinner. And you, my dear, how are you? You were right not to go for a walk. It's a miserable day. I've caught cold. Formerly, I used to walk from one side of town to the other, putting up with *considerable* cold and heat, and never caught cold. Now, in this life of stoves and overcoats, with rubbers and an umbrella, a fellow always has a drippy nose. I was at your house, Morentín. I had to see Don Juan."

"I believe my father is coming here tonight."

"I'm glad. We have to *discharge* a little matter. A fellow has no choice but to search out good business deals with a lamp, because a fellow's needs pile up like sea foam, and in this life—we live like marquises!—every satisfaction costs an arm and a leg."

"Then you've got to earn lots of money, Tor, lots and lots," said Fidela with a cheerful air. "I admit that I'm crazy about the vile metal, and defend it against sentimental people, like this Morentín here, who is all for spiritual and ethereal things . . . Material interests . . . how disgusting! Well, I'll go over to the side of sordid positivism, yes indeed, and I'm becoming terribly miserly, terribly attached to the ochavo and still more to the centén, and especially to the thousand-peseta banknote, which is my delight."

"Perfectly charming!" said Morentín, watching Don Francisco's ecstatic face.

"So now you know it, Tor," continued the lady. "Bring me home lots of pretty silver, heaps of lovely gold and reams of banknotes, not to spend on vanities, but to keep. What a joy! Morentín, don't laugh; I say what I feel. Last night I dreamed that I was playing with my dolls, and that I had set up a bank for them. The dolls came in to change banknotes, and the doll that says 'mama' and 'papa' did the changing, discounting twenty-seven percent on silver and eighty-two on gold."

"That's the way, that's the way!" exclaimed Torquemada, laughing immoderately. "That's filing toward the inside of the house, like silversmiths do, *considerably*, and then sweeping it in."

During dinner, where Donoso was also a guest, Don Francisco was in fine fettle, voluble and cheerful.

"Since Donoso and Morentín are close friends," he said during the second or third course, "I can *manifest* that this entree, or whatever it's called—Cruz, what's the name of this?"

"*Relevé* of lamb, Roman style."

"Well, if it's Roman style, I'd like to send it to the Nuncio, and I'd kick that damned cook out. Why, this is nothing but bones."

"You suck on them, silly," said Fidela, "and they're marvelous."

"I'd say that sucking doesn't exactly make a good first course, so there! Oh well, got to have patience. Now then, señor, as I was saying. . ."

"Come now, come; tell us who hit you for a loan today."

"Did someone ask you for a loan today?" said Donoso. "We all know that borrowing is the evil of our times. We live in the midst of beggary."

"Begging for loans is an incipient form of collectivism," opined Morentín. "Nowadays we are in the period of martyrdom, of the catacombs. Later the right to beg and the obligation to give will be recognized; law will protect the beggar, and the principle of everything for everyone will triumph."

"That principle is already *under consideration*," said Torquemada, "and at this rate there will soon be no other way of living than by that blessed begging for loans. I pride myself on being able to head them off, for they almost never catch me; but the one today, because it had to do with an orphan lad, the son of a very respectable lady, who paid her debts with such punctuality—goodness, she was punctuality personified—well, because the lad was very well-mannered and very hard-working, I let myself be taken, and gave him three duros. What do you think he wanted them for? To publish a volume of poetry."

"A poet!"

"The kind that makes verses."

"But, my dear man!" observed Fidela. "Three duros for printing a book! To tell the truth, you haven't spent much."

"Well, that little angel must have been very grateful, for he's written a letter thanking me, and in it, after flattering me madly, he calls me . . . goodness, he uses a term I don't understand."

"Well, what is it?"

"Forgive my ignorance. You know already that I haven't had advantages, and here *inter nos*, I confess my ignorance of many words that were never used in the neighborhoods and among the people I used to associate with. Tell me the meaning of the word that young fellow called me, wishing, no doubt, to say something complimentary. . . Well, he told me that I'm his . . . Maecenas" (laughter). "So take me out of this doubt that's been tormenting me all afternoon. What the devil does that mean, and why am I anybody's Maecenas?"

"My dearest man," said Fidela joyfully, placing her hand on his shoulder, "Maecenas means a protector of letters."

"Well, I'll be . . . ! And to think that I've protected letters without knowing it! Unless they were letters of exchange. That's just what I said to myself, it had to be something to do with laying out cash. I never heard that term, or anything the least like it. Mae . . . cenas. That is, to invite those good-for-nothing poets to supper. Well, sir, that's fine. And what does a fellow get out of being a Maecenas?"

"Glory."

"You might say, approval."

"Approval? What the devil! Glory, man."

"Well, approval, public opinion, if what's said is in praise of me. . . *I'm bound to declare*, in all sincerity, on *my own behalf* as I'm a truthful man, that I don't want the glory of puffing poets. It isn't that I despise them, mind you! But there's something here inside me that's more compatible with prose than with verse. The men I like, with apologies to present company, are scientific men, like our friend Zárate."

And when he named him, a chorus of praise arose from the table. "Zárate, oh, yes indeed! What a worthwhile young man! How much he knows for one so young!"

"He's not so young, my dear. He's of our time. He was a classmate of Rafael's and mine at the university. Later he went into the Faculty of Science, and we into law."

"Know a lot, I should say he does!" exclaimed Torquemada, displaying an admiration that he was accustomed to confer on very few persons.

Cruz, who had left the table a short time before to take a look at her brother, came back saying, "Well, your prodigy Zárate is right here. He's just come in, and is talking with Rafael."

All of them heartily welcomed the sage's appearance, especially Don Francisco, who sent him a message via Pinto to come and have a cup of coffee or a brandy, but Cruz had the coffee sent to the blind man's room so as not to deprive him of this interval of distraction. Morentín offered to "change the guard" so that Zárate could come to the dining room, and went off to Rafael's room. During the moment when the three friends were together, Morentín said to the sage, "Go on, old chap, go and have coffee. Your friend is calling for you."

"Who?"

"Torquemada, my dear chap. He wants to explain to you what 'Maecenas' means. I thought I'd die laughing."

"Zárate has just been telling me," said Rafael, who had completely recovered from his disturbance of the afternoon, "that he met him on the street yesterday and . . . let him tell you."

"Well, he stopped me, we greeted one another, and after asking I don't remember what about the atmosphere and after I answered something or other, he comes out with this question: "Tell me, Zárate, you who know everything: when children are born, or rather, when children are about to be born, or, to wit, when—"

Pinto opened the door, saying very hurriedly, "You're to go, Señor Zárate."

"I'm going."

"Run along, run along. You'll tell us later."

And when he was alone with Morentín, Rafael continued the tale.

"This is the most amusing extravagance yet of our wild boar, who, blinded by vanity and swollen with his savagery, which flourishes amid opulence like a thistle in a garbage dump, thinks that nature is as stupid as he. Listen, and first make sure that no one can hear us. He divides human beings into two great castes or families: poets and scientists" (loud laughter from Morentín). "And he wanted Zárate to give his opinion about an idea he has. You'll see what the idea is, and you'll laugh yourself off your feet, old boy."

"Be quiet, be quiet. I've laughed so much I'll have stomachache. I've eaten very . . . Go on, do; this is absolutely divine."

"You'll see what the idea is. He thinks that there can and should be certain—I don't remember the term he used—rules, procedures, something like that, so that the children a man has will *come out* to be scientists and under no circumstances poets."

"Hush," roared Morentín, in the convulsions of unrestrained laughter. "I'm going to, I'm sure to have stomachache."

"Are you all crazy in here?" said Cruz, her face appearing at the door with an expression of lively apprehension upon it. Ever since the blind man's insane hilarity early that morning had filled her soul with uneasiness and perturbation, she could not hear laughter without a shudder. What a strange thing! And tonight the one who was laughing was Morentín, having caught it, no doubt, from his poor sick friend, who by that time, it seemed, was enjoying a gentle and soothing kind of merriment.

ELEVEN

Zárate? Who is this Zárate?

Let us recognize that in our time, a time of uniformity and a physical and moral leveling process, generic types have become outworn and that, in the slow twilight of the old world, those traits represented by large portions of the human family—classes, groups, moral categories—are gradually disappearing. Persons born more than twenty years ago, for instance, can remember perfectly that a real military type used to exist, and that every warrior who had been seasoned in the civil wars proclaimed his status by his martial appearance, even though he wore civilian clothes. There were many other types, "ringers for each other" as is popularly said, established by very particular conformations of the human countenance and by ways of behaving and dressing. The miser, for example, had the traits and facial characteristics of his caste and could not be confused with any other kind of man, and the same can be said of the "Don Juan" type, either those who aim high or those who expend their efforts on servant girls and nursemaids. And the exaggeratedly pious person had a face, and a way of walking, and clothing, that were like no others, and the same sort of characterization could be observed in those who sucked human blood, moneylenders, vampires, etc. All this is gone now, and scarcely any types are left who betray the class to which they belong, unless it be bullfighters. Mannerism is disappearing from the world scene, which is probably a good thing for art, and nowadays no one knows who anyone is except by studying the question carefully, family by family and person by person.

This tendency toward uniformity—corrected to some degree by the great progress humanity is in process of achieving, with the progress of industry and even with the lowering of tariffs, which has made good clothing more common and cheaper—has caused great confusion in our minds in the matter of types. Daily we see personalities who, from their dashing appearance and mustached faces, seem to belong to the military genus, and what are they? Why, judges of the lower bench, or piano teachers or Treasury officials. We find well-dressed and even elegant men, whose company is very agreeable and even charming, who can give anyone at all a tremendous surprise, for one thinks that they are idle men-about-town and they turn out to be inveterate usurers. We frequently see a big robust young chap who looks like a horse trainer and turns out to be a pharmacist or a professor of canon law. And one who gives every appearance of going about adoring saints and bearing candles in processions, is a marine painter or a member of the City Council.

But nowhere is the transformation more noticeable than in the pedantic type, formerly one of the most characteristic, even after Moratín portrayed the entire group in his character "Don Hermógenes." Just as the poet has lost his traditional appearance, for there are no longer flowing locks, nor pale countenances, nor languid attitudes, and one can see poets with all the look of a respectable wholesale grocer, the pedant has got lost in the process of moving his furniture from the Muses' old house to this new home that we live in, and we don't yet know whether it is Olympus or what the devil it is. At this stage in the game, where is the hilariously amusing hunchback of *The Defeat of the Pedants*? In the limbo of aesthetic history. What is most confusing nowadays is that the current pedants are not as amusing as those others were, and since they do not possess amusing qualities, there is no way to recognize them at first sight. Nor does the pure literary pedant exist any longer, with his plethora of Greek and Latin and his incorrigible garrulousness. The modern pedant is dry, diffuse, peevish, pugnacious, incapable of amusing anyone. He commonly takes in the whole field of literature and politics, physiology and chemistry, music and sociology, by virtue of that close relationship which now reigns among the arts and sciences and by virtue, too, of the brand-new interpenetration and connection among the parts of human knowledge. It need hardly be said that the modern pedant affects very different forms in his outer appearance or aspect, and there are some who look like ticket-scalpers, or sportsmen, or grave persons of the sort who tend to be patrons of religious brotherhoods.

Well then: learn who Zárate is. A man of the age of many other men, thirty-two, good-looking, well-dressed, exceedingly obliging, a terrible busybody, with a cheerful face and ingratiating glance; able to play the gallant to ladies and handy consultant to unintelligent gentlemen; journalist by spells, candidate for several university chairs, in hopes of transferring from the Corps of Archivists to the Faculty of Letters; his appearance every inch that of a son of good family, whose parents give him an allowance of twenty duros a month and pay his clothing bills; frequenter of the theater as member of a claque; a man who half-knows two or three languages, an easy speaker, flexible in thought and, in a word, the most tiresome, prattling, and turbulent pedant God ever sent into the world.

Of all the people who went to the house, Zárate was the one Don Francisco liked best, for the young man had succeeded in winning the miser's benevolence by flattering him outrageously most of the time, patiently listening to him always, and volunteering to satisfy whatever doubts the good gentleman had, of whatever kind they were. For a man in a state of metamorphosis who, finding himself in an unknown world at the age of fifty-odd, was obliged to learn very quickly in order to fit into his new sphere, Zárate was simply priceless, for he was a living encyclopedia, who instantly enlightened on any page at which he was opened. The least of it was the vocabulary our man was acquiring by dint of attention and study; he already possessed a very respectable little fund of locutions. But he lacked that multitude of elementary facts possessed by every man who goes about in frock coat and a hat; a bit of history, no more than an idea, so as not to confuse King Ataulf with Ferdinand the Seventh; a bit of physics, at least enough to be able to say *the gravity of bodies* when a chair falls over, or *the evaporation of liquids* when the soil dries up.

Hence Zárate was, for the good Don Francisco, a very mine of easy, circumstantial, and inexpensive knowledge, for it meant that he did not even have to buy a manual of useful facts or take the trouble to read it. But he did not easily deliver himself into the hands of the sage, for thus he considered him; whenever he consulted Zárate about his doubts on murky points of history or meteorology, he was extremely careful not to let his crass ignorance show. So what did the sly rascal do? Why, he discreetly encouraged the other to talk, drawing the honey

of knowledge from his encyclopedic brain to his loquacious lips, and
then the avid ignoramus would eat that honey without laying himself
open to humiliation.

In response to this astute game by his friend, that scamp Zárate,
who possessed a few grains of shrewdness amid his pile of garrulous
knowledge, treated him with extreme consideration, agreeing with
whatever stupid pronouncements he uttered, affecting to think him a
marvel of discourse, although free from certain marks of erudition that
he would acquire when he felt the need for them. That night the two
of them stayed at the table alone, for Donoso had gone off to Fidela's
sitting room, where Morentín's mama and the marquis of Taramundi
were already present, and Zárate lost no time in covering the Torque-
mada-brute with a thick layer of adulation, with which he lulled him
so as to gain ascendancy over him later.

"You must already have heard about the Home Rule question," he
said.

To escape from the dilemma Don Francisco emitted a few grunts,
for he had no idea what that was, and Zárate had to chat on for a
while and mention Ireland and the Irish before the other found himself
on firm ground.

"Do you believe," continued the pedant, "that Gladstone will get
his way in the end? The matter is grave, very grave, for in that country
tradition has unbelievable strength."

"Simply immense."

"And do you believe that it's possible? You—please allow me to say,
for I say everything I feel—have the clearest judgment of anyone I
know, and an accurate eye for any question in which great interests
enter into play. Now, you know that Gladstone—"

With this peg to hang onto, for he had learned some surprising tidbits
in *El Imparcial* that morning, Don Francisco took the words out of his
adviser's mouth and, sparkling with erudition, his head thrown back
and his tone emphatic and bold, permitted himself to say, "That Gladstone . . . what a man! Every morning after his chocolate, he takes an
axe, cuts a tree in his garden, and splits it for kindling. Really, a man
who splits kindling is a pretty powerful *entity*."

"And you don't think that he'll find great difficulties with the House
of Lords?"

"Oh, yes indeed! How can there be any doubt of it? The Lords, *in the vernacular* Twelve Peers, as I understand, are like the Senate is here, and the Senate, *velis nolis*, always tries to slow things down. And by the way, I've read that Ireland is a country that has excellent potatoes, which constitute, *so to speak*, the chief food of the Irish classes—*in the vernacular*, populace. And that drink they call *whisky*, I believe they make it out of corn, and that they use a lot of that grain to feed pigs—pardon the reference—and also to feed little children and old folks."

TWELVE

At this point the living encyclopedia took the floor to launch upon a very boring disquisition on the introduction of the potato into Europe, to which Torquemada listened with genuine fascination; and as the sage, in his unbridled rambling, then leaped to Louis XIV, they found themselves thrust feet-first into the French Revolution, a subject much to Don Francisco's taste, for he was anxious to learn about a matter that was mentioned so often in every polite conversation. They spoke for a long time, and there was even a bit of controversy, for Torquemada, *without wishing to go into the question too deeply* (a phrase he had recently aquired), loathed the revolutionaries and the guillotine. The other, in his desire to flatter, had to give way a little, adopting a modernist position by saying, "It's true, as you know very well, that the legend of the French Revolution is withering a bit, and as the idealism that used to surround many of the figures in that period fades, we see the wickedness of their characters exposed."

"Well, of course, old fellow, of course. What I say . . ."

"Tocqueville's studies . . ."

"Why, what doubt can there be about it? And it's quite clear now that many of those men, who were later adored by the ignorant majority, were first-class rogues."

"Don Francisco, I recommend that you read the work of Taine."

"Why, I've read it . . . No, I'm a liar; I haven't read that one; it was another book. I have a very bad memory for the materialism of things when it comes to reading. My head, *velis nolis*, has to work on studies of a different kind, eh?"

"Naturally."

"Well, I always say that *after action there must necessarily be re-*

action. If that's not so, just look at Bonaparte—*in the vernacular,* Napoleon—the one who gave us his brother, 'Joey Bottles'—the conqueror of Europe, you might say, a man who began his career as a mere artilleryman and then . . .''

Zárate had some things to say about Napoleon that were a great novelty to Don Francisco, and the ruffian heard them as if they were gospel, at last venturing to express an idea which he laid before his hearer with complete solemnity, placing before that hearer's eyes a perfect doughnut formed with the thumb and index finger of his right hand.

"I believe and maintain—it's a *thesis* of mine, Señor de Zárate—I believe and maintain that those extraordinarily great men, *considerably* great in power and in crime, are crazy."

He was tremendously pleased with himself, and the other, who was well versed on modern topics, gleaning all his knowledge from newspapers and magazines without learning anything thoroughly, disgorged the opinions of Lombroso, Garofalo, etc., which Torquemada fully approved, appropriating them for his own use. Zárate then took up the topic of the discrepancy that often exists between ethics and genius, and cited the case of Chancellor Bacon, whom he praised to the skies for his intelligence and dragged through the mud for his conscience.

"And I suppose," he added, "that you've read the *Novum Organum.*"

"I believe I have, back when I was a boy," replied Torquemada, thinking that those "organs" must be like the ones in the church at Móstoles.

"I say that because you, in the intellectual sphere, mind you, are an extremely apt pupil of the chancellor's, but in the ethical sphere, no, mind you!"

"Ah, well, I'll tell you, my teacher was an uncle who was a priest, and he used to stuff ideas into my noggin the way you'd stuff a capon, and I'm of the opinion that my uncle had read that other fellow and knew him by heart."

In this delightful chat, time passed very sweetly, without either of the two conversationalists getting tired; and God knows how long the conference would have lasted had not Don Francisco's attention been distracted by more serious matters with which he had to deal without delay, involving other persons who had been summoned to the house for the purpose. These were Don Juan Gualberto Serrano, Morentín's father, and the marquis of Taramundi, who, along with Donoso and Torquemada, formed a conclave in the study.

When he was left alone, Zárate fell like a plague of locusts on the other groups in the house, and it is worth noting that although some people, considering him an oracle, put up with him and even listened to him with pleasure, others fled from him as from a pestilence. Cruz could not abide him, always trying to place the greatest possible distance between her person and that blessed man's torrential wisdom. Fidela and Morentín's mama had to withstand the storm, which began with Edison's phonograph and passed through Goethe's elective affinities, the same writer's theories of color, Bizet's operas, Velázquez's and Goya's paintings, decadentism, measurement of seismic movements, psychiatry, and the papal encyclical. Fidela chatted gracefully about everything, making a charming show of her ignorance as well as of her very daring personal opinions. On the other hand, the Señora de Serrano (who belonged to the Pipaón family, grafted onto the secondary branch of the Trujillos) was so short on vocabulary that she knew how to say only "entirely." For her it was a phrase made to order to express admiration, acquiescence, boredom, and even the desire to accept a cup of tea.

Cruz managed to persuade her brother Rafael to come to the sitting room, and once he was there it seemed that the poor blind man's spirits were settling down after that day's neurotic disorders. He spent the evening well entertained and even cheerful, nor did any symptom of his strange mania appear in him, which greatly reassured his friend Morentín, whom that afternoon's disturbance had filled with anxiety.

It was almost eleven o'clock when Fidela, tired out, showed a desire to leave the company. Since all were close friends, they declared abolished—with perfect unanimity, as Zárate expressed it—any sort of etiquette that might cause trouble to the owners of the house.

"Entirely," said Morentín's mama with profound conviction.

And he, after having said goodnight to Fidela, who went to her bedroom almost asleep on her feet, proposed a game of bézique to the marquise of Taramundi. It was twelve-thirty, and still the conference that the grave elders were holding in the study had not ended. What could they be talking about? The other guests knew nothing, nor in truth did they care to find out, though they suspected that it had to do with business transactions on a grand scale. When they emerged from the study, the members of the conference spoke of meeting again at Taramundi's house on the following day, and all beat a retreat. Morentín and Zárate went off, as usual, to the Café Suizo and had a conversation on the way which ought not to remain undisclosed.

"I saw you, I saw you," remarked Zárate, "doing the Lovelace. This one's not going to escape you, Pepito."

"Quit it. Rafael gave me such a bad moment! Just imagine . . ." and he described the scene in a few words. "I've had, in cases like this, some very formidable guardians, but I'd never had to deal with a blind Argus before. And that rascal can see a long way off! But with Argus or without him, I'll keep trying, as long as I don't see any danger of involving myself in scandal. After all . . . for Mama's sake, she's such a good friend."

"Entirely," replied Zárate, in whose brain the sound of that overworked adverb seemed to have stuck.

"Tell me, what do you think of complex characters?"

"Are you referring to Fidela? I don't think she's more complex than other women. All characters are complex, or polymorphous. You only see monomorphism in idiots, that is, with characters all of a piece, as they're usually employed in dramatic art, which is almost always conventional. I recommend that you read the articles I wrote for the *Revista Enciclopédica*."

"What's their title?"

"*On the Dynamic Measurement of the Passions*."

"I'll give you my word not to read them. Such intellectual reading matter is not for me."

"I take up the electrobiological problem."

"And to think that we live, and live perfectly well, without knowing all that twaddle!"

"It's because you're ignorant that you're groping your way in the matter we might call 'psychofidelian.' "

"What d'you mean?"

"Come now, stupid,"—and here both stopped in the middle of the sidewalk, with their coat collars up and their hands in their pockets—"have you read Braid?"

"And who is Braid?"

"The author of *Neurypnology*. Why, you don't know anything. Well, I assure you that I see Fidela's case as autosuggestionism. Are you laughing? Well, now, I'll bet that you haven't read Liebault either."

"No, old chap, I haven't read him, either."

"So you haven't a clue to the phenomena of inhibition, nor what we call 'dynamogeny.' "

"And what has all that farrago to do with—"

"It has to do with Fidela. Didn't you notice how she was falling asleep tonight? Well, she was in a state of hypotaxia, which some call 'enchantment' and others 'ecstasy.' "

"I only saw that the poor girl was sleepy."

"And doesn't it occur to you, you great brute, that without realizing it, you exercise a psychomesmerizing effect on her?"

"Look here, Zárate" (suddenly losing his temper), "go to the devil with your great long words, which you don't understand yourself! I hope you burst from an overdose of undigested science!"

"Witless!"

"Hopeless pedant!"

"Romancer!"

The last note of their dispute was uttered by the glass door of the café, which closed behind them with a creaking noise.

THIRTEEN

Cruz was the only person in the house who knew what Torquemada, Serrano, and Taramundi were doing those days with so much serious-ness and mystery, for her friend Donoso, who held no secrets from her, had informed her about the plans which were sure to increase fabu-lously, in a very short time, the already rich capital of the man whose fate had become linked with that of the Aguila sisters. And this news, so opportunely acquired by the lady, gave her extraordinary strength of spirit to continue opening a breach in Don Francisco's miserliness and to obtain from him the accomplishment of her plans for reform, for she was always concerned with the aggrandizement of the whole family, and especially that of its head.

Her natural courage having been strengthened by these ideas, and by another which had certainly not been Donoso's suggestion, she tackled Torquemada, catching him in his study one morning when he was most involved in the labyrinth of numbers, written on different pieces of paper, which were before him.

"What's the good word, Crucita?" said the skinflint in a tone of alarm.

"Why, I've come to tell you that we simply cannot go on living in these cramped quarters," she replied, going straight to the point, trying to intimidate him with the rapidity and energy of her attack. "I need this room, which is one of the best in the house."

"My study? But, Lord . . . Christ! Do I have to go and work in the kitchen?"

"No, señor. You will not go to the kitchen. On the third floor you have the room on the right, which isn't rented."

"The rent's worth sixteen thousand reales."

"But from now on it isn't going to bring you anything, because you're going to use it for offices."

In the face of this arrogant onslaught, Don Francisco was confused and stammering, like a bullfighter who has been knocked down and cannot quite get up off the ground.

"But, my dear, what do you mean by offices? Is this by any chance the Ministry of State, or, as they say in France, External Affairs?"

"But it is the ministry of your great affairs, my dear sir. Ah! I know all about it, and I'm glad, I'm very glad to see you moving in that direction. You'll be rolling in wealth. I promise to make good use of it, and to present you to the world with the dignity you deserve. No, you mustn't put on that innocent yokel's face, which you employ to pretend that you're ignorant of things you know quite well" (seating herself familiarly). "There are no mysteries with me. I know that you have the contract for Virginia and Kentucky tobacco, and also for Boliche. I'm well satisfied. You are a man, a great man, and I don't say it to flatter you, nor to have you thank me for the trouble I've gone to on your behalf, taking you away from a sordid and petty life to bring you into this large-scale one, so well suited to your immense mercantile talent." Torquemada listened to her stupefied. "In short, you need a very large office. Let's see: where will you keep the two clerks and the bookkeeper you mean to bring in? In my room? In the room where we store clothes?"

"But—"

"But me no buts. Begin by installing your office on the third floor, along with your private study, for it really isn't appropriate for you to receive, in front of your clients, people who come to see you about some confidential matter. The bookkeeper must have a room to himself. And the cashier's office, won't that need another room? And the telephone, the files, the copy press, and the room for the orderly? Do you see why you need space? To operate on such a grand scale and live meanly simply cannot be allowed. Is it dignified for you to have your clients waiting in the corridors, half dead with cold, like that banker whose name I can't at the moment recall? Ah! If I didn't exist, Señor Torquemada would be making a fool of himself every minute. But I won't allow it, no indeed. You are my creation" (charmingly), "my masterpiece, and sometimes I have to treat you like a little boy, and slap you, and show you good manners, and not let you play tricks."

Don Francisco was furious; but Cruz got the better of him with her arrogance, with her brutal logic, and the skinflint was unable to defend himself against her authority, which he had so often recognized.

"But—*admitting the thesis* that we do get the tobacco contract— all I've got to say is that I've been *cherishing the idea* for some time, and it might well come to something. All right, *starting from the principle* that it would be a good idea to make the study larger, wouldn't it be better if I took over the room next door?"

"No, señor. You're going upstairs with all your gear to make millions," said the lady in an authoritarian tone which came perilously close to insolence, "because I'm going to throw this room and the one next door together by pulling down the wall."

"What for, for the love of Christ?"

"To make a billiard room."

His sister-in-law's daring and expensive project made such a tremendous impression on the ruffian that he was within a hair's breadth of losing control and striking her. Indignation kept him mute and overcome with rage for a short time. He searched for a term that would be tough and at the same time courteous and, not finding one, scratched his head and slapped his knee.

"Well," he grumbled at last, rising to his feet, "I've no doubt left that you've gone crazy . . . stark raving crazy, *so to speak*. A billiard room, so's a bunch of good-for-nothings can turn my house into a café!

You know perfectly well that I don't know how to play any game . . . I *just merely* know how to work."

"But your friends, who also work, play billiards—a pleasant, honorable, and very hygienic pastime."

Don Francisco, who in those days, with gleanings from every sphere of enlightenment, had taken a fancy to hygiene and talked about it without making much sense, burst out laughing.

"Billiards hygienic? What a ridiculous thing to say! And what do billiards have to do with effluvia?"

"Whether or not they have anything to do with them, there will be a billiard room; because it is indispensable in the home of a man like you, who is destined to be a financial power of the first magnitude, of a man who will necessarily see his house invaded by bankers, senators, cabinet ministers—"

"Be quiet, be quiet. I don't need any of those *powers*. Why, I'm just a poor man scratching for a living. Come now, *let's be fair*, Crucita, and let's not lose sight of the real *objective*. It's true that I ought to show myself to advantage, and I've done that already; but not a bit of luxury, of ostentation, not a bit of showing off. Look here, at this rate we'll soon be out of house and home. And, say, d'you want me to make the living room and dining room bigger, too?"

"That too."

"Well, request denied, by Christ, and that's the end of the story. I won't take out a single brick, even though you get angry with me. Look, I've had enough. I'm the master of my house, and nobody gives orders around here except . . . yours truly. There's going to be no tearing down, *in the vernacular* expansion. Let's not aim so high, and then there'll be peace. I recognize in you a talent that's *sui generis*, but I won't hand you an advantage . . . and I'll keep the banner of economy *erect*. Period."

"If you think that you're convincing me with that show of authority," said the lady imperturbably, gradually becoming bolder, "why, what you are denying now you'll have to grant later; and what's more, you really want to do so."

"Me? That's what you think."

"Haven't you told me that you can compromise if circumstances require it?"

"Yes, but I won't compromise with losing my shirt. The most I'll do, the very most . . . Look, I say that when we have an increase in the family, I'll consent to fix up the house, not on the scale that you're asking for, but on a different scale that's more in agreement with my small means. And now we've finished with that."

"Ah, but we're just beginning, my dear Señor Don Francisco," replied Cruz, laughing, "for if you have to have hopes of an heir before I can seize the demolishing pickax, I'll have the masons come today."

"So she's already . . . !" exclaimed Torquemada, opening his eyes very wide.

"Already."

"Are you telling me officially?"

"Officially."

"All right. Now, the presence of that *desideratum*, which I felt to be a sure thing, because logic is logic, and one event brings on another event, isn't enough reason for me to authorize anybody to seize a pickax."

"But I don't forget that I have the responsibility of seeing that you live according to your means," said the lady resolutely, "and I have to be more papist than the Pope, and look out for the dignity of the household, my dear sir. No matter what happens, I have to see to it that Don Francisco Torquemada has the image in society that he deserves. And, to say it once and for all, Donoso has included you in the tobacco contract at my suggestion; and it will be because of me, make sure you know it, exclusively because of me, because of this gift I have for being in the thick of everything, that Señor Torquemada will be a senator—a senator—and will move in the sphere that is fitting to his great talent and his splendid capital."

Torquemada was not appeased even by this shower of praise, but continued to protest and grumble. But his sister-in-law had a power of suggestion over him, no doubt owing to her clever brain or habit of governing, which tamed the will of the rough skinflint, though without subduing his intelligence. He did not consider himself beaten; but when in fact he tried to reject his sister-in-law's decisions, he felt inwardly inhibited by an inexplicable compulsion. That woman with her penetrating eyes, her trembling lip, and her elegant turn of phrase, to whom there was no possible reply, had with remarkable boldness set herself up as dictator of the whole family; she was the genius of command, she was authority itself, and in a confrontation the superiority of brute force succumbed to the higher jurisdiction of the intellect.

Cruz ruled and would always rule, whatever the flock entrusted to her care; she ruled because, since the day she was born, heaven had endowed her with powerful energies, and because by battling with her fate during long years of poverty, those energies had been tempered and strengthened until they were colossal, irresistible. She was government, diplomacy, administration, religious dogma, armed forces, and moral force, and against this combination of authorities or principles the wretches who came under her iron rule were helpless.

At last the lady retired from Don Francisco's study with a dictatorial flourish, and he remained there, exercising, to the serious detriment of the carpets, his right to kick them furiously, and venting his anger with a spate of gross expressions.

"Cursed be your soul forever and ever, amen, dammit! By Christ, at this rate, before long they'll leave me mother-naked. Damn, why did I let that *element* into my house, and why didn't I bust my halter when I saw they were pulling on it? And they can't say, mind you, that I don't treat them well, or that I let them go hungry. Certainly not, mind you! Hunger, never. Economy, always. But this lady, she's prouder than Napoleon, why can't she let me run my house the way I want to and according to my own flipping logic? Damn her, how she has to rule, and how she gets me under her thumb, leaves me unable to act, *just merely* bewitched! I don't know what that freak has, she leaves me breathless; I want to breathe in defense of my interests, and I can't, and when she's through with me I'm like a child. And now she wants to sweet-talk me with the coincidence that there's going to be an heir! That's a hot one! Why, I knew that was a certainty, with a hundred thousand pairs of dammits! Why, it's my own son who's coming back, because I wanted him to, and because it was decreed by the Most High, or the Most Low, or whoever it was! Despot, boss-woman, *grand-vizier-lady* and captain-generaless of all the administration in the world, some fine day I'm going to get my good sense back, I'll get unenchanted, and I'll grab a stick . . ." (tearing his hair). "Oh, what kind of a stick will I grab, wretch that I am, if I'm afraid of her, and when I see that her lip's trembling I'll already be hiding under the table! The stick I'll grab will be St. Joseph's staff, because I'm a good fellow and all I'm good for is to put together numbers and get money out from under stones. That's a talent nobody can take away from me. But she's better than I am at running things, and at inventing argu-ments that leave a fellow senseless. I've never seen any female as smart, nor do I think there's another one under the sun. But who did I marry, anyway, Fidela or Cruz, or both at once? Because if one of them is, properly speaking, my wife—with respect—the other is my tyrant, and tyranny and women, both together, are what this devilish marriage machine is made of. Well, on with the dance, and let's live to earn the blessed penny, which I'll put away where my illustrious, my respectable, my aristocratic . . . consorts . . . can't get a whiff of it."

ONE

Everything planned and ordered by the person representing irresistible intelligence and will in the internal government of Torquemada's house was carried out, nor could the skinflint's grumblings prevent it, for he was impotent to struggle against his sister-in-law's fierce resolution; nor did the show of passive resistance prevail with which he attempted to delay, if not to stop, installation of the counting room and offices on the third floor of the house, thus depriving him of a handsome rental income. But Cruz swept all before her when she said "I'm off!" and in four days, with herself as foreman, and contractor, and architect, the remodeling was finished; and Don Francisco himself, while grunting and protesting in the bosom of the family, declared it good in the presence of outsiders.

"It's an idea of mine," he would say, showing his friends the spacious counting room. "I've always liked to work with space to spare, and to make my employees comfortable. Hygiene has always been one of my *objectives.* Just see what a fine study I have . . . and this other room, for people who want to speak to me privately. On the other side—just step this way—is the room for the bookkeeper and the copying press . . . the two clerks, in there . . . then, the telephone . . . I've always been in favor of modern improvements, and even before they brought us this fancy invention I felt that there ought to be some way to send and receive messages over long distances. Now look at the cashier's department. What independence! What convenience of operations! *I profess the theory* that, just because times are so bad, and business isn't what it used to be, a fellow has to work hard, and open up new sources, and take in a lot of territory, which can't be done without establishing oneself according to modern demands. That's the way I always *propend*; and since I know what those demands make necessary, I've decided to spread out both upstairs and downstairs, for society demands comforts for our own sake as well as hers. We must sacrifice ourselves for our friends, and though I've never had a cue in my hand, I've decided to install a billiard table in my house—lovely thing. The table is really elegant and cost me a pretty penny. Since I'm the one who makes all the decisions in the house, from the most *considerable* to the most minimal, I've spent a few days with everything topsy-turvy—"

Crucita's entrance made him break off, silencing the garrulity with which he expressed himself when he was far removed from her authoritarian and despotic person. But the lady, who with exquisite tact knew how to conceal her power over him in public, as she took the words of the master of the house out of his mouth, employed them in this diplomatic form:

"Well, now you can see the dance our Don Francisco has led us. A billiard room and reception rooms downstairs, offices here. What an upheaval, what confusion! But at last it's done, and as quickly as possible. Just think; it was his idea, and he oversaw the work himself. You can see that he's a man of initiative and that he likes to be exceptional, and distinguish himself nobly. As he says, 'You can't operate on a grand scale and live on a small one.' This Don Francisco is quite a person. May God give him health to turn his plans into realities. We sisters help him, we try to help him, but oh, dear, we're of so little use! We're used to a modest existence, and would prefer to live and die in a corner. He sweeps us by main force to the lofty sphere of his vast ideas. No, don't say it's not true, my friend. Everyone knows that you are modesty personified. He hides his talents. . . But those tricks of his—the tricks of an extraordinary man whose point of pride is to be taken for an ordinary one—don't work. Is what I'm saying the truth or isn't it? Superior intelligences glory in supreme humility."

Needless to say, these words were received with a chorus of assent, followed by another of praise for the great man and his multiple aptitudes. But he, making a show of false laughter and putting on the bewildered-yokel face that he held in readiness for these occasions, inwardly heaped curses on his tyrant, blaming her with all the weight of his anger for the bills he was having to pay to carpenters, masons, furniture dealers, and other *leeches of the rich*, in addition to the loss of rent for the third floor. And after their friends had seen the entire remodeling job, repeating downstairs in Fidela's and Cruz's presence all the hyperbole they had uttered upstairs, once he was alone in his room, the usurer let off steam with a number of kicks and an equal number of imprecations under his breath:

"How that puffed up know-it-all bosses me around! And the fact is, she has such a gift of gab that you fall for it and it drives you crazy . . . because she's sucking the marrow out of my bones with her sweet-talk, and she doesn't let me do what I damn well want to, which is to economize. What a piece of bad luck has hit me! To earn so much *dough* and not to be able to use every bit of it in new business deals, so that I could see such a big pile, such a big pile of . . . ! But with this house, and with these ladies of mine, my cashboxes are as leaky as a basket. The money comes in on one side and goes out in a thousand places, all because of a supposition, because of this crazy notion that I'm a *power*. To hell with the mania of being a power! And how about the bright idea she and my friend Donoso came up with last night, that they're going to make me a senator *velis nolis*? I, I, Francisco Torquemada, a senator, and on top of that, Grand Cross of the Most Worthy Whatsit! Good Lord, I'd do better to laugh at it and then, in defense of my pocketbook, let them do whatever they like, including setting me up like a straw man to advertise their vanity to the whole world."

Summoned by Fidela, he had to tear himself away from his meditations. They showed him samples of material for portieres, for floor coverings and carpets. But he refused to choose anything, delegating his sumptuary opinions to the two ladies and saying merely that he would prefer whatever was most reasonable in price. At last he and Don Juan Gualberto Serrano rushed out of the house toward the Ministry. The Ministry! How well he was received there, and how he enjoyed going! And not because the servility of the doormen flattered him (for when they saw him come in with Donoso they rushed at the doors as if trying to open them with their heads); nor was it the flattering friendliness of lower-grade employees, who sought opportunities to serve him, attracted by the odor of wealth that emanated from his person. He was not vain, nor did he give importance to futile external details. In that administrative hive he was chiefly delighted by the queen bee, *in the vernacular* the minister, a man who, because he was unprepossessing in manner, highly practical, not an easy speaker, and very confident in his management of numbers, resembled our skinflint

in ideas and character, for he too was the skinflint of the public treasury, a merciless collector, nemesis of the taxpayer, in whom he always saw an enemy to be resolutely pursued and harassed. This man
had not made his political career exclusively by speech; he was, rather,
a man of action, in the sense that bureaucratic formalities can be
considered action. He and Donoso behaved toward each other with
the familiarity of old colleagues, and Don Juan Gualberto Serrano addressed him in the familiar form, a sign of old acquaintance dating
from their primary studies. After the third or fourth private conversation with his cronies and the minister, Torquemada succeeded in
overcoming the timidity he had felt in the early days, and very soon
was as much at ease in His Excellency's study as in his own home. He
was exceedingly careful about everything he said, so as not to let slip
some grammatical blunder, and very soon observed that, thanks to his
dexterity and discretion, none of those present, including the minister,
spoke better than he did. This was in general conversation, for when
business was being discussed he was far ahead of the rest of them,
presenting questions with clarity and precision, using unadorned figures with inescapable logic; nor could he be successfully contradicted
by anyone. To achieve this the skinflint spoke as little as possible,
avoiding offering his opinion on any subject that was not in his *field
of competence*; but if the conversation entered the area of parsimony,
now on a small scale, now on a large or financial one, our man enlarged upon the subject, and everyone listened to him open-mouthed.

The result of all this was that the minister saw in him special aptitudes for managing interest, and though he was a man little given
to flattery, heaped compliments and praise upon him, with the pecu-
liarity that he was wont to employ the same terms that Cruz used
when she wished to play hob with the household budget. You would
have thought that the lady and the minister had made a pact to soft-
soap him, the difference being that she did it with the perverse intention of spending his returns on vanities and fripperies, while the other
offered him all the increase in earnings compatible with the interests
of the State.

To speak plainly and forthrightly, be it known that the minister,
whose name is superfluous here, was an extremely honorable man,
and that his defects (for, being a man, he had to have some faults)
were not those of greed or desire for personal gain. No one had ever

been able to accuse him of exploiting his position in order to get rich. In his vicinity, no sharp practices occurred with his consent; those who grew richer than was reasonable were sent off to manage as best they could in a sphere inferior to the office and tertulia of His Majesty's councillor. As for Donoso, we are well aware that he was of impeccable integrity, a man of formula, to be sure, and a rabid proponent of administrative orthodoxy, to the point that his honorableness and scrupulosity had caused not a few victims. He did not become rich, but he would have set fire to half of Spain to save the Treasury money. The same could not be said of Don Juan Gualberto, a man whose conscience was so elastic that many droll things were told of him, some of which must be withheld, for their very enormity makes them unconvincing. He never looked out for the State, which he considered to be a great *son of a*—; he always looked out for private interests, either in the essential concept of the "I myself" or in an altruistic and humanitarian form, such as protecting a friend, defending a company, business establishment, or any sort of entity. The fact is that in the five famous years of the Liberal Union's existence, he achieved considerable wealth, and then that pesky revolution and the Carlist War completed the job of feathering his nest. If we are to believe what malicious gossip said, both verbally and in print, Serrano had swallowed up whole pine forests, many square leagues of pine trees, all at one gulp, with his fabulous stomach. And, to get rid of the overload, he had amused himself (following the adage about the devil finding work for idle hands) by supplying to soldiers shoes with cardboard soles, or giving them moldy beans and rotten codfish to eat; little pranks which, at most, at the very most, raised a bit of noise in a few newspapers; and owing to the mischievous coincidence that those newspapers did not have the best reputation for truth-telling, because they had written a great many lies about that campaign, no one thought of carrying the matter to a formal inquiry by the courts, nor did the possibility of such an inquiry cause any fear whatsoever in Don Juan Gualberto, who was a first cousin of various directors-general, a brother-in-law of judges, a nephew of magistrates, and a more or less close relative of an infinite number of generals, senators, councillors, and grand panjandrums.

Therefore, in the meetings we are talking about, the only one who spoke of morality was Serrano. While the others never even thought about that fancy word, it was constantly on Don Juan Gualberto's lips, and he was wont to say:

"For we, be it understood, represent and try to represent a great principle, a new principle. We are here to fulfill a mission and to fill a vacuum, the mission and vacuum of introducing morality into tobacco contracts. *Both Greeks and Trojans* know that until now . . ." (Here he painted a horrific picture of such contracts in the *now-past historical moment.*) "Well, from now on, if our plans merit the approval of His Majesty's Government, taking into account the reliability and respectability of the persons who are placing their intelligence and their capital at their country's service, that service, that income, will be established upon bases . . . upon bases . . ."

Here the orator got stuck, and Don Francisco had to finish his sentence for him as follows:

"*Under* the basis of honest business and total disclosure, as you might say, for we *propend* toward profit for ourselves as much as we can—within the law, mind you!—and profiting the government more than *both Greeks and Trojans* have done before, be they called Juan, Pedro, or Diego, without *Machiavellianisms* on our part, but without allowing *Machiavellianisms* on the government's part either, giving a pull here, slackening there, with the *objective* of *skirting* the difficulties and *discharging* our business, within the strictest interest and the strictest morality—everything very *strict*, as you might say—for I uphold the thesis that *the viewpoint of morality* is not incompatible with *the viewpoint of business.*

THREE

Simply because he had entered that broad terrain of large-scale business, finding himself dealing openly with the State itself, Don Francisco did not abandon the murky transactions—one might rather say underground transactions—in which our man had been engaging since his apprentice days, when, in confabulation with Doña Lupe, he had occupied himself with personal loans at interest rates that would have swept into their coffers all the hard cash in the world if anyone had paid them with strict punctuality. In his new life he turned down several sharp dealings of a dirty and dishonest kind, for it wasn't the thing to get mixed up in such operations when a fellow considered himself a gentleman and a person of circumstance; but he maintained others religiously, because he saw no reason to throw out of the window the beautiful *liquid cash* they brought him. But he was secretive about them, hiding them as one hides a shameful defect or revolting deformity, and did not speak openly even to Donoso on this subject, so sure was he that his good friend would look unkindly on him when he found out—what the reader is going to find out right now—that Don Francisco Torquemada was the owner of six pawnshops, the most central and best-regarded in Madrid; and I say "best-regarded" because they offered cash promptly and for a fairly long term at the rate of one real per duro monthly, that is, at sixty percent a year. He was absolute owner of four of them, with day-to-day operations carried on by an employee who had a share in the earnings, and in two of them a capitalist partner, collecting fifty percent. What with one and another, our man salted away the trifling sum of a thousand duros a month with no more effort than that of examining a worn and ill-written account book for each establishment.

To examine these squalid accounts and inform himself about the progress of the undertaking, he would shut himself in his study for a couple of mornings each month with the individuals who ran the *establishments*. To explain the mystery, he invented any number of stories which for some time deceived all the members of the family, until at last Cruz, with her shrewdness and keen nose, by dint of studying the appearance of those types, tying up loose ends, unexpectedly discovering some aspect and guessing the rest, uncovered the whole enigma. The skinflint, who was also clever at certain things and had a bloodhound's sense of smell, instantly perceived that his sister-in-law had torn away the disguise, and awaited her more dead than alive with fear, expecting the attack that must surely come in the name of morality, of decorum, and other trifles of the same sort.

Indeed, having chosen a favorable occasion, she confronted him one morning in his study on the third floor, without witnesses. Every time he saw her come in, Don Francisco trembled, for on all her visits, Cruz brought some tale to mortify him and rip him to pieces. The sly creature was like a ghost who appeared before him just when he was most unconcerned and happy. She rose as from a trapdoor, upsetting him with her grave smile, leaving him stripped of ideas and opinions, quite speechless. Such was the dominating power of her face and ideas.

That morning she entered on cat feet; he did not see her until she was in front of his desk. Sure of the fascination she exercised, the tyrant used no preamble; she went straight to the point, always with courteous and flattering expressions, at times affecting familiarity and fondness, at other times resolutely stripping off the mask and showing her despotic countenance, whose tragic beauty made Don Francisco's hair stand on end.

"You know already what I've come for. No, don't play the yokel with me. You are very clever, very quick-witted, and you can't pretend that I don't know . . . what I know. Why, I can see it in your face. The knowledge is oozing out through every pore."

"Damned if I know what you want to tell me, Crucita."

"Yes, you do. Bah, to try to fool me with such tricks! There's no use trying to hide things from me. Don't be frightened. Do you think I'm going to scold you? No, señor, I understand how things are, I understand that one can't break off routines all at once, or change one's habits in a short time. However, let's speak plainly: that sort of business is unsuitable to the position you now occupy. I won't argue about whether or not it was legitimate at other times in your life. I respect history, my dear sir, and respect unworthy ways of earning money when it wasn't easy to do so in any other way. I admit that what was had to be as it was; but today, Señor Don Francisco, today, when you need not lower yourself—take note of what I said—lower yourself to such a vile terrain, why don't you sell the leases of those . . . establishments, leaving them in the dirty hands that were born to occupy them? Your hands are nice and clean now, and you yourself realize as much. The proof that you feel degraded by this business lies in the secrecy you're trying to wrap it in. Ever since you married, you've been playing this comedy so that we won't find out about it. Well, your efforts at secrecy have come to nothing, and here I am, well aware of everything, without anyone's having said a word to me."

The ruffian did not dare defend himself with a flat negative, and, striking the table with his fist, confessed openly.

"So? Is there anything special about this *expedient?* Am I going to throw my profits out the window? You tell me to sell them! But how? For some ridiculous amount? I'll never do that. When a fellow's earned what he's earned with the sweat of his brow, he doesn't sell at a loss. Now then, my fine lady, we've talked enough."

"Don't lose your temper, for there's no reason to. No one knows this, Fidela does not suspect it, and you may be easy in your mind, I'm not going to tell her. If she were to find out, the poor girl would be terribly upset. Donoso doesn't know it either."

"Well, let him know it, dammit, let him know it!"

"It may be that some busybody has taken the tale to him, but he wouldn't have believed it. He has such a high opinion of his friend that he doesn't listen to any of the calumnies that are told about you, placed in circulation by those who envy your prosperity. No one but myself knows about these sordid dealings of your past, and if you insist on continuing them, I will keep the secret, I will even help you to keep it, for myself and the family, the shame that attaches to all of us."

"All right, all right," said Torquemada impatiently, feverishly, feeling an urge to pick up the heavy inkwell and heave it at his tyrant's head, "now we know. I'm master of my affairs and I'll do what I please with them."

"That seems fair to me, and I will not be the one to oppose it. How can I oppose it when I look out for your interests more than you do yourself? Very well. Even though you pay no attention to me when I suggest that you cleanse yourself of that leprosy of vile usurious moneylending, I will continue to offer you, with the help of our friend Donoso, business dealings that are as clean as a whistle, business that offers as much honor as profit. I repay evil with good. It doesn't matter to me if you squeal in protest when I try to lead you along the way of righteousness; whether you like it or not, the righteous road is the one you must take. Why, in the end you'll be convinced that I am your oracle! And you'll have no choice but to follow my inspirations, and you'll end up by not even breathing without my permission."

She said this last so charmingly that the ruffian could not help bursting into laughter, though anger still sparkled in his eyes. The lady abruptly turned the conversation in another direction, coming out with what the skinflint least suspected.

"By the way," she told him, "although I'm very much put out with you because you value your old conduct as a moneylender more than the decorum of your present position, I'm going to give you a piece of good news. You don't deserve it; but I'm so good, so compassionate, that I will repay your bites with a hug, a moral hug, and if you like with a kiss, a moral kiss, mind you!"

"What is it, what is it?"

"Then let Señor Don Francisco be informed that I've found a buyer for the land you own out there in Ventas del Espíritu Santo."

"Why, I already had a buyer for it, my girl! A fine piece of news Doña Crucita is giving me."

"Simpleton, I know what I'm talking about! The buyer to whom you refer is Cristóbal Medina, who offers one and one-fourth reales per foot."

"That's right; and I'm holding off giving it to him, waiting till somebody offers me two reales."

"A lovely piece of business. You bought that land, that is, it was made over to you on a debt, at the rate of two hundred-odd pesetas per fanega."

"Correct."

"And last week, Cristóbal Medina offered you a real and a half per foot and I . . . I, at *the present historical moment*, offer you two reales."

"You!"

"No, my dear man, don't be materialistic. What could I offer? Am I going to build houses on it?"

"Ah! Your friend, that Torres? I get it, he's an enterprising chap, hardworking as can be. I like him, I like that fellow."

"Well, last night I saw him at the Taramundis'. We talked: he told me that he has no objection to taking all the land at two reales a foot, paying one-third down in cash and securing payment of the other two-thirds by a note to be paid on the dates agreed upon, as construction progresses. In short, he's writtten me this letter, in which he sets forth his proposition and adds that if you agree, the deal is made as far as he is concerned."

"Here, let's see the letter," said Torquemada, uneasy and eager, grabbing out of Cruz's hands the letter which she, with the coquetry of a woman doing business, held out to him.

And he rapidly scanned the four sides of the folded sheet, assimilating *in a brief historical moment* the principal points it contained. "Payment in cash of one-third . . . Construction of a palace surrounded by gardens to be called 'Villa Torquemada,' which, on an architect's valuation, will be offered as payment for the second third . . . Mortgage on the land itself to guarantee the third payment, etcetera . . ."

"And don't I deserve a brokerage fee for acting in this business?" asked Cruz gaily.

"The business, though it's not considerable, isn't bad, no, *as a general thesis.* I'll read it at leisure, I'll make my calculations."

"Don't I even deserve to have the name of Torquemada, now united to the house and name of Aguila, erased from the wretched placard that says 'Pawnshop' "?

"But what's that got to do with . . . Bah! You see risks where none exist. That business is as honorable as any other, as much so as the very reverend Bank of Spain. The difference consists in the fact that you don't see pawned capes hanging in the magnificent windows of the bank. My word, what importance you give to appearances! They're your *beau ideal.* I keep an eye out, not for appearances, but for substance."

"Then I'll tell Torres to give up the deal about the land, for you're a regular shylock and will play some trick on him. Why, when I want to be disagreeable, I can be really disagreeable. You don't know what you have to deal with in me. Either we follow the constitutional path, that is, the path of decorum, or we'll have seven quarrels every day."

"Crucita of all the devils, and the almighty Bible, and the Bible in verse, and the double-damnation of the archipelago . . . I mean the archpanjandrum of Seville! Don't you say anything to Torres except that he's to see me this very afternoon, because his proposition suits me down to the ground and I want us to negotiate and come to an understanding."

"Very well, my dear sir. Calm yourself. Sit down. Don't pound the table until it breaks, for you'll have to buy a new one, and you'll lose money."

"It's just that you don't let me live the way I want to. *To recapitulate:* I'll cover up the matter of the pawnshops."

"No matter how much you cover it up, the business will still smell bad. Sell them, I said."

"Keep cool, now. *Let's be fair.* We'll have to wait for a good opportunity. We'll compromise. Look, let me keep on for a while with that

. . . with that *vineyard*, and I'll agree to let you have the season ticket that, on account of . . . I mean, because they're in mourning, the Medinas are giving up at the Prince Alfonso Theater."

"But we've already taken the season tickets."

"Without my permission?"

"Without your permission. Don't pull your hair; if you do you'll go bald. It was outrageous that you wouldn't give permission, when Fidela likes it so much. The poor girl needs to spread her wings, hear good music, see her friends."

"Curses on the opera and the dog who invented it. Crucita, don't put any more pressure on me. Look, I'm about to explode and . . . I can't stand any more of this. You're dragging me down to bankruptcy. It's no use my working like a slave, because every coin I earn is a coin the two of you spend on trinkets and gewgaws. To curb my ladies Aguila, I'd have to make them a deal of the following *tenor:* give them the season ticket, yes, but deducting it from their board and clothing."

"That can't be, for we're not going to go to the theater with empty stomachs, or dressed like freaks."

"It's no good, no good, you're ruining me. Because the season ticket at the Opera brings on thousands and thousands of expenses—*in the vernacular,* fancy jewelry, gloves, I don't know what-all. Very well, my girls, very well; some fine day I'll have to pawn my overcoat. That's the direction we're going in."

"The day you have to do that," said Cruz gaily, "I'll take in sewing."

"No, don't joke about it. If things go on at this rate, my life will be mighty short . . . and I tell you, I can't guarantee to maintain the family."

"I'll maintain it. I know how to live without having anything to live on."

"Then you could live today the way you did back then."

"Circumstances have changed, and we're rich now."

"We have a reasonable income—*let's be fair*—a good income."

"So, I take that into account, and try to have us live well."

"Leave me alone, for God's sake. Your . . . manifestations are driving me crazy."

"Remember what I've said. Prepare yourself for another one," said the firstborn Aguila, smiling and proud, preparing to depart.

"For another . . . ! By blessed San Caralampio, who defends us against mothers-in-law! For you really are a mother-in-law, *so to speak*, and the worst and most unbearable one in the whole human family."

"And what I have waiting for you is the biggest thing of all, my dear son-in-law."

"Holy Virgin, be with me. What is it?"

"The time's not ripe yet. The victim is worn out by today's temper tantrum. Despite the fact that I brought him the wonderful deal about the land. And the rascal isn't even grateful to me!"

"Yes, I am. But look here, tell me what new bite you're going to take out of me."

"No, because you'd take fright. Another day. Today I'm satisfied with the season ticket and the hope of getting rid of the ignominy of the pawnshops. Some other day we'll continue, my Señor Don Francisco Torquemada, presumptive Senator of the Realm and Grand Cross of Charles III."

And when he saw her leave the skinflint cursed her under his breath, at the same time as he recognized, with brutal sincerity, her absolute control over him.

THREE

It was not for motives of fleeting vanity that Cruz del Aguila desired the pomps of aristocratic life, but for those of noble ambition, for she wished to encompass with prestige and honor the obscure man who had rescued the illustrious ladies from poverty. She really had no ambitions for herself; but the family must recover its rank and, if it was possible, aspire to a higher position than that of former times, to confound those envious souls who commented on its social resurrection with vulgar jests. Cruz proceeded in this plan with pride of breeding, as a person who looks out for the dignity of her people, and also with a feeling of lofty vengeance against relatives she loathed, who after having denied them help during their period of penury, now tried to make her and her sister look as ridiculous as possible because of the marriage with the moneylender. By raising him high and making the man into a personage, and the personage into an eminence, she and her sister would be winning the game, and the darts of slander would turn against those who had thrown them.

When the marriage became public knowledge, naturally there were the inevitable comments among the Aguilas' former friends and among their relatives, both those residing in Madrid and in the provinces. And there were even a few who, after the first surprise, made charitable comments about the matter; there were some who took it as comical, treating it like a music-hall turn, and the most implacable of all were that blessed cousin of theirs, Pilar de la Torre Auñón, and her husband, Pepe Romero, with whom Fidela and Cruz had long been on bitter terms owing to family squabbles, which took a turn toward legendary hatred when the Romero in question assumed the court-ordered administration of the two estates in Córdoba, "El Salto" and "La Alberquilla." Well, when they learned that Torquemada was buying back the estates, placing them in more favorable conditions in the probable case that the court of disputed claims would return them to their owners, the Romeros raised their hands in horror and promptly began to rain insults in very bad taste upon the unfortunate ladies. It must be added that Pilar de la Torre Auñón's husband had two brothers, one married to the niece of the marquis of Cícero and the other to a sister of the marquise of San Salomó. They were, moreover, relatives of the count of Monte Cármenes, of Severiano Rodríguez, and of Don Carlos de Cisneros. Pepe Romero and Pilar de la Torre lived in Córdoba, but, along with the other Romeros, spent the autumn months and sometimes part of the winter in Madrid. It is easy to understand that the poisoned darts against the poor Aguilas and the idiot who had freed them from poverty emanated from the house where all this group of Romeros was gathered.

Because Madrid, though fairly populous, is small when it comes to the circulation of injurious gossip, it all became known, and there was no lack of officious women friends to carry to Cruz, one by one, all the nasty slanders that were being forged in the Romeros' tertulias. And in these gatherings there was invariably someone who knew, either by sight or hearsay, Torquemada the Worse, a man notorious in certain unwholesome and turbid areas of society. Villalonga and Severiano Rodríguez, who knew of him through their unfortunate friend Federico Viera, described him as a regular musical-comedy usurer, as a grotesque and dismal being who drank blood and smelled bad. Some said that the haughty and selfish Cruz had sacrificed her poor sister, selling her for a mess of pottage; others that the two ladies, in association with that sinister individual, intended to establish a pawnshop on the Calle de la Montera. The most remarkable thing was that when Torquemada, by the months of February and March, began to frequent the houses of the *grand monde*, and many of those who had positively flayed him alive did not find him either as grotesque or as horrible as legend had painted him, this opinion gave rise to great polemics about the fellow's authenticity. "No, he can't be that Torquemada of the southern quarters of the city," said some. "Either he's a different one or we'll have to believe in reincarnation."

As Don Francisco began to make a place for himself in society, these whispers lost their asperity and gradually died down, for little by little the skinflint was gaining partisans and even admirers. But a nest of malicious gossip always remained: the intimate circle of the Romeros, who did not forgive and would never forgive, for the proud Cruz tried to ruin them every time she got the chance.

This was the reason why the noble lady tried in every way to ennoble the man who was her creation and her masterpiece, the yokel turned townsman, the savage transformed into a person, the vampire of the poor made into an important financier, as decent and ostentatious as any of the others who suck the State's colorless blood and the blue blood of the rich.

And what things the Romeros said about him and about them, even after Don Francisco had gained the superficial admiration of many people, who saw nothing but the external aspect! That all the money he had was the product of the vilest rapine and cruel usury . . . That he had filled the cemeteries of Madrid with suicides . . . That all those who jumped off the Viaduct pronounced his execrable name just as they took the tumble . . . That Cruz del Aguila also engaged in money-lending on used clothing in good condition, and that she had the whole house filled with capes . . . That the man had not given up his cheese-paring habits, and that he kept the poor Aguila sisters on a diet of lentils and fried blood . . . That all the jewels that Fidela wore came from the pawnshop . . . That Cruz made Don Francisco's frock coats out of dead men's clothes, which she turned for him . . . That Cruz had a share in almost all the booths in the flea market, and dealt in old shoes and broken-down furniture . . . That Fidela, whose innocence bordered on imbecility, did not know the origins of that clown they had given her as a husband . . . That, despite her simplemind-

edness, she allowed herself the luxury of three or four lovers, that her
sister knew about it and winked at it, and that they were Morentín,
Donoso (at his sixty years of age), Manolo Infante, and a certain
Argüelles Mora, a grotesque type resembling a gentleman of Philip IV's
time and a bookkeeper in Torquemada's office. Zárate and the little
footman, Pinto, were involved with the older sister . . . That she cut
Don Francisco's nails, washed his face, smoothed his shirt collar every
morning before she launched him on the street, to make him look
respectable, and taught him how to greet people, instructing him in
everything he had to say, according to circumstances. . . That secretly
Cruz and the usurer between them had positively stripped a number
of noble families who were a bit hard up, by lending them money at
two hundred and forty percent . . . That Cruz collected the cigarette
butts of those who smoked in her house to send to the flea market in
an enormous basket, and that she also collected bread scraps to sell to
some people who made chocolate, the cheap kind that costs two and
a half reales. . . That Fidela dressed dolls on special order for toy shops,
and that poor Rafael was given only pap to eat, and a plate of broth
at night . . . That the blind man had put a cartridge of dynamite or
gunpowder under the bed of the married pair, which was discovered
with the fuse already lighted . . . That the eldest Aguila, among other
dirty business dealings, owned part of a garbage dump in Cuatro Caminos, and got half the pigs and chickens as her share . . . That Torquemada bought Cuban bonds at three and a half percent of their
value, and that his was the money behind a company of swindlers,
disguised with the label of Redemption from Military Service and Sub-
stitutes for Overseas.

All this gradually reached the ears of Cruz, who, although she was
indignant at first, passing some very miserable hours and shedding a
few tears, at last came to the point of accepting it with philosophical
calm; and when Don Francisco went out into the great world with his
frock coat of English cut, his manners really quite easy, his speech
fluent and his personality surrounded by a certain amount of respect,
rubbing elbows after all with cabinet ministers and gentlemen of influence, the lady was eventually able to laugh at her relatives' spiteful
outbursts. But while such stupid malevolence caused her to scorn them
all the more, she felt an even greater desire to smash them flat and
flaunt under their very noses the real opulence of the resuscitated

Aguilas and the obvious prestige of the "opulent capitalist," for that was what the flatterers now called him. And so they would keep on nipping at her, and she would continue to rise, or rather to raise the puppet that overshadowed them, until she had built him an enormous tower from which the Aguilas could gaze upon the Romeros as miserable little worms trailing their slime along the ground.

FOUR

Summer was approaching, and there was nothing to do but think of going to some cool place, at least for the dog days. A new battle was begun by Cruz, in which she found the enemy more resistant and emboldened than usual.

"Summer," Don Francisco was wont to say, "is the season *par excellence* in Madrid. I've spent my whole life here, and I take to it perfectly. A fellow's never more comfortable than in July and August, free of colds, eating well, sleeping better."

"About yourself I have nothing to say," objected the lady, "for among the many gifts with which you were endowed by Divine Providence, you also have the gift of health that is proof against extremes of temperature. Nor do I say it for myself, because I adjust to everything. But Fidela cannot spend the summer months here, and you are a ruffian if you allow her to."

"My poor Silvia, may she be in heaven, was also bothered by *calorific* weather, especially when she was in the last months, and we stuck it out here. With the earthenware water jug always cool, the balconies shut during the day and a little stroll at ten o'clock at night, we had us a fine time. There'll be no thinking about going away for the summer, my lady. I can compromise with anything but that *inveterate* foolishness of sea bathing, or river bathing, that is the *encumbrance* of so many families. Everybody's going to stay in Madrid because I have to stay in Madrid, fine gentleman though I am, to organize this folderol of the tobacco, which, by the way, doesn't seem to be such a straightforward business as your friends described it to me in the beginning. And you're not to mention the subject again. This time I won't give in. So—ting-a-ling—meeting adjourned."

Cruz, determined that the trip would take place, did not insist that day; but on the next, Fidela having been well instructed, Don Francisco's redoubt of avarice was attacked with such overpowering force that in the end he had no choice but to surrender.

"I'm giving in very much against my will," said the skinflint, chewing the ends of his mustache and assuming a martyred air, "to make Fidela happy. But let's be reasonable. We're not going away for more than twenty or thirty days, mind you! And all of it, my lady, will have to be done with as little expenditure as possible. We're in no shape to put on princely airs. We'll travel second class."

"But Don Francisco!"

"Second class, with a round-trip ticket."

"That's impossible. Goodness, I'll have to take command. In second class! It is intolerable for you to forget the decorum of your name to such a degree. Leave everything connected with the trip to me. We won't go to San Sebastián or Biarritz, which are places of ostentation and show; we'll install ourselves modestly in a little house in Hernani. I've already spoken for it."

"Ah! So you, all on your own, had arranged . . . ?"

"All on my own. And for all of that, and a great deal more which I'll keep to myself for now, you have reason to be grateful to me. So hush."

"But—"

"I'm saying that we'll speak no more about it, and that I'll take care of everything. Now, if it were left to you, we'd travel in the dog kennel. That's a fine way to respond to public opinion, which sees you as—"

"What does it see, what can it see in me, dammit to hell! but a poor fellow, a martyr to your fancy ideas, a man who's a prisoner here, with fetters and handcuffs, and who can't live in his element, that is, saving money . . . the *mere* economy of the penny that a fellow earns with his blessed sweat?"

"Hypocrite . . . joker! Why, you don't spend one-tenth of what you make," answered the autocrat spiritedly. "You've got to spend more, lots more. Start preparing yourself, for I'm going to be implacable."

"Kill me and be done with it, for I'm such a fool that I don't know how to resist you, and I let you strip me and beat me and flay me alive."

"Now we're starting again. And I warn you that your children will take after me, I mean they'll take after their mother. They will be Aguilas, and they'll have all of my personality, and my thoughts."

"My son an Aguila!" exclaimed Torquemada, beside himself. "My son to think the way you do . . . my son stripping me of everything I own! Oh! Señora, leave me in peace, and don't utter such heresies, because I don't know . . . I feel capable of . . . Leave me alone, I say. This is too much. I'm blinded, my blood's going to my head."

"Goodness, how foolish! Why, what more could you want?" said the lady, observing him smilingly and maliciously from the door. "He'll be an Aguila . . . pure Aguila. We'll see . . . we'll see."

Don Francisco could put up with anything save the thought that his son-to-be would be a different person from Valentín himself, reincarnated and returned to the world in his pristine form and character, so sensible and gentle, with all the talent in the world for mathematics. And the poor simpleton believed this so firmly that if Cruz had insisted on her joke, the spell that held his will subject to hers would certainly have been broken, and the miser, regaining his freedom, would have laid a vengeful hand on the tyrant who tormented him. The idea drove him quite wild. His son, his Valentín, an Aguila instead of that lovely little Torquemada who was wandering around in glory awaiting his new departure for the world of the living! No, jokes could go so far and no further. He spent the whole of that afternoon sunk in sad meditation about the matter, and at night, after working all alone in his study upstairs, he went into his private sitting room on the same floor, where he kept the chest of drawers we have encountered before and upon it the boy's photograph, though it was now completely divested of its appearance as an altar. Striding from one corner of the room to the other, the usurer gave all the twists and turns imaginable to the idea so unfortunately expressed by his sister-in-law.

"My word, to say that you're going to be an Aguila! Did you ever see such insolence?"

He looked fixedly at the portrait and the portrait said nothing; that is, its sad little face expressed no more than a silent and prudent concern. Since his papa's social and financial success had increased, Valentinico spoke very little and, as a rule, responded with only a yes or a no to Don Francisco's questions, though it is true that he no longer spent his nights in that room, battling against invincible insomnia or the fever of numbers.

"Can't you hear what I'm telling you? That you'll be an Aguila. That's right" (believing that he saw a slight negative indication on the portrait's face), "you won't. Of course; that's what I said. What that fine lady is thinking about is perfectly absurd."

He returned to his study and spent more than half an hour casting up accounts, thereby heating his brain. Suddenly, the numbers that were before his eyes began to dance in a frightful whirl that rendered them illegible, and from the midst of that dust which swirled as if blown by a hurricane, Valentinico emerged, capering, and confronting the author of his days (all this in the middle of the paper), told him, "Papa, I want to go bye-bye on the train."

The good man struggled for an instant with that playful image, and at last wiped it out by passing his hand over his eyes and throwing back his heavy head. The orderly approached to tell him that the ladies, already seated at table, were expecting him for dinner. Torquemada grunted when he heard the servant say that he had already been called three times, and at last rose and stretched, and with the step and gestures of a drunken man descended to the ground floor by the service stairs that had been built for the purpose. On the way he kept saying to himself, "So he wants to have a lark on the train . . . Bah! Whims of his mother. He hasn't even been born yet and the two of them are already spoiling him."

FIVE

During the month of May and part of June, Don Francisco devoted body and soul to the company formed for exploitation of the tobacco contract, and with Donoso's help, each man emulating the other in activity and intelligence, they set up all the administrative machinery, which, if it corresponded in fact to its perfect organization, would necessarily work like a charm. Torquemada, as principal stockholder, was responsible for the higher administration of the business. Donoso was in charge of the company's relations with the State and all intra-office matters. Taramundi handled the purchase of tobacco in Puerto Rico and Serrano in the United States, where he had a cousin who owned a brokerage firm in Brooklyn.

They agreed that everything must be working properly before he left for his summer vacation, for in December the first consignment of Boliche tobacco was to be made, and in February, the Virginia. A formal contract to supply both types of leaf had already been awarded them in May, not without protest by others who had made, or thought they had made, a more advantageous offer to the Treasury; but since they were discredited people and with a deplorable history in such business, no one was surprised when the minister decided against them, taking advantage of some quirk or other in the law. Once the four principal actors had come to an agreement about things—for although there were other participants they had nothing to do with running the affair, owing to the fact that they had put minor capital sums into it—nothing was left to do except work like slaves to make the business come out neatly and cleanly. In the days that preceded the summer's expedition, Torquemada and Don Juan Gualberto Serrano came to an agreement in private about a few matters having to do with the purchase of bulk tobacco in the United States, and this stayed between the two of them without Donoso's or Taramundi's knowledge. The reason for this was that Don Francisco, with his instinctive knowledge of humanity, *under the aspect of give and take,* had seen from the first moment what the mainspring of that business was, understanding that to proceed in one way or another would determine whether the *liquid assets* would be merely good or of such a kind that one could thrust one's arm in them up to the elbow. Scarcely had the skinflint nudged Don Juan Gualberto's inclinations in this matter when the other responded with five words: "Here's the man we need." And with this exchange of expressions, Serrano went off to London, where he was going to confer with his cousin, and Torquemada left for Hernani with the family. The Taramundis installed themselves in San Sebastián. Donoso did not leave Madrid because his wife, whose host of illnesses had become still more complicated, could not move, nor would it have helped her to do so, for nowhere could she hope to find relief.

Dear Lord, how bored Torquemada was in the provinces, and what a miserable humor he was in, always picking a fight with *them* over trifles, complaining about everything, finding the water bad, the food tasteless, the people boring, the sky horribly ugly, the air harmful! His center was Madrid; away from that Madrid in which he had spent the best years of his life and earned so much money, the man was lost. He missed its Puerta del Sol, its streets—Carmen, Tudescos, and the little Callejón del El Perro—its Lozoya water, its variable climate with scorching days and freezing nights. He was consumed with homesickness as well as the impossibility of pursuing the fugitive coin, of giving orders to this or that agent. He loathed resting; his nature demanded the constant preoccupation of business and the infinite fidgeting involved in the very anxiety about the outcome of things, the fury of losing, the sadness of making only a little, the delirium of making a killing. He counted the days as they passed, the days of that torture his plaguey consorts had brought him; he abominated the idle society that surrounded him, so many insubstantial idlers, so many people whose only thought was to ruin themselves financially. For him, the acme of extravagance was giving money to innkeepers and hotelkeepers and those good-for-nothing bathing attendants who held on to the ladies so that they wouldn't drown. San Sebastián horrified him: it was all a continuous looting operation and a thousand tricks to plunder the citizens of Madrid who were about to spend a year's income in two months. Fidela and Cruz kept him there for three days, and he nearly fell ill of misery and repugnance.

In Hernani he would go walking by himself, working out in his noggin the whole edifice of numbers that constituted the tobacco business as well as other embryonic deals, such as the arrangements made by the ruined House of Gravelinas with its creditors. Fidela, who knew how ill her husband tolerated a stay in a resort, tried to cut it short, but Cruz refused because the climate in the North suited Rafael very well, and since they had been in Hernani the mental disorders we already know about had not been repeated. The family divided itself into two couples: Cruz went walking with the blind man, Fidela with her husband, and tried to distract him by calling attention to the beauties of the fields and landscape. The ruffian was not insensible to his wife's kindness or her attentions, and spent some pleasant times chatting with her in the meadows and woods. But during these indolent wanderings Torquemada was like the exile who thinks only of the motherland, and could speak of nothing without bringing up the subject of Madrid and those wretched business affairs of his. Fidela was pleased to have him do this, and told him over and over, with childish mischievousness: "Yes, Tor, you'll have to earn lots of money, but lots and lots, and I'll keep it safe for you."

She was so insistent on this idea that Don Francisco took his wife into his confidence as he had never done before, telling her everything that he felt and thought and the causes of his joys as well as his sorrows. He began by declaring himself satisfied with the way fate had treated him, for his earnings were increasing like sea foam. But what good was that, if the family had set itself up in such luxury that it was impossible to save? Every day of the week Cruz came up with some new extravagance to waste money on. What was the use of describing in detail that *uninterrupted series* of mad extravagances, if Fidela knew them already? It was no use for him to live in magnificence, though from force of circumstance he adapted himself to it in the end. His *beau ideal* was to reinvest his considerable earnings, reserving only a very minor part of them for day-to-day expenses. To see the money come in by cartloads and go out by saddlebags cut him to the heart and filled his head with somber and pessimistic thoughts. A struggle to the death had been unleashed between him and Cruz; he recognized himself as very inferior to her in intelligence and power of expression, but he believed, in this case, that he had right on his side. The worst of all was that Crucita controlled him and was able to impose her economic standards, completely defeating him every time she *placed under consideration* the question of new expenses. He would writhe with rage, like the devil who is depicted at the feet of Saint Michael, and the impudent creature would trample his head and do exactly as she pleased with his money.

In short, he considered himself to be a most unhappy man and felt so embittered that he lacked even the spirit to feel happy about being a father when the time came. Fidela was circumspect in replying to his plaints, assuring him that for her part she would not mind in the least living in modesty and obscurity; but since Cruz was arranging things in a different way, she must have her reasons for it.

"She knows more than we do, dear Tor, and the best thing is to let her do what she wants. For the sake of your business itself, you ought to breathe an atmosphere of ostentation. Frankly, Tor: would you have made the money you have by living like a pauper on the Calle de San Blas? Why, every duro my sister spends is spent to bring you twenty more! And, above all, that person you call a tyrant is as much a wizard as Merlin, and to her despotism we owe, first, having come out of that dreadful poverty alive, and then, finding ourselves living in abundance and with you turned into an influential man. Don't be foolish. Close your eyes and give in to everything my sister says and proposes."

In all this, and in further things she said, she revealed her almost

superstitious respect for Cruz's authority and the impossibility of rebelling against anything, large or small, that the autocrat of the family
might propose. Hearing her, Torquemada sighed, and thought with
deep discouragement that in no case would his wife help him to throw
off the yoke. A slight indication of this was enough to make Fidela
protest with infantile fear. She—oppose her sister's judgments and decisions? Before she did that, the sun would come up in the west.

"No, no, Tor. The one who rules, rules. I repeat that all those things
that bother you are really what you need, and what we all need."

Between complaints, the usurer came out with another idea that
also tormented him. Before expressing it he hesitated for a time, fearful
that his wife would greet it with laughter. But at last he took the
plunge with the most delicate spontaneity:

"Look here, Fidela, everybody has his little ways and his *idiosyn-
crasity*, as our friend Zárate says, and I assure you that I don't want
my son to turn out to be an Aguila. Of course I know that Cruz is
dying to have the baby be like you two, like her, a little spendthrift,
ostentatious and with a lot of whims of the prodigal aristocrat. But
I'd rather he wouldn't be born at all than be born like that. Of course,
I'm of the opinion that both of you are deceiving yourselves if you
expect that the new Valentín will be the spit and image of your family,
because my heart tells me that he'll be a Torquemada of the finest
quality, that is, the very same Valentín as before in body and soul,
with the same cleverness and the very same looks as the other time."

SIX

Fidela was stupefied, unable either to support or combat such an idea,
and merely said, "It will be as God wills. What do we know of the
designs of God?"

"Yes, we do know," said Torquemada, getting angry. "There has to
be justice, there has to be logic, because if there weren't, there'd be
no Supreme Being, nor Christ to prove it. My son is coming back. Ah,
you didn't know that prodigy! But if you had known him, you'd want
it the same as I do, and you'd be sure of it, given the fact that things
ought to happen according to the law of fairness. You'll see, you'll
see, what a talent for mathematics. He's just pure mathematics, and
knows all the problems better than the teacher. To speak to you

frankly, hiding none of my thoughts from you, I'd say that I simply must associate certain phenomena with the gifts of my son Valentín. Didn't you tell us that a couple of nights ago you had some very strange dreams, seeing that they seemed to be putting figures made of eight and ten numbers in front of you, and that then you went through a wood and found fourteen nines that came out to meet you and barred the way so you couldn't go any farther?"

"Yes, yes, it's true that I dreamed that."

"Well, there you are," said Torquemada, his eyes sparkling with joy. "It's he, it's he who has your soul and all your veins full of those blessed numbers. And tell me: don't you feel right now as if enormous quantities, quadrillions or something like that, were rising from your body into your head, *in the vernacular* cerebral region? Don't you feel a really devilish movement of multiplications and divisions, and all that about the square root and cube root?"

"Yes, I do feel something like that, in a vague way," answered Fidela, allowing herself to be influenced by the idea. "But I don't feel any of the part about the roots. Numbers that seem to climb up to my head, yes."

"See, see? Didn't I tell you? I knew I couldn't be mistaken. And isn't it true, too, that everything you calculate comes out right? As if you had the pure spirit of mathematics and the science of sciences inside you."

"I wouldn't go as far as that!" answered Fidela doubtfully. "I don't make calculations because I'm no good at calculations."

"Then start right now to add up quantities; try it and you'll see."

Don Francisco rubbed his hands, adding by way of synthesis, "Let's agree that he's not an Aguila, that he'll be who he is and nobody else."

Husband and wife meant to say something more about this strange matter, but they were distracted from their talk by a carriage full of people that was approaching the town from the San Sebastián road, and heard joyous voices loudly greeting them. They were seated in a meadow near the road, at the foot of a sturdy chestnut tree, and when the charabanc passed in front of them, they recognized some friends' faces among the crowd on the box and the lateral seats.

"Oh, Morentín!" said Don Francisco.

And Fidela: "Ah, Infante, Malibrán!"

And they started off in the direction of the town, some half a kilometer away, taking rather a long time to arrive because in those months the lady was not distinguished for the rapidity of her movements.

At the house they found the friends who had come from San Sebastián to descend upon them: Morentín with his mama, Manolo Infante, Jacinto Villalonga, Cornelio Malibrán, two of Pez's sons and one of his daughters, Manuel Peña and his wife Irene, and one or two more unknown to history.

"And do we have to feed this whole crowd?" asked Don Francisco in anguish.

"Of course, my dear; we have no choice. But they'll divide up. You'll see how some of them will go to Severiano Rodríguez's house, or to General Morla's."

"We'll always be stuck with the ones that talk the loudest and eat the most. And Zárate hasn't come, who's the only one of all this bunch I really like, because he's such a scientific young man."

The ladies spent a very pleasant afternoon of visiting, and Don Francisco could talk business with Morentín, who gave him news of his diligent papa, now ready to leave London for Spain. Rafael was stimulated by his friends' chatter, listening with special pleasure to Infante and Villalonga, who told any number of amusing stories about the society of Biarritz and San Sebastián. There was also talk of politics, and at nightfall they departed with the same cheerful hubbub they had brought with them.

Though the afternoon was agreeable for the poor blind man, his sister noticed that he was very restless that night, with signs of reversion to the old manias which had seemed forgotten. He chattered mechanically, laughed disproportionately, and mentioned Morentín's name at every moment in order to hold him up to ridicule and make fun of what he said.

"But isn't he the friend you're fondest of? Why have you taken this absurd antipathy to him now?" said his sister Cruz when they were alone and she was giving him his supper.

"He was my friend. He is one no longer, nor can he be. And mark my words: I was afraid he'd turn up here. It was absolutely logical that he should come, attracted by his evil thoughts."

And in the remarks that followed he displayed, rather than antipathy, an insane hatred so violent in form that Cruz felt her fears of earlier days renewed, and prepared to spend a restless night in the unfortunate young man's company. Indeed, no sooner had her sister and Don Francisco retired than she went to Rafael's room, which was a ground-floor chamber with a window opening on the garden, wreathed in honeysuckle; and, finding him very wide awake and disinclined to sleep, she proposed that the two of them chat until they both became sleepy. Since it was August, the night was very hot. Rather than tossing and turning in bed, they would spend their time enjoying the out-of-doors, breathing the sweet-scented air of the garden and listening to the song of the frogs, which were intoning their garrulous hymn to the warm night in a neighboring pond.

Rafael joyfully accepted his sister's proposal. Once she was seated near the window—acting quickly and authoritatively so as to give him no time to think about his answers—she went straight to the point:

"Look here, Rafael. You're going to tell me right now, plainly, but very plainly, without circumlocutions or attenuations, why your affection for Morentín has turned to loathing. What has he done to you?"

"To me, nothing."

"What has he said to you?"

"Nothing."

"I won't stand for subterfuges. You must tell me plainly and immediately. Some time ago, a long time before we left Madrid, I began to notice that you got very nervous every time you talked about him. Come now, tell me everything, Rafael. I beg you in the name of God."

"Morentín is an egotist."

"And that's the only reason you hate him?"

"And a scoundrel."

"What has he said to you? You talked about something. Don't deny it."

"I don't need to have Pepe show me the ugliness of his soul. For I see it with the eyes of my own . . . and with the light of my thoughts . . . but so clearly!"

"Come, now, you're beginning to exaggerate. Let's see, one of your friends who visited you today, Manolo Infante, or Peñita, maybe Malibrán, who is very naughty and has the worst tongue in the world, has told you something horrid about poor Morentín."

"No; no one has told me anything."

"Try to think, Rafael. Malibrán, it was Malibrán. But my dear boy, why do you pay attention to that fatuous fellow with his viper's temperament and his poisonous tongue?"

"I swear to you on the memory of our mother," said Rafael in solemn tones, "that Malibrán has told me absolutely nothing about . . . well, about the painful matter which is the cause of my loathing for Morentín. But now I understand. Dear sister, you have come to question me tonight, and now I'm the one who is asking questions. Answer me quickly, plainly: has Malibrán said something, somewhere, about . . . that?"

"About what?"

"About that. Don't pretend you haven't heard. The idea that torments me also torments you. I see it all very clearly by the light of my reason. What I guessed with only the resources of my logic the world is already saying, perhaps trumpets it shamelessly, and that scandal has reached your ears. Tell me, tell me. Malibrán, or some other loose-lipped person, has said something at the Romeros' house, or the San Salomós', or maybe the Orozcos'."

"But . . . what?" asked Cruz, terrified, trying to hide her ideas from the blind man's perspicacity.

He did not see her mortal pallor; but he noted an opaque tone in her voice, which for him was as sure a sign as the whiteness of her countenance, and Cruz's voice betrayed astonishment, anger, shame.

"Very well," added Rafael after a short pause. "I'll say it in plain words. Rumors of scandal have come to your ears. Someone, whoever it is, spreads this scandal in the homes of our enemies, also perhaps in those of our friends. Without having heard it, I know what it is, just as I have seen it without seeing it. Why make a mystery of it? What they are saying is that my sister Fidela has a lover, and that that lover is Morentín."

"Be still," cried Cruz in an access of fury, placing her hand over his mouth with such force that she seemed to be striking him.

"I'm telling the truth. The scandal has reached your ears. Don't deny it."

"Very well, I don't deny it. Malibrán is the one who has permitted himself to insult us with this dreadful calumny. And we've had him here today! Thank goodness he went to the Cíceros' house for dinner, for if I see him at my table, I don't know . . . I think that I myself . . . He said it in Biarritz, and in Cambo and in Fuenterrabía. I know it through a person who is incapable of deceiving me and has warned me about it. Dishonor that has a basis in fact is sad enough, but dishonor that arises by spontaneous combustion and spreads and grows without the existence of the slightest fact to justify it, is something that drives one mad."

"But—I'll tell you if you won't be angry—I don't believe that that dishonor is as baseless as you seem to think."

"But you . . ." (indignantly), "you believe . . . you, too!"

Furious, she caught him by the arm and shook it violently, the only way she knew to reply to the vile insinuation.

SEVEN

"Keep calm, and let me express everything I'm thinking about," added Rafael with a great sigh, for he, as well as his sister, was out of breath. "In conscience I must tell you that the thing is perfectly logical. Let me speak. The thing is the product of social life, of the corruption of customs, of the disorder of the moral idea. When our sister married, I said, 'This has to happen,' and it has happened just as I thought. From this dark cave of my blindness I see everything, for to think is to see, and nothing escapes my sure logic, nothing, nothing at all. That dishonor was an unavoidable thing. We had all the elements at home for it to arise. Naturally, it has arisen, and no one has been able to avoid it. Yes, I know already what you're going to tell me."

"You do not know, you do not know," replied the lady in a firm and haughty tone. "What I must tell you is that our sister is as pure as the driven snow. Under no circumstances would I doubt her perfect, her absolute chastity; still less can I doubt her, living, as I do live, always at her side. None of her actions, or even her most hidden thoughts, are unknown to me. I know what she thinks and feels as well as I know what I think and feel. And nothing, absolutely nothing, exists that could serve as a foundation for such a vile supposition."

"I concede that on the ground of facts there is no reason to—"

"Nor on any other grounds."

"On that of intention, on that of wanting it to happen."

"Neither on that ground nor on any other does the slightest shadow of a blot exist. Fidela is purity itself; she loves and respects her husband, who within his crudeness is very good to her and to the whole family. Don't let me hear you say such a foolish thing again, Rafael, or I won't promise to treat you with the gentleness I customarily use with you."

"All right, all right; don't get into a huff. I admit that you are right insofar as my sister is concerned. And can you give me the same assurance about Morentín's intentions?"

"How can I do that? To me, he has always seemed decent and fastidious."

"Well, I do know him, because we have been through adventures together in times which will never return; and now, in the files of my memory, those adventures are very instructive for me. I assure you that quiet corruption, the kind which is not felt, which devours noiselessly and sometimes without the slightest scandal, is harbored in his soul. Although Morentín has said nothing to me, I know that he means to dishonor us, that he believes that victory is certain sooner or later. If he makes no boast of having succeeded already, neither will he honorably deny it when he is congratulated on a conquest which some people probably think has already taken place, and everyone, everyone, considers probable. Oh, it is horrifying to think that, were my sister a saint and Morentín a model of virtue, the world, which pays heed only to the composition of this marriage and the showy life you lead, will always consider what Malibrán has said as an incontrovertible fact! And now you can no longer avoid having the infamous rumor spread and grow. Nor will you succeed in rectifying what you believe to be an error . . . and which probably is one for the moment."

"Not for the moment, forever. You, too? It really seems that you are on the side of the slanderers. This is intolerable, Rafael. Is it or is it not a calumny? Well, if it is a calumny, if the innocence of our sister shines like the sun—and before I would doubt her I would doubt that a just and merciful God exists—if she is chaste, I say, and if those who calumniate her are deserving of the pains of hell, the truth will shine forth sooner or later, and the world will have to recognize and respect it."

"It will not recognize it. The world proceeds to judge people and things with a logic that it has created itself. I concede that it is a logic constructed out of artifice, but it exists . . . and just try to deprive public opinion of its unworthy idea. You cannot, you cannot. To avoid this, it would have been preferable to keep on living in modest obscurity after that unfortunate wedding. But in the whirlwind of society, in the midst of such ostentation, by cultivating old social contacts and seeking new ones, there is no way to remove ourselves from the overall atmosphere, my dear sister. The overall atmosphere surrounds us; in it float the pleasures and satisfactions of vanity; poison also floats there, the microscopic bacillus that kills us, amid all these joys. A young and beautiful woman, sensitive, surrounded by adulation, without domestic occupations; an old and ridiculous husband, brutally selfish and absolutely devoid of personal attractions . . . anybody knows . . . draw the inference. If it isn't true yet, it will be. The world sanctions it before it happens, and authorizes it, and even seems to decree it, as if, in that hidden constitution of the modern conscience, there were an article that expressly demands it. I have been aware of this for some time; it was one of the most serious drawbacks that I saw in my sister's marriage. Now we must suffer in silence."

"No, I will neither suffer nor be silent," replied Cruz, overcoming the uneasiness caused her by that subject. "I despise slander. God willing, this will never come to Fidela's ears; but if it should come, she will despise it as I do, and as you do. I forbid you to speak of this; still more, I forbid you to think . . ."

"To think! Forbid me to think! That indeed is something which cannot be. I think of nothing else. It is the only thing in which I can occupy myself, and were it not for the exercise of my mind, how would I, a poor blind man, conquer the weariness of my darkness? I promise to tell you everything as I discover it."

"No, you will not, you cannot discover anything," the lady said nervously, anxious to dispute him. "And whatever you think about will be your product exclusively, the product of your poor little bored, idle, mischievous mind. I forbid you, Rafael; yes, I forbid you to think about that."

The blind man smiled without saying a word, and his sister sighed, turning over in her mind the sentences she had spoken before, along with others that she tried to speak, but the first word stuck in her throat. Thus a fairly long period of time passed, and the pair were about to break out in new arguments when they heard a noise in the upper rooms, where the married couple slept, and soon heard Don Francisco's heavy step descending the stairs. Cruz went out to meet him, fearful that something untoward had happened, but he reassured her by saying, "It's nothing. Fidela is sleeping like an angel; but, with the heat and a plaguey mosquito that's been giving me the dickens all night, I haven't been able to sleep a wink, and so finally, tired of the heat of the bedclothes, I'm coming down to take the air in the garden."

"Tonight is oppressive and sultry, which is very rare in this part of the country," observed Cruz. "Tomorrow there'll be a storm and it will turn cooler."

"What a night!" murmured the skinflint. "And for this a fellow left Madrid, where it was so comfortable!"

He went out into the garden in his shirt sleeves, with a jacket thrown around his shoulders, his silk skullcap on the back of his head. From the window where the brother and sister sat, silently breathing the warm, honeysuckle-scented air, they could see Don Francisco's big black shadow as he walked slowly up and down, and could hear his little cough and the squeak of the gravel under his authoritative tread.

The night was all serenity, warmth, and solemn poetry. The air, motionless and as if intoxicated by the smell of fields, drowsed among the leaves of the trees, scarcely moving them with its light breath. The deep sky, moonless and cloudless, was illuminated by the stars' silvery light. In the earth's dark foliage, in groves, meadows, orchards, and gardens, crickets broke the peaceful silence with the metallic whirring of their wings, and the toad, with melancholy rhythm, gave forth the high peeping sound that seems to mark the decline of eternity's grave pendulum. No other voice but these sounded, in heaven and on earth.

For a long time Cruz and Rafael sat contemplating the shadows of the garden and the figure of Don Francisco, who was walking to and fro, also in measured rhythm, from one end of the garden to the other, passing and repassing like the soul of an unburied sinner who comes asking to be interred. Motivated by a very peculiar state of mind, and also affected by the poetic serenity of the night, Cruz felt intensely sorry for that desperately homesick man. She thought that, since it was through him that the noble family of Aguila had emerged from horrifying poverty, it ought to repay him by giving him the happiness he deserved. And instead of trying to do this, she, the ringleader, vexed him by raising him to social heights that were repugnant to his habits and his character. Would it not be more humane and generous to let him cultivate his miserliness and take pleasure in it, like a reptile in slimy mud? Because, in addition to all this, the poor man, removed from his natural sphere, suffered the nibblings of slander, and though he was ceasing to be ridiculous in one way, he was so in another. Was it not all her fault, because she had set herself to raise a man of the lower classes and had tried to make a gentleman and a tycoon out of a boor? This pricking of her conscience, and the extreme compassion that she felt toward her brother-in-law at that solemn hour of the summer night, moved her to speak to him affectionately. Leaning out of the window, she said to him, "Don Francisco, aren't you afraid that the night breeze will do you harm? You mustn't trust the warm weather too much in this part of the country."

"I'm all right," answered the skinflint, approaching the window.

"It seems to me that you've gone out without enough clothing. Goodness, you mustn't catch a grippe or a bad cold on us."

"Don't worry. That would be something, to run away from that nice heat in Madrid, as pleasant as it is and, no matter what they say, very hygienic, and for a fellow to come here and fall ill in the humid heat of this region, as extremely aquatic as it is."

"You had better come in here, and the three of us will keep one another company until we're sleepy."

Rafael also approached the window. At that moment, as if Cruz's feelings had transmitted themselves to him by some magnetic mystery, he too felt sorry for the man he hated.

"Come in, Don Francisco," he told him, reflecting that the hungry family of nobles had deceived the man who helped them, using him to redeem themselves and, after making him unhappy by taking him out of his proper element, had covered him with more ridicule than the family had incurred by associating with him. He felt a desire to reconcile himself with the ruffian, though always keeping his distance, and to return to him in the form of sympathetic friendship the material protection he received from him.

Since both brother and sister insisted upon his joining them, the skinflint could not be insensible to these demonstrations of affection and entered the house, grumbling about the climate of the Basque Country, about its food and, especially, about the confounded rains that were, without a shadow of a doubt, the worst in the world.

"You are out of your element here," said Rafael, who for the first time in his life spoke to him pleasantly. "You cannot live far away from your beloved business."

When she heard this, Cruz had an inspiration, and instantly leaped from thought to deed.

"Don Francisco, would you like it if we left tomorrow?"

The vacation-weary businessman was so surprised by the proposal that he could not believe that his sister-in-law was speaking in earnest.

"You're trying to get my dander up, Crucita."

"And really," added Rafael, "for all we're doing here, it's not even cool; on the other hand, there are lots of mosquitoes and another kind of worse vermin—demanding and embarrassing friends."

"That's the gospel truth."

"I propose that we leave tomorrow," said the elder sister resolutely. "That is, if Don Francisco wants to . . ."

"If I want to! Sweet Christ, do you think I'm in this cursed country because I want to be? Or am I here to make you happy and in obedience to the demands of horrible, filthy fashion?"

"Tomorrow, let's," said the blind man, clapping his hands.

"But . . . are you speaking seriously, or are you just trying to make me feel worse?"

"Seriously, seriously."

And, convinced that it was not a joke, the skinflint became so happy that his eyes shone like stars in the sky.

"So, tomorrow! Crucita, old girl, you couldn't have decided anything I'd like better. I was just like *the soul of Garibaldi* here, bored and with nothing to do, looking at earth and sky and remembering my affairs in Madrid the way a fellow who's enjoyed divine glory would remember it if he found himself shut up in the depths of hell. So, tomorrow, Rafaelito? What a pleasure! Excuse me; I'm like a youngster who's been let out of school. Blessed work is a vacation for me. I don't enjoy this stupid life in the country, nor do I enjoy the salt water of San Sebastián, and this silly folderol of bathing and little walks simply wasn't made for me. Greenstuff is for folks who like to eat it, and the *natural* countryside is just plain foolishness. I say that there oughtn't to be any countryside, but all cities, all streets and people. Leave the sea to the whales. Oh, my dear Madrid! So, really, tomorrow? Another year the family can come without me, if they want expensive cool air.

I'll stick to my cheap hot weather. They can say what they like; after the fifteenth of August, Madrid cools off *outstandingly* at night, and it's a pleasure to go out and take the evening air on the heights of Chamberí. What I say is, now that the melon season has begun, and that delicious new wine—Christ! If it weren't for the noise and letting Fidela sleep, I'd start packing right now. What time does the San Sebastián train pass through? At ten. Well, as soon as it's light we'll order the carriage and be away in a flash. You mustn't go back on your word, Crucita. You're the boss, but don't deceive us with doses of honey—*in the vernacular*, promises—because I deserve the reality of this return to Madrid for the patience with which I've come to these miserable lands, with no more *objective* than shifting the family around and acting tony, by a hundred thousand bibles! Tony! Always that blessed *bon ton*, which I think is a pretty toneless tone."

EIGHT

So they left that morning, to the surprise and mystification of the whole colony, among which there was inevitably some malicious idler who sought a reason for that sudden return, which rather resembled a flight, and discovered nothing less than a serious matrimonial disagreement. The fact is that they all returned happily to Madrid, and Torquemada was merry as a cricket. How joyfully he observed the smiling face of his dear city, its sunny streets and dusty promenades, for there still had not been a drop of rain! And what marvelous, stinging heat! Let nobody tell him there were more hygienic places in the world. For effluvia, Hernani, a place which, to make it even more disagreeable, had the name of an opera. Lord, whoever heard of towns having the same names as operas!

He plunged into the waves of his business like a thirsty duck returning to the pond; but since many persons in the official element and the *private element* were still away from the city, he did not find the full occupation he would have wished. However, his pleasure was great; and to complete it, Cruz did not trouble him with new plans for expansion. Another happy novelty was that Rafael had become gentler in his dealings with the skinflint, and even seemed to want to have him for a friend. Before the trip, the only words they had exchanged were the indispensable ones, a greeting in the morning and a few meaningless phrases about the weather at night. After the return from Hernani they sometimes kept each other company, and the blind man showed him consideration that bordered on affection. He listened to him calmly and even asked his opinion about current matters of politics, or some event of the day. But the most peculiar aspect of all this was that Cruz, that good woman who had so ardently desired peace between the two brothers-in-law and had always encouraged them to compose their differences, now seemed uneasy when she saw them peacefully chatting together and did not leave them alone for a moment, as if she feared that one of them was going to let something slip. It should be mentioned that during that time (September and October), Cruz's opinion about her unfortunate brother's mental state was more pessimistic than ever, despite the fact that the poor fellow no longer behaved oddly, or laughed for no reason, or became irritated.

"If we have him settled down now and he gives us no trouble," Fidela would tell her, "why do you worry?"

"A sultry calm often presages great storms. I prefer to see him nervous and talking a bit too much than to have him shut himself up in this brooding spleen, with suspicious appearances of good judgment in the little he says. Well, it's in God's hands."

During all of September Don Francisco had the pleasure of not seeing many persons who ordinarily frequented his house, and who were still wandering about seasides and watering places, some of them in Paris; and the only exception to that exodus—Zárate—heightened his pleasure, for that worthy, owing to the impecuniousness that commonly accompanies wisdom, summered for only two or three weeks in nearby El Escorial or Colmenar Viejo. The skinflint spent some very good sessions with his friend and *scientific* consultant, the two of them almost alone every night, chatting about fascinating subjects, such as the Eastern question, chemical fertilizers, the spherical shape of the earth, the papacy's relations with the kingdom of Italy, the fisheries of the Grand Banks of Newfoundland. During that period of fruitful progress, Don Francisco learned some very droll expressions, such as *Penelope's web*, also discovering why such a thing was said, *the sword of Damocles*, and *the Greek calends*. In addition, he read *Don Quixote*, parts of which he had known since boyhood, straight through, and appropriated a large number of instances and sayings, such as *Sancho's caps, let sleeping dogs lie, the reason of the unreason*, and others which the clever chap applied very well, with truly Castilian sly wit, in conversation.

Chatting away as they did, they spoke of Rafael, and Zárate pointed out that his apparent mental stability did not inspire confidence in his sister, to which Don Francisco replied that his brother-in-law was not quite right in the head, and that sooner or later there was going to be some kind of big *contingency*.

"Well, I have an opinion concerning this," said Zárate, "that I venture to consult you about on condition that you will maintain absolute secrecy. It's a personal opinion of mine; perhaps I'm mistaken, but I won't relinquish it as long as events do not demonstrate the contrary. I believe that our young man is not insane but is pretending to be, as Hamlet pretended to be, so that he could act as he wished in the course of a family drama."

"Family drama! There's no family drama here, or family comedy either, friend Zárate," replied Don Francisco. "It's only that the aristocratic gentleman and yours truly have been on bad terms. But now it seems that he's giving way, and I go along with him. Naturally, it's preferable to have peace in the house. That's the reason of the unreason, and I say nothing of the troublesomeness and foolishness of my brother-in-law. *Let sleeping dogs lie.* For the rest, I also think that at times in the past his insanity has been pretended, like the madness of that gentleman you mentioned so aptly."

And he was left with a doubt as to who that "Hamley" might be; but he refrained from asking, preferring to give the impression that he knew. But from the name and the fact that he pretended to be mad, he rather imagined that the fellow in question must have been a poet.

"I'm very glad that we're in agreement on this point, Señor Don Francisco," said Zárate. "I find many points of resemblance between our Rafael and the unhappy Prince of Denmark. Yesterday, for instance, the poor blind man was talking to himself, and said things that reminded me of the celebrated soliloquy 'to be or not to be.' "

"Yes, in fact he did say something like that. I noticed it, and the *points of resemblance* did not escape me. For I observe and say nothing."

"Yes, that's exactly what needs to be done, observe him."

"The poor thing has a good deal of the poet in him, hasn't he?"

"Yes, indeed."

"And when we say poetry, we say not much good sense, brains addled."

"Exactly."

"And by the way, friend Zárate: I'm surprised that poets have so many different names. They're called *druids*, they're also called *bards*. Believe me, I nearly died laughing when I read an article they've *dedicated* to that young fellow I sponsor, and the damned critic calls him *bard* here and *bard* there, and covers him with so much praise that it stinks. I'd call the verses that that young fellow writes *boredoms*, for nobody in his right mind can understand them and you get lost in the fancy talk. Everything's said backwards. Oh well, *let sleeping dogs lie*."

The pedant greeted this sally with enthusiasm, and they went on to another subject, which probably had something to do with socialism and collectivism, for next day Torquemada walked the streets of Madrid transformed into a scholar on those subjects. He found *points of resemblance* between certain doctrines and the evangelical principle, and wrapped his absurdities in phrases he had half understood and used with doubtful application.

Don Juan Gualberto Serrano, who returned at the end of September, brought him very good news from London. Purchases of leaf would be made by persons exactly right for the purpose, who were very experienced in that trade and would know how to adjust themselves to the indicated prices even if they had to make do with sweepings from the warehouses. On that score they had only to think about making piles of money. He also proposed another business deal based on operations with English bankers using Spanish funds, and the moment he suggested it Torquemada pronounced it absolute nonsense. In principle, however, the combination was a good one, and after the skinflint had thought it over for two or three days he found a new practical development, which he proposed to his friend, and Serrano thought it so excellent that he embraced him enthusiastically.

"You are a genius, my friend. You have seen the matter under its sole positive aspect. The plan I had in mind was chaos, and you have brought order out of that chaos, a world of order. This very day I'm going to write to the inventors of this combination, Proctor and Ruffer, and I'll tell them how you see the matter. I'm sure they will think it marvelous, and we'll set to work immediately. It's a matter of a half-million reales clear profit every year."

"I won't say no. Write to those gentlemen. You know *my line of conduct* already. Under the conditions I propose, I'll go in, I should say I will."

They discussed this complicated matter for a long time, agreeing about everything and upon everything, and when Serrano was saying good-bye, for he was lunching that day with the president of the Council (as he did almost every day), he told Torquemada, beaming, "I think that other thing's a foregone conclusion."

"And what's *that other thing?*"

"But don't you know? Hasn't Cruz told you?"

"She's told me nothing," replied Don Francisco distrustfully, suspecting that *that other thing* was a new attempt on his pocketbook which the ruler of the household intended to make.

"Ah! Well, consider it done."

"But what? By the almighty Bible!"

"Really, have you no knowledge?"

"What I have is my heart in my mouth, dammit! Shall we bet that this time it's the bombshell she warned me about? Come on, I'm already starting to lock up my money box good and tight."

"No, you won't have to spend much money . . . a little luncheon for your sponsors . . . a dozen telegrams . . ."

"But what is it, for the love of God?"

"Why, we're putting you up for senator."

"Me? But how, life term or . . . ?"

"Elective. The life term will come later. First we thought about Teruel, where there are two vacancies; then about León. Why, you'll be representing your native district, El Bierzo."

"Some plague that is, that'll fall upon me. God preserve me from clients from El Bierzo, and the whole of Léon coming to me begging."

"But, aren't you pleased?"

"No. What do I want to be a senator for? It doesn't bring in anything."

"My dear man, yes. These posts are always profitable. At least, you lose nothing, and you might gain something."

"And even *somethings?*"

"Yes, señor, and even lots and lots of *somethings.*"

"All right. Like Sancho, I accept the island. We'll go to the Senate—*in the vernacular,* Upper Chamber—and if they twist my arm I'll have a few things to tell the country. My *desideratum* is the considerable reduction of expenses. Economies from top to bottom; economies in every social sphere. Let's have done with this *Penelope's web* of our administration, and let's level off that budget, over which is suspended, like a *sword of Damocles,* the prospect of bankruptcy. I would undertake to set Treasury straight in two weeks, but for the purpose I'd demand a very radical plan of economies. That will be the *condition sine qua non,* the chief of all *conditions sine qua nons.*"

NINE

Don Francisco was in great haste to have it out with his sister-in-law about that matter, and on the following morning at breakfast, he timidly interrogated her.

"I didn't want to say anything to you until the pie was out of the oven," answered Cruz, smiling. "To be sure, I'm not at all happy with the way we went about it, and think that we really weren't up to doing it. Monte Cármenes and Severiano Rodríguez had promised us that one of the vacancies for life senator would be for you, and after a lot of lobbying and consulting they tell us that the president has other obligations and I don't know what else. They can't haggle about a life senatorship with a man like you, nor can they satisfy you by putting a miserable little credential in your hand, a credential that nowadays is within the grasp of any unimportant professor or the first intriguer to arrive on the scene. And the Treasury Minister is just as indignant as I am. He had a row with the president. . . There's a lot of talk about it!"

"I didn't know," said Torquemada in stupefaction. "They've had arguments about my life senatorship. How stupid can they be? I haven't the slightest need to be a senator, or to sit on those benches. It's just that I'd like the pleasure of telling some home truths, but real truths, eh? *As for the rest,* I don't aspire to it, *neither near nor far.* My *line of conduct* is to work away at my business, without putting on airs. And if they want to give that sugarplum to someone else, then let them give it, and I wish him well."

"I thought about not accepting it, but they'll take it as a slight, and that won't do. We'll be, I mean you'll be, an elective senator, and you'll represent your native district."

"Villafranca del Bierzo."

"Province of León."

"I can already see the flock of long-hungry brethren that's going to descend on me like a plague of locusts. You'll take over the job of receiving them, and sending them off with a good dose of soft soap. Your gift of gab will stand you in good stead for these matters."

"All right, then, I'll take over that department. What would I not do to keep you happy and replete with satisfactions?"

"Oh, Crucita, old girl!" said Torquemada, turning pale. "Now I can see the dagger falling."

"Why do you say that?"

"Because when you flatter me and smile at me, it's because you're coming at me knife in hand, asking for my money or my life."

"Ah, don't you believe it! For some time now I've been very kind to you. I don't recognize myself. You can see that I'm letting you accumulate your fabulous earnings in peace."

"It's true that ever since we came back from that confounded Hernani you haven't played the tune of new extravagances, and *hence* of new expenses. But I'm trembling, because after the calm come thunder and lightning, and since you threatened me a while ago with something really big . . ."

"Ah, yes, that one! The big thunderbolt is still under discussion here," pointing at her forehead with her index finger. "It's a very serious step, and I haven't quite decided."

"God help us, and the Virgin be with us, with all the almighty bibles in the world! And what devil's kind of an idea are you *cherishing?*"

"You'll know in good time," replied the lady, going out the far door of the dining room and smiling graciously on him from the doorway.

And it was true that the household ruler, though she had not renounced her grand project, had placed it in the file of the doubtful and contingent. To speak plainly, ever since the trip to Hernani her firm intentions for greater things had been shattered. The dreadful slander which had been brought to her ears and which, far from fading away in Madrid, continued to circulate and was increasing, perfidiously gaining currency, was what had made her decide to retreat, and caused something like remorse for having taken the family out of obscurity after the marriage with the miser. Would they not have been happier, would he not have been happier, without a doubt, in a peaceful mediocrity, their daily bread well assured, within four walls? This idea tormented her for days and even for weeks and months, and she was on the verge of undoing everything she had done and of proposing to her slave that they should all go to live in some small town, where the only frock coat they saw would be the mayor's on the day of the patron saint, where there were no elegant and depraved young men, envious and gossiping old women, politicians in whom parliamentary life corrupts all forms of life, ladies who enjoy hearing talk about other women's frailties so as to make their own more respectable, or, in a word, so many forms and styles of moral laxity.

She vacillated for some time, spending her nights in painful meditations, until at last her spirit decided to go forward along the path she had envisioned. The force of acquired momentum made a sudden stop impossible, for it would mean a shock with serious consequences. The least dangerous course was to continue upward, always in search of greater heights, with a majestic eagle's flight, scorning pettinesses from below and hoping to lose sight of them in the distance. Her mind became excited with these ideas, and exaggerated ambitions bubbled in it, whose realization, besides raising her family to new heights, would serve to confound utterly the vile Romeros and the whole despicable tribe of envious people.

Meanwhile, Fidela was completely unaware of these internal struggles of her sister's and the unpleasant fact that motivated them. She had become, owing to her interesting physical condition, a precious object of extraordinary delicacy and fragility, whom everyone protected even from the air around her. They were not far from putting her under glass. Her appetite for sweetmeats eventually took the form of the most extraordinary whims. She wanted those dragées known as "sweet peas" for dessert; sometimes she had a taste for the most vulgar things, like dried chestnuts and coarse olives; she usually supped on fried birds, which had to be served to her with little red caps made of radishes; she ate prodigiously of watercress seasoned with butter. She asked for sugar wafers at all hours of the day, toasted pine nuts after her chocolate, and at eleven, gelatines and little turnovers besides.

The months went by without her learning of the dreadful rumors that some of her friends, or enemies, had caused to circulate about her, supposing her to be unfaithful. She was as ignorant of the slander as she was innocent of the ugly sin they imputed to her, attenuating it with excuses no less odious than the sin itself. Her purity and limpidity of soul were truly angelic, for neither did it occur to her that such things could be said, nor did she ever dream of the danger of the rumors that circulated so closely around her. One would have thought that she had no desires except to live well in a vegetative way, at an infinite distance from all psychological problems. Judging her with the frivolity of a superficial sage, one of those who gobble up magazines and newspapers but do not observe life or see the essence of things, that fool of a Zárate said, "She's stupid, a being completely atrophied in everything that isn't purely organic life. She is ignorant of the affective element. The passions are a dead letter for this beautiful peacock or Angora kitten."

And Morentín did not believe that categorical opinion, promising himself many joys after *that*—her pregnancy—was over. But Zárate, who was one of the few who denied the voices of slander, tried to discourage the other's hopes, assuring him that motherhood would awake in Fidela instincts contrary to any distraction, making her stupidly chaste and incapable of any feeling except care for the child. The two friends disputed this subject hotly and eventually fell out, reproaching each other with fatuity on the one side and pedantry on the other.

Don Francisco cared for his wife like the apple of his eye, regarding her as an infinitely frail vessel within which all the mathematical combinations that would transform the world were being worked out. She was the incarnation of a God, of a new Most High, the Messiah of the science of numbers, destined to bring us the infallible dogma of quantity and renew with it societies half decayed by the debris of the many centuries of poetry they had been exuding. He did not express it like this, but those, *mutatis mutandis*, were his feelings. And Fidela repaid the miser's over-scrupulous care with a cold, sweet, watered-down affection that lacked all intensity, the only form of tenderness she had in her, and which she expressed in very strange ways, sometimes resembling those that one uses to pet domestic animals, sometimes like the love of a child for a parent.

Her family loves had always been centered on Rafael. But in those days she paid no particular attention to her brother, nor did she worry about whether he ate well or not, or if he was in a good humor. It is true that her sister's care relieved her of all concern about the blind man, and he, since the wedding, did not spend as many hours as before in pleasant intimacy with Señora de Torquemada. A certain detachment had been initiated between them, which was observable only in imperceptible incidents of word and deed and noticed only by the very shrewd, very perceptive Cruz.

One afternoon when Torquemada returned from his business errands, he found Fidela alone in her sitting room, crying. Cruz had gone out shopping, and Rufinita, who spent occasional afternoons there keeping her stepmother company (a company, be it said in passing, very much to Fidela's taste), had not come that day, which annoyed the miser greatly.

"What's the matter, what's wrong with you? Why are you alone? And that confounded Rufina, what's she thinking about not to come and chat with you? For all she has to do at home! Come on now, why are you crying? Is it because they didn't want to give me the life senatorship?" (denial by Fidela). "I was sure that wasn't it. When all's said and done, the elective office is just as good, though, to tell the truth, this business about the senatorship *doesn't really fill a void for me*. Fidela, tell me why you're crying or I'll get really angry, and I'll say bad things to you, *Bibles* and *Christs*, all those rough words I use when I get mad."

"Well, I'm crying . . . because I feel like it," replied Fidela, bursting into laughter.

"Bah! Now you're laughing, *from which it can be inferred* that it isn't anything."

"There is something . . . family matters . . ."

"But what is it, for goodness' sake?"

"Rafael. . ." murmured Fidela, beginning to cry again.

"What about Rafaelito?"

"My brother doesn't love me any more."

"So that's it. And what does it matter to you? I mean, how do you know it? Has that *individual* started his foolishness again?"

"This afternoon he said some things to me that . . . that offend me, that he has no right to say."

"What has he said to you?"

"Things. We started to talk about the theater performance last night. He said such clever things. He was laughing and reciting. Then he spoke about you. No, don't think he spoke ill of you. On the contrary; he praised you. That you're a wonderful character, and that I don't deserve you."

"He said that? Well, you certainly do deserve me."

"That you're to be pitied."

"Hello, hello! He probably says that because of the way your sister plunders me, and the way she has me cleaned out."

"That's not the reason."

"Then why, dammit!"

"If you say awful things, I won't speak another word."

"I'm not saying them, dammit, double-dammit! Your little brother is starting to annoy me again; I repeat that he's starting to annoy me, and in the end it'll be necessary to avoid *any point of contact* between him and me."

TEN

"Well, all of a sudden he started to say things to me," added Fidela, "in a tragic tone, phrases very similar to those Hamlet said to his mother when he discovered . . . ."

"What? And who's this *Hamley*? Christ! Who is this *individual* who's starting to annoy me so much, for Zárate, too, always drags him in at every shake of a lamb's tail. *Hamley!* To hell with *Hamley!*"

"He was a prince of Denmark."

"Yes, the one who went around finding out about *to be or not to be*. Tomfoolery! I know that already. And what does that rascal have to do with us?"

"Nothing. But my brother's not right in the head and he said to me what Hamlet said to his mother . . ."

"Which must have been quite a mouthful, too."

"It wasn't very nice. Look, this happens in one of Shakespeare's most beautiful tragedies."

"Whose? Ah! The one who wrote *The Maidens' Consent*."

"No, darling. How ignorant you are!"

"All right, the author of . . . of . . . Well, whoever he was, it doesn't matter much to me, and knowing that this Hamley is an invention of poets, it doesn't interest me at all. Devil take him. Let's talk about something else, girlie. Don't pay any attention to your brother, and whatever he tells you don't listen to him. And your sister?"

"She's gone shopping."

"Oh, my God, what a pain I have right here!"

"Where?"

"In my blessed pocket. Shopping! Farewell to my *liquid assets*. Your sister and I are going to come to a bad end. What projects is she *cherishing*? What new *encumbrances* are awaiting me? I'm trembling, because quite a while ago, before our summer trip, she promised a thunderbolt, and I'm beating my brains out wondering what can it be, what can't it be."

Fidela smiled impishly.

"You know it, you minx, you know it and don't want to tell me for fear of your sister, who has you scared to death, just as she has me and the whole terrestrial globe."

"Maybe I do know it, but it's a secret, and it's not up to me to tell you about it. She'll tell you."

"But when? While I'm waiting for this cataclysm of my interests, there isn't a *historical moment* that isn't painful for me. I can't live, I can't breathe. But what is it? Is it something that's going to leave me stripped naked?"

"My dear man, of course not."

"Is it about an *encumbrance* and does it mean that I can't economize? What the devil, a fellow can't live this way! This life is a purgatory for me, and here I am, paying for all the sins of my life . . . which aren't very many. By the Bible! There's only the natural and consanguineous sins of a man who's swept everything into his house that he could. And now my little sister-in-law is sweeping everything out."

"Don't exaggerate, Tor."

"Are you or aren't you going to tell me what it is?"

"I can't. Cruz would be angry with me if I took away from her the pleasure of the surprise she wants to give you."

"Don't talk to me about surprises. Let things come at their natural pace."

"And besides, if I tell you, I'm invading an area that isn't mine, and attributions which . . ."

"That's nonsense, all nonsense. I order you to tell me, or there'll be a real *fracas* in the house."

"Don't be such a ruffian. Come here; sit down beside me. Don't wave your hands about or act vulgar, Tor. Look, I don't love you when you behave like that. Come here . . . give me your paw" (taking his hand in hers). "Now, stay here quietly talking like a gentleman, without saying anything foolish or ugly. There, there."

"Get the doubt over with."

"Do you promise you'll keep the secret and pretend to be surprised when my sister . . . ?"

"I promise."

"Well, look. An aunt of ours, the poor thing's dead now . . ."

"May God have her in His blessed glory. Go on."

"My aunt, Doña Loreto de la Torre Auñón . . ."

"At her service."

"Marquise of San Eloy . . . I say, marquise of San Eloy."

"I catch on, yes."

"The poor lady died suddenly, leaving very little money. The title belonged to Mama, but it came to her during that time of our misfortune, and the least thing we cared about was the marquisate of San Eloy, for the first step that had to be taken was to pay the taxes for transmission of titles of the realm."

"What the devil, dammit! now I know, I know . . . Christ! And what your sister wants now is to . . ."

"Is to bring back the title, for which one has to institute proceedings and pay something called a half-benefice tax."

"Benefices and benedictions and the almighty Bible in verse! And she expects me to pay! No, a thousand times no. This I won't allow. I rebel, I mutiny."

"Be calm, Tor. But, my dear, there's no alternative to taking the title before the Romeros do, for they're after it too. Just imagine— those wretches, marquises of San Eloy! I'd rather die, darling Tor. Summon your courage and face up to the expense."

"Let's see . . . just a moment . . . let's find out," said Torquemada breathlessly, wiping the sweat from his face. "How much might this cost?"

"Oh! I don't know. It depends on the time that has elapsed, on the importance of the title, which is very, very old, for it dates from 1522, from the reign of Emperor Charles the Fifth."

"Fine rascal he was! He's responsible for my having to swallow these things. Might it cost . . . five hundred reales?"

"My dear man, no; the title of marquis for five hundred reales!"

"Will it cost two thousand?"

"More, ever so much more. The State charged the marquis of Fonfría for his title, according to what Ramoncita told us last night . . . I think it was eighteen thousand duros."

"Brrr!" shouted Torquemada, starting to pace frantically up and down the room like a wild beast. "Well, from this minute, I'm telling you that the title can stay where it is till *the Greek calends* in the afternoon if they expect me to take it out of there. You two are going to rip out my liver. Eighteen thousand duros! And for a label, a piece of vanity, a sucker trap! Look at the good it did your aunt, that old Doña Loreto, to be a marquise. She died without a real in her pocket. No, no, Francisco Torquemada has reached his limit, the flipping limit of his patience, his compliance, and his prudence. No more purgatory, no more doing penance for sins I haven't committed; no more throwing the blessed fruits of my labors out the window. Tell your sister to come to her senses, that if she wants to be a marquise let her order her patents of nobility from one of those copyists in some cubbyhole, for it's all the same; what more is the government than a great copyist whose establishment is always open?"

"But it's not my sister who's to be the marquise. The marquise is going to be me, and, naturally, you the marquis."

"Me a marquis?" exclaimed the miser with an explosion of laughter. "Look, me a marquis!"

"And why not? Aren't others marquises?"

"Others? And did those others have a grandfather who lived from the noble task of doing an operation on pigs that made their voices squeaky? Ha, ha, I could die laughing!"

"That doesn't matter. In no time, any one of those who deal with almanacs of nobility can make you a genealogical tree proving you're a lineal descendant of King Mauricat."

"Or King Mauridog. Ha, ha! But tell me honestly . . . joking aside" (stopping in front of her with arms akimbo). "Do you have the whim of being a marquise? Would you like to have that little coronet? In a word, is it a question of *to be or not to be* for you, like the man said?"

"Don't you believe it: I don't have that particular vanity."

"So it's all the same to you whether you're a marquise or *Plain Jane?*"

"Just the same."

"Well, if you don't *cherish that idea* of wearing a coronet, and neither do I, then why this stupid expense of . . . ? What's that thing called?"

"Duties and half-benefices."

"I never heard that fancy word."

"And you'll have to pay a bit more for it because now it turns out, according to what Cruz was told by the person in the Ministry of State, the marquis of Saldeoro, you know? that Aunt Loreto used the title without paying for the rights, and they've been owing since the time of Charles the Fourth."

"Hell's bells! My goodness, I'm going crazy," exclaimed Don Francisco, slapping himself smartly on the head. "And they want me to . . . pull that out . . . I'd sooner pull out my fingernails. *In a word,* no, no, a thousand times no! I rebel . . . duties and half-benefices . . ." (furiously) "I say no . . . duties . . . San Eloy . . . Charles the Fourth. No, and no. Look, I'm spitting with anger, can't you see? Half-benefices . . . I say no . . . half-benedictions . . ." (raising his voice) "Fidela, I can't live like this. When your sister tackles me about this piece of extortion, I'm going to take and . . . *in a word,* I'll kill myself."

"Tor, don't take it like that. Why, for you the expense is a mere trifle."

"A trifle! Oh! What a pair of women you are! How you torment me, how you make my blood boil! Half-benefices . . . duties . . ." (repeating it as if to fix the words in his memory) "San Eloy . . . Charles the Fourth . . . Listen, Fidela, if you want me to love you, we've got to rebel against that monster, your sister. If you come over to my side, I'll stand fast . . . but you have to be on my side, on my team. I can't do it alone; I know I won't have the courage. I have it when I'm alone, but as soon as she stands in front of me with that trembling lip, I just fall apart. Duties . . . halves . . . Charles the Fourth . . . those cursed benefices . . . Fidela, shall we rebel, yes or no?"

Somewhat alarmed by the excitement she observed in her husband, Fidela went over to him, caressed him, and led him to the sofa.

"But, Tor, why are you making such a fuss?"

"I tell you that we'll rebel, for see here, this half-marquisate of San Eloy doesn't mean a blessed thing either to you or to me . . . I mean half-benefices; what I say is, if all that doesn't matter a bit to us, let her buy the marquisate and she can strut around with it all she wants."

"Silly boy, the marquisate is for you to show off with. You're enormously rich; you'll be richer still. A rich man, a senator, a person of the highest reputation in society. The title is made to order for you."

"If it didn't cost money, I wouldn't say no."

"My dear, things cost what they are worth. Look at it sensibly. . . And there's another reason that my sister has taken into account. If the sparkle of a coronet doesn't dazzle you, wouldn't you like to see it on your son's little head?"

The fierce moneylender was so disconcerted when he heard this, that for a good while he was unable to pronounce a word. And his wife, observing the good effect her argument had produced, reinforced it as much as she could within her small store of rhetorical means.

"All right; I concede that it wouldn't be a bad thing for my son to have a marquis's coronet. A boy who's so worthy of it! But the truth is, I've never known mathematicians to be marquises, and if they are, they'd have to invent titles for them with some *point of contact* with science; to wit: it wouldn't be so bad if our Valentín was called marquis of Squaring the Circle, or something like that. But that doesn't sound good, does it? You're right. Don't laugh . . . I'm sort of upset by the idea of that brutal expenditure, that will wipe out half a year's liquid assets . . . benefices, halves . . . Charles . . . duties . . . My head's turning round and round. There's nothing for it . . . rebellion . . . If it weren't for you, I'd run away from home before Cruz faced up to me with that nonsense. Of course, for my son's glory I'd do anything. Listen to what I've just thought of. Compromise. Persuade your sister to put off the business about the marquisate until the child's born; no, no, till we've got him a little older."

"That can't be, darling Tor," replied Fidela sweetly, "because the Romeros are also negotiating concession of the title, and it would be shameful for us if they snatched it away from us. We have to forestall their intrigues."

"Well, they'll have to forestall my death—Christ!—which I think isn't far off with these shocks I'm getting! Fidela, your sister will send me to my grave at the most unexpected *historical moment*. We can fix everything if you'll back me up and help me in the defense of my *interest*, because at the rate we're going, believe me, we'll very soon be the marquises of Copper Penny."

He could say no more because his daughter Rufina came in, and the moment he saw her he discharged all his anger on her, scolding her for being late. It was all her fault. The poor girl paid the piper, and the man who was all cowardice and unease in the face of Cruz's formidable authority vented his rage in a vulgar tirade against a weak creature linked to him by the law of obedience. Fortunately for Señora de Quevedo, the tyrant came home, and the sound of her footsteps outside the door sufficed to produce absolute silence in the sitting room. Don Francisco returned to his study on the upper floor, grumbling very much under his breath, and until dinnertime his brain never ceased to shuffle the ideas that were tormenting him. Half-duties . . . benefices . . . San Carlos . . . San Eloy, Valentín . . . scientific marquises . . . ruin . . . death . . . rebellion . . . half-benefices.

ELEVEN

Neither peace nor charity could save him now, for the household ruler, in her lofty designs, had resolved to add to the Torquemada coat of arms the heraldic beasts of the marquisate of San Eloy, and the stars would fall from the sky before she would fail to achieve that resolution. Precisely at the *historical moment* of the above-mentioned conversation between Don Francisco and Fidela, the heraldic artist and the investigator of genealogies were up to their elbows in the matter, that is, manufacturing a coat of arms for the miser, which in fact was not difficult for them, since the name of Torquemada had a noble ring to it, an authentic combination of elements and one very suitable for finding origins as old as Jerusalem. Cruz swept all before her and, before talking with her brother-in-law, had made all the arrangements for the swift execution of her prideful idea—her desire to get ahead of those disgusting Romeros only increasing her haste. She asked to have the petition activated in the Office of Grace and Justice, arranged to have all the necessary family trees and letters patent prepared as quickly as possible, and nothing was left to do but to firmly impose the *encumbrance* on the ruffian, as the most suitable thing both for the family and himself.

This time Cruz found him more stubborn than ever, for the sheer scale of the plunder made his blood boil, giving him the courage for defense. For reinforcement the lady had to call in Donoso, who earnestly informed him of the advantages of being a marquis and how remunerative that expense would be, for his social reputation would increase along with the coronet, translating itself sooner or later into financial benefits. The poor man was only half convinced, and groaned as if they were pulling all his teeth at once with the most primitive instruments. As a result of his anger he was ill for five days, a rare thing in his vigorous nature; he lost weight and acquired a great many white hairs. Cruz went out of her way to please him and return serenity to his troubled spirit; she disguised her tyranny, tried to anticipate his slightest desires, and indeed did so in the minor details of life. But not even this was effective: the poor man surrendered kicking and screaming and accepted the half-benefices with repugnance, exhausted by the struggle and lacking the courage to mount a full-scale rebellion against despotism.

His presentation in the Senate and the acquaintanceships he made there distracted him a bit from his low spirits. The president of the Council, to whom he had to present his thanks before his credentials were approved, told him very cordially that he had been eager to see him there and that persons like himself (like Señor Torquemada) were those who worthily represented the country, something which the miser believed to be absolutely correct. He saw himself treated with consideration and courtesy, saw that he was praised—why deny it?—and that the president, as well as all the gentlemen of the presidential table, welcomed him with great respect. When he returned home after his first flight in spaces that were new to him, Cruz watched his face, trying to discover the effects of that atmosphere of vanities, and observed certain oozings of satisfaction that augured well for the future. She interrogated him about his impressions; she made him tell about the session and its incidents, and saw with pleasure that the good man had taken note of everything and hadn't missed a trick. It goes without saying that the lady congratulated herself about all this. In her eyes shone a maternal joy, or rather, the pride of a hardworking teacher who sees progress in the most rebellious of her students.

In order to understand Torquemada's extraordinary luck and how right Cruz was to push him, *velis nolis*, along that path, suffice it to say that soon after he had taken his seat in the Senate, with his credentials easily approved, clean as a whistle, there was a vote on the secondary railway line called "Villafranca del Bierzo and Mines of Berrocal," which had been held up since the previous session of the legislature. It was a project eagerly desired by the inhabitants of El Bierzo, for they believed it to be a source of inexhaustible riches. And what happened? The people of the district attributed the project's rapid success to the influence of the new senator (whom they supposed to have great power), and raised a tremendous fuss over "El Bierzo's favorite son." Don Francisco had indeed done something in favor of the project: he had approached the Commission and spoken to the minister along with another prominent citizen of León, but this did not cause him to believe that he was author of the miracle or anything like it, nor did he conceal his surprise when he saw himself the object of so many ovations. For you have no idea of the fulsome telegrams he was sent from the district, nor of the panegyrics intoned in his honor by the mayor in City Hall, the apothecary among his friends, the political boss in the middle of the street, and even the priest in the holy pulpit. And there was a letter in *El Imparcial* which told of the effect caused by the news in that sensible town, describing how all the highly sensible inhabitants had lost their senses; how they had formed a street procession carrying a bad portrait of Don Francisco, wreathed in laurel, that they had got hold of somehow; how they fired off rockets that thundered in the air, expressing their gratitude with those rockets' explosions, and how, at last, they acclaimed him hoarsely, calling him "father of the poor," "foremost glory of El Bierzo," and "savior of the province of León."

For Cruz to learn of these things and go wild with joy, was all one.

"Do you see, my dear sir? If it weren't for me, would you have these satisfactions? What a man! He has hardly taken the first steps, and successes sprout out of the ground."

Hearing these flatteries and the whole chorus of congratulation sung by his friends, Don Francisco smiled out of one half of his mouth and wept with the other half, fluctuating between the prickling of satisfied self-esteem and the fear that all these praises would eventually result in new *encumbrances*.

Though still on a small scale, the suspicious miser's forebodings lost no time in coming true, for on the following day four parties of strolling musicians invaded the staircase, and the doorman had to threaten them with a broom to get rid of them, distributing tips at the rate of one duro per orchestra, on Cruz's recommendation. And in a few days, alas, the multitude appeared. As it began with only a few, it seemed child's play at first, but it grew and grew and soon caused terror to look upon. First came two married couples, the kind in which the husband wears corduroy and the wife green petticoats, one asking to have their son excused from military service and the other for return of the postal operation which the intrigues of the government had taken from them. There was also a torrent of folk from Astorga in country breeches, bringing gifts of pastries and asking *the Bible and all* for some minor employment, forgiveness of taxes, permission to make charcoal, expediting a request—some baldly demanding alms, others asking alms disguised by a thousand ingenious tricks. There followed others who, though village folk in essence, presented themselves as gentlemen, aspiring to all sorts of crooked deals; one asking to have the whole city council of some place or other fired; another, a post in the Treasury Office of the province; still another, to have the highway right-of-way altered.

After each group of importuners came another and another, with very strange commissions. A good number of Leonese residing in Madrid—*maragatos* and turkey-sellers and outrageous nuisances—also fell upon the house, asking protection from the law or demanding all sorts of illegal dainties, giving the most ingenious twists and turns to their requests. Let one individual serve as an example: he sent Don Francisco a little project, very well drawn up to be sure, for "a monument to be built in Villafranca del Bierzo to perpetuate the glory of her favorite son," etc. And others sent verses, odes asking for loans, and begging pentacrostics, or proposed that he should buy an old painting of souls in purgatory that looked a terrible mess. Torquemada shook them off with a certain degree of brutality, passing the buck to his sister-in-law, who faced the storm with Christian forbearance and treated them nicely and smiled at them, giving them a bit of sweet talk to make them go away sooner. The folk from his native town had so lofty an idea of Don Francisco that they turned pale when they laid eyes on him and stood open-mouthed, as if in the presence of an emperor or the Pope. All had high hopes of the visit and came convinced of success, for in Villafranca it was said that anything one asked of Don Francisco was sure to be done, in every sphere of the government of the realm, that the Queen herself took no decision whatever without consulting him, and invited him to eat at her table very frequently. Well, they had such a hyperbolic idea of Torquemada's riches that some were amazed not to see cartloads of money coming in through the carriage entrance of the house. Among those dressed in dark corduroys and green petticoats were two or three who had known Don Francisco when he was a lad running barefoot through the middens of Paradeseca; and there was even a hag who, throwing her arms around his neck, greeted him with expressions similar to those of the country wench in the comic play: "Come here, my boy—you old donkey!"

TWELVE

The poor man was becoming greatly annoyed with that flood of clients, and when he encountered someone from his district, the hairs in his mustache stood on end and his face assumed such an expression of ferocity that the visitor's spirits were quite dashed. At last he told Cruz to close the door to all such good-for-nothings, or to allow to enter, after careful inspection, only those who brought something, whether it was sausages or chocolate . . . or even chestnuts and acorns, which he liked very much.

Meanwhile he was becoming accustomed to parliamentary life, and, having been elected to this or that commission, ventured to enlighten his fellows with some useful idea, always in case it dealt, mind you, with fiscal matters. Indeed, he would have been very happy if his pocketbook had not been assailed, ever since he had taken his place on the red benches of Parliament, with requests for money in one form or another. That drove him wild. It was really too much. Lord, a fellow couldn't shine according to his merits without having his lean pocketbook bled at every moment! Now it was a little subscription to print the speech of any one of those *individuals*, again a collection to erect a monument to some Juan, Pedro, or Diego of antiquity—if it wasn't to build one to some modern personage, the kinds of fellows who become famous by talking their heads off or turning everything topsy-turvy. And at every moment, *victims* from here, there, and everywhere; contributions for victims of floods, of shipwrecks, and widows and orphans of somebody or other. It was a constant leakage, which amounted to a terrible liability at the end of the month. Heavens, at that price he didn't want the satisfaction of being a father or a grandfather to the country. How that rascally country charged for the honors she conferred on her famous sons! He was so sick of being a *famous son* that one night, when he came home in a vile humor because the marquis of Cícero had diddled him out of forty duros for the restoration of some damned cathedral or other, he told Cruz that he wouldn't put up with any more of it, and that some fine day he'd throw his credentials into the middle of the circle—*in the vernacular* hemicycle—and let someone else take over. To complete his despair, that same night his tyrant took it into her head to inform him that she proposed to offer a dinner for eighteen, and that others would follow it weekly, for the purpose of inviting different persons of high degree. All the stubborn miser's protests were in vain. Banqueting was inevitable, and banqueting there would be. The decorum of the new statesman demanded it, and instead of raging like a lion, he ought to be grateful to her and glad that he had persons at his side who cared so religiously for his dignity.

But, Lord, if they went down that road he would soon come to *the road to the poorhouse*! Dinners for fourteen and eighteen and twenty persons! Ever since October the food budget had been rising. It was an overwhelming daily expense which badly frightened Don Francisco, for he was accustomed to the meanness of the twelve or thirteen reales of expenditure in Doña Silvia's day. But with the *new regime* of invitations, the sum would increase until it attained a figure that would keep the Seven Sleepers awake, and even the Seven Sages of Greece, whose slumber was eternal. Why, the good man would have a stroke any day now from the indignation it caused him; he was consumed with grumblings, and the satisfactions of the public figure and great financier were embittered by that endless outflow of his *liquid assets*. How much better to gather it all together and use it in new business dealings, living very modestly but comfortably, without banquets, which always endangered the health, and dressed with simple decency by a clever tailor, the kind who turns the cloth and uses it again! This was the logical thing, and the sensible thing, and *the perfectly obvious thing*. Why so much luxury? Where did Cruz get the idea that in order to engage in large-scale finance one had to invite so many ne'er-do-wells to dinner? And what did those diplomats go there for, spluttering bad Spanish and talking endlessly of horse races, the opera, and other absurd trifles? What liquid benefit was brought him by those people, and the minister's brothers, and General Morla, and so many others who did nothing but complain about the government and find everything in very bad shape? It was true that he also found everything in terrible shape, for any policy that did not consist of economy across the board, *come what may*, was playing with dolls, and he said this in front of twelve or fourteen guests at his table, who ended up agreeing with him.

Toward the end of the year the tobacco business was going without a hitch, for Serrano's relative who made the purchases in the United States was a man who understood the business, sticking strictly to instructions given by the manager. In short, the first shipments went into the storage facilities without difficulty, and when one shipment or another gave rise to doubts or hesitations, because the tobacco looked like garbage that had been swept up from the streets of Madrid, orders were given to accept it thanks to the actions of Don Juan Gualberto, who had a remarkably sharp eye for these things. Donoso did not intervene in anything having to do with deliveries. The profits, according to Torquemada's calculations, would be phenomenal in the first year. Serrano lost no time in proposing another deal to him: to buy up all the shares of the Villafranca and Mines of Berrocal Railway, with which action a good many birds would be killed with one stone, for the people of El Bierzo would see it as a new triumph by their idol, and he and his cronies would make an excellent deal by unloading the shares after causing them to rise, by the arts that are applied to such combinations, to enormous heights. With this and the arrangement with the House of Gravelinas, whereby the incumbent duke was assigned a pension for his lifetime plus ten years, with Torquemada and his business associates keeping all the real estate (which would be sold piece by piece, payment being received in shares issued by the ducal house), the miser's fortune increased like sea foam, in an extraordinary mathematical progression, quite apart from his innumerable deals of other kinds, buying and selling of bonds so shrewdly carried out that he was never mistaken in his calculations of the rise and fall of shares; and his orders on the Exchange were the key to almost all the large-scale operations that took place there.

Among these joys, the great event approached, eagerly awaited by the miser, for he thought he saw in it the compensation for his sufferings over the useless extravagance with which Cruz was trying to gild the bars of his cage. Very soon now the delights of fatherhood would sweeten the sorrows of the usurer, constantly thwarted in his attempts to accumulate wealth. The good man also wanted to resolve that cruel doubt: would his son be a Torquemada, *as he had the right to expect*, if the Supreme Maker behaved like a gentleman? *"I'm inclined to believe* that He will," he said to himself, in a regular flood of fine language. "Though it could well be that that busybody, Nature, will *muddle up the matter* and the baby will turn out to have Aguila instincts, in which case I'd ask the Lord God to give me my money back . . . I mean, not the money, the, the . . . There's no expression for that idea. We'll soon emerge from the *dilemma*. And it could just as well be a girl, and be like me, devoted to economy. We'll soon see. *I'm inclined to believe* that it will be a boy, and *hence* another Valentín, *in a word*, Valentín himself *under his very own aspect*. But those two don't believe it, undoubtedly, and that's why expectation *reigns in everyone*, as when folks are waiting for the lottery to be drawn."

Fidela no longer left the house, nor could she move about. And they counted the days, both desiring and fearing the one that would bring the great event. There were errors in the calculations. It was expected for the first half of December, and nothing happened. The twentieth came and went; confusion and fear. At last, on the twenty-fourth, beginning at dawn, the solution of the tremendous enigma announced itself with horrible discomfort and apprehension on the lady's part. Since Quevedito was not considered to be sufficiently competent to bring Torquemada's heir into the world, one of the eminences of obstetrics had been engaged in good time; but the case must have appeared a bit difficult, for the eminence proposed the aid of another eminence. When both doctors had conferred, they declared that the birth was an extremely tricky one and requested the collaboration of a third eminence.

The master of the house chewed his mustache and rubbed one hand over the other, now overcome by panic, now by rosy hopes, and did nothing but pace to and fro, and go up and down from the counting room to the sitting room without managing to decide anything, on that critical day, in connection with his vast business affairs. His closest friends went to inquire and keep him company, and he had harsh words for all. He had certainly not been pleased with the invasion of doctors, and said to Quevedito, who was acting as assistant, when he caught him alone:

"All this business about bringing in so many doctors is only Cruz's meddlesome ways, for she always *propends* to do everything on a grand scale, even if it's not necessary. If the seriousness of the case demanded it, I wouldn't hesitate over the expense. But you'll see that we don't need so many people. You'd be enough and more than enough to get her through her trouble. But, my boy, the boss is the boss. She's *refractory* to modesty and moderation, and good theories don't work with her . . . duties and half-benefices . . . I don't know what I'm saying . . . She'll ruin me in the end with so much folderol . . . San Eloy . . . And what do you think? Will we come out of this fix all right? San Eloy . . . I'm sure that by tonight we'll have Valentín in the house . . . And if I get what I want it'll be a coincidence that it's the same night . . . half-benefices . . . that our Redeemer, *in the vernacular* Jesus Christ, came into the world, or in other words the promised Messiah . . . Go on, go in the bedroom, don't leave her for a moment . . . I'm just about crazy . . . Imagine bringing those three medical *individuals* here, they'll send me such bills . . . ! Well, it's all in God's hands. I can't breathe till I see . . ."

THIRTEEN

By nightfall the case appeared as one of the most dangerous and difficult possible. The three eminences held a solemn consultation, and were on the point of sending for a fourth celebrity. At last it was agreed to wait, and Torquemada, who was nearly out of his skin with pure fidgets, succumbed to the fear of danger and declared himself willing to have more *medical personnel* brought in if necessary. The prospective mother became calmer early in the evening, though the case was still serious; favorable symptoms appeared, and the men-midwives even ventured to cheer the grieving family with rosy hopes. Don Francisco's face was the color of wax; you would have thought that his mustache was not in its proper place, or that his mouth had become twisted. Sometimes heavy drops of sweat stood out on his forehead, and at every instant he put his hand to his waist to pull up his trousers, which were slipping. A few people came in, awaiting the event, and went to the drawing room, prepared to unleash demonstrations either of joy or of grief, according to the turn the occasion might take. The miser fled the drawing room, horrified by the idea of having to perform social duties, and in one of his flittings about the house alighted in Rafael's room, finding him quietly seated in an armchair talking of literary matters with Morentín.

"Ah, Morentín!" said Don Francisco, greeting him coldly. "I didn't know that you were here."

"We were saying that there's no cause for alarm. We'll soon be able to offer you congratulations. And I will offer them twice: first, for what you're waiting for . . ."

"And second?"

"For the marquisate of San Eloy. I meant to hold back, so as to give you the two congratulations at once."

"I don't need them," replied Don Francisco harshly. "San Eloy . . . half-benefices . . . Ideas of this fellow's sister, who's always inventing claptrap to take us out of the *status quo* and put me, humble as I am, in high places. Imagine, me a marquis! And what blessed use is that title?"

"None is more illustrious than the title of San Eloy," said Rafael, somewhat nettled. "It dates from the time of Emperor Charles the Fifth, and persons of great merit have worn that coronet, such as Don Beltrán de la Torre-Auñón, grand master of the Order of Santiago and captain-general of His Majesty's galleys."

"And now they want to send me to the galleys! San Eloy . . . Oh, fine marquises we are! We'd be much better off if we didn't have anything to fill the pot, like *certain and particular* titled folks who live by trickery. My *beau ideal* is not the nobility; I have a *sui generis* way of looking at things. Rafael, don't get mad at me if I sound off against the dead-broke aristocracy whose only *desideratum* is to humiliate the unfortunate lower classes. I'm a poor man who's managed to secure the *classic* daily bread and no more. It's a sad thing to have what I've earned with so much hard work spent on marquisates. Nor do I have anything in common with that sonofa ——— who commanded the king's galleys. Don't take it in the wrong way, Rafaelito. You know I don't say it to offend your ancestors . . . with all respect . . . No doubt they were very decent *individuals*. But I'd give up the marquisate any day for what it costs and a ten percent surcharge, if there's anybody who wants it. Hey, Morentín, I'm selling the coronet. D'you want it?"

The two friends laughed: Rafael reluctantly and the other most heartily, for every demonstration of coarseness on Don Francisco's part filled him with glee.

"But all of that," said Torquemada when they had finished, "is of no importance *as a parallel* to the great struggle we're in now. Just let Fidela come out of this in good shape and I'll face up to everything, even the half-benefices."

"I foresee events," stated Rafael with serene conviction, "and I prophesy that Fidela will come out of her trouble safe and sound."

"May God hear you. . . I believe the same."

"Misfortune will not come to you from that quarter, nor will it come today, but from a different quarter and in days that are still far off."

"Bah! Now you're playing the prophet," said Morentín, trying to temper with his laughter the seriousness that the blind man was imparting to his words.

"For the moment," added Torquemada, "let today's prophecy come to pass. I congratulate myself that Rafael is right. But what a long time it's taking, Most Holy Virgin of La Paloma! And for this they have to bring in three star practitioners! What are those fine gentlemen doing that nothing's happening? Because I'm the first to *render tribute* to science. But let's see its practical results. What, does everything have to be theory, Señor Morentín?"

"I agree."

"Lots of theory, lots of Greek terms, and this one orders one thing and the other the opposite; and the treatments are like *Penelope's web*, today it's done and tomorrow it's undone. If the sick person dies, that's no excuse for not paying the *Galen's* bill. No indeed! And *I profess the theory* that the worms ought to pay those bills. Don't you agree with me? Right: the worms, who're the ones that come out ahead. Here we are in an *expectant attitude*, saying 'will it be, won't it be,' and these fine medical gentlemen as cool as cucumbers. And *I'll be frank with you*: I'm so nervous that . . . look . . . my hands tremble and I even get tongue-tied. My son-in-law Quevedo was enough and more than enough; that's my humble *point of view*."

He left the room without hearing what Rafael and Morentín were expressing about their respective points of view, and in the hall encountered Pinto, to whom he administered several cuffs to the head, the reason for which neither the aggressor nor the victim had a very clear idea. Whenever Don Francisco became out of sorts or very nervous, he vented the effluvia of his wild anger on the innocent ears and cranium of the little footman, who was a dear chap and bore patiently the buffets he was paid to receive. Good treatment by the ladies of the house and having as much as he wanted to eat compensated for the brutalities of his master, who, when he was in a good mood, would come to terms with him about certain matters of espionage, to wit:

"Pinto, come here. Is Señorita Cruz in the sitting room? Who just came in, Señor Donoso or the Señor Marquis of Taramundi? Listen, boy, come and tell me upstairs when Donoso leaves, without anybody knowing it, see? Listen, Pinto: Señorita Cruz will ask you if I'm upstairs, and you tell her that I have visitors."

That day the hardness of his knuckles was such that the boy began to cry.

"Don't cry, my lad," said the miser, suddenly softening. "I didn't mean to do it; it was just out of pesky habit. I'm out of sorts. What's going on? Has any one of those plaguey doctors come out of the bedroom yet? Stop crying, I tell you. If the mistress comes out of this in good shape, you can count on a new livery. Go see who's in the drawing room. It seems to me that Morentín's mama has come in, *entirely*. And Señor Zárate, has he come? No? Well, I'm sorry for that. Find out carefully, discreetly, where Señorita Cruz is, if she's still in the bedroom, or in the drawing room, or in her room, and hurry and tell me. I'll wait for you here. Go in acting stupid, as if you thought they'd called you. I can't stand this. You, too, want us to come out of this all right, and for it to be a boy, don't you?"

Drying his tears, the good Pinto answered that he did, and went off to carry out the commissions his master had charged him with. And Torquemada continued to wander through the halls, slowly at times, his eyes fixed on the floor, as if he were searching for a coin he had lost; at other times fast, his face turned up to the ceiling as if he expected a shower of gold to fall from it. When he heard knocking at the door, he would hide in the nearest available room, fleeing from visitors, who either irritated him or made him furious.

But one person did come in who was very welcome, and he rushed toward him joyfully, allowing the other to embrace him and give him a couple of hugs.

"I really wanted to see you, friend Zárate. I'm—we are—in terrible anguish."

"What," said the sage, feigning consternation, "can't we congratulate you yet?"

"Not yet. And I've had three first-class practitioners come, eminences all three of 'em, and one of them is the foremost man-midwife on the terrestrial globe."

"Oh, then there's nothing to fear! Let us quietly await the results of science."

"D'you really think so?" said Torquemada, now completely exhausted, leaning against the walls of the corridor like a drunken man unsure of the ground under his feet.

"I trust in science. But perhaps the case is a difficult one? Maybe the family is frightened for no reason. Is the patient in the first stage? And the offspring, is it presenting by the head or the breech?"

"What's that you say?"

"And haven't they thought of bringing an instrument that's often used in Germany, the *sella obstetricalis?*"

"Shut up, man. What's the function of those instruments? Please God, everything will be natural, as it is with poor women, who make short work of it without the help of practitioners."

"But rarely, Don Francisco, do you find a good childbed without the aid of practical women, *vulgo* midwives, who in Greece were called *omphalotomis*, just imagine, and in Rome *obstetrices.*"

He had not finished pronouncing these imposing terms when they heard a tumult deep inside the house, hurried footsteps, voices. Something tremendous was happening; but it was not easy to surmise at the moment whether it was good or bad. Don Francisco stood there like a corpse, not daring to investigate for himself. Zárate took several steps toward the drawing room; but he had not yet reached it, when they clearly heard someone say, "It's over, it's over."

FOURTEEN

"What is it? By the beard of Christ Almighty!" cried Torquemada, spitting out the words.

"It's over, it's over," repeated the servants, scurrying about; their happy faces announced the good news.

And at the door of the sitting room, where he ran like a streak of lightning, Don Francisco found himself squeezed in an iron grip. It was Cruz's, who in her wild joy kissed him on both cheeks, saying, "It's a boy, a boy."

"I knew I couldn't be mistaken!" exclaimed the miser, feeling the lump in his throat grow tighter. "A boy . . . I want to see him. Half-benefices . . . Oh! Science . . . bibles . . . Valentín, Fidela. Good for the three eminences."

Cruz would not let him enter the bedroom. He would have to wait a little while.

"And what's he like? Strong as a bull. . ." added the happy father, who, without knowing exactly how, was dragged off to the drawing room and there embraced by a multitude of persons who relinquished him and caught him again like a ball, and smeared his face with saliva. "Thanks, ladies and gentlemen. I appreciate your *manifestations* . . . San Eloy . . . science . . . three foremost aces of medicine. Thanks very much . . . you're welcome. It hasn't caught me unprepared. I knew it had to be . . . of the masculine sex—*in the vernacular,* a male. Excuse me, I don't know what I'm saying. Hey, Pinto, I want to invite everybody to a drink. Go to the tavern and have them bring some Cariñena wine. What an idiot I am! I don't know what I'm saying . . . The almighty Holy Bible and champagne . . . Ladies and gentlemen, a thousand thousand thanks for your *attitude* of sympathy and . . . approval. I'm very happy. I'll be the *Maecenas* of everybody. Bring on the brew, I mean sherry. I knew how the *occurrence* was going to turn out. I had it figured out, I figure out everything . . . My dear Zárate, come on, another hug. Science! *Praise* . . . *be* to science! But it's just as I said; we didn't need so many doctors. It has been a *merely* natural and spontaneous birth, *so to speak.* We're happy . . . Yes, ladies and gentlemen, happy . . . *entirely;* you're right, *entirely.*"

He went in to congratulate his wife. After having lavished caresses on her and taken a look at the baby when they were washing him, he reemerged, radiant.

"He's the same, the very same Valentín," he told Rufinita, giving her yet another hug. "How good God is to me! He took him away from me; now He's giving him back! There are designs that only a few know; but I know about them. Now, what would be very nice for us would be to have all these people clear out."

"But more are coming. The whole house will be filled with them."

And, once again in the drawing room, he heard, among the chorus of congratulations, comments about the extraordinary coincidence that Torquemada's son should be born on the birthday of the Son of God.

"You'll see. It's the designs, the lofty designs."

"Happy Christmas Eve, Señor Don Francisco, the great man, the lucky man, the Almighty's spoiled child."

Amid so much flattery he did not forget to go and receive the congratulations of Rafael, who received him with chilly cordiality, very happy that his sister had given birth successfully, but he made no mention of the new being who had come to perpetuate the dynasty. Don Francisco did not like this at all, and told him with a haughty air and in a loud voice:

"A boy, Rafael, a boy, so that your house and every bit of the nobility of old times, older than the Eternal Father's beard, can be represented in coming and future centuries. I suppose you'll be happy about that."

The blind man nodded without saying a word. Morentín had gone to the drawing room, adding his voice to the chorus of praise and congratulations. The household ruler thought it very appropriate to improvise a supper for all present, with the dual motive of celebrating the birth of God's Son and that of the successor to the house and estates of Aguila-Torquemada. Since the confusion and feverish activity of that day had not allowed anyone to think of festive meals, at ten o'clock the whole corps of servants was desperately trying to hurry up the supper, which, owing to the occasion, the date, and the place it was being celebrated, had to be a splendid one.

Torquemada was not in favor of *filling the craws* of that whole crowd, and in his poor opinion they would have fulfilled their obligations by inviting the most intimate friends, like Donoso, the Mo-

rentíns (both father and son), and Zárate. But Cruz, to whom he somewhat timidly imparted his restrictive standard with regard to invitations, replied drily that she knew very well what the circumstance
demanded. *To recapitulate*: Christmas Eve was celebrated there with
an improvised banquet, by forty-five persons *and then some*—that is,
about fifty in round numbers—eating and drinking *like wild beasts*,
according to Torquemada's comment. The master of the house was
sensible enough to drink champagne only in homeopathic doses, and
thanks to this precaution he behaved like a gentleman, letting no
untoward expressions fall from his respectable lips and speaking to
everyone in the fine and measured language that was to be expected
from his character and social position. There were frequent toasts both
in prose and verse until long after midnight, and Zárate wound up the
evening by addressing Don Francisco familiarly and prophesying that
he would be master of the whole earth, and that under his sway the
problem of air travel by balloon would be solved, and all the isthmuses
would be cut through for greater fraternity among the seas, and all
the continents would be joined by means of revolving bridges. Others
offered a toast for the marquisate of San Eloy, which would very
shortly acquire more luster with a grandeeship of Spain (first class),
and someone even requested, with all respect, that the Señores de
Torquemada give a grand ball on the day of Epiphany, to celebrate
the happy event.

When the dinner guests had departed, Don Francisco could hardly
stand on his feet for fatigue, his head felt like a coach lamp and his
spirits somewhat depressed. The sun of his happiness was clouded over
by the thought of the enormous expense of that supper, and of those
that would come *on the heels of it*, for the tyrant had invited everyone
present for the whole of the following week until New Year's Day,
distributing them in batches of up to twelve a day. "At this rate,"
thought Torquemada, "this house will be Lhardy's, and I the chump
par excellence." He went to bed shortly before dawn with half his
mind rejoicing and the other half agitated by terrible anxieties. Was
it a joke about the grand ball, or had they said it in earnest? When
Cruz heard it she had laughed, but without protesting, as he would
have protested had he dared. That and the twelve guests every day
kept him from sleeping, for the other half of his mind, the cheerful
and frolicsome half, also rebelled against rest. He got up without hav-

ing slept, and the first thing his eyes fell upon was a pair of wenches, in whom he instantly recognized the zoological characteristics of wet nurses.

"Hello!" said he, addressing them. "And how are we fixed for milk?"

Cruz had had them sent previously from Asturias, entrusting the responsibility to a doctor friend of hers. They were two superb milk animals, chosen from among the best, dark-skinned, with black, abundant hair, very pronounced udders, and firm footsteps. While the miser was visiting his wife and baby, Cruz was negotiating with that pair of cows and the churlish villagers who had accompanied them.

"Which one did you choose?" Don Francisco asked her later, for he wanted to be informed about everything.

"What do you mean, which one? You really are wandering in your wits, my dear sir. Both of them. One permanently, and the other as a replacement, in case the first fails us."

"Two wet nurses, two!" exclaimed the ruffian with all the hairs on his head and in his mustache standing up like a hairbrush. "Why, one wet nurse, just one, is the scourge of God in a house, then two . . . help me to take it in, two . . . are the same as if the earth were to open and swallow us."

"How little it takes to frighten you. Is this the way you look after the welfare of that blessed little sprig that God has given you?"

"But why does my little sprig need two wet nurses, Christ, sweet Christ? Four breasts, dear Lord, four breasts! And to think that I didn't even have one from my mother, for they raised me on a she-goat!"

"That's why you're always so stubborn!"

"But look here, Crucita. *Let's be fair.* Who did you ever see that had two wet nurses?"

"Whom have I seen? The king and queen, the king . . ."

"And do you think we're *crowned heads, so to speak?* Am I *perchance* a king, an emperor, even in a play, with a cardboard crown?"

"You are not a king, but your dignity, your name, demand royal intentions and royal acts. No, I'm not laughing. I know what I'm saying. We are entering a new period. Now you have a descendant, now you have an heir, a crown prince."

"Oh, sure, I have all of that."

And he was unable to say more, for anger made his blood boil and choked him. Seated in the dining room, he amused himself by biting his fingernails while they brought him his chocolate. Seeing him in such a bad humor, Cruz took pity on him and tried to explain the reason for that new period of greatness that the family was entering. But Don Francisco listened to no arguments but those of his avarice. Never had he felt in his soul such a desire for rebellion, nor such an inability to carry it from thought to deed, for the fascination that Cruz exercised on him was even greater and more irresistible since Valentín's birth. It can be understood that the household tyrant used this to consolidate her control and make it invulnerable against any kind of rebellion. The poor miser groaned as his chocolate passed from the cup into his stomach, and as Cruz encouraged him to let her know his thoughts, the poor man tried to speak, but the words simply refused to emerge from his lips. He tried to bring to them the vulgarly expressive terms that he had been accustomed to use in the free period of his life, but only fine concepts and words came into his mouth, the language of that opulent slavery in which he was wasting away, cramped by a personality that bound in chains all the ferocity of his own.

"I'm not saying anything, my lady," he murmured. "But we can't go on like this. You'll see. I am economy *par excellence*, and you are *extravagance personified*—three doctors, two nurses . . . grand ball . . . daily invitations . . . half-benefices . . . in short, our expenses are *pullulating*."

"What *pullulate* are your avaricious thoughts. What does all this mean compared to your enormous income? Do you think I would increase expenses if I saw that your profits were decreasing the least little bit? Have things gone so badly for you under my guidance and control? Well, glorious days are in store, my friend . . . But what's wrong with you . . . What's the matter?"

The miser was weeping, no doubt because the last piece of chocolate-soaked bread had stuck in his throat.

· PART III ·

ONE

The new year began auspiciously. It might be said that the Wise Men had brought the miser as many goods of a material kind as the fantasy of the most ambitious man could imagine. Money rained upon him faster than he could pick it up; and on top of all this, he and Tara-mundi each held half of the winning ticket in the lottery at the end of December, and none of the business transactions he undertook, either by himself or as a member of a group, failed to bear fruit in the form of rich returns. Never had Lady Luck been more lavish with him, nor heeded less the unequal way in which she distributes her favors. Some attributed it to diabolical arts, and others to designs of God, precursors of some catastrophe; and though there were many who envied him, some looked upon him with superstitious fear, as a being whose nature harbored some infernal spirit. An infinite number of persons tried to entrust their interests to him, in the hope of seeing them increased in a short time, but he did not consent to handle funds for anyone, with the exception of two or three families who were very close friends.

Although in the sphere of business he had reason to swell to bursting with satisfaction, in the purely domestic sphere the situation was not the same, and the poor man had been devoured by intense melancholy ever since the beginning of the year. Household expenditures were now princely: an increase in domestic staff of both sexes; liveries, another carriage, this one exclusively destined for the mistress and the nurse with the child; dinners for twelve and fourteen persons; replacement of furniture; vastly expensive green plants to decorate the rooms; season tickets to the Comedia as well as the Opera; enormous luxury in outfits for the nurse, who went out transformed into an empress in her regional costume, with more coral necklaces draped on her mighty torso than she had hairs on her head. As for Valentinico, nothing more need be said: by a few days after his birth he had, on the debit side, more expenditure for clothing than his papa in the fifty-odd years of his life. Rich laces, silks, hollands, and the finest flannels constituted his apparel, no less luxurious than that of a king. And the usurer could not oppose these superfluities because his last stores of energy were depleted, and the tyrant's sway in the new order of things had broadened to such a point that in Cruz's presence he dared not even breathe.

On Epiphany there was a great dinner, and that night a solemn reception, attended by hundreds of persons of prominence. There were too many to fit into the house, and it was necessary to make a reception room out of the billiard room, decorating it with tapestries whose value would have been sufficient to maintain two dozen families for several years. It was true that Don Francisco had the satisfaction of seeing in his house ministers of the Crown, senators and deputies, many titled persons, generals, and even scientists, with no lack of *bards* and a reporter or two, which made the marquis say to himself in the words of Sancho, "Though you give me a good island, it has cost me a lashing." The licentiate Juan de Madrid described the splendid soiree in the most exotic terms imaginable, concluding by begging for its repetition in affected language. The Romeros made a joke about it that circulated throughout society, making everyone who heard it laugh. They said that the master of the house couldn't attend because . . . "he had gone to wait for the Wise Men."

The winter months passed with no more novelty than a few indispositions of Valentinico's, characteristic of his age. Really the baby did not seem to be of a very healthy nature, and a few intimates of the house did not hide their unfavorable opinion about the robustness of the heir to the coronet. But they were very careful not to say so after a disagreeable incident occurred between Don Francisco and his son-in-law Quevedito. The latter was talking one morning with Cruz about whether or not the nurse's milk was superior, about the infant's feeble constitution, and, unbosoming himself with medical sincerity of everything he was thinking, permitted himself to say, "The child's a freak. Have you noticed the size of his head, and those ears that hang like a hare's? And the legs haven't acquired their natural shape, and if he lives, which I doubt, he'll be bowlegged. I'll be very much mistaken if we don't have a little marquis of San Eloy who's a perfect idiot."

"So you belive that . . .?"

"I do, and I say that the freak . . ."

Don Francisco, who at that time had acquired the habit of listening from behind doors and curtains, spying on his sister-in-law's ideas in order to protect himself against them, surprised this brief dialogue from behind a portiere, and when he heard the word "freak" repeated, was too impatient to restrain himself; he entered the room at a bound, seized the young practitioner around the neck and, squeezing it with the laudable intention of strangling him, shouted, "So my son is a freak? Thief, quack! You're the freak! Your soul is bowlegged and eaten up with envy. My son an idiot! I'll choke you so you won't say it again."

Cruz succeeded, with great difficulty, in extricating Quevedo and calming Torquemada's fury.

"I'm speaking no more than the truth," murmured Quevedo, red as a pepper, pulling his shirt collar into place where his father-in-law's nails had torn it. "Scientific truth above all else. Out of respect for this lady I don't treat you as you deserve. Good-bye."

"Get out of my house and don't come back. To say that he's a freak! He has a big head, yes indeed—all full of terrific talent. The idiot and the big-ears is you, and your wife's another idiot. What do you bet I disinherit her?"

"Calm youself, friend Don Francisco," Cruz told him, hanging on his arm, for he was trying to run after his son-in-law and grab him again.

"Oh, yes indeed, my lady, you're right," he answered, falling breathless into an armchair. "I did behave to him like a brute. But just imagine his saying that!"

"All he said was that the baby is a bit sickly. The part about the freak was a joke."

"A joke? Well, let him come back and tell me it's a joke and I'll forgive him."

"He's already gone."

"Notice that Rufina doesn't look favorably on a male child. Naturally, before I married the girl thought that everything was going to be hers after I closed my eyes—don't think she didn't. She got very angry with me *in connection with* my marriage. Oh, that little thing

is terribly selfish! I don't know who she takes after. D'you think I ought
to forbid her the house?"

"Oh, no! Poor girl!"

The tyrant had to make no little effort to get these ideas out of his
head. At first, so as not to contradict him openly in everything, she
did not insist unduly, but after a few days had passed she did not leave
the subject alone until she had succeeded in having the doors of the
house reopened for the ejected couple, daughter and son-in-law. Rufina
did indeed return, but Quevedito broke off relations with his father-
in-law and, refusing to retract his medical opinion, continued to insist
that the infant was a case of abnormal development.

Business affairs, which during those months consumed the better
part of Torquemada's time, did not prevent him from devoting some
time at least, in the evenings, to the great work of his progressive
enlightenment. He was in the habit of reading some good book in his
study, the *History of Spain* for example, which in his opinion was the
indisputable basis of knowledge, and would spend some time consulting dictionaries and encyclopedias, where he could satisfy his doubts
without having recourse to Zárate, who confused him with his dizzying flow of scientific knowledge. By this practice, and by redoubling
his attention when he heard well-educated people speak, his style and
language became refined to the point that, in this third phase of his
social evolution, it was not easy to recognize in him the man of the
first or embryonic phase. He spoke reasonably correctly, avoiding affected ideas or those which smelled of the midnight oil, and indeed,
had not his lessons begun so late in life, he would have become Donoso's rival in refined and adequate expression. What a pity that the
evolution had not caught him at the age of thirty! Even so, he had not
wasted his time. Serving as his own critic and laying modesty aside,
for it has no place in soliloquies, he would say to himself, "I speak
ever so much better than the marquis of Taramundi, who says something stupid every few seconds."

His appearance was very different as well. There were persons who,
having known him on the Calle de San Blas, or at Doña Lupe's, thought
that he was a different man. The habit of wearing good clothing, of
constantly rubbing shoulders with well-bred folk, had endowed him
with a varnish in which appearance covered up reality. Only in fits of

rage did the brute show through, and then, ah, then, he was the coarse fellow of former times, as rough in words as in actions. But he avoided with exquisite care any occasion for becoming angry, so as not to lose his savoir faire in the presence of persons to whom he owed consideration for his own purposes. His worldly successes were extraordinary, indeed almost miraculous. Many who had made fun of him in the first stage of his evolution now respected him, considering him to be a man of exceptional shrewdness in business—something about which they were not mistaken—and the glitter of gold fascinated certain persons so much that they held him to be quite an extraordinary man. Ideas which in any other mouth would have been foolishness, in his were clever sallies and strokes of wit.

Though at first the marquisate sat rather awkwardly on him, like a pair of pistols on a statue of Christ, it eventually soaked (so to speak) into his person, his manners, even his clothing, and habit did the rest. The only thing lacking for complete adaptation of the title to his plebeian appearance was accomplished by the comparisons of public opinion, for it easily found means to explain why this head or another displayed a coronet, while others, equally rude both inside and out, wore it, either through inheritance or royal favor, no less dashingly than the former moneylender.

TWO

We know without having to be told it by the licentiate Juan de Madrid or any other society chronicler, that by three or four months after giving birth, Señora de Torquemada was extremely beautiful, as if a rapid physiological crisis had given new and vigorous sap to her somewhat faded beauty, causing her to flower with all the splendor and freshness of May. Her color improved, its opaline transparency changing to the warm tones of lightly-fuzzed fruit at the beginning of its ripening; her eyes acquired brilliance, her glance animation, her movements rapidity, and in the moral sphere her transformation was no less real for being invisible, for her spoiled attitudes gradually changed to seriousness and her mischievous imagination to calm judgment. Her life was consecrated to the heir of San Eloy, who, while in the first few days he was no more than a live doll to his mother, to be washed, dressed, and played with, became over the course of several months what nature ordains, master of all her affections and the sacred object on which all the most serious and beautiful of a woman's functions are employed. No one could have any idea of the way Fidela carried out her maternal mission without having seen it. There never was a mother who could outdo her in care and solicitude, or who was more aware of her responsibilities. From exaggerated caresses, which at first produced a convulsive tenseness in her, she progressed by gentle degrees to that truly protective love that is a guarantee of life for the feeble creatures who enter it threatened by a thousand dangers. The fear of falling ill and dying before her son grew up cured her of her extravagant taste for sweetmeats, and she gradually became accustomed to healthful food and consistency in meals. She did not read novels any more, nor had she time to do so, for there was no hour of the day when her attention was not engaged in some important task, sometimes the toilets of the baby and his nurse, sometimes the clothing of both; and then there was putting him to bed, and watching over his sleep, and seeing whether he was nursing well or not, and whether all his little functions were going along regularly.

She went nowhere, and was seen only very occasionally in the box at the Comedia for an hour or a little more, since she did not have the patience to stay there stupidly listening to something that interested her not at all and assailed by a thousand horrifying ideas, for example, that the nurse, when she put him to bed, had not left him properly covered, or that the hour for taking the breast had passed because the silly girl had fallen asleep. She was on tenterhooks, impatient for Tor to come and take her home. She trusted no one, not even the most assiduous and careful maids, nor even her sister. Her tertulia served exclusively to ask innumerable questions about subjects concerning motherhood, with this or that lady; everything else was a matter of indifference to her. Let no one think that the monotony of her conversation was irritating, for she had the gift of endowing everything she said with her inborn originality and gaiety. She was, in short, the delight and admiration of all the family's close friends. On this subject, Donoso said one day to his friend Torquemada, "You are a lucky man in everything, in absolutely everything. What extraordinary virtues are the cause of God Almighty's protection and favor? You have such a wife that, if you looked for another like her with a hand lamp all over the earth, you couldn't find one. What a woman! All the money you possess isn't as valuable as the last hair on her head."

"She's a good girl, yes, a very good girl," replied the miser, "and there's no complaint on that score."

"Or on any other. It would be a fine thing if you complained, when it seems that money doesn't know how to go anywhere except into your pocket. And by the way, my friend, they say that you and your associates are definitely going to take over all the shares of the Leonese railway."

"That's what we've agreed on."

"And that is why I've observed that two or three individuals in the Leonese colony here in Madrid are wildly enthusiastic about it, and they talk of offering you a banquet and I don't know what else."

"Banquet me because I'm going about my business? Well, if they pay for it . . ."

"Naturally."

Morentín continued to be an all too persistent visitor to the House of San Eloy, and, under the pretext of keeping his friend Rafael company, spent long hours there both in the afternoon and at night. But the fact is that the blind man secretly loathed him, and became very nervous when he heard his voice. Cruz, for her part, was not pleased by such assiduity. But neither of the two could find an excuse to get rid of him or even to succeed, by some discreet stratagem, in making him reduce his visits to the level strictly indicated by social practice. One afternoon, by familiar custom, he entered Fidela's sitting room and then Valentinico's room, adjacent to the matrimonial bedroom, and stood there entranced, watching the marquise of San Eloy at the height of her maternal functions, showering her with hyperbolic praise and using the most extravagant forms of gallantry, after having tried the commoner forms of flattery with deplorable success.

"Because, Fidela, you are one of those rare examples in history, in sacred and profane history; don't laugh. I know what I'm saying. The man who possesses you must have the greatest influence in the court of divine judgment, for if not, how did they happen to give him the winning number, the select creature, the *ne plus ultra?*"

"Goodness, I'm not nearly as grand as you think. On a certain occasion I allowed myself to say that I was very clever. How often I've

laughed about that boast! For now I feel that I'm worthless and that
I have no talent at all. Don't think that I say it out of modesty. Modesty continues to seem foolish to me. Now that something very pleasant, with a great deal of responsibility, lies ahead of me, I understand
that I can't aspire to what I want."

"Don't tell me that you are not modest. Everyone knows very well
what he is worth. But there is one thing which, no doubt because of
the distraction your maternal duties have caused, you haven't noticed
as yet."

"What?"

"That you're very, very beautiful just now. Heavens, a degree of
beauty that makes a man despair. Believe me: when one looks at you
one suffers from vertigo, and I can almost say light-blindness. It's like
looking at the sun."

"Then put on smoked glasses," said Fidela, beginning to laugh and
showing the two strings of pearls that were her incomparable teeth.
"But why, if your mind is smoked over, too?"

"Thanks very much."

"No, now I feel like speaking sincerely. Making a show of immod-
esty, I will tell you that if I'm worthless in—what's the phrase?—the
opinion of others, I know that as far as beauty goes . . . it's true that
I'm very lovely, isn't it? Don't think I'm going to blush to hear you
say it. Why, I'm tired of knowing it."

"Your sincerity is another charm that I hadn't noticed before."

"You don't notice anything. You pay attention only to yourself, and
since you look from such a short distance you can't see yourself."

"It's so true that I've never looked at myself that I don't know what
I'm like."

"I belie√e that, because if you did know, you wouldn't be the way
you are. I'll give you that."

"Well then, what am I like?"

"Oh, I'm not the one to say it."

"Since you are so sincere in criticizing yourself, you should be so
when judging others."

"I don't like to praise people, and since you are one of those who
still cultivate modesty, if I cover you with praise you might believe
that I'm flattering you."

"I'll believe no such thing, but only that you're doing me justice."

"No, no, for surely if I tell you what I think, you'll turn red like one of those timid boys, and will never return to my house for fear that my praises will make you blush."

"I swear to you that I won't stop coming back, though you compare me with the angels in heaven."

"Well, I was thinking about comparing you with them. See how right you were."

"On the score of purity?"

"And on that of innocence. Ever since the time when you were a student and flirted with the landladies of the boarding houses where your classmates, the ones you studied with, lived, you have not made one step of progress in the art of the world, nor in knowledge of the persons with whom you deal. Now see whether you are still in a state of innocence and if you merit praise. You have succeeded in learning many things, not all of them, to be sure, terribly useful. But a sure touch for knowing the degree and kind of affection to which you should aspire in your friendly relationships is not yet possessed by Pepe Morentín. You are very much a child, and if you don't learn this quickly, I believe that my Valentín will get ahead of you."

Disconcerted, the offstage Don Juan pretended not to understand and defended himself with jesting exclamations; but inwardly he was tormented by the attack on his pride administered by the high-minded lady. She had made her speech standing up, with her child in her arms, walking him up and down and giving him little pats on the back.

"You employ ironies that leave me confused," said Morentín at last, for he could no longer form his features into an appearance of amusement, and abruptly became serious.

"Irony, I . . .? Bah! Pay no attention to me. It's only that I look upon you as on a child, and certainly not one of the best mannered. Today's youth, and I call youth the men from thirty to forty years of age, needs a schoolboy type of severe discipline in order to circulate freely in society. Such men do not know what real refinement or delicacy is, and they are, shall we say, a generation of very well-dressed fools who know a bit of French. I don't know who it was who said here in the house the other night that there are no ladies left."

"The marquise of San Salomó."

"Precisely. Perhaps she is right. It's doubtful that there are, at any rate. What is undoubted is that there are no more gentlemen, unless some old gentleman or other of the previous generation can be called so."

"Do you really believe that? Oh, what wouldn't I give to belong to the previous generation, though my head were full of white hairs and my life plagued with rheumatism! If that were so, would you be kinder to me?"

"Am I unkind, pray? This is not unkindness, Morentín, it's age. Don't laugh, I am old, older than you think—if not in years, in what suffering has taught me."

Suddenly Fidela changed her tone, leaving the other disconcerted and unable to think of anything to say. Wildly kissing the baby, she burst out in the following cries:

"But have you ever seen, Morentín, a sweeter face than the face of my precious little monster, king of scamps and the angels' little helper? Have you ever seen such beauty, or such adorableness, or such naughtiness as his? This is worth more than the whole world. See that pretty little hair that stuck to my lips when I kissed him? Well, this little hair is worth more than you in body and soul, much more, something like ten billion times more . . . raised to a cube root . . . I'm a mathematician too. And he's worth more than all of past, present, and future humanity. So . . . farewell. Say goodbye to him, darling" (taking the baby's hand and waving it). "Say bye-bye, bye-bye, silly."

She went into the adjoining room and Morentín left the house, embittered and weary. At that moment his self-esteem was like a showy flowering shrub which a savage foot had brutally trampled.

THREE

The dashing young man's discouragement was of long standing, for, spoiled by easy triumphs, he imagined that God had made the world for the enjoyment of bristol-board Don Juans, and that human passions were a game or sport destined for the solace of young men who, in addition to the title of Doctor of Laws, possessed credentials as a representative of the country, sufficient income to live well, a horse, good clothing, etc. His hopes, which at the beginning were very flourishing and nourished exclusively by his vanity, and which she had in no way encouraged, had already withered before the conversation that has just been recounted. Whenever he had occasion to speak to his friend in private, the man would cautiously try again, but she would stop him in his tracks, rubbing his face in ironic and pointed replies no less harsh than nettles. What chiefly disconcerted the good Morentín was the compromised position in which, as regarded public opinion, he had been placed by Señora de Torquemada's resistance, for since it was almost an article of faith that she had chosen him in retaliation for all the sorrows of her marriage to an "impossible" man, how could he have the effrontery to say to public opinion, "Señores, she isn't retaliating with me or anyone else, for there is no adultery or anything resembling it, either in fact or intention. Abandon this slanderous idea, if you don't want to be called imbeciles as well as ill-wishers."

And surely he would have added, "I'm doing everything I can. But it's no use. As far as I'm concerned, everyone who's acquainted with me knows that I was perfectly willing. But it's one of two things: either she simply doesn't like me, which I find extremely humiliating, or she is taking refuge in virtue. I incline to believe this last as less uncomplimentary to myself, and would have no hesitation in proclaiming that, if I don't please her, it's a sure thing that no other man will please her either, though he were to be brought down from heaven especially for her. No, señores, this time I was off the mark. I believe, like Zárate, that the cerebral lobe governing the passions is atrophied in her case. Ah, the passions! They are what make women fall; but they also ennoble and exalt them. A woman without passions can be a beautiful doll, or a very useful broody hen if she is a mother. I admit that no battle seemed easier for me to win last year, when Fidela reappeared to the world married to that barnyard turkey. This is the first time that, thinking I was going to embrace a woman, I fetched up smashing against a statue. Patience, and try another woman. When a chap thinks that he's passed up some very pretty possibilities to follow this deceptive trail! So I give up, and console myself with the thought that if the god of battles—amorous ones—hasn't given me the victory this time, it's because he's steering me away from a great danger. I sense the incubation of a drama in the House of San Eloy, and my mother's son flees from drama as from the cholera. This is what Serrano Morentín, professional adulterer, declares and maintains."

It must be added that although Don Juan Gualberto's only son was incapable of virtue in higher degree, he was also inept in evil categorically performed. Because he had a little of everything he also had his bit of conscience, and after bandaging the wounds to his self-esteem with restorative optimism, he began to think how iniquitous were the errors of public opinion regarding Fidela. But no one could destroy the hard concretion formed with evil thoughts and society's false logic. Like certain calcareous conglomerates, the slander hardened with time, and in the end not a soul could break it with all the hammers of truth. Morentín was quite ready to go and say to everyone willing to listen, "Señores, it's not true. There's virtue in her, real virtue, and not its pretense." But no one would believe it! These are fine times to believe voices that try to restore reputations, not destroy them. That little bit of conscience which the gallant gentleman could call upon in very grave matters of morals argued his culpability, for when the rumors began, his conviction of eventual victory was one reason why he did not deny them with the energy and indignation that justice demanded. He let the story circulate, though it was false, because he believed with absolute certainty that events would make it true. Events gave the lie; therefore, it was they which were guilty, not he. However, as Morentín left the House of San Eloy that day, greatly cast down in spirit, he thought that, in conscience, and proceeding with noble gentlemanliness (of which he also possessed his little bit), he ought to make a supreme effort to stifle such gossip and tear it up by the roots.

Not ten minutes had passed since Morentín left Fidela's sitting room when Rafael came in, led by Pinto.

"I know already that that trifler has gone. I was waiting for him to leave before I came in," he said to his sister, who returned to the sitting room with the baby in her arms.

"Yes, 'the brave Malek-Adel has left for Palestine.' Sit down. It's too bad you can't see this precious thing. He's so happy today that he does nothing but laugh and pull my ears. And why is God's little good-for-nothing so cunning today?"

"Let me touch his face. Come closer."

Fidela brought the baby close to her brother, who kissed him and patted his cheeks. Valentinico puckered up his face.

"What's that, my angel? Mustn't cry."

"It frightens him to see me."

"Nonsense! This little wretch isn't afraid of anything. Now he's look-ing at you fixedly, very fixedly, with startled eyes, as if he were saying

'How serious my uncle is today!' Isn't it true that you love your uncle lots, little king, pontifex maximus, Virgin Mary's little kitten? He says yes, that he loves you ever so much, and he respects you and he's your humble servant who kisses your hand, Valentín Torquemada y del Aguila."

Seeing that Rafael had fallen into melancholy silence, she thought that she would cheer him up a bit by telling him about the little tricks the baby performed with remarkable precocity.

"You don't know what a rascal he is. The minute he sees a woman he throws himself into her arms. This one's going to be very much attracted to the fair sex, yes indeed, and quite a lover. Every woman he sees he'll want for himself. Beginning right now" (giving him little pats in the appropriate place) "I'll have to be teaching him not to be so enthusiastic about the ladies. Isn't that right, my darling, that you like the pretty girls ever so much? He can't stand men. The only one he gets along with is his father. When he puts the baby on his knee to play horsie, he laughs and laughs. And do you know what the little wretch does? He takes his watch. He has a mad desire to steal watches. He's also learned the trick of putting his hand into his father's pocket, and honestly, he starts to pull out duros and pesetas and throw them on the floor, laughing when he sees them rolling."

"Symbolism," said Rafael, emerging from his taciturnity. "Poor angel! If he persists in that trick, within twenty years, heaven help us!"

Whenever he was with his sister, either in the sitting room or the baby's room, the poor blind man's sensations and even feelings underwent abrupt changes, passing from expansive contentment to deep and exhausting depression. It was a constant variation, like the movements of a weathercock on a stormy day. Rafael had some hours when he tremendously enjoyed listening to his sister in the little tasks of her motherhood, other hours when that same picture (or rather, in his case, a sonata) of domestic happiness filled his heart with venom. The reasons for this: before Valentinico's birth Rafael was the baby of the family, and in the period of poverty, a baby spoiled to the point of exaggeration. Of course, his sisters continued to love him, but the new life and the tasks demanded by a great household distracted them in a thousand ways. They waited on him, they cared for him; but he was not, as in other times, the principal person, the center, the axis of their lives. The heir of San Eloy came into the world to a great pealing of bells, and although the two sisters continued to have affection and attentions for Rafael, these were never equal to those they lavished on the baby; a very natural thing, for although both he and his nephew were weak, Rafael was a grown man and there could be no thought of curing him of his hopeless affliction or making him stronger, while Valentín was the mere beginning of a man, a hope that had to be protected against the myriad dangers that surround childhood. The eternal subordination of past loves to the loves and interests of present and future!

This was how Rafael thought of it during his melancholy reveries, filled with deep bitterness: "I am the past, a past that weighs heavily upon them, that gives them nothing, that offers them nothing; the child is the smiling present, and a future which is interesting because unknown."

His constantly working imagination interpreted quite commonplace occurrences in the light of his idea. He thought he noticed that his sister Cruz, when she took care of him, did so more out of obligation than affection; that on some days the sisters served his dinner in a great hurry, while they could spend hour after hour feeding porridge to the youngster. He also imagined that his clothes were not treated with as much care as before. Occasionally, buttons were missing or rips appeared, which troubled him. On the other hand, the two ladies and the nurse would spend whole days on the baby's little garments. About all this, of course, he maintained absolute silence, and would rather have died than offer a complaint. His sister Cruz noticed a funereal sadness about him, a gloomy laconism and the kind of sigh that seems to pull out half the soul in a single breath. But she did not question him for fear he would come out with one of his well-worn themes. "Let sleeping dogs lie," she told herself, speaking like Cervantes and like Don Francisco.

FOUR

They did speak at length on the subject of Morentín, and while discussing the best stratagem for avoiding his steady visits, agreed to make use of Zárate. Rafael had wished to forbid him the house without more ado; but Cruz did not agree to this, so as not to offend Señora de Serrano Morentín, one of their best and most loyal friends. The best thing would be to have Zárate address the following hint to him: "Look, Pepe, I don't know why, but Rafael has taken a dislike to you, and gets excited every time you sit beside him. It would be better if you stopped going there for a little while. The ladies don't want to tell you for fear you'll take it amiss. But I, a friend of yours and a friend of theirs, advise you . . . ," etcetera. Once this plan had been agreed upon, Cruz could hardly wait to ask the pedant for his friendly mediation, and the pedant did such a good job of his commission that the other appeared at the house only very infrequently, and always at night when a number of friends were on hand. The comments exchanged by sage and gallant, when the former transmitted the ladies' desires, are not a matter of public knowledge, but it is easy to surmise that each man offered a version very different from the official explanation for that courteous dismissal.

And a great weight was lifted from Rafael when he knew for certain that his old friend would not visit him with such frequency. But his sadness did not diminish, and Cruz, after giving the matter much thought, decided that his conscience was troubled because he had been so malignly convinced of Fidela's guilt, and had been so wrong about it. Indeed, Rafael seemed to be dissuaded from the evil thoughts that his insane logic, the logic of a pessimistic and self-absorbed blind man, had suggested to him. One night he confessed as much to Cruz, adding that although he had changed his despicable conviction insofar as Fidela was concerned, he maintained it with regard to Morentín, who was a sinner in intent, for he pinned all his pride on being an adulterer without dramas, and a corrupter of families with discreet scandal.

"And, so that you'll see that my logic never deceives me," he added, "I will tell you that my sister's defamation, far from ceasing now, is increasing and acquiring credibility, because the world does not recover, cannot recover, the stone that it has thrown."

"Very well," replied the eldest sister, trying to cut him short. "Pay no attention to that, and scorn evil talk."

"I do scorn it, but it always exists."

"That's enough about that."

"Indeed it is."

When he was left alone, his head sunk on his breast, he plunged into dark and cavernous thoughts: "Am I the one who is mistaken? No, because I surmised this attack by public opinion against the honor of my house, and I was right. Though my sister has behaved as she was bound to do, accomplishing the greatest marvel of all time, this only means that our breed is a very select one . . . yes, indeed . . . superior blood, uncorrupted amid this sink of iniquity."

He got up abruptly and, as if he believed that his sister Cruz was still there, said with great emphasis, "But did I see the danger or did I not?"

He soon fell back into the chair. His sadness turned into acute scorn for himself; his self-esteem, much more potent than Morentín's and better founded, was not so easily cured after a fall, and he felt as though he had plunged from the highest point of his pride to the deepest part of his conscience.

"Yes, yes" he thought, elbows on knees, his hands clutching his head as if he were trying to pull it off, "I want to deceive myself with flattery, with praises of myself; but above all these blandishments rises my reason, telling me that I'm the most benighted fool God ever put into the world. Mistaken in everything! I firmly believed that my sister would be unhappy, and she is blissful. Her happiness knocks down all this logic, which I store in my poor broken-down brain like rusty scrap iron. I firmly believed that the absurd, unnatural marriage of the angel and the beast would have no offspring, and this hybrid manikin, this monster, has come of it—for he is a monster, he must be, as Quevedito says. What a representative of the Aguila line! What a marquis of San Eloy! This is revolting. If the social cataclysm doesn't come soon, it must be that God wants society to decay gradually and pulverize everything into garbage to make future growth more fertile" (heaving a great sigh). "The truth is that I don't know what to feel. I am obliged to love the poor child, and sometimes it seems to me that I do love him. Is he responsible for having come to destroy all my logic? And if he is a hybrid, and monstrous, and will grow up marked by cretinism and sickliness, at least he has served to light the fire of maternal love in his mother, which will purify her. The height of misjudgment, for me, would be to have the child grow up intelligent and strong . . . I'd need only that to make myself believe that the deformed and sickly person is I; and in that case . . ."

A light rap on the door cut short his musings. It was Fidela with the baby in her arms.

"Here's a visitor," she said, "a gentleman who asks if Señor Don

Rafaelillo is visible. Can we come in? Come on, my darling. Tell him that you're angry, but very angry, because he hasn't come to see you today."

"I was thinking of going just now," replied the blind man, cheering up. "Come. Give me your hand."

Fidela carried him off to her room, where they embarked on a long conversation which she warmed with her lively wit and he cooled with his deadly sadness. They contended on the terrain of words, he producing lead and his sister quicksilver. The dialogue alternately languished and ran headlong, responding to very different ideas. More than once Fidela tried to place the child in her brother's arms, but Rafael refused, fearful, he said, of letting him fall. When Valentinico was barely a month old, his uncle enjoyed playing nursemaid: he picked him up, juggled him about, told him all sorts of affectionate nonsense, and did not put him down until the baby, by rubbing his eyes with his fists or breaking into screams, asked to be given to someone else. But after some time had passed, Rafael began to feel a brutal aversion to his little nephew, which he was unable to fight down by any process of reasoning. The sensation of his powerlessness to overcome that insane impulse was as strong and clear in his mind as that of the fear it caused him. Fortunately it lasted only a short time, but even in its almost instantaneous brevity it was sufficiently intense to make him suffer horribly, a suffering aggravated by the struggle he had to carry on with himself. One afternoon he felt such instinctive loathing for the baby that, as he hastily relinquished him to avoid an act of savagery, he nearly let him fall.

"Maximina, for God's sake come here!" he shouted, getting to his feet. "Take the baby, quick. I'm leaving . . . He's very heavy . . . he tires me . . . I'm choking."

And delivering the baby into the hands of his nurse, he left the room, trembling and gasping, feeling his way along walls and stumbling over furniture. It was impossible to gauge the duration of that savage impulse, but there is no doubt that it was extremely short, and as soon as it was over he felt an overwhelming desire to cry; he shut himself in his room and threw himself down in his easy chair, seeking solitude. In that solitude he found that he could do nothing but minutely analyze that strange phenomenon, investigate its origin, and determine the forms in which it manifested itself. And he knew it better through retrospective observation of his soul than in the moment he suffered the attack, for it was a lightning flash of confusion and fear, in which the tremendous destructive impulse was mingled with the panic of his conscience, terrified by the crime.

"The cause of this," he told himself, with the sincerity of a solitary philosopher, "can be nothing but a terrible access of envy. Yes, that's it; it has been born in my soul like a tumor. Envy of the little fellow, because my sisters love him more than me! I can express it plainly in the inner solitude of my conscience. Naturally the child is the hope of the house, of possible future glories, and I am an outworn, useless, dead past. But how has such a vile feeling arisen in my soul and such a new feeling in me, Lord, for I never felt envy of anyone? And what does it mean when the feeling of envy suddenly goes away and I can love the little fellow again? No, no, it doesn't go away, no. After the attack is over there's always a certain amount of hostility left in me toward that manikin, and though it's true that he inspires pity in me, it is also true that I want him to die. Let's analyze the matter with care. Have I ever wanted him to live?" (pause). "I don't know. It must have been a very few times, and my memories of this moment or another tell me that most of the time I think that the unfortunate creature would be better off in heaven, or in limbo—yes indeed, in limbo. And another symptom that I see in myself is the absolute conviction that God has done a very bad thing in sending him here, unless he has come as punishment for the ruffian, and to embitter the last years of his life. However that may be, little Valentinico . . . I'll tell myself clearly, as I ought to say things to myself, in the confessional of my conscience, which is like going on one's knees before God and uncovering our whole soul to Him . . . I can't stand Valentinico . . . I recognize that we're two of a kind in infantile candor. I talk, he doesn't; but both of us are equally childish. If I, being as I am, were now at the breast and had a wet nurse of my own, I would be no more of a man than he is, even though, as I clung to the breast, I worked out inside my head all the philosophies in the world" (pause). "Why does it cause me such profound irritation to see that my sisters live only for him, and worry about his clothing, his feeding, whether he sleeps or not, as if the fate of all humanity depended on it? Why, when I hear them fussing over him, and singing to him, and tossing him in their arms, do I rage inside because they don't do the same to me? This

is infantile, Lord; but it is as I say, and I can't help it. I confess the
whole truth to myself, omitting nothing, and when I do so I feel relief,
the only possible relief" (long pause, meditation). "I don't know what
is happening to me, or how the accursed attack begins. It breaks out
suddenly, like an explosive charge. It invades my whole nervous system in less time than it takes to tell it. If the attack catches me with
my nephew in my arms, I have to bind my willpower with bands of
bronze not to fall on the poor baby and smother him under my body.
Or sometimes I have the idea of hurling him against a wall with the
terrible strength that develops in me. One afternoon I even put my
hand around his neck; I could do so easily, for our little heir apparent
isn't exactly fat; I pressed a little, only a little. What saved him was
the cries he gave and the illusion that I had—the hallucination that
I heard him say, 'Uncle, don't.' It was a frightful second. My conscience won out by a jot, by the thousandth part of a hair's breadth,
which was the distance that separated me from the crime. I fear that
on another occasion my willpower will not reach the critical point,
and that impulse will win out, and that, when I realize the act of
savagery I've committed, it will have happened and I'll be able to do
nothing about it. I regret it, I will regret it very much; I will die of
shame, of terror. And when he and I meet in limbo, victim and executioner, we will laugh at our quarrels here on earth. What misery,
what pettiness, how stupid it is to fight over who is greater! 'Valentín,'
I'll tell him, 'do you remember when I killed you because I didn't like
your being greater than I? Isn't it true that you, in the first stirrings of
your will, wanted to destroy me, and pulled my hair trying to hurt
me? Don't deny it. You were very naughty: your father's lowborn blood
could not be denied. If you had lived you would have been the avenger
of the dishonored Aguilas and would have tortured your mother, who
sinned, sinned gravely, in becoming your mother. Admit it: my sister
ought not to have married your brute of a father, nor ought I to have
been your uncle. And even admitting that the marriage had to take
place, you ought not to have been born, no indeed. You were an absurdity, an error of nature" (pause). "And I'll also tell you that on
the night you were born I had terrible feelings of jealousy, and when
your father came to tell me that you'd taken it into your head to be
born, I could hardly stop myself from showering him with insults. So
you see . . . Now you and I are equal. Neither of us is more than the

other, and both of us are spending eternity in this impalpable form, wandering through endless gray spaces, with no other distraction than describing curves, nor any other plaything than ourselves, tearing through masses of opaque light in the midst of chaos."

FIVE

His sister Cruz often extricated him from these painful trances with the abrupt force of her positive reasoning. Using a measure of affection and a measure of severity in her language, she would calm him. One afternoon when Rafael was with Zárate in the sitting room, he was suddenly assailed by his mad impulse. The nurse had placed the sleeping Valentín in his arms, to go in search of some articles of clothing in the adjoining room. No sooner did he feel the weight of the tender babe than his face changed, his lips trembled as if attacked by mortal cold, his face flushed, his arms contracted convulsively.

"Zárate, damn it, Zárate, where are you? For the love of God . . ." he shouted hoarsely. "Take the baby, grab him, man, grab him quickly. If you don't I'll smash him on the floor. What are you doing? I can't hold out any longer. Zárate, grab him. My God!"

The sage rushed to him, caught the baby almost in mid-air; he woke up howling, and when the mother hurried in, she saw her brother lying back on the sofa in epileptic convulsions. But he recovered rapidly and, with nervous hilarity, trying to stretch his muscles and return his altered face to serenity, said, "It's nothing . . . nothing. This attack I have . . . it's foolish. It seems as if I grow very, very strong, that I'm a Hercules, or else that I turn to rags and can't stand up. I don't know . . . What a strange thing! It's over, I'm all right now. I want to be alone. Have them come and get me, take me away from here. And the baby—has anything happened to him? Poor little thing. These little creatures are so delicate! Ninety-eight of every hundred perish . . ."

The elder sister also hastened to the scene, and with the pedant's help took him to his room, where a short time later he was chatting peacefully with his friend and recalling episodes of their student life together. At about nightfall he asked to be taken to Fidela's sitting room again, and there a pleasant conversation ensued, for Cruz entered saying, "It seems to be a foregone conclusion that the Leonese are going to offer your husband a monumental banquet, because of his initiative about the railway line."

And Zárate, who was one of those involved in the affair, confirmed the news, adding that some eighty persons had already subscribed and that the organizing committee had agreed not to limit the party to *the Leonese element*, but that everyone who wanted to do so could subscribe and attend, for thus the manifestation would assume a truly national character, a public and solemn homage to the extraordinary man who was placing his riches and intelligence at the service of public interests.

As he was saying this, and before Fidela and Cruz could add any commentary, Torquemada and Donoso arrived.

"So, Tor, they're going to give you a great big din-din?" said his wife. "I'm glad. These solemnities ought not to be held exclusively for literary men and poets."

"I don't know what's the good of these fancy meals. But they insist on it, so what can I do? *My line of conduct* will be to eat and keep my mouth shut."

"That you will not," said Cruz. "For you'll have to give quite a little speech."

"I?"

"Yes, you. My dear Tor, the spice of these banquets lies in the toasts."

"They'll do the toasting. But I . . . to speak in front of so many well-informed people!"

"You are no less so," observed Cruz. "And you can easily say wonderfully witty things, if you want to—things with practical value and true eloquence, in the English style."

"I won't open my mouth in front of many important men and so many eminences, in any style at all."

"You'll have no choice, my dear Don Francisco," remarked Donoso, "but to say a few words. No matter how much people agree that there will be no toasts, someone has to speak, at least to explain the reason for the occasion, and naturally you will have to make a speech of thanks—a simple manifestation without pretensions to elegance, a few phrases from the heart."

The infant suddenly laughed, and everyone, Torquemada first of all, taking it that he was laughing about his papa's speech, echoed his baby merriment.

"God's little wretch, laugh, go on, about the itty-bitty speech Tor's going to make. Isn't it true that you know how to talk better than he does? Stop it, now, and you and I will go and boo him."

"You have no choice," said Zárate, giving himself over to flattery, "but to offer us your thoughts about certain and specific matters which are agitating public opinion. Indeed, all of us are anxiously waiting for it, and to deprive us of a chance to hear your words would mean defrauding the hopes of all of us who are to gather there."

"Well, *I start from the principle* that in a closed mouth enter no flies. Let them ramble on as long as they want, and if I see that they're praising me unduly, I'll tell them laconically that I'm not impressed by flattery, that I'm very practical, and that they should leave me in peace, so there."

"Prepare yourself," said Cruz, who on that occasion as on all occasions was the ruling voice, though she made no great show of it. "Think carefully about the reason they're giving you the banquet. Pay attention to this point and that; make sure of the order in which you want to say things; select the phrases that seem most suitable to you; choose your words, and I'll wager my head that you'll make a really notable speech, and leave all the orators who may be present gasping."

"I doubt very much, Crucita," stated Torquemada, seating himself on the sofa beside the blind man, "that good oratory, like what we hear in the Chamber, will ever come out of this mouth, which is very stupid *on its own account*. But, in case I've no choice but to have a go, I'll do it so as to leave the family flag well planted."

"I also," remarked the blind man, who until then had said nothing, "feel in my heart, like my sister Cruz, that you are going to turn out to be a first-rate orator. Once you've decided to grow, my dear sir, you will grow in every sphere. And if on that night you speak halfway decently, the crowd who hears you will go out saying that you're the equal of Demosthenes, and will believe it; that's the way public opinion is formed. Whatever the marquis of San Eloy does and says will be taken today as delightful, because it is said and done in the atmosphere of success. Ah! If you would follow my advice, I would rise to my feet, after everyone had spoken, and say, 'Señores . . .' "

Cruz tried to interrupt him, fearing some scornful outburst; but he paid no attention, and, encouraged by Don Francisco himself, who urged him to express his thought with absolute frankness, he continued as follows:

" 'Señores, I am cleverer, infinitely cleverer than you, though many of those who hear me are adorned with academic degrees and official labels which I lack. Since you are casting dignity aside, I will cast away modesty, and tell you that I richly deserve the cult of adulation that you render me, a shining golden calf. Your idolatry would turn my stomach if I did not keep it well fortified against all possible repugnance. What do you praise in me? Virtues, talent? No; riches, which in this pitiful age are the supreme virtue and wisdom *par excellence*. You praise my money, for I have been able to make it and you have not. You all lead lives full of deceit, some in the sorry traffic of political and bureaucratic life, others in the religion of living on borrowed money. You envy me, you see in me a superior being. Very well: I am one, and you are a bunch of useless dummies, clay figures modeled with a certain amount of skill; I'm made in the style of Alcorcón pottery, but not in clay, in pure gold. I count for more than all of you put together, and if you wish to test the fact, make a trial of me, put your shoulders under my throne and carry me in procession, for it is no exaggeration to carry your idol through the streets. And while you are acclaiming me deliriously I will low, for I repeat that I'm a calf, and after congratulating myself on your servility, seeing you crowded beneath me, I will open my four legs and reward you with a copious evacuation, in the clear understanding that my manure is ready money. I pass five-duro coins and even banknotes when I want to present my friends with the efforts of my belly. And you fall all over yourselves to pick it up; you gather up this precious manna, you—' "

He became so overexcited, gesticulating and raising his voice, that Cruz had to cut short his speech, begging him to stop talking. His listeners either took it as a joke or became very serious, as if to indicate that they seconded the censure, and Donoso in particular was very glad that the elder sister had succeeded in shutting her brother's mouth. Torquemada, however, praised the speech and, patting the orator on the knee, told him, "Good, very good, Rafaelillo. The *synthesis* of your speech seems excellent to me, and if I had my way I'd *pronounce* it, if I could find a really tricky vocabulary, so as to be able to say those awful things in a language with a double meaning, the kind that says what it doesn't exactly say. But you'll see how the poor calf won't pronounce anything but a great big *moo*."

His brother-in-law's approbation excited Rafael still more, and he would have continued in that raving torrent of words had not Cruz, with great effort, led the conversation to another topic. Zárate outdid himself, chattering about a thousand things which he dragged in by the heels, and Rafael had something to say about all of them, expressing very amusing opinions, now on the new theories of degeneracy, now on the bankruptcy of the Panama Canal Company, anarchists, or the Shah of Persia's diamonds. At dinnertime Rafael and Cruz spoke of his desire to move to the third floor of the house, for his room on the main floor was very warm and somewhat cramped, and on the upper floor there were two very handsome rooms overlooking an interior courtyard which were not being used, and where the blind man could live more independently. The elder sister had not wanted to consent to the transfer because downstairs she had him nearer her to watch over him and give him personal care; but Rafael insisted so much that at last, after consulting with Don Francisco, the move was authorized, and it was arranged that Pinto would sleep in the adjacent room to take care of the young master. Rafael seemed very happy with this change of lodgings, for upstairs he had two very ample rooms in which he could easily walk about; he would not be bothered by street noise and would be farther from the hubbub of the house, which was unbearable on the nights when there were receptions of grand dinners. Joking with Torquemada, he said, "I'm going upstairs where you are. What apostasy! To install myself so close to the golden calf! What turns the world takes: I, who was the calf's worst enemy, now request hospitality in his sacristy."

SIX

The banquet in honor of the great man was held early in May, and I swear that there is no need to investigate the details of the festive affair, for the press of Madrid contains, in its numbers of those days, minute descriptions of everything that occurred there. The place was one of the roomiest in Madrid, large enough for two hundred persons to eat at two or three very long tables; but since there were more than three hundred subscribers, no matter how eager the proprietor was to accommodate them, the fact is that they were packed in like sardines. Although they could manage pretty well with one hand, the other had to go into their pockets. By seven o'clock the hall was already in ferment, and the members of the organizing committee, among whom, needless to say, Zárate was one of the most active, hurried hither and yon to place everyone and try to make the allocation of seats obey a criterion of rank. Scattered about the hall were politically important personages, military officers of high rank, engineers, a professor or two, bankers and men of wealth, journalists poor in pocket though rich in talent, an occasional poet, and, here and there, various persons as yet unknown to fame, important landowners and financiers, in short, very distinguished people, some with titles of aristocracy, etc. As Donoso correctly observed, the serious element of society predominated.

While the diners were getting settled, much confusion and hubbub reigned in the hall. Some of them, already seated and with napkins in place, were chatting and laughing; others left one spot to go and sit in another, near the group of friends most to their taste. The decorations in the room were of the kind usually employed for such solemnities: swags of foliage, large plaques with the coats of arms of the provinces, the worse for wear after much use in festivals; national flags hung in the manner of bathing costumes put out to dry. All this belongs to the patriotic wardrobe of City Hall, which generously makes it available, thus contributing to the splendor of the feast. Some plaques were added, through Zárate's initiative, with the names of the chief towns in each district of the Province of León, and in the center of the large room, at the head end of the tables, was a big engraving of the beautiful cathedral of León with the motto, on badly painted ribbons, of *pulchra leonina*.

The different chroniclers of that splendiferous festivity agree in stating that it was five minutes past the hour of seven-thirty when Don Francisco entered, accompanied by his court: Donoso, Morentín, Taramundi, and one or two more who are not named. There is no agreement, however, about indications of the miser's appearance, for while one newspaper speaks of his pallor and evident emotion, another states that he entered smiling and with a rather high color. Although it does not appear in accounts of the event, we may certainly say that when Don Francisco was seated in the place of honor, all the guests sat down too, and the soup began to be served. It was a pleasure to see those tables and those rows of gentlemen in frock coats, some bald, others with abundant hair, almost all of them with an air of positively Chinese gravity. There were few representatives of the youthful element, but no lack of hubbub and cheerfulness, for among three hundred persons, even though they be of a serious bent owing to their age and circumstance, there are sure to be a few wits who know how to enliven the most boring acts of life.

Tucked away at one end of the lateral table, at the farthest possible distance from its head, were Serrano Morentín, Zárate, and the licentiate Juan de Madrid, this last with the worst intentions in the world, for he was preparing to take note of all the foolish statements and solecisms that the grotesque miser, the object of so extravagant an homage, was sure to pronounce in the course of his speech of thanks. Morentín, with the gift of prophecy, announced in advance some of the ideas that Don Francisco was bound to express, and even the words he would use; Zárate assured the others that he knew the main lines of the speech, deducing them from the questions his friend had asked him in recent days, and all three, along with others who joined the group, were licking their lips with pleasure, awaiting the amusing comedy that was to be offered them at the hour of the toasts. Naturally, the more ridiculous things the ruffian said the more enthusiastically they would applaud him, to push him along the path of foolishness, and would laugh all the more, and have as delightful a time as in those theaters that offer one-hour comedy programs.

But this sentiment of mocking hostility did not predominate in all the groups. Near the center of one of the tables, Cristóbal Medina, Sánchez Botín, and their cronies expressed their curiosity as to what San Eloy would or would not say in his reply to the toasts.

"He's a rough man," said one, "a hard-working man and, as such, does not speak with ease. But what intelligence, señores! What practical sense, what calm judgment, what an aim he has to hit the center of the target in every matter!"

And elsewhere:

"Let's see what this Don Francisco comes out with. He won't speak long. He's a very shrewd character, who hides his thoughts, like all superior intelligences."

Meanwhile, the miserly marquis was experiencing different emotions. He ate little, and praised none of the dishes. They all tasted alike to him; they were, compared to his coarse gastronomic criterion of potatoes and meat salad laced with onion, the same old messes, just as in his own house, but cooked with less care, and all of it on a large scale. At first he did not worry in the least about the peroration he had to give. His neighbor, an old Leonese gentleman—a rich land-owner, a senator, and known to be very religious—occupied him by chatting about things and persons in El Bierzo, and drew his thoughts away from the literary effort that all those brilliant orators assembled in the hall were going to impose upon him. But by the third course our man had begun to think about it and to refresh the ideas he had brought from home for the purpose, which already were no less wilted than the flowers on the table. They escaped him as quickly as they came into his mind, bringing other, fresh ideas which seemed to arise in the overheated atmosphere of the immense dining room: "Sweet Christ!" he thought, trying to cheer himself up, "if only I don't forget the words that I've studied so carefully; if only I don't make a mistake in terms, saying one thing when I mean another, we'll come out all right. Francisco Torquemada is responsible for the ideas, and what I must pray to God is not to get my words mixed up."

Although his intention had been not to drink a drop, so as to keep his head absolutely clear, he had occasionally had to break his prom-ise, and when the roast meat was served—chicken or young turkey, and harder than a saint's foot—and then a salad with no onions in it, tasteless and limp, he felt as if vapors were rising to his head and that his vision was clouding over. What a strange thing! He saw Doña Lupe, seated halfway down one of the central tables and dressed exactly like a man, with the shirtfront like a folded piece of stiff paper, white tie, frock coat, flower in the buttonhole. He took his eyes off the strange figure, and a little later looked again. Doña Lupe had gone away. He searched for her, examining each face one after another, and finally found her again in one of the waiters who was serving platters of food, and who, with servile amiability, was smiling exactly as she did. There was no doubt that it was indeed the Turkey Lady, with her prim mouth and lively eyes. Undoubtedly she had emerged from her tomb at the patriotic call of the Leonese faction, leaving some parts of her person behind in her haste, to wit: the knot in her hair, the cotton wad that replaced her lost breast, and her whole body from the waist down.

When he saw the waiter at close quarters, the resemblance was so exact that Torquemada felt a kind of fear. "Goodness me!" he thought. "My head is swimming with these things, and I'll get into a terrible mess. Come now, come; I've already forgotten every last thing I wrote last night. And, mind you, it was good! I've certainly covered myself with glory; I can't remember a syllable."

He looked anxiously for Donoso among those who occupied places of honor on one side of him or the other, like the apostles in the picture of the Last Supper, and noticed that his friend's place was empty. Donoso would have been very helpful to him at that moment, for only with his encouragement would he recover his serenity, and with serenity his memory.

"What's happened to Don José?" he asked, very uneasily.

He was soon informed that Donoso had had to leave the table, for he had received word that his wife was at death's door. This was no small blow to the miser, for he had only to look at Donoso for his ideas to become refreshed, and fine words and an elegant mode of speech, slow and ceremonious, would return to his mind.

Well, sir, he had no choice but to get out of the predicament as best he could. He would try to concentrate all the energies of his brain, without ceasing to listen to the chat of the two apostles on either side of him. Before long some of what he had jotted down on the previous night came to his mind; but his ideas appeared in two or three forms, because first he had written something that did not please him and had torn the page and written it again, and torn it again . . . Heavens, it was a regular centipede. But by good luck he remembered perfectly a few rhetorical formulas he had heard in the Senate, and which had stuck in his noggin like lichens on a rock . . . And then, something had to be left to the inspiration of the moment, yes indeed.

They served a sort of cake, and Don Francisco never found out whether it was ice or fire, for it burned on one side and on the other set his teeth on edge as if he were eating snow. He was unaware of the passage of time, and soon saw that between him and the guest on his right the waiter's hand was being inserted with a bottle in it, and that champagne was being poured into his glass. At the same instant he heard a noise of corks popping and an uproar, a deep, penetrating murmur. One of those individuals rose to his feet, and for the space of half a minute nothing was heard but the shushing noises of those who called for quiet. At last a relative silence was produced, and . . . off went the little speech on behalf of the organizing committee, explaining the object of that homage.

SEVEN

To tell the whole truth, the first speaker (a director of companies, whose name is superfluous here), a dark-complexioned, heavyset man, spoke very badly, though the morning newspapers, paying tribute to courtesy, said otherwise. How vulgar he was! He hoped that they would excuse him for making use of the floor, assuming representation of the organizing committee, he, so humble; he, so unimportant; he, undoubtedly, the last and least . . . but because he was the last he was speaking first, to give thanks to the illustrious man who had deigned to accept, etc. He enumerated the battles that had had to be fought against the great man's modesty, a terrible struggle in which modesty defended itself spiritedly, and how they had almost had to drag there the marquis of San Eloy, this hardworking man, this man of isolation and solitude, this man of fruitful silences, a man who fled from social luster and the trumpet blasts of fame. But to no avail. It was essential, for the good of society itself, to extract him bodily from his place of retirement, bring him to a place where he could receive the compliments he deserved . . . "to surround him with our affection, our homage, our . . . our . . . praises, señores, so that he will know how much he is worth, so that society can express its tremendous gratitude to him for the benefits it has received from his powerful intelligence. That is all." (Great applause; the orator sits down very red in the face, wiping the sweat from his countenance. Don Francisco embraces him with his left arm only.)

The hubbub produced by the first speech had not subsided when far away, at the opposite end of the hall, a tall, dried-up gentleman arose. He must have been famous as a brilliant orator, for his speech was preceded by a murmur of anticipation, and the whole grave assemblage licked its collective lips with satisfaction over the sublime things it was soon to hear. Indeed, the poor devil was a regular electrical machine. He spoke with his mouth, with his arms, which resembled windmill blades; with his trembling hands, which almost touched the ceiling; with his clutching fingers, with his whole flushed face, which flashed fire; with his eyes, which almost bulged from their sockets; with his eyeglasses, which alternately fell and were replaced on the bridge of his nose by the same hand that was trying to pierce the ceiling. Such were the excesses of his emphatic and kaleidoscopic speech that, if it had lasted more than fifteen minutes, everyone would have left the place with Saint Vitus' dance. What an accumulation of idea upon idea, what a whirlwind of figures, running along like derailed railway cars, which as they collide are heaped one upon another; what a furiously lofty tone, from the very first moment, so much so that there was no possible gradation, and his oratory was a delirious succession of special effects! And because that engineer (I don't know whether he graduated in Madrid or in Liège), an initiator of public works that were as grandiose as they were impracticable, spouted a frightful amalgam of rhetoric of an industrial and constructive kind, and everything was coal here, red-hot boilers there, spirals of smoke that wrote upon the blue of the sky the poem of manufacturing, the hum of wheels, the crackling of winches; and after this, dynamos, calories, the force of cohesion, the vital principle, chemical affinities, all winding up in the rainbow, the dewdrops that break down solar rays into their component parts, and I don't know what else, good God, emerged from that mouth. And after all this, he still had not said anything about Don Francisco, nor was any relationship apparent between the guest of honor and all that taradiddle about dewdrops, dynamos, and winches.

Without abandoning his vertiginous style and epileptic gesticulations, he briskly made the transition. He represented Humanity as coming to blows with Science, so to speak. Science yearned to redeem Humanity, and Humanity was obstinately insistent on not letting herself be redeemed. Naturally, nothing could be accomplished until men of action appeared. Without them our lady Science was impotent. At last—hosanna!—the man of action appeared. And who, you will say, was the man of action? Why, Don Francisco Torquemada (hearty applause as a salute to his name). After a short panegyric about the distinguished Leonese gentleman, the orator sat down, deluged by enthusiastic cries. He sank breathless into his chair like a workman who has fallen off a scaffolding with all his bones broken, and has to be taken to the hospital.

A parenthesis followed, full of noise, laughter, and witty sallies.

"Let Don So-and-So talk, let Señor Such-and-Such talk."

The audience found itself in that pleasant psychological state from which all the agreeableness and wittiness of this sort of event are derived. Each person present felt touched by the dash of humor that seemed to spread through the enormous dining room. After this man and that were encouraged to speak, a short, bald gentleman rose to his feet, not without many protests on his part. The moment had arrived for the wit to appear, for in the solemnity of a banquet, to make the picture complete, there must always be a recreational portion, a speaker who deals jocosely with the same questions the others have dealt with seriously. The one chosen to fill this void was a former journalist, a magistrate for a short time, then a government-sponsored deputy in Parliament, and at some periods in his life a dealer in crating materials for the shipment of tobacco. His reputation as a wit was such that, even before he spoke, his hearers were helpless with laughter.

"Señores," he began, "we have come here with very wicked motives, with the naughtiest of intentions, and I, because my conscience demands it, ask the governor, who is present here, to send us all off to jail" (laughter). "We have brought the most excellent Señor Marquis of San Eloy here under false pretenses. He came to honor us with his company at this poor table . . . and now it turns out that we offer him a menu—which some call 'bill of fare'—of speeches, a real indigestive medicine to make the meal disagree with him."

The preamble was very amusing, and then he went into the main part of his speech, saying, "None of those here present knows who the marquis of San Eloy is, and I, who do know, am going to tell you about him. The marquis of San Eloy is a poor fellow, and it is we rich and powerful men who are honoring him" (laughter). "He's just a poor chap who happened to be passing by, and we've invited him to come in here, and he does so and takes part in our celebration . . . No, don't laugh; I said he's a poor little chap, and I'm going to prove it to you. The man who, possessing riches, dedicates them to building humanity's good, is not rich. He is merely a trustee, an administrator, not of his own riches but of ours, for he dedicates them to bettering our moral and material situation" (applause, though the line of thought convinced no one).

He continued to string together foolish statements and to play with paradoxes until he finished by comically offering his protection to the "Administrator of Humanity," Don Francisco Torquemada. Impossible to mention everything that was subsequently said, in various registers; there were speeches that were good and short, others that were long, diffuse, and totally without substance. One gentleman spoke in the name of the province of Palencia, the neighboring one to León, assuring the gathering that there was no need for so many railways, though he had no quarrel with them, mind you, and that capital ought to be employed on irrigation canals. Another spoke in the name of the army, to which he belonged, and still another in the name of the merchant marine. Someone also expressed some lofty sentiments in the name of the aristocratic class and in that of the college of notaries, and the governor expressed his regret that Señor Torquemada was not a native of Madrid, an idea against which the Leonese gentlemen present protested angrily; but the governor insisted on his idea, assuring them that León and Madrid lived in perfect harmony. A man from Astorga leaped into the fray, calling Madrid his second homeland, the first homeland of his children, and ended by bursting into tears; and another, who had come from Villafranca del Bierzo, declared himself to be the nephew of the priest who had baptized Don Francisco, which was the most moving detail of the whole occasion. Thanks to a very welcome maneuver, some plaguey poets were prevented from reading the verses they were on the point of producing, with the most treacherous intentions in the world. Owing to the high standing of the persons assembled there, and the serious object of the ceremony, it was deemed not in character to read poetic compositions. And at last the culminating moment drew near. The hero of the festivities, mute and pale, was already turning over in his mind the first sentences of his speech. In the brief instants left to him, he summoned up his courage and fixed firmly in his mind certain rules that he had determined to follow, namely: not to cite specific authors without being absolutely certain of the quotation, to express vaguely and with equivocal phrases everything over which he did not have absolute control, to always stay between two viewpoints without saying either black or white, as a man who errs more on the side of reserve than garrulousness, and to gloss over, as if walking on hot coals, every delicate point of the kind that cannot be placed in any less than knowledgeable mouth without the risk of saying something absurd. Having made this mental preparation, and entrusting himself to his literary idol, Señor Donoso, whom he believed that he bore within himself in essence, like a second soul, he stood up and waited quietly for the august silence he needed in order to begin. Thanks to the diligent scribes whom the narrator of this story took to the banquet, at his own expense and risk, the most brilliant paragraphs of that notable speech have seen print, as will be observed by those who continue to read.

EIGHT

"Señores: I am not going to make a speech. Even though I might like to, and you . . . I mean that although you might like to hear me make one, I could not do so, because of my poverty . . ." (murmurs) "my poverty of oratorical resources. I am an unpolished individual, *eminently* a worker, and come from the people, an artisan *par excellence* of honest business" (hear, hear). "Do not expect more or less flowery speeches from me, for I have not had time to learn the art of oratory. But, gentlemen and friends, I cannot fail to respond to what your courtesy and my gratitude demand of me,[1] and so I must offer a few badly expressed . . . manifestations which, though poor in style and crude as literature, will be the sincere expression of a grateful heart, of a noble heart, a heart that beats,[2] now and always, in rhythm with every gentlemanly and generous feeling" (hear, hear).

"I repeat, do not expect pretty speeches or eloquent periods from me. My flowers are numbers; my eloquence, action" (applause). "Action, señores. And what is action? You all know what it is, and I don't need to tell you. Action is life, action is what is done, señores, and what is done says more than what is said. *It has been said. . .*" (pause). "It has been said that speech is silver and silence is golden. Well, I will add that action is all Oriental pearls and magnificent diamonds" (warm approval).

"*I take satisfaction* in answering the gentlemen who have preceded me on the floor, and as I do so" (pause), "*I am bound to declare* that I would by no means have accepted this undeserved homage that you

[1]Expression learned from Donoso two days previously.
[2]He tries to recall the end of a paragraph heard in the Senate, and at last pulls it out as well as he can remember it.

offer me had I not been obliged to it by considerations of one sort or another, and that motives of vanity have not brought me here, *even remotely*[3] . . . to the point that . . . my spirit . . . well, my absolute purpose was to prevail in *the line of conduct* that I have always observed, and to establish myself in the thesis that we must resist everything that *propends* toward personal aggrandizement . . . for personalities, señores, have more than sufficient representation *at the present historical moment!*[4] And now it is time to glorify deeds, not persons; principles, not entities, for I recognize their merit, señores, I recognize it; but now it is time to place deeds, action, the great principle of action, above the personal individual" (raising his voice), "each in its own element, and in the circle of their own operations" (hear, hear; bravo).

"Who has the honor of addressing his modest words to you at this moment? Why, he is only a poor workman, a man who owes everything to his own initiative, his own hard work, his honesty, his constancy. I was born, as you might say, in the greatest indigence, and with the sweat of my brow I have made my bread, and I have lived, skirting difficulties day after day, always fulfilling my obligations and *discharging* my business transactions with the very strictest morality. I have certainly been no angel; I have made no pact with the devil, as some *wrongly and foolishly*[5] believe" (laughter). "I do not have the gift of miracles. If I have reached the point where I am today, I owe it to the fact that I have two virtues, and I am proud of them, with your approval; two virtues. What are they? *Behold them:* work, and conscience. I have worked in an *uninterrupted series* of . . . of . . . *economico-financial* tasks, and I have practiced good works, doing all possible favors to my fellow men, and *forging* the happiness of all persons within reach of my actions" (hear, hear). "This has been my *desideratum,* and the idea I have *cherished* always: to do all the good I could to my fellow beings. For business, *in the vernacular* activity—take note, señores—has no quarrel with charity or with more or less suffering humanity. There are two elements that complement each

[3]The speaker, now getting fairly warmed up, believing himself on firm ground and in control of all the phraseology of the Senate, becomes confused and does not succeed in finishing the sentence.

[4]At last finding his way out of the labyrinth.

[5]Adverbs he had picked up in the Senate the day before.

other, two *objectives* that come together in one *objective*; an *objective*, señores, of which we have a picture in our consciences, but which resides in the Most High"[6] (huge, noisy, and enthusiastic applause).

"But if I declare that it was always my *line of conduct* to do good to all, without distinction of classes, to all, *Greeks and Trojans alike*, I can also tell you that, as a working man *par excellence*, I have never, never *given rise* to sloth nor protected evil people—for that, mind you! would be neither charity nor humanity but lack of practical sense; that would mean *giving the greatest possible rise* to idleness. You can say of me anything you like, but let it never be said that I was the Maecenas of laziness" (delirious applause).

"*I have always started from the principle* that each man is master of his own destiny; and the happy man will be he who knows how to forge his happiness, and unhappy he who does not know how to forge it.[7] One need not abandon oneself to fate. Ah, fate; foolishness, idiocy, *dilemmas, antinomies, Machiavellianisms!* There is no ill luck except that which a man brings on himself by his own errors. Everyone who wants to possess *material interests* has only to seek them. Seek and ye shall find, as the man said. Except you have to sweat, move, sharpen the old bean, *in a word* work, now in this job, now in the other. But to live a self-indulgent life with promenading and junkets, chatting in casinos or getting mixed up with fine wenches" (laughter) "doesn't earn the daily bread . . . and the bread is there, there it is, look at it, there.[8] But you have to go and grab it; because it, the bread, can't come looking for us. It hasn't any feet, it stays there very quietly waiting for man to come and grab it, man, to whom the Most High has given feet to run after his bread, intelligence to know where it is, eyes to see it, and hands to grab it" (bravos and frantic clapping).

"And so, if you spend your time on amusements, you'll have no bread, and when hunger forces you to rush out looking for it, others smarter than you will already have grabbed it—the early birds, the ones who know how to spend all the hours of the day in *classic* work, those who knew how to *discharge* all their tasks at the proper time,

[6]A phrase distorted out of another that he had read in a newspaper on the previous day.

[7]The orator, encouraged by the applause, now speaks with a serenity and easy flow of words that many a man might envy.

[8]Feeling inspired and launching fearlessly into improvisation.

leaving nothing until tomorrow; those who put themselves the question of *to eat or not to eat*, like the other fellow whom you know better than I do, and I don't have to name him; just as the other one, as I said, put the question of *to be or not to be*" (admiration, clamorous applause).[9]

"Señores, let us be practical. I'm practical and proud of it, setting the mask of modesty aside, for it's been put on and taken off so many times that it's falling off our faces in little pieces" (noisy applause and cries of "yes, yes"). "Let us be practical, I say; all of you ought to be, and I, an old fox, recommend that you be practical. Be practical if you don't want your life to *display the characteristics* of a *Penelope's web*. If today you weave your well-being with *elements* greater than your means, that is to say, your possibilities, tomorrow the *deficit* will oblige you to unravel it . . . and you will always have *the sword of Aristotle* hanging over your heads" (whispers). "I mean . . ."[10] I said Aristotle because . . ." (He laughs and everyone laughs with him, expecting a joke.) "I have a real mania for that philosopher, who is the most practical of them all." (Yes, yes.) "He's my man; I have him in my thoughts at every hour of the day. And as *I'm of the opinion* that Damocles, the one with the sword, was a son of a . . . or no one knows what he was . . . Does anybody in the audience know who that fellow Damocles was?" (laughter, cries of "No, no . . . we don't know"). "Well, I'm fed up with all those ways of speaking, and I've decided that the famous sword was Aristotle's . . . I mean, I dub him a knight because he's the man I'm devoted to, he's my idol, señores, the most glorious man of ancient Greece and the Golden Age of all times" (bravo, hear, hear).[11]

"Excuse the digression, and let's return to the thesis. Let's pay more attention to action than to words; let's work, work a lot and speak little. Work always, *in accordance* with our needs and with *the valuable accompaniment* of all the elements that *accompany* us. And, having made these manifestations, which I believe were called upon

[9] The speech is commented upon favorably in all the groups, and in some with warmth and enthusiasm. Here and there ardent praises are heard: "What a clever chap! He may be crude, but what shrewd judgment he has, what practical sense!"

[10] The speaker instantly realizes his error, but cleverly corrects it at once.

[11] Enthusiastic comments in the audience. "But what a rascal he is!" "He knows something about everything." "What native wit!"

by my presence in this august place . . ." (corrrecting himself) "and I call it august because so many scientific, political, and private eminences are here assembled . . ." (hear, hear; bravo) "having made these declarations, I go on to make the question concrete. To what does this dinner *respond*? What particular *objective* leads you to honor me, humble as I am? Because you have seen in me a man who is active by nature, a man ready to preside over the great advances of the century, to bring them to the level of practice. I place my humble intelligence and accumulated wealth at the service of our country; I do not look out for my interest, but to the general interest, to the public interest of Humanity herself, for the poor thing is much in need of being looked out for. *Behold me* ready to undertake very important work, with no ambition for private lucre, believe me, and to favor my native region by bringing the locomotive *with its plume of steam* across the fields. If I did not idolize science and industry as I idolize them, if progress were not my *beau ideal*, I would not sponsor the locomotive; I would sponsor the cart and would envision no other *link of union* between towns than the Astorga stagecoach or the Ponferrada stagecoach. But no, señores; I am a child of my century, of the eminently practical century, and I patronize the local stagecoach, or better still, the whole world's stagecoach: namely, the locomotive" (frantic applause).

"On with science, on with industry.[12] The word is being transformed by progress, and today we are amazed to see the marvelous brightness of electric light where before there were nothing but oil lamps, tallow and stearine candles, and refined petroleum.[13] From which I draw the conclusion that modern things are making an end of old stuff. What a great truth it is, señores, that *the new will kill off the old . . .* as . . . the fellow you all know said, and said very well!" (prolonged applause).

"I, señores—I don't tire of repeating it to you—am an extremely humble man, a very plain man, with very few brains" (cries of "no, no") "not very bright" ("no, no") "with little education; but no one

[12]Those in the group of critics at times laugh shamelessly and at times conceal their hilarity, applauding noisily in unison. *Morentín*: "This animal really has a sort of eloquence. He brays quite oratorically."

[13]The orator, without ceasing to talk, says to himself, "I'm doing fine. I think I'm showing myself to advantage. How sorry I am that Donoso can't hear me!"

is more punctilious than I. Would you like me to *define* my moral and religious *attitude?* Well, I tell you that my dogmas are work, honor" (murmurs of approbation) "love for my neighbor, and good habits. I start from these principles always, and that is why I have been able to carve out an independent position. And don't think that I ignore, *so to speak,* the sacred dogma of our elders. No; I know how to *render to Caesar the things that are Caesar's* and to the Most High . . . the things that are His. Because no one is a better Catholic than I, as God well knows, and no one is more ready to defend *venerated beliefs.* I adore my family, in whose . . . *focus,* in whose bosom I find my happiness, and I assure you that it's only a step from my home to Heaven . . ." (tenderly) "I ought not to speak of these things, which belong to *the private element* . . ." (cries: "yes, yes; go on"). "But my family, that is, the circle of the domestic hearth, is first in my heart and I think of it constantly, and cannot omit from my thought those portions of . . . No, I won't go on; don't let me go on . . ." (great emotion on the audience's part).

"Of politics I say nothing to you" (cries of "yes, yes"). "No, no, señores. I still haven't found out what parties we have, or what they're good for" (laughter). "I will never be in the cabinet, nor will I distribute appointments . . . No, no . . . I see that government employees *pullulate,* and that no one makes up his mind to *castigate* the budget. Of course, they don't castigate it because this hurts the castigators themselves" (laughter). "I wash my hands: I *make a boast* of obeying the man who rules and of not *infringing the laws.* I respect *Greeks and Trojans alike,* and do not haggle over the *obol* of taxes.[14] *By dint of* being a practical man, I don't engage in systematic opposition, nor do I engage in *Machiavellianisms* of any kind whatever. I am *refractory* to intrigue, I cherish no idea but the good of my country, be it provided by Juan Pedro, or Diego" (hear, hear).

"To conclude, señores . . . for you must be tired of listening to me" (no, no). "And I'm tired of talking too, for I'm not used to it, nor do I know how to express myself with all the peculiar brilliance, nor . . . nor with the correct prose . . . which . . . Anyway, señores, I conclude

---

[14]In the group of critics. *Morentín:* "Have you ever seen such a delicious fool?" *Juan de Madrid:* "What I see is that he's a first-class satirist." *Zárate:* "Yes, he's making fun of everyone here."

with manifestations of my gratitude for your manifestations . . . for this *holocaust*,[15] for this magnanimous and veritable homage. I say it and repeat it; I don't deserve this; I am unworthy of offerings that are so . . . sublime, and which have no *point of contact* with my modest merits. Don't attribute to me *characteristics* that I don't possess. The truth before everything else. In the question of the railway I have done no more than obey the impetus of an illustrious and particular friend of mine, here present, and whom I do not name in order to protect his *considerable* modesty." (Everyone looks at the marquis of Taramundi, who lowers his eyes and blushes slightly.) "This friend is the one who has pushed the whole matter of the railway line, and he is responsible for[16] the *coronation of success*, for, although he has not appeared publicly at all, *behind the scenes* he has managed everything very neatly, so that I can indeed tell you that he has been . . .[17] hold onto your hats, señores, the *Deus ex machina* of the Villafranca to Berrocal railway." (Very noisy applause. The Leonese clap their hands sore.)

"Now . . .[18] there's nothing left for me to tell you except that my gratitude will be eternal, and in no sense ephemeral, no, and that everyone present, without distinction between *Greeks and Trojans*" (laughter), "will find me unconditionally at their disposal. I don't say it to praise myself; but I know how to judge, and no one is better than I at serving my friends and helping them in . . . what they need, that is, that in *any little thing* in which they need my modest cooperation, they have only to command, in the certainty that in me they will have a humble servant, an intimate friend, and . . . a companion, ready to offer them . . . all the *disinterested* cooperation, all the favor, all the moral and material support, all the confidence in the world . . . always with my heart and soul . . . And so I offer you, with the best will in the world, my fortune, my person, and everything that I am and everything I am worth. That is all." (Frantic applause, delirious acclamations, cries, hubbub. Every man on his feet, clapping unceasingly, with an astonishing amount of noise. The ovation is endless.)

---

[15]Smothered laughter in the group of critics.

[16]The orator prepares to spout the elegant phrase he has learned a few days earlier, and of whose effect he is confident, if only he can manage to say it without making a mistake in pronunciation.

[17]Pausing to remember the phrase before launching it.

[18]The orator's face shines with joy, for the phrase came out exactly right.

NINE

Those nearest to him hastened to embrace the triumphant orator, and all was delirium. What hugs, what commotion, what emotion! They practically dismembered the poor man, who, with a face shining as if it had been smeared with grease, his eyes sparkling, his smile convulsed, was no longer capable of responding to such noisy demonstrations. And then all the diners came to him in a straggling troop, jostling one another, and all of them crowded around him, some with fraternal effusion and a certain affection, the result of the noise, the applause, and that emotional contagion which is produced in large gatherings. Don Juan Gualberto Serrano, his voice breaking, red as a turkey cock and sweating freely, said merely, "Colossal, my friend, colossal."

And another assured him that he had never heard a speech he liked better.

"And how it showed the practical man, the man of action!" said a third.

"What we have here is the apostle of common sense. That's the way to think and talk. My most enthusiastic congratulations, Señor Don Francisco."

"Sublime. Let me give you a hug. Oh, what fine things you told us!"

"And you knew how to speak to the heart as well. What a man! Goodness, after this we'll make you a cabinet minister."

"I? Stop right there," replied the miser, who was getting annoyed by so much hugging. "I said three or four courtesy phrases, that's all."

"Three or four phrases, eh? Then say three or four thousand magnificent, tremendous ideas. Another hug. Frankly, it's been astonishing."

Among the last to arrive was Morentín, who embraced him with pretended affection and the smile of a man of the world, saying, "But, very good! What an orator you turned out to be tonight! Don't take it as a joke; you're an orator, and one of the great ones."

"Stop it . . . for the love of God."

"An orator, yes indeed," added Villalonga, with the serious expression he knew how to assume on such occasions. "You have said some very good things, and very well spoken. My congratulations."

And then came Zárate, who embraced him weeping, actually weeping, for in addition to being a pedant he was a consummate actor, and told him, "Ah, what a night . . . what emotions! My congratulations in the name of science . . . yes . . . of science, which you have praised as no one else could. What a witty synthesis! The whole world's stagecoach! Splendid, my friend. I can't help it; tears come to my eyes."

And when he took his leave of everyone, more hugs, more handshakes and new effusions of praise. Astonished by this extraordinary success, Don Francisco even began to doubt that it was real. Suppose they were pulling his leg! But no, they were not laughing at him, because, really, he had spoken feelingly; he knew it and told himself so, modesty aside. He would never cease regretting that the great Donoso had not heard him.

His more intimate friends went home with him, and another ovation awaited him there. Reliable news of the great success had reached them, and the moment he entered the drawing room all those ladies rushed to embrace him. Cruz and Fidela, who had heard about the serious illness of their friend Señora de Donoso before Don Francisco's arrival and had had a very unhappy time of it, quickly changed from sorrow to jubilation as soon as they saw the hero of the evening enter, and thought only of adding their voices to the chorus of congratulations.

"I'm not surprised by your triumph, darling Tor," his wife told him. "I knew perfectly well that you would speak splendidly. You still haven't realized that you're very talented."

"I expected a success, I did indeed," said Cruz, "but I didn't think that it would be so great. I don't know to what else you can aspire now. You have everything; it seems that the whole world is lying at your feet. Gracious, what can you ask for now?"

"I? Nothing. Only that you don't have the idea of enlarging our circle, my lady. We have enough circle already. No more, now."

"No? " said the household ruler, laughing. "You"ll see. Why, we're just beginning . . . Prepare yourself."

"But do you still . . .?" murmured Torquemada, trembling like a leaf on a tree.

"We'll talk about it tomorrow."

These fateful words embittered the brand-new orator's satisfaction and he spent a restless night, not only because of the nervous excitement brought on by his *apotheosis*, but because of his implacable tyrant's menacing hints.

Next day Torquemada tried in vain to elicit congratulations from Rafael. A slight indisposition kept him in his room on the third floor, and he let no one see him except his sister Cruz. The morning newspapers more than satisfied the great man's oratorical vanity, praising him to the skies and acclaiming, in agreement with the opinion of the moment, his practical sense and energy of character. All day long there were frequent visits from personages *both private and public*, a diplomat or two, directors in the ministries of Treasury and Internal Affairs, generals, deputies and senators, and two cabinet ministers, all singing the same song: that the orator had said things with *a great deal of substance* and that he had succeeded in *dotting the i's*. It seemed that the only ones still to come were the king, the Pope, and the Emperor of Germany himself. The Church did not lack representation in that jubilee, for the very reverend provincial of the Dominicans, Padre Respaldiza, and my lord bishop of Antioch also arrived to cense the miser, and exhausted the vocabulary of praise.

"Blessed," said His Lordship with evangelical unction, "are the rich who know how to employ their treasures in a Christian way to the benefit of the needy classes."

When the last visitor had departed the great man gave a sigh of relief, enjoying the solitude of his home and family. But his contentment was short-lived, for Fidela and Cruz confronted him in hostile fashion. Fidela said nothing, assenting with her expression to everything her sister said in a facile and haughty tone. From the very first words, Don Francisco turned livid, bit his mustache, nibbling off more than half of the pepper-and-salt bristles that composed it, and clutched his arms or his knees, a prey to terrible nervous apprehension. What new bite would the ruler take out of his considerable *liquid assets*, which were, rather, solid ones? Well, it was the most awful thing imaginable, and the miser thought he could almost feel the house coming down and burying him in the ruins.

In the arrangement about the Gravelinas debt, the ducal palace, assessed at ten million reales, was one of the first properties destined to be put up for auction. It was said that it would be difficult to find a buyer, unless the duke of Montpensier himself or some other member of the royal family might be tempted, and negotiations were going forward to have the government acquire it for the office of the Presidency. Such a fine and lordly property could belong only to the State or to some prince. And imagine the ideas of that demon in female form and oracle of the practical and cautious man *par excellence*, the firstborn Aguila! Judge of her audacious plans by the response given her by Don Francisco, as he breathlessly swallowed saliva that was bitterer than gall.

"But have the two of you gone crazy, or have you decided to send me to a madhouse? To have me take over the Gravelinas palace, that mansion of crowned heads—that is, that I buy it—unless the papal nuncio buys it first!"

He burst into insolent laughter, which made the ruling lady believe that this time she would find in her subject a resistance difficult to overcome. At first, as the branding iron entered his flesh, the miser felt strong, and his heavy breathing and the blows of his fist upon the table would have inspired terror in the heart of anyone less courageous than Cruz.

"And what do you say?" Don Francisco asked his wife.

"I? Why, nothing. But goodness, in the deal with the duke's estate, including the palace and the country properties, you've made an enormous amount of money! Take the palace for yourself, Tor, and don't pretend you're a poor little wretch. Heavens, suppose I figure it out for you and prove to you that if you buy it, it's going to cost only about six million?"

"Stop, stop. What do you know?"

"And in the last instance, what are six millions to you, or even ten?"

Don Francisco looked at her indignantly, spluttering expressions which somewhat resembled barks; but once that brutal explosion of avarice had passed, the poor man completely collapsed, feeling, in the presence of the two ladies, the cowardice of some helpless rodent caught in a trap impossible to break. Cruz saw that the battle was won and, out of consideration for the vanquished foe, gave him an affectionate talking-to, placing before him the material advantages that that purchase would bring.

"There's nothing for it; we'll end up in poverty . . ." said the miser with bitter humor. " 'From the bell tower of San Bernardino forty centuries look down upon us.' All right, all right, bring on the palaces. Oh, my old house in the Calle de San Blas, if only I could see you again! Tell them to notify the funeral parlor; tell them to bring my coffin; I'm going to die today. I won't survive this blow; I'm dying! I said it already in my speech: *the new will kill off the old.* I ask you, my fine ladies of palace and coronet, what are we going to use to fill those immense halls, that look like the Hippodrome, and those galleries that are longer than Lent? Because everything will have to measure up."

"Why . . . very simple," answered Cruz calmly. "You know that Don Carlos de Cisneros died last week."

"Yes, señora . . . and so?"

"His gallery is going to be sold at auction."

"A gallery; and what do I want galleries for?"

"My dear man, the paintings. He has first-rate ones, worthy to be hung in royal museums."

"And I've got to buy them! I!" murmured Don Francisco, whose brain had turned soft from so many blows, and who was entirely bemused.

"You."

"Oh, yes, Tor!" said Fidela. "I just love good paintings. And Cisneros had magnificent ones, of Italian, Flemish, and Spanish masters. But how stupid you are, for that always represents money!"

"Always money," repeated the miser, who had been reduced to a state of idiocy.

"Of course; the day that you don't feel comfortable with the paintings you can sell them to the Louvre or the National Gallery, and they'll pay their weight in gold for the Andrea del Sartos, the Giorgiones, the Ghirlandaios, and the Rembrandts, Dürers, and Van Dycks . . ."

"And what else?"

"And to round out everything else, take over the duke's armor collection, for it has priceless historical value, and, according to what I've heard, the valuation is most low."

"I say that the *Most Low* himself has entered my house, and you two are his helpers. So, armor too! And what kind of a show am I going to make with all that old iron?"

"Tor, don't joke," said Fidela, caressing him. "It's a pleasure to own

these historic treasures and show them off in our home to the admiration of persons of taste. We'll have a superb museum and you'll be
famous as an enlightened man, a real prince of arts and letters; you'll
be a sort of Medici . . ."

"A what? What I'd willingly buy right now is a rope to hang myself
with. You can believe me: if I don't kill myself, it's for my son's sake.
I need to live to protect him from the poverty you're bringing him to
and the misfortune you're *occasioning* him."

"Silly, be quiet. Look, if I were you, I'd also keep the Gravelinas
archive; I'd take it away from the government, which wants to buy
it. What an archive!"

"It's probably full of rats."

"Unbelievably precious manuscripts, unpublished plays by Lope de
Vega, signed letters of Antonio Pérez, Saint Theresa, the Duke of Alva,
and the Great Captain. Oh, what beautiful things! And then there are
Arabic and Hebrew codices, the rarest of books . . ."

"And I'm to buy that too? Oh, what a delight! What else? Shall I
buy the Segovia Bridge as well, and the bull statues of Guisando? So,
manuscripts, that is, a bunch of bibles? And all so a few good-for-
nothing poets can come and take notes and tell me that I'm ever so
enlightened. Oh, my God, how my heart hurts! You two don't want
to believe it, but I'm very ill. Any day now I'll kick the bucket in one
of these attacks and you'll be my widows, widows of the man who's
sacrificed his saving nature to make you happy. But I can't stand any
more, any more at all. I'd cry like a baby if the *focus* of my tears
hadn't dried up with all these shocks."

He rose to his feet as he said this and, stretching as if to ease his
limbs, emitted a great roar, followed by an obscene ejaculation, and
then his arms fell to his sides with so much force that dust flew out of
his frock coat. Even in the last twitchings of his willpower, now vanquished and moribund, he still had to rebel, and, confronting Cruz,
he told her, "This is a dirty trick . . . to loot me like this, to *dilapidate*
my money so stupidly! I want to consult with Rafael about this extortion, yes, with Rafael, who used to seem the craziest one in the
family and now is the sanest. He's gone over to my side, and now he'll
defend me. Bring Rafael here. I want him to know about this horrible
goring. The horn, poor me, has gone right into my heart . . . Where's
Rafaelito? He'll say . . ."

"He doesn't want to leave his room," said Cruz serenely, having emerged victorious. "Let's go to dinner."

"To dinner, Tor," repeated Fidela, hanging on his arm. "Silly, don't be such an old beast. Why, you're a perfect angel, and you love us very much, as we love you."

"Brrr!"

TEN

Donoso's wife was very ill, desperately ill. The news that reached the home of the marquises of San Eloy that morning (on a certain day in April which was destined to be memorable) reported that all hope was lost. The viaticum was brought to her during the afternoon, and the doctors were sure that the good lady's inveterate martyrdom would come to an end before the night was over. In her, science was losing a clinical document of indubitable importance, and hence the College of Physicians might have wished for her life not to be extinguished, a life so painful for her and so fertile in experimental instruction for science.

Fidela and Cruz ate hastily and perfunctorily so as to go to Donoso's house. It was arranged that Don Francisco would stay at home looking after the baby. His mother could not go without apprehension unless his papa promised to mount guard with exquisite vigilance. Cruz also charged him to look after Rafael, who had seemed unwell for several days, though his mental disorder appeared to present considerable improvement and he was much calmer. The miser was very grateful that he had been ordered to stay behind, for he felt greatly dejected and melancholy, with little desire to leave the house and still less to watch anyone die. He yearned to be alone, to meditate on his unhappy fate and stir up his spirit in search of some consolation for the bitter tribulation of having to buy the palace and all that old canvas and rusty armor.

The two ladies departed, after telling him to send word at once if anything out of the way occurred, and, calling for some papers to be brought from upstairs, he began working in the sitting room. The baby was asleep, closely watched by his nurse. All was silence and sweet tranquillity in the house. The servants were chatting in the kitchen. On the second floor, Argüelles Mora, the bookkeeper, to whom Torquemada had entrusted an urgent piece of work, was writing all alone. The orderly was dozing on a bench in the hall, and from time to time the clatter of Pinto's feet could be heard as he went upstairs or down by the servants' staircase.

After Don Francisco had been scribbling pothooks at the table in the sitting room for a quarter of an hour, he saw Rafael come in, led by Pinto.

"Since you don't come up to see me," the blind man told him, "I've come down."

"I didn't go up because your sister told me that you weren't feeling well and didn't want to see anyone. *Contrariwise*, I was anxious to see you and have a little chat with you."

"So was I. I know that night before last you had a great success. They've told me all about it."

"It was fine. As they were all friends, they applauded me madly. But I don't let myself be carried away by flattery, and know that I'm a poor *artist of bookkeeping* who hasn't had time to educate himself. Who could ever have told me, two years ago, that I was going to make speeches in front of so many cultivated and professional people! Believe me; while I was speaking, *deep down inside* I was laughing at the nerve I had and how foolish they were."

"You must be satisfied," said Rafael calmly, fingering his beard. "You have reached the top in a short time. There aren't many men who can say as much."

"It's true. Confounded top!" murmured Don Francisco with a sigh, mulling over the sufferings that had accompanied his rise to the heights.

"You are a happy man."

"No, I'm not. Say that I'm the unhappiest of individuals and you'll be right. The man isn't happy who's kept from doing as he likes and living according to his nature. *Public opinion* thinks me fortunate, envies me, and doesn't know that I'm a martyr, yes, Rafaelito, a real *martyr of Golgotha*, I mean, of the *cross* of my house, or, in other words, a tormented man, like those that are pictured in engravings of the Inquisition or of Hell. *Behold me* tied hand and foot, obliged to carry out all the ideas *cherished* by your sister, who's decided to make me into a duke of Osuna, a marquis of Salamanca, or the emperor of China. I rage, kick, and don't know how to resist, because either your sister knows more than all the fathers and grandfathers of the Church, or she's *Pope Joan* in the shape of a lady."

"My sister has made a tremendous success of you," replied the blind man. "She is a true artist, an incomparable master, and will still do marvels with you. There's no potter like her in the world: she takes a piece of clay, kneads it, and . . ."

"And makes the piece . . . Heavens, even if she wanted to make a Chinese vase of me, I'd always come out an Alcorcón cooking-pot."

"Oh, no. You are no longer a cooking-pot, my dear sir!"

"I think that I am. Because look here . . ."

Stimulated by the silent peace of his dwelling, and further stimulated by something that was stirring in his soul, the miser felt, at that *historical moment*, a great desire to unburden himself, to reveal all his inner self. The strange thing was that Rafael felt the same desire, and had come downstairs determined to spill out the most intimate secrets of his mind to the man who was his irreconcilable enemy. And so their implacable rivalry had come down, in the end, to a burning desire to confess, and to communicate their respective sorrows to each other. Hence Torquemada told him the dilemma he was in, to have to *take on* a palace and a *raft* of old paintings, *disseminating* money and being deprived of the ineffable joy of piling up his profits so as to amass a fabulous capital sum, which was his *desideratum*, his *beau ideal*, and his *dogma*, etc. He complained bitterly about his situation, described his sufferings and the misery that entered his breast every time that he approved a considerable expense, and the other tried to console him with the idea that such expense would be fabulously profitable. But Torquemada was not convinced and continued to heave tempestuous sighs.

"Well," said Rafael, lounging in the easy chair, his face turned upward and his arms extended, "I assure you that I am more unhappy still, much more, with no other consolation than to see the end of my sufferings close at hand."

Don Francisco observed him carefully, marveling at his perfect resemblance to a statue of Christ, and quietly waited for the explanation of those sufferings which were greater than his own.

"You suffer, my dear sir," continued the blind man, "because you cannot do what you want, what your nature demands of you, which is to make and keep money; since you are a miser . . ."

"Yes, I am," agreed Torquemada in a regular delirium of sincerity. "So I am, and so what? I feel like being one."

"Very well. It is a taste like any other and ought to be respected."

"And you, why do you suffer, for heaven's sake? Unless it's because of the impossibility of regaining your sight, I don't understand."

"By this time I'm accustomed to darkness. It's not that. My suffering is purely moral, like yours, but much more intense and serious. I suffer because I feel superfluous in the world and in my family, because I have been mistaken about everything."

"Well, if being mistaken is a reason for suffering," replied the miser spiritedly, "then nobody's unhappier than your humble servant, because *yours truly*, when he got married, thought that your sisters were two little ants capable of holding onto the Bible itself, and now it turns out that . . ."

"My mistakes, Señor Marquis of San Eloy," stated the blind man without changing position, pronouncing his words with gloomy solemnity, "are much more serious, because they affect the most delicate part of the conscience. Pay close attention to what I am going to tell you, and you will understand the magnitude of my errors. I opposed my sister's marriage to you for various reasons."

"Yes, because she's got blue blood and I have . . . well, the kind that couldn't be more plebeian."

"For various reasons, I say. I accepted the wedding very unwillingly; I believed that my family was dishonored, my sisters degraded."

"Yes, because I put people off by smelling of onions and lent money at interest."

"And I firmly believed that my sisters were falling toward an abyss where they would find shame, disgust, and despair."

"Well, I don't think that the . . . damned abyss has suited them badly."

"I thought that my sister Fidela, having married at the urging of my sister Cruz, would reject you after the first week of marriage, that you would inspire loathing in her, aversion . . ."

"Well, I think that . . . my goodness!"

"I thought that both of them would be unhappy and that they would abominate the monster they were trying to tame."

"Monster's going a bit far, old fellow!"

"I thought that you, despite the teaching talents of 'Pope Joan,' would never fit into the society into which she wished to bring you, and that each step taken by the upstart in that society would make you still more ridiculous and bring shame to my sisters."

"I think I'm not out of place . . ."

"I believed that my sister Fidela could not escape certain stimuli to her imagination, nor condemn herself to insensitivity during the best years of her life, and, applying the logic that exists in society for cases of marriage between a young and beautiful woman and an old, disagreeable man, I believed, as firmly as one believes in God, that my sister would commit a crime that is very common in our society."

"Old fellow, old fellow . . ."

"I believed it, yes indeed; I confess my vile thoughts, which were nothing more than the projection of social thought on my spirit."

"So, you got it into your head that my wife would step out on me . . . Well, look here, I never thought any such thing, because one night my wife said to me . . . in confidence, *just between her and me*, 'Tor, the day I come to hate you I'll throw myself off the balcony into the street; but fail you, never. In my family adultery is unknown and will always be unknown.' "

"Of course she would think like that, but her salvation is not owed to that idea. To continue: I believed that you would not have children, for it seemed to me that nature would not sanction so absurd a union, nor bring a hybrid being to life."

"Hey, do me the favor not to call Valentín names."

"Well, my dear sir, none of these beliefs of mine has been anything but a tremendous error. I begin with you, who have proved me absolutely wrong, because not only does society accept you, but you adapt yourself admirably to it. Your wealth increases like sea foam, and society, which is never so pleased as with the man who brings it money, does not see you as the vulgarian assaulting the heights but as a superior being, endowed with great intelligence. And they make you a senator, and admit you everywhere, and fight for your friendship, and applaud and glorify you, without paying attention to whether what you say is stupid or wise, and the aristocracy flatters you, and the middle class acclaims you, and the State supports you, and the Church blesses you, and each step you take in the world is a success, and you yourself are beginning to believe that your crudeness is refinement and your ignorance enlightenment."

"I don't believe that, no, Rafaelito."

"Well, if you don't believe it the others do, and it's the same as if you did. You are held to be an extraordinary man. Let me go on; I know very well that . . ."

"No, Rafaelito; they can hold me to be anything they want, I say and declare that I'm a brute . . . of course, a brute *sui generis*. As for earning money, that's true, mind you! Nobody can beat me at it."

"Then you already have one great quality, if earning money in heaps is a quality."

"*Let's be fair*: in business—I don't say it to boast about myself—I'm miles ahead of all those other fellows out there. They're a lot of fools, and I thumb my nose at them. But outside of business, Rafaelito, let's agree that I'm an animal."

"Oh, not as bad as that! You know how to assimilate social forms; you are beginning to identify with your new position. However that may be, you are held to be a prodigy, and people praise you to the point of exaggeration. Your speech the other night, and your great success, prove it. Speak to me perfectly frankly, with your hand on your heart, as you would speak to a literary confessor: What is your opinion of your speech and all those ovations at the banquet?"

ELEVEN

Torquemada rose to his feet and, quietly approaching the blind man, placed his hand on his shoulder, and in a grave voice, like one who reveals a very delicate secret, told him, "Rafaelito, dear old fellow, you are going to hear the truth, just exactly as I feel and think it. My speech was nothing but an *uninterrupted series* of empty phrases, a few sentences I picked up from the newspapers, one or another little expression that stuck to me in the Senate, and a few other shreds of good speaking from our friend Donoso. I made a salad out of all that— heavens, it made no sense at all—and let it out just as it occurred to me. What an effect it caused! I'm of the opinion that they were applauding the moneyed man, not the *palaverer*."

"Believe me, Don Francisco, the enthusiasm of all those people was genuine enthusiasm. The reason is quite clear: believe me—"

"Let me speak. I believe that all those who heard me, except for a *nucleus* of two or three, were stupider than I am."

"Certainly; stupider without excepting any nucleus. And I will add: the greater part of the speeches that you hear in the Senate are as empty and badly put together as yours; from all of which it can be deduced that society proceeds logically by praising you, since for one reason or another, perhaps because of that marvelous aptitude for bringing other people's money into your house, you have a value of your own that is very great. There are no two ways about it, my dear sir; and I come to the same conclusion: that I have made a crass mistake, that I have been the appallingly stupid one."

When he reached this point he began to lose that sad serenity with which he customarily spoke, and placed more vehemence in his voice, greater vigor in his gestures.

"Since the day of the wedding," he continued, "and for many days before it, a formidable battle was waged between my sister Cruz and me; I defended the family's dignity, the splendor of our name, tradition, the ideal; she defended positive existence, eating again after suffering so much hunger, the tangible, the material, the transitory. We have been fighting like lions, each on his own terrain, I always against you and your grotesque vulgarity; she always in your favor, raising you, purifying you, making you into a man and a personage and restoring our house; I, always pessimistic; she, a furious optimist. In the end I have been defeated all along the line, because everything that she thought of has come to pass beyond expectation, and out of all that I thought and held to be true, nothing is left but dust. I declare myself vanquished, I surrender, and since defeat pains me, Señor Don Francisco, I cannot be here any longer."

He made a movement as if to rise, but Torquemada turned toward him, holding him in his chair.

"Where do you have to go? Stay quiet there."

"I said that I was going to my room. I'll stay for another little while, for I have not finished expressing my thoughts to you. My sister Cruz has won. You were . . . who you were, and thanks to her you are . . . who you are. And you complain of my sister, and invent nicknames, and make fun of her! Why, you ought to place her on an altar and adore her."

"I'll tell you: I recognize . . . I'd put her in the Holy of Holies if she'd let me capitalize my earnings."

"Oh! To make my sister's work even more astonishing, she even corrects your avarice, which is your principal defect. Cruz has no other *objective*, as you say, than to surround you with prestige and power. And how magnificently she has achieved her aim! That certainly is practical talent and ruling genius! Of course, there is something in my ideas that lies outside any error, and it is the fundamental idea: I hold that there can never be nobility in you, and that your successes and your worth in society are purely visual effects, like the stage sets in a theater. Only the money you know how to earn is real. But, though your triumph is pure farce, it is a fact which confounds me, because I held it to be impossible; I recognize my sister's victory, and declare myself the greatest of fools." (Rising abruptly to his feet) "I must go . . . farewell."

Once more Don Francisco held him back, forcing him to sit down.

"You are right," added Rafael gloomily, folding his hands. "I still must say the most important thing, the confession of my chief error . . . Yes, because my sister Fidela, who I thought would hate you, has taken the very highest path and is a model of wives and mothers, something which makes me very happy. I will say, putting my whole soul into my words, that I did not expect it; I had my logic, which now seems to me like a barrel organ with a broken bellows. I try to play it and wheezings emerge instead of music. Yes, indeed, and now that I've begun to confess I also confess that the baby, who by coming into the world has contradicted my ideas and made a fool of me, is hateful to me . . . yes, indeed. Ever since that hybrid creature was born, my sisters pay no attention to me. Before, I was the baby; now I am a sorry object who is a nuisance everywhere. Knowing this, I wanted to go and live on the third floor, where I am less of a bother. I will keep climbing until I reach the attic, the natural residence of old junk. But this will not happen, for I will die first. No one can take this logic away from me. And by the way, Señor Don Francisco Torquemada, will you do me a favor, the first one I have asked of you in my life, and the last as well?"

"What?" asked the marquis of San Eloy, alarmed by the mournful tone his brother-in-law was assuming.

"To have my body taken to the pantheon of the Torre-Auñóns, in Córdoba. It's an expense that means little to you. Ah, one more thing! I was forgetting that it will be indispensable to restore the pantheon. The west wall has collapsed."

"Will the restoration cost much?" asked Don Francisco with all the seriousness in the world, unsuccessfully trying to hide his reluctance to make that unlooked-for expenditure.

"To leave it in good condition," replied the blind man in the glacial tone suitable to a comptroller, "I calculate about two thousand duros."

"It's a lot," agreed the miserly marquis, heaving a sigh. "Come down a little; no, come down forty percent at least. You can see that to take you to Córdoba would cost a good bit. And as we're marquises, and you belong to the *classic* nobility, there's no way you can be deprived of a first-class funeral."

"You are not generous, you are not noble or a gentleman, trying to haggle about the posthumous honors that I believe I deserve. This request that I've made was made as a test. Now I know that I am not mistaken: you will never be what my sister is trying to make of you. The ear of the moneylender of the Calle de San Blas will always stick out of the ermine mantle. All logic has not been lost, Señor Marquis Consort of San Eloy. All that about the pantheon and taking me to Córdoba is a joke. Throw me onto a garbage heap; it's all the same to me."

"Here, take it easy. I haven't said that I . . . But, my boy, are your wits wandering, or have you taken the notion to make fun of me, *so to speak?* Why, you're not going to die, nor is that the way to . . . In case of accident, mind you! I wouldn't jib at . . ."

"To a garbage heap, I say."

"No, old fellow. What would people think of me? Tonight you seem to be taking turns at being *poetic* and having some fun with me. But what's this, are you going at last?"

"Now I really am going," said the blind man, standing up. "I'm returning to my room, where I have something to do. Ah, I was forgetting! I take back what I said about hating the baby. It only happens at brief instants, like a lightning flash. And then I'm calm again, and love him, believe me that I love him. Poor child!"

"He's sleeping like an angel."

"He'll grow up in the Gravelinas palace, and when he sees in those great rooms the arms of the Great Captain, of Don Luis de Requeséns and Pedro de Navarro and Hugo de Moncada, he'll believe that they're saints in his own church. He will not know that the House of Gra-

velinas has turned into a decent sort of flea market, where the spoils
of the hereditary nobility are piled, buried in garbage. What a sad end
for a lineage! Believe me," he added with gloomy bitterness, "death is
preferable to the sorrow of seeing the most beautiful things that exist
in the world in the hands of the Torquemadas."

Don Francisco was about to answer him; but he refused to listen,
and went out groping his way along the walls.

TWELVE

Pinto led him slowly to his room on the third floor, and on the main
floor the miser was left filled with confusion about the extravagant
ideas he had just heard from that blessed brother-in-law of his. From
confusion he soon passed to concern, and, fearing that he might be ill,
went upstairs and knocked on the closed door with a discreet tap of
the knuckles.

"Rafaelito," he told him, "are you going to go to bed? *I incline to
believe* that you're not very easy in your mind tonight. Do you want
me to send for your sisters?"

"No, there's no reason to do that. I feel very well. A thousand thanks
for your concern. Come in. I'll go to bed, yes indeed; but tonight I
won't undress. I feel like sleeping in my clothes."

"It's very warm."

"Cold is what I feel.'

"And where's Pinto?"

"I sent him to bring me a little sugar-and-water."

The blind man was already in shirtsleeves, and sat down, crossing
one leg over the other.

"Do you need anything else? What are you waiting for, to go to
bed?"

"For Pinto to come and take my boots off."

"I'll take them off for you if you want."

" 'Never was a knight . . . so well served by kings,' " quoted Rafael,
stretching out one foot.

"That's not right," said Don Francisco, trying to show off his erudition, as he removed the first boot. "You say 'ladies,' not 'kings.' "

"But since the one who serves me now is not a lady, but a king, I've
said 'kings.' *Welladay*, as you say, the great men of a new stamp."

"King? Ha, ha! Your sister gives me that high-and-mighty treatment too. The times are strange."

"And she's right. The monarchy is a useless formula; the aristocracy, a shadow. In their place the dynasty of the Torquemadas, *vulgo* the newly-rich moneylenders, reigns and governs. It is the empire of the capitalists, the patriciate of those papier-mâché Medicis. I don't know who it was who said that the impoverished nobility seeks plebeian manure to fertilize it and be able to live a little longer. Who said that? Let's see . . . You, who are so erudite . . ."

"I don't know . . . What I do know is that *the new will kill off the old*."

"As Seneca says, isn't it?"

"Heavens, not Seneca. Don't fluster me," observed the marquis, taking off the second boot.

"Well, I can add that the wave of manure has risen so high that humanity has begun to reek. Yes, indeed, and it's a pleasure to escape from it . . . Yes, these ever-so-modern kings irritate me, indeed they do. When I see that they are masters of everything, that the State rushes into their arms, that the people flatter them, that the aristocracy asks them for money and even the Church falls prostrate before their insolent rudeness, I feel like starting to run and not stopping till I've reached the planet Jupiter."

"And I'm one of those deuced kings! Ha, ha!" said Don Francisco gaily. "Well then, as a sovereign, though my blood and line are plebeian from away back, I order and command you not to say any more foolish things and to go to bed and sleep like a top."

"I obey," replied Raphael, lying down on the bed fully dressed. "I wish to announce, after thanking you—a lordly marquis!—for having deigned to be my *valet de chambre* tonight, that from now on I'll be submission itself and *obedience personified*, and that I won't give the slightest trouble either to you, my illustrious brother-in-law, or to my good sisters."

He said this smiling, his arms encircling his head in a pose resembling that of Goya's reclining Maja.

"Fine. And now . . . to sleep."

"Yes, indeed; sleep is invading me, a healing sleep, which I think will not be short. Believe me, my friend Señor Marquis, that the weariness I feel demands a long sleep."

"Then I'll leave you. So, good night."

"Good-bye," said the blind man with so strange an intonation that Don Francisco, already at the door, felt obliged to turn around and look back at the bed, in which the descendant of the Aguilas was, except for his clothing, a perfect image of Christ in the sepulcher, just as it is carried in procession on Good Friday.

"Do you need anything else, Rafaelito?"

"No . . . I mean, yes . . . now that I remember . . ." (sitting up) "I forgot to give Valentín a kiss."

"How foolish! And you're getting up because of that? I'll give it to him for you. Good-bye. Go to sleep."

The miser left the room, and instead of going downstairs went into the office where the bookkeeper was working. As he heard Pinto's footsteps a little later, he called to him. The little footman told him that Don Rafael was still awake, and that after drinking part of the sugar-and-water had sent him downstairs for a cup of tea.

"Well, take it to him right away," his master ordered, "and don't budge from the room until you see that he's really asleep."

A period of time elapsed which the miser could not measure. He and Argüelles Mora were checking a long account when they heard a dull, heavy sound, which could just as well have been nearby as some distance away. Seconds later, shrieks from the concierge's wife in the patio, cries and servants' running feet all over the house. Half a minute more and they saw Pinto come in, breathless, his features convulsed.

"Señor, señor . . ."

"What, by a thousand bibles?"

"Out the window . . . patio . . . young master . . . Boom!"

They all rushed downstairs. Dashed to the ground, dead.

· 4 ·

TORQUEMADA
AND SAINT PETER

· PART I ·

ONE

The first glimmerings of a slow, bleary dawn, typical of a dawn in January, slipping through skylights and transoms inside the former Palace of Gravelinas, gradually awoke all things from the sleep of darkness, extracting them, one might say, from black nothingness to pictorial life. In the armory, the morning light endowed the plumes of casques and helmets with the first touch of color: then it modeled with firm strokes breastplates and backplates, brassards and corselets, until it surrounded all of the gallant figures, in whom it was not difficult to see a semblance of living beings, for the outer skin of burnished iron is the body of a monstrous and terrible person, and inside that empty space, who knows if a soul may be hiding! Anything is possible. The mounted figures, shield on arm, in a posture for jousting rather than warfare, could be taken for enormous toys that History played with as a child. It could be observed in some of the standing warriors, when daylight had fully revealed their forms, that the mannequins, dressed in their heavy steel garments, were supremely bored, tired of the immobility that wasted their cardboard muscles and of the feather duster that had cleaned their faces Saturday after Saturday for thousands of weeks. Their rotting hands, some with a finger missing and the others stiff, could not have held the lance or the two-handed sword had not these been tied on with stout cord. Up under the roof of that beautiful museum, the white banners with St. Andrew's crosses on them hung gloomily, dustily, raveled, remembering the happy times when they flapped in the breeze on the brave galleys of the Tyrrhenian and Adriatic seas.

The morning light took possession of the splendid archive in the wink of an eye or the opening of windows. In the broad space with its lofty roof, cold as a tomb and solitary as a temple of wisdom, it was only rarely that a living person entered, aside from the manservant in charge of cleaning or some erudite scrutinizer of bibliographical rarities. Shelves with metal grilles over them covered the wall all the way up to the molding, and through the little apertures of the wire netting, the backs of parchment volumes, the edges of bundles of yellowing papers tightly tied together, and other kinds of manuscripts could be dimly seen. As the awakening light poured in, the latest-to-bed mouse of those solitudes cautiously retired to his home: the little scamp was happy and surfeited, as was his whole family, for parents, children, nieces, nephews, and grandchildren had supped in love and good company on one of the Great Captain's most interesting letters to King Ferdinand the Catholic, and on part of a very curious *Inventory of Jewels and Paintings* that had belonged to the Viceroy of Naples, Don Pedro Téllez Girón, the Great Duke of Osuna. These and other shocking feasts occurred because the cat who occupied the library had died of a sudden colic, and the owners had not bothered to fill the position by appointing a new cat or governor of those dusky realms.

The broad windows of the archive and armory looked out on a patio separating them from the main part of the palace, which, because many and diverse persons slept there, was invaded somewhat later by the light of day. But at last the large and sumptuous mansion was brought wholly to life, and almost from one moment to the next, repose changed into movement and nocturnal silence into innumerable stirrings that emerged here and there. The patio of the armory was connected by a long corridor, rather resembling a tunnel, with the coach houses and stables, which the last duke of Gravelinas, a conscientious sportsman, had had built new, with all the refinements and little touches of English taste in these important matters. It was there that the first noises and stirrings of daily routine arose, steps of men and animals, the soft stroke of a hoof and the harsh clatter of clogs on the wet paving stones, voices, oaths, singing.

In the first patio a multitude of servants appeared through several different doors; women who lighted charcoal braziers, drip-nosed children who, with a scarf around their necks and a piece of bread in their mouths, emerged to give the first hop and skip of the day on the pavement or the grass. A man with a face like a bishop's, in a silk skullcap, cloth slippers, and a striped vest, an old coat tossed over his shoulders, called to the stragglers, hurried up the lazy ones, administered pushes to the children, and offered to all the example of his activity and diligence. Minutes after his appearance he could be seen at a ground-floor window shaving himself with as much care as haste. His imposing face shone like the sun when he reemerged, having washed with care, to go on giving orders in an authoritarian tone and a French accent. A woman whose tongue was very free and whose accent was pure Andalusian was arguing with him, making fun of his exhortations to haste; but at last she had no choice but to submit, and then and there pulled a very handsome youth bodily out of bed and, dragging him off by one ear, made him plunge his mug into cold water, then washed and dried him thoroughly. After combing his hair with maternal zeal, she put on his hard, shiny shirtfront and a white cravat that kept his head as rigid as the knob on a cane.

Another youth appeared with a pipe in his mouth, his left hand inside a footman's boot as if it were a glove, and a brush in his right hand. Paying no heed to the Frenchman, or the Andalusian woman, or the others, he began to shout irritably, yelling in the middle of the corridor, "Dammit! Damn and double-damn, this is a thieves' kitchen! I'd like to see the pig who's pinched my boot polish! They steal a fellow's polish, and his blood, and the damned marrow right out of his bones!"

No one paid him the slightest attention. And in the middle of the patio another servant, in clogs and apron, yelled furiously, "Who took one of the sponges out of the stable? My God, this is what goes on every day, and there's no authority here, or *ministration*, or law and order!"

"Take your sponge, you villain," cried a woman's voice from one of the upper windows, "and use it to wash the soot off you."

She threw down the sponge, and it hit him in the face with such force that if it had been a stone it would have broken his nose. Laughter and chaffering, and that confounded Frenchman hurrying everyone along with paternal suggestions. He had already donned, atop the heavy undershirt, his shirt with its starched and shining dickey, and was preparing to finish dressing, not without aiming admonitions at scullery maids and flunkies, exhorting them all to breakfast quickly and well.

The hallways in that part of the house converged, on the opposite side of the patio, in a large hall or lobby which on one side gave access to the kitchen and on the other to the room used for ironing and mending clothes. At the far end a broad door, covered with heavy baize, gave access to the extensive halls and chambers of the ducal dwelling. In that large space, which the servants simply called "the big room," one woman was lighting heating stoves and footwarmers, another braziers, and a manservant, with an apron that came down to his feet, was placing several pairs of boots in a straight line, which he then proceeded to clean in strict order.

"Hurry, hurry, the master's boots," said another manservant, who hurried in from the door at the back. "These, nitwit, the heavy ones. He's already up, and there he is hopping around the room and cursing like anything."

"Well, let him wait," answered the man who was doing the cleaning. "I'll make 'em shine like gold. He can't do the same with the itch he has in his soul."

"Shut up," said a third, adding a friendly kick to his words.

"What're you eating?" asked the shoe-shiner, seeing that the other was chewing something.

"Bread, and a few little scraps of truffled tongue."

From the nearby kitchen came a hearty smell of coffee. There the servants went, one after another, and the cleaner of boots, with his left hand stuck inside one of them, stretched out his right to take a few slices of exquisite cold meat from a plate presented to him by a scullion. The Frenchman guzzled heartily and all the others imitated him, chewing away for all they were worth, some half dressed, others in shirt sleeves and with their tousled hair uncombed.

"Hurry, hurry, *mes amis*, for at nine o'clock we all have to go to mass. You heard what was said last night. All the servants, and dressed in uniform."

The doorkeeper had already squeezed into his livery, which covered him to his feet, and rubbed his hands together as he asked for good hot coffee. The *valet de chambre* advised not leaving the Señor Marquis's chocolate until the last minute.

"*Uncle Tor*," said a hoarse voice, which must have belonged to one of the stable hands, "only likes the cheap, three-real kind, made with brick dust and acorns."

"Silence!"

"He's a man, you might say, of low extraction, and if he were to please himself he'd eat like a poor man. He eats like the rich so's they won't gossip about him."

"Shut up, you! Who wants coffee?"

"I and us . . . Listen here, 'Bizconde,' get out the bottle of brandy."

"The lady has said we mustn't take *morning nips.*"

"Get it, I said."

A scullion in a white chef's hat, with a squint to boot, handed out little glasses of brandy, hastening to pour it, as did the others to drink it, so that they would not be caught by the chef, who usually turned up in the kitchen at that hour and was a bad-tempered man, a sworn enemy, like the lady, of *morning nips.* The Frenchman urged sobriety "so your breath won't smell"; but he himself drank three glasses, saying as he finished the last, "My breath doesn't smell; I get rid of it with a mint drop."

Just then the sudden and vibrant trilling of a bell made them all jump as if seized by panic.

"The lady! The lady!"

Some ran off to finish dressing, others to continue the tasks in which they had been engaged. One girl, who must have been chief chambermaid, rushed up to the door leading to the rest of the palace and gave the cry of alarm from there:

"Get busy, good-for-nothings, and hurry and dress! If someone doesn't show up he'll have to explain things to the lady."

A second trill of the loud bell swept her away like the wind, through innumerable galleries, salons, and corridors.

TWO

"It's the mass that's said on the eleventh of each month, because it seems that it was on the eleventh that a brother of the ladies, who suffered with his eyesight, jumped off the balcony," said the Frenchman to his companion and crony, the chef, who had just come in, along with two helpers carrying heavily loaded baskets with the day's shopping in them.

Indifferent to everything that was not his job in the house, he knocked the dottle from his pipe and put it in his pocket, preparing to change his gentleman's clothes for the white uniform of the captain-general of the kitchens. He dressed in the other Frenchman's room, and there he kept his pipes, his supplies of tobacco, and a good reserve of cold meats and liquors for his personal use.

While the butler was brushing his frock coat, the chef was going over the accounts of the day's shopping in his notebook, touching up numbers.

"There," he murmured. "The eleventh. That's why we have ten places for lunch. So, there's a mass? That's not for me. I'm a Huguenot. Now I remember: that clergyman was just ahead of me. I was hurrying and passed him on the corner. He must have gone in through the main door."

"Eh, Ruperto!" cried the other, going out into the hall. "Father Gamborena is already here, he's going to do the mass, and you haven't lighted the heating stove in the sacristy."

"Yessir, it's lighted. Saint Peter, as the master the marquis calls him in fun, hasn't arrived yet."

"Run. Find out about it. See if all the altar service is ready . . . cloths . . . wine."

"That's Joselito's job. What have I got to do with the priest's clothes or the cruets?"

"You'll have to do the work of two," the Frenchman said officiously, donning his frock coat and straightening his collar. "If a man doesn't look after everything personally, things get into such a mess!"

He hurried off toward the rooms of the palace proper, which on that side began with a large square gallery overlooking a patio. On the walls were old woodcuts in mahogany frames and bird's-eye-view maps of battles; the floor was covered with red-and-yellow-striped hemp matting, like a faint whiff of the colors of Aragón; the windows were shaded by very elegant stained-glass inserts with the coats of arms of the families of Gravelinas, Trastamara, and the Grimaldis of Sicily. At the end of this gallery a very graceful staircase led to the inhabited rooms, properly speaking, of the sumptuous dwelling. On the lower floor there were only reception rooms, the rotunda, the state dining room, the conservatory, and the chapel, restored in exquisite taste by the Aguila sisters. The good Frenchman was heading in that direction when he saw, coming through the great transverse hall that starts at the vestibule and main door of the palace, with hat in hand, a priest of medium height, bald and ruddy-faced. The servant made him a deep bow; the priest answered with a nod and went into the sacristy, at whose door a footman in a livery heavy with braid was awaiting him. The Frenchman, uneasy until he learned that nothing was lacking in the chapel, exchanged a few words with this footman; then he aimed a few pleasantries at a chambermaid who was climbing the stairs burdened with clothing; then he went to cast an eye over the small dining room and, while there, heard a coach draw up to the door. The stamping of horses' hooves on the paving could be heard, and then the noise of the carriage door closing.

"It's La Orozco," said the Frenchman to his second-in-command, who already had the table prepared for the guests who might wish to have breakfast there after mass. "She's a lady with quite a history, isn't she? She and the marquise are as thick as thieves."

Indeed, from the door of the small dining room he saw a slender lady come in, dressed in deepest mourning, who with the freedom of intimate friendship went upstairs without being announced. Then came two more ladies and a gentleman, who entered a reception room on the ground floor. From moment to moment the bustle of the numerous servants increased, and it was pleasant to see the picturesque coats, the white shirtfronts, and the elegant frock coats of the whole lot of them. At nine o'clock Cruz del Aguila descended the stairs, arm in arm with her friend Augusta, and on the staircase they lamented the fact that Fidela, abed with a stubborn attack of influenza, was unable to attend mass. They went into the salon, and from the salon to the chapel along with the other ladies who were occupying seats of honor in the presbytery. The rest of the space was filled by the servants, men, women, and children. The lady went down the list, with the aid of her lorgnette, to see if anyone was missing. The only ones not present were the chef and the head of the family, the very excellent Señor Marquis of San Eloy.

Who, at the moment the mass began, emerged from his bedroom so out of sorts, and with his temper in such disarray, that he was fearful to see. His feet shod in heavy, shining boots, his black silk skullcap pulled down to his ears, clad in a heavy dark dressing gown, he erupted into the corridor by hops and jumps, coughing noisily and spitting furious remarks under his breath. He descended to the stable patio by an inner staircase and, not finding any of the *employees of that section* there, unloaded the whole stream of invective on a poor old man who had a humble temporary job, and who was at the moment sweeping up rubbish and loading it in a wheelbarrow.

"But what's all this, dammit! One of these fine days I'm going to put every one of you out in the street, sure as my name's Francisco! Drones, good-for-nothings, wasters of other folks' money, rascals, leeches on the State! And you didn't even send word to the veterinary to have him come and see the swollen leg on Boby—Boby, the sorrel saddle horse—and the glanders on Marly, the Norman bay, the draught horse. If they go and die on me, dammit all! I'll take the cost out of your hides. So there's a mass? The things that woman invents to make all the servants go woolgathering and take the staff away from their jobs! Dammit, double dammit!''

Then he went into the big room, which was a sort of place of rendezvous for all the servants, and, seeing no one there, continued into the interior of the ducal residence, grumbling and coughing and hawking; he took two or three turns around the gallery of pictures and battle maps; at last, in the middle of an oath that got lodged between his teeth, with part of the epithet outside and half inside, stuck to his sputtering tongue, he found himself near the chapel door and heard a sonorous tinkling twice and thrice.

"There, now they're elevating the Host," he grumbled. "I won't go in. And who says I have to, by the confounded Bible?''

He returned to his room, where he finished dressing, donning a frock coat, overcoat, and top hat; and, grasping his heavy woolen gloves in one hand and in the other his stick with the staghorn handle, which he had retained from his days of struggle, he again descended the stairs just as the divine office was ending and the servants were hastily filing out, each to his own department. The ladies, two solemn gentlemen, Taramundi, Donoso, and young San Salomó, who had served as acolyte for the mass, went upstairs to see Fidela. Don Francisco made his escape to save himself the bother of greetings, for that morning he was in no mood for fine manners. When he saw that the coast was clear he hurriedly entered the sacristy, where no one was left but the officiant, already divested of chasuble and alb and addressing himself to a bowl of excellent coffee flanked by toast and butter, which a pretty little page had placed, on a silver tray, on top of the chest of drawers where the vestments were stored.

"I got to mass late," Don Francisco told him brusquely, with nothing more in the way of greeting or courteous preliminaries, "because they didn't let me know in time. You can see for yourself what a household this is! Anyway, I decided not to come in so as not to interrupt. And, believe me, I'm not well, no indeed; I'm not well. I ought to have stayed in bed."

"And who forces you to rise so early?" said the priest without looking at him, taking his first sip of coffee. "Poor fellow, he gets up to seek a miserable daily wage, and to bring a couple of rolls and half a pound of meat home to the Palace of Gravelinas!"

"That's not it, dam . . . that's not it. I get up because I can't sleep. You can believe me, I haven't shut an eye all night, Señor Saint Peter."

"Really? Why?" asked the priest, with half a piece of toast in his mouth and the other half in his hand. "And, incidentally, why do you call me Saint Peter?"

"Didn't I tell you? I will, one of these days. It's a story from my good times. I call the good times those times when I had less folderol than now, when I used to sweat gall and vinegar to earn money; the times when I lost my only son, well, not the only one; I mean . . . well . . . when I wasn't acquainted with all this ridiculous pomp of nowadays, and when I hadn't had to grieve over so many vicissitudes. That was a terrible vicissitude when my boy died, but even so I had a quieter life, and was more in my element. I had sorrows there too, but I also had times when I was alone with myself, goodness, when I rested in an oasis . . . an oasis . . . oasis." Entranced with the word, he repeated it three times.

"And now tell me, why did you not sleep last night? Was it perhaps . . .?"

"Yes, yes it was; I couldn't sleep because of what you told me when I went off to my room last night, as the sum and accumulation of that long private talk you and I had. That's why!"

THREE

"Good, good, very good!" exclaimed the priest, bursting into laughter and dipping the toast in his coffee repeatedly so as to eat it first and then drink with a good appetite.

What a man he was! His body was on the small side, but hard and strong, dressed in a very clean soutane; a weatherbeaten face, all crisscrossed with very fine parallel wrinkles, in rows that started from his eyes and went toward his forehead and from his mouth to his chin and cheeks; his complexion bronzed and ruddy like a seaman's, one of those who have faced the tempest and have reached old age amid the inclemencies of sky and water, dividing their existence between faith, which emanates from above, and fishing, which is taken from below. That man's most characteristic feature was his glossy baldness, which began where the wrinkles on his forehead began to be more widely spaced and ended near the nape of his neck, a spacious, shining convexity like a pilgrim's water-gourd, burnished by time and friction. A little fringe of very curly gray hair encircled it in a horseshoe shape, ending above his ears.

Now that I recall it, something else about him was as characteristic as his baldness. What was it? His black eyes, of a positively angelic sweetness, the eyes of a young Andalusian girl or a handsome little boy, and a gaze that had sparks of celestial regions in it, incomprehensible regions guessed at rather than seen. To complete this very attractive face, something must be added. What? A slight touch of Mongolian race or resemblance in the features: the lower lids full and flat to his face, the brows a little twisted, the mouth, chin, and cheeks flat too, as if they wanted to appear on the same plane, an indefinable impression of Japanese malice in his smile or the slyness of a Chinese face, taken from teacups. Yet the good Gamborena was a Spaniard, from Alava near the Navarrese border; but he had spent a large part of his life in the Far East, fighting for Christ against Buddha, and Buddha, angered by religious persecution, had stared at him for years and years, until some of the typical traits of Buddha's face became imprinted on his own. Can it be true that people come to resemble what they constantly see? It was merely a vague family resemblance, almost nothing, which as often seemed to become accentuated as to vanish, according to the intention with which he looked at one or the sleekness of his smile. Apart from this, his whole head appeared to have been carved and painted, like a venerable image which religious devotion keeps clean and shining.

"Ah!" exclaimed the saintly Gamborena, raising his eyebrows, which caused the two series of fine curved wrinkles to stretch halfway up his cranium. "Some day my lord marquis of San Eloy had to hear the essential truth, the truth that doesn't get twisted or corrupted by fashionable manners."

Don Francisco, lifting his eyes to the ceiling and heaving a huge sigh, exclaimed in his turn, "Ah!"

The two gazed at each other for a little while, and the priest finished his breakfast.

"All night," said the skinflint at last, "I have spent my time tossing and turning in bed as if the sheets were a bramble patch, and thinking about it, about the same thing, about what you . . . manifested to me. And I couldn't wait for daylight in order to get up and hurry to find you and ask you to explain it to me, to explain it to me better."

"Very well, right this minute, my dear Señor Don Francisco."

"No, no, not now," replied the marquis mistrustfully, looking toward the door. "It's something that you and I ought to talk about all by ourselves, mind you! Right now . . ."

"Yes, yes, we might perhaps be interrupted . . ."

"And besides, I have to go out . . ."

"To run after business affairs. Poor day laborer of your millions! Go on, go on, and leave your health out there in the street, that's all you needed."

"You can believe me when I say," replied Torquemada disconsolately, "that I don't have good health, or even half-good health. I used to be a regular oak, with a solid, hard grain. Now I feel as if I'm turning into a reed, that the wind shakes me and dampness has started to rot me from below. What is this? My age? It's not so very great, you might say. Is it the aggravation, the sorrow it causes me not to be the real boss in my house, and to see myself in this golden cage with a female lion tamer who waves the red-hot iron bar at me at every turn? Is it the worry of seeing that my son's well on the way to being an idiot? How can anyone know! I don't. Probably it's not just one cause, but the sum of all the other causes that has brought on this situation. I have to admit that I'm at fault, because of my weakness; but it does me no good to recognize it *a posteriori*, because it's no use crying over spilt milk, and because I didn't know how to avoid it *a priori*. A fellow can't do anything but give in and succumb *velis nolis*, cursing his fate and consigning himself to the devils."

"Softly, softly, señor marquis," said the ecclesiastic in a tone of paternal severity tempered with gaiety, "that business of consigning yourself to the devils is something I will not allow or consent to. What a gift to the devils! And what am I here for, if not to snatch their prey from that infernal gentry, if perchance they succeed in catching you in their claws? Take a bit of care! Restrain yourself, and for the moment, since you're in a hurry and my obligations are calling me, I'll say no more. Leave it for another night when you and I are alone."

Torquemada dug both fists into his eyes as if to stimulate his vision, weakened by insomnia. Then he gazed like a purblind man, seeing dots and circles of different colors, and at last, when the clarity of his eyesight had returned and his brain was clear, he put out his hand to the priest, saying in a hearty tone and manner, "Well then, good-bye. Keep well."

He left the room, and calling for his carriage our man lost no time in emerging on the street, fleeing from the slavery of his gilded home. And it was not an illusion of his, no indeed. Really, once he crossed the wrought-iron gate of the Gravelinas palace and felt on his face the free atmosphere of the public street, he breathed more easily, his head cleared. He felt that his mercantile talents were sharper and clearer, and the oppression in the pit of his stomach, that constant symptom of bad health, was less painful. That is why he had said with all his heart, improperly using the recently acquired word, "The street is my oasis."

No sooner had the skinflint left the sacristy than Cruz entered. You would have thought that she was spying out the other's departure in order to slip in herself.

"There he goes, there he goes; he's off sailing those streets, that poor fisher of coins!" she said gaily, as if continuing a dialogue begun the previous day. "What a man! How he hankers to increase his riches!"

"You must let him do so," said the priest sadly. "If you take away the pole he uses to fish for wealth, he'll die raving, and then who will take responsibility for his soul? Let him fish, let him fish, until God is ready to bait the hook with something that will move him to abhor his trade."

"Really, unless you, who are so skillful at instructing savages, toss a rope around him and bring him in tied hand and foot, who can tame him? And first of all, dear father, was the coffee to your taste?"

"Delicious, my dear."

"Naturally, you'll have lunch with us."

"My dear, I can't. Excuse me for today."

And he reached for his hat, which was not a typical priest's hat because it had a flat brim.

"Well, if you're not lunching, I won't let you go so soon. That would be a fine thing! Come, sit down again for a little while. I'm the boss here."

"I obey. Have you something to tell me?"

"Yes, indeed. The same thing as always: that I'm counting on you to soften that wild man and make this life of constant unpleasantness more tolerable."

"Oh, dear daughter!" exclaimed Gamborena, preceding his speech by turning his incomparable gaze upon her, as the most persuasive argument. "I have spent my life preaching the gospel to savages, spreading Christianity among people who were raised in idolatry and barbarism. I have sometimes lived among races whose chief characteristics were cunning, lies, and treason; at other times, amid blood-thirsty and ferocious tribes. Very well: there, with the patience and courage imparted only by faith, I have been able to succeed. Here, in the midst of civilization, I mistrust my abilities. What a strange thing that is! And it is because here I've encountered something even worse, much worse than barbarism and idolatry, which are the result of ig-norance: I find hearts that are profoundly damaged, intelligences turned away from the truth through innumerable errors that are set into the depths of your souls, and that you cannot get rid of. Your errors give you, in a way, the character and appearance of savages. But savagery for savagery, I prefer that of the other hemisphere. I find it easier to create men than to correct those who, being too fully formed, make it impossible to know what they are."

The good priest said all this seated beside the sacristy chest, with his elbow resting on the edge of it and his head in the fist of his right hand, expressing with a certain air of refined indolence the little taste he had for those battles with the savages of civilization. The lady listened to him entranced, fixing her eyes on the preacher's eyes, and, if it can be put that way, drinking in his glances or assimilating the thought in them before it was formulated by his mouth.

"Since you say so, it must be true," said the lady, feeling a tightness in her breast. "I understand that the domestication of this good man is a hard piece of work. I cannot undertake it; neither can my sister; she doesn't even think about it, nor does it matter to her that her husband is a ruffian who constantly places us in a ridiculous light. You, who have come here so opportunely, as if you'd fallen from heaven, are the only one who can . . ."

"I certainly want to! Difficult tasks are just the ones that tempt me, and seduce me, and carry me away. Easy things? Nothing doing! I have a military, a warrior temperament! Yes, my dear, what did you think? Listen to me."

His imagination aroused and his pride inflamed, he stood up in order to express more easily the things he had to say.

"My character, my temperament, my whole being are made to order for fighting, for hard work, for difficulties that seem insuperable. My companions in the Order say—you're going to laugh—that, when His Divine Majesty decided to have me come into this world, at the moment I entered life (for our highest aptitude is imprinted on our souls when we are born), He was still wondering whether to send me into the military or into the Church. This vacillation on the part of the Supreme Author of all things was, they say, imprinted on my being, and the brief moment when I was held between those sovereign fingers was sufficient for the purpose. But at last Our Father decided for the Church. For a divine trice the possibility existed that I would be a great warrior, a destroyer of cities, a conqueror of peoples and nations. But I turned out to be a missionary, which in some ways is a life work similar to warfare, and here I am, having won for my God, with the flag of the Faith, portions of land and humanity as large as all of Spain.

FOUR

"Though the difficulty of the project in which my good Croisette wishes to engage me frightens me a little," he continued, after leaving time, by means of a pause, for the lady to express effusive admiration, "I am not intimidated. I clutch my glorious banner and head straight for your savage."

"And you will conquer him . . . I am sure of it."

"I will tame him, at least; I promise you that. Last night I fired a few arrows at him, and the good man let me know today that they reached a sensitive spot."

"Oh, he has a high opinion of you. He looks upon you as a superior being, an angel or an apostle, and all the fierceness and arrogance he uses with me and my sister change to mildness in your presence."

"Whether out of fear or respect, the fact is that he is impressed by the truths that he hears from me. And I tell him no more than the truth, the truth plain and unadorned, with all the uncompromising harshness that my evangelical mission demands. I do not compromise; I despise elastic concessions insofar as Catholic morality is concerned. I attack evil energetically, deploying against it all the rigors of doctrine. Señor Torquemada will hear very good things from me, and he will tremble and look inside himself, also taking a few quick glances toward the beyond, which is all mystery for him, toward eternity, where all of us, great and small, must go in the end. Leave him, leave him to me."

He took several turns around the room, and during one of them, paying no heed to his noble interlocutor's admiring exclamations, he stopped in front of her and commanded silence with a deliberate movement of both extended hands, a movement which could equally have been that of a preacher or an orchestra conductor; and all this to tell her, "Wait a bit, wait a bit . . . and don't get excited so soon, my dear, because a few pebbles will strike you, you too; for not all the blame is his, indeed it is not; you and your sister are also to blame, you more than your sister."

"I do not consider myself free from blame," said Cruz humbly, "either in this case or in other cases in life."

"Your despotism, for despotism it is, though extremely enlightened; your zeal to rule autocratically, going against his tastes, his habits, and even his evil machinations, imposing on him a grand style that is repugnant to him, and expenditures that make his blood run cold— all this has placed our savage on a level of ferocity so great that we will have quite a job taming him."

"It's true that I'm just a little despotic. But that brute knows full well that without my rule he would not have reached the heights where he is now, and where, believe me, he is very pleased to be when his avarice is not involved. Who made him a senator, who made him a marquis and a man of prominence, respected by great and small? But perhaps you will tell me that these are vanities, and that I have fomented them at no profit for our souls. If you tell me this, I will have nothing to say. I recognize my error and abdicate, yes indeed, abdicate the rule of these realms, and will retire . . . to private life."

"Gently. Judgment and opportunity are needed for everything, and chiefly for abdications. Continue your rule until you see . . . Any disturbance in the established order would be very harmful. I will define my goals, paying heed only to the moral order of things. I do not concern myself with the rest, and whatever has to do with this world's goods, either remotely or close at hand, simply does not exist for me. For the moment my only command is that you be gentle and loving toward your brother, for the Church has made him your brother. You must not be . . ."

Cruz, unable to curb her imperious and argumentative nature, interrupted the clergyman in this wise:

"But it is he, he who makes a mock of the brotherly relationship! For four months now we haven't spoken to each other, and if I say something to him, he lets out a bellow and turns his back. Today he is more vulgar when he speaks than when he doesn't. And you must know that, outside the house, he never mentions me except to say horrible things about me."

"Horrible . . . nasty words," said Gamborena, a trifle weary of the subject and seizing his hat with a decisiveness that indicated an intention to leave. "There is one kind of bad language that is no more than a habit of using words mindlessly. It is a bad but not a very bad thing; it is an effervescence of vulgar verbal play whose intention is sometimes merely a joking one. In many cases this accursed vice is not rooted in the heart. I will study our savage *under that aspect*, as he says, and will show him the use of the muzzle, a most useful object to which not everyone becomes accustomed; but, once one has overcome the bother of it—ah!—eventually it brings great benefits, not only to the tongue but to the soul. Good-bye, my dear. No, I can't stay any longer. I have things to do. No, no, I won't come to lunch, and that's that. If I can, I'll come this afternoon to chat for a while. If not, until tomorrow. Good-bye."

All the noble lady's wheedling to keep him there was useless. She stayed in the sacristy for a moment, as if the thoughts that the venerable Gamborena had expressed in their recent conversation were holding her there, exercising on her a melancholy pressure. Ever since Rafael's tragic death, sorrow had been a persistent tenant in the Aguila family; its installation in the Palace of Gravelinas, so full of worldly and artistic beauties, had been like entering a somber realm of tedium and discord. Fortunately, merciful God had granted the ruler of that ill-assorted family the consolation of a peerless friend, who combined a pleasant social manner with apostolic mastery in everything concerning spiritual matters: an angel, a pure soul, an inflexible con-science, and a luminous intelligence for which neither human life nor the social organism held any secrets. The eldest Aguila received him like an envoy from heaven when she saw him enter her palace two months before the scene we have described, coming from I don't know what Polynesian islands, or Fiji, or the fifth circle of Hell . . . or let us say the fifth circle of Paradise. She clung to him as a drowning man clings to a plank, trying to have him come and live in the house, but, when this proved to be impossible, she attracted him with all sorts of delicate lures to have him there at lunchtime and at dinnertime, to ask his advice about everything and bask in his beautiful preaching, and lastly to be entranced by the tale of his marvelous feats of evan-gelization.

The first piece of information about Father Luis de Gamborena that we find when we begin to investigate his history goes back to 1853, a time when he was no more than twenty-five years of age and was serving as familiar to the bishop of Córdoba. Nothing is known of his youth, and it is certain only that he was from Alava, of a rich and noble family. The Aguila parents took him as their chaplain and brought him to Madrid, where he lived with them for two years. But God called him to greater endeavors than the obscure chaplaincy of an aristocratic house, and, feeling in his soul a burning desire for he-roic works and the holy ambition to propagate the Christian faith, trading luxury for privations, a quiet life for danger, health and even life itself for glorious immortality, he decided, after long thought, to leave for Paris and enlist in one of the missionary legions with which our cautious civilization attempts to tame the barbarous African and Asiatic hordes before unsheathing the sword against them.

The young enthusiast lost no time in seeing his wishes fulfilled, and, having joined a congregation whose name is not important to my tale, was sent off to preach in Zanzibar, and from there to the vicariate of Tanganyika, where he began his campaign with an excursion to the upper Congo, becoming notable for his physical resistance and his un-wearying zeal as a soldier of Christ. He spent fifteen years in tropical Africa, working with mystical courage, if the term applies; he had become a lion of God, holding cheap the extremes of climate and human ferocity; intrepid, tireless, first in battle, great catechist, great geographer, explorer of vast territories, of labyrinthine jungles, of pestilent lakes, of harsh rocky solitudes, taming everything in his path to implant the Cross by shoves, by blows, by any means he could, in nature and in the souls of those barbarous regions.

FIVE

Then he was sent to Europe as member of a commission, half religious and half mercantile, whose purpose was to arrange a very important colonial agreement with the king of the Belgians, and the good father discharged his diplomatic task so well that here, there, and everywhere he was praised for his many talents. "Commerce," they said of him, "is as much indebted to him as is faith." The congregation decided to use such exceptional aptitudes once again, and sent him off to its missions in Polynesia. New Zealand, land of the Maoris, New Guinea, the Fiji Islands, the Torres Strait archipelago were the theater of his heroic labor for twenty years, and if these seem many in the life of a worker, they were few indeed for the foundation, an almost miraculous achievement, of hundreds of Christian communities and proselytizing and charitable establishments in the innumerable islands, atolls, and reefs that are sprinkled over that immense ocean, as if a childish hand had amused itself by scattering to left and right the rubble of a broken continent.

After his sixtieth birthday, Gamborena was recalled to Europe. They wanted him to rest; they feared risking such a useful life by exposing it to the rigors of that constant struggle with men, beasts, and storms, and sent him to Spain with the peaceful and sedentary mission of organizing the collection of missionary funds on a practical basis. He went to live in the Irish hospice, the parent foundation of the congregation to which he belonged, and within a few weeks of his residence in the capital and court of Spain he reencountered the Aguila ladies, thus renewing his old and affectionate friendship with that noble family. He had known Cruz as a little girl; she was six years old at the time he was chaplain in the household. Fidela, much younger than her sister, had not yet been born at that time; but he accepted both of them as old friends and even spiritual daughters, permitting himself to address them familiarly from the very first interview he had with them. They soon let him know of the terrible vicissitudes the family had undergone during his absence in remote places: its ruin, the death of their parents, the days of wretched poverty, the marriage with Torquemada, the return to prosperity, the freeing of part of the Aguila properties, Rafaelito's death, increasing wealth, the acquisition of the Palace of Gravelinas, etc., after all of which the good man was as well informed as if he had never left Madrid during that whole period of incredible misfortunes and happy changes.

Needless to say, the two sisters looked upon him as an oracle, and they eagerly savored the nourishing honey of his advice and doctrine. Cruz, especially, deprived of all real love by the very particular direction that fate had taken in the course of her life, felt for the good missionary a profound adoration, all purity, all idealism, like the expansion of an imprisoned and wounded soul which glimpses joy and freedom in ultraterrestrial things. She would have liked to have him in her home all day, caring for him as for a child, showering on him all the love that poor Rafael had left unrequited. When, urged on by the two ladies, Gamborena would start to relate the marvelous episodes of his missions in Africa and Oceania, a Christian epic worthy to be sung by an Ercilla if not by a Homer, both ladies were entranced. Fidela listened like a child hearing tales of magic; Cruz in ecstasy, her soul bathed in mystical beatitude and in astonishment before the greatness of Christianity.

And he did his best, out of his great store of talent, to fascinate them and make them feel deeply all the interest of his tale, for though he knew how to summarize admirably, he also described events with wonderful details which amazed and captivated his hearers. They could almost have believed that they were experiencing what the missionary was telling them, such was the descriptive power of his words. They suffered with him in the emotional passages, they rejoiced with him in his triumphs over nature and savagery. Shipwrecks, in which his life was in imminent danger, when he was saved miraculously from the storm-tossed waters; sometimes in the rushing currents of rivers as broad as oceans, at other times on inhospitable coasts, sailing in old steamships that smashed against the reefs or caught fire in the midst of ocean solitudes; treks through unexplored equatorial lands, under a scorching sun, through rough places and inaccessible paths, fearing encounters with wild beasts or poisonous reptiles; installation among the members of a tribe, and the description of their barbarous customs, of their terrifying faces, of their primitive clothing; the efforts at evan-gelization, in which he used diplomacy, sweet persuasion, delicate tact, or defensive sternness, according to circumstances, aiding incipient trade or making use of it himself; the difficulties of learning the different dialects of those regions, some sounding like the cries of four-footed animals, others like the chattering of parrots; the dangers that arose at every step, the horror of wars between different tribes and the massacres and ferocious reprisals, with the awful sequel of enslavement; the thousand incidents of slow victory, the joy of finding a soul well disposed to Christianity amid the savagery of those races, the docility of some after their conversion, the backslidings of others and their false acceptance; everything, in short, coming from that mouth and that picturesque form of expression made the most enjoyable tale that can be imagined.

And how well the narrator knew how to combine the grave and the gay to vary his tale, which sometimes went on for hours and hours! The ladies could scarcely restrain their laughter when they heard him tell of his difficulties after he fell into the hands of a horde of cannibals, and the ingenious tricks he and other priests employed to foil the ferocious gluttony of those brutes, who wanted to string them up on a spit and serve them as human roast beef, no less, in their horrible festivities.

And, to top it all off and make sure that the two ladies' burning curiosity was satisfied in every particular, the missionary would yield the floor to the famous geographer, the eminent naturalist, who studied and experienced on the spot, in palpable reality, all the planet's beauties and all the marvels God had placed on it. Nothing was more fascinating than to hear him describe the full-flowing rivers, the perfumed jungles, the proud trees untouched by the axe of man, free, healthy, extending their foliage over hills and plains larger than many a nation of Europe; and then the multitude of birds that lived in that thick immensity, birds of many colors, of an infinite variety of forms, chattering, lively, clothed in the brightest plumage that imagination can dream of; and then to explain their habits, the warfare between the different ornithological families, all of them avid to live and fighting over the resources of the enormous forested areas. And then, what about the monkeys and their terrifying gangs, their amusing expressions and the almost human ingeniousness with which they pursued flying and creeping creatures? That was an endless tale. Nothing having to do with fauna was unknown to him; he had seen and studied it all, the voracious crocodile, denizen of greenish pools or stinking canebrakes as well as the never-to-be-catalogued horde of beautiful insects which exhaust the patience of scholar and collector alike.

And, so as to omit nothing, the splendid flora, explained and described with more religious than scientific emotion, as demonstrating the infinite variety of God's works, completed the enchantment and admiration of the two ladies, who, by a few days after those wonderful lectures, felt that they had seen the five parts of the world and even a little bit more. Cruz, more than her sister, drank in all the spiritual manifestations of that beautiful person, stored them away in her soul to keep them safe and to mingle them eventually with her own feelings, thus creating a new life. Her pure and ardent adoration of the divine friend, counselor, and teacher, was the only bloom in an existence that had become arid and mournful; a single flower, yes, but one of such beauty, of a fragrance as exquisite as that of the most beautiful flowers that grow in the tropical zone.

SIX

Within its opulence the Torquemada family—or the San Eloy family, to speak in terms of mundane etiquette—lived quite apart from the hurly-burly of parties and soirees, giving the lie to its high position in the outside world, although within doors there was nothing that could indicate meanness or cheeseparing practices. Since Rafaelito's dreadful death, the two Aguila sisters had not gone once to the theater, nor did they have any very obvious connection with what is usually called high society. In the evenings their tertulias were limited to half a dozen very intimate friends. Their dinners, which were among the very best as to quality, were extremely modest affairs as far as the number of guests was concerned: it was a rare occasion when more than two persons, in addition to the family, sat at their table. Parties, dances, or musicales with a buffet or liquid refreshment were never seen in those splendid but solitary spaces, which was a great satisfaction to my lord marquis, who consoled himself thereby for his many frustrations and tantrums.

And there were, and are, few houses in Madrid better arranged for displaying aristocratic superfluities. The Palace of Gravelinas is the former mansion of the Trastamaras, constructed solidly and in doubtful taste in the seventeenth century, restored at the end of the eighteenth (at the time of the family's union with the houses of San Quintín and Ceriñola), after plans brought from Rome; restored again during the latter years of Queen Isabella II's reign on the Parisian model and enlarged with magnificent annexes for the servants, archive, armory, and everything else that fills out a large and lordly residence. Naturally, enlarging the house, after the decree that put an end to primogeniture, was an insane move, and the last duke of Gravelinas paid dearly for it, for he was a practical example of disentailment by reason of his vast expenditures. In the end that fine gentleman had to succumb to the law of the century, which means that the propertied wealth of the historically famous families is gradually passing into the hands of a second aristocracy whose patents of nobility are lost in the shadows of some shop, or the crannies of the moneylending business. Gravelinas is living out his days in Biarritz, existing on a small pension allowed him by the syndicate of his creditors, which permits him some modest expenditures and even a mild fling or two to help him remember his former splendor.

Within the parish of San Marcos, and between the Calle de San Bernardo and that of San Bernardino, the Palace of Gravelinas, today Palace of San Eloy, occupies a very large area. Someone has remarked that the only bad thing about this princely mansion is the street on which its severe facade faces. This street, because it is so ordinary, is like a hypocritical contradiction of the extraordinary beauties and refinements within. In order to reach the broad carriage door, one has to pass by hideous second-hand clothing shops, low taverns and wineshops, and ironworks that are vestiges of the ancient ironmongers' trade. On the streets beside and behind the palace the Gravelinas outbuildings, occupying a very large city block, deprive the public street of all variety and make it look like a dismal small town. All that is lacking are gardens, and this form of relaxation was severely missed by its present female inhabitants though not by Don Francisco, who detested with all his heart everything belonging to the vegetable kingdom, and who at any time in his life would have exchanged the best of trees for a chest of drawers or a night table.

The installation of the Cisneros picture collection in the reception rooms of the palace conferred upon it a sumptuary and artistic importance which it had not formerly possessed, for the Gravelinas family had owned only period portraits, neither many nor good, and during their time the palace had had only some frescoes by Bayeu, one good ceiling—a copy of a Tiepolo—and a number of decorative paintings by Maella. The Cisneros collection came into the palace as into its own proper place. The ample rooms became filled with pictures of the first order, with paintings on wood and canvas of great merit, some of them famous in the world of art dealers. Cruz had used the greatest possible care in placing these jewels, taking advice from experts to give each object its proper importance and most suitable light, and this resulted in a museum that could well rival the famous Roman galleries of Doria Pamphili and Borghese. At last, after seeing all that had been done and observing the crush of foreign and Spanish visitors who requested permission to admire these marvels, the great skinflint Torquemada was eventually glad that he had kept the palace, for though its worth as architecture was not great, the land it stood on was immensely valuable and would be still more so in the near future. As for the Cisneros collections and the armory, he soon became re-signed to their acquisition, for, according to the opinion of intelligent folk, critics, and the like, all of that stuff, painted cloth and colored wood, had a real and positive value, and it could well be that within a relatively short time he could sell it for double or triple what it had cost.

There were two or three pieces in the collection, Mother of God! before which the above-mentioned critics stood openmouthed; and an *individual* even came from London, commissioned by the National Gallery to buy one of them, offering the trifling sum of five hundred pounds. It seemed fabulous to him. The painting in question was a Masaccio, which at one time was believed to be of doubtful attribu-tion, and was at last declared authentic by a bunch of experts—*in the vernacular,* antiquarians—who came from France and Italy to see it. The Masaccio! And what was it, dammit? Why, a little bit of a picture which at first sight seemed to represent the inside of an inkbottle, all black, with only the torso of one figure and the leg of another standing out against the darkness. It was *The Baptism of Our Redeemer;* and as for him, according to a remark made by the then legitimate owner of the treasure, his own mother wouldn't have recognized him. But this mattered little to Torquemada, and all the Masaccios in the world could rain upon his house and he would extol their value, concerned only with business and not with art. But others, such as a Paris Bordone, a Sebastian del Piombo, a Memling, a Fra Angelico, and a Zurbarán, were also held to be of great value, and these, along with all the other paintings, and the vases, statues, and tapestries, formed a sort of *America* of enormous value for Don Francisco. He regarded the paintings like stocks or bonds of powerful and well-administered companies, quoted easily and favorably in all the markets of the globe. He never paused to contemplate works of art or to scrutinize their beauty, admitting with genial modesty that he *didn't understand anything about daubs*; he stood in ecstasy, with an attention resembling that of an artist, only before the inventory that a skillful restorer, or *museum rat*, had made for his guidance, adding to the description and critical and historical analysis of each canvas or panel its probable value, after consulting the catalogues of foreign dealers, who trafficked for sums involving millions in ancient and modern *daubs*.

An immense, fascinating house, noble, rendered holy by art, venerable by its lineage! The narrator cannot describe it, for he would be the first to lose himself in the labyrinth of its rooms and galleries, enriched with all the marvelous things invented both yesterday and today by art, luxury, and vanity. Four-fifths of it had no other inhabitants than those of the realm of fantasy, some dressed in clothing of varied form and color, others naked, showing their beautiful muscular structure, which made them seem like men and women of a different race from ours. Today we have nothing but faces, thanks to the dreadful clothes with which we hide our diminished anatomies. All of that ideal world was perfectly preserved by the eldest Aguila, who personally supervised the cleaning operations, assisted by an army of servants who were particularly skillful, as persons trained to work in picture galleries, palaces, and other European "Americas."

Be it said, in conclusion, that the ruling lady, when she joined in a tight embrace the riches of Gravelinas with those of Aguila and Torquemada, would not have considered her task of restitution complete had she not finished the job with the kind of domestic staff appropriate for such a house. A palace like that one, a family of such lofty lineage in patents of nobility and in money, could not exist without an interminable flock of servants of both sexes. So the lady organized the *personnel* by letting herself be carried away by her instincts of grandeur, within the very strictest order. The section of stables and coach houses, as well as the kitchens and dining room, were organized without omitting the slightest detail appropriate to a family of princes. And in different departments, the host of lady's maids, footmen, pages, upstairs and downstairs servants, doorkeepers, ironing women, etc., made up, along with the sections previously mentioned, an army that in a pinch would have sufficed to defend a fortified castle.

This superabundance of servants was chiefly what made Don Francisco's blood boil, and although he compromised on the purchase of old paintings and rusty suits of armor because of the good return they might bring him in the fairly near future, he could not get used to the presence of so many lazybones who nibbled away and destroyed the household; what they ate every day was enough to feed half the world. This indeed was the principal reason why the poor man felt so sour in those days, but he swallowed his bitterness; though he suffered a great deal, he was also insufferable to everyone else. When alone or with the good Donoso, he let off steam, protesting about the *plethora of servants* and the fact that his house was a *faithful copy* of governmental offices, full of do-nothings who only went there to idle away their time. He understood full well that he could not live like a poor man, as in a three-peseta boarding house; of course not. But as for exaggerations, he would have none of them, for *from the sublime to the ridiculous is only a step.* And it is also obvious that in governments where the vice of overemployment has grown out of hand, disaster is certain. Were he to rule the household he would follow a system *diametrically opposed* to Cruz's. Few servants, but *appropriate* ones, and a great deal of vigilance to keep everybody on the straight and narrow, spending what was designated and no more. What he said in the legislative chamber to all who would listen, he also said to his family: "Let's remove *fifth wheels* from the administrative vehicle to make it move better. But this sister-in-law of mine, devil take her! what does she do? She turns my *domicile* into an *administrative center* and makes my head spin, for there are days when I believe that they are the masters and I *the very last pariah* in that whole mob."

SEVEN

Few friends visited the Palace of Gravelinas daily. Needless to say that Donoso was one of the most faithful, and that his friendship was as much valued as ever, although, it is only fair to state, he had been supplanted by the famous missionary to the Indies insofar as affection and admiration were concerned. As for ladies, there is no evidence that the household was visited assiduously by other than the marquise of Taramundi and the Señoras de Morentín, Gibraleón, and Orozco, this latter a more intimate friend than those previously mentioned. The old schoolgirl friendship between Augusta and Fidela had become so close in recent times that they spent almost all day together, and when the marquise of San Eloy was kept at home by different illnesses and ailments, her friend did not leave her side, and amused her with gay conversation.

Though we need not refresh old memories now, all who read these lines probably know that the daughter of Cisneros and wife of Tomás Orozco, following a certain lamentable tragedy, remained in obscurity and retirement for a few years. By the time we see her reappear in the House of San Eloy, Augusta's abandonment of social life was not as absolute as before. She had aged, if this term applies to an all-too-visible progression into maturity, but without detriment to grace and beauty. Her black hair was sprinkled with premature white, which she did not try to hide with dyes and cosmetics. Her graceful body was the same as in happier times and continued to maintain a charming mean, neither thin nor fat, and was extraordinarily agile and flexible. And as for the rest of her description, it can only be remarked that her beautiful eyes were perhaps bigger, or at least seemed to be, and her mouth . . . the same. It was known for being as large as it was bewitching, with a set of teeth whose perfection cannot adequately be described by the comparisons with marble, mother-of-pearl, and pearls that rhetoric has lavished on those inner decorations of beautiful mouths ever since the dawn of poetry. Though she was two years younger than her friend and had very few, almost invisible gray hairs to comb, Fidela seemed the elder. She had grown thinner and more unhealthy-looking, her opaline complexion was more transparent, and the bridge of her nose had sharpened to the point that one could certainly have used it to cut something not very tough. There were granular red spots on her cheeks, and her thin and almost colorless lips allowed too great an expanse of her pink gums to show when she smiled. In those days she possessed a type of distinction that we might call Austrian, for she recalled Charles V's sisters and other illustrious princesses who live in effigy in museums all over the world, their noses aristocratically sharp-pointed. She was a very elegant whiff of Gothic painting, and had a certain family resemblance to one of Quentin Massys' best pictures—a *Descent from the Cross*—in the San Eloy collection.

And so . . . the day after the mass, first chronological link in the chain of this tale, Augusta entered the house shortly before lunchtime. She found Cruz in one of the lower rooms, doing the honors of the house for an important visitor, a member of the Academy and a great scholar, who was examining the paintings. A famous painter who had been given permission to copy the Paris Bordone had set up his easel in the rotunda, and a third art enthusiast, a little farther off, was reproducing a Tiepolo cartoon in black and white. It was an extremely busy day for the eldest Aguila, for her highborn sense of dignity obliged her to look after and entertain the admirers of her museum, taking care that they lacked for nothing. As for the academician, he was a man of easily aroused enthusiasm, and when he was standing in ecstasy contemplating the details of a painting, you would have had to toss a bomb at him to bring him back to his senses. Cruz had already endured two hours of artistic rapture, with mental excursions through the Italian museums and side-flights through the pre-Raphaelite cycle, and was beginning to tire. Two-thirds of the collection was still to be examined. To make matters worse, she had another scholar in the archive, a bibliophile more patient than Job, who had gone there to examine "the Sicilian papers" in order to clear up a weighty historical point. She had no choice but to look after him as well, and to find out whether the archive would offer him unrestricted access to all the paper material kept in those ancient depositories.

After inviting the academician to luncheon, Cruz delegated her functions to Augusta for a moment, and while the latter was carrying them out temporarily with admirable accuracy—for she knew by heart the collections that had belonged to her father, Don Carlos de Cisneros—her friend went to have a look at the scholar in the archive, whom she found diving into a sea of papers. She invited him also to partake of luncheon and, while the academician and the painter were locked in an artistic dispute over whether a little painting they had both seen and instantly adored was or was not a Mantegna, returned to the rooms where she had left her friend and had a short whispered conversation with her.

"Look, my dear, if Fidela is lunching in her room I'll stay with her. I don't care for the society of such scholars as these."

"I thought that Fidela would come downstairs today, but if you like, the two of you can be served upstairs. I'm the loser. I'll be alone among two guests and my old savage, Don Francisco; I'll need God's help and a bit more to take care of my dear brother-in-law's foolish statements. He is awful, and since we've been estranged he usually tears off the mask of refinement and, by letting all his vulgarity show, often places me in very ticklish situations."

"Do what you can. I'm going upstairs. Good-bye. Have fun."

She went up, as energetic, gay, and agile as a little girl, and in the first room on the upper floor found Valentinico, crawling on all fours on the carpet. The nursemaid, who was a robust mountain girl, pretty and clean, was holding him up with an arrangement of straps, tugging on him when he strayed too far, and guiding him if he took an unsatisfactory direction. The youngster was howling, moving his four limbs with animal delight, drooling from the mouth and trying to hug the floor and rub his face on it.

"Brute," Augusta told him forthrightly, "stand up on your two feet."

"He just doesn't want to, señorita," said the nursemaid timidly. "Every time I pull him up he gets furious, and nobody can handle him."

Valentín, still in his turtle's position, stared fixedly at Augusta.

"Aren't you ashamed to go on all fours like the animals?" Augusta said to him, bending to pick him up.

Holy Mother of God! At the mere attempt to lift him from the floor where he was crawling, the little boy went wild, flailing his legs and arms wildly—and for a moment his hands really did seem like paws—and made the room ring with his screams, throwing back his head and clenching his teeth.

"Goodness, stay there, stay there on the blessed floor," said Augusta, "you little toad! You're a pretty fellow, you are! Go on, cry, cry, you ridiculous little creature, to make yourself uglier than you are already."

The naughty little boy insulted her in his monosyllabic language, which was savage, primitive, and of a ferocious simplicity, for no one could hear more than pa . . . ca . . . ta . . . pa . . .

"That's right, tell me something. The devil himself couldn't understand you. You'll never talk like real people. It's unbelievable that you're a child of your father, who is all intelligence and sweetness. Oh dear, what a pity!"

Lady and nursemaid exchanged glances of sadness and compassion.

"Yesterday," the girl said, "he was very good. He let his mama and his auntie kiss him, and didn't throw down the plates at dinner. But today we're at our wits' end with him. He breaks everything he touches, and the only thing he wants to do is crawl like a little animal, imitating dogs and cats."

"I think this one will never have other models. How sad! Poor Fidela! That's right, darling, make noises like a pig. Little by little you're making progress. Grunt, grunt . . . that's right, learn that fine language."

The nursemaid pulled on his reins, for the rascal was going after a Japanese vase that was placed on the lowest shelf of a corner cupboard, and would certainly have broken it into splinters. His childish savagery made terrible inroads on the crockery supply in the house, and on the many precious objects in it. They changed his clothes frequently and yet he was always dirty from dragging his tummy along the floor; his oversized head was full of bumps which made it even uglier than did its great size and his huge ears; saliva drooled in strings over his chest, and his hands, which were his only pretty feature, were always as black as if he knew no other amusement than playing with coal.

EIGHT

The heir to the combined estates of San Eloy, del Aguila, and Gravelinas had been, in the first year of his life, a delusion for his parents and the object of false hopes for the whole family. They thought that he was going to be pretty, that he was so already, and in addition lively and intelligent. But these hopes began to dissipate after the baby's first serious illness, and Quevedito's prophecies, which came to pass with terrifying regularity, filled all their hearts with anxiety and distress. The growth of his head began before he was two years old, and soon after that his ears became longer and his legs twisted, accompanied by a great reluctance to stand on them. His eyes became very small during that crisis in his life, and moreover they were cold and dull, without the slightest animation or spark of charm. His hair was straight and sickly in color, like cornsilk. They thought that his ugliness would be concealed by putting it up on curlers; but the little scamp, in his fits of convulsive rage, tore off the papers and locks of hair with them, so that it was decided to shave his head.

His habits were the strangest imaginable. If he was left alone for an instant, he crawled under the beds and crouched in a corner with his face jammed against the wall. He felt no enthusiasm for playthings, and when they were given him he would bite them until they broke. He rarely allowed anyone to caress him, and only with his mama was he less aloof. If someone picked him up, he would throw back his head and express a desire to be released by extremely violent arm movements and kicks. His last defense was the bite, and the poor nursemaid's hands were riddled with them. It had been easy to wean him, and he ate a great deal, preferring soupy, greasy foods, or those loaded with sugar. He liked wine. He loved to play with animals, but he had to be deprived of this pleasure because he tortured them terribly, whether they were rabbits, doves, or dogs. It was virtually impossible to make him take medicines during his illnesses, and he never went to sleep unless he had his hand thrust into his nursemaid's bosom. There were times when his mama was able to cure him of that wicked habit of crawling on all fours. He would walk on two feet, staggering, as long as they permitted him the use of a little whip, stick, or cane, with which he hit everyone mercilessly. They had to take great care not to lose sight of him, for he would strike the bibelots and porcelain figures in his mama's boudoir. The house was full of headless bodies and shards of beautiful porcelain.

And this was not the only depredation he committed when he walked on two feet, for he also had the charming habit of stealing whatever objects were in reach of his hand, whether valuable or not, and would hide them in dark places—under the beds, or inside some forgotten Chinese vase in the anteroom. When they least expected it, the servants who did the cleaning would find large collections of heterogeneous objects: buttons, pieces of sealing wax, watch keys, cigar ends, cards, valuable rings, snaps, coins, gloves, hairpins, and pieces of molding torn from the gilded chairs. He frisked across the nap of carpets on all fours like a lamb nibbling on young grass, and rooted into all the corners. These were his joys. When the ladies were tired of the attacks of fury that came over him if he did not get his way, they would let him carry on freely in that savage condition. They didn't even want to think about it. Poor things! What reasons must God have had to give them that sad and distressing little beast as an emblem of the future!

"Hello, darling, how are you?" said Augusta, entering Fidela's room and hastening to kiss her. "I found your son out there, turned into a hedgehog. Poor thing! What a shame he's such a brute!"

As she saw that the cloud of sadness on her friend's face was about to condense into tears, she quickly tried to clear away her thoughts with consoling words:

"But, silly, who tells you that your son won't change one of these fine days? And furthermore: I believe that his intelligence will soon awaken, maybe a superior intelligence . . . There are such cases, lots of cases."

Fidela expressed with movements of her head her deep-seated pessimism on the subject.

"But you're wrong, very wrong, to be so mistrustful. Believe it, because I'm telling you so. Precocity in children is a very deceptive trait, an illusion that time sweeps away. Just think about what really happens. Those children who talk and chatter at a year and a half, who at two make speeches and tell you very clever things, change later and get stupid. I've seen many examples of the opposite. Children who seemed to be freaks turned out later to be men of extraordinary talent. Nature has her whims—let's call them that because we don't know what to call them. She doesn't like to have her secrets discovered, and gives some big surprises . . . Just a minute. Now that I remember . . . Yes, I've read about a great man who during his first years was just like your Valentín, a regular little beast. Who is it? Ah, now I remember. Victor Hugo, no less!"

"Victor Hugo! You're out of your mind."

"I've read it, anyway. And you must have read it too, only you've forgotten. He was just like yours, and his parents complained at the tops of their voices. And then came his development, the crisis, the second birth, you might say, and that big head of his turned out to be full of all the genius of poetry."

Augusta insisted on the point with such affectionate and ingenious arguments that in the end the other believed her and felt better. It must be said that Augusta Orozco had great persuasive power over Fidela, and this had its roots in the very intense affection that Fidela had come to feel for her in recent months; rather, it was idolatry, a sort of spiritual submission, similar in a sense to what Cruz felt for the saintly Gamborena. Is this not a strange thing, this similarity of effects, when the causes or the persons are so different? Augusta, who was no saint, not at all, exercised absolute spiritual domination over Fidela; she fascinated her, to express it in more comprehensible terms; she was Fidela's oracle in everything related to thinking, her master-spring with regard to feeling, the consolation of her loneliness, the cure for her sadness.

Necessarily housebound because of her feeble health, Fidela would have liked to keep her intimate friend beside her morning, noon, and night. The other, loyal and undeviating, dedicated all her free time to her. If she was late on an occasional day, the little marquise felt that her ailments were worse, and nothing gave her consolation or distraction. Messages and little notes were her only alleviation when the favored one was absent, and when Augusta came in, after having played truant for a morning or a whole day, Fidela visibly came to life, as if she passed from shadows to light both in body and soul. This is what happened that morning, and the pleasure of seeing her friend increased her credulity a hundredfold, causing her to receive like a voice from heaven that whole farrago about the monstrosity of Victor Hugo's childhood and other farfetched examples which the compassionate deceiver pulled out of her brain. Then the questions began:

"What have you been doing since yesterday afternoon? Is anything going on at home? What's being said out in the world? Who has died? Is there anything new about the scandal of the Guzmán girls, Eloísa and María Juana?"

For Augusta told her all the social tidbits and the gossip and intrigues that circulated in Madrid. Fidela did not read newspapers, but her special friend did, and always came well supplied with happenings. Her conversation was extremely agreeable, witty, sprinkled with paradoxes and original ways of expressing things. And in those conversations there was no lack of racy and cutting gossip, for which Augusta possessed more than average aptitudes, and she cultivated them with implacable anger on occasion, as if she had to vindicate with her tongue offenses by other tongues more hurtful than her own. We would have to know, for the total study of the intense friendship that united the two women, whether Augusta had told her friend the truth of her tragedy, unknown to the public and discussed in worldly circles with such different opinions, by vague indications and according to the intentions of each person who spoke of it. It is almost certain that the tragic lady and the comic lady (high comedy, that is) had spoken of that mysterious affair, and that Augusta did not hide from her friend the truth or part of the truth that she knew; but there is no evidence that she did so, for when we find them alone they do not talk about it, and only by veiled references on the part of the marquise of San Eloy can it be assumed that she knew about this black spot—and what a black spot!—in the life of her idolized friend.

"Well, look here," Fidela told her, returning to the same subject after a short digression, "you've convinced me. I accept the fact that my son is so difficult, and, like you, I have hopes of a transformation that will turn him into a genius . . . no, not so much as that, but into an intelligent and good person."

"I wouldn't accept that. My hopes are not limited to so little."

"Because you're very paradoxical, very intense. I'm not; I'm contented with very little, with what is reasonable, you know? I like the middle ground in everything. I've already told you; it's a burden to me that my husband is so rich. Please God we may never be poor, not that; but so much wealth makes me sad. The middle ground is best, even in one's intelligence. Listen, my dear, don't you think it would be better if you and I were a little stupider?"

"Oh, what a joke!"

"I mean that you and I, because we are too clever, have not been, nor are we now, as happy as we ought to be. Because you have a great deal of natural cleverness, Augusta; so have I, and as this is not good— don't laugh—since great cleverness only serves to make us suffer, we try to counterbalance it with our ignorance, avoiding as much as possible knowing about things. For goodness, learning is a dreadful bore! And as long as we succeed in not knowing wise things, we manage not to know them and can be stupid, very stupid indeed."

"That is why," said Augusta gracefully, "I haven't wanted to lunch downstairs. We have two scholars at the table today. I've already told

Cruz not to count on me, for I don't want any scholarship to stick to me."

"A very good thought. It's a pleasure to be a bit primitive, and not to know anything about history, and to think that the sun revolves around the earth, and to believe in witches, and have one's mind full of superstitions."

"And to have been born into a community of shepherds, and spend your life carrying bundles of firewood."

"No, I wouldn't go as far as that."

"Conceiving and giving birth and raising healthy children."

"I'd like that."

"And then watching them go for soldiers."

"I wouldn't like that."

"And growing old amid rough tasks, with a husband who's more like a domestic animal."

"Bah!" said Fidela. "And what would that matter to us? I have an idea about that, which I may have mentioned to you at one time. Look: I spent all last night thinking about it. It seemed to me that I was a great *philosophress*, that my head was filled with an infinite number of great, self-evident truths, truths that, if they were written down, would have to be accepted by humanity."

"And what is your idea?"

"I've already told you. But I've never felt so much conviction in myself as now. I say and maintain that love is foolishness, the greatest idiocy into which a human being can fall, and that the men and women who succeed in avoiding it by all possible means are the only ones who deserve immortality. How can it be avoided? Why, very easily. Would you like me to explain it to you, my dear idiot?"

Alternating between laughter and compassion, Augusta listened to her friend's arguments. At last, good humor won the day; both of them burst out laughing. The marquise was just preparing to expound her thesis further when a servant came in with luncheon. The thesis fell under the table, and no one gave it another thought.

NINE

Until the next one came along. Fidela's theses followed one another with startling rapidity, and if one was extravagant, the next was still more so. Her weak memory did not allow her to retain today what she had said yesterday, but the contradictions endowed the innocent ramblings of her spirit with even greater charm. After lunching with something less than indifferent appetite, she had the little boy brought to her, and he, by one of God's miracles, was not as savage when in his mother's arms as Augusta had feared. He let Augusta hug him and even answered with a certain amount of sense the questions they asked him. It is true that the sense depended in large measure on the interpretation given to his primitive attempts at speech. Fidela, the only person who understood them, and was as proud of the fact as if she had learned one of the languages of the Congo, translated with all the good will in the world, and almost always got very pretty answers from him.

"He says that if I let him have the whip he'll love me more than Rita: ta, ta, ca . . . Just look at what a rascal he is. And that he won't hit me: ca, pa, ta . . . Just look at what a scamp he is. He already knows how to treat nicely the people who help him, the ones who encourage his little tricks. Why, you can say what you like, but this is a mark of intelligence."

"Of course it is. Why, in the end," said Augusta playfully, pinching his legs, "this little blockhead is going to turn out with an intelligence that will leave all of humanity crosseyed!"

Valentinico laughed, excited by her tickling, opening his huge mouth from ear to ear.

"Goodness, darling, don't open that bulkhead so wide. You're frightening us. Is it possible that, when you start to grow, that pillar-box you have for a mouth won't get smaller? Tell me, my little rough diamond, whom do you take after with that soup plate of yours?"

"Yes, it is strange," said Augusta. "Yours is quite small, and his father's isn't surprisingly large. Mysteries of nature! But look, take a good look; all this part, from the nose up, and between the brows, and the prominent forehead, is exactly like his father . . . But what's he saying now?"

The little boy took part in the conversation, spilling out a string of harsh sounds, like those you might hear among a band of monkeys or parrots. He slid down to the floor, returned to his mother's lap, sticking his legs out toward Augusta's lap, without ceasing his unintelligible chatter.

"Ah!" exclaimed his mother at last, overcoming the difficulties of interpretation with great intellectual effort. "Now I know. He says . . . you'll see what a tease he is . . . he says that . . . he loves me ever so much. See, see that he knows how to talk? My little brute is very naughty and very clever. He says he loves me ever so much. It couldn't be plainer."

"Well, my dear, I can't make any sense out of those noises."

"Because you haven't spent your time studying primitive languages. The poor little fellow explains himself as best he can: ta, ca, ja, pa . . . ca . . . ta. He says he loves me ever so much. And I'm going to teach my little savage to pronounce clearly, so that I won't have to scramble my brains by translating. Come on, loosen that little tongue."

Whatever the sense of what Valentinico was trying to express, the fact is that on that occasion he displayed a docility, a filial love, which left both women marveling. Nestled against his mother's bosom, he petted her with his dirty little hands, and his face bore an expression of contentment and placidity that was very rare in him. Fidela, who suffered from a persistent oppression and fatigue in her chest, at last tired of that heavy weight; but when she tried to put him on the floor, or into the nursemaid's arms, the little boy became terribly upset, and farewell docility, farewell gentleness.

"Don't cry, my treasure, they'll give you your whip, two whips, and you can play around here for a bit. But don't break anything."

Fortunately the tantrum was not one of his noisiest; the heir of San Eloy staggered out of those rooms and soon could be heard imitating the asthmatic howling of a sick dog who lived on the lower floor of the house. Cruz, who had emerged from her second session with the scholars with a blinding headache, had the nursemaid take the child to a room some distance away, so that he would not bother them with his inharmonious cries, and went in to see her sister.

"I'm only so-so," Fidela told her. "The shortness of breath bothers me a little. And how are you?"

"I'm out of my mind. And we have art and erudition for a while yet! Holy Virgin, what a nuisance!"

"Because you," said Augusta pertly, "don't have that charming father of mine to handle the amateurs and all those annoying art fanatics. Papa was never bothered by anyone, because he had the gift of bothering everyone else. No one could outlast him, and whenever someone who was extraordinarily tiresome turned up, he would begin to take out one precious object after another so quickly, and string together such rapid, fantastic, and incoherent observations about them all, that no brain could withstand them, and the most tedious of them rushed out with no desire ever to return. You can't use that system, for which one needs a sly and wicked character, and besides, you need to reserve all your talent for other things, more difficult things maybe . . . Let's see . . . tell us what happened during that lunch of yours, and what prodigies of fencing you've had to perform to parry some wild blow . . . from the distinguished man. Doesn't the newspaper call him that every time it speaks of him? For I'd swear that the distinguished man has been up to his usual tricks."

"Marvel, if you like. He has behaved very correctly and sensibly," replied the elder sister, sitting down for a little rest. "He didn't say a word to me, which I was very glad of. But goodness! when I saw that he was taking part in the conversation, I was frightened to death. 'The game's up,' I thought. 'Here it comes.' But God inspired him, no doubt. Everything that he said was so much to the point that . . ."

"Oh, wonderful!" exclaimed Fidela, radiant. "Poor dear distinguished man! Why, I always say that he's very clever when he wants to be."

"He said that the most complete chaos reigns in the arts and sciences today."

"The most complete chaos! Fine, bravo."

"That everything is chaos, literature is chaos, criticism of arts and letters the most absolute chaos, and that no one knows what he's doing."

"Did you ever . . .?"

"Well, he must know! And then, they say that . . ."

"Those two gentlemen were positively dumbstruck with admiration and praised his opinions highly, agreeing that the part about chaos was true and more than true. Fortunately he didn't say much more than that, and his laconism was interpreted as a concentration of ideas, as a miserly measuring of thought and a way not to squander eternal truths . . . So . . . I can't waste any more time here. My duties as cicerone call me."

Her sister and her sister's friend tried to keep her with them, but she was not to be won over. Unfortunately for all three it was a very disagreeable day, and there was no hope that the two illustrious scholars of art and history might go and take a little walk to clear their heads. It was snowing, and there was a furious wind; sky and earth vied with each other in gloom and dirty color. The snow, which was falling in violent squalls of tiny snowflakes, did not whiten the ground and turned into mud as it fell. The cold was intense in the street and even inside well-heated rooms, for its sharp nose poked through every crack it found in window frames and chimneys and balconies, mocking at weather stripping and laughing at heating stoves. The three ladies were astonished by the furious wind that beat against the windowpanes; they looked out and amused themselves by observing the difficulties of the passersby, who wrapped themselves to their ears in vain, for the wind carried away both capes and scarves, and sometimes their hats. This, and their efforts to avoid falling, made both men and women seem like strange figures in a fantastic dance on the Siberian steppes.

"Goodness, what a dreadful day," said Cruz very disconsolately. "And to make it entirely ill-fated, our friend the priest can't come today."

"Of course, he lives so far away!"

"And if he were to be caught in a blizzard! No, no, he mustn't go out, poor man!"

"Send the carriage for him."

"Yes, and have him send it back empty and come on foot, like the other day when it was pouring rain."

"But do you think," asked Augusta, "that that man is cowed by windstorms or any other sort of storm?"

"Of course not . . . but you'll see that he won't come today. My heart tells me that he won't."

"Well, mine tells me that he will," said Fidela. "Would you like to bet on it? And my heart never deceives me. For several days now, the rascal has been right about everything. It's a proven fact: every time it hurts, making my breathing difficult, it turns into a prophet. It doesn't tell me anything that doesn't come true."

"And now it will tell you to step back from the balcony and try not to catch cold. That's right: catch cold, and then you'll start to complain, and have bad nights, and be tired and cough constantly."

"And if I catch cold, so much the better!" answered Fidela in the voice and tone of a spoiled child, letting herself be led to the sofa. "My heart tells me that soon I'm going to catch cold, such a cold, that no embers will be able to warm me. There, now I'm shivering. But it's not important, no. It's already passing. It was just a gust, a little kiss the wind in the street sent me through the frosty windowpanes. Go on, run along, for your scholars are impatient, and the one who's viewing pictures is missing you dreadfully."

"How do you know?"

"Why, through my second sight. What? Don't you believe in my second sight? Well, I'm telling you that Father Gamborena is on his way here. And if he's not already coming in the street door, he'll do so very soon."

"What do you bet he's not?"

"What do you bet he is?"

The elder sister hastened out, and shortly returned, laughing.

"So much for your second sight! He hasn't come, nor will he. Look, just look how the snow is falling now."

It must have been pure chance! Who could doubt it? Less than ten minutes had elapsed when they heard the great missionary's voice in the next room, and all three hastened to meet him with great laughter and enthusiasm in their joyful hearts. The good cleric had left his enormous umbrella and his hat downstairs, and the small amount of snow that had stuck to his cassock had melted in the time it took him to climb the stairs. As he entered, he took off his black gloves and shook one finger of his right hand with a show of pain.

"My dear," he said to Fidela, "your son has bitten me."

"Lord!" exclaimed Cruz. "Was there ever a greater scamp? I'm going to kill him."

"It's nothing, my dear. But he did sink his teeth into me. I tried to pet him. Luckily his little teeth didn't go through the glove. But goodness, what a child you two have!"

"He bites for fun," said Fidela sadly. "But we must cure him of that ugly habit. No, he doesn't do it out of naughtiness, you can believe that."

TEN

"Of course, I'm sure it isn't naughtiness," said the missionary graciously, "but the instinct is certainly not a good one. Goodness, what a temper!"

"For the kind of day we're having, and the bad condition of the streets," observed Cruz, without taking her eyes off the priest, who was huddling close to the fireplace, "your shoes aren't very wet."

"It's because I possess the art of stepping between patches of mud worse than those in Madrid. It's not in vain that one has learned to pick one's way over the reefs of Polynesia. I know how to avoid potholes, as well as slippery places and even abysses. What did you think?"

"Now, today," said Fidela, "you simply mustn't go without eating. And you'll eat with us, if you prefer us to the scholars downstairs."

"Today he's not to go, he's not to go. Because we won't let him," said Cruz, observing him with a tenderness that seemed almost maternal.

"He's not to go," repeated Augusta, "even though we have to tie him by one foot to make sure of him."

"Very well, my dear ladies," replied the priest in an expansive tone, "do with me as you will. I turn myself over to your every whim. Give me a meal, if you care to, and tie me to the leg of a chair if that is your wish. The severe weather relieves me of duties in the street."

"And the best thing you could do would be to stay here tonight," added Cruz. "What? What have you got to say? We don't eat people here. We'll prepare the room upstairs, where you'll stay like a prince, or rather like a lordly cardinal."

"That I won't accept. I'm more accustomed to sleeping in bamboo huts than in ducal houses. Which doesn't mean I can't resign myself to staying here if my presence were to be needed for something."

Cruz urged him to take off his outer cassock, which was very damp and quite unnecessary in the well-heated room, and he agreed, letting the illustrious lady pull at his sleeves.

"Now, would you like something to eat or drink?"

"But, my dear, what sort of idea do you have of me? Do you think I'm one of those gluttons who have to be feeding their stomachs at every instant?"

"A bit of cold meat, a little glass of something . . ."

"No."

"But I would like something," said Fidela with childish volubility. "Have them bring us some wine, at least."

"Port?"

"As far as I'm concerned, whatever you want. And I'll have a little sip with these good ladies."

Cruz left the room, and Gamborena spoke of Valentinico again, stressing the need to bring him up a little more strictly.

"It really pains me to punish him," replied Fidela. "The poor little angel doesn't know what he's doing. We'll have to wait until he has a clearer idea of good and bad. His mind is a bit obtuse."

"And his teeth very sharp."

"But that child—right there where you see him—" said Augusta, "is going to be intelligent."

"Then you know more than I do! Father Gamborena, please don't put on that gloomy face when my son is being discussed. It pains me very much when people have a bad idea of my darling little brute, and it pains me still more to have people think that it will be impossible to make a man of him."

"But, my dear, I haven't said anything. Time will bring a solution."

"Time . . . death, perhaps . . . Are you referring to death?"

"My dearest girl, I haven't spoken of death at all, nor even thought of it."

"Yes, yes. That solution of which you speak," added Fidela in a low, emotional voice, "is death. Don't deny it. You meant that my son will die, and then we'll be free of the sadness of having, as our only heir, a . . ."

"I haven't thought any such thing, I assure you."

"Don't deny it. Just look, today I'm in good form. I guess people's thoughts."

"Not mine."

"Yours and everyone's. That solution of which you speak will bring . . . but I will not see that time, for before that I will have had mine, my solution. I mean that I will die before then."

"I'll not say that you won't. Who knows what the Lord has in store? But I never announced anyone's death, and if I occasionally speak of it, I do so without giving a dreadful emphasis to my words. What we call death is a common and very natural event, an indispensable stage in the totality of life, and I consider that neither the fact nor the name ought to frighten any person of upright conscience."

"Now you see why it doesn't frighten me."

"But it does me, I admit it," declared Augusta, "and the father may say of my conscience anything he likes. I won't take offense."

"I have nothing to do with your conscience, dear lady," replied the priest. "But if I had something to say I would not hold my tongue, even if you did take offense."

"And I would receive your reprimands with resignation and even with gratitude."

"Scold us all you like," said Fidela, nibbling at the cold meats and pastries that had just been brought her. "I've got over my bad humor. And I'll say more: if you wish to speak to us about death and give us a good sermon on the subject, we'll listen to you . . . even gladly."

"That you won't," said Augusta, offering the missionary a glass of port. "Don't let anyone talk to me about death or anything to do with that mystery, which begins in our cemeteries and ends on judgment day. I tell my family that when I die they must cover my ears tight, so that I won't hear the trumpets of the Last Judgment."

"Lord, what a dreadful thing to say!"

"Do you fear the resurrection of the body?"

"No, señor. I fear the Last Judgment."

"Well, I do want to hear the trumpets," said Fidela, "and the sooner the better. I'm as sure that I'm going to Heaven as that I'm drinking this delicious wine."

"So am I . . . that is, no . . . I have my doubts," said Augusta. "But I have faith in divine mercy."

"Very good. Trust in mercy," said the priest, "if, and when, you have attained merits to deserve it."

"I am attaining merits."

"You can find fault with any woman, Señor Gamborena," observed the marquise of San Eloy in a slightly jesting yet tasteful tone of seriousness, "all except this one, who is Catholic to the marrow of her bones, who organizes solemn religious ceremonies, presides over charitable committees, and is a collector of funds for the Pope, for missions, and for other pious purposes."

"Very well," said the priest, falling in with the marquise's jesting seriousness. "You need only one thing, then."

"What?"

"A bit of Christian doctrine, the elementary kind, the kind that is taught in schools."

"Bah! I know it by heart."

"Indeed you do not. And if you like, I'll examine you here and now."

"My dear man, no. To go so far as to examine me . . . One might well forget some little thing."

"To forget the letter doesn't matter in the least, if the principle, the essence, is stamped upon the heart."

"It is on mine."

"I venture to doubt it."

"And me too," said Fidela, delighted with the turn the conversation was taking. "This girl, surreptitiously, is a terrible heretic."

"Oh, what a joke!"

"Not I. I believe everything that Holy Mother Church commands; but I believe in lots of other things too," declared Fidela.

"Such as?"

"I believe that the machinery, that is, the governing, of the world is not functioning as well as it should, and that the President of the Council, up there, has been neglecting the affairs of this lowly planet just a teeny bit."

"Are we making sacrilegious jokes? You do not feel deeply what you are saying, my dear daughter; but even though you do not feel it, you are committing a sin. A sentence does not cease to be blasphemous just because it is uttered as a joke."

"There, that's telling her!"

"But you can't tell me," continued the marquise of San Eloy, "that all this business of life and death is well governed, especially death. I insist that people ought to be allowed to die when they want to."

"Ha, ha! How lovely! Then no one would want to die."

"Ah! I don't agree, and excuse me," said Augusta seriously. "All, absolutely all living beings, even though they lived for thousands of years, would come to the point of being tired. There would not be a single human being who wouldn't, at last, have a moment when he says 'No more, no more.' Even the stubbornest egotist, the one most wedded to enjoyments, must end by hating his own self and dismissing it for good. Then there would be voluntary death, summoned rather than feared, without old age or illnesses. Come now, Father, tell me if this wouldn't mean arranging things better than they are now. Let God come and see!"

"He has already seen, and He knows that both of you have intelligences as faulty as your hearts. I don't want to follow you along that path of monstrous philosophizing. You are joking sacrilegiously."

"Sacrilegiously!" exclaimed Fidela. "No, Father. We are joking, and that's all. Certainly, when God made things as they are, He did well. But I stick to my argument: I am not criticizing divine authority, but I'd be glad if this business about choosing when to die became established."

"That is the same as defending the greatest of abominations: suicide."

"I don't defend it, indeed I don't," said Augusta, turning pale.

"Well, I . . ." remarked the other, struggling to express her thoughts, "though I don't defend it, don't attack it either . . . I mean . . . wait a moment . . . that if all the means of taking one's life were not so disagreeable, I think that . . . I mean . . . that I wouldn't find it so bad."

"In the name of Jesus!"

"No, Father, don't be upset," said Augusta, coming to her friend's aid. "Let me complete her thought. Her idea is not a foolish one. Suicide is acceptable in the following form: a woman—or a man, speaking also on the part of men—goes to sleep and maintains, through a very deep sleep, the will, the power, I don't know what to call it, of sleeping for centuries and not waking ever, ever again."

"There, that's exactly it! How well you've expressed it!" exclaimed Fidela clapping her hands, her eyes sparkling. "To sleep, until the trumpets wake one up."

Gamborena very deliberately took a chair and placed it opposite the two ladies, both of them within reach of his hands, one on each side of him; and in a familiar and kindly tone, given even greater charm by the sweetness of his gaze, he delivered the following philippic:

ELEVEN

"My daughters, even though you were not to permit me to do so, I, both as a priest and friend, can and must upbraid you for that habit of mocking and parading, with elegant humor and literary touches, the gravest questions of morals and the Catholic faith. This is a vice acquired in the very high social sphere in which you live, and arises out of the habit of sprinkling your conversation with sparkling and dazzling ideas to divert and amuse yourselves, just as in the legitimate verbal games of society—supposing that they are honorable, which is a great deal to suppose. I do not need your permission to tell you that everything you have expressed about death and our purposes, both here and in the other world, is heretical, and in addition stupid and exaggerated to a degree, and that, in addition to lacking any Christian meaning, it is not in the least amusing. The innumerable imbeciles who frequent your tertulias and soirees can praise this subtle concept all they like, corrupt men and shameless women—some of the women, I don't say all. If you want to say something amusing, say it about matters pertaining to the temporal order. Make judgments lightly, and with originality, about things concerning the theater, the dance, or horse races or bicycle races. But in nothing having to do with conscience, in nothing that touches upon the grandiose plan imposed by the Creator on the creature, may you say anything that is out of harmony with what the last little girl, in the humblest and poorest school, knows and says. There is something very sad here, and it is that the upper classes are those which have most forgotten pure and eternal doctrine. And do not tell me that it is you who protect religion, strengthening worship with splendid ceremonies or organizing charitable brotherhoods and committees; in most cases, you merely surround Almighty God with official and worldly pomp, denying Him the homage of your own hearts. You want to make Him one of those constitutional monarchs we have nowadays, who reign but do not govern. No, and I am not saying this specifically for you two, but for other women of your class; so much ostentatious religion does you no good; external homage is not acceptable unless you accompany it with the surrender of your hearts and the submission of your intelligence. Be simple and childlike in matters of faith; render to intelligence what belongs to intelligence, and to God that which is and will always be God's."

The two ladies listened in absorption, drinking in with their own eyes the sweetness of the missionary's eyes, at the same time as they absorbed through their ears the ideas he expressed and welcomed them in their thoughts. During the brief pause that ensued the two ladies scarcely breathed, and he continued quietly, becoming a little more severe:

"You upper classes, or, to speak more plainly, you rich people, are deeply corrupted in your hearts and your intelligence, for you have lost your faith, or at least you are well on the way to losing it. How?

Because of the constant contact you have with trivial philosophizing. Philosophizing, in former times, did not cross the boundary that separates you from the lower classes; philosophizing was at that time a plebeian thing, a vulgar thing, and was usually personified in persons and types of persons who were profoundly disagreeable to you; bearded, ill-smelling scholars, uncombed poets who didn't know how to eat decently. But, ah, all that has changed. Philosophizing has become refined, has become elegant, has slipped in through your doors, and you give it shelter and flirt with it. You despised it before, now you pay it homage, and think that your tables are not sufficiently honored if you do not seat two or three disciples of Satan at them daily, and your soirees do not seem sufficiently elegant if you do not invite to them the whole horde of unbelievers, heretics, and atheists. You, the upper and wealthy classes, bored, tired because you do not have a glorious role to play in present-day society, have lowered yourselves to politics, like the sick and sad nobleman who, not knowing what to do for amusement, lowers himself to joking with the servants. Philosophizing, tired of living in cellars and among cobwebs, has risen into politics to find something to do there, and all of you have met on that common ground and have become friends. Then, falling into familiarities in bad taste, you take philosophy to higher levels, to your drawing rooms, and there the vile subject infects you with its perverse ideas, deadening the faith in your hearts. It is true that you possess a nominal faith, but only as an emblem, as a mark of class to defend yourselves with in case your rights are attacked and your positions menaced. We find the proof of this in the very latest habits of noble folk. Tell me: is it not perfectly obvious that your devotions are superficial and that there is nothing underneath them but indifference and corruption? You yourselves have laughed, this Christmas season, at the hostesses who offered a 'midnight mass with dancing to follow.' You yourselves have organized charitable concerts, and accept the theater and the lottery as instruments of charity with the same audacity as you carry theater into the church. All this is very well as long as you amuse yourselves, which is the supreme, the sole, aspiration of your souls."

The two ladies relaxed from their strained attention, each heaving a sigh from the depths of her breast, and Gamborena, after distributing pats on the hands of each, continued his discourse and ended by saying benevolently, "We must return to religious simplicity, my dear ladies; we must cleanse our hearts of every impurity and not allow frivolity to slip in where it does not belong, and where it is totally out of place. Do you want to be elegant ladies? Be as elegant as you like, without mixing God's word or Catholic doctrine into your epigrammatic gossipings. Let charity, worship, devotion, be serious things, not one among many subjects to show off the naughtiness of one's thoughts. If a woman has no faith, let her say so and stop playing comedies that deceive no one, and still less Him who sees everything. If she does have faith, let her learn how to have it simply; let her be like children when they learn Christian doctrine and like the humble and poor in spirit in practicing it, leaving all clever tricks for the devil, for he is the great talker and master of chitchat, and the one who wins in the end as a result of all these vanities of conversation. High lineage and wealth are often a heavy burden for souls who wish to rise still higher, and a great obstacle for those who seek simplicity. The trick is, my dear ladies, to achieve those ends without making a display of money and lineage, though there do exist some cases, but we will not speak of this because it is exceptional and extraordinary. If a person knows whom he is dealing with and the kind of times he lives in, he will not commit the foolishness of saying, 'Imitate those who, though they were noble and rich, tried to be poor and humble.' That you must not do. We live in very prosaic times, with a great deal of wretchedness and pusillanimity. Human willpower is diminishing visibly, like a tree that is turning into a shrub, and from a shrub to a potted plant. It can't be asked to perform great actions, just as the weakly pygmy cannot be commanded to don the armor of the heroic García de Paredes and walk away in it. No, my daughters, I am never going to tell you to be heroines, for you would laugh at me and you would be right. You are both dwarves, and no matter how much you preen yourselves, though you put on plumes of pride and high heels of vanity, you can never reach full size. That is why I tell you: since you are so very insignificant, try to be good Christians within the limitations of your spiritual means; continue to be aristocratic and rich; reconcile religious simplicity with the ostentation that your social position demands; and when the moment comes for you to pass out of this life, if you have been successful in purging the impurities that invade your hearts, you will not find the gates of eternal joy closed against you."

The ladies heard this homily with deep emotion, and were almost on the point of tears. When the missionary had finished, repeating the affectionate pats on his listeners' hands, Augusta merely sighed. Fidela appeared to be a bit frightened, and when she recovered from her fright, her mischievousness abruptly broke out in one of those remarks that the priest had just been criticizing:

"But if I can't purify myself completely, really completely, I hope that there will be a bit of latitude with me, and that you will open the heavenly gate for me."

"I?"

"Yes, you, you, for you have the keys."

"I?"

"My husband says so, and believes it, and because he believes it he calls you Saint Peter."

"It's a joke."

"And won't I deserve a bit of indulgence?"

"God alone gives indulgence."

"Well, look here, no one can get it out of my head that I'm going to need it soon, very soon."

"Oh, don't say such a thing!"

"You may both believe me. For several days I've been thinking about that, about my approaching death, and now, while you were speaking, the idea got into my head that I'm almost on the point of it, but never mind . . ."

"How foolish!"

"But I'm not frightened. On the contrary, I regard it with such serenity . . . To die . . . to sleep for a long, long time! Isn't that right, Father? Isn't that right, Augusta?"

Cruz entered the room at that moment and, having heard part of what her sister was saying, scolded her gently, observing the expression on her face. This must have seemed highly symptomatic of illness, though not enough to make her feel alarm.

"Of course, you spend all afternoon chatting, and then come the breathlessness and feeling of oppression. Don't do anything but listen, and speak as little as you can; especially, don't start to defend the innumerable foolish things that come into your mind, because when you argue you run out of breath, and there! you see . . ."

"I'm not so bad," said Fidela, breathing with difficulty.

"No, you're not so bad. But if I were you, I'd go to bed. You can see what kind of a day it is. With all the precautions in the world, and constantly putting wood in the fireplaces, we can't keep you from getting chilled. Isn't it true, Father, that she ought to go to bed?"

Her sister's insistence, seconded by Gamborena, led her to bed, where she felt better. After she had had a little nap, she became very cheerful and chatty. Augusta, who had not left her side, told her more than once to stop talking.

Nothing worthy of being recounted happened during the rest of the day. Gamborena and Cruz chatted in Fidela's sitting room and the latter, in her bedroom, amused herself with Valentinico and her faithful friend. After nightfall, a short time before the dinner hour, the little marquise of San Eloy awoke from a short and quiet sleep, breathing easily. How well she felt! So Augusta thought when she approached the bed and leaned over her. The nurse carried the little boy off to feed him, and then Fidela, caressing her friend's hand, told her in the most natural tone of voice in the world, "I have to tell you something."

"What?"

"I want to confess."

"Confess!" exclaimed Augusta, turning pale and hiding her perturbation. "But have you gone crazy?"

"I don't know why wanting to confess has to be a sign of craziness."

"But, my dear . . . they'll think you're ill."

"I don't know whether I'm ill or well. I don't know anything except that I want to confess . . . and the sooner the better."

"Tomorrow."

"Don't talk about tomorrow. It would be better tonight."

"But what kind of an idea have you had . . .?"

"Just an idea, you've said it yourself, an idea. Is that bad?"

"No . . . but it's an alarming idea."

"Well, so much the better. Do me the favor of telling my sister. Or tell Tor . . . No, you'd better tell my sister."

TWELVE

At the same instant that this was happening, Don Francisco was returning from the Senate, bringing with him his friend, a physician and senator, whom he had invited to dinner less for the pleasure of his company than to have him take a look at his wife, and thus to receive a free consultation about the irksome and persistent, though not serious, malady from which she suffered. The senator figured among the medical eminences and wanted to be a political eminence as well, for which purpose he had taken social reforms upon himself, pronouncing pompous and dreadfully boring discourses that Torquemada took delight in, for he found them in perfect agreement with his own ideas about such subjects. They had made friends in the corridors of the Senate, and almost always sat together in the Chamber. The doctor was a very agreeable man, and Don Francisco was extremely fond of refined men as long as they were disinterested and did not attack his pocketbook with the weapons of refined courtesy, like certain *individuals* whom our miser could not stomach.

And so the doctor-senator saw my lady the marquise, questioned her with exquisite delicacy and charm, and his opinion was reassuring to the family. It was all nothing more than anemia and a touch of hysteria. Quevedito's treatment struck him as admirable, and the desired improvement would have to be expected at his hands. He did not permit himself further comment than to recommend *rustication* when the summer arrived, residing in a mountain region far from the sea. Then they all dined in very high spirits; but Cruz observed in Augusta a sadness that was a very rare trait in her, for generally she enlivened the table and entertained her fellow diners wittily. Torquemada was loquacious, trying as hard as he could to shine in front of his friend, who brought up social problems willy-nilly between one course and another, and thereby caused a heated argument, for the doctor resolved the question by political means, the missionary by religious ones, and my lord marquis deplored exaggeration of all kinds. The two ladies, wretchedly bored, refrained from offering their opinions on so dull a matter.

When the meal was over, Augusta hastened to the bedroom and whispered to Fidela, "Cruz says tomorrow . . ."

"My sister did not say that."

"What do you mean?"

"No, because you haven't said anything to her yet. Look, I know everything and see everything from here. It's no use fibbing to me. And if you don't tell her right away, I'll have to tell her myself."

Cruz's unexpected presence in the bedroom, slipping in like a ghost, cut the dialogue short. At first, observing something strange in the attitude of both women, she thought that they were discussing some prank. She asked a question, they answered her, and at last she learned the truth about her sister's whim. Confess! When? Right away, right away! But what was the hurry? Her attempt, either real or feigned, to take the matter as a joke, had no more result than to confirm the other in her stubborn wish. It can easily be understood that that sudden desire for confession, since the lady's illness was no worse, made the family uneasy. Cruz went and told the story to Gamborena, and he told it to Don Francisco, who hurried to the bedroom in great alarm and said to his better half, "But what *phenomena* have got into you? Why, the doctor says that they're *reflex phenomena, exclusively reflex.* What's the point of this talk about confessing? You have plenty of time. My friend has gone, but I'll call him if you want . . . No, that won't be necessary. The fewer doctors that show up here, the better. Quevedo will be here very shortly, and among us all we'll convince you of how foolish you are."

Fidela, urgently interrogated by everyone, could not declare any dangerous symptom without lying. She had not a trace of fever, as Don Francisco proved again and again, for he considered himself a good taker of pulses. The only thing she felt was the oppression in her chest, the difficulty in breathing, as if an iron corset were pressing on her rib cage, and something else which, she thought, was pressing against her throat, like an internal noose to which she constantly raised her hands, believing that with them she could feel a large swelling there.

"But haven't I a huge lump here?"

"No, my dear, you haven't anything. It's all apprehension."

"*Reflex phenomena.*"

"Go to sleep, and you'll see."

"That's what I want to do, sleep, and see what's there beyond. But I think that I won't sleep a wink all night."

Quevedito, who had come in at about this time, found nothing new in her condition that ought to be a cause for alarm; but the invalid's low morale and the strange restlessness of her spirit at last aroused his concern, and he proposed to his father-in-law that Doctor Miquis be called into consultation on the following day. Meanwhile, Cruz was trying to convince Gamborena of the inadvisibility of going home on such a bitter and disagreeable night, and he did not insist, as on other occasions, on going off and facing the wind and cold. More than the troubles and even dangers of the journey, vague forebodings that his presence there might not be unnecessary kept him in the ducal mansion. At last he consented to sleep in the "cardinal's room" that had been prepared for him on the upper floor, and Cruz begged him to try to obtain from Fidela before he retired, with his all-powerful authority, postponement of the confession until the following day. No sooner said than done. The good priest went to the door of the bedroom, and from there, with persuasive affection in his voice, told the sick woman, "Do you know that your sister won't let me go home? I'm resigned, because the streets are icy: both horses and humans are afraid of sliding and breaking our legs. The thought you've had, my daughter, seems like a good one to me, a very good one. But precisely because you're no worse, you want to make your confession leisurely, when you're rested, like an obligation that you can perform at any time and in normal circumstances. Fine, just fine. But I am tired, you need to sleep, and since you have me here in the house, let's leave it till tomorrow. Sleep, dear child, go to sleep quietly. Good night."

A short time later Augusta took her leave, kissing her friend again and again and promising to come early next morning. Peace and quiet reigned in the household, but not in the heart of Cruz, who could not rest, and laid herself down like the duty officer when there is danger of an uprising. Don Francisco spent all night watching over his wife. He would enter the room on tiptoe and approach the bed like a ghost. The poor girl dozed for a few brief periods, but her sleep was short and far from restful.

"I'm awake," she said on one occasion. "Although you see me with my eyes closed, I'm not asleep, no. And how eager I am to have a good sleep, a long, long one!"

"Is there some new phenomenon, my dear?"

"No, nothing more than this awful feeling of oppression. If I didn't have that, I'd feel very well."

And later:

"My darling *distinguished man*, don't be frightened, this is nothing. Just a moment when my breathing stopped, and I thought I was choking."

"Do you want another spoonful of medicine?"

"No, not now. I think that all these potions are bad for me. Goodness! What awful things I dreamed in the minute I fell asleep! That our Valentín had torn out his eyes and was playing with them. And then he gave them to me to keep . . . Ta . . . ca . . . pa . . . ca . . . And what are you doing, why don't you go to bed, my poor little *distinguished man?*"

"As long as you're awake, I'll keep watch," said her husband, seating himself beside her. "I pride myself on being cautious and vigilant, and I'm *foresight personified.*"

"Why, nothing's the matter with me, I feel very well . . ."

"But we must *propend* to have you better. I've thought of a plan. Sometimes a fellow knows more than this flock of doctors who *pullulate* around here."

"If only I could go to sleep! But you'll see. By no later than tomorrow I'm going to have a long, long sleep . . ."

"When I can't sleep I start to add up figures, and to pull in and out of all the corners of my brain the arithmetic I learned when I was a boy."

"Well, I add things too, and the only sum I come up with is the thousand five hundred minutes that are left until I can sleep. What a head I have! See? Now I think that I feel sleepy. I'm breathing easily, and the lump in my throat has gone up to my eyes. My eyelids are heavy. Tor, my *distinguished man*, I assure you that Valentín will have a lot of talent, not talent for business, like you, but for poetry and for . . ."

She fell asleep. At daybreak, after several short periods of torpor, she had a slight attack of breathlessness. Torquemada became alarmed, but she reassured him, saying, "Dearest *dis—dis—tinguished man*, don't be frightened. It's nothing. I want to breathe, and my nose tells me to . . . breathe through my mouth . . . and my mouth . . . to breathe through my nose . . . and in this argument . . . See? Now it's over . . . now."

After full daylight came, she slept about two hours and woke up cheerful and loquacious, asking if Augusta had come. Her sister hastened to bring her breakfast, tea with milk, which she drank eagerly. Torquemada had gone off to rest, and Gamborena was preparing to say mass. The dawn of that day was stormy and glacial, like its predecessor, which did not keep Augusta Orozco from appearing in the palace, assiduous and apprehensive, a short time before mass was said, which she heard with great calmness and devotion. At nine o'clock, as Gamborena was having breakfast in the sacristy and the harsh screechings of the heir apparent, and the noise of the blows he was delivering with his stick to benches and chairs, resounded in the down-stairs halls, Augusta went up to the bedroom and chatted with Fidela about pleasant and agreeable things that made her laugh. During the best part of this enjoyable conversation, the priest entered saying cheerfully, "My young friend, just now you are superfluous here. Fidela and I have to have a little talk."

The lady left the bedroom, and marquise and missionary were left alone. The confession was long, though not as long as the sleep that she desired.

THIRTEEN

"What now?" Augusta asked the priest, in Cruz's sitting room, while the latter was spending a little while with her sister. "After the confession, are we going to have viaticum?"

"*Are we going to have!* You speak of it, my friend, as if you were talking about a garden party or a cotillion."

"No, that's not it. I mean . . ."

Torquemada suddenly entered, asking the same question: "What now? *Have we got viaticum?*"

"We'll wait until she requests it," said Augusta, "or until the doctors tell us that it's expedient. I find her quite well, and see no cause for alarm. Poor little angel!"

"She's a saint," said the miser in a solemn tone, "and it would be neither just nor equitable to have her die so soon, when there are any number of men and women in the world who are confoundedly un-necessary."

"Only God knows who ought to die," added the priest, "and whatever He decides is correctly decided."

"Yes; but it's not so easy for a fellow to resign himself just like that, *willy-nilly*," replied Torquemada, becoming annoyed. "I should say not! I admit that all of us are mortal, but I'd ask the Most High for a little more logic and political consistency, I mean mortiferous consistency. This much is clear. Those who ought to die, don't die, and have seven lives, like cats, and they'd do a *signal service* to all of humanity if they'd take off for the other world."

Gamborena did not answer and went off to pray in the chapel.

A short time later Fidela, who had stayed in bed on the recommendation of the whole family and on the orders of Quevedito, asked them to bring her the child, who, though at first he sulked because they would not let him play his inane games in the downstairs halls, lost no time in accepting the company of his mother, the only person to whom he ever showed any affection. Tired of running around the bedroom brandishing his whip, he insisted on being put on the bed, and crawled all over it on hands and knees, imitating the dog and the pig; and sometimes he crawled hastily toward the head of the bed and let his mama kiss him, and sometimes down to its foot, biting the bedspread and uttering "gru-gru" noises to make Augusta believe that he was some terrible little animal who was going to eat one of her hands.

"He's adorable," said Fidela, enchanted with his game. "Don't tell me that this child is going to be stupid. What he's got is a lot of mischievousness, and in him this animal naughtiness prefigures the intelligence of the grown man."

She would wiggle her feet inside the sheets so that he could bury his face in the hump in the bedclothes, with the leaps and attacks of a hunting animal, and then he would stand up with legs wide apart, and then sniff the air, squatting on his hindquarters and supporting himself on his hands, and then, at last, would sit down and rub his little muzzle with movements like those of a trained bear tired of amusing people. But his chief diversion was to frighten the people who stood around the bed and his mama herself, barking at them, pretending to butt them, with his mouth open in all its frightening width. It is true that he never really ate them, but he made them think that he would, to judge by the cries of alarm with which they greeted his furious attacks. Finally he stretched out at full length beside his mother and, resting his face against hers, stayed for a long time gazing at her very fixedly, without uttering a grunt or any word whatsoever. Augusta was amazed by the fact that Valentinico's gaze was less sullen and perverse than usual, but she made no comment about it.

"Why, this child of mine is so good!" said Fidela delightedly. "Now he's whispering such clever little secrets into my ear! Ta, ta, pa, ca . . . that he loves me very much, and other very pretty things, very very pretty things."

More than once Cruz put him on the floor to keep him from bothering his mother; but he, with a tenacious attraction that was the strangest thing about that memorable day, managed to get back on the bed. You would have believed that he understood the need to be quiet and good in order to receive those honors. No one had ever seen him so subdued, nor noticed such a sweet expression in the ta, ca, and pa that he constantly pronounced, nor had he ever had the patience to stay there quietly, with his little muzzle very close to his mother's face, letting her caress him and hearing from her lips the tender words that surely he was unable to understand. He fell asleep for a while, and Fidela would not let them take him away from her. She too slept, with a serenity which all felt was a good omen, and indeed that little sleep would have done her good had it been longer.

Owing to the delay in Doctor Miquis's visit, for he could not come until the afternoon, Cruz and Don Francisco were extremely anxious, both of them eager to draw hope from the famous doctor's visit. Before he arrived Fidela had another mild attack of respiratory distress, followed by a very brief collapse, of which only Augusta, the only person present at the time, was aware. Valentinico climbed up on the bed again, and although a short time before a certain amount of gentleness could be observed in his eyes (unless this was the effect of the benevolent opinion of those watching him), they soon noticed in them the peculiarly combative expression that they usually had. Perhaps this had to do with his small body, contrasting as it did with the large head and a sort of catlike coloring in his dark pupils. No one knows. But they all said, and Augusta first of all, that that was not the innocent and seductive gaze of a child. What a devilish little creature he was! He took it into his head to lie like a dog at his mother's feet, and to warn off with grunts everyone who approached, showing his teeth and preparing to bite whoever tried to do so, even his very own father or his aunt.

"How spirited he is!" said Fidela. "How he defends his mother! This is real intelligence, this is love . . . But goodness, no one is hurting me, darling! Be quiet and don't move much, for you're bothering me."

Miquis entered just then, and they carried off the savage child, whose howls protested his inability to be present during such an important visit. It was long, and very protracted was the examination which that peerless physician made of his illustrious patient. He encouraged her with his courteous and compassionate words, then showed himself noncommittal with the family, and at last, when he and Quevedito were alone, they spoke more or less as follows:

"But what in the world are you thinking of? What are you doing? Are you an utter fool?"

"I? What . . .?" stammered Torquemada's son-in-law, turning pale. "Why are you saying that to me, Don Augusto?"

"Because you're a blind man if you can't see that this poor lady is very ill indeed. A fine time to let me know, when it's already . . .! It's possible there's still time, but I doubt it. The cardiac depression is so severe that I fear a collapse, and if the collapse comes with the intensity I expect, there's nothing to prescribe, unless it be the viaticum."

Quevedito wiped the sweat from his face. His color ebbed and flowed, and he did not know what reply to give to the terrifying words of his friend and master, who continued, "But why are you giving so much digitalis? Enough of that, enough, and prepare injections of caffeine and ether, and inhalations of oxygen . . . to be ready for what's sure to come tonight."

"Then you fear . . ."

"I hope I'm mistaken. But don't commit yourself with the family by making optimistic statements which, unfortunately, might be illusory. Don't give them hope."

"Do you fear that the collapse . . . ?"

"Has already begun. I've recognized it in the irregular pulse, in her face, which is becoming distorted or seems about to become distorted . . ."

"I hadn't observed . . ."

"Then what good is medical divination, the art of seeing beyond phenomena in the almost invisible traces that they leave in the organism? I'll return tonight. Don't leave the patient's side, and observe everything that happens minute by minute."

"So you'll come back?"

"Yes. I feel that our treatment will get nowhere and that the poor lady won't last the night."

These lugubrious words disconcerted the good Quevedito so much that, when the other doctor had left and Cruz, feeling anxious, came to consult with the house physician, he could not hide his distress. He was almost at the point of bursting into tears. He responded jerkily to Cruz's and Don Francisco's eager questions, struggling between professional veracity and family feeling.

"A bad diagnosis . . . why hide it? Bad . . . bad. It would be worse to give you hopes, for . . . But we mustn't lose them yet, no, no, not that . . . No more digitalis. We'll have to give her injections . . . inhalations . . . we'll see tonight. I think Miquis exaggerates the degree of seriousness. These high-toned doctors are like that. They make a great to-do about the simplest thing, so that they can come out of it saying . . . But the seriousness exists, a relative seriousness . . . and it's better to be prepared."

FOURTEEN

Cruz's first thought, as she bravely recovered her composure in the face of danger, was to call immediately on the chief medical eminences of Madrid. After listening to his son-in-law, Torquemada flung up his arms and began to vent all his anger on Miquis:

"That man's crazy. That man's a rascal who wants to exploit us. He sees that there's *dough* in the house and says, 'This is the spot for me.' No, no, out with famous doctors, who don't know anything at all. To say that there's serious danger! Where and why? Heavens, just by looking at her you can tell that it's only *a few little smidgens* of reflex phenomenon, a neglected cold, the vapors, and the little indispositions it leaves behind. This is a swindle, a plot, *so to speak*."

He soon changed his mind, *compromising* on their bringing in as many important doctors as might be necessary, and then his excited brain came up with the most extravagant ideas: for example, that of calling a famous folk healer from the Calle de La Cava de San Miguel. He knew him and could testify to his marvelous cures. Nothing would be lost, therefore, by bringing him in, for if he did not cure he did no harm; his entire therapeutics consisted of well water and massaging the stomach and torso with a brush made of herbs. The man was so confused that he soon laughed at his own advice, and again raised a doubt as to the medical profession's competence to cure anyone.

The news of the marquise of San Eloy's grave illness circulated among the friends of the family with astonishing rapidity, and also reached the Senate before the end of the session; hence Don Francisco was assaulted, during the early evening hours, by a multitude of friends both political and private who, with emphatic demonstrations of feeling, gave him a bad time for longer than his grief and desire for solitude were willing to accept. He paid heed to no one, not even to those who, giving themselves airs as optimistic prophets, assured him of a happy ending to the illness. The skinflint cursed everything, his friends as well as science, cursed both fate and the *so-called . . . lofty designs of . . . whoever-it-is*. Even the company and consolatory remarks of Donoso, his friend and in a certain sense his teacher in enlightenment, irritated him on that unhappy night. He refused to eat a mouthful, and when the unwelcome visitors began to depart, he wandered from one part of the palace to the other like a madman strolling among ghosts, for that is exactly the way he viewed the religious or pagan figures, some nude, some ill-dressed in *sheets* or *bedspreads*, which peopled salons and galleries.

Meanwhile Fidela had passed, during the melancholy transition from day to night, through different fluctuations, at moments desperately ill and at other moments so much improved that the family did not know whether to fear or hope. Augusta did not leave her bedside; the hands of one woman, intertwined with those of the other, confirmed at those critical moments the intense love against which death itself could not prevail.

"You feel better now, much better, don't you? Don't think that you've frightened us very much. It's perfectly obvious that it's nothing."

"That's right, it's nothing," said Fidela, recovering the vivacity of her speech. "If I could keep on feeling as I do now . . . I feel well; I'm breathing easily and—what a strange thing!—my memory has been so refreshed that I see everything very clearly, and any number of things that I had forgotten, insignificant things, come to my imagination now as if they had happened yesterday."

"Really? How amusing! But look, don't talk much. You know that the doctors want you to keep your mouth shut. Not talking is easy medicine."

"Let me talk a little bit. Why, it's what I like best in all the world! Chatter . . . my passion."

"All right, I'll let you have a bit of chatter. If Quevedo and your sister find out, they'll scold me."

"Goodness, what a strange thing! I was bragging about my memory, and now it's slipped away from me . . . Nothing . . . I'd meant to ask you something, and I've forgotten. But it was only half a minute ago that I had it right here, on the tip of my tongue!"

"Then leave it for later."

"Ah, now I have it! You'll see: just a few words. Tell me something. Do you think that the dead come back?"

"Look, my dearest girl," answered Augusta, feeling a chill in her heart, "don't speak of the dead. Heavens, what foolishness comes into your mind!"

"And why is it foolishness? I'm asking you if you believe that people who die . . . come back to the world of the living. Listen, I think that they do, and that one shouldn't laugh at the fairy tale about souls in purgatory."

"I don't know anything about that. Do be still, or I'll call Cruz."

"No, no! She'd give me an awful scolding! I believe that when one is a free spirit one can come and go as one pleases. What I don't know is whether you'll be able to see me as I see you . . . And take care not to do anything naughty . . . For look, I'll be watching you."

Augusta was trembling. An instinctive terror took hold of her and, as there was little light in the room, she seemed to see specters arising from those shadows, specters who slowly and terrifyingly drew nearer.

"What do you think about this?" insisted Fidela, a trifle uneasily. "At some time in your life, under very serious circumstances—do you know what I mean?—have you ever seen the image of some beloved person who had died? Because it seems to me that it's an indispensable condition for the person to be beloved, very much beloved, before the fact of seeing that person, seeing him or her as I see you, can be true."

"Bah, bah! Will you stop talking if I tell you the thing you'd most like to hear? Very well, if you'll stop talking I'll say yes. But don't ask any more questions. If one loves very much, then . . . There, that's enough. All this might keep you awake, and you must sleep, my poor darling."

"Why, I want to go to sleep too. That's what we're talking about, silly. I like your answer! Those who sleep, dream, and the person who dreams lives in dreams, and his sleeping self may perhaps be his visible image. There's a philosophy for you! Ah, don't let Father Gamborena hear us! A fine sermon he'd spout at us! Yes, to sleep, sleep."

She closed her eyes, and Augusta, after pulling up the covers around her throat, kissed her tenderly and lulled her to sleep as one does with children. Cruz entered the room on tiptoe, and when she had been told how quiet Fidela was, went out again. Just then three eminences, in addition to Miquis and Quevedito, were holding a consultation, and there was great anxiety in the family to know the outcome of the scientific discussion. Unfortunately the eminent medical team confirmed fully and categorically Miquis's opinion about the seriousness of the illness and imminent danger. The much-feared catastrophe might be delayed for a day, two days, or occur at the most unexpected moment, that very night.

Cruz tried to consult with Torquemada about whether to bring the viaticum without loss of time; but Don Francisco, through Donoso, whom he was using to carry out these consultations, refused to offer his opinion about so grave a matter. His dejection and pessimism deprived him of the quiet reflection needed to solve any problems whatsoever. Gamborena, meanwhile, under the pretext of visiting the sick woman, entered her bedroom. He saw that she was asleep; he waited. A short time later, Fidela awoke. She was very happy to see the missionary, and told him that she wanted to make her peace with God.

Everyone left the room, and Gamborena, as was natural, took advantage of this excellent opportunity to suggest the administration of the sacrament. There was not perfect agreement about the hour, because the sick woman said, "Tomorrow." Cruz did not want to go against her wishes by showing haste, and the priest compromised, giving a resourceful interpretation to the word "tomorrow."

"Very early then, very early. That's best. It's ten o'clock at night."

At about eleven o'clock, when the much-feared collapse had already begun, Don Francisco went to the bedroom. The same terror that invaded his spirit gave him an ardent desire to see the heartbreaking spectacle of that precious life about to be extinguished in the flower of its youth, a horrific flaunting of logic, common sense, and even the laws of nature, which are *sacrosanct*, yes indeed, *sacrosanct*, unless they let themselves be influenced, mind you! by the whims that come from above. Ashen and bewildered, he gazed at his beloved wife, unable to articulate a word or a complaint, and there he stayed like a statue, feeling, even more strongly than he had felt the terror of entering the bedroom, the terror of leaving it. He found neither the word nor the movement to take himself away from there. At last Augusta, who was weeping bitterly, took him by the arm, telling him between her sobs, "Go away, Don Francisco, this is affecting you too deeply."

The poor man found himself outside the room when he least expected it, and silently, his hands clasped behind his back, his lips pursed, his teeth tightly clenched, as if he would never in all his life utter another word, he went to his study on the main floor, which was empty because Donoso was also upstairs, dealing with something having to do with the imposing ceremony that was being prepared.

FIFTEEN

The marquis of San Eloy shut himself into his room like a fugitive creeping thing which feels secure only in the crack that shelters it; but since that crack was, in this case, of fairly large size, the poor man passed the time by measuring his misfortune, by walking it from one end of the room to the other as if, by stretching it and pacing it up and down, he could make it less profound. Truly, it was a wicked thing—he was on the verge of saying "a raw deal"—well, a tremendous injustice, for Cruz ought to have been the one condemned to die, because of her age and the fact that she wasn't the least use in the world, instead of the other one dying, the good, sweet Fidela. What a blunder, my God! And he had the guts to say so in the Eternal Father's face, as he would say it to the nuncio and the Pope himself, to have them go and tell Him.

"What was the reason for Fidela's death? What is the reason?" he repeated furiously, turning his face toward the ceiling as if he expected to find his interlocutor's face painted there. "Is this fair? Is this merciful and divine? Divine! Some divinities those are that they have up there! Well, I'll tell *His Lordship* that He hasn't convinced me, and that all this business about infinitely wise, infinitely . . . I dunno, I take it all with a grain of salt. Well, now, I don't like to fawn on powerful folks, those who are above me. Fawning just doesn't agree with my character. We've got to have dignity. And what is prayer but fawning; that is, kissing the rod that breaks our backs? I . . . after all . . . would pray if it were necessary, if I knew that I'd find mercy; but

. . . fat chance of that . . . mercy! Ah, only a fool could swallow that! That's obvious. Any mercy there is, they can throw it right in my face. What else? How can I forget the case of my first Valentín, that bit of angel that they took away from me in the most awful and uncivilized way, scuttling all the laws of nature, and no prayers or alms or anything did me any good? Go on, let others fawn! A fellow's no fool, a fellow's not a nobody, a fellow's not just an insect."

Tired of striding up and down, he sat in a chair, elbows on the table, and covered his eyes with both hands.

"Dammit!" he said. "I think I must be raving. With what I'm going through, it's no wonder. Even if everybody in the house went crazy with praying we wouldn't accomplish anything, for the illness, at this point, is one of those that's hopeless. Poor little Fidela is dying. She's dying without a hope of cure. Maybe she's died already. To save her, That One would have to do a little miracle, and as for that . . . He does do favors . . . but miracles . . . A fellow can't be sure it's true He does them. Favors, yes; but these giveaways are only for extra-pious folks and church mice. A fellow can't descend to their level, mind you! To be sure, if they'd promise me that . . . I'd make myself humble, I certainly would. But, by a hundred thousand bibles! to leave me holding the bag as they did in Valentín's case . . ."

He began to walk up and down again, transfixed with grief and terror, tormented by the picture of his dying wife, present in his mind with all the traits and shades of pure reality. He could see her, he was seeing her as if he had her before his eyes. How much better it would have been for him not to go into the bedroom, to have stayed outside . . . saving himself the pain of seeing her dying and the torment of keeping that vision, that photograph in his brain, which would not be blotted out if he lived a thousand years! Unconscious, no longer able to see anyone, perhaps already glimpsing things in heaven, poor little Fidela was dying unawares, her eyes sunken, the pupils dull and blank, rolled upward as if they were trying to look at the inside of her skull; her mouth panting, the lips contracting and expanding like the mouths of fish in a fishbowl; a purplish circle around her mouth which disfigured her face horribly; her skin damp from the cold sweat that covered it; her hair stuck to her temples, also looking dead, false, like a wig that has slipped to one side, out of place; and, finally, the motionless body already sunk in inertia, no longer reacting. Only in her fingers did a little muscular life remain, expiring in slight contractions. Such was the pitiable image which Don Francisco had seen, and which had remained stamped on his mind with sufficient force to transfer it from his mind to reality.

Some time passed, he was unable to say how much, in that painful musing, feeling deeply, seeing clearly what he did not want to see, struggling to blot out the picture when it grew too lifelike and to bring it to mind anew when it vanished, for though it was painful to see, he felt disconsolate when he did not perceive it; and to his other torments was soon added the torment of doubt. Had she already died, or was she still alive? Nothing in the world would have induced him to return to the bedroom. Why did they not inform him of her death, if indeed it had taken place? It was probable that she still lived. Had they brought her the viaticum? No, because he would have heard noises of people stirring, and the mournful tinkling of the bell. The palace was large, but not so large that a ceremony of such a nature could take place without his knowledge. He thought he heard a strange bustling noise. They had come from the parish church! It must be extreme unction, for it could not be the viaticum.

Then he listened carefully to the noises that sounded in the immense building. At times so profound a silence reigned that everything seemed dead, everything quiet and mute, like the figures in the paintings that adorned the ducal mansion; at times he heard the hurried footsteps of servants hastily running up or down the stairs as if in search of something very urgent. He was tempted on more than one occasion, when he heard the step of some servant passing his lair, to go to the door and ask . . . But no. If he was told of the death, how could he bear to hear it? And besides, all the servants had become so hateful to him that he did not want to have anything to do with them, and if perchance they answered him rudely, he would have a hard time to keep himself from kicking them. At last his anxiety grew so great that he opened the door a crack. Opposite him was a broad, well-lighted gallery. How much sadness was expressed in its golden spaces! Footsteps could be heard, indeed, but very far away, upstairs, up there, where what was happening . . . was happening. At the end of the gallery he saw an enormous nude figure, with its head near the ceiling and its great legs above a door. It was a canvas by Rubens, which Don Francisco thought the most irritating thing in the world, an ugly, stupid fellow chained to a rock. Folks said that he was Prometheus, an individual of mythological antiquity. The fellow must have played some very bad tricks, for a big bird was eating his gizzard, a torment which in the opinion of the marquis of San Eloy he richly deserved. A bit closer to him he saw a nymph whom he also found irritating: almost naked, the shameless hussy, with her breasts in full view, and as stiff as if she had swallowed a chocolate beater. Torquemada could not remember her name, but she too had something to do with Greeks and Trojans. Suddenly he wanted to go out with a cudgel and start hitting the statue (a copy of the Daphne of Naples), which decorated the far end of the gallery, and to break it in pieces to make that hussy stop pointing her provocative finger, or laughing in his face. But it would have been madness to break it, valuable as it was.

Just then he heard the sound of footsteps on the staircase, and closed the door in fright. "Now they're coming, now they're coming to tell me." Then he remembered that he had given his valet strict instructions not to bring him messages, that he did not want to know anything or see anyone. "*Welladay*, that's why not so much as a fly comes to my room. They're afraid of me."

By this time it was about two o'clock in the morning. The noise in the upper story of the house grew louder. Don Francisco felt intensely cold, tossed another coat on top of the one he was wearing, and continued to walk. "Surely," he said to himself, "it has already happened. I can almost see it. Cruz must be going wild with grief . . . and she feels it, I don't doubt that she feels it. But she won't be the one to come and tell me. Donoso, maybe. No, not he; he won't leave his beloved Cruz's side for a moment, to console her and make both of them—ah, how well I know them—start thinking about arrangements for the funeral. Donoso won't come. Neither will Augusta, for she really will be grief-stricken. She loved her so much! Ah, now I have it! The right one to give me the sad news is the priest, my Señor Gamborena, who must be upstairs too, spouting Latin. Fat lot of good that'll do! We'll see what holy religion is good for. This Saint Peter or Saint Pete, whom I take to be the gatekeeper of the heavenly abodes, can't or won't keep people who ought not to die from dying. Sure, what they want is to carry off more and more people up there. They don't care who it is. At the bottom of all this saintliness there's a lot of selfishness, so to speak. Oh, yes, the holy Gamborena will be the one ticked off to bring me the news. When he doesn't bring it, it means that she's still . . ." He went to the door and laid his ear against it. He heard nothing. "Maybe the missionary won't come to tell me anything either! Heavens, I'm bursting with anxiety. Maybe in the end I'll have to go upstairs and . . . Let's walk a bit more."

He had taken a few dozen turns around the room when he heard footsteps. His heart nearly leaped out of his chest. Yes, those were Gamborena's footsteps. He would have known them among the thousands and thousands of footsteps of a marching throng. Even the good clergyman's way of walking revealed the grave news of which he was the messenger, and before his arrival he was already announcing it with his feet, with their solid, rhythmic tread, with the noise of his shoe soles on the flooring. At last the footsteps stopped at the door; it was opened with ceremonious slowness, and Torquemada saw appear in the rectangle, like a luminous shape in a black frame, the figure of the foreign missionary, his face like an old carving with its warm, bronzed patina, his bald head shining, his body all in black, his eyes with an angelic expression. Don Francisco fixed his own upon him, his look saying, "I know . . . I know." And the priest, in an emotional, solemn voice, a terrible voice, which sounded in the miser's ears like the crackling of worlds breaking apart, told him, "Señor, it was God's will!"

· PART II ·

ONE

It is a proven fact that, moments after receiving the news of the death, to which the reverend Gamborena added some extremely sad details, Don Francisco stretched out his arms and then one of his legs—in the vernacular, lower extremities—and fell flat on the floor in a spasmodic attack very like the one that came over him when he witnessed his first Valentín's death. A number of servants rushed to their master's aid and held him down, and with the greatest difficulty succeeded in carrying him to his bedroom, where he was given a series of rubdowns that would have sufficed for an ox, until Quevedito could take charge of him. The fit passed, and in the morning, after a short rest, Señor Donoso was able to go and see him and discuss with him a subject as important as the lady marquise's burial and funeral honors. The good friend of the household was uniquely qualified to deal with these questions, and explained and discussed them with an aplomb and a vocabulary which anyone might have envied for the highest purposes of state. Don Francisco was emphatically in no mood for discussions, and tried to cut short his friend's oratorical flights.

"It has to be a first-class funeral? I understand that. But I don't see the need to make it so very showy. Of course it must be in harmony with our . . . comfortable . . . position, but you know that I don't like pomps or Oriental luxuries. Because what you're proposing is like a kind of . . . satanic pride . . . or something like an apotheosis that . . ."

"It is not that, my dear Don Francisco. It's an homage, the only homage that we can pay to the beloved remains of that angel."

He then said that Cruz wished to endow the burial and funeral with all the sumptuousness possible, but she was making no decisions without knowing the opinion of the person who ought to make all the arrangements in the house, and when Torquemada heard this he expressed himself with astonishing candor, discharging the whole contents of his heart and his conscience.

"My friend, I'll be frank with you. If it were a question of our burying her, my illustrious sister-in-law, we ought to do it no matter what the cost, because of the saying 'If your enemy flees, give him a silver bridge.' "

"For God's sake, my friend!"

"Let me finish, dammit! I'm saying that when a good disaster comes to somebody, that is, a disaster that brings rest and peace, it doesn't matter to spend lots of money on the burial. But when the disaster is a bad one, one of the kind that hurts, eh? then to spend too much on funeral honors is piling one bad thing on top of another and combining grief with grief. Because, to recapitulate: you will not fail to recognize, if you think about it, that insofar as logic is concerned, and establishing the principle that one of them had to die, it shouldn't have been Fidela but her sister. It seems as clear as crystal to me."

"It's neither clear nor unclear: it is simply blasphemous, for only God knows and decides who is going to die. Let us accept His designs."

"Let's attack . . . I mean, let's accept everything you like. I accept, mind you, when and if it's proved to me that those designs don't include a perfectly obvious negation of . . ."

"That's enough, my dear marquis; I cannot let you continue along that absurd train of thought. With the grief you feel, your head is just a trifle upset."

"That could well be, for such a terrible blow would upset anyone. Let's not talk about it any more, and you are authorized to represent me in any arrangements about the burial. I admit the reasons you have brought forward. Is it appropriate to have pomp? Then let's have pomp, a whole lot of pomp, and on to the next one . . . I mean, no more of 'em."

With so broad an authorization, and with so much money in hand, Cruz and Donoso arranged everything just as they pleased, and each outdid the other in suggesting what should be done to make everything sumptuous and impressive, the most beautiful combination possible of the elegant and the mortuary. The preparations began that very morning with febrile activity, and the house was invaded by tradesmen of this and that branch of business among all the branches having to do with funeral matters. The invitations were as simple as they were elegant; the most magnificent hearse in Madrid was selected; wreaths of phenomenal richness were ordered; and finally, the funeral chapel was prepared with all the sumptuousness of which so splendid an abode was capable. The great salon was floored in black. On the walls were hung Tristan's six colossal canvases of *The Martyrdom of St. Agatha* and other religious and mystical subjects of impressive appearance; on the far wall a magnificent altar with the triptych by Van Eyck, and under it an *Ecce Homo* by the "divine" Morales. Murillos and Zurbaráns formed its accompaniment on either side. The lower part of the room's four walls was upholstered in black with a narrow gold border, and two other altars were set up with very fine sculptured images, Juan de Juni's *Christ Tied to the Column* and Gregorio Hernández's *Mater Dolorosa*. The benches that were placed around the room, made of walnut and studded with nails, were also a masterpiece of antique carpentry and came from the Cisneros collections. Prominent on the three altars were fabulously valuable reliquaries, marble reliefs, and magnificent bronzes. Donoso, along with two other friends of the household who were artists or amateurs of refined taste, supervised the task, aided by an infinite number of servants, sewing women, carpenters, etc. Cruz and Augusta would go to look and offer an opinion, but they could not be there all the time. All of the former's immense willpower did not suffice to distract her from her terrible grief. She gave orders that no expense be spared which might increase the splendor of that homage, inadequate as it was to the merits of the poor dead girl.

Everyone worked so hard that morning that before two o'clock all was in place, arranged beautifully and with supreme artistry, and amid it all and raised above the rest, under the splendid canopy of the imperial bed, Fidela was sleeping her *long, long* sleep with that absolute abandon, as solemn as it is sad, of an inert thing, the faded image of what once had life and movement. Dressed in a simple habit of the Virgin of Sorrows, with a white headdress and black gown, her face scarcely disfigured, serene and all but smiling, her appearance demonstrated to the utmost degree the resemblance between sleep and death. Hundreds of candles spread a reddish light over the room and reflected a feeble glow on the dead woman's face, light's last offering to darkness.

That afternoon innumerable wreaths, some of monstrous size, were delivered, with a varied abundance of very beautiful flowers. The silk ones were an elegant imitation of natural flowers, brought from far-off climes. Proud of the permanence of their tints and their deceptive freshness, they envied the other flowers the rich aroma they did not possess, and which, since they were nearby, they stole from the fresh ones. The live flowers could not conceal their desire to wilt, tending to languish in that warm, somnolent atmosphere. Violets and pale roses joined their mournful colors to the affectedly elegaic tints of the artificial blooms, and the decaying fragrance of natural flowers mingled with the factory odor of the artificial ones. This mixture of odors became mingled with that of burning wax, and the result was indefinable, a vague sensation of the mysterious chemistries by which life decomposes and decomposition becomes life again.

A large number of the public (understanding by "public" the host of friends) came in the afternoon to sign the lists. Some went upstairs to admire the funeral chapel, in which there were great comings and goings all afternoon. To avoid crowding it was arranged, as in royal palaces, that the public could enter by the great gallery and exit through the rotunda, thus passing, in a little space, through the most beautiful parts of the building. Footmen in mourning livery maintained adherence to the rules of traffic, which only very intimate friends were allowed to infringe. As can easily be understood, there was no lack of busy journalists, the kind who can slip through the eye of a needle. They were going to take note of all that magnificence in order to write about it in the newspaper. Nothing escaped those rascals, who were concentrating on prolixity of description and on collecting names of persons and personages. The licentiate Juan de Madrid, who made an appearance there, wrote a description of the house and the marvels contained in it, omitting no precious scrap of biographical information about the House of Torquemada-San Eloy. At the main entrance of the house the visitors' signatures already filled a fabulous number of sheets of paper, and the pile of visiting cards was so large that it seemed like something that had rained in, a hailstorm of paper or something resembling one.

TWO

On the morning of the burial, and half an hour before the procession set out, all the balconies on the street were replete with people. There was reason for their curiosity, since it was rare that the serenity of those districts was disturbed by so much hurly-burly and movement. The appearance of the funeral coach, drawn by eight black horses wearing plumes, caused a real sensation. That day all the children played truant from nearby schools; their cries and antics filled the street with joy, and in the midst of so much cheerful hubbub the ridiculous, unwieldy black coach and its ill-aligned steeds seemed almost comic, no doubt from contagion by the onlookers' good cheer. The children, with great agility, ran in front of it and behind it, and when the carriage stopped, the footmen with their powdered wigs had to shoo them away with slaps to free themselves from their annoying curiosity. This and the Senate carriage, looking like something in a Mardi Gras parade, and the crowd of different vehicles that were coming from both ends of the street, kept the municipal police busy, for there were not nearly enough of them to supervise such a complicated task.

Inside the house, the invasion of sad-faced persons dressed in mourning grew larger by the minute. Everyone visited the funeral chapel, whose atmosphere it was impossible to breathe for long without growing dizzy. Nuns from different congregations were kneeling in prayer. Gamborena and other priests had been saying mass in the oratory from dawn until nine o'clock. The servants had not had a chance to rest since the previous night, and exhaustion rather than grief was stamped on the men's freshly shaved faces.

Senators, important businessmen, political leaders and more or less genuine friends went to visit Don Francisco in his study, after rehearsing the sighs they were going to emit and the doleful phrases that the circumstances demanded. They found him dressed in deepest mourning, very clean, his face sagging and showing signs of sleeplessness, his hair neatly combed, clumsy in word and gesture.

"Thank you, thank you, señores," he told them, expressing himself in set phrases. "There's no consolation, nor can there be."

And to the next visitor he said the same thing: "A tremendous misfortune, unexpected . . . Who could have expected it, when the natural thing would have been . . . ? I appreciate these manifestations. But there's no consolation, nor can there be. *Let us attack*, I mean let us accept the designs . . . Señores, I appreciate these manifestations. There's no consolation, that's true, there is none. Consolation is a myth. I didn't believe that this misfortune would *transpire* now. It has taken me by surprise. What alternative do I have but to resign myself and accept *the accomplished facts?"*

Meanwhile, a new outbreak of childish glee took place on the street with the appearance of the entire clergy of San Marcos Church, the great cross and huge processional candles, the three parish priests dressed in full vestments and then, in two flanking lines, a couple of dozen others in surplice and biretta. The constant movement of the carriages forced them to disperse, stumbling here and there over the numerous children and a flock of goats which at that moment, by awful coincidence, happened to pass by en route to the dairy shop at Number 15. And such heated discussions arose among the coachmen and the municipal police and the goatherd that the priests had to hear things very different from the liturgy they were about to chant. In the confusion, the bassoon player could not avoid being carried away by the human wave to a considerable distance from the clergy, suffering several squeezings of his person and not a few bashings of his mournful instrument. At last, order restored, the parish party entered the palace and went up to the funeral chapel. The youngsters would have given part of their future life to follow them upstairs and poke their noses into everything, seeing the bier, which was said to be like a monument, and hearing the priests' singing. While they were intoning responses in front of the imperial bed, the florists vied with each other (for there were two, and they were bitter rivals) to place their wreaths in such a way as to make them more visible and more impressive. And the newsgatherers took notes on everything they saw, also lending an ear to the flower-makers' hints about having their businesses mentioned in the newspaper; and the servants set themselves in motion; and Donoso issued autocratic orders to clear the salon; and the priests went downstairs, the employees of the funeral business went upstairs; and the corpse was carried down on the shoulders of four footmen in black liveries. The palace became filled with a grave, whispering murmur, more of footsteps than of voices, and on the broad staircase, in the lower gallery, and in the vestibule, people were so crowded together that the footmen who were carrying the coffin had to stop two or three times before they reached the street.

It was a formidable task to get the mournful procession moving, for the wretched florists spent more than a quarter of an hour exhibiting their wreaths on the coffin and the four columns of the carriage. The effect was very beautiful, with so many flowers of so many gentle colors, and the splendid ribbons with gold lettering hanging from them here and there. Since there was not room for all of them on the coach, the rest were placed in an open landau which was to follow immediately after the hearse. The police had managed to control traffic on the public street, clearing it as best they could of stubborn bystanders and shameless little boys. Thanks to this, the poor folk from the Asylum of San Bernardino, the children from the School of Christian Doctrine, the nuns of the Slaves of Mary and other communities who formed part of the cortege, could be placed in two lines. Donoso was everywhere at once, and the first thing he did was to place the clergy at the head of the procession. Then the funeral carriage was set in motion, which produced an ah! of admiration or satisfied curiosity all along the street, for really it was a lovely thing to see the slow gait of the eight horses and the noddings they made with the black plumes they wore on their heads. And the white-haired coachman with tassels on his tricorne hat was the greatest admiration of the urchins, who could not understand how he managed so many reins on that high box where he was sitting, like a king on his throne.

The mourning party, headed by my lord bishop of Andrinopolis and composed of persons of high social position, followed the landau with the wreaths in it; then came many and diverse persons and then an infinite number of luxurious carriages. The inhabitants of the neighborhood, who crowded balconies and windows, did not grow weary of that interminable parade, and would have wanted it to last all night. The procession stopped at every instant because of the obstructions that its forward portion encountered in such a narrow street. Once in the Calle de San Bernardo it proceeded more easily, drawing the curiosity of the indifferent crowd. Donoso did not cease to glance backward, observing the masses of people who were following the mourners and the snakelike undulation of the line of carriages.

"It's a demonstration," said the bishop, sad-faced, "a real demonstration."

While the funeral procession was crossing all of Madrid, en route to the Cemetery of San Isidro, astonishing the passersby with its extraordinary sumptuousness and the importance of those participating in it, the Palace of Gravelinas fell back into a sort of silent lethargy, like a body overcome by exhaustion and fever. The noise made by those who were removing the funeral objects from the salon stopped a few hours after the procession had departed. The servants took exquisite care to avoid any unnecessary noise and, under instructions from the butler, managed to place upon their faces and movements the gravity and moderate grief demanded by the circumstances. Augusta and Señora de Morentín were with Cruz in her sitting room. Don Francisco, in his study, wanted no more company than that of his daughter Rufina, whose eyes were red from so much crying. Father and daughter scarcely spoke.

One would even say that time passed with a certain reluctance in that atmosphere of grief, as if trying to make the cadences of its progress or the inevitability of its inflexible divisions less noticeable. Since the day before her sister's death, Cruz's imagination, beside itself with anxiety, had calculated time with enormous errors, and on the morning of the funeral it seemed to become absolutely motionless. The procession had not been gone from the house ten minutes when the inconsolable lady, seeing in her mind's eye the cortege's progress through the streets of Madrid, was thinking as follows: "Now they've reached the Cuesta de la Vega. Everyone, or almost everyone, is taking leave of the procession . . . without counting those who have slipped away as it passed along the streets. Now they're going down toward the bridge, hastening the pace a bit . . . I don't know why they have to go so fast."

She allowed an hour and a half to pass, her mind lulled in that painful reflection, and at the end of this time she said again: "How fast, how fast they're going! All the solemnity of the ceremony is lost if they're in such haste! It's easy to see why! The poor parish priests want to come back soon, because they're used to having dinner at twelve on the dot. Now they're arriving at the cemetery. . . They're going terribly fast. How bad the pavement must be! With so much dampness, ah! I'm afraid that the good father's cold will get worse. I certainly told him not to go. Dear Lord, we must always have some worry to torment us! But that is life. Thy most holy will be done. Now they're taking her down from the carriage. All of them go inside. Requiem mass . . . Jesus, what a quick mass! Now it's over. Not even a military mass in the field would be shorter. Goodness, what they want is to finish up and go home. How sad! Now they're carrying her into those inner courtyards. Now they're setting her down next to the tomb; everyone gathers around; one can't see anything. Now the earth is receiving her in its bosom. It seems to caress her, to welcome her. . . Go away, leave, all of you, and let her be, for the earth is kinder than you are. Now they're putting on their hats and leaving. The few who are left are covering my poor sister's resting place with an enormous stone, heavy as eternity. The official mourners and those who have accompanied the body have met at the gate and are exchanging courtesies. Then they return in their carriages, talking of business, of last night's theater premiere, or the singer Massini's sore throat. How fast they drive! It's time for lunch. . . Out there the poor gravediggers, a short distance from the dirt that has been excavated and the solitary stone, sit on the ground, take out their lunchboxes, and are having their lunch too . . . One must live. . . . "

The intimate friends returned to the house. Donoso, who was bringing the elegant little velvet box with the key to the vault, went straight to Don Francisco's room and embraced him, and then, in an admiring tone which revealed as much affection as pride, told him, "It was a demonstration, a real demonstration."

THREE

The marquis of San Eloy, deeply wounded by the blow he had received, paid the tribute that his grief exacted from physical nature, for sooner or later his bodily robustness, which, with the wear and tear of the years, was already on the wane, was bound to fail. As he said, *that little affair* cost him a month's illness, and he found himself obliged to give up business and *cobble himself up a bit* in order to continue his activities as a minter of fortunes. That troublesome symptom which he was wont to call *a swelling in the head* grew worse, and this, added to his almost absolute loss of memory after meals, made him feel really desperate. But worst of all were the dizzy spells that attacked him unexpectedly and prevented him from going to the Senate and even from leaving the house. Deaf to the advice of Quevedito, he administered purgatives to himself, which soon made his trouble worse. He paid less heed to the doctor than to the friends who recommended this and that remedy. He tried them all, and if one of them gave him an illusory and coincidental improvement he considered it to be an excellent, infallible panacea. Disillusionment soon set in, and then he would try other drugs, always rejecting an examination by a physician, for he could not abide doctors. "Just as misfortune makes a fellow into a philosopher," he would say, "illness makes us professors of medicine. I know more than all those quacks, for I observe myself, and I know when it's time to *open the valves* and when not to."

It was in the realm of morale, rather than in the physical sphere, that the inroads of the recognizable illness that was eating away at him were most clearly visible; for though he had always been an irritable man, at that period in his life his ill temper was unbearable. He quarreled with everyone, great and small, with family members and servants; his daughter and son-in-law needed Christlike patience to put up with him, and his bad qualities—miserliness, mistrustfulness, cruelty to his inferiors—increased to a degree that frightened everyone who came into contact with him. His pessimism could not be confined to the domestic sphere and spilled over into the public one, in politics as well as business. All those who had dealings with him were thieves; cabinet ministers were bandits who deserved to be hanged without mercy; senators were fakers and wretches, and the world was a great hell . . . that is, the only admissible hell, for the other hell spoken of in bibles did not exist; it was just part of the slop used by mysticism and obscurantism to try to bamboozle humanity . . . to get money out of people.

These symptoms were followed by what he called *stomach weakness*, which he tried to cure with meat extract, gelatines, and succulent broths. He improved a little, but then came horrible dyspepsias, indigestions, and colics that made him feel sick unto death. Good wines, mixed with meat extracts, agreed with him, and he put so much thought on this remedy that for a few days he tried to invent a specific liquor, a true elixir of life, and spent a great many hours pouring liquids from one bottle to another and straining out various mixtures, like an apothecary in a comedy. Those illusions, too, vanished like smoke. At last the good man had no choice but to turn himself over to the medical profession, which, though it could not cure him, improved his condition a little and allowed him to return, though very cautiously, to his mercantile campaigns.

And how ill and down-in-the-mouth he seemed to those who had not laid eyes on him during that month of illness! His body no longer had the rigid stiffness of former times; his legs seemed made of cotton; his face was muddy in hue and had deep furrows in it, and resembled a mask like those that are used to frighten children. Another new feature made him look even more unlike himself, and it was that, since in recent days it had bothered him to shave, he decided at last to *take expeditious measures* and let his beard grow; and so he did not have to think about that daily ordeal of soap and razor, scraping away at his skin. His beard was sparse, lopsided, and graying, and seemed an untidy mixture of rabbit fur, horsehair, and bunches of dirty fleece, which, along with the freckles and blotches on his parchmentlike cheeks, made of him the most miserable figure imaginable.

Although he was able to go out to attend to his business and take a turn or two around the realm of large-scale negotiations, he no longer possessed the winged buskins of Mercury nor the caduceus with which, by touching it to this and that, he used to make money sprout from stones. This infuriated him. He sought the cause of his mercantile impotence in external causes or in blind destiny, and on his way home would emit sparks and flashes of lightning, or something like them, from his eyes. If his dear Fidela were alive, that would be a different story! But to hell with those practical jokes played on high! Imagine, to have taken her and left the other one, that insufferable female, Cruz, here on earth. . . The more he thought about it the less he understood it. It was for this reason that his house, instead of being an oasis, was something *diametrically opposed*, and he never found consolation or peace or satisfactions there.

If he turned to look at his son, his heart sank to his toes, for he saw that the child was more brutish every day. After the death of Fidela, whose maternal love gave her exquisite tact in dealing with him and awakening sparks of intelligence in him, there was no longer any hope that the little beast would become a person. No one knew how to tame him; no one understood that strange and barbarous language of his, which resembled the tongue of wild beast cubs or Hottentot babes rather than the tongue of angels. From the first hour of his orphanhood, the wretched child seemed to want to declare his rights to savage independence by roaring furiously and crawling around on the carpets. He seemed to say, "Now I haven't the slightest interest in ceasing to be a beast, and now I'll bite, and howl, and kick all I want to." Fidela, at least, had faith that her son would awaken to reason. But alas! No one believed in Valentinico now; he was abandoned to the hazards of an animal life, and that ironic contrast between his monstrousness and the opulence of his cradle was accepted with resignation. Neither Cruz, nor Gamborena, nor Donoso, nor the servants, nor he himself, the afflicted father, had any hope that the poor little savage's physical or moral nature would change. It could not be, it could not be. And although convinced of the impossibility of having an intelligent and prepossessing heir, the miser loved his son, felt united to him by a profound affection which would not have altered had he seen him wallowing in a sty and eating cabbage stalks. He loved him and marveled because he loved him, either ignorant or forgetful of the laws of vital linkage that parental love establishes.

It was a source of further unhappiness for the good Don Francisco that he no longer had the escape of falling into a brown study, heating his brain as he had formerly done and evoking, by a process similar to the trances of mysticism, the image of the first Valentín, in order to lose himself in it, give it an imaginary life, and bring it to a communion and association that were very close to his own personality. These *sprees* of thought, for that is what he called them, purified and *converted into essence of angel*, did not produce the consoling effects he was pursuing, for—you would have thought the devil had a hand in it!—when he evoked the first Valentín, the second would come to him, the poor little monster with his ill-shaped head, his brutal face, his menacing mouth and teeth, his harsh and primitive language. And no matter how hard the distraught father tried to *intoxicate himself* and distill, in the alembic of his thoughts, the idea of his other son, he could not, dammit! he could not. The picture of the beloved and intelligent child had been wiped out. The most he could manage was to make the second Valentín, the ugly one, who did not even seem like a human child, speak in a voice that was like the other's, and say, "Papa, don't torment me any more. Why, I'm the same one, I'm myself and the other one too! Is it my fault that they've given me this shape? I don't recognize myself, nor does anyone recognize me, either in this world or the other. I'm both here and there. . . There and here they take me for a beast, and I am, I am. . . I can't remember any more the intelligence I used to have. There's no intelligence left. That's all over, and now, dear Papa, put me in a golden manger with a good ration of barley and you'll see how fast I eat it."

Don Francisco emerged from these spiritual duckings more dead than alive, with his brain feeling as if it were wrapped in cobwebs, which he tried to remove by rubbing his eyes, and it took him hours and hours to recover from the ordeal. His health was failing in a very obvious manner, and he was also losing the confidence in his inner fiber which had sustained him in the deepest crises of his existence. It gave way to the old distrust, to pathological apprehensions and manias, with some elements of flight instinct and persecutory mania. But his chief torment in those bitter days was the hatred—now unbounded and with many tragic aspects—that he felt for his sister-in-law. Since his widowerhood had broken all relations between them, suspending social formulas, the only link that had previously united them, Torquemada never spoke to Cruz, nor did she ever try to address him, and if it was necessary to deal with something concerning domestic matters or interests, Donoso readily agreed to be intermediary and carry messages to and fro. He would gladly have smoothed rough edges, but it was a vain hope. Though he found Cruz disposed to make peace, the other was like a hedgehog, who turned into a bristling ball as soon as he was touched. While his wife was alive, her love had led him to compromise, and compromise simply meant submitting to the will of the woman who ruled; but after Fidela's death, his obstinate character found an easy way to escape tyranny by breaking off relations. For, and he knew it very well, by conceding the honors of speech to his enemy, which was the same as confronting her, he was lost, because the wretched woman fascinated him with her arguments, and then she would eat him up as the snake eats the baby rabbit. Hence he thought it preferable not to expose himself to the dangers of fascination: no contact, no familiarities, not even a greeting, so as not to let her put her oar in and get her own way.

Sometimes Father Gamborena acted as "papal legate," and Torquemada feared him more than he did Donoso, for Gamborena always ended by preaching him sermons that depressed him and filled his spirit with anxiety and dread.

One afternoon, when Don Francisco had recovered considerably from his ailment and had returned to the exercise of his business, he returned home earlier than usual, escaping from the cold outdoors, which was dry and penetrating, and found the missionary in the downstairs gallery, walking up and down and reading his breviary.

"What an opportunity, and what a fortunate thing, my dear marquis!" he exclaimed, holding out his arms to embrace him, whereupon the other coldly crossed his.

F O U R

"Why?"

"Because I had determined not to go home without seeing you, and lo and behold, my lord marquis has returned early, perhaps owing to the cold, though we might well believe that God sent him home half an hour earlier than usual so that he could hear what I have to tell him."

"Is it so urgent? Let's go in."

"Is it urgent? You will soon see. Extremely urgent. I was just thinking that you weren't going to escape me tonight without putting up with a new headache from this poor priest. But what can we do? Each of us has his job. My Señor Don Francisco's job is to make money, mine is to utter truths, even though these may be, because of their elementary simplicity itself, troublesome ones. Prepare yourself and have patience, for this afternoon I'm going to be a bit hard on you."

As he lounged in an armchair opposite the priest, Torquemada's only answer was a grunt, thus signifying that he was ready and arming himself with patience as with a breastplate.

"Those of us who exercise this difficult ministry," said Gamborena, "are obliged to employ harshness when gentleness is not effective, shall we say. You know me. You know how much I respect and love this noble family, and you, and everyone. In my dual role as preacher of the gospel and friend, I am permitting myself, therefore, to speak plainly. I am like that; you can take me or leave me. When I am called upon, I come in through the same door I leave by if I am thrown out. If you dismiss me I'll go away quietly because I will have done my duty, but sad if I have not achieved the moral purpose that I desire. And I am also warning you that I don't go in for pretty phrases when it is a question of serious errors to be corrected, and I observe rebellion or stubbornness in my hearer. To speak more clearly: I pay no attention to social hierarchies, nor to respectabilities, no matter what they may be, because there is no head that does not have to bow before the truth. And so my Señor Don Francisco must not be surprised if I treat

· 486 ·

him like a schoolboy in the matter that brings us together here . . .
No. you mustn't be frightened: I have said 'like a schoolboy' and I
don't take it back because, though in the world I am nothing, I am
the master now owing to my ministry, and one of the most demanding
of masters. And you, sitting opposite me, with the moral question that
lies between us, are not my lord marquis, nor the millionaire, nor the
highly respected senator, but everyman, a miserable little sinner without name or rank, who needs my teaching. And that is what I am
going to do, and if I administer a slap that hurts, you must put up
with it and mend your ways."

"Where is the fellow going to end up, I wonder?" said Torquemada
to himself, swallowing hard and wriggling in his chair.

And then aloud, with a certain amount of irritation:

"Very well, my dear sir, hurry up and tell me what . . ."

"But you know it! Shall we make a bet that you know it?"

"Some bothersome commission from my dear sister-in-law. Let's see.
Go ahead and state the question."

"The question I am stating is that you are gravely offending God,
and also offending society, by nurturing hate and pride in your heart
. . . hate, yes indeed, against that saintly woman, who has done you
no harm. Quite the contrary, she has been a ministering angel to you;
and this dreadful loathing with which you repay the favors you have
received from her, and that arrogance with which you banish her from
your presence and your company, are horrible sins with which you
blacken your soul and prepare it for eternal punishment."

The missionary said this with such supreme conviction, with such
energetic emphasis in word and gesture, that he seemed actually to be
knifing him, slashing at him with a long, sharp sword. The other staggered, utterly confounded by the blows, and for the moment did not
know what to say, nor to do anything but put his hands to his head.
But he lost no time in coming to himself, and all of a sudden the bile
and resentments of his unhappy times returned. Moreover, he was in
a bad mood that day because he could not find a solution for a certain
piece of business: this and other causes abruptly awakened the crude
man in him. It was an infinitely sad spectacle to see that man reappear, take a stand, and reply with calm insolence: "But what business
is it of yours, Señor Priest, whether I speak with my sister-in-law or
not? Who lets you into things that have nothing to do with conscience,

but with the free will of *the individual's rights?* This is too much, dammit! I won't stand for this, nor would any person of halfway decent circumstances and intelligence stand for it."

"I stand by what I said, Señor Marquis," the other replied firmly. "I am speaking as a father of souls. You reject exhortation. Well and good, you must take the consequences. Repeat it, repeat that you do not deign to listen to me, and you will see how quickly I leave you in peace, I mean, at war with your conscience—with your conscience!— a specter which, to be sure, does not have a very pretty face."

"No, I haven't told you to go," stammered Torquemada, recovering his equanimity. "Speak if you wish. But you won't convince me."

"Will I not?"

"No. Because I have my reasons for breaking off all contact with that lady," said the miser, returning to his normal self and searching his mind for fine phrases. "I do not deny that the *distinguished* Señora del Aguila has *carried out many beneficial reforms* in the house; but she is the reason that economies here are like *Penelope's web.* What I save in a year, she scatters to the winds in four days."

"Always meanness, always the habits of poverty! I maintain that without Cruz's guidance you would not have come to possess what you possess. The reason for this hatred, my dear sir, is not the distribution of miserable coins. What goes on in the soul of my lord marquis of San Eloy he does not even know himself, because, knowing so many things, he does not succeed in reading his own soul. But I know it, and I am going to tell it to you very plainly. These mysteries of the human spirit do not customarily reveal themselves to the knowledge of those who harbor them, but rather to the penetration of those who see them from outside. The cause of the diabolical aversion you profess toward your sister is her superiority, the sublimity of her intelligence. Everything in her is great; in you everything is petty, and your ability to earn money, a secondary art composed of trifles, feels humiliated before the greatness of Cruz's thoughts. You are (let's see if I can express it) in this matter of business the simple workman who does the job, and she the superior brain that conceives admirable plans. Without Cruz you would be nothing but a miserable moneylender, who would have spent his life amassing a paltry fortune with the blood of the poor. With her you have accomplished everything, and have clambered into the highest social circles. But it is a very common thing

in life that the ambitious man, once he has triumphed, does not recognize the power that raised him from the dust to the clouds, especially
if this ambitious man is merely an instrument, and the power that
raised him is intelligence. The hatred of the lower members for the
head is an old story in the social body. There are examples both large
and small, in human organizations and in families, and this example
that I have in front of me is so clear that if you yourself do not see it,
it is because you do not wish to see it."

"Well," said Don Francisco, helpless before the priest's resounding
eloquence, "I assure you that I do not *harbor* . . . no, I cannot *harbor*
such a feeling. Nor do I see so much intelligence in Señora Doña Cruz.
To think up my senatorship and the marquisate, and to invent the
purchase of these *Americas of good taste*, one doesn't have to be the
daughter of the Seven Sages of Greece, or the grandmother of the Nine
Muses, so to speak. Certainly she is no fool. *I'm bound to declare* that
she has a certain gift of the gab, and that when she comes out against
a fellow with all the hokey-pokey of her *oratorical ability* she'd drive
the Divine Word himself out of his mind."

"I do not want to get into a discussion on that point, nor do I need
to prove to you that you are conscious of your inferiority to Cruz, for
that consciousness is perfectly clear. Do you admit that the hatred
exists?"

"She must be the one who *harbors* it."

"No, not she; you . . ."

"All right then," said Torquemada more calmly, acknowledging
himself beaten, "I confess that we don't like each other much, neither
she me nor I her. But the *bone of contention*, the argument that you
adduce . . . oh, that I will not admit! I have my complaints, I have
reasons that *vouch for my conduct* in this matter. I will *pass over* her
propensities toward ostentation, and mention only her desire to go
against my *prerogative*, not to allow anything to be done that I order
in the house, as if everything that I ordered was a *deficiency*. That's
all. She has a grudge against me, a grudge that's *sui generis*, as if she
believed that I, by giving orders for this or that, would outshine her.
For her, there's nothing good or commonsensical except what she *dic-
taminates*."

"That's not true, that's not true. Goodness, Señor Don Francisco, let
us go from words to deeds and, now that we've recognized where the

wound lies, let us try to cure it radically," the priest said gently, placing his hands on the marquis's knees. "It is necessary, without loss of time, to kill that hatred, destroy it, smash it, like a poisonous reptile whose bite brings death."

"Well, as for me . . . the one who hates is her, not me."

"The one who hates is you; and the initiative for reconciliation must come from you. But in order to facilitate it, I propose that each of you sacrifice some of your self-pride. Therefore, let us not have vexing scenes, nor explanations. You will meet at table one of these days, and you will speak to each other as if nothing had happened."

"Agreed," said Don Francisco. "But beforehand, set forth *a line of conduct.*"

"That is up to the two of you. As a priest, I try to make peace, I propose it, I seek it. I speak to hearts, not to interests. Both of you must think about God and recognize each other as brother and sister, and live in harmony and love. Once this is achieved, deal at leisure with the prerogatives of each, and the household budget, economizing, and all those unimportant details. Keep in mind that, if reconciliation is purely external and for form's sake, if you have merely come to an agreement or *modus vivendi*, to pretend cordiality of relations before the world, and rancor continues to be hidden in your heart, nothing will be gained. You will deceive society but not God. Without purity of will, my dear Señor Don Francisco, you cannot aspire, I have told you so on another occasion, to eternal treasures."

"Ah, I don't believe you!"

"Yes, yes, and you will tire of being evil before I tire of scolding you and exhorting you. To sum up, my dear sir: it is not enough for you to stage-manage a reconciliation with your sister-in-law, and talk to her, and come to an agreement about running the house. It is essential that you pardon her for any offenses you think you have received at her hands, and that hate be changed into love, into brotherly affection."

"And if I can't manage that," asked Torquemada with the most vivid curiosity, "what will happen to me?"

"You know it very well, for although you are ignorant of many essential things, I do not believe that you have forgotten the ABCs of Christian doctrine."

"Sure, sure," remarked the miser, attempting a humorous freethinker's pose, "heaven is for those who love and hell for those who hate. No matter how much you preach at me, Father, you won't convince me that I'm going to hell."

"That . . . you will see."

"No, I'm already sure of it. I should think not! Me, go to hell! On a certain occasion you told me that the gates of heaven wouldn't open for me, and . . . well, that really affected me. I spent some wakeful nights, racking my brains and saying to myself, "Dammit! What have I done not to be saved?"

"It would be better to ask yourself, 'What am I doing to deserve my salvation?' I am forced to repeat it to you, Señor Marquis: toward this eternal purpose you are doing nothing, or are doing the opposite of everything you should. Do you have faith? *No, Father.* Do you believe what every good Christian is obliged to believe? *No, Father.* Do you stifle your evil passions, do you exile rancor from your soul, do you love those whom you ought to love? *No, Father.* Do you put a brake on your selfishness, doing all possible good to your fellow humans? *No, Father.* Do you distribute among the needy the enormous riches that you have left over? *No, Father.* And the man who behaves in this way, the man who now, approaching the end of his life, does not take care to purify his conscience and cure it of such rottenness, dares to say, 'Let them open the gate of the heavenly mansions to me, for there I will go, ready to push at it with my filthy hands or bribe the gate-keeper, for that's why God made me a millionaire, and a marquis, and a distinguished person.' "

FIVE

Don Francisco laughed, pretending to enjoy the joke, but his laughter was purely external; inwardly, God knows, something resembling a lively little devil was wandering through his whole soul, causing him fright and perturbation.

"Laugh, laugh, and put on airs as a philosopher and a strong spirit," Gamborena told him, "and we'll see what you have to say later on."

"But where did you get the idea, Señor Missionary, that I'm not a believer?"

"Do you fulfill your obligations to the Church?"

"Well, I have to admit that . . ."

"What are you waiting for? My word, you must be a mere boy and bursting with health, to say as others have said, 'There's time, plenty of time.' "

"No, I know that there isn't plenty of time," said the skinflint with sudden seriousness, and feeling that his affected laughter was turning into painful contractions of the facial muscles. "This machine of mine is breaking down, and there's something here inside that . . . that . . ."

"Say it right out, something that terrifies you. Naturally, you see the loss of material possessions, the end of life. Those unfortunates who cannot see the beyond see a void—a void, alas!—which certainly has nothing pleasant about it . . . Well, Señor Marquis, do you want, yes or no, the last days of your life to be quiet ones; do you want, yes or no, to prepare yourself to regard with a serene mind the final outcome, or the transition from the finite to the infinite? Answer me quickly, and here I am at your disposal."

"Well, to tell the honest truth," replied the marquis of San Eloy, anxious to give in but trying to find a way to do so without sacrificing his pride, "I accept whatever solution you set forth. It's going to be a little bit hard for you to convince me of certain things. It's not for nothing that sorrow has made a fellow a philosopher. Here where you see me, I'm very scientific, and though I never had an education, as a mature man I've looked at things a lot and studied men and natural phenomena. I take a good look at the practical phenomenon wherever I can catch hold of it. Well, then, if that's what being good is all about, I'm a regular cupcake. Do I have to give something to the needy? Well, that's no problem. So . . . now you've got your savage converted."

"One step at a time. It's not as easy as that. But I don't wish to nag you. For today I'll be satisfied with your good intentions. I will be your conqueror and will attack you with all the arms I can find in my evangelical arsenal."

"Agreed," said Don Francisco, reassuming the air of a supercilious senator discussing a point of administration or a small detail of politics. "It's agreed that, from today, my objective is to earn heaven, eh? To earn it, I say, and I know very well what earning's all about."

"Mind, it's not the same as earning two or three or a thousand or a hundred thousand duros in a business operation. Money is earned by intelligence, by stratagems, sometimes by treachery and evil tricks; heaven is earned by good deeds, by purity of conscience."

"It's all very easy, to my mind. And here you have me, ready to obey you in anything you want to command in the sphere of dogma and conscience."

"Very well."

"But a fellow's always a philosopher, and scientific . . . a fellow can't help that. I haven't a jot of the poet in me, thanks be to God. I set myself to thinking and work out according to my lights the phenomenon of this world and the next. Doubt gnaws at me, and, frankly, a fellow doubts without suspecting it, without wanting to. Why does a fellow doubt? Why, because he exists, of course. Let's be scientists, not poets. The poet is a simpleton with a turn for pretty words, a blockhead with flowers growing on him, d'you understand me? Well, then, I'll go on. We're going to make an agreement, Señor Gamborena."

"An agreement? There's no agreement here except that you are going to place your conscience in my hands and let yourself be guided by me."

"That's just what I mean," and, as he said this, the marquis brought his chair close enough to the priest's to give him little pats on the knee. "Francisco Torquemada is ready to be ruled by Father Gamborena, like the smallest child in the kindergarten, as long as Father Gamborena will guarantee him . . ."

"What's this about guaranteeing?"

"Hold on. I'm very plain when I speak about business. It's my inveterate custom to make everything very clear and to tie up all the loose ends."

"But the business of the soul . . ."

"The business of the soul, so to speak . . . I'm alluding to the entity that we call soul, which we suppose to be a large, fat capital, the foremost among all capitals."

"Good, good."

"And, naturally, when dealing with the placement of that fine capital and making it secure, I have to discuss all the conditions with a great deal of care. Consequently, I'll hand over to you what my conscience demands . . . Good . . . But you'll have to guarantee me that, once you have my entire conscience in your power, the gates of eternal glory will have to open to me, that you'll have to open them yourself, since you have the keys to do so. Let there be honesty and good faith on both sides, mind you! Because, frankly, it would be very sad, my very dear Señor Missionary, if I were to hand over my capital and then it would turn out that there were no such gates, nor any such glory, nor Christ who established them."

"So, nothing less than guarantees?" said the cleric, losing his temper. "Am I, perchance, some commission agent or stockbroker? I don't need to guarantee eternal truths. I preach them. The sinner who does not believe in them has no basis for improvement. The business man who doubts the security of that bank in which he deposits his capital will have to go and settle accounts with the devil eventually. You must have faith, and if you have it you will find the guarantee in your own conscience. And lastly, I don't stand for jokes in this area, and, so that we will understand each other, forget the tricks, the habits, and even the language of business. If you don't, I will believe that you are a lost cause and will abandon you to the sorrows of your old age, to the fears about your bad health, and to the terrors of your conscience filled with shadows."

Pause. Don Francisco leaned back in his chair and passed his hands over his eyes.

"Imbue yourself with the great truths of doctrine, so easy, so simple, so clear that even the intelligence of a child understands them," said the missionary kindly, "and you will not need to have me guarantee anything. I could say 'Answer for your improvement and the gates will open.' First things first. But you, like a good egotist, want to have guaranteed earnings in advance. I'm going to leave you to think about it."

The priest rose to his feet, but Torquemada seized him by the arm, forcing him to sit down.

"A little while longer. Let's agree that I'll reconcile with Cruz. The idea is acceptable. A fellow has to start somewhere."

"Yes, but let it be with your whole soul, true reconciliation, not merely in outward appearance."

"Well, look here, it's going to cost me a little trouble, if it has to be on those terms and with all the stiffness of conditions *sine qua nons*. But I'll do what I can, and for the moment, let's speak over and over about these things, which absorb me more than they seem to. I believe that a fellow should think about all that and prepare himself for what-ever may befall. And in the end, my very reverend Señor Saint Peter, you'll open the gate for me, because it's not for nothing we're friends and—"

"I am not the heavenly gatekeeper," said Gamborena, cutting him short, "nor, even if I were, would I open the gate for someone who doesn't deserve to come in. Your head is full of ridiculous fairy stories, of irreverent and absurd tales."

"Well, now that we're talking about tales, I'm going to tell you a very old one that maybe will interest you. The why and the how and the when of that habit I have of calling you 'Saint Peter.' "

"Out with it, out with it."

"You're going to laugh for sure. It's really foolish. Stuff of our imagination, which is a real comedian. It seems impossible that a fellow, being so scientific and not having a speck of the poet in him, would let himself be swindled by that madcap. Well, this happened many years ago, when I was a poor man or not far from it, and my son fell ill of that filthy disease that carried him off, an attack to the brain, in the vernacular meningitis. Not knowing what to do to make God save my son, and having my suspicions that the Lord himself as well as all the saints had an eye on me because I was a little bit overbearing with the poor, it occurred to me that by changing my conduct and becoming compassionate, those gentry upstairs would take pity on my affliction. I was generous and even openhanded and extravagant. D'you think they paid any attention to me? As if I'd been a dog . . . And then they say . . . ! I'd better shut up."

"Charity must be practiced constantly and systematically," said the priest with gentle severity, "not in particular cases where one is in difficulties, like those who put money into the lottery because they are avid to win. Nor ought one to do good out of calculation, nor is heaven a ministry to which one sends briefs in order to secure a position. But let's leave this subject and go on with your story."

"To get back to what I was saying: I went out one night, desperate and turned into a demon, I mean terribly grieved, because the boy was gravely ill. I was determined to give alms to every poor man I found in my path. And that's what I did, you can believe me. I distributed a good number of five- and ten-céntimo coins, in addition to the big donations I had made that morning in my house on the Calle de San Blas, forgiving odds and ends of rents and taking the heat off late-paying tenants . . . awful people, goodness, really awful people, parenthetically speaking. Well, as I'm saying, I was walking along the Calle de Jacometrezo, and right there, near the Postigo de San Martín, I found an old man who was begging, trembling with cold. The poor fellow was in shirtsleeves, and you could see his hairy chest, his naked feet, and the little clothing he did have on him was in rags. I felt terribly sorry for him. I spoke with him and had a good look at his face. And here's the first part of the humor in this tale, for if it weren't for the joke, in the vernacular coincidence, it wouldn't be worth telling."

"Are there two parts to the humor?"

"Two. The first coincidence is that the man reminded me of a Saint Peter, an image that lots of people were devoted to, which you can see in the church of San Cayetano, first chapel on the right as you go in. The same bald spot, the very same eyes, his hair curly around the bald spot, all his features—in short, Saint Peter to the life. And I used to know and associate with the image of the apostle just as I did with my best friends, because I was steward of the brotherhood he was patron saint of, and in my younger years I had a certain amount of devotion to him. Saint Peter is the patron saint of fishermen; but since there aren't any seafaring men in Madrid, we moneylenders got together to pay homage to him, for, in a certain sense, we're fishermen too. But to go on. The fact is that the poor ragged beggar was just like, exactly like, the saint of our brotherhood."

"And did you give him alms?"

"I'll say! I gave him my cape. Well, what did you think? I don't stop with half measures."

"That was well done."

"But, let's be fair. I didn't give him the cape that I was wearing, but another old one that I had at home. It was good enough for him."

"All the same, it was a meritorious act, yes indeed, I should say so!"

"Well, that man's face stayed so present in my memory, that years and years passed and I couldn't forget him; my fortunes and position changed, and always with that confounded saint fresh and vivid in my noggin. Well, sir, time passed and one day, when I was least thinking about it, he shows up again in flesh and blood, with a soul, with life, with a voice, the same entity, though in a very different dress. There you have the second part of the humor of the tale. My Saint Peter was you."

"That certainly is amusing. So I resemble . . .?"

"The man who asked me for alms that night, and, therefore, the holy apostle in question."

"And did that Saint Peter have keys?"

"I should say he did! Silver, and good solid ones."

"Then we don't resemble each other in that."

"The face is the same, that bald spot, those wrinkles, the way the hair grows around the bald spot, the eyes as if lighted up from within, and all the features, mouth and nose and even the tone of voice. Only that man didn't shave and you do. But what a fantastic resemblance, Lord! The day that you first came to my house I got frightened, believe me that I got frightened, and I told Fidela about it, yes, I told her, 'This man is the devil.' "

"Jesus!"

"No, it was a manner of speaking, no more than a manner of speaking. But it set me to thinking, and the whole thing turned on my wondering if you had, or didn't have, keys."

"I don't have any," said Gamborena lightly, getting to his feet. "But as far as conscience is concerned, it's the same. Don't be disturbed. The Church has the keys, and the One who can open those gates transmits power to me and to all of us who exercise this divine ministry. So get ready to enter. Are we agreed that the reconciliation will take place?"

"We're agreed. But are you leaving already?"

"Yes, for you're about to have dinner. It's very late. Real reconciliation. We'll soon speak about the rest, for it seems to me that neither of us wants to put off the matter for too long."

"No. From now on, the matter will be under consideration. And you can speak of it whenever you want to."

"Good. Farewell. Your tale has amused me. We will have to repeat the matter of the cape, I mean, that I will ask you for it again, and you will have to give it to me."

"Agreed."

"If not, there will be no keys. And believe me, my friend, that gate cannot be opened with a picklock."

SIX

The reconciliation was in truth a colossal effort, and to bring it to a satisfactory conclusion, as Don Francisco said, the good Gamborena had to intervene again with more diplomacy than religion, aided by the excellent Donoso and by Rufinita. At last Cruz and Torquemada sat down to table together one day, and peace was made, both showing themselves disposed toward agreement, though always holding back on the serious points of the schism that separated them. To everyone's delight, my lord the marquis had a good appetite that day and ate some of everything that was brought to the table, and nothing did him any harm, a strange thing, for his digestive processes had become quite difficult.

The missionary was not wholly convinced, and he as well as Donoso suspected that the rapprochement was not really substantial but merely apparent, and that the hearts of both parties remained distant from each other. This was confirmed in practice several days after the *modus vivendi* was established, for Don Francisco demanded, and wanted to carry out, such things that the negotiators themselves took fright. He wanted to fire two-thirds of the servants, no less, leaving only what was indispensable for the care of the two adults and the child, and mercilessly wielding the sickle of economy against the employees needed to clean and care for the artistic treasures. Cruz, whose ambitions as an autocrat had waned considerably, agreed to everything. The loneliness in which the deaths of her beloved brother and sister had left her had tempered her pride, inspiring in her indifference and even scorn for extravagant vanities. She was grieved, indeed, that the works of art would not receive the devotion they deserved; she found her illustrious brother-in-law's meanness very hard to endure, for, with one foot in the grave, he was tarnishing his name and his house by saving sums that were insignificant compared with his immense riches. In other circumstances Cruz would have confronted the matter energetically, sure of emerging victorious; under these circumstances she did not wish to put up a fight and, with the melancholy gravity of an emperor retiring to Yuste, said to her good friends Gamborena and Donoso, "Let him do exactly as he likes. It's only right that that brute should recover possession of his avaricious desires in his last years. What can be gained by pestering him? To embitter the last days of his life and leave him ill-prepared for death. No. After me, him, and after him the deluge. Poor House of Gravelinas! If I had my way I'd go into a convent, for I am good for nothing now, nor do I wish to interfere in anything."

Really, like a heroine who had exhausted her powerful energies in a formidable struggle, Cruz was at that time completely drained of will-power, ill with discouragement. She had done so much, had created so many marvels, that it was only fair to let her rest on the seventh day. The ingratitude of that man, her pupil, her creature, did not embitter her life as much as it should have, no doubt because she had counted on it and because her great spirit felt even more lofty when she observed the distance that his ingratitude placed between the artist and her work. Moreover, the time came when the noble lady began to look more toward divine than earthly things. It was a natural evolution of her life under the circumstances in which she found herself, alone, with no one to love but her little nephew (and him she loved with ineffable pity), with all her ambitions realized, the House of Aguila restored and vengeance on other family members, which in her mind assumed the character of inflexible judgment, satisfied. All temporal things were, therefore, accomplished and more than accomplished; it was time to look toward the other side of our lives' dark paths. Solitude, grief, even her age, which was now well past forty, led her to this, and if anything was lacking to accelerate the evolution, it was given her by constant association with the great missionary, the example of his virtue, and by hearing him preach the purification of the soul and the joys of immortality.

Very soon after Fidela's death, Cruz devoted herself to reading the mystic writers, and became so enthusiastic about this pleasure that she could no longer do without it for many hours of the day and night. She was entranced by the Spanish mystics of the Golden Age, not only because of the luminous path that they opened before her eyes but because she found a certain aristocratic touch in the style that ravished her spirit, always attracted to whatever was noble. That kind of literature, apart from being holy in its ideas, was worthy, select, and majestic in its form.

She lost no time in progressing from thoughts to actions, dedicating the morning hours and the early hours of the night to religious exercises in her chapel, losing herself in meditations and spiritual exercises. From acts of pure devotion she easily progressed to evangelical work, and since the *modus vivendi* had separated her capital from Torquemada's, she could freely devote her income to charity. And certainly she practiced it with a discretion and good sense that could serve as a model for all of aristocratic Christendom. Truly, to what could that woman, so intellectual and so well acquainted with the world, turn her hand and not have it come out perfection itself? Though charitable organizations were not much to her taste, she did not avoid the frequent necessity of belonging to them . . . but she saved her energies and the better part of her resources for campaigns that she undertook alone, without fanfare or any sort of publicity. She dressed simply, made few social visits, and her carriage was very well known in the poorer quarters of the city. It need hardly be said that Gamborena, delighted with his pupil's efforts, brought her information and news of shameful poverty or horrifying evils so that the lady would find half her work done for her, and would not have to exert herself so much.

She might well have wished to demonstrate her evangelical spirit to the degree of divine virtue that the lives of saints offer us. But it was not her fault that the regularity of life in our refined century makes certain extremes impossible. The noble lady felt strong enough to imitate Murillo's Saint Elizabeth by washing the scabby, and believed herself as much a Christian and as much a lady as she. But it would not have been easy to satisfy such ambitions; Gamborena himself would not have permitted it, for fear her health would suffer. But her imagination grew more feverish every day, and her strong willpower, no longer having other things to feed upon, showed itself in that sort of imaginings, to her own glory and that of the Christian idea.

However, Cruz did not neglect certain obligations pertaining to the house which, according to the *modus vivendi*, were her responsibility. The heir's personal cleanliness, his meals, his clothing, his games, were all overseen and arranged by the lady with maternal solicitude, and she would have done the same with his education had education been possible for that hapless monster, who day by day became harder to control, more stupid, and more lacking in every childish charm. But although his Aunt Cruz took exquisite care of him in the material order of things, so that he felt no lack of a mother in that respect, the same was not true in other orders of existence, for Valentinico no longer had anyone who understood him, or who could translate his barbaric language, or who believed in his future as a human person. Totally lacking in intelligence and sensitivity, the poor savage did not realize the void that his good mama had left around him, for she had caressed him with all her heart, always seeking the soul in the eyes of the little animal. Of Don Francisco let us not speak. Though he also loved him as flesh of his flesh and blood of his blood, he regarded him as a hope absolutely dashed, and his love was, as it were, formal and given out of obligation.

Meanwhile the heir continued to grow, and his head seemed ever larger, his legs more twisted, his teeth sharper, his habits more gross and his temperament harsher, more perverse, and cruel. He gave a great deal of trouble in the house; his aunt devoted such patience to him that there was no room left in her heart for love. If he fell ill she cared for him zealously, trying to save him, and the monstrous child rapidly recovered from all his spells of illness, and emerged from every one of those crises closer to the earth and to animality. The only thing in which he made some progress was his speech, for eventually the nursemaid taught him to articulate a good many syllables and to pronounce, though imperfectly, the easier words in the language.

Barely a month after the *modus vivendi* had gone into operation, Don Francisco, embittered by his ailments, which grew worse at the beginning of the spring, began to violate it, altering some of its chief bases. Though at first he was well content not to have Cruz interfering in things, he took the notion to meddle in matters that were the absolute responsibility of the lady. In her economies concerning servants, he thought he saw desires to make things difficult for him, depriving him of service while the other got more of it for herself. Moreover, it infuriated him to see the crowd of clerics and pious women who took the palace and chapel by assault at every hour of the day. For the chapel was his, and frankly, they ought to have the consideration not to use it except on Sundays and days of obligation. The noise of so many devotions annoyed him, and the organ, and the singing of the young girls who went there entirely too often, under the pretext of religion but really to see one another and rub elbows with their sweethearts. Goodness, he didn't want his chapel to be a hotbed of scandal.

These and other uncouth remarks which the marquis of San Eloy let fly one morning, gross in his speech and angry in his manners, were protested by Father Gamborena, who at last had to lose his temper. The other also got angry, for he was suffering horribly from stomachache; both raised their voices, the missionary lost all restraint, the skinflint replied with extremely bitter words, mingled with the groans of his long-standing illness, and at last the priest told him, "Today you are impossible, Señor Marquis. But excuse yourself with your illness, and perhaps I will have nothing to reply to you. Yes, I do; I will reply that you simply must call a doctor, the best doctors, and must place yourself in their hands. Your illness beclouds your soul and obscures your reason. The sick man is forgiven for the foolish things his ailment makes him say. It is not he who speaks, but his sick kidney, his churning bile."

"That's what I say, Señor Gamborena, it's the bile, and since it's so easy to keep it in its place, why am I ill? Ah! Because health isn't possible with this life I lead. I have no one to take care of me, no one to take an interest in me. If my Fidela were alive, or my Silvia, if both of them were alive, I'd sing a different song. But here I am, abandoned in my own house, in the middle of this palace that weighs me down and oppresses me. For you can see, I've sacrificed myself on the altar of domestic peace, and nobody sacrifices themself on the altar of my well-being. How am I going to be healthy with the food they serve in this house, that would take away the appetite of a brace of gluttons? They're killing me; they're murdering me bit by bit, and when a fellow's suffering and bursting with pain, then they come along with an organ and nuns' chanteys that make my blood boil, and grate on my guts."

SEVEN

Cruz, in the doorway, heard the end of this tirade and entered hastily, forcing herself to assume a conciliatory and smiling expression and tell him, "But we haven't changed cooks, and the meals are the same. Put the blame on your stomach, which is in bad shape at the moment. If you want to cure it, complain about your fits of temper rather than about the meals, which are excellent. But they'll be changed in any way you like. Tell me what you feel like eating and you shall have it."

"Leave me, leave me in peace, Crucita mine," replied the marquis, flinging himself onto a sofa. "Why, I don't feel like eating anything; everything repels me, even the wine with meat juices that I invented, and which is the most appalling brew that ever entered a Christian's mouth!"

"You'll see how Chatillon will eventually please you, preparing little dishes that are pleasing to the palate and easy to digest. As for the noise from the chapel, the organ will be stilled and we'll take our music elsewhere. We're here to make you happy and spare you annoyances. You give the orders, and we'll all bow to them."

The crusty millionaire was appeased by these words of humility and affection, and after Cruz had departed he again remained alone with Gamborena, who recommended patience as the only relief for his troubles, while the medical profession tried to determine whether it could or could not cure them permanently. It could well be that science, since the illness was very deep-rooted and the sick man's health much broken, would not emerge victorious. The safest thing was to take the most pessimistic view, to consider as inevitable, and within a short space of time, the end of all these pains and to prepare oneself for a better life.

"So I have to die from this illness?" said Torquemada, flying into a temper. "Then I'm on death row, so to speak, and have nothing to think about but my funeral services?"

"Others will take care of that. Think about what is most important for you. The language of truth must be spoken to a man of firm character like yourself."

"Sure, and the priest's job is to rub a fellow's nose in death . . . Look here, Señor Missionary, I'm ill, very ill, but those who are anxious to see me going out of here feet first needn't get so excited, for if I make up my mind not to die, there'll be never a bit of it. I can stand an awful lot, and I'm made of timber that doesn't bend or splinter. None of the superdoctors or all the petty clergy in the world are going to push me into passing on until the whole thing comes at its own pace. And as for those who think they're going to inherit from me, they'd better make themselves comfortable, because they have a long wait ahead. So there's nothing to do but leave those who hate us well off? I'm still going to put up quite a fight. Of course, when the time really comes, and Nature says 'this is it,' I won't make a fuss. Let's be honest: I won't make a fuss, in principle, you understand. But not yet, not yet, dammit! and keep your prayers for when they're asked for, dammit! for when circumstances call for them, double dammit! What are you, anyway? A spiritual clerk, who comes to bring service when he's called upon. But as long as you're not sent for, you have no horn to blow or candle to hold in this funeral; I mean, it's not a question of a funeral, mind you! but something diametrically opposed to one."

"Very well, my dear Don Francisco, very well!" said the priest gently, realizing that it was imprudent to contradict him in such a hypochondriacal crisis. "You will send for me. I am always at your disposal. I hope that I will soon see you relieved of your complaints and, in consequence, that these rages of yours, which go to your head and becloud your judgment, will calm down. Go and rest, and we will talk another day."

They did talk, day after day, without making much progress, for, far from improving, the sick man grew worse and became impossible to deal with. Neither Donoso nor Gamborena could do anything with him, and the latter observed disconsolately that the matter of that conscience of Torquemada's was taking a bad turn, and how likely he was to lose the game if Infinite Mercy did not open new paths in the most unexpected places.

The marquis of San Eloy's illness grew so much worse that during the whole month of April he did not have a single good day, and had to abstain completely from business, becoming all the more irritable because of his idleness, and cursing himself merely to think that he was no longer earning money and that his capital was stagnant and producing nothing. It was a rare day that he did not vomit up his food. What a strange thing! He ate with a fairly good appetite, trying to keep within the strictest sobriety, and, an hour later, wham! dizziness, nausea, retching, and . . . Frankly, it was a nasty practical joke either by Nature or his internal economy.

"Ah!" he would exclaim, feeling his stomach and ribs, "I don't know what's got into this confounded economy of mine; you'd think it was a madhouse. There's no government here inside, and the organs do exactly as they please, with no respect for established order or accomplished fact. What the devil is the matter with this body, that it doesn't want to be fed, and rejects the good food I give it? Without a doubt there's some leaven of revolution or anarchy in these innards of mine. But my mister stomach had better be careful, because these phenomenal excesses can be tolerated once or twice, but I could well find a medicine that'll put the screws on this organ of mine, which is giving me the very dickens and making me . . . ouch, ouch . . .!"

His bad temper was not constant, for it was often interrupted by fits of tenderness which seemed like real attacks because they were so exaggerated. There were some days when he was so sentimental that he did not appear to be the same man, and his endearments almost always fell upon Rufinita, who at that time never left his side by day or night.

"My darling daughter, you're the only person who really loves me. Who but you takes an interest in me? That's why, curse it! I love you more than anyone else. You don't do or say a single thing to annoy me and bother me, like other personalities who, it seems, are studying the way to tickle my temper and make it burst out. You're the model of all good daughters and an angel, as one might say, although, let's be fair, I don't believe that there are angels or seraphs. But I love you with my whole soul and I'm telling you so with my heart in my hand; if I regret my passing for any reason, it's for your sake, for though you've got that little husband of yours, you're going to be left alone, very much alone. See . . . my eyes are filling up with water, and I'm drooling."

Rufina, who was as good as gold, would console him and pay him innumerable small attentions, trying to drive all pessimistic ideas from his mind, and from his heart his unextinguishable hatred for other people in the family.

"No, my darling daughter," he would say, biting the handkerchief that he held, "don't tell me that Cruz is good. You judge everybody by the prism of your own self, you angel, but your tender heart deceives you. That woman is not good. I reconciled with her to please my friend Donoso and that blessed man Gamborena, and also so as not to be an obstacle to the settlement and separation of interests. You can see: we've become friends again, and have contact with each other, and I treat her considerately and give in to her meddling ways and her whims as an arbitrary woman. For days now I haven't eaten anything except what she tells me to."

Rufinita would return to the charge, extolling Cruz's merits and her intelligence and her unassailable rectitude, and the usurer would seem at last, if not convinced, on the way to being convinced. He heaped loving words upon his daughter until, once that mysterious eddy of his hypochondria had passed, waves of bitterness again invaded his soul.

"How you all insist that I'm so very ill!" he would say, pacing up and down the room. "And that Quevedito, your husband, will manage to make me so in the end if I pay any attention to his confounded science. He knows about as much medicine as I know about gelding mosquitoes. Just look at the diet he wants to put me on now! Not to take anything but milk: milk in the morning, milk at night, milk in the wee hours. Milk! As if I were a suckling babe . . . Because, let's be impartial, what interest do you all have in my continuing to be ill? Let's have no talk about my dying, for that's not the question, the question is my being very ill. What are you getting out of the fact that I'm shut up in this blasted room and can't go out to discharge my business? Ah! You'll see, you'll see some day ever so many years from now, when I close my eyes . . . ever so many years, you'll see . . . What a blow it'll be for you when you find out that there aren't any fat sheep, that the wealth you thought was so choice is nothing but a piece of bread, as you might say, because what was earned yesterday by work has been lost today by loafing! Of course, others go and swipe all the business, and meantime here I am, bored to confounded tears and looking out for my stomach and my economy and my goddam guts to see if the . . . I dunno . . . is going to pass through them or not pass through them. It's horrible to live like this, seeing the pile that I built with my sweat melting away, and that what I'm losing others are winning; they're carrying off the meat and leaving me nothing but the bone."

For another symptom of his illness, in addition to those bouts of tenderness which broke the monotony of his devilishly bad humor, was the stubborn idea that, because he could not work, not only was his fortune lying idle but inaction was destroying it to the point of nothingness, as if it were a liquid mass left out in the open to evaporate. In vain did his friends employ the most elementary logic to divest him of such an absurd idea, but it clung to his brain with such force that neither logic, nor plain examples, nor reasoning, nor teasing, could cure the strange ailment of his imagination. The pesky idea tormented him day and night, and he could find no other procedure to choke it off than to postpone his death for a considerable time, to call himself cured and plunge once more into the feverish press of business.

The man went from bad to worse, and a day came when the mere attempt to eat produced indescribable discomforts in his stomach and kidneys, cardiac oppression, and dizzy spells. One night, after struggling against insomnia, he fell into a stupor that more resembled a drunken torpor than sleep, and toward morning awoke with a start, as if the elegant canopy of the bed he was sleeping in had fallen on him. A terrible idea assailed him, like a bolt of lightning that flashed right through his head. He jumped out of bed in the dark and lighted the lamp. The idea did not vanish with the light; on the contrary, it seized upon his confused mind all the more strongly. "It's as clear as that light there, it's pure evidence, and I'm the stupidest man in the world not to have discovered it before. I'm being poisoned! Who is the criminal? I don't even want to think about it. But the accomplice is that wretched, filthy Chatillon, that *furrin* cook . . . Thank God, I can see it all as plain as day; every day they give me a little, a few drops of . . . whatever it is. And that's why I'm dying without realizing it. There's no doubt of it. If it's not so, let them do an autopsy on me right now, and they'll see what my *physiognomy's* like. Why, I can feel the bitter taste of that filthy poison in my mouth! The taste comes up in my mouth, it comes up all the time. And will those wretches be able to deny it?"

The dreadful hours of anguish, fright, and convulsive dismay that he spent, until the light of the newborn day visited him, were indescribable. He alternately piled on the bedclothes, chilled to the bone, and threw off the heavy eiderdown, burning with heat. And the idea that was drilling into his brain descended through the current of his nerves to the great sympathetic nerve, and there the horrid thing dug in, producing an unspeakable feeling of anxiety and a torture like that of Prometheus. "I'm thinking with my stomach . . . Well, they must have got turned around, for yesterday I was digesting with my head."

The morning light cleared his brain a little, bringing doubt to his mind, which under the circumstances was consoling. It might be true or it might not. The poisoning might or might not be a fact. Sometimes he persisted in his awful idea, sometimes rejected it as the most absurd notion that could appear in a sick brain. At last, what the devil, reason began to recover its rights and win out over the insubordinate thoughts that had raised the cry of rebellion in that unlucky dawn. "Poison me? How ridiculous! Why in heaven's name would they do that?"

EIGHT

He rose, his chocolate was brought to him, and as soon as it was placed before him he was assailed by awful repugnance, and the terrible idea arose in his mind like a demon playing hide-and-seek. "Here I am," it told him. "Don't drink this concoction if you want to live."

"Ramón," said Torquemada to his valet, "I don't want the chocolate. Tell that fraud Chatillon to drink the nasty stuff himself, and kick the bucket once and for all . . . Listen: beginning tomorrow, have them bring me all the kitchen gear and a spirit lamp; I'll make my chocolate up here, myself."

His stubborn monomania suggested a logical procedure to him, thus: "But what am I getting so upset about, if it's so easy to prove? A couple of days will be enough to truly convince myself of whether or not they're poisoning me. It's terrifically easy. I won't rest until I can be sure . . . absolutely sure."

He called for his carriage. To avoid questions and officiousness on the part of Cruz, who would surely be surprised and alarmed to see him go out so early in the morning and would attempt by all possible means to keep him from doing so, he tried to take advantage of the time when the lady was attending her first mass of the day. Wouldn't she be cross when she learned that the invalid had taken to the streets in the exercise of his free will! And what a fuss the confounded woman would make! "To go out so early, and without breakfast! And your health is so delicate!" "Your health is delicate too . . . but it's your conscience that's unhealthy. I'll give you something to fuss about." And before the mass was over he slipped away like a schoolboy, causing no little surprise to the servants, who, when they saw my lord marquis go out at such an early hour after his long period of incarceration, believed that his illness had affected his mind.

He ordered the coachman to take him to the outskirts of the city, without designating any particular place; he yearned to breathe fresh air, see new faces—that is, faces different from those he saw daily in his house—and give space to his spirit and his eyes. It was a beautiful morning, the sky clear and sunny, the atmosphere unclouded. No sooner had the carriage taken him to the outlying boulevards than Torquemada felt that the placidity of that beautiful day in May was seeping into his soul; and, as he advanced toward the suburbs, everything that he saw, earth and houses, trees and persons, appeared before his eyes as if nature had been given a coat of good cheer, or been newly painted. That was the way the miser regarded what he saw: the passersby, country folk who lived in those outlying areas, seemed happy people who walked along the street or highway proclaiming by the expression on their faces, rather than by words, the joy they felt on so supremely beautiful a day.

From the heights of Vallehermoso he told the coachman to drive down to the groves of Virgen del Puerto, and there he decided to risk a little walk. Leaning on his stick with the staghorn handle, he covered considerable distances, delighted to observe that he was strong enough to do so, though he limped a little; his legs were not a model of reliability, and the soles of his feet hurt. To make him even happier, he felt no discomfort at all in his stomach, nor in his gut, nor anywhere. Why, he couldn't even feel that he had a stomach! To be sure, there is nothing as healthful as morning walks, nor anything that undermines one's nature more than taking and filling one's body with disgusting medicines. Of course, it was the family's fault that his illness had reached such a point, for it would have been no more than a slight indisposition had they not surrounded him with such stupid cares and precautions, if they hadn't made his head swim with so many petty little doctors talking about the pylorus and diathesis, and so many soothsaying priests talking about death.

"By the almighty Bible!" he exclaimed when he had spent an hour limping among those solitary groves. "Why, haven't I an appetite? Yes, there's no doubt of it. Either this is appetite or I don't know anything at all. An appetite it is, and one of the best. The signs are surefire. Why, right now I'd eat . . .! Let's see, I wouldn't eat anything very heavy, but some good garlic soup or rice with codfish; I surely would put that away. See, I was right not to have the chocolate at home. As soon as the stomach gets out on the street it's a new man, it's a new stomach, so to speak, and gets its independence back. Good, good . . . How I'm laughing at Cruz now, and Donoso, and Saint Peter himself, with his keys and all, and at that thief of a cook, and that whole gang in my house and palace! Oh, you Gravelinas mansion, just you wait, I'll fix you! I'll tear you down to make you pay for what you've made me suffer inside of you, after I've disposed of all the *wealth of the Americas*, and I'll sell the ground it stands on, which is worth a lot.

And let Cruz and that fellow with the keys go and say their masses and recite their litanies somewhere else. Hell's fire, this is really too much! I'm certainly getting a tremendous appetite! It's a ravenous appetite, the kind a fellow has when he's a boy and comes home from school. Why, I could eat half a sheep! But oh, my! Just remembering those French messes that Chatillon makes, it seems that this stomach of mine is starting to feel cheated, and I feel those ticklings that come just before wanting to vomit . . . No, no, down with the bastard race of Chatillons and all his crew. I'll fix you, you great rascals, if, as everything seems to indicate, it turns out that . . . But maybe you're not the guilty ones. What interest could you have in my turning up my toes so soon? We'll have to look for the initiative of the crime somewhere else. But what a terrific appetite I have! What better symptom of what I suspected and discovered? My stomach's pealing like churchbells ever since it got away from that lowdown action . . . and, with its cheerful tolling, is telling me to eat, to eat and not be afraid, free at last from priests and pious women who poison the soul as well as the body. And what if I, Francisco Torquemada, marquis of San Eloy, went into one of those mean little taverns like there are near the municipal washplace, and asked for a plate of tripe or some salt pork with tomatoes? What would public opinion have to say? Ha, ha! What would the Senate say if it found out such a thing? Ha, ha! What's certain is that I'm getting rejuvenated. The fellow who said that all this stuff about religion is bunk spoke the truth, and that there's nothing but Nature . . . Nature is man's mother, and doctor, and teacher, and sweetheart."

No action that was not perfect folly could be the consequence of his disordered thoughts, and instead of returning home he spent a long time thinking about where to find the food that his stomach, with youthful energy, was demanding. Suddenly, like the donkey who smells his stable, he gave a start and turned the attention of his eyes and soul toward the huddled architecture of Madrid, which is visible from the hill where he was, with a hundred cupolas and towers: Vistillas, the Toledo Gate, the churches of San Francisco and San Cayetano, the Charity School of San Fernando, and so on. He felt an attraction for the places where he had spent the best years of his life, working like a slave, certainly, but in tranquil independence, those delicious southern districts of the city, so prolific, so honorable, so carefree, and with as much joy in the streets as there was charm in the people. To want it and decide upon it was the work of a moment, and the coachman started off up the Calle de Segovia, with orders to stop in the Plaza de Puerta Cerrada.

As soon as my lord marquis stepped down from the carriage people began to notice him, and when he walked slowly up the Calle de Cuchilleros, leaning heavily on his stick as if he were walking with three feet, both men and women emerged from the doors of their narrow shops to look at him. Most of them did not know him; though his face had changed a great deal in recent times, the appearance of the inhabitants had changed still more. In the years that had passed since the usurer Torquemada transferred his life and activities to other spheres, there was almost a whole new generation among us. But someone among the older folk must undoubtedly have recognized him; the rumor flew about the neighborhood, and more and more persons came to their doors every minute. Torquemada walked along the whole street on the odd-numbered side, recognizing the principal shops, which offered little or no change. On the opposite side he saw the house where the great Doña Lupe had lived, and this memory produced a fleeting emotion in him. If the Turkey Lady were still alive, how happy she would be to see him, and how her cotton breast would rise and fall!

On both sides of the street he recognized the shops, as one recognizes familiar faces one has not seen for a long time, and these could well be called historical, for they were Madrilenian of the purest descent: poultry shops where live birds were sold, the bootmaker's with his blown-up sample pigskins, the woodturner's, the glazier's with its shining glass, like artillery pieces in a military museum; the famous eating-house of "Sobrinos de Botín," the knife shops, the workshop and looms for making reed mats, and at last the narrow staircase, with its ancient wine cellar underneath, like a cavern hollowed out of the foundations of the Plaza Mayor. He stopped before it for an instant, but the meddlesome curiosity of a group of women who had come out of the door of the tavern made him perform an about-face and start down the street again. Don Francisco had been very friendly with the owner of that wine shop in former times, but by now the establishment had passed into new hands. "The truth is," thought the marquis of San Eloy, heading for Puerta Cerrada again on the even-numbered side of the street, "the truth is that folks are dying off; one today, two to-morrow. But the world doesn't come to an end, no, and others and still others come, and those who were children yesterday are around here today, running the establishments." From the dark interior of a poultry shop, its floor bloodstained and covered with feathers, some women emerged who apparently recognized him; at least it seemed so, from the fright that was painted on their faces and the astonishment with which they crossed themselves. Rumor ran like a train of gun-powder, and before he had reached the syringe shop, a few voices were pronouncing the name of Torquemada. He paid no attention and kept reminding himself that he was a national figure, as rich as Croesus, and that familiarities with such people were not the thing. He stopped for an instant before the shop window where all kinds of enema devices and clysters were displayed in shining variety, and, a little farther on, decided to ask about the only friend he still had in that neighborhood, and to invite himself to have a bite to eat in his establishment if he was lucky enough to find him there. It would be funny if Matías Val-lejo had died during the year that had passed since the last time they saw each other! "It might well be, for . . . it happens every day that others die before a fellow dies himself."

He stopped to contemplate the dirty glass window of a tavern in which he saw the usual pot of beans in a red sauce that would stop a fellow in his tracks, the golden sardines, the yellow rounds of hake, the pork chops smeared with tomato sauce, the strings of sausages with that dusty sheen and purplish cast that prove their Spanish origin; and my lord marquis was asking himself whether that tavern was Vallejo's or not, when . . .

NINE

Lo and behold, Matías Vallejo himself stood before him and, doffing his cap with an equal measure of respect and pleasure, told him, "My dear Señor Don Francisco, you here in these neighborhoods, you hav-ing a look at this poverty!"

"Ah, Matías! I was thinking about asking after you. Is this your house? And where's the shop?"

"Come, come with me," said that uncouth man, pulling him by one arm, for which purpose he had to push and shove to break the circle of curious onlookers that instantly formed.

The person of Matías Vallejo was composed of a regular friar's paunch, covered with a black-striped green apron; below it, a pair of feet that scarcely fitted inside some vast carpet slippers, and above, a head that was exactly like a large tomato with eyes, mouth, and nose. In addition to all this, a hearty affability, a roaring laugh, and a watery, gentle gaze denoting the peace of his conscience, a lot of strong wine, and a sedentary life. With this man, who at the time was sixty years old and would grow older if he did not explode one of these days, like a wineskin bursting at the seams with the pitch running out, Don Francisco had had a very close friendship in former times. In the days of his greatness he was the only person from that part of the city with whom he had some slight contact. Matías Vallejo, breaking all the rules of etiquette, had appeared two or three times in the Calle de Silva and the Palace of Gravelinas to ask financial aid from his long-time friend, and Torquemada had graciously given it to him without interest, an unheard-of circumstance of which there is no other example in the great man's history. It is true that Vallejo retired his note faithfully and paid interest out of gratitude; he was a good man both by nature and by circumstance, after his somewhat crude manner.

So, as I say, they carried him off almost bodily to the shop, and from the shop to the room behind it, and sat him down next to an ill-painted wooden table with sticky rings of muscatel left by the bottoms of cheap glasses, which a woman swiped away at, rather than washed, with a rag. Vallejo, his daughter and son-in-law, and two other persons who were in the room, were rendered quite stupid by so extraordinary and important a guest, and did not know what to say to him or what courtesies to pay him in order to do the honors and leave the household banners flying. They bustled about in embarrassment; the woman stemmed the invasion of inquisitive neighbors who tried to slip in behind Don Francisco; Vallejo laughed, wheezing like a bellows; and his son-in-law scratched his head, doffing his cap and putting it on again.

"Goodness gracious, Don Francisco here! What a surprise to have you come and honor this poor shop . . . you, a lord marquis!"

Formerly Torquemada and Vallejo had used the familiar form of address to each other. But Vallejo realized that new times bring new customs and, biting his tongue as if to punish himself, swore to take more care in the future.

"Well, I was taking a walk," said Don Francisco, quite moved by the hospitality of those good people, "and I said to myself, I said, 'I'm going to go and see if that poor fellow Vallejo has died already, or if he's alive.' I've been very ill."

"I heard that you were . . . and believe me, I was really sorry."

"But now I'm in the convalescent stage, in full convalescence, thanks to my decision to take the air and . . . get away from doctors and apothecary shops."

"Sure . . . Why, there's nothing like good fresh air and country life. What I say is that you, you blue-blooded folks, who take care of yourselves more than you need to, don't really live."

"No, because the kind of fellow I am doesn't let go of life as easily as that. By the almighty Bible! Look here, Matías, just as an example, this very day I've given death such a kick in the pants that . . . dammit, I just told it to go to hell . . . Ha, ha! And tell me something: could I have lunch here?"

"Well, hail Mary! By blessed Saint Christopher! The things you say! Nicolasa, by golly, he wants to have lunch! Colasa, and you, Pepón, he's lunching here! What an honor! Just a minute, let's see . . . are there any partridges? If not, send out for some. We've got a suckling pig that'll make you lick your fingers."

"No, not suckling pig."

"Colasa! What are you doing? His Excellency wants to have lunch! It's more of an honor than as if it was the emperor of all of the Germanies and all the Russias."

You would have thought they had gone crazy. Vallejo was crying with joy and jigging with contentment. He himself cleaned the table again with his green apron while Nicolasa brought embroidered tablecloths and napkins from the supply they kept stored away in a chest, for the tavern service was not suitable for such a great personage. It must be mentioned that tavern and shop composed Vallejo's establishment, that both businesses were administered jointly, and that both connected through the back room.

"There's everything," said Vallejo to his friend, "pork chops and veal chops, cured pork loin, poultry, bream, ham, lamb, squid in its own ink, suckling pig, red sausage, good Candelario sausage and as much of it as you want, why, strike me pink, as much as you like!"

"You haven't mentioned something that I've seen in your window, and that really made me want it when I saw it. It's a whim. What I'd really like, Matías, and I think it will agree with me wonderfully . . . Can't you guess? Why, beans, give me a plate of stewed beans, by gum, for it's time for a fellow to be of the people, and go back to the people, to nature, so to speak!"

"Colasa! D'you hear? He wants beans—an eminent senator—beans! For heaven's sake, what a plain man and . . .! But you'll also have an omelet with ham, and then some salt pork . . ."

"For the moment just those little beans, and then we'll see what the stomach says, for surely it's going to thank me for this food, so nutritious and . . . honest. Because I'm of the opinion, Matías, that all the Spanish and Madrid seasonings put together suit folks' stomachs better than the thousand and one messes that my French chef makes; they'd ruin the health of the bronze horse in the Plaza Mayor."

"You said it, by golly! Nothing can get the idea out of my head that all of Señor Don Francisco's illness was just an overdose of those confounded plasters, and too much of those cursed sauces, that seem made up in an apothecary's shop rather than for the table. To put a fellow's innards right, Señor Marquis, there's nothing better than lean salt pork and honest wine. I'm not going to tell Your Excellency, since your stomach's a little delicate, to eat pork, you'll pardon the reference, but I have some veal chops here that would raise the dead, if they're broiled on a grill."

"We'll have a taste of them," said the great man, beginning to eat the beans, which tasted positively heavenly to him. "I can't believe that I'm eating this with such an appetite, and that it's agreeing with me so well. Why, Matías, it's as if they'd taken out my stomach overnight and given me a new one. Your beans are delicious. I don't know how many years it's been since I had some. I'd like to bring my chef here to learn how to cook. For—you won't believe it—he costs me forty duros a month, without counting what he makes by cheating, which is probably a million, believe me, a million."

Matías did the honors for his guest by eating with him, to stimulate him by example, which was extremely persuasive. They were also brought different wines to choose from, and the two preferred a vintage Valdepeñas that was worthy to speak on equal terms with God. After he had enjoyed the beans, the marquis noted joyfully that his stomach, far from feeling strain or indifference, demanded more, like a school-boy released from confinement who rushes out to do all sorts of wild tricks. Bring on the omelet with ham or the first-quality sausage; bring on those chops like cartwheels, nicely grilled and resting on a cushion of tomato sauce; and, especially, more Valedepeñas to season all that substance in a fellow's craw and digest it well.

All those who entered the back room, either to see Señor Matías or with the intention of eating something at the other tables, stood stupe-fied in the presence of Señor Torquemada with their mouths wide open, some because they did not know him, others because they had known him all too well. And the respect inspired in everyone by such a great person kept them speechless, until Vallejo, halfway through the meal, growing cheerful with wine and self-satisfaction, told them, "Blas, and you, Carando, and you, Higinio, don't be *pusillaminous* or hang back. Pull up to the table, for the Señor Marquis feels no shame in associating with you, and he's a very democratic and very dis . . . dissolute gentle-man."

They sat down, and Don Francisco made them one of those grave bows that he had learned in his aristocratic period. Matías made the introductions in bluff style:

"This Blas is the Astorga carrier, and despite his appearance he's worth at least thirty thousand duros. Higinio Portela is the nephew of that Deogracias Portela who used to keep the poultry shop in La Cava . . . d'you remember?"

"Oh! yes, I remember . . . and . . . Deogracias . . . To your health."

"And this Carando is an ass, pardon the reference, for he used to have the business of disposing of dead animals, but because he got involved in a lawsuit with the Gonzálezes in Carabanchel Bajo, he lost his shirt. In short, all of us here—a thousand duros more, a thou-sand duros less—are a bunch of poor ragamuffins in comparison with your greatness, with the terrific richness of a man who, so to speak, has more millions in his coffers than hairs on his head."

"Mustn't exaggerate, mustn't exaggerate," said Don Francisco, af-fecting modesty. "Don't believe the statements of the common herd. I've worked hard, and I intend to work still harder, to repair the damage this confounded illness has brought me. Praise be, today I've been rejuvenated and, to judge by the appetite I'm eating with and how well it agrees with me, I feel as if I'd never been sick or ever will be again all the days of my life, which are going to be a lot of days, lots and lots."

TEN

They raised their glasses and drank to the health of the most democratic of great men and the least high-and-mighty of plebeians turned wealthy, although those who drank did not use these words or anything resembling them: the idea existed only in their crude intention and the roar with which they expressed it. Torquemada felt flooded with youthful joy; very well satisfied with the way his stomach was behaving, he did not know which to praise more, the excellent flavor of everything he was eating, or the cheerful openheartedness of those simple, loyal people who were entertaining him so heartily. However, though he recognized the need to repay their compliments verbally, he also thought, and the opinion was a correct one, that in such a place and with such persons he must uphold the dignity of his position and his name, using the fine language that he had learned, not without effort, in political and aristocratic life.

"Señores," he said, searching his noggin for noble ideas and choice expressions, "I am most grateful for these manifestations, and take real satisfaction in being seated among you and in partaking of these succulent and gastronomic victuals. I do not conceal my origin. I was of the people, and I will always be of the people. You probably know that in the Chamber I have defended the working classes and common people. For the nation to prosper, there must not be antagonism between classes, and Greeks and Trojans must fraternize."

"See, see," exclaimed Matías, who had turned red, or rather the color of blackberries, with enthusiasm. "This man is saying the same thing to you today as I said to you yesterday. The classes have to grab hands, the great ones and the working folks, so's we can have public order and national prosperity."

"The fact is," said Torquemada, spiritedly tackling the meat, "that there are many points of contact between your ideas and mine."

"If all those folks on top," began the man named Carando, "were like those of certain great houses that I know about! I don't say it because Señor Don Francisco is here present with us; I said it yesterday, too. For the fact is that there are rich folks and not all of them are like the family of the gentleman who's listening to me. There's no fear that any poor person in this district will die of hunger while that Señora de Aguila is alive, 'cause she goes from garret to garret finding out where there are open mouths to fill and naked bodies to clothe. I've seen her, and in my tenement house on the Calle del Nuncio there's lots of folks that owe their lives to her."

"It's true, " added the man named Higinio. "And I can bear witness to it, too. She got the son of some neighbors of mine off military service, and bought the daughter her sewing machine."

"Sure, sure," said the marquis of San Eloy without meeting their eyes, realizing that he must maintain not only his dignity, but that of the whole family. "My sister-in-law, Cruz del Aguila . . . She's a saint."

"Well, may she live a thousand years, and let's drink the first glass of muscatel to her health."

"Thanks, señores, thanks. I also drink to the health of that *noble lady*," said Don Francisco, thinking that his private quarrels with her should not be made apparent in outside society. "Ah! She and I are so fond of each other! I let her do exactly as she pleases, for she has such talent and such . . . Whatever changes are *implemented* in my palace, she's the one who makes them. And if some difference or *discrepancy* arises between us, I compromise and sacrifice my desires on the altar of the family. There's no other woman who *scores higher* in overseeing a large number of servants. Mine are like the armies of Xerxes. D'you know who that fellow Xerxes was? A king of Persia, a country that's off somewhere near the Philippines, who had so many troops of all kinds that when he reviewed them, he spent at least seven months watching them come along or pass by . . . Anyway, señores, and you, Matías, my *particular friend*, let's leave my little sister-in-law to her prayers, cosy as can be with God, and let's get to *the reality of things*. I'm very much given to what's real, what's true, I'm realism *par excellence*. What delicious veal! Blessings on the cow that gave you birth and gave you suck and the confounded slaughterman who bled you to make you tender! *I profess the principle* that veal's better than steer and steer's better than heifer. In short, señores: I'm very pleased to be here. I'm stuffed to bursting but my stomach's not rising up to my chin, and I'm happy, so happy that I wouldn't move from here, if the thousand things I have to *undertake* didn't call me elsewhere. This is an *oasis* . . . d'you know what an oasis is?''

"Sure! That fine eating-house they've put up in La Bombilla, that has a sign saying 'At the Oasis of the River.' ''

"That's not correct," said Torquemada, beginning to suspect that he had eaten more than was prudent and had had a bit too much to drink. "It absolutely isn't correct, because *oasis* is something on land, and a river, well . . ."

What happened then was what is inevitable in meals offered by plain, hospitable people with good hearts and little refinement; and it was that the moment Don Francisco showed the slightest reluctance to load his stomach, they all fell upon him, yelling like madmen to encourage him to go on gobbling up everything in the establishment.

"Goodness, to turn up your nose at bream! D'you think it's not as good as the fish your Frenchy cook fixes? Well, I won't let you look down on our poverty! You've got to taste it, just taste it. You'll see how delicious . . . Why, today's your day off! Believe me, Don Francisco, I wish I had your stomach. What's wrong with that rascal is that it's got dirt in it on account of all those lousy apothecary's medicines you've put in it, and you get rid of dirt by eating good things and drinking fine wine. Don't be scared, Señor Marquis, for it's the belly makes the feet go and not the other way around. Nosiree, you don't go out of my house turning up your nose at the bream, by golly! Then for later on I've got some capons that would make the Holy Trinity itself sit up and take notice! Get along with you! Drink up, do yourself some good."

A great deal of character and willpower were necessary to resist these suggestions by a hospitality that was as cordial as it was inappropriate, and at that moment Torquemada lacked both, for he had abdicated all power of decision regarding the people who were his equals in birth and upbringing. And, because the discomfort he was beginning to feel was still minor, and its effects were lessened by the gluttonous instincts that had been awakened in him by those victuals so much to his taste, he agreed to everything, and on with the party. The guests' chitchat distracted him from feeling apprehensive and did not allow him to hear the signals his stomach was sending from time to time. But even so, when the capons reached the table he drew the line, for really he felt a weight on his stomach that worried him. Capons! *Get thee behind me, Satan.* What he did eat, however, was the fresh and well-seasoned lettuce salad, and *between times* he drank glass after glass of a number of different wines, which he gulped down mechanically without noticing what he was doing.

"The truth is," he said, "that everything's agreeing with me. A little sensation of heaviness, but that's all. I'm feeling very happy, rejuvenated, *so to speak*, and ready to repeat the spree every day of the week. If the folks at my house could see me they'd be amazed and dumbstruck. And I'd tell them, "Sure, I've got the proof. Just look at this mister stomach of mine, that before couldn't carry on the digestion of a *mere* cup of chocolate, and now . . . It's enough for me to get out of your orbit to find myself in perfect shape, and my stomach's the first to congratulate itself on being in *another sphere of action*, very different from the one in which . . . Because it's very plain that there's a crime and that . . ."

For the first time words failed him and his thoughts grew vague. For an instant he clawed at the air. But fortunately this passed, and when he returned to himself my lord marquis complained of shortness of breath.

"That's nothing but wind," Matías told him. "A little glass of Anís del Mono, and you'll see how it unloads you. Colasa!"

While the anisette was on its way, Matías applied to the sick man the elementary medication of pounding him on the back with the palm of his hand. But he did so with such good will and desire to obtain an effective and quick response, that Torquemada had to tell him, "Here, here, man, don't be so rough. D'you take me for a bass drum? Ow, ow! Now I think it's easing a little. It's wind, just wind that's got stuck . . . Brrr . . . !"

He tried to ward off the storm by attempting to bring up belches, which stuck halfway and left him worse off than before. The confounded anisette gave him some relief shortly after he drank it, and he was again able to speak and express his happiness.

"I *concur* with your ideas. I mean, I think the same as you do about the . . . Eh! Say, you, what were we talking about? Heavens, all my memory is slipping away. . . Damn, how I forget things! Eh! Say, you, what's your handle? Imagine, me forgetting your name!"

"Matías Vallejo, at your service," replied the host, who felt inclined to informality after so much eating and drinking. "What? Is that spell coming on again? What's this, Francisco my boy? You old rascal! It's only some cussed wind! Get rid of it, get rid of it quick, for heaven's sake . . . Come on, now!"

And he fell to slapping him on the back again. While the other was administering this medicine Don Francisco leaned forward, rigid and distended, like a full sack that has been stood on end and is starting to fall over.

"That's enough. I tell you that it's enough. You've got a hand like one of those rammers they use to pave the streets . . . dammit! Now I've got my memory back. Now I know what I was going to tell you, fellow guests . . . because one of you said that we ought to give something to my coachman, who's waiting for me outside . . . and I . . . exactly . . . I said, "Señores, I *concur* with your ideas, or, *in other terms*, I also think that we ought to give something to that drunken coachman of mine."

"That's true," grumbled Matías. "I didn't remember. Colasa!"

"And *in this vein*, I'll go on to tell you," continued Don Francisco, displaying obvious difficulty in staying upright, "that I don't feel very well, you might say. I feel as if I've swallowed the cross of Puerta Cerrada, which we could see through the window here . . . Hey, I can't see it! Where did that blasted cross go? Cruz? I said Cruz, and I don't take it back."

"Francisco, my fine old friend!" exclaimed Matías, violently hugging Don Francisco, for in one of his teeterings he had bumped into the other man. "I love you like a son. Now, to clear our heads, let's have coffee . . . Colasa!"

"Mocha," said Torquemada hastily, making efforts to open his eyes, which seemed determined to close. "Coffee. . ."

"With rum, or cane brandy?"

"There's cognac too."

"Señores," murmured the marquis of San Eloy, bellowing rather than speaking, "I feel awful, just awful. The fellow who says I feel well isn't doing justice to truth . . . to the truth of the matter. I've been eating like the greatest gobbler of all gluttons . . . but I swear by all the confounded bibles in the world that I've got to digest it, so they won't say at my house that . . . so she won't laugh at me, the other one, the . . . Confound my memory! Say, Matías, tell me, what's her name?"

"Who?"

"That one . . . the sister of my departed . . . I've forgotten her name. Listen, you, just a little while ago I was looking at her through the window . . . over there."

"Sure . . . the cross of Puerta Cerrada."

"Ah! It's called Puerta Cerrada . . . that's the cross . . . no, it's the other one . . . and Puerta Cerrada is the cross that I have inside my body and can't get rid of . . . cross of the devil, and gate of heaven that doesn't want to open . . . and closed gate of hell. Say, what's the name of that pig of a priest? The one of the munitions or messions or missions or whatever they're called. Tell me what his handle is. I want to tell him a thing or two. It was between him and that two-faced hellcat of Gravelinas that they figured out the plan to poison me. And they did it . . . You see . . . what they've done to me. They made me swallow this whole house. How am I going to get it out of me now, dammit, dammit, double dammit?"

He fell over on the opposite side from Matías, and landed against a chair that kept him from falling to the floor. They all rushed to help him. They did not know whether to set him upright or lay him down by placing two or three benches in a row. He writhed in horrifying convulsions, grunting like a pig. At last, brrr . . . ! The whole floor of the room was too small for everything that came out of that miserable body.

"Colasa!"

ELEVEN

"This man is really sick," said Matías to his friends. "And what'll we do? What the devil shall we give him?"

"Let him get it all out."

"Oh, my God! What is this? Where am I? What a calamity! I thought . . . What a shame that I ate that meal! Matías, señores, I'm terribly ill."

This was the first thing that Torquemada said after his horrible fit, and although the oppression in his stomach was eased by vomiting, very severe pains in the gastric region soon began to torment him.

"A cup of tea . . . Colasa!"

"And I was feeling so great! And the meal had tasted so fine! D'you know what hasn't been good for me? The heat. It's terribly stuffy in here . . . and because you were all talking at once, and made a noise pounding on the table with the glasses . . . Ow, what a terrible pain! It seems as if my innards are twisting and turning. They can say what they like, this is natural. Because, believe me: a fellow has his bits of *scientific* knowledge and knows how to distinguish natural illnesses from artificial ones. There are *pathological phenomena* that are the work of nature and others that are the *end product* of our enemies' hatred. I'd swear I have a fever. Matías, d'you know how to feel a pulse?"

They suggested taking him home, and he resisted the idea. He could not sit up straight, and his head was heavy as lead. He held it up with both hands, his elbows resting on the table.

"I won't go home till this upset is over. The pain isn't so bad now. But I can tell you that my memory's slipping away from me again. Would you believe that I can't remember the name of my house? That is, the name of that pig of a duke I bought it from has gone right out of my head, that crook, that show-off . . . Gosh! My coachman's name is gone too. They must be frightened to death at home, and my—can't remember that either—that woman, and the priest and Donoso . . . will think I'm dead. The fact is that I can't remember why I got the crazy whim of going out so early in the morning. It must have been a sudden idea, some urgent business. . . Goodness, I can't find the *concordance*. What I do have well fixed in my memory is that there are a lot of paintings in my house, and the Masaccio, the famous Masaccio, that the English offered me five hundred pounds for, and I wouldn't give it to them. . . Let's see if all of you can help my memory. Did I go out because you called me, to buy the picture gallery that belonged to that *individual*—can't remember his name either—Doña Augusta's papa? Or did I go out because an idea occurred to me *sui generis*, and I rushed off without knowing what I was doing?"

"Go home . . . Please go, Señor Don Francisco," said Vallejo, who, with the fright he had received, was recovering the use of his mental faculties. "They must be worried about you there."

The others were of the same opinion and supported Vallejo's arguments, for he wished to see his establishment free of this complication.

"My house is a long way off," said Torquemada very disconsolately, again tormented by severe pains. "I can't answer as to whether I'll get there, or whether I won't die on the way. How are they going to take me? On a stretcher? Ah, You're right—in my carriage! I hadn't remembered that I have a carriage now. . . How funny that is! Just now I was thinking that I lived on the Calle de la Leche, that I was poor, as you might say, and that I hadn't married those highfalutin Aguilas yet. But, d'you know what I say? If they take me anywhere, let it be to my daughter Rufina's house, for she loves me like the apple of her eye. Though, if I'm going to be frank with you, I'm beginning to suspect that Cruz loves me too, and that the priest—now, there's a name I can't remember—has promised me the salvation of my soul, if and when I give him a very strict accounting of all the sins that appear on the debit side of my conscience, which, I assure you, aren't very many, and if you want me to confess right now, I'll spit it all out. . . Seems to me it's a day to spit everything out. So I'm going home? My house is very big, I can see it now, as if I'd left it just a minute ago. Although you people uphold the *opposite thesis,* I say and repeat that I have a fever of at least eighty degrees, for fever is also measured in degrees, like the *heat column* of thermometers. I'm very grateful for your fine hospitality, and *deplore* with all my heart the fact that the menu, *in the vernacular* fare, did me harm, which has been a nasty trick by my stomach, for if it had behaved itself decently, by this time I would have had that meal as well digested as a baby's pap. But after all, there'll be another time, because I believe it's an incontrovertible fact that I'm going to have a digestion like clockwork. I'll soon get the upper hand of this mister stomach of mine, and if I can't do it by fair means I'll do it by foul. It's scandalous *to the highest degree* that an individual can't attend to his business because of the whims of his goddamned stomach, and can't go to the Senate Chamber, where there's so much, so much business to *undertake,* and then having to give up food . . . though if you'll permit me to tell you everything I think, I'll say that if this organ of mine *persists in its destructive campaign,* I'll fix it with the simplest and most effective rule. What do you think I'll do? Why, not eat. That's right: *not eat.* What does that nuisance want? For me to give it food only to vomit it up again? I'll take its rations away, that's what, I'll empty the trough. I'll wipe out all the luncheons and dinners in the budget with a stroke of the pen. You'll see how it'll have to give up then, and beg my pardon, and ask me for something to eat. But I won't give it anything, no. Don't laugh. When a fellow wants to do a thing, it gets done. Hurrah for most blessed willpower! When a fellow makes up his mind not to eat he doesn't eat, and I swear and promise that I won't eat ever again in my life."

All of them applauded the joke, and, *placed under consideration* again, or rather, placed upon the dirty boards of the tavern table, the question of whether or not he ought to go, and if so where, the hapless marquis said that they could take him wherever they wanted, adding that he was unable to move, and that his legs had turned to cotton, and that his body felt like a trunk full of rocks. At last, Matías and Carando half carried him to the carriage, which drew up to the very door of the tavern, and with no little difficulty managed to shove him inside, all of them taking a very courteous leave of him and feeling delighted that so great a calamity was out of their hands.

Well, the fuss that was raised in the Palace of Gravelinas when the carriage arrived and the doorkeeper and the other servants saw their master, lying back like a corpse, with his eyes closed and emitting foam and terrible groans from his contorted mouth! There was great disquiet in the house, owing to the strange circumstances of his departure as well as the length of time the marquis had been absent. Cruz and the friends who had come when they heard the news feared some accident. The arrival of the carriage, and the pitiable state in which the sick man had arrived, confirmed their fears. But they thought only of getting him out of the vehicle and putting him to bed. Four of the strongest servants took charge of this difficult operation, transporting him through galleries, up staircases, and through antechambers to his bedroom. The poor man had lost consciousness and did not move a finger. Cruz immediately sent for doctors, and the most elementary household remedies were applied to bring him back to consciousness and reawaken life, if any was left in that miserable, inert body. When they tossed their heavy burden on the bed, the spring mattress bounced as if it were trying to throw him off.

Quevedo hastened in, panting, and examined him on the spot. Before this, Donoso, who luckily had been in the house when the carriage arrived, had examined him, but he was unable to determine the true state of his unhappy friend's condition.

"I think he's not dead," said Donoso to the doctor, fearing a response that would deprive them of all hope.

"No, he's not dead . . . but he won't recover from this."

· PART III ·

ONE

By the use of powerful emetics, they managed to make the great Madrid skinflint's ramshackle physiological machine operative again; but even so, all night and part of another day passed before he recovered his memory and recognized his surroundings. By the following afternoon, therefore, he was relatively improved and was described as such in the visiting lists, which soon became covered with hundreds of signatures illustrious in politics and banking. A suggestion on the part of the attending physician to call upon Dr. Miquis was unnecessary, for the patient himself, as soon as he had recovered consciousness and the power of speech, asked to have him come. The famous doctor ordered a tentative course of treatment and an exploratory diet, for he was not yet certain of the illness that had to be combated. The physical picture was still obscure and the symptoms did not clearly demonstrate the morbid character of the profound organic change that had occurred. In his private conversations with Quevedito, Miquis made reference to an intestinal problem, also to cancer of the pylorus, but nothing could be firmly stated yet, except for the seriousness and eventual near-uselessness of scientific efforts.

During his resurrection, for it can well be called so, poor Don Francisco expressed himself in the emotional and sentimental register that went so well with his physical weakness and the flagging of his faculties. He took it into his head to ask forgiveness of all and sundry, to grow emotional over the least thing, and to express vehement affection toward all the persons who came to his bedside to console him. With Rufinita he was syrupy-sweet: he squeezed her hand, calling her his *angel*, his *hope*, his *glory*. He was on the best of terms with Cruz and never ceased praising her talent and governing gifts, and he called Gamborena and Donoso *pillars of the house*, peerless friends, the kind you find none of in the world.

· 527 ·

Showing through all these sentimental manifestations, an intense feeling of fear could be observed in the patient's mind. His self-pride tried to conceal it, but it was apparent in his deep and frequent sighs, his profound attention to every whisper that was heard in the bedroom, the expression of alarm in his eyes when he was asked questions. He took extraordinary pleasure in being encouraged with announcements that he was getting better, and asked everyone his or her own opinion, as well as that of others, about his illness. One morning, when he was alone with Dr. Miquis, he took his hand and gravely told him, "My dear Don Augusto, you are a man with a great deal of science and respectability, and will not deceive me. I am somewhat *scientific*; that is, in my nature the scientific side dominates the poetic side, you understand, I'm sure. In consequence, I deserve to be told the truth. Is it certain that you believe I'll be cured?"

"Why should I not believe it? Yes, señor, have confidence, stick to your regimen and . . ."

"And about how long? About how much time, my dear Señor Don Augusto? Will it be a month before you say I'm well, or will I have to wait a little longer?"

"It's not easy to pinpoint . . . but it will be soon. Lots of rest, and don't worry about going back to business."

"No?" said the skinflint in a deeply disconsolate tone. "Well, if the medical profession wants me to cheer up, let me think about my business and count the days that are left before I can plunge into it again up to the eyebrows. Oh, my friend and very wise physician, I beg you by what you love most in all the world to make an effort and polish up your science so as to cure me soon, soon! Read whatever needs to be read, study everything that needs to be studied, and have no doubt that the emolument will be such that you'll have no complaints of me. I know what you're going to tell me: that you know everything already and haven't anything to learn. Ah, science is infinite! One can never possess it all. It occurs to me that maybe in the archives of this house there's some old paper with this or that prescription to cure this trouble I've got, prescriptions that doctors nowadays don't know about. Great Heaven! Who can tell me that the ancients didn't know about some herb juice, salve, or something of the sort, that modern doctors are ignorant of? Think about it, and of course you know that you have the archive at your disposal. It cost me an arm and a leg, and it's too bad that we can't find a cure for me there."

"Who knows?" said the doctor benevolently, to console him. "It may be that among the Naples and Sicily papers there's some recipe of an old alchemist or necromantic healer."

"Don't laugh at magic, or at those types who used to tell fortunes by looking at the stars. Science is something that has no end . . . no beginning either . . . And now that we're talking about science, tell me: what the devil is this thing that I've got? Because, thinking about it these days, I believe that . . . it's gotten into my head that my illness is a fake, a slight indisposition, and that you medical gentlemen think the same, but, to keep up scientific appearances . . . you've got me here, with all this stage scenery of staying in bed and diet and . . . bibles. I feel fine now, just fine. Will you admit, yes or no, that there's nothing wrong with me?"

"Not so fast. Your illness may not be very serious, but neither is it a slight indisposition. We'll overcome it by taking care of it."

"So I can count on . . . ? Do you assure me that . . . ?" asked the marquis of San Eloy with lively apprehension.

"Just be calm and have confidence in me and in God, first of all in God."

"I have that already . . . Why, is the Lord God going to leave me in the lurch, without having given Him cause for it? If you help Him with the resources of the medical profession, the Lord won't mind my returning to my usual occupations. Yes, my dear Don Augusto, you will do humanity a favor by curing me. I have a plan! Oh, what a plan! It's an idea that wouldn't occur to anyone except yours truly. You don't understand about this, nor will I trouble you by explaining it to you. Everyone has his kind of knowledge, and in my branch of it I'm absolutely unbeatable. Make me well and the business world will tremble with this operation that I've got inside my head. The matter is so important that I'll be satisfied just to be well for the time I need to move the pieces on the board and make my great play. And then, I wouldn't mind falling ill again. A parenthesis, Señor Don Augusto, just a parenthesis of health . . . But no, it would be a pity if I'd kick the bucket after carrying out the operation, so those who come after me would get all the good out of it. That's not fair. Admit that it's not fair."

Miquis saw that he was so possessed with his idea, and was so much alarmed by the shining of his eyes and the restlessness of his hands, that he thought it prudent to cut the conversation short. And since there was no better way to calm him than to cater to his desires, the doctor took his leave, giving him assurances of recovery. Naturally, this would come sooner or later depending on whether the patient speeded his improvement by repose of body and spirit or delayed it by his impatience. And the less he thought about financial operations the better. There was plenty of time.

The fact is that our man was overjoyed with the doctor's visit, and his hopes cheered him sufficiently to endure the dreariness of the dietetic regimen and being confined between sheets. When speaking to Cruz, he told her, "That Don Augusto is a great man. He assures me that it's all a question of a few days. You could certainly give me a little more to eat, which I promise to digest *velis nolis*. We certainly don't want mister stomach to go back to his old tricks! My bellyaches aren't as strong now, and as for fever, I haven't got any. The only thing I recommend is that you look out for the cooks and scullions, because . . . they could let too many condiments slip in, and something would turn up and poison me . . . *in principle, so to speak*. No, I'm not saying that they's poisoning me *motu proprio*, like that rascal Matías Vallejo and those fool friends of his, who stuffed me with a lot of disgusting things practically by force. No, I know that you'll look out for that . . . *I cherish the conviction* that there's nothing to worry about with you on hand. Well, just arrange it among all of you to get me well in a few days, because, I want you to know, it's very important for the family and I can almost—almost—go so far as to say for the nation and all of humanity. For if this confounded *pathological phenomenon* gets a stranglehold on me, I don't know what will become of the little fortune I've put together with so much effort, and it could even happen that my children, in the near future, if I continue to be so feeble, won't have anything to eat."

Cruz burst out laughing and, forgetting for a moment that under the circumstances she must place the pious lie before the truth which she, as supreme intelligence of the family, always professed, warned him in an authoritarian tone, "Don't think so much, don't think so much about interests that will necessarily stay here on earth, for although you're not in danger of death, God forbid, your situation is one of the sort that must be considered as a providential warning; therefore, you must turn your eyes to the interests of the beyond, to eternal interests, if only to get used to them gradually. Let's see, now: do you still think that you haven't much money, or do you plan to take it to the other world to start a bank or credit institution in the regions of eternal bliss?"

"Whether or not I found credit institutions when I'm in divine glory is no business of yours. I'll do exactly as I please, my fine lady," he said, and, like a scolded child, dived into the depths of the bed and covered his face with the sheet.

TWO

Either in the morning or the afternoon, Gamborena never failed for a single day to visit him, showing great affection for the poor invalid, to whom he spoke in the language of a friend rather than a spiritual adviser. The things that he did occasionally say to him in this regard were so delicately put, and so carefully enveloped in general concepts or concepts of health, that the other received the suggestions without becoming alarmed. Once Don Francisco's head was clear, Gamborena amused him by telling him fascinating cases and incidents concerning missions, which the other heard with as much delight as if he were being read novels or travel books. They were so much to his taste that more than once he had the missionary sent for before the hour when he usually visited, and would ask him for "a story," as sick children do to the nurse or nursemaid who is taking care of them. And Gamborena, believing that because the sick man's imagination was imprisoned it would be easy to gain ascendancy over his mind, told him splendid episodes of his evangelical epic: his work in the vicariate of Ubangi, Equatorial Africa, right in a country of cannibals, when the priests, after officiating, would take off their vestments and work as masons or carpenters in the construction of the modest cathedral in Brazzaville; the terribly dangerous mission in the country of the Banziri, the most ferocious of African tribes, where some priests suffered martyrdom and he succeeded in escaping by a miracle of God, with the aid of his keen intelligence; and, lastly, the moving odyssey of his labors in the remote islands of the central Pacific, the archipelago of Fiji, where in a short time seventy churches were founded and ten thousand Kanakas converted to the Catholic faith.

Of course, the fact that Torquemada heard these stories with lively attention and profound interest did not mean that he believed them or took them for real and positive events. He thought, rather, that all of them had occurred on another planet and that Gamborena was an exceptional person, a historian, if not an inventor, of those sublime yarns. He supposed them to be tales for grown-up children or sick old men.

We do not know how the conversation gradually got around to the territory on which the priest wished to confront his friend, but the fact is that one afternoon, when he saw that Torquemada was relatively quiet, he brought up the subject this way:

"It seems to me, my dear sir, that we ought not to put off that matter of ours for very much longer. Several days ago you told me that your head was very weak; today it is strong, from what I can see, and it is in your interest that we talk."

"As you wish," replied Torquemada, mumbling his words and assuming a slightly childish accent. "But if I'm to be frank with you, I can't see such a hurry. I think that there's no question that I'm going to come out of this illness: I feel well. I expect to get well very soon."

"So much the better. What, do we have to wait till our last hours to prepare ourselves, when there will be no time left and the medicine arrives too late? Come, my dear sir, I won't wait any longer. I'm doing my duty."

"But I don't have any sins, what the devil!" exclaimed Don Francisco, half serious and half joking. "The only sin I had I told you about the other day. That I was struck by the idea that Cruz wanted to poison me. Nobody's free of one bad thought."

"Very well . . . And aren't there any more? Search your mind carefully, search it."

"No, there's nothing else. Even if you get angry, Señor Gamborena of my sins . . . not of my sins, because I haven't any . . . Señor Gamborena of my virtues . . . even though you'll be shocked, I have to tell you that I'm a saint."

"A saint! Congratulations. The next thing you'll do will be to ask that I be your penitent, and you my confessor."

"No, because I'm not a priest. Being a saint is something else. I call myself a saint because I do no harm to anyone."

"Are you sure of it? I certainly will not refuse to recognize as truth what you have just told me, if you prove it to me. Come now, I'm waiting for the demonstration. Would you like to have me start you off? Well, here goes. You have only one vice, only one, which is avarice. Convince me that a man who is avaricious and grasping to extremes can be a saint, a man who knows no love but money, or any desires except to bring home everything he finds out there; convince me of this, and I will be the first to request your canonization, Señor Don Francisco."

"Bah, bah! Dammit! Now you're playing on the key of avarice and sums and percentages! Words, words, words. You priests—*in the vernacular, ministers of the altar*—may understand theology, but you don't understand one thing about business. Let's see: what's wrong with my bringing money home, if the money lets itself be brought? And why does this great operation that I have in mind have to be a sin? A sin for me to propose to the government converting *the external debt into internal debt*! Let's see, my fine friend, do the Council of Trent, the Church fathers, or the fellow who wrote the Bible, who I guess was Moses, have anything to say about that? What the devil, why, the conversion of the *external* into *internal* debt is a great thing for the country! Tell me, Señor Saint Peter, what does God gain if exchange rates are so high? Well, if I manage to bring them down, and benefit the country and all of humanity, then how am I sinning, by all the holy bibles? But I know, I know what my lord the minister of the altar is going to tell me. That I'm not carrying out this operation for the benefit of humanity, but for my own profit, and that what I'm looking for is the commission that I and the other bankers who're in on the deal are going to knock off. But to that objection I reply with a question: on what tablets of the law, in what missal or in what Christian or Mohammedan doctrine does it say that the workman mustn't charge anything for his work? Is it right that I should risk my *assets* and tramp the streets from one government office to another like a drudge, without *realizing* a percentage that corresponds to the size of the operation? And tell me: isn't it also charity to do good to the State? What is the State but an oversized fellow creature? And if it's admitted that I like to have folks do for me what I do for the State, don't we have here a clear and obvious case of *do unto others as to yourself?*"

"Holy, holy, holy . . . hosanna!" exclaimed Gamborena, laughing, for what could the priest do but take it as a joke? "Goodness, your illness has made you very witty. I confess that your explanation has amused me. But look, I'm not entirely convinced, and I greatly fear that, what with these conversions of debts and so much 'sacrifice' for the State and the exchange rates and humanity, my dear Don Francisco is going to wind up in the deepest of hells, where Satan's book-keepers will finish balancing his accounts, for they are there to take care of those and other sorts of liquidations. Hell, yes indeed! One must say it plainly, even though you are frightened by the word. Those who in life did not know how or did not want to do anything but accumulate riches, those who had no compassion on the poor and consoled not one afflicted person, fall headlong there. Hell, yes indeed! Do not expect from me anything but the naked truth, with all the strictness of doctrine. Offenses done to God, who is eternal goodness, are eternal forfeits that must be paid."

"Bah! Now you're giving me bad news," said Torquemada, affecting a joking tone and completely cowed. "So what? Do I have no choice but to believe in the existence of that *center* all full of flames, and in devils, and that all of it is to last eternities?"

"Why, of course, you have to believe it."

"Agreed. If it's an obligation, a fellow has to believe. So that I can't even *place it under consideration* . . . but have to believe it all, lock, stock, and barrel, I mean . . . believe it with my eyes shut?" The missionary nodded affirmatively. "All right. Then it's time to believe. Let's agree that there is a hell, but that I'm not going to go there."

"You will not go provided you try not to, by the means which I propose to you, and which constitute the most elementary part of the doctrine that I profess and want to inculcate into you."

"Then inculcate whatever you think necessary, for here I am, ready for everything," said Don Francisco, with a resignation which the missionary took to be a very good sign. "What must I do to be saved? Explain it quickly and with the plainness that has to be used in business. I, as the good Christian that I am, want and need salvation. I ought to try for it simply because it's in keeping with my dignity. It would be too bad for people to say . . .! All right, let's save ourselves, Señor Gamborena. Now tell me what I have to *do* or what I have to *give* to obtain that result."

THREE

"What do I have to *do* . . . what do I have to *give!*" repeated Gamborena, frowning. "You always have to treat this matter as though it were a mercantile operation. How much better it would be for you to forget your habits and even your language as a businessman! What you have to do, my dear sir, is to cleanse your soul of all that leprosy of avarice, to be good and humane, to pay more attention to the innumerable sorrows that lie all around you so as to remedy them, and to persuade yourself that it is not fair for one person to possess what so many others lack."

"In a word, that there are a lot, an awful lot, of poor folks. I've been poor too. If I'm rich now, I owe it to my own efforts. I've never broken into anyone's strongbox, nor have I gone out on the highroad with a musket. And there's something else: all those poor folks who *pullulate* out there, I didn't make them poor. But don't you people say that it's very beautiful to be poor? Leave them alone, leave them alone, and let's not interfere to take their divine poverty away from them. Which is no *obstacle* to my having a clause in my will to distribute charity, though the truth is that I've never liked to *foment* idleness. But I'll leave something to help a hospital or whatever they want, dammit! Excuse me, it just slipped out . . . And I'll leave something to the holy clergy for masses for myself and my two beloved wives, for it's only fair to let the church rabble eat . . . It's true, there's a lot of poverty in the parish priesthood."

"That is very good," said Gamborena gently, "but it is not all that I want. I do not see that these offers come from the heart. It seems to me that you are making them as an act of mere politeness, like paying a visit, like leaving a visiting card when one sets out on a journey. Alas, my friend, when you depart on the supreme journey, you are going to bear such a weight on your soul that it will cost you a bit of trouble to take flight."

"Weight? Weight?" murmured the miser sadly. "Why, I won't be able to take anything I own with me, and every bit of it will have to stay here!"

"That is what you regret, that wealth stays here and that there is no use thinking about transporting it to eternity, where it is absolutely unnecessary. The riches that are appreciated there have another name: they are called 'good deeds.' "

"Good deeds! And with good deeds can I be sure of . . . ?" said Torquemada, abandoning his attempt to strike a bargain.

"But I do not see those good deeds in you, for you are all hardness of heart, selfishness, and avarice."

"Hardness of heart? I don't believe you're right about that, Señor Gamborena. I love my children, and especially my first son, I adored him; I loved my two wives, my Silvia and the one I lost this year."

"Heavens, what an admirable trait that is! To love one's children! Why, even the animals love theirs! If my lord marquis of San Eloy lacked such a primitive feeling, he would be an egregious monster . . . To love one's wife, one's life companion, the woman who gave you social position and an illustrious name! Well, I should hope so! And when God took her away you grieved, that is true; but you also raged, protesting because Cruz did not die instead of Fidela. That is, you would have been happy to see your sister-in-law die."

"Man alive, I wouldn't go so far as to say happy. But if the *dilemma* were to be posed as to the two of them, I wouldn't have hesitated for a moment."

"Stop talking about dilemmas. You have confessed to me that you desired Cruz's death."

"Well, yes, I . . ."

"Your hardness of heart is clearly shown. And your covetousness, your avarice . . . a person would have to be blind not to see them, and you yourself must recognize those horrible sores on your soul and confess them."

"All right, I've confessed . . . Let's get on with it. A fellow's the way he is, and can't be any other way. Only when a fellow's getting to the end does he see things clearly, and since he no longer has interests on this side, naturally, he calls on those of the other side. And the worst of it is that they come at us with this stupid bore about good deeds when we no longer have time to . . . *verify them*, either bad or good."

"You still have time."

"That's what I think too," said the marquis with a certain gleam in his eyes, "because I'm not going to die of this illness. I've got time, right?"

"Certainly, and we'll start to make the most of it at once."

"How?"

"By your giving me your cape."

"Ah! So you want that little old cape of mine? Ha, ha!"

"Yes, yes; but let's be sure we understand one another. I want the new one."

"What's this? The new one?"

"The brand-new one, the Number One cape. On that occasion, I forgive you for having given me an old rag that you had no use for. Today you must give me the garment that you care about most."

"Gosh!"

"And, moreover, I want your frock coat, your overcoat, your waistcoat, in short, the very best clothing that my lord marquis possesses."

"You're going to leave me mother-naked."

"Then you will have lightened your load."

"Well, wouldn't the man look dandy with all my clothes on . . . and wouldn't he be warmly dressed, for God's sake?"

"No, I don't want those clothes for myself. You can see: I am well dressed and need nothing. I ask them for others who have no clothes at all."

"In short, I have to dress a lot of people."

"And warm their stomachs, give them what you have absolutely no need of now. But it has to be with an outpouring of love, as when that Don Francisco we were talking about gave me the old cape."

"All right then, *formulate, formulate* your proposal."

"I will formulate it, never fear. For if I did not offer you the solution, I know very well that the shrewd businessman who is listening to me would 'change his cape for a smock,' as the saying goes, and . . ."

"Out with the formula."

"Ah, not so fast! Let me think about it carefully. But don't go back on your word later. The cape I want is made of such fine cloth that, with the amount it is sold for, many miseries will be relieved, many. Poor folk, an infinite number of poor folk, half of humanity, will be very fortunate."

"Here . . . wait a bit," said the marquis of San Eloy, greatly alarmed. "There's no need to hurry so much, Señor Missionary. I'm against these *professional* exaggerations, and if I *overstep myself*, then I won't be a saint but a madman, and madmen don't go to heaven but to limbo."

"You will go . . . where you deserve to go. You will see all the paths ahead of you. Choose the one that suits you best, because that is what your free will is for. With purity of heart, with love for your fellow man, with charity, you will go there above very easily, and with their opposite, there below without a doubt. And do not believe that your salvation is certain just because you've given me your cape, if along with that piece of cloth you do not offer me your soul."

"Then . . . ?"

"But even though an outpouring of love must precede the act, there are cases in which the act produces the outpouring, or at least helps to do so. Hence you always come out the winner. And now I'll stay no longer, my friend."

"But don't go until we at least come to an agreement about the *bases* . . ."

"Leave that to me, I will take care of the bases. For the moment, more conversation isn't good for you. We have talked enough. Rest now, and be calm and have confidence in God's will. Tonight, if you feel well, I'll come back for another little while. Good-bye."

Don Francisco was very suspicious about that matter of *giving away his cape* and, indeed, could not understand what the devil the blessed Gamborena meant by "cape." And it might well be that, if he placed an enormous value on the garment, there would be no way to come to an agreement with him. He wanted that evening to come in order to confer again with the priest about that matter, and to establish the bases in question for himself. But unfortunately, at about nightfall he was attacked by extremely violent pains in his belly, with such spells of retching and nausea that the poor man thought he was dying, and his fear made his illness doubly severe; and his combined fears and nausea, forming a powerful combination, caused the whole family to believe that the marquis of San Eloy's last hour was at hand. Miquis hurried to the scene and ordered injections of morphine and atropine. At about ten o'clock the storm subsided, but the sick man was exhausted, befuddled, with trembling feet and hands, his face as altered as his spirit was shaken, unable to utter anything that made sense. He was eager to eat something, and then repelled by the very thing he had asked for. In view of the gravity of his illness, the family succeeded in persuading Miquis to spend the night there; Rufinita and Cruz decided to sit up with the sick man; and Donoso, as the most reliable person for the task, took charge of preparing his friend for those acts and dispositions which, owing to the seriousness of the situation, could not be further postponed. Before taking this step he had to confer with the good doctor, who promised to prepare the way for him at the first opportunity that presented itself.

Indeed, when he was summoned to the bedside by Don Francisco, who wanted to cheer himself up with the presence of the eminent physician, Augusto told him, "Señor Marquis, don't be frightened. We have had a setback. But we'll get the cart rolling forward again."

"You wouldn't be alluding to the funeral cart."

"Oh, no!"

"Because, though I feel terrible tonight, I don't think that . . . What's your opinion? Speak frankly."

"My opinion is that, though there's no danger for the moment, it might be that it will take you several days to recover. On Saturday we agreed to wait for an improvement so that you could peacefully satisfy your . . . noble desire to come to terms . . . well, to come to terms with your conscience, like a good Christian. Now I think that, instead of waiting for an improvement—an absolutely certain improvement, but it might be two or three days—we really ought to perform that act, for . . . this act which, as experience proves, is as beneficial for the body as for the soul . . . That is, if you see fit . . ."

"Yes, yes," murmured Don Francisco, who was left breathless and felt a mortal cold that soaked into his very bones. For an instant he thought that the ceiling was falling on him like a tombstone, and that the room had become profoundly dark. His immense panic left him speechless and even incapable of thought.

FOUR

"That means," he stammered, ten minutes after having heard his doctor's words, "that . . . well, I'd already suspected it when I saw that you were here at such a late hour. What time is it? No, I don't want to know. When the doctor stays here all night, it's a sign that things aren't going so well. Isn't that right? And now, after what you've told me . . . !"

Donoso intervened with all his diplomatic skill, corroborating the doctor's statements.

"Why, we're merely proposing, my dear friend, that you not postpone what you thought about several days ago . . . such a beautiful act of piety, so sweet, so consoling. If we're proposing to do it ahead of time, I say, it's because *everyone is well aware* that it offers equal advantages to body and spirit. Those who are ill, after performing these elementary duties, feel stronger, feel happier, become more cheerful and acquire great resolution, and this means that the illness, *in an almost total number of cases,* subsides, yields, and on many an occasion disappears completely. *I profess the theory* that we ought to perform it while we are well, or at least fairly well, so as not to have to do it hastily and unsatisfactorily."

"Agreed," said Don Francisco, sighing deeply, "and I have also heard that many serious invalids found improvement simply by performing the commandment, and there was even someone who was given up for lost . . . now I remember . . . the baker in La Cava Baja, who was half dead already, and the holy viaticum was a resurrection for him. He's still out there somewhere, in perfect health."

"There are thousands of cases, thousands."

"Well, it's probably a coincidence," said the sick man, smiling gloomily, "but the fact is that just talking about all that makes me feel a little bit better. If I were drowsy, I'd sleep a little while before . . . but it's not likely I'll be able to sleep. I want to talk to Cruz. Call her."

"Here I am," said the lady, stepping out of the dark corner where she had been hiding. "We'll talk all you like."

After the others had left the room and Cruz had seated herself beside the bed, she prepared to hear what her illustrious brother-in-law had to tell her. But, as he allowed a certain amount of time, and then more time, to pass without saying a word, or giving any other sign of consciousness than an occasional sigh which he heaved with great difficulty from his suffering breast, the lady rose to her feet to look closely at his face and, placing her hand upon his, said tenderly, "Courage, Don Francisco. Think only of God, believe me. Whatever may be the result of this crisis, consider as concluded everything having to do with this wretched world. And if you get better? Then it will have been to the glory of God, and to render Him homage in the latter days of your life."

"I am thinking, I am thinking about Him," replied Don Francisco, articulating the words with difficulty. "And you, Crucita, who are so intelligent, do you believe that the Lord will listen to me?"

"To doubt divine mercy! What an aberration! Sincere repentance wipes out all sins. Humiliation is the antidote to pride; abnegation and generosity are the antidote to selfishness. Think about God, ask Him for grace . . . and grace will come. The conscience will light up, the soul will be transformed, will burn in ardent love, and the ardent desire to be pardoned will suffice."

"You have said abnegation, generosity," murmured Torquemada in an almost inaudible voice. "I want you to know that Father Gamborena asked for my cape. Do you know what the cape is? Well, I've given it to him. I'm here waiting for him to establish the bases . . . Then I'll talk with Donoso about the provisions of my will and I'll leave . . . What do you think? Ought I to leave a lot for the poor? In what form, under what conditions? Don't forget that sometimes everything you give them winds up in the taverns, and if you give them clothing it winds up in the pawnshops."

"Don't drag the matter down to such a petty level. Do you want to know what I think?"

"Yes I do, and right now."

"You know already that everything I think about is big, on a very big scale."

"Big scale, yes."

"You have amassed an enormous capital; with your skill, you've succeeded in bringing vast sums of money into your house, most of which ought to have remained elsewhere; but you've brought them here, I don't know how, but undoubtedly by pretty sharp practices. Such immense wealth ought not to belong to a single person; that is what I think, that is what I believe, and that is what I say. Since my sister's death my ideas on this subject have changed; I have meditated a great deal on the things of this world and on the ways to find eternal salvation in the other, and I have seen clearly what I did not see before . . ."

"What . . . ? Tell me."

"That the possession of exorbitant riches runs counter to divine law and human justice, and is a very evil burden to our spirits, a very bad leaven for our bodies."

"Then, you . . . ?"

"I? Nowadays I spend everything that is left over after my needs are satisfied to help the poor. I mean to reduce those needs to the most modest level possible for the rest of my life, and when I do this I will designate a larger amount to pious purposes. In my will I'm leaving everything to the poor."

"Everything!"

Don Francisco's stupefaction was demonstrated by repeating the word "everything" at intervals of lugubrious precision, like the intervals between the tolling of bells that announce a funeral.

"Everything!"

"Yes, señor. You already know that in my ideas, in my personal way of looking at things, there is no room for half measures, or meannesses, or compromises. I have given everything to society at a time when my only concern was the dignity of the family, of your name and mine. Now that the pomps I have acquired are vanishing like smoke, I will give it all to God."

"Everything!"

"I am returning it to its true owner."

"Everything!"

"We've talked about me more than I deserve. Now let's talk about you, which is the most important thing just now. You ask for my opinion, and I give it to you as I have always done, with absolute frankness and, if I may do so, with the somewhat arrogant authority which you used to call despotism, and which was merely the conviction that I possessed the truth in everything having to do with the family's interests. Formerly I looked after your dignity, your rise in society, placing you in a position to increase your fortune. Now, in these days of disillusionment and sadness, I am looking after your soul's salvation. Before, I was determined to lead you to social heights, serving as your guide; now, my whole desire is to bring you to the mansion of the just . . ."

"Quick, tell me. What must I do . . . ? Everything!"

"I believe in conscience," said Cruz in a ceremonious voice, drawing closer to him and receiving the pallid gaze of the miser's eyes directly in her own, "I believe in conscience that, after reserving for your children the two-thirds designated by law, giving equal shares to each, you should turn over the rest, that is, the remaining third . . . entirely . . . to the Church!"

"To the Church," repeated Don Francisco without budging. "So it can take care of distributing it. Everything! To the Church!"

Raising his arms with a kind of priestly solemnity, he let them fall heavily upon the sheets.

"Everything . . .! To the Church . . .!" The remaining third . . . And this way can they assure me that . . . ?"

Without noticing what the expression of this last concept meant, Cruz continued to develop her ideas as follows:

"Think it over carefully, and you will see that, in a way, it is a restitution. Those extremely large sums originally belonged to the Church, and you are merely returning them to their owner. Don't you understand? Listen to a word from me. So-called disentailment, which really ought to be called despoilment, snatched the Church's property to turn it over to private persons, to the bourgeoisie, through sales that were really nothing but gifts. From that wealth which was distributed in raw form has arisen this whole world of business, of contracts, of public works, a world in which you have trafficked, absorbing large sums of money which were sometimes in one set of hands, sometimes in another, and which for the most part have eventually come to rest in yours. The current changes direction very often, but the wealth it carries in one direction or another is the same, for it was taken from the Church. How happy the man who, possessing it temporarily through the whims of fortune, is virtuous enough to return it to its legitimate owner! So, now you know what my opinion is. As for the manner of making the return, Donoso can inform you better than I. There are any number of ways of doing it and distributing it among the different religious institutions. What is your answer?"

Cruz asked this question because Don Francisco had fallen silent. But the fear that he might have lost consciousness was unfounded, for the sick man had heard his sister-in-law's opinions very clearly. It was merely that his spirit had fallen into such a brown study that it had no strength to give any external sign. He had closed his eyes; his face looked like death. Peering inside himself, he mused, "Now there's no doubt; I'm dying. When this one starts playing that tune, there's no hope. Everything to the Church! All right, Lord, I'm satisfied as long as I can be saved. But now, if I'm not saved, it'll mean there's no justice in heaven, as there's none on earth."

"What is your answer?" repeated Cruz. "Have you gone to sleep?"

"No, my dear, I'm not asleep," said the poor man in such a feeble voice that it seemed to come from the depths, and without opening his eyes. "It's just that I'm meditating. I'm asking God to take me to His bosom and forgive my sins. The Lord is very good, isn't He?"

"So good that . . ."

The emotion felt by the noble lady choked her voice. At last Torquemada opened his beady eyes, and he and she regarded each other in silence for an instant, confirming in that exchange of glances their respective convictions about infinite goodness.

FIVE

They gave him chilled champagne, chilled consommé, the only nourishment he could tolerate, and he spent something like an hour very quietly, speaking from time to time in a cavernous and muffled voice. Calling Gamborena to his side, he told him in a whisper, "The cape . . .! Everything . . . everything that's left . . . for you, my dear Señor Saint Peter. Donoso already has instructions."

"Not for me. I don't want to neglect making a clarification. Cruz advised you, entirely on her own, to do what Donoso has just informed me of. I have nothing to do with that. I preach the saving word, I exhort souls, I point out to them the path of salvation, but I have nothing to do with the distribution of material goods. When I asked for your cape I meant that you must not forget the needy, or the hungry, or the naked, in your arrangements. I never thought that my request would be interpreted as a proposition, as a desire that the cape, or the value of the cape, should come into my hands for me to tear up and distribute the pieces. These hands have never touched anyone's money, nor have they ever received a bequest or legacy from any dying person. Give your money to whomever you like. I will say one more thing, which I have already announced to Señor Donoso. My congregation does not accept testamentary donations, or anything at all in the way of inheritance; my congregation lives from alms, and even to receive them it has minimum figures which can in no case be changed."

"According to that," said Don Francisco, recovering his lively spirit for a moment, "don't you want . . . ? For I've already decided . . . everything for the Church. And you, Señor Saint Peter, will be the one who . . ."

"Not I. There are others more suitable than I for that assignment. Neither I nor my brothers can receive responsibilities of that kind. I praise your decision, I think it exceedingly useful for your soul; but others will receive the offering, and will know how to use it for the good of Christianity."

"So . . . you don't want . . . ? But I agreed thinking of you, of your congregation, which is all made up of saints. What does Donoso say? What does Cruz say? But you won't leave me. You will tell me that I'm going to be saved."

"I will tell you that when I know that I can say it."

"Well, what are you waiting for, holy man of God?" Torquemada replied impatiently, thrashing about between the sheets. "Now, now, after the sacrifice I've just made . . . everything, good Lord, every-thing . . .! Now don't I deserve to be told, to be promised . . . ?"

"Have you made this decision for reasons of charity, with ardent love for your fellow creatures and true zeal to alleviate the sufferings of your fellow man?"

"Yes, señor."

"Have you done so with your soul fixed on God and believing your-self unworthy of being forgiven for your sins?"

"Of course."

"Look here, Señor Marquis, you can deceive me, but not God, for He sees everything. Are you very sure of what you say? Are you speak-ing with your conscience?"

"I'm very honest in my dealings."

"This is not a deal."

"Well, whatever you want to call it. I've decided to be saved. Nat-urally, I believe everything that God commands us to believe. It would be a fine thing if now, so close to the end of my life, I should come out and say that I didn't believe this or that point! Begone doubts, so that fears can be gone too. I have faith, I want to be saved, and it seems to me that I'm demonstrating it by giving the remaining third of my assets to Holy Church. She'll administer it well; there are very sharp men and many good administrators in the different religions. Oh, my money will be in very good hands! How much better than in the hands of a spendthrift and stupid heir, who would spend it on nastiness and stupidities! I can see already that they'll build chapels and cathedrals, magnificent hospitals, and posterity won't say 'Ah, the skinflint! Ah, the miser! Ah, the shylock!' but 'Oh, the splendid, oh, the generous great man! Oh, the upholder of Christendom!' That third is better off in ecclesiastical than in secular hands, the hands of extravagant and slovenly men. Don't worry, Señor Saint Peter. I'll appoint a committee of *appropriate* people, presided over by my lord bishop of Andrinopolis. And meantime, I'm counting on you. Don't abandon me. Don't give me ifs, ands, and buts about entering the celestial realm."

"There are no such ifs, ands, and buts," said Gamborena with exquisite kindness and gentleness. "Be sensible, and turn yourself over to me with absolute confidence. What I'm saying is that your decision, Señor Don Francisco, though it is good . . . extremely good . . . is not enough, not enough. You need something more."

"But . . . Lord, still more!"

"You mustn't think that I'm haggling over the amount. Even though that remaining third were a sum of as many millions as there are sands in the sea, it would not be sufficient unless the act signified, at the same time, a spontaneous movement of the heart, if the offering of a purified conscience did not accompany it. This is very clear."

"Yes, very clear. I *wholeheartedly agree* with those ideas."

"Because, my friend," added the priest with great charm, rising to his feet to peer more closely into Torquemada's face, "I do not even dare to suspect that you are thinking of effecting your entrance into heaven by bribing me, the guardian of the gate. If you should think such a thing, Señor Marquis of San Eloy, you would not be the first. Many believe that if they slip the saint a little tip . . . But no, you are not one of those. You have already turned your eyes to God, withdrawing them forever from the vileness of temporal and outworn possessions. You already have the divine light in your conscience; I see it, I recognize it. Tonight, during a brief period of rest, we will wind up being very good friends, in agreement about everything. You will be greatly consoled, with your soul serene, free, full of confidence and love, and I will be satisfied and happier than a lark."

Torquemada had closed his eyes, looking inside himself, and answered only with slight movements of his head the earnest exhortations of his friend and spiritual father. The latter took advantage of the excellent opportunity offered by the sick man's relative quiescence and, exhorting him with persuasive and affectionate words, accustomed as he was to taming the most recalcitrant human beasts imaginable, within half an hour had softened him so much that no one recognized him, nor could he have recognized himself if he could have seen himself from the viewpoint of his old character.

Then he rested for a few hours, and very early in the morning the priest came and tackled him again, fearful that Torquemada would slip through his fingers. But no, he was well secured, humble, and with the slightly petulant coyness of a sick child. His personality was completely altered, with nothing remaining but cinders, his fierce independence destroyed. He was transformed by the certainty of his approaching end; undoubtedly it worked upon his spirit in the same way as the illness acted upon his body, devouring it, with effects like those of fire, and reducing it to ashes. His querulous voice aroused profound emotion in all who heard it. His testy disposition and gross and inappropriate expressions no longer tormented the family and servants. All was concord, pity, pardon, and love. Death had achieved this good result merely by knocking at the sinner's door. Exhausted by the illness that was consuming him from hour to hour, he scarcely had strength to pronounce a few words, of love for his daughter and Cruz, of paternal goodness for the other persons around him. He did not move; his ashen face was sunk in the pillows and his eyes were sunk into his head, and he spoke with them rather than with his tongue. You would have thought that with those eyes he was begging pardon for his selfishness. And with them he also seemed to be saying, "I'm turning over everything to you, my soul and my riches, to do with them whatever you like. Now I am nothing, I no longer count for anything. Here I am, turned into dust, and as dust I beg you to blow on me, to strew me to the winds and scatter me through space."

Very late in the morning they brought him the sacrament, without fanfare, in the presence of only the closest family and friends. The ducal mansion seemed more beautiful than ever that day, providing a splendid frame for the moving ceremony and for the grave gathering that filed through the vestibule and the spacious galleries, filled with representations of human beauty. The servants, much fewer in number since the *modus vivendi*, were present, dressed in their best uniforms. The chapel, which resembled a golden live coal with its myriad lighted candles, was filled with nuns both white and blue, with ladies in black mantillas. An altar was placed in the sick man's bedroom, with the Van Eyck triptych that had presided over Fidela's funeral chapel. The entrance of the viaticum produced profound emotion in everything contained within that princely habitation, in absolutely everything, whether alive or represented, persons and things, art and humanity. As the Divine Majesty entered the bedroom, the sum of emotion became more intense, accentuated by the silence that enclosed the solemn act both within and without. The priest's voice sounded, in the midst of that peace, with loving quietness. The flickering flames of the torches cast a yellow light, like old gold, on the scene and its figures. When he received God, Don Francisco Torquemada, marquis of San Eloy, seemed like a different person. He was not the same man as before, nor even the same as the previous night, with his ashen face and lusterless eyes. Either because of the lights' reflection or from some internal cause, the fact is that the skin of his face recovered the colors of life, and his gaze the vivacity of his best times. It expressed a deep respect, a simplicity of spirit which was close to childish timidity, an indefinable compunction which could equally well have meant all of the love of his soul or all the terrors of animal instinct.

After the ceremony came the noise of departure, footsteps, prayers, the tinkling of the bell. The procession descended the staircase and, again passing through the great gallery, left the house, and everything in the palace returned to its normal appearance.

A great many people had gathered in the chapel: some entered eager to pray, others to admire the artistic beauties that adorned the altar. Meanwhile the sick man, after talking briefly but satisfactorily with Gamborena, Cruz, and Donoso, in affectionate, innocent, simple language, congratulating himself from the bottom of his heart for what he had done and receiving their congratulations very joyfully, felt a sudden desire for rest, as if the religious ceremony had had an intensely sedative effect on his exhausted body. Closing his eyelids, he slept so quietly and deeply that at first they thought him dead. But no: he was sleeping like an angel.

SIX

Family and friends were overjoyed to see the poor invalid resting, though they felt that a fatal outcome of his illness was inevitable. All of them were in the room adjoining the bedroom, waiting to see the result of such a long sleep. Although Cruz and Donoso displayed some uneasiness, Augusto Miquis lost no time in setting their fears at rest, telling them that the patient's sleep was one of those that bring repose and the repair of the organism, a desirable phenomenon in the course of the illness, though it would not dispel the imminent and inescapable danger. It would be well, therefore, not to disturb such a sleep, the precursor of certain, though brief, improvement. They waited, not without a certain lack of confidence in what the doctor had told them, and at last, very late in the afternoon, hearing Don Francisco give a great shout, they all hastened to his bedside and saw him stretching and yawning. He stretched out his arms as far as he could, and with a smiling face told them, "I'm better . . . much better. Try giving me something to eat, for damn my eyes if I'm not a little bit hungry."

A chorus of satisfaction and praise was heard all around the bed, and they soon brought him a few spoonfuls of something, and on top of that a sip of sherry.

"Look here, all of you. I haven't eaten with such a good will for a long time. I've really got an appetite. And I think that this nourishment will agree with me."

"What do you have to say now?" asked Cruz, elated and triumphant. "Is it or isn't it proved that doing our duties as Catholic Christians always brings us something good, even without counting the good of the soul?"

"Yes, you're right," replied Don Francisco, feeling that the delight of his family and friends was spreading to him. "I believed it, too, and that's why I was in a hurry to receive the Lord. Blessed be the *Supreme Being*, who has given me this improvement, this resurrection, *so to speak*, because if this isn't resurrection I don't know what is! And I had heard tell about really miraculous cases . . . sick folks given up for dead who returned to life and health simply with a visit from His Divine Majesty. There are such cases, and it could well be that I'm one of the most sensational ones."

"But simply because we have an improvement," said Donoso, who did not want him to chatter so, "you must be quiet and not talk too much."

"Friend Donoso, are you going to come out with your cautiousness and your priggishness? Why, if I were put to it, I'd be capable of . . . What d'you bet that I can get up and go to my office . . . ?"

"That you absolutely cannot do."

"Good Lord, what nonsense!"

And all their hands were held over him as if to hold him down, in case he really meant to *implement* his insane idea.

"No, don't be scared," said the invalid, affecting docility. "You know that I never act precipitately. I'll stay right here in bed until I'm really well. And believe me, as I believe in God and reverence Him, that I feel better, a lot better, and that I'm on the way to being well."

"I think, Señor Don Francisco," said Gamborena affectionately, "that the best way to express your gratitude to God Almighty, who has deigned to visit you today and be with you in body and blood, consists in acceptance of what He determines, whatever its outcome may be."

"My good friend and teacher is right," replied Torquemada, opening his arms to the priest. "I owe my health—I mean, this improvement— to you, to you. I conform to anything that the Lord wants to decide with respect to me. If He wants to kill me, let Him kill me; I won't complain. If He wants to cure me, so much the better. I mustn't turn up my nose at life either, if the blessed Lord wants to give me lots more years of it . . . Oh, Father, how fine it is to be on good terms with God, to tell Him all a fellow's sins, to recognize all the black spots in a fellow's character, to recall that a fellow's never been soft-hearted, and, in short, to be filled with good will and divine love. Because, *to give only one example*, God made the world and then suffered for us. That's *obvious*. Therefore we ought to love Him, and do, and feel, and think, everything that the good father tells us. Agreed, agreed. Give me another hug, Señor Gamborena, and you, Rufinita, hug me too, and hug me, Cruz and Donoso. There, now I'm happy, because I realize that I'm a good Christian, and together we'll give thanks to the Almighty for having cured me, I mean helped me. May it be as He wishes, and His will be done."

"Good, good."

"How good the Lord is! And how evil I've been until now, not to have declared it and recognized it *a priori*! But it's never too late to mend, right?"

"Right."

"Long live Christ and His holy Mother! And I, wretch that I am, who doubted His infinite mercy! But now I have no doubts; I see it very clearly. And I'll not go back, mind you, on anything I conceded and decided! The Lord has illumined me, and now I must *follow a line of conduct* that's *diametrically opposed . . ."*

None of those present thought that he ought to talk so much, nor did they like to see him so excited. They gave him a little more broth and sherry, which agreed with him quite as well as the dose he had taken before, and, by previous agreement on the family's part, left him alone with Donoso, who wished to take advantage of his improvement to speak to him about the terms of his will and arrange the last details, so that everything could be taken care of that same day. They spoke quietly together, and Torquemada confirmed his decisions about the manner of distributing his immense riches. His good friend made several suggestions which he accepted without hesitation. As Torquemada was a man who never failed to have objections to anything that he had not thought of himself, Donoso regarded such meekness with suspicion.

"Everything, everything you want," Torquemada told him. "Have the will drawn up, *conceived in the terms* you think proper. In any case, the testamentary arrangements can be modified in the future, or whenever a fellow feels like it."

Donoso said nothing, and continued to take notes.

"That doesn't mean that I'm thinking of changing it," added Don Francisco, who seemed completely recovered, so easily was he speaking. "I'm a man of my word, and when I say 'done!' the operation is closed. No, I don't want in the least to break off my relations with the Lord God, who has behaved so well toward me . . . I should say not! I am who I am, and Francisco Torquemada doesn't go back on his word. One-third, every little bit of it, for Holy Church, distributed among the different religious institutions that dedicate themselves to teaching and charity. It's understood that that will be after my demise . . . of course."

They dealt with some other matters connected with the appointment of executors, and Donoso, with all the information well in hand, urged Torquemada to be quiet, to stop talking, and was almost on the point of recommending mental prayer; but he did not say so.

"Agreed, my dear Don José María," replied the sick man, "but since I feel so well, the active man in me cannot be denied. Admit to me that I have seven lives, like cats. Come on, I'm going to get away with this one. No, of course I'm very grateful to His Divine Majesty, because to whom do I owe the health that I'll recover? The truth is that on my side I did everything that was asked of me, and I'm very happy, but very happy to be a good Christian."

"I say the same as Gamborena, that one must conform to the will of God and accept from Him what He wishes to send us, life or death."

"Exactly, that's what I say and maintain too, in *motu proprio*, and God's will right now is for me to live. I feel it in my soul, in my heart, in my whole *economy*, which tells me, 'You will live so that you can carry out your great project.' "

"What project?"

"Well, when I opened my eyes after that fine healing sleep, I felt that I had my usual energies of thought and willpower. After I came back to life, my dear Don José, my head filled up with ideas that I've been *cherishing* for some time, and a little while ago, while I was hugging the whole family, I was thinking about the combinations that will make the deal possible."

"What deal?"

"That's right, play the fool! Don't you know? The project that I'll present to the government to convert the *external* debt into *internal* debt . . . It will be the way to wipe out the floating obligation of the Treasury, and we'll achieve unification of the national debt on the basis of *single perpetual internal income, bringing the interest down to three percent.* You know already that the Cuban mortgage notes are included in the conversion."

"Oh, yes, a great project," said Donoso, alarmed by the excitement of his friend's brain. "But there's time to think about it. To do so the government has to ask permission of Parliament."

"It will ask, man, it will ask, and Parliament will give it. Don't worry about that."

"I'm not worrying; I say that we ought not, for the moment, to think about those things."

"But come now. Since I feel so much better and on the way to recovery, I see God's will so clearly that I can't be mistaken. And the Lord, they can say what they like, is giving me back my life so that I can carry out a project so beneficial to humanity, or, *to give only one example*, to our dear Spain, a nation of which God is particularly fond. Let's see: isn't Spain *the Catholic nation par excellence?*"

"Yes, indeed."

"Isn't it just and natural that God, that is, Divine Providence, should want to do her a big favor?"

"Certainly."

"Well, there you are. That's the reason why the Supreme Maker doesn't want me to die."

"But do you think that God is going to bother just now about whether the external debt is converted into internal debt?"

"God runs everything, directs everything, small things as well as large. Gamborena has said so. God gives both evil and good, according to what's appropriate, to individuals and nations. He gives to the birds the seeds or straw that they eat, and to *collectivities* . . . either a whack when they need one, *to wit* the Flood, and pestilences and calamities, or some benefit, so that they can live and prosper. D'you think that God can regard with indifference the trials of this poor nation, and the fact that we have to exchange at twenty-three percent? Poor commerce, poor industry, and poor working classes!"

"Yes, very well. I like that logic," Donoso told him, thinking that it would be worse to contradict him. "There is no doubt that the Author of all things wants to favor Catholic Spain, and for the purpose, what better than straightening out her Treasury Department?"

"Exactly," added Torquemada emphatically. "I don't know why His Divine Majesty can't look out for financial matters, as a good father looks after the different works that his children are engaged in. This is a very strange thing, you pious men: as soon as a fellow talks about money, about blessed money, you all put on a very sour face. By the Bible, either the Lord pulls the strings for everybody or for nobody! You've got the military, whose job is to kill folks, and they talk to us about *the God of battles*. Well then, why, dammit! can't we have *the God of treasuries* too, *the God of budgets, of business, or of sums and percentages?*"

SEVEN

"As far as I am concerned," replied Donoso, "there can be that God and as many others as you see fit. We will talk about conversion at length, and now rest, rest, until you've recovered your health completely. Don't talk too much, and don't converse more than is absolutely necessary. I'm going to the lawyer's to take him these notes. Everything can be finished by tonight, and we'll read it and sign it whenever you say."

"Fine, my dear friend. Everything will be done according to what we decided yesterday . . . or day before yesterday; I no longer remember. You know that my word is sacred, absolutely sacred, as you might say."

Donoso departed, not without letting the family know about the cerebral hyperactivity displayed by Don Francisco, so that they could all try not to add fuel to that dangerous symptom. This they promised, but when they went in to see the patient they found him calmer. He did not talk of business matters, but of his acceptance of the Lord's will. The man was truly edifying. His beady eyes sparkled feverishly, and his hands accompanied his words with expressive gestures. Cruz spoke to him of mystical things, of God's infinite mercy, of the marvels of eternity, and he answered in short sentences, showing himself to be in agreement with his illustrious sister in everything she said, and adding that God punishes or rewards individuals and nations according to the merits of each. "Naturally, He protects and even pampers the nation that professes the truth and is a good Catholic country. That's obvious."

He spent all the early part of the night in relative tranquillity, and at about nine-thirty the witnesses to the will arrived, for Donoso did not wish to postpone its reading and signature; although it was very probable that Don Francisco would be inclined to the task next day, the opposite could also occur and he might not be right in the head. Gamborena was of the same opinion: the sooner the formality of the will was out of the way, the better. With the witnesses gathered in the salon awaiting the lawyer, Donoso gave them an idea, in general terms, of that document's structure and contents. The testator began with the solemn declaration of his religious beliefs and with his reverence for Holy Church. He ordered that his funeral rites be modest in the extreme and that he be buried beside his second wife, Her Excellency . . . etc. He left to his children, Rufina and Valentín, two-thirds of his fortune, designating equal parts, that is, exactly one-third, to each. This equal division of the two-thirds required by law between the two children, one of the first wife and the other of the second, was Cruz's idea, which was praised by all as one more proof of the illustrious lady's greatness of soul. Were a liquidation of community property made, Valentín's part would necessarily be larger than Rufinita's. It was simpler and more generous to divide equally, setting forth the terms of the disposition clearly in order to avoid disagreements between the heirs. In another clause Donoso was named Valentín's guardian, and the necessary precautions were taken so that the testator's desires would be fully carried out.

And, lastly, the remaining one-third of the capital was devoted entirely to works of piety, a committee being named which, with the help of the executors, would proceed to distribute it among the religious institutions designated by the testator. Once they had been informed about the terms, the witnesses discussed the size of the capital that Señor Don Francisco was leaving here on earth as he set off for the other world. Opinions were divergent: some allowed themselves to name sums that were more than fabulous; others said that it was all sound and fury, signifying nothing. The good friend of the household, proud of being able to give information about the matter that was very close to the truth, stated that the marquis of San Eloy's capital would be not less than thirty million pesetas, which figure was heard by the others with their mouths hanging open, and when their astonishment permitted them to speak, they extolled perseverance, astuteness, and good luck, the basis of that fabulous pile of gold.

When the lawyer had arrived, the reading of the will took place, and during it the testator displayed great serenity, making no remark except for a couple of short phrases alluding to the document's excessive length. But everything comes to an end in this world: the last word of the will was read and everyone signed, Torquemada with a somewhat tremulous hand. Donoso did not conceal his satisfaction at having successfully carried through an act of such transcendental importance. The sick man was congratulated on his improvement, which he corroborated verbally by attributing it to God's mercy and His inscrutable designs, and they left him to rest, for he well deserved to do so after such a long and boring session of reading.

After the lawyer came the doctor, who urged repose on Don Francisco, prohibiting any disturbing thoughts and assuring him that the less he thought about business the sooner he would be well. He made a few arrangements in the not improbable case that phenomena of extreme gravity should appear, and took his leave, indicating to the family his readiness to return at any hour he might be called upon, and adding that he had little confidence in that misleading and probably false improvement. With these prophecies in mind, Cruz, Rufinita, and the priest prepared to sit up with the sick man. Torquemada continued to look very composed, but he was wakeful and wanted them to keep him company and talk to him. He repeated how sure he was of a quick recovery and, happy to have made his peace *with God and men*, based many optimistic plans on those cordial relations.

"Now that we're marching in step, we've got to do something that will cause a sensation."

These pleasant hopes lasted a very short time, for in the small hours of the morning, after a very short doze, he felt ill. Great restlessness and prickling of his skin kept him tossing restlessly in bed for a long time, and assuming the strangest postures. He cursed and swore, forgetting his newborn Christianity, blaming the family, the valet, saying that the fellow had put itching powder on the sheets to prevent him from sleeping. Suddenly he experienced very severe pains in the belly which made him burst out into dreadful cries and double up and twist about, clenching his fists and tearing at the sheets.

"Why, this," he said, foaming at the mouth with rage, "is nothing but weakness. The stomach's rebelling against not getting enough to eat. Curse that doctor! He's killing me. And I'm so hungry I could eat half a roast kid right now!"

Quevedo gave him injections and they fed him some chilled broth. But he had not finished swallowing it when horrible retching and deadly nausea demonstrated that his hapless stomach was incapable of receiving nourishment.

"But what the devil have you given me here?" he said, in the midst of his nausea. "This tastes absolutely hellish. You're trying to finish me off and you're going to succeed, because I haven't anyone to look out for me. Lord, Lord, confound them, confound our enemies!"

From that moment onward he had no rest either of body or spirit; his eyes bulged, his mouth was unable to pronounce a charitable word.

"Well, this damned setback! Somebody's cheating here. No, I won't give up no matter what. Have them call Miquis . . . Some bill that faker's going to hand me! But if he doesn't cure me, he'd better look out. These doctors charge an arm and a leg. What will the nation say, what will humanity say, what will the Supreme Being himself say?

Look, if he doesn't cure me I won't pay him. Eh, Cruz! Now you know it. If *by any chance* I die, you mustn't pay the doctor's bill . . . Let him grab a musket and go off to Sierra Morena, the bandit! Oh, my God, how terrible I feel! *Behold me* anxious to eat and unable to put a swallow of water into my body, because the minute I drink it my whole *economy* gets up in arms and a battle royal starts up inside me."

Sitting up in bed, he at times raised his arms, throwing his head backward, and at times doubled up, curled like a ball, his face between his hands, his elbows touching his knees. Gamborena came close to the bed to urge patience and acceptance upon him. Don Francisco looked him in the eye and addressed him as follows:

"And what do you say to me about this, Señor Friar, Señor minister at the altar or minister of the flipping Bible? What do you tell me now? You and I have certainly made fine fools of ourselves. I was getting along so well! And all of a sudden, by Christ, all of a sudden I get this attack, which . . . anybody could say that death's after me. This is a cheat, a real swindle, yes, señor . . . I won't shut up, no I won't . . . I feel like saying it: I'm a plain-spoken man . . . Ow, ow! My soul seems to want to pull right out of me. You rascal! I know what you want; to skedaddle out of here and leave me turned into a heap of garbage. Well, you can go jump, because I won't let go of you. That's all we need, my lady soul, you fickle thing, you bitch, you slut, to have you gallivanting out there in the world! No, no . . . you can go jump, I'm the one who's in charge of my confounded self, and all your airs and graces don't bother me a bit, you strumpet! What are you saying, Señor Gamborena, my *particular friend*? Why are you looking at me like that? Are you one of the ones who thinks I'm going to die too? Well, the Lord, your master properly speaking, has told me that I won't, and you and all those priest fellows that are already licking their lips thinking about the millions of masses they're going to say for me . . . take it easy, señores, you're going to have a long wait."

Really, the good missionary did not know what to say to him, for though his first intention had been to upbraid Don Francisco for that ridiculous and bestial spate of language, he soon realized that his mind was unhinged and that he had no realization of, nor was he responsible for, those dreadful statements.

"Brother," he told him, squeezing his hands, "think about God, about His blessed Mother. Accept the divine will, and these shadows that are trying to invade your mind will disappear. Prayer will bring back your serenity."

"Leave me alone, leave me alone, Señor Missionary," replied the miser angrily, thoroughly upset, beside himself, "and go to the devil. Where's my cape? You certainly might give it back . . . I need it, I'm cold, and I haven't worked all my life just to have the bishop and a bunch of lazybones cover themselves with my clothes."

They all listened to him in consternation, not knowing what to say to him or what measures to use to keep him quiet and resigned. Just as he had rejected Gamborena, he rejected Rufinita, saying, "Get away from me, you greedy creature. D'you think you can butter me up with your blarney, you hellcat? You're licking your lips and getting your claws ready! And all to grab that *third*. Well, there's no *third*. Clean off your mug; you've got egg on your face. You're just like that other one, who used to turn up her nose at me, and now the hypocrite wants to chuck me under the chin, her excellency the vulture lady, rather than eagle lady, who's been in seventh heaven ever since I got sick. To try to snare a *third* for those church-going gluttons! That rosary-stringer, that Saint Peter's housekeeper!"

EIGHT

As soon as Miquis saw him, he felt inwardly that Torquemada was a dead man. A day, with an hour's difference more or less, was all that separated him from fathomless eternity. And when palliatives were prescribed, simply to make his last moments less painful, Torquemada told him angrily, "But what are you thinking about, doctor? Why can't you take this stupid illness away from me? I can see now that either you fellows don't know a thing or that you only want to cure poor folks in the hospitals, who don't do humanity a damned bit of good. So a rich man falls into your hands? Why, split him right down the middle . . . That's right; divide the wealth, so that nations will be weakened and there's never a proper budget. I say, 'We live to even things up,' and you, doctors of medicine, say, 'We even things up by killing folks.' But some day you'll get what's coming to you. And there's something else: if somebody really wanted to save me, he'd give me a poultice for my stomach. Because what I say is, isn't there any way to feed a fellow except by eating? *In my opinion*, a fellow can certainly live without eating. And I'll go further: what's eating good for? For fomenting a vice—gluttony. Just give me a poultice and you'll see how I feed myself by the leaking of liquids, *in the vernacular* by absorption. Nothing comes to their minds; I have to think about everything myself, and if it weren't for my natural intelligence I'd be a lost man, and at the least little slip in attention you'd have that crazy soul of mine flying away and leaving me here in the lurch."

They applied the poultices, though it was only to make him believe that something was being done, and the poor man became a little quieter, though his disconnected chatter continued.

"Listen to me, Father," he said to Gamborena, clasping his hand, "the only decent person around here is my son, poor Valentín, who because he can't talk is incapable of hurting me or wanting me to die. I'm going to leave everything to him on the day that the Lord is pleased to decide that I'll go up to heaven, a day that's still a long way off, I don't care what they say. They can liquidate the community property so that that leech Rufina doesn't suck up what's not hers, and as for the cape, that is, the free third, I'm telling you that it's coming back to my hands, though this doesn't mean that I won't give you something, some practical thing: to wit, a waistcoat in good condition."

And to Donoso, who also came at his summons, he said, "I've changed my mind about everything we arranged, and there's plenty of time to revoke it. All that the law allows, and a little bit more that I'll manage with special transactions, is for Valentín, that rough little chunk of angel in a state of brute savagery, but there's no evil in him. Oh, God's poor little donkey loves his father such a lot! Yesterday he was saying, 'Pa, pa, ca, ja, la, pa,' which means 'You'll see how well I hang on to everything for you.' Of course, with a good family council to take care of feeding him and keeping him clean, the interest can keep on accumulating and the capital increasing. And then, when he's of age, my little man can be anything he wants, except a spendthrift, for he certainly shows no signs of that. He'll be a hunter and eat only vegetables. And he won't care for the theater or poetry, because that's where men get lost, and he'll hide the money in a jar so that even God can't see it. Oh, what a son I have, and what a joy it'll be to work for a few more years, many years, to fill his piggy bank to overflowing!"

By morning the mental confusion was checked, but the gastric and nervous symptoms had taken on a character of open rebellion which presaged the end of life. Once the doctor had pronounced the fatal opinion, the medical profession declared itself beaten. Only God could save him, if that was His holy will, but in Miquis's opinion He would have to perform a miracle to accomplish it. Whether a miracle or a favor, the stubborn Cruz did not despair of obtaining it, and she proceeded to discuss and put into practice all the means inspired by faith to implore divine mercy for the health of His Excellency my lord marquis consort of San Eloy, etc. Alms were distributed in considerable quantity, innumerable masses were said in different churches and oratories, the papal benediction was requested by telegraph to Rome, and lastly, as a supreme outpouring of piety, it was decided, with prior permission from the bishop, to expose the Host in the chapel of the palace. After mass had been said by Gamborena, the Divine Majesty remained exposed in a magnificent monstrance with a glass-windowed gold case adorned with precious stones which, along with the other sacred vessels, had come, like the palace, from the liquidation and sale of the Gravelinas assets. A large number of priests and nuns kept vigil over the sacrament, watching in pairs until relieved. The chapel was decorated with the best treasures in the palace, and a multitude of candles was lighted. All was quiet and devotion in the sumptuous dwelling; visitors entered it as if it were a church, for as soon as they set foot in the vestibule all noticed something moving and solemn, and their nostrils were assailed by a cathedral atmosphere. All this that I am describing took place in the first half of May, shortly before the Feast of San Isidro, Madrid's great day.

Gamborena, who had come to stay in the house for the duration, spent all the time that his service in the chapel permitted in the patient's bedroom. Seated beside the bed, he read his breviary, without neglecting the sick man, and if Torquemada muttered or asked for a drink, he would leave the book on the bedspread to answer or help him. In the morning Don Francisco's weakness and taciturnity were as great as his agitation on the previous night. He answered only in monosyllables, which were more like grunts, and kept his eyes closed as if overcome with invincible lethargy or fatigue. It was the exhaustion of muscular and nervous energy, the total depletion of the machine, whose parts no longer meshed properly and scarcely moved. By contrast, his mental faculties appeared clearer when for a brief instant sleep allowed them to appear.

"My dearest friend, my brother," said Gamborena, stroking his hands, "do you feel better? Are you conscious?"

Torquemada nodded his head affirmatively.

"Do you restate what you declared to me yesterday, do you submit to God's will and believe in Him and His divine mercy?"

A new affirmative nod, using the same language of gesture.

"Do you renounce all vanities, do you strip yourself of egotism as of a stinking garment, and humble, poor, and naked, do you ask pardon for your sins and greatly desire to be admitted to the celestial mansions?"

Having received no response, the missionary repeated the question, adding some very appropriate remarks. Suddenly the unfortunate Torquemada opened his eyes and, as if he had heard nothing of what his confessor was telling him, came out with a different tune in a hollow voice, gasping for breath between every few words.

"I feel very weak . . . but with those poultices they've given me I'll improve, and I won't die, I won't die. I have the conversion operations all worked out."

"For the love of God, don't think about that! Think of Jesus and His Most Holy Mother."

"Jesus and Most Holy Mother . . . How good they are, and with what pleasure I pray to them to give me life!"

"Ask them to give you immortal life, the true health that is never lost."

"I've already asked for it . . . and my prayers, and yours, Father, and Cruz's . . . and everyone's have reached heaven . . . where they pay a lot of attention to what sincere people ask for . . . I pray, but my mind wanders sometimes . . . because things from my youth, that I'd forgotten, come into my head. That's certainly strange! Just now I was remembering something that happened . . . 'way back there . . . when I was a boy . . . and I could see it as clearly as if I were in that *historical moment.*"

And gathering strength little by little, he continued:

"This happened the day I arrived in Madrid. I was sixteen. Another lad and I came together . . . his name was Perico Moratilla, and later he went for a soldier and died in the war in Africa. Handsome lad! Well, as I'm telling you, we got to La Cava Baja with the clothes we stood up in and not a penny between us. What were we going to eat?

Where would we spend the night? We managed to get some crusts of bread out of an old woman who kept a poultry shop, the widow of a man from the Maragato country. Moratilla had a big piece of soap in his knapsack, that somebody had given us before we reached Galapagar; we tried to sell it and couldn't. Night came, and, well, we made our bed curled up next to the market stalls in the Plazuela de San Miguel. We slept like tops till early morning, and when we woke up we took it into our heads to have our revenge on filthy humanity for leaving us in such a fix. Before God's sun was up, we went to the staircase in the Plaza Mayor and smeared soap on every step from halfway up right to the top. Then we stationed ourselves down below to watch people fall. Very early, men and women started to pass by and slip, thump! It was something to laugh at. They rolled down like cannonballs, and some of them even shot over to the Calle de Cuchilleros . . . One broke his leg, another smashed his head, and there was a woman who rolled down with her petticoats up over her head. I never laughed so much in my life. Since we couldn't eat, we fed ourselves with fun. The things boys do! It was a wicked thing. So take note, and there's a sin that I didn't tell you about because I didn't remember it."

NINE

Gamborena did not answer. He was distressed by the lack of religious unction displayed by the sick man, and the rebellion of his spirit against his inevitable death. Either he did not believe in it or, believing, he was rebelling against divine judgment, possessed by diabolical fury. The missionary was a stubborn man and would not relinquish his prey so easily. He observed Torquemada's face, trying to penetrate his thoughts with his shrewd gaze and to see what ideas were stirring under that yellowish skull, what images under the closed eyelids. A man who had had much practice in those matters and was very expert in catechizing both healthy men and dying ones, he suspected that the evil spirit, making a mock of the precautions taken against him, had slyly won over the will of the unhappy marquis of San Eloy and had him in his clutches, ready to carry him off. The good priest prepared to fight like a lion. Having examined the terrain and chosen the weapons, he drew up a plan whose logical structure can be understood by the following reasoning: "This poor wretch is all egotism, with his bit of pride and overweening love of riches. Accursed Satan has caught him through his egotism, an enormous weight, a monstrous bulk; it is greed that gives him his ardent desire to live. He adores his own self, his very own personality, and as long as he has the hope of remaining in it, just as he is, he will not accept death, and will allow neither compunction nor divine grace to enter his soul. Let him lose hope, and his egotism will be weakened. It is hard, and sometimes inhuman, to take their last hope from the dying, to cut the slender thread with which instinct clings to the material things of this world. But there are cases when it must be cut, and I do cut it, yes indeed, for I regard it, in all conscience, as the only way to snatch from the accursed devil what must not be his, no, a thousand times no . . . It will not be his."

Reasoning thus, he prepared to act quickly.

"Señor Don Francisco," he said, shaking him by one arm.

He did not respond until the third shake.

"Señor Don Francisco, listen to me for a moment."

"Leave me alone . . . I was thinking . . . Goodness, I was seeing myself back then . . . when I entered the Royal Corps of Halberdiers and put on my uniform for the first time."

"Haven't we, perchance, anything more profitable to think about?"

"Yes. I feel well, and I'm thinking about my affairs."

"And aren't you afraid that soon you will feel ill?"

"You've told me that I'm going to get well."

"That is always said to console poor invalids. But the truth should not be hidden from a man of such courageous character and superior intelligence."

"Won't I be saved?" asked Don Francisco suddenly, opening his eyes wide.

"What do you understand by being saved?"

"Living."

"We're not in agreement. Being saved is not that."

"D'you mean that I *must* die?"

"I don't say that you *must* die, but that the end of your life has arrived and that it's urgent that you prepare yourself."

Stupefaction paralyzed Torquemada's tongue, and for quite a long while he fixed his eyes upon his confessor's face.

"So . . . there's no getting out of it?"

"No."

The priest pronounced this "no" with the calculated energy that the case demanded, in his opinion, believing that he was carrying out a duty of conscience within the powers conferred by his lofty ministry. It was like an axblow. He believed that he must administer it, and did so without the slightest compunction. For Torquemada it was as if a formidably strong hand were squeezing his neck. His eyes rolled upward, a low moan came from his mouth, and both body and head sank farther into the softness of the bed, or at least it seemed that they did.

"My brother," Gamborena told him, "at these moments, joy is more appropriate for a good Christian than sorrow. Consider that you are abandoning the miseries of this execrable world and are going to enjoy the presence of God and eternal bliss, the glorious prize of those who die in loathing of sin and love of virtue. It will suffice if you direct all your thoughts, all your faculties, to Divine Jesus and offer Him your soul. Courage, my son, courage to renounce outworn possessions and all this earthly rottenness, and have fervor, love, soul fire to ascend to the bosom of Our Father, who is sure to receive you lovingly in His arms."

Don Francisco said nothing, and his confessor feared that he had lost consciousness. With his eyelids closed, his brow furrowed, his mouth clamped shut, with one lip flattened over the other, the sick man had become visibly altered in a very short period of time. His skin was like brown paper and gave off a mousy odor, a symptom commonly observed in death by starvation. Was he asleep or had he fallen into a profound collapse, the precursor of eternal sleep? Whatever it was, the fact is that when he crawled into himself like a frightened snail who hides inside its shell, he saw vague images and felt emotions that disturbed his soul, by now almost detached from matter. He thought that he was walking down a road, at the end of which was a not very large door. Rather, it was quite small, but how beautiful! The frame was silver and the door itself (for it had only a single panel) was of gold, studded with diamonds; there were diamonds, too, in the hinges, on the knocker, and the plate around the keyhole. And the builders of that door had made it all with coins, not melted down but stuck on, nailed one on top of another or fastened no one knew how. He saw very plainly the die-stamp of Charles III on the pale doubloons, the American and Spanish duros, and among them the exquisite little coins called *veintiuno y cuartillo*. The miser was gazing at the door without daring to place his trembling hand on the knocker, when he heard the lock creak. The door was being opened from the inside by the blessed Gamborena. It did not open sufficiently for a person to go through, but enough to see that the good missionary was dressed like the Saint Peter in the moneylenders' brotherhood, in which he (Don Francisco) had been chief steward. His shining bald head, his gentle eyes were easily recognizable from outside. Torquemada observed that he was barefoot and that he wore over his shoulders quite an old cape with red revers.

The doorkeeper regarded him smiling, and he smiled too, moved by fear and hope, saying, "Can I come in, master?"

TEN

Gamborena called to him so many times, speaking with his mouth almost touching his ear, that at last he answered, as if awakening from sleep, "Yes, master, yes. I've been left wondering if . . ."

"What?"

"If you were going to let me in or not. Let's see . . . Do you have the keys there?"

"Don't think about the keys and tell me in a few words if your desires to enter are sincere, if you love Jesus Christ and long to be with Him; if you recognize your sins, the dreadful vice of avarice, your cruelty to your inferiors, your absoute lack of mercy for your fellow man, the tepidness of your beliefs."

"I recognize," said Torquemada in a low voice that could scarcely be heard. "I recognize . . . and confess."

"And now, all your thoughts are for Jesus, and if some idea or desire of the kind that caused you to stray in life comes to disturb that peace, that sweet resignation with which you await your end, you will reject it, you will reject that sentiment, that idea."

"I do reject it . . . yes . . . Jesus," murmured the sick man. "But are you going to open? Tell me whether you're going to open. Because if not . . . I'll stay here and . . . though it's no small job . . . converting the external debt and the Cuban notes into internal . . ."

"My son, heap scorn on all that rubbish."

"Rubbish! You call it rubbish?"

He continued to grumble, very much under his breath. His words were unintelligible. His speech was like the deep gurgling of a spring at the back of a cave.

Disconsolate and troubled, Gamborena was certain that the battle continued to be joined between him and Satan, with the two of them disputing possession of a soul almost ready to take flight into the infinite. Who would win? The cleric's mind, endowed with poetic gifts, saw the formidable battle represented in images. On the other side of the bed, next to the wall, was the devil, all the more treacherous for being invisible. The Christian priest was prompting Don Francisco on his left, and the enemy of everything good on his right. Gamborena had the heart on his side. He placed his hand upon it and could hardly feel it beating. He tried to call upon Torquemada's mind, in hopes that he still might answer, but the mind either refused to respond or no longer exercised authority over speech. The inarticulate groans, the crude ironic expressions that played over the dying man's cold lips, sounded in the priest's ears as if inspired by the enemy who was battling fiercely on the other side of the bed.

Dusk was falling, and the missionary had to abandon his combat post on one front to go to the chapel and reserve the sacrament. During this impressive ceremony, which was attended by the family, the servants, and many friends of the household, the good father fervently elevated his spirit to Omnipotent Majesty, imploring support and aid to emerge victorious in the tremendous fight. He commended the unhappy sinner's soul with sorrowful prayers and asked grace on his behalf through the marvelous means that only God knows and employs, compensating for the helplessness of human means. The good priest's emotion was visible in his grave face and the sweetness of his gaze. When the ceremony was over, he could observe that many of those present had faces flushed from weeping.

And then he returned once more to the field of battle. In the short time that the ceremony of reservation lasted, the poor invalid's face had altered so much that Gamborena would not have recognized it had he not been accustomed to such changes in the human countenance at times like this. If each transformation of the features could be expressed in periods of time, and if facial disintegration were represented by ages, Don Francisco Torquemada was already nine hundred years old, like Methuselah.

Last-minute remedies were discontinued by agreement between the family and the doctor, for they merely serve to dispute death for a few moments, tormenting the patient uselessly. Science had nothing left to do there: this was clearly shown by the withdrawal of Miquis and his departure through the great gallery toward the street, a departure in which a certain sadness could be observed, but resolution too, like that of a man who regrets not having triumphed in one place and goes to another where he does expect to triumph. Science dismissed, the rest belonged to religion, and all believed that it was a very important part. Gamborena and a Sister of Charity occupied the two sides of the bed, soon to be a deathbed. The family retired to the sitting room next door.

Don Francisco opened his mouth eagerly, as if asking for water, which the nun gave him. His breathing was labored, with an irregular rhythm that was terribly painful to listen to. A moment arrived when the almost instantaneous cessation of stertor made them think that he had died, and they were about to make the mirror test when Torquemada breathed again, relatively strongly, and spoke a few words: "External and Cubans . . . my soul . . . the door."

He looked at them. But undoubtedly he did not recognize them. Turning his head toward the nun, he said, "Are you going to open up or not? I want to come in . . ."

Gamborena sighed. His uneasiness increased sharply as he observed in the dying man's glance the ironic expression usual in him when he spoke of things beyond the grave. The missionary spoke some very emotional words to him, but he appeared not to understand them. His eyes, which in the depths of the purplish sockets reflected scarcely any light, no longer focused on any object and wandered uncertainly, seeking . . . God knows what. Gamborena saw that the foundation of that personality was about to extinguished.

On the other side of the bed, the nun was telling him fervently to invoke the name of Jesus and, showing him a bronze crucifix, placed it to his lips for him to kiss. They could not tell whether he did so, for the movement of his lips was imperceptible. When they administered Extreme Unction the sick man did not know it. A short time later he had another moment of relative lucidity and replied to the nun's exhortations, perhaps without conscious thought.

"Jesus, Jesus and I . . . good friends . . . I want to be saved."

Gamborena's hopes returned, and what he could no longer achieve by addressing a soul almost detached from the body, he tried to do by fervently invoking the Divine Judge, who was soon to sit in judgment upon it; he thought he felt a slight pressure from the ice-cold fingers. To what the missionary said to him, speaking very close to his face, Torquemada responded with tremors of his hands, which might well have been a kind of language. A few murmurs, groans or simple acoustic phenomena of breath slipping through his lips, or air in the larynx, were translated by Gamborena in various ways. Sometimes, confident and optimistic, he translated, "Jesus . . . salvation . . . pardon." At others, pessimistic and in despair, he translated, "The key . . . bring on the key . . . External . . . my cape . . . three percent."

This extremely painful situation lasted two hours or a little more. Just before dawn the two religious were sure that the end was approaching and redoubled their efforts as death watchers, and as the nun was exhorting him with great vehemence to repeat the names of Jesus and Mary and to kiss the holy crucifix, the poor miser took his leave of this world by saying, in a perfectly audible voice, "Conversion."

A few minutes after he had said it, that soul turned its face toward eternity.

"He said 'conversion'!" observed the nun joyfully, clasping her hands together. "He meant that he was converted, that . . ."

Touching the dead man's forehead, Gamborena coldly gave this response: "Conversion! Is it the conversion of his soul or that of the public debt?"

The nun did not fully understand the concept, and both, kneeling, began to pray. What the doughty overseas missionary was thinking about as he raised his prayers to heaven he never told, nor can the layman guess.

In the presence of the mystery that covers, like a somber cloud, the frontiers between the finite and the infinite, the layman must be content with saying that at that immensely solemn moment, the soul of the marquis of San Eloy approached the gate, whose keys are held by . . . whoever holds them. Nothing was seen, but a squeaking of metal in the lock was heard, yes indeed. Then the sharp sound, the formidable slam that shakes the spheres. But here an immense doubt enters the picture. Did the gates close after the soul passed through, or did they close and leave it outside?

Not even Gamborena himself, the "Saint Peter" of this world, though he knows so much, can dispel this doubt for us. The layman, pausing heart in mouth before the impenetrable veil that hides the most feared, and at the same time the most beautiful, mystery of human existence, abstains from expressing a verdict that would be disrespectful, and confines himself to saying, "Torquemada might well have been saved."

"He might well have been lost."

But he does not affirm one thing or the other . . . mind you!